THE READER'S DIGEST

GREAT WORLD ATLAS

THE READER'S DIGEST ASSOCIATION

LONDON · SYDNEY · MONTREAL · CAPE TOWN

THE READER'S DIGEST GREAT WORLD ATLAS

Prepared and Published by The Reader's Digest Association Limited. Planned under the direction of the late

FRANK DEBENHAM

O.B.E., M.A., D.SC. (HON.), EMERITUS PROFESSOR OF GEOGRAPHY, CAMBRIDGE UNIVERSITY

The Reader's Digest expresses its gratitude to the following
who have generously contributed to and advised on the preparation of this Atlas:

Academy of Science of the U.S.S.R.

P. J. Adams, B.SC., PH.D., F.G.S., Institute of Geological Sciences

J. B. Allen, B.SC., PH.D., F.G.S., Institute of Geological Sciences

W. R. Aykroyd, C.B.E., M.D., SC.D.

John Bartholomew & Son Ltd.

Andrew Boyd, M.A.

British and Foreign Bible Society

British Broadcasting Corporation

British Medical Association

Maurice Burton, D.SC.

Wm. Collins, Sons & Co. Ltd.

J. G. Cook, PH.D., F.R.I.C.

F. W. Dunning, B.SC., F.G.S., Institute of Geological Sciences

F. V. Emery, B.LITT., M.A.

Food and Agriculture Organization of the United Nations

General Register Office

Geographical Projects Ltd.

Madeleine Glemser, M.A.

Greater London Council

Michael Hart, M.A.

Cdr. H. R. Hatfield, R.N.

Information Service of India

Institute for Strategic Studies

B. Gyrth Jackson, M.SC., School of Agriculture,
University of Cambridge

E. A. Jobbins, B.SC., F.G.S., Institute of Geological Sciences

H. C. King, PH.D., M.SC., F.R.A.S., F.B.O.A.

H. A. G. Lewis, Esq., Directorate of Military Survey
(War Office and Air Ministry)

Lick Observatory

Longmans, Green & Co. Ltd.

N. B. Marshall, M.A., British Museum (Natural History)

R. J. Marston, B.SC., PH.D., F.G.S., Institute of Geological Sciences

Ministry of Agriculture, Fisheries and Food

Ministry of Health

The Rev. Vernon P. Mitchell

Patrick Moore, F.R.A.S., Director, Armagh Planetarium

Mount Wilson and Palomar Observatories

National Institute of Oceanography

B. M. Nichol, O.B.E., M.B., CH.B.,
Nutrition Adviser, Government of Nigeria

K. P. Oakley, D.SC., F.B.A., British Museum (Natural History)

Office of the South African High Commissioner

The Rev. E. G. Parrinder, M.A., PH.D., D.D., London University

E. Penkala, Esq.

The Polar Institute

The Rev. B. M. G. Reardon, M.A.

C. S. Roetter, LL.B.

C. A. Ronan, M.SC., F.R.A.S., Royal Society

Royal Geographical Society

Scientific Liaison Office, Australia, New Zealand, Canada

Scottish Office

Peter Small, Esq.

P. R. Smithson, B.SC., F.R.MET.S.

Robert Spencer, B.A., British Trust for Ornithology

United Nations, London Information Centre

B. B. Waddy, D.M., London School of Hygiene and Tropical Medicine

G. R. Wadsworth, M.D., London School of Hygiene and Tropical Medicine

The Wellcome Foundation Ltd.

The Wellcome Museum of Medical Science

Bernard Workman, M.A.

World Health Organization

Norman C. Wright, C.B., M.A., PH.D., D.SC., F.R.I.C., F.R.S.E., Deputy-
Director-General, Food and Agriculture Organization of the United Nations

Yerkes Observatory

Acknowledgment is also made to the numerous authors
and compilers of technical books and journals to which reference was made
in the preparation of this Atlas

CONTENTS

From the centre of the Earth

to the outermost limits of space

PARADISE IS SOMEWHERE IN THE FAR EAST. JERUSALEM IS THE CENTRE OF ALL NATIONS AND COUNTRIES, AND THE WORLD ITSELF IS A FLAT DISK SURROUNDED BY OCEANS OF WATER. So the monks, map-makers of the Middle Ages, saw the world they lived in.

Today, our knowledge of the world has increased through travel and exploration and scientific discovery. This Atlas has drawn on the sum of that knowledge—knowledge that has been accumulated through many life-times of research.

We look at THE FACE OF THE WORLD, starting with a view of our Earth in space. The following maps made from sculptured models show in relief how our world would appear to an observer at a point some hundred miles above the Earth's surface. The peaks of the great mountain ranges show in sharp contrast to the worn surfaces of older rocks and the flat plains formed by the great rivers. The levels of the ocean floor tell the history of submerged lands and of yet unexplored deeps. Here, a new dimension has been added to standard map-making.

Next come THE COUNTRIES OF THE WORLD. Towns and cities, rivers and railways can all be found easily, for the colouring is subdued and the text clear and definitive. Together with the relief maps they complete a picture of the landscape of our Earth and of the places where we live.

The third section portrays THE WORLD AS WE KNOW IT. Incurably inquisitive, man searches continually for knowledge about our world and about other worlds beyond. He now knows that he is only one of many forms of life on the thin crust of a planet revolving round the Sun—a minor star at the edge of the Milky Way. A multi-million starred galaxy, the Milky Way is itself only one among a million other galaxies moving in the black infinity of space where traditional concepts of north and south are meaningless.

It is a vision that dwarfs the globe on which we live and makes man seem very small; but it also gives him a new importance. For on this tiny planet life has been created and developed, and as yet we do not know whether the delicate balance of conditions which has made evolution possible on this planet has ever been repeated on any other.

The marvel of this creation cannot be told by any single map or chart. Each feature in the third section of this Atlas has been devised to illustrate a facet of it—our place in the universe, the mystery of our neighbours in space, the world beneath our feet, the evolution of life, the creatures around us, the growth and disappearance of civilizations, the beliefs of man, and his migrations. Each subject is linked to another: climate to cultivation, cultivation to food, food to health, for none of the world's problems can be seen in isolation. All are related to and interwoven with one another.

This Atlas, in presenting geographically the facts about Earth and life and space, also offers many pointers towards exploration in the future which lies before us.

THE EDITORS

THE FACE OF THE WORLD

CONTENTS

Pluto

Neptune

Uranus

Saturn

THE SUN AND ITS PLANETS—AS VIEWED
FROM A POINT IN SPACE

THE Sun dominates and dwarfs its solar family of nine major planets and at least a thousand tiny planets called "asteroids". Jupiter, the Sun's largest dependent planet, is but a speck by comparison with it, and the volume of Jupiter is roughly 1,300 times that of Earth. The Sun contains over 99·87 per cent of the entire mass in our Solar System. Yet, despite their comparative smallness and the enormous distances of empty space that separate them from the Sun and from one another, the Sun keeps its planets under strict control.

Revolving round it continuously in elliptical orbits, these planets are held near the Sun by the pull of gravity, and kept from being drawn into it by the speed with which they move through space. The closer they are to the Sun, the faster they move. Mercury—at an average distance of 36 million miles, the planet nearest to the Sun—averages only 88 days to travel right round it, moving at a speed of nearly 30 miles a second. The Earth, whose average distance from the Sun is 93 million miles, needs exactly one year to complete its orbit, travelling at a speed of 18·5 miles per second, or roughly 66,600 miles per hour. Pluto, the most distant known planet, about 3,666 million miles from the Sun, takes just over 248 years at a speed of a mere three miles a second to make one journey round it.

Moving at different speeds, in separate orbits, and at varying distances from the Sun, the planets, as viewed from the Earth which is itself moving, *appear* to be changing constantly in size and brightness. Venus, well known as the Morning Star or Evening Star, comes as close to the Earth as about 25·5 million miles, and goes as far away as 160 million miles.

Life as we know it cannot exist on any other planet in our Solar System. Mercury is so close to the Sun that the temperature on its sunlit side is estimated to be of the order of 400°C. Venus, about twice as far from the Sun as Mercury is roughly 25 million miles closer to it than the Earth, and probably has a maximum surface temperature of 440°C. Of the planets farther than Earth from the Sun, Jupiter, Saturn (its semi-transparent rings made up of fine particles, dense enough to throw a shadow over the planet's surface), Uranus, Neptune and Pluto are all too cold, and their atmospheres

THE SOLAR SYSTEM

Jupiter

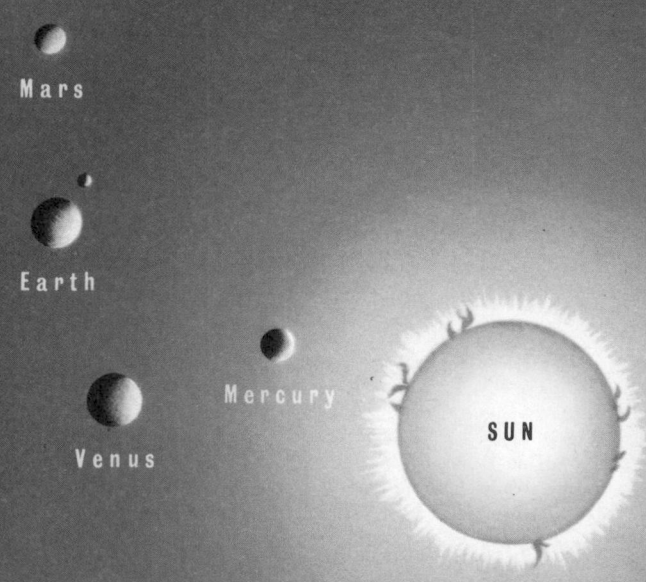

Mars

Earth

Mercury

Venus

SUN

contain high concentrations of poisonous gases—helium, hydrogen, methane and ammonia. Some form of life is thought to exist on Mars, but, to live in the planet's thin, icy air, is probably a form of primitive vegetation.

The Earth is the only member of our Sun's family known to support living creatures. Alone among the planets in the Solar System—though not perhaps among those belonging to the millions of sun-like stars in the Universe—the Earth's composition and distance from the Sun seem to have provided exactly the right conditions in which evolution to an advanced form of life could develop.

The life-giving energy of the Sun, the source of all the heat and light in our Solar System, is generated by nuclear reactions in its interior, which raise the temperature deep inside it to about 14 million degrees Centigrade. So tremendous is the radiation rate of the Sun's energy, that it loses some four million tons in weight every second. Yet, despite this rate of loss, it is estimated that the Sun will survive as a source of energy for at least another 8,000 million years.

DISTANCE OF PLANETS FROM EARTH (IN MILES)

	MOON	MARS	URANUS
Maximum	253,000	247,000,000	1,946,000,000
Minimum	222,000	34,000,000	1,594,000,000
	MERCURY	JUPITER	NEPTUNE
Maximum	136,900,000	597,000,000	2,891,000,000
Minimum	49,100,000	362,000,000	2,654,000,000
	VENUS	SATURN	PLUTO
Maximum	160,900,000	1,023,000,000	4,506,000,000
Minimum	25,700,000	773,000,000	2,605,000,000

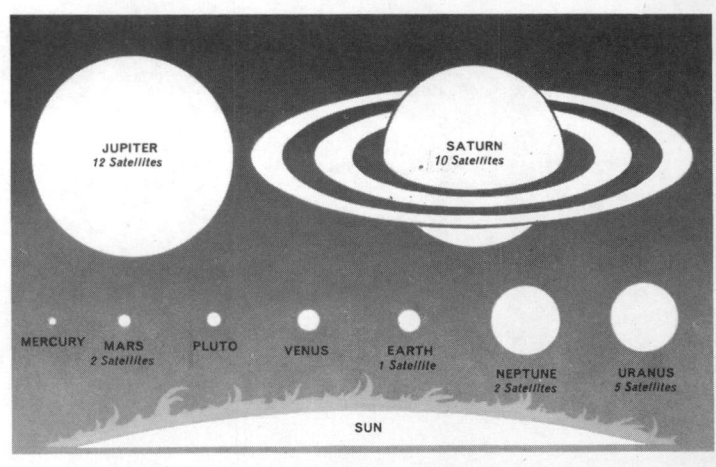

JUPITER
12 Satellites

SATURN
10 Satellites

MERCURY MARS
2 Satellites

PLUTO VENUS EARTH
1 Satellite

NEPTUNE
2 Satellites

URANUS
5 Satellites

SUN

SOUTH POLE AND NORTH POLE

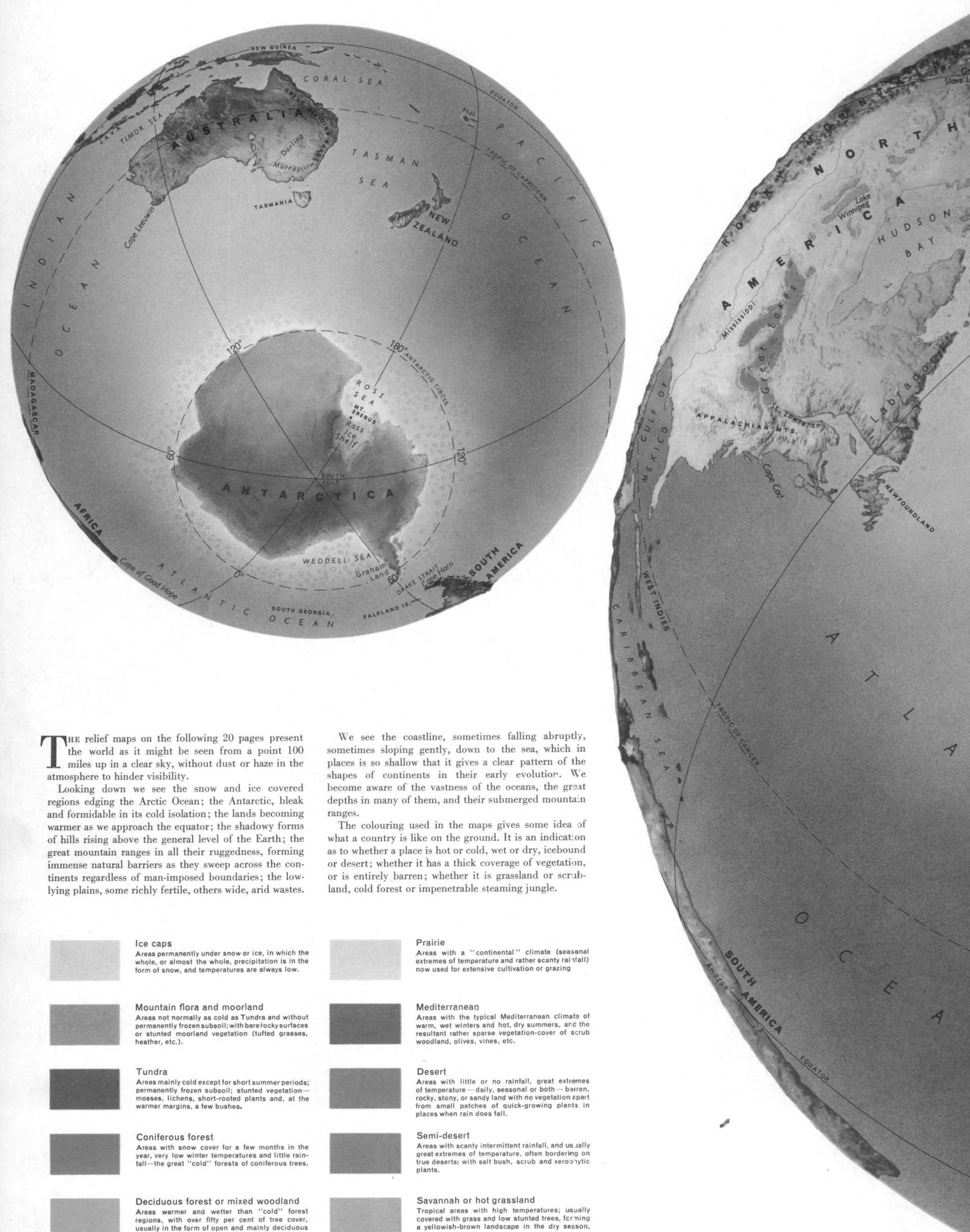

THE relief maps on the following 20 pages present the world as it might be seen from a point 100 miles up in a clear sky, without dust or haze in the atmosphere to hinder visibility.

Looking down we see the snow and ice covered regions edging the Arctic Ocean; the Antarctic, bleak and formidable in its cold isolation; the lands becoming warmer as we approach the equator; the shadowy forms of hills rising above the general level of the Earth; the great mountain ranges in all their ruggedness, forming immense natural barriers as they sweep across the continents regardless of man-imposed boundaries; the low-lying plains, some richly fertile, others wide, arid wastes.

We see the coastline, sometimes falling abruptly, sometimes sloping gently, down to the sea, which in places is so shallow that it gives a clear pattern of the shapes of continents in their early evolution. We become aware of the vastness of the oceans, the great depths in many of them, and their submerged mountain ranges.

The colouring used in the maps gives some idea of what a country is like on the ground. It is an indication as to whether a place is hot or cold, wet or dry, icebound or desert; whether it has a thick coverage of vegetation, or is entirely barren; whether it is grassland or scrubland, cold forest or impenetrable steaming jungle.

Ice caps
Areas permanently under snow or ice, in which the whole, or almost the whole, precipitation is in the form of snow, and temperatures are always low.

Mountain flora and moorland
Areas not normally as cold as Tundra and without permanently frozen subsoil; with bare rocky surfaces or stunted moorland vegetation (tufted grasses, heather, etc.).

Tundra
Areas mainly cold except for short summer periods; permanently frozen subsoil; stunted vegetation—mosses, lichens, short-rooted plants and, at the warmer margins, a few bushes.

Coniferous forest
Areas with snow cover for a few months in the year, very low winter temperatures and little rainfall—the great "cold" forests of coniferous trees.

Deciduous forest or mixed woodland
Areas warmer and wetter than "cold" forest regions, with over fifty per cent of tree cover, usually in the form of open and mainly deciduous woodland.

Temperate grassland or woodland
Rather wet areas in the middle latitudes, with no extremes of temperature; over fifty per cent grassland and the rest mainly mixed woodland.

Prairie
Areas with a "continental" climate (seasonal extremes of temperature and rather scanty rainfall) now used for extensive cultivation or grazing

Mediterranean
Areas with the typical Mediterranean climate of warm, wet winters and hot, dry summers, and the resultant rather sparse vegetation-cover of scrub woodland, olives, vines, etc.

Desert
Areas with little or no rainfall, great extremes of temperature—daily, seasonal or both—barren, rocky, stony, or sandy land with no vegetation apart from small patches of quick-growing plants in places when rain does fall.

Semi-desert
Areas with scanty intermittent rainfall, and usually great extremes of temperature, often bordering on true deserts; with salt bush, scrub and xerophytic plants.

Savannah or hot grassland
Tropical areas with high temperatures; usually covered with grass and low stunted trees, forming a yellowish-brown landscape in the dry season, and reviving in the wet season.

Tropical forest or jungle
Areas of great heat and moisture and very luxuriant vegetation.

8

9

EURASIA

ARCTIC OCEAN

SEVERNAYA ZEMLYA

Mys Chelyuskin

Gory Byrranga
Poluostrov Taymyr

Nordvik

Khatanga

NOVOSIBIRSKIYE OSTROVA

LAPTEV SEA

EAST SIBERIAN SEA

O. VRANGELYA

CHUKOTSKIY KHREBET

Uelen

Mys Navarin

ST. LAWRENCE I. (U.S.A.)

Tiksi

Sredne Kolymsk

Sylgy Ytar

Anadyr

KOLYMSKIY KHREBET

BERING SEA

KOMANDORSKIYE OSTROVA

Verkhoyansk

KHREBET CHERSKOGO

Kolyma

Indigirka

Igarka

Yana

VERKHOYANSKIY KHREBET

Lena

Okhotsk

KHR. DZHUGDZHUR

Petropavlovsk-Kamchatskiy

Kamchatka

Mys Lopatka

KURIL'SKIYE OSTROVA

Nizhnyaya Tunguska

Vilyuy

Vilyuysk

Yakutsk

SEA OF OKHOTSK

Yenisey

Srednе Sibirskoye

Aldan

Nikolayevsk

TATARSKIY PROLIV

SAKHALIN

LA PEROUSE STRAIT

Ploskogorye

Olekminsk

Lena

Kirensk

SEVERO-BAYKAL'SKOYE NAGORYE

STANOVOY KHREBET

Amur

Khabarovsk

SIKHOTE-ALIN

Tomsk

Krasnoyarsk

Yenisey

Tulun

Angara

Chita

YABLONOVYY KHREBET

Shilka

TA HINGAN LING

SIAO HINGAN LING

Sungari

Otaru

Sapporo

HOKKAIDO

Hakodate

osibirsk

p'yevsk

Novokuznetsk

Barnaul

Ob'

SOCIALIST REPUBLIC

Ozero Baykal

Irkutsk

Ulan Ude

Kyakhta

Manchouli

Hulun Chih

Manchuria

Ozero Khanka

Harbin

Vladivostok

SEA OF JAPAN

TSUGARU KAIKYO

SADO-SHIMA

Niigata

Tokyo

Kyzyl

TANNU OLA

Kosogol

Selenga

Kerulen

Changchun

HONSHU

Yokohama

UKHA 4,784

Ubsa Nor

Jirgalanta

Jibhalanta

Ulan Bator

Shenyang

An-tung

Hungnam

P'yongyang

Seoul

Inch'on

Pusan

Niigata

Yokohama

Nagoya

Kochi

SHIKOKU

Kyoto

Kobe

Osaka

ungaria

Urumchi

Turfan

MONGOLIA

Gobi

Changkiakow

Peking

Tientsin

PO-HAI WAN

Talien

Shantung Pen.

Hiroshima

Fukuoka

KYUSHU

Lop Nor

Ansi

Ordos

Hwang Ho

Paoting

Taiyuan

Hwang Ho

Tsinan

YELLOW SEA

CHEJU-DO

Nagasaki

Kagoshima

EAST CHINA SEA

ALTYN TAGH

NAN SHAN

Tsaidam

Ch'ing Hai

Changyeh

Lanchow

MIN SHAN

CH'IN LING SHAN

Sian

Loyang

Kaifeng

Suchow

NANKING

Nanking

Shanghai

NAN SHAN

Tsaidam

Sian

Tung-T'ing Hu

Red Basin

Chengtu

Ichang

Wuhan

Anking

Po-yang Hu

Hangchow

Wenchow

TROPIC OF CANCER

betan

Lhasa

Brahmaputra

RANGE

MO-SVERDS 29,028 MAKALU

KANGCHENJUNGA BHUTAN

Darjeeling

Patna

Ganga

KHASI HILLS

Shillong

Silchar

Salween

Mekong

Paan

Ipin

Chungking

Changsha

Nanchang

Kanchow

Changting

Foochow

Taipei

STRAIT OF FORMOSA

RYUKYU RETTO

PACIFIC OCEAN

Yangtze Kiang

NAGA HILLS

BURMA

Tali

Myitkyina

Kunming

Hengyang

Kwelyang

Amoy

Swatow

Tainan

TAIWAN

Paoshan

Si-Kiang

Canton

Hong Kong (Br.)

NAN LING

100 0 100 200 300 400 500 Miles

11

EUROPE

NORWEGIAN SEA

NORTH SEA

ATLANTIC OCEAN

FÆRÖERNE (DAN.)

ROCKALL

SHETLAND
Lerwick

ORKNEY

Cape Wrath

ST. KILDA

HEBRIDES
THE MINCH
I.O. SKYE

Inverness

Aberdeen

Dundee

Glasgow
Edinburgh

Newcastle

UNITED

Londonderry

DONEGAL BAY

REPUBLIC OF IRELAND

Sligo

GALWAY BAY

Dublin

Limerick

Belfast

IRISH SEA

Liverpool
Manchester

Leeds

Hull

Sheffield

SNOWDON

KINGDOM

Cork

Cape Clear

ST. GEORGES CHANNEL

PENNINES

Birmingham

Swansea

Cardiff
Bristol

London

Plymouth

Southampton

ISLES OF SCILLY

Thames

ENGLISH CHANNEL
STR. OF DOVER

CHANNEL ISLANDS (BR.)

Cherbourg

Brest

Le Havre

Calais

Lille

Amiens

Rouen

FRIESISCHE IN.

Namsos

Trondheim

Molde

Bergen

Stavanger

Lindesnes

Kristiansand

Larvik

Drammen

Oslo

SKAGERRAK

Skagen

DENMARK

Aalborg

Aarhus

Esbjerg

Schleswig

Kiel

HELGOLAND

København

Odense

Malmö

SJÆLLAND
FYN

JYLLAND

Lübeck

Hamburg

Bremen

Hannover

Amsterdam

s'Gravenhage

Arnhem

Rotterdam

Antwerpen

NETHERLANDS

Bruxelles

BELGIUM

Liège

Köln

Dortmund

Essen

Düsseldorf

WEST GERMANY

Braunschweig

Berlin

Leipzig

Dresden

Rhein

Frankfurt

Karl Marx Stadt

Trondheim

Ostersund

Storsjön

Faluna

Gävle

Uppsala

Stockholm

Örebro

Karlstad

Vänern

Norrköping

Jönköping

GOTLAND

ÖLAND

Göteborg

Halmstad

Hälsingborg

Karlskrona

BORNHOLM

Szczecin

Gdynia
Gdańsk

Kalinin

BALTIC

Umeå

Vaasa

GULF OF BOTHNIA

Pori

Turku

HVENANMAA

O. KHIUMA

O. SAREMA

EAST GERMANY

POLAND

Poznán

Łódź

Wrocław

Wisła

Katowice

Kraków

SUDETY

Ostrava

Praha

Plzen

CZECHOSLOVAKIA

Brno

BESKID

LUXEMBOURG

Luxembourg

Reims

Nürnberg

Regensburg

Strasbourg

VOSGES

Stuttgart

München

SCHWARZWALD

Donau

Linz

Wien

Bratislava

Salzburg

AUSTRIA

Graz

HUNGARY

Budapest

Balaton

Szeged

Debre

Nancy

Paris

Le Mans

Orléans

Dijon

Seine

Rennes

Nantes

Tours

Loire

FRANCE

La Rochelle

ILE D'OLERON

Limoges

Bordeaux

Clermont Ferrand

MONT DORE

Massif

Central

CEVENNES

Saône

Basel

Bern

Zürich

SWITZERLAND

Genève

L. Léman

JURA

ALPS

Lyon

MONT BLANC

Grenoble

Rhône

Avignon

Nîmes

BODENSEE

Innsbruck

Milano

Torino

Verona

Padova

MONTE ROSA

Genova

ALPS

Trieste

Venezia

Zagreb

Sava

YUGOSLAVIA

Zagreb

Beograd

Sarajevo

Toulouse

Bayonne

Bilbao

PYRENEES

Andorra

Perpignan

Marseille

Toulon

Nice

MONACO

Livorno

LIGURIAN SEA

Firenze

SAN MARINO

Ancona

APENNINES

Pennina

DALMATIAN ISLANDS

ADRIATIC

Dubrovnik

Titograd

ALBANIA

Bari

Durrës

Tirane

CORSE

Ajaccio

Bastia

ELBA

Roma

Napoli

VESUVIO

Taranto

KÉRKIRA

IONIAN ISLANDS

La Coruña

Cape Finisterre

CORDILLERA CANTABRICA

Valladolid

Porto

DOURO

Madrid

Tajo

Zaragoza

Barcelona

SIERRA MORENO

Guadalquivir

Valencia

Cartagena

MALLORCA

Palma

MENORCA

IBIZA

ISLAS BALEARES

SARDEGNA

Sassari

Cagliari

TYRRHENIAN SEA

I. LIPARI

Palermo

Messina

SICILIA

Catania

ETNA

BAY OF BISCAY

PORTUGAL

SPAIN

Lisboa

Sevilla

Granada

Málaga

STRAIT OF GIBRALTAR

Cádiz

Tangier

Gibraltar (Br.)

Tetuan

MEDITERRANEAN

IONIAN SEA

Alger

Melilla

Oran

Mostaganem

Blida

Skikda

Annaba

Bizerte

C. Bon

PANTELLERIA

Tunis

LAMPEDUSA

Valletta

MALTA

Meknès

Fès

Tlemcen

Constantine

Sousse

Kairouan

MOROCCO

Ain Sefra

Hauts Plateaux

ATLAS

Sfax

Gabès

ILE DE DJERBA

Colomb Béchar

Laghouat

Chott Melrhir

Touggourt

TUNISIA

Tripoli

El Goléa

Ouargla

Grand Erg Occidental

ALGERIA

Gadames

Misurata

Benghazi

JABAL AKHDAR

Sirte

GULF OF SIRTE

Agheila

LIBYA

Tripolitania

Cyr

Cape T

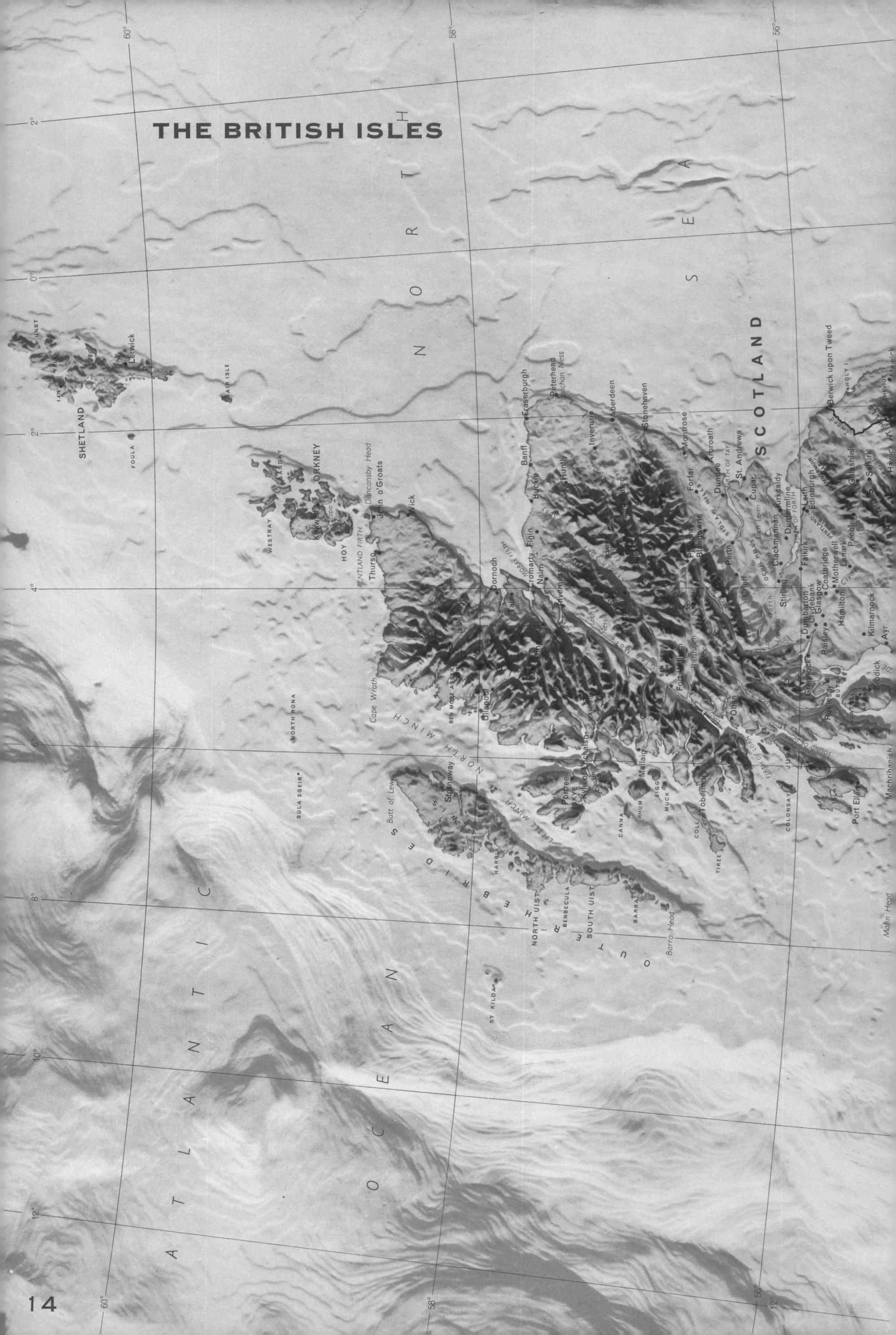

THE BRITISH ISLES

SCOTLAND

NORTH SEA

ATLANTIC OCEAN

SHETLAND
UNST
Lerwick
FOULA
FAIR ISLE

ORKNEY
WESTRAY
KIRKWALL
HOY
PENTLAND FIRTH
Duncansby Head
John o'Groats
Thurso
Wick

Cape Wrath
NORTH RONA
SULA SGEIR
NORTH MINCH
BEN MORE ASSYNT
Lairg
Dornoch
Tain
Dingwall
CROMARTY FIRTH
Cromarty
Nairn
Inverness
Elgin
MORAY FIRTH
Buckie
Banff
Fraserburgh
Peterhead
Lochan Ness
Aberdeen
Stonehaven
Inverurie
Huntly

Butt of Lewis
Stornoway
LEWIS
HARRIS
LITTLE MINCH
Portree
SKYE
CUILLIN H.
Kyle of Lochalsh
Mallaig
EIGG
MUCK
RHUM
CANNA
Fort William
Oban
Montrose
Arbroath
FIRTH OF TAY
Dundee
St. Andrews
Cupar
Kirkcaldy
Forfar
Perth
Crieff
Blairgowrie
Pitlochry
Rannoch
SIDLAW HILLS
OCHIL HILLS
Loch Leven
Dunfermline
Clackmannan
Stirling
FIRTH OF FORTH
Leith
Edinburgh
Falkirk
PENTLAND HILLS
Dumbarton
Clydebank
Glasgow
Paisley
Coatbridge
Motherwell
Hamilton
Lanark

NORTH UIST
BENBECULA
SOUTH UIST
BARRA
Barra Head
TIREE
COLL
Tobermory
COLONSAY
JURA
Rothesay
BUTE
SOUND OF JURA
Campbeltown
Port Ellen
Machrihanish
Mohn Head

ST KILDA

OUTER HEBRIDES
INNER HEBRIDES

Berwick upon Tweed
HOLY I.
Galashiels
Selkirk
Peebles
Kilmarnock
Ayr

14

CANADA

ARCTIC

OCEAN

BEAUFORT
SEA

CHUKCHI
SEA

O. VRANGELYA

Cape Lisburne

Point Barrow

Cape Bathurst   AMUNDSEN
GULF

PRINCE
PATRICK
ISLAND

QUEEN   ELIZ

PARRY   ISLAND

MELVILLE   ISLAND

BANKS   ISLAND

VISCOUNT MELVILLE SOUND   PRINCE

WAL

ISLA

SVERD

BROOKS   RANGE

CHUKOTSKIY KHREBET

U. S. S. R.

ST. LAWRENCE I.
(U.S.A.)

BERING STRAIT

Mys Dezhneva

KOTZEBUE SOUND

Kotzebue

Nome

Seward
Pen.

NORTON
SOUND

Yukon

Tanana

Fort Yukon

Circle

Eagle

Dawson

VICTORIA   ISLAND

CORONATION
GULF

Coppermine

Bathurst
Inlet

Aklavik

Fort Good Hope

Norman Wells

Great Bear
Lake

Port Radium

MT. McKINLEY

Fairbanks

Tanana

Holy Cross

Iliamna
Lake

ALASKA   RANGE

ALEUTIAN

BRISTOL BAY

Alaska   Peninsula

Anchorage

MT. SANFORD
16,208

Seward

Cordova

Kodiak

KODIAK I.

AFOGNAK I.

COOK INLET

Kenai
Pen.

GULF   OF   ALASKA

ST. ELIAS MTS.

Whitehorse

Skagway

Juneau

Sitka

ALEXANDER
ARCHIPELAGO

Fort Selkirk

SELWYN RAN.

R   O   C   K   Y

COAST   RANGE

Fort Simpson

Fort Providence

Hay River

Great Slave
Lake

Yellowknife

Fort Smith

CARIBOU MTS

Slave

Peace

Uranium City

Lake Athabasca

Fort Chipewyan

Athabasca

Reindeer
Lake

Dubuq

C   A   N   A   D   A

DIXON ENTRANCE

Prince Rupert

QUEEN
CHARLOTTE
ISLANDS

QUEEN CHARLOTTE
SOUND

Cape Scott

HECATE STR.

Skeena

Kitimat

Prince George

Fraser

Peace River

Lesser Slave
Lake

Grande Prairie

Fort McMurray

Beauval

Flin Flon

The Pas

MT. ROBSON

Yellowhead Pass

Edmonton

N. Battleford

North Saskatchewan

Prince Albert

Saskatoon

South Saskatchewan

Lake
Winnipeg

Yorkton

Assiniboine

PACIFIC

OCEAN

VANCOUVER

ISLAND

JUAN DE FUCA STRAIT

Cape Flattery

MT. OLYMPUS
7,955

WASHINGTON

COAST   RANGE

Kamloops

Vancouver

Victoria

PUGET
SOUND

Seattle

Tacoma

Olympia

Nelson

Trail

Kicking Horse
Pass

Banff

Calgary

Fernie

Medicine Hat

Hanna

Swift Current

Regina

Moose Jaw

Lethbridge

Bran

Weyburn

Cot

CASCADE   RANGE

Portland

Salem

Cabo Blanco

Columbia

Grand
Coulee
Dam

Spokane

Columbia   Plateau

BLUE MTS.

Columbia

SALMON RIVER MTS.

Sage
Plains

Boise

Cape Mendocino

Eureka

Klamath Falls

MT. SHASTA
14,161

Twin Falls

Snake

Helena

Butte

BITTERROOT MTS.

BIG HORN MTS.

Great Falls

Billings

Fort Peck
Reservoir

Missouri

Yellowstone

Minot

Garrison
Reserve

Lead

BLACK
HILLS

Rapid City

U   N   I   T   E   D

Great Salt
Lake

North Platte

S   T

100 0   100   200   300   400   500
Miles

70°

170°

160°

150°

80°

170°

180°

170°

160°

150°

140°

130°

120°

110°

60°

50°

40°

130°

120°

110°

40°

50°

60°

70°

16

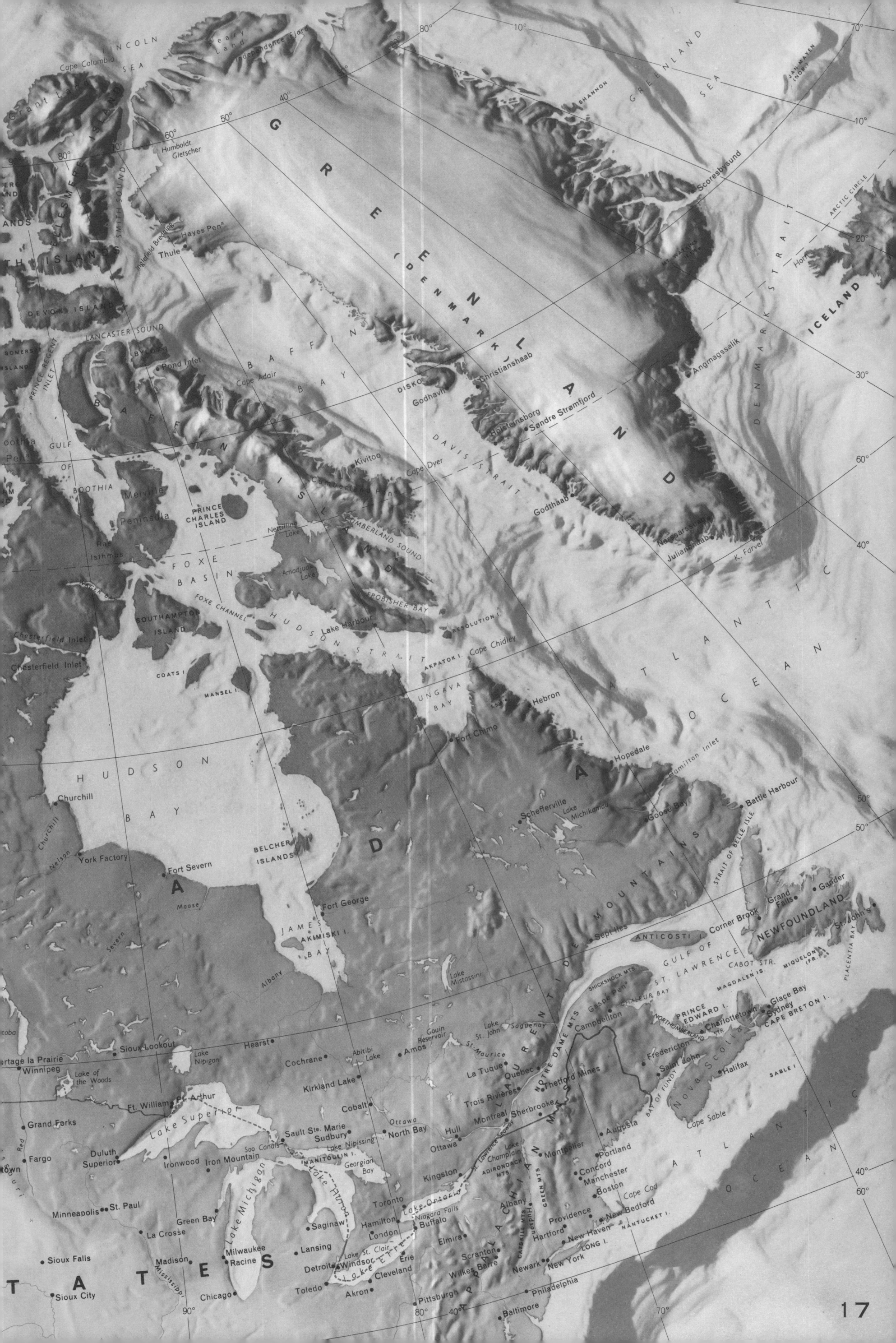

UNITED STATES
OF AMERICA
AND MEXICO

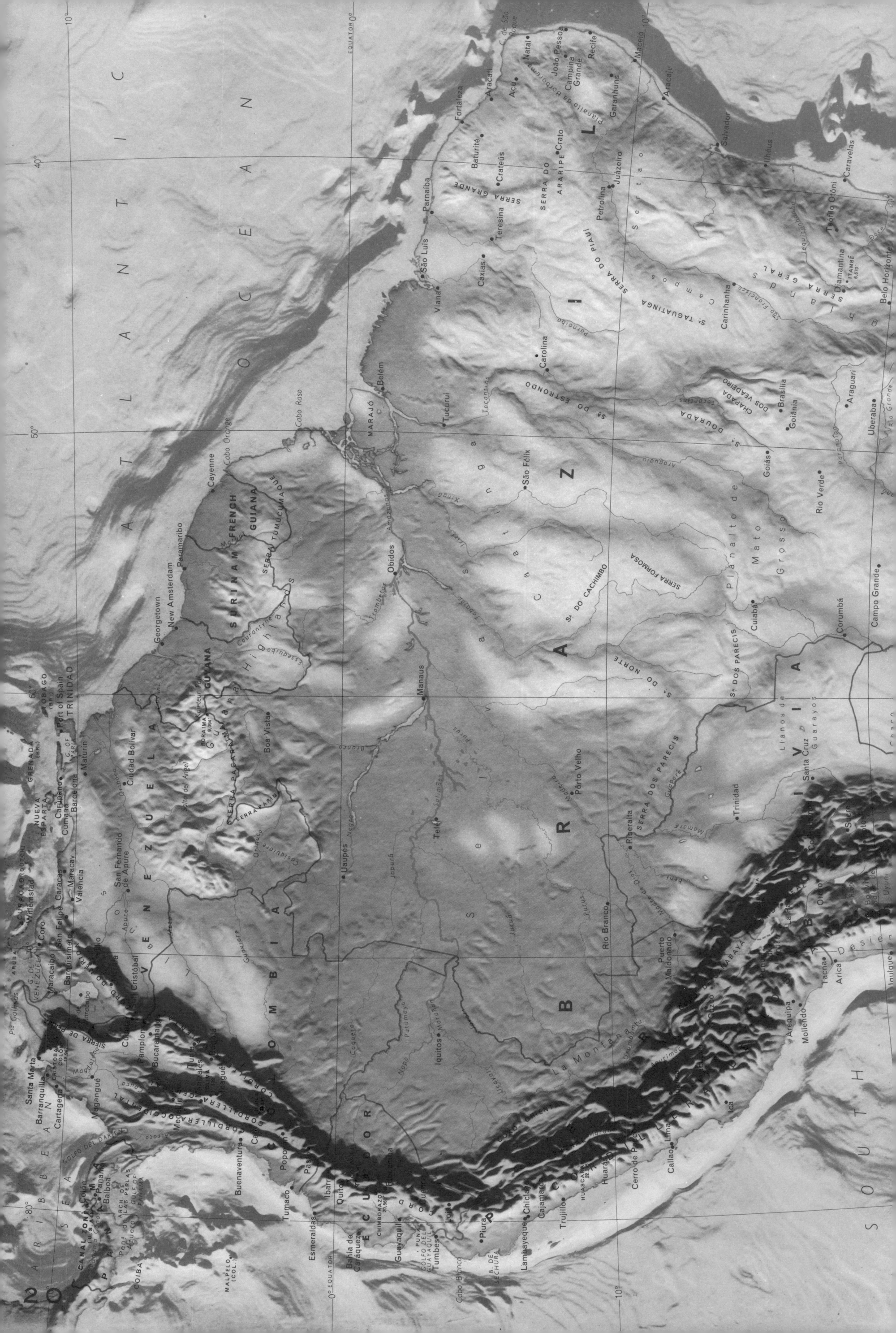

A T L A N T I C   O C E A N

EQUATOR 0°

B R A Z I L

Recife
João Pessoa
Campina Grande
Natal
Garanhuns
Maceió
Aracati
Açu
Fortaleza
Salvador
Ilhéus
Caravelas
Teófilo Otôni
Baturité
Crateús
Parnaíba
Teresina
Caxias
Viana
São Luís
SERRA GRANDE
SERRA DO ARARIPE
Crato
Juàzeiro
Petrolina
Carinhanha
Diamantina
ITAMBÉ
Belo Horizonte
SERRA DO PIAUÍ
Planalto da Borborema
Sertão
Caatinga
St TAGUATINGA Campos
São Francisco
SERRA GERAL
Carolina
Belém
Tucuruí
Sr DO ESTRONDO
CHAPADA DOS VEADEIRO
Brasília
Goiânia
Araguari
Uberaba
Rio Grande

MARAJÓ

São Félix

M A T O   G R O S S O

Cuiabá
Corumbá
Campo Grande
Rio Verde
Goiás
Planalto de Mato Grosso
SERRA FORMOSA
St DOS PARECIS
Sr DO NORTE

Cabo Roso
Óbidos
Amazonas
Manaus

GUIANA FRENCH GUIANA
SURINAM
Cayenne
Cabo Orange
SERRA TUMUCUMAQUE
Paramaribo
New Amsterdam
Georgetown
Guiana Highlands
Courantine
Essequibo
GUIANA
RORAIMA
Boa Vista
Ciudad Bolívar
SIERRA PACARAIMA
SERRA PARIMA

TOBAGO
Port of Spain
TRINIDAD
GRENADA
NUEVA ESPARTA
Cumaná
Carúpano
Barcelona
Maturin

V E N E Z U E L A
San Fernando de Apure
Maracay
Valência
Caracas
Maracaibo
Coro
Barquisimeto
San Felipe
Barinas
San Cristóbal
Pamplona
Bucaramanga

C O L O M B I A

Iquitos
Uaupés
Teté
Solimões
Juruá
Purús
Rio Branco
Porto Velho
Riberalta
Puerto Maldonado

P E R Ú

B O L I V I A
Trinidad
Santa Cruz
Llanos de Guarayos
Mamoré
La Montaña

CARIBBEAN SEA
Santa Marta
Barranquilla
Cartagena
Magangué
SIERRA DE PERIJÁ
Medellín
CORDILLERA OCCIDENTAL
CORDILLERA CENTRAL
CORDILLERA ORIENTAL
Buenaventura
Popayán
Pasto
Tumaco
Ibarra
Quito
Esmeraldas
Bahía de Caráquez
Guayaquil
GOLFO DE GUAYAQUIL
Tumbes
Piura
Lambayeque Chiclayo
Cajamarca
Trujillo
Callao Lima
Huaraz
Cerro de Pasco
Arequipa
Mollendo
Tacna
Arica
Iquique

E C U A D O R
CHIMBORAZO
0° EQUATOR

PANAMÁ
CANAL ZONE
Colón
Panamá
Balboa

SOUTH

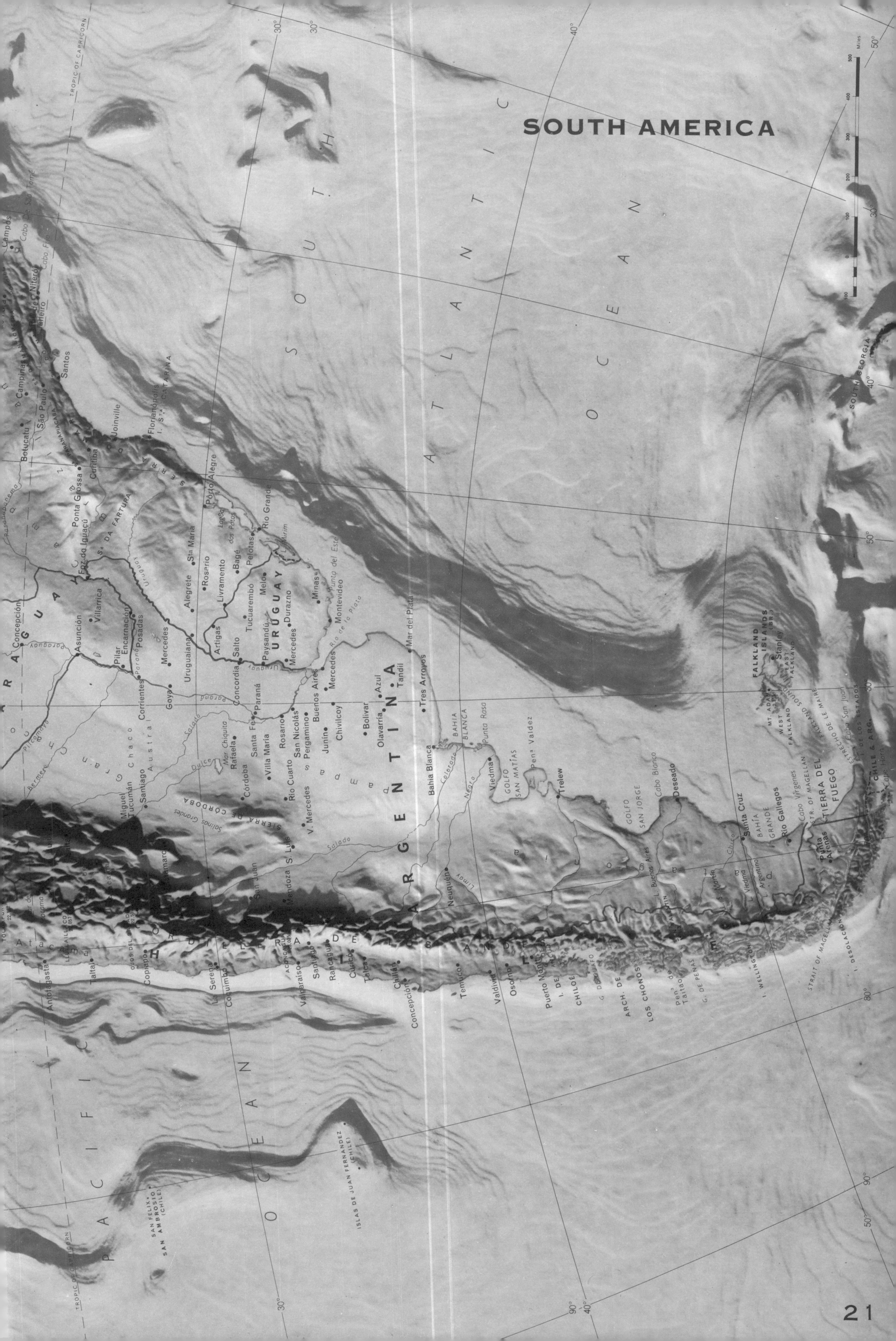

SOUTH AMERICA

Miles
500
400
300
200
100
0

SOUTH ATLANTIC OCEAN

SOUTH GEORGIA

FALKLAND ISLANDS (BR.)

Stanley
WEST FALKLAND
EAST FALKLAND

Campos
Cabo de São Tomé
Niterói
Cabo Frio

São Paulo
Botucatú
Santos
Campina

TROPIC OF CAPRICORN

Joinville
Curitiba
Ponta Grossa
Florianópolis
I. STA. CATARINA

Foz do Iguaçú
SERRA DA FARTURA
Villarrica

PARANÁ

Pôrto Alegre
Rio Grande
Bagé
Pelotas
Lagoa dos Patos
Sta. Maria
Rosario
Alegrete
Livramento
L. Mirim

PARAGUAY
Concepción
Asunción
Encarnación
Pilar
Posadas
Corrientes

URUGUAY
Artigas
Tucuarembó
Salto
Paysandú
Melo
Durazno
Minas
Mercedes
Montevideo
Punta del Este

Mercedes
Uruguaiana
Goya

Paraná
Santa Fe
Rafaela
Río de la Plata
Mar del Plata

ARGENTINA
Buenos Aires
Mercedes
Chivilcoy
San Nicolás
Pergamino
Junín
Rosario
Villa María
Bolívar
Olavarría
Azul
Tandil
Tres Arroyos

Miguel
Tucumán
Santiago
del Estero
Córdoba
Río Cuarto
V. Mercedes
SIERRA DE CÓRDOBA
Mar Chiquita
Dulce
Salado

San Juan
Mendoza
S. Luis
Neuquén
Limay

Bahía Blanca
BAHÍA BLANCA
Colorado
Punta Roja
Viedma
Negro
GOLFO SAN MATÍAS
Pen. Valdéz
Trelew
Cabo Blanco
GOLFO SAN JORGE
Deseado

Santa Cruz
BAHÍA GRANDE
Río Gallegos
Cabo Vírgenes
STR. OF MAGELLAN

TIERRA DEL FUEGO
CHILE & ARG.
Punta Arenas

CORDILLERA DE LOS ANDES

Copiapó
Serena
Coquimbo
Valparaíso
Santiago
Rancagua
Curicó
Talca
Chillán
Concepción
Temuco
Valdivia
Osorno
Puerto Montt
I. DE CHILOÉ
CHILOÉ
ARCH. DE LOS CHONOS
Pen. de Taitao
G. DE PENAS
G. de San Martín
STRAIT OF MAGELLAN

Antofagasta
Taltal

SAN FÉLIX
SAN AMBROSIO (CHILE)

ISLAS DE JUAN FERNÁNDEZ (CHILE)

PACIFIC OCEAN

TROPIC OF CAPRICORN

21

AUSTRALASIA

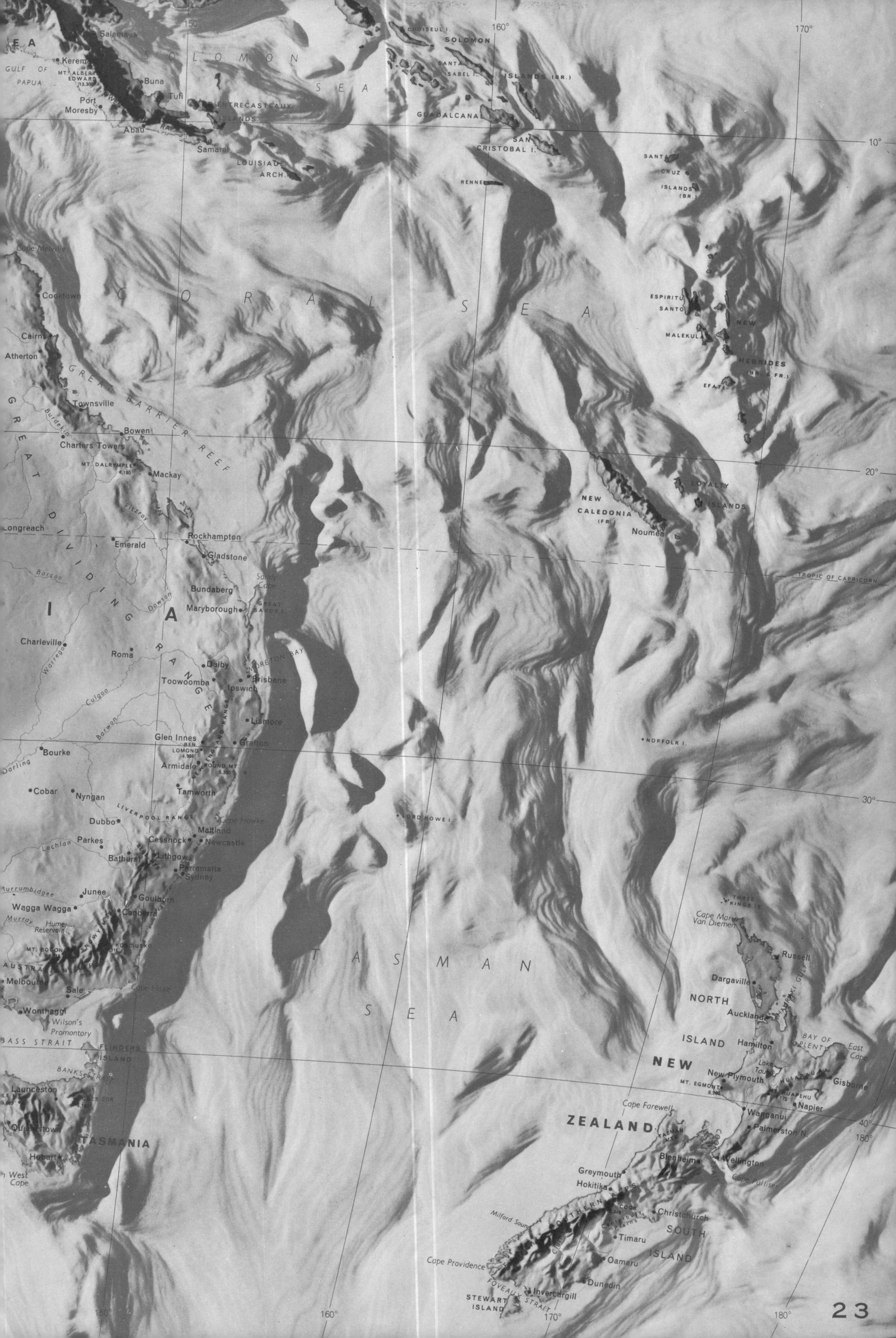

THE FAR EAST

NORTHERN AFRICA

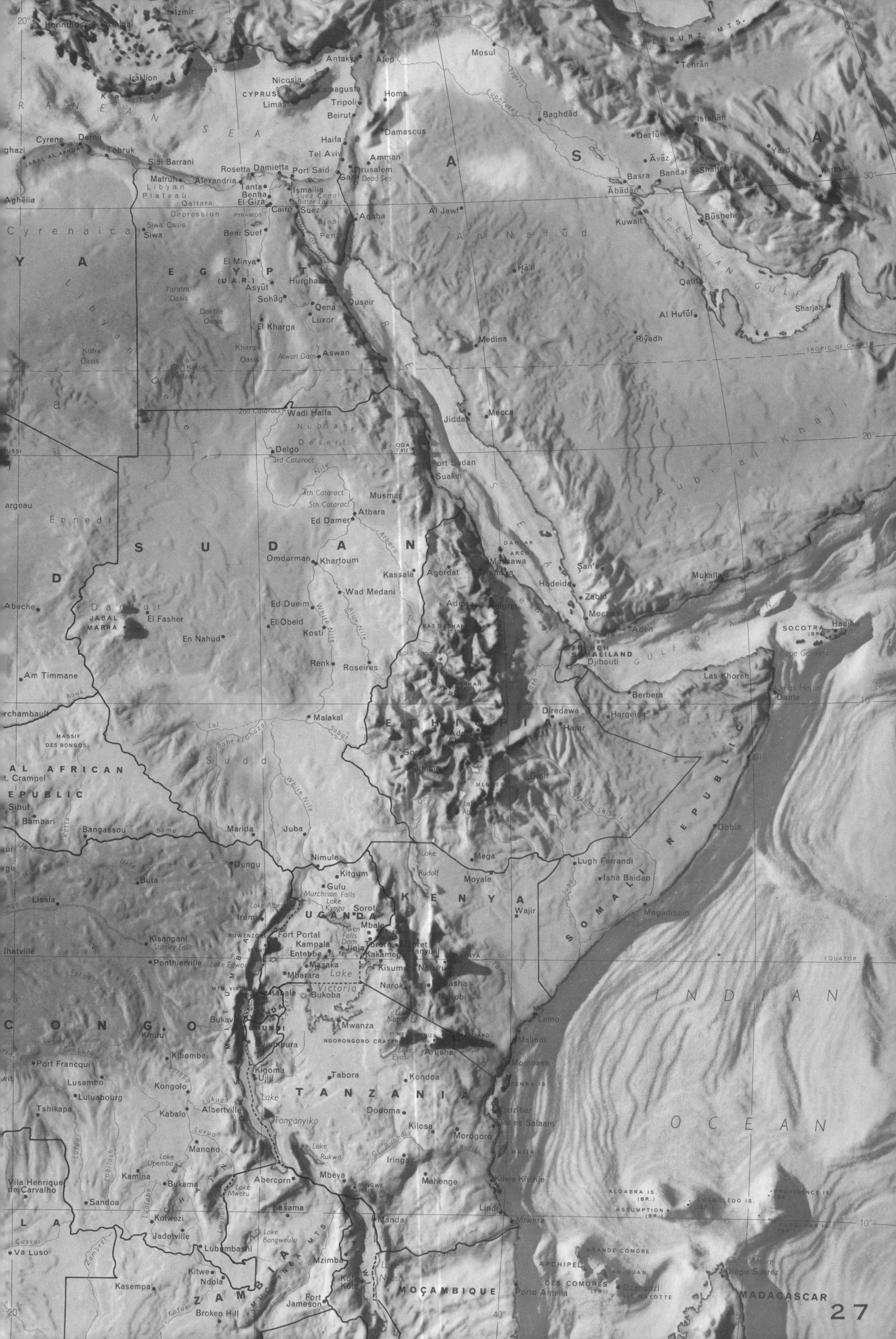

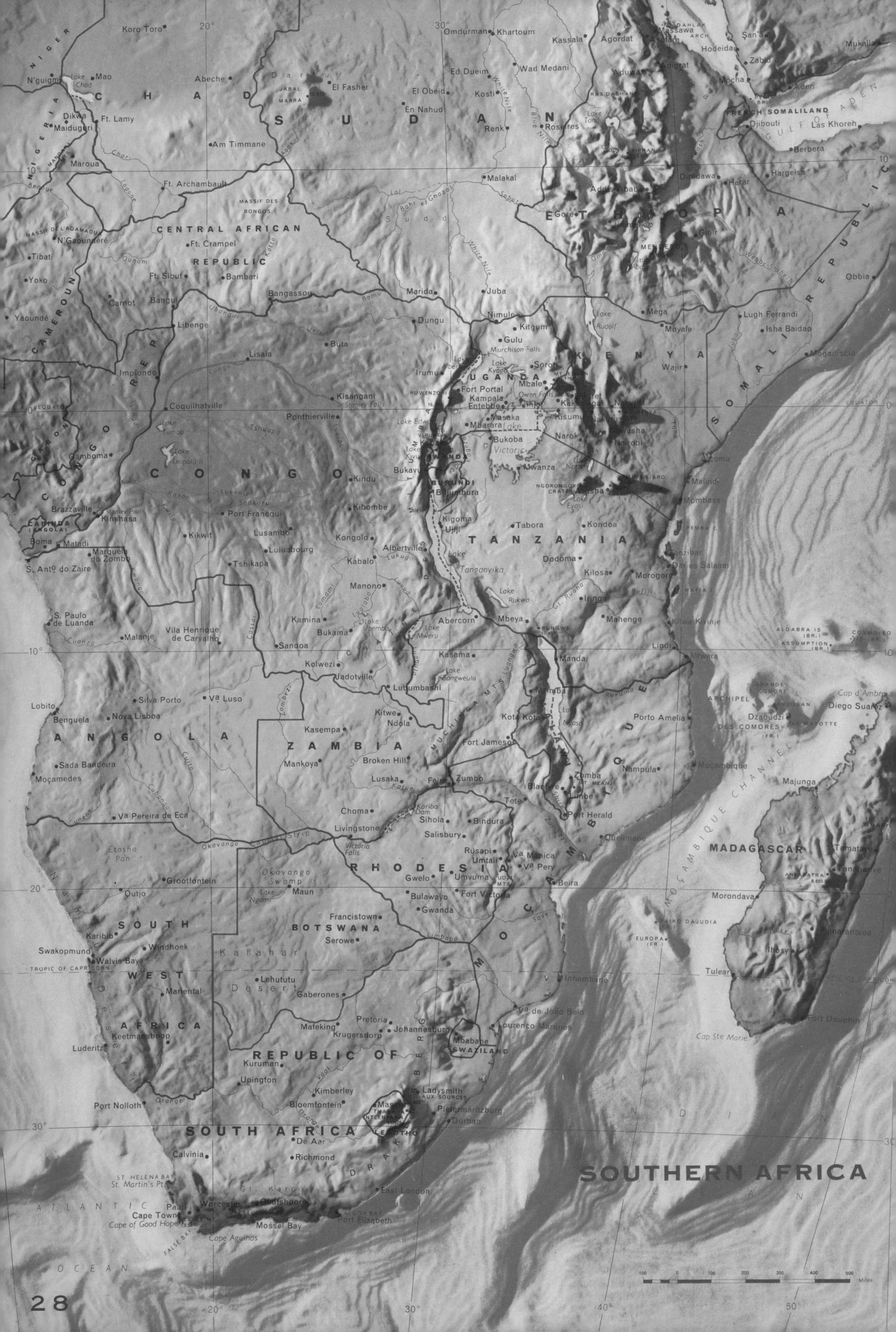

THE COUNTRIES OF THE WORLD

CONTENTS

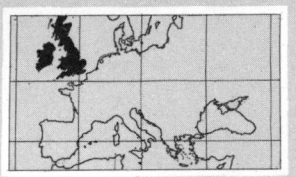

THE BRITISH ISLES

UNITED KINGDOM (ENGLAND: SCOTLAND: WALES: N. IRELAND)
AREA: *94,207 sq. miles.* POPULATION: *54,965,000.*
ENGLAND AREA: *50,327 sq. miles.* POPULATION: *45,374,000.*
WALES AREA: *8,016 sq. miles.* POPULATION: *2,701,000.*

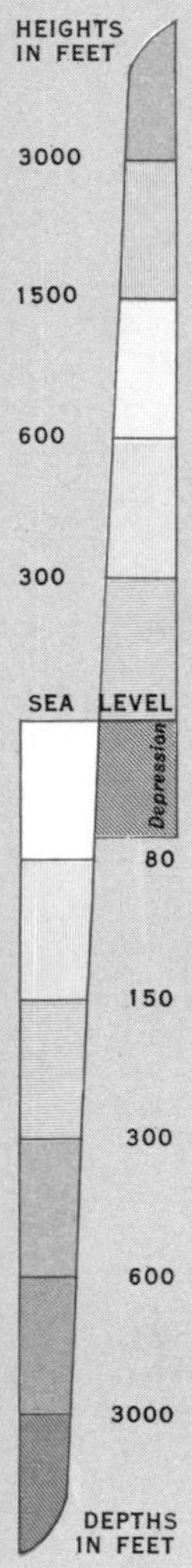

HEIGHTS IN FEET
3000
1500
600
300
SEA LEVEL
Depression
80
150
300
600
3000
DEPTHS IN FEET

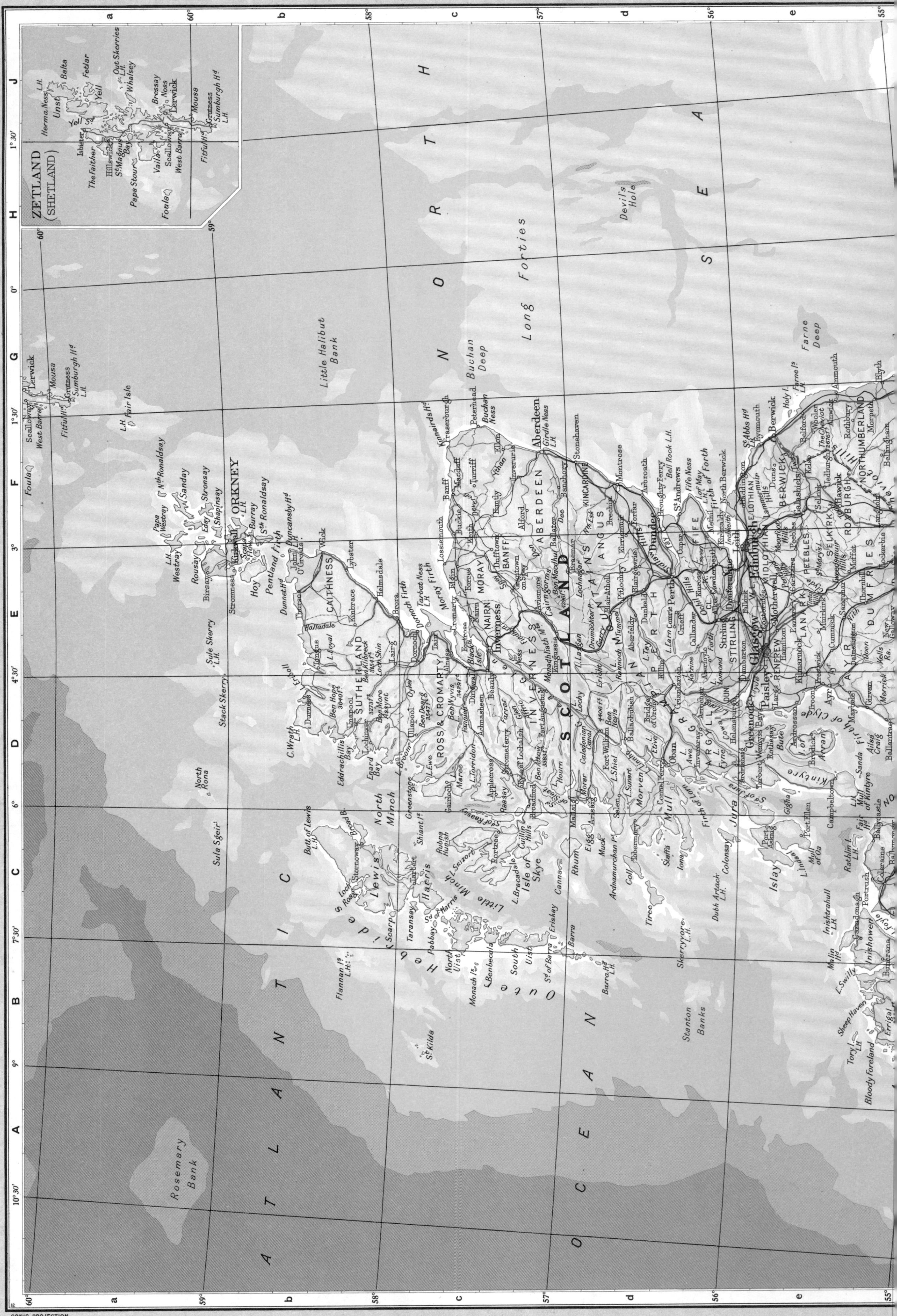

ZETLAND (SHETLAND)
ORKNEY
SCOTLAND
N O R T H S E A
A T L A N T I C O C E A N
Long Forties
Rosemary Bank

CONIC PROJECTION

SCALE: 1 INCH TO 39 MILES

MAIN ROADS
RAILWAYS

The British Isles, having regard to their relatively small area, show a structural variety matched by few European countries. A line drawn north-eastwards from the Exe to the Tees roughly separates Great Britain's ancient uplands (stretching from the Scottish Highlands to the moors of Devon and Cornwall) from the more recent rock formations found in the gentler slopes of the Cotswolds and Chilterns, East Anglia and the Weald. Signs of a one-time connection with the Continent are evident in the south, the fens of East Anglia having their counterpart in the low-lying flats of the Netherlands, and the chalk cliffs of Dover and the granitic cliffs of Cornwall in the coast of northern France.

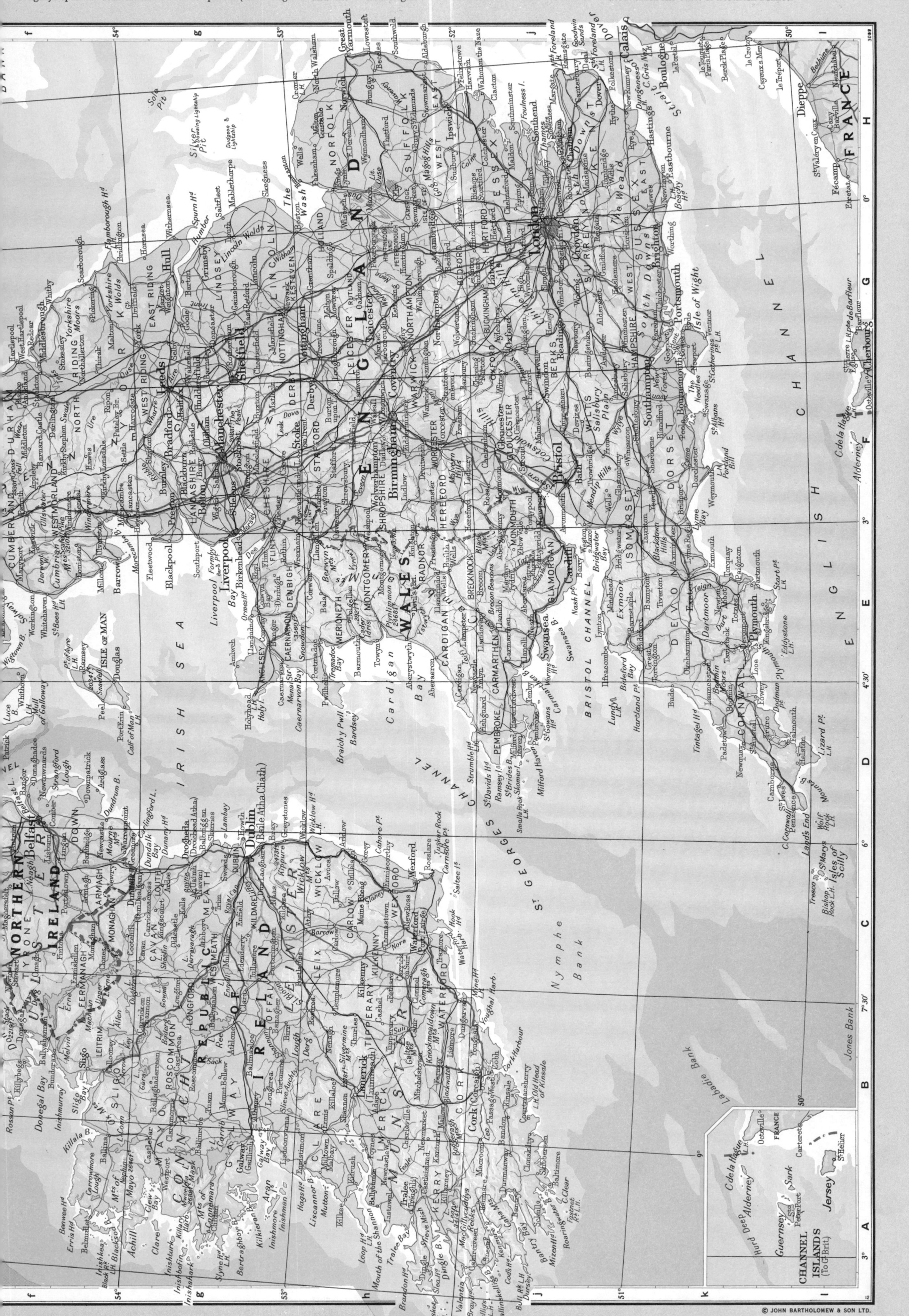

SCALE IN MILES

STATE BOUNDARY
COUNTY BOUNDARIES

© JOHN BARTHOLOMEW & SON LTD.

SCALE: 1 INCH TO 39 MILES

31

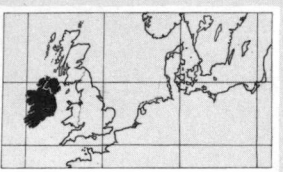

IRELAND

NORTHERN IRELAND AREA: 5,459 sq. miles. POPULATION: 1,484,000. CAPITAL: Belfast (population: 402,900). REPUBLIC OF IRELAND AREA: 27,135 sq. miles. POPULATION: 2,880,752. CAPITAL: Dublin (population: 568,271).

By comparison with England and Wales, Ireland is fairly compact in shape. Apart from the stretch of coast running from Dundalk Bay to Dublin, the island is almost entirely surrounded by uplands which, especially

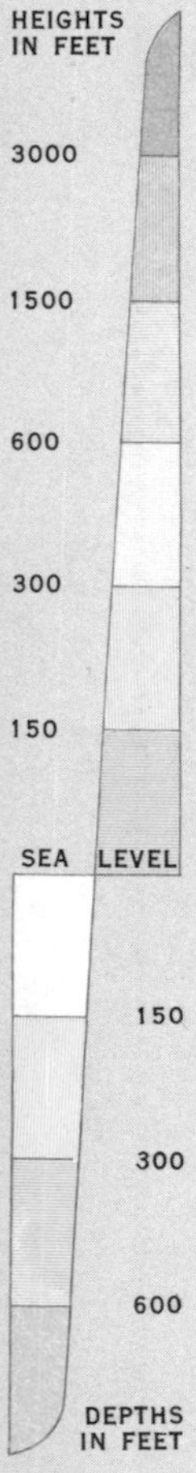

HEIGHTS IN FEET

3000

1500

600

300

150

SEA LEVEL

150

300

600

DEPTHS IN FEET

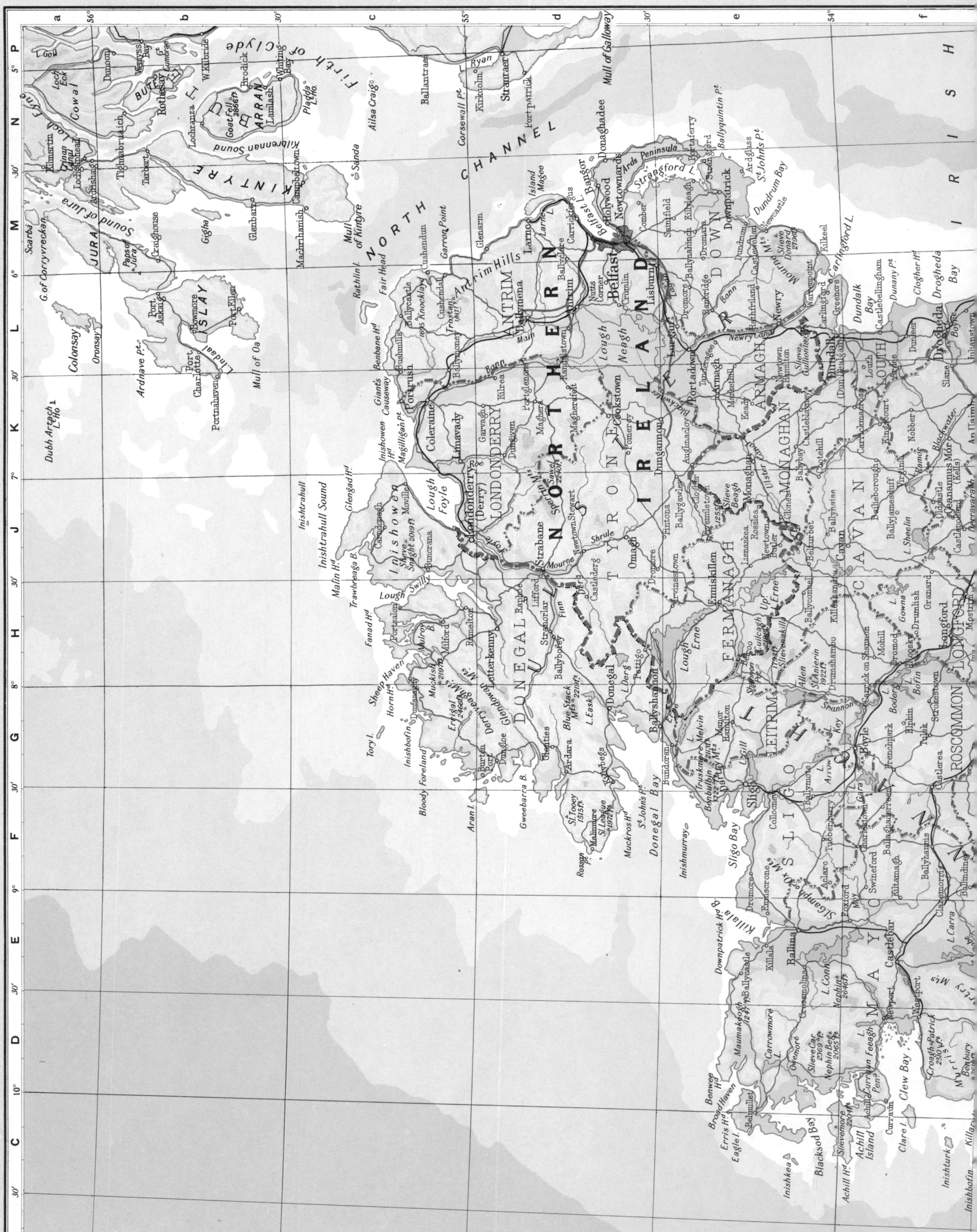

32

CONIC PROJECTION

SCALE: 1 INCH TO 20 MILES

MAIN ROADS

RAILWAYS

on the jagged west coast, often rise sheer from the sea. Inside this upland enclosure is an extensive lowland area covered with lakes, moors, and low-lying bogland; though even this region is interrupted by groups of hills. The land level of the plain is low, averaging about 300 feet above the sea. The Shannon (240 miles long) is Ireland's principal river and the longest in the British Isles. Draining the central plain, the river flows southwards through a series of loughs before reaching the huge estuary by which it flows into the Atlantic. The Shannon estuary is one of a number of rias, or drowned river valleys, which cut far into Ireland's west coast.

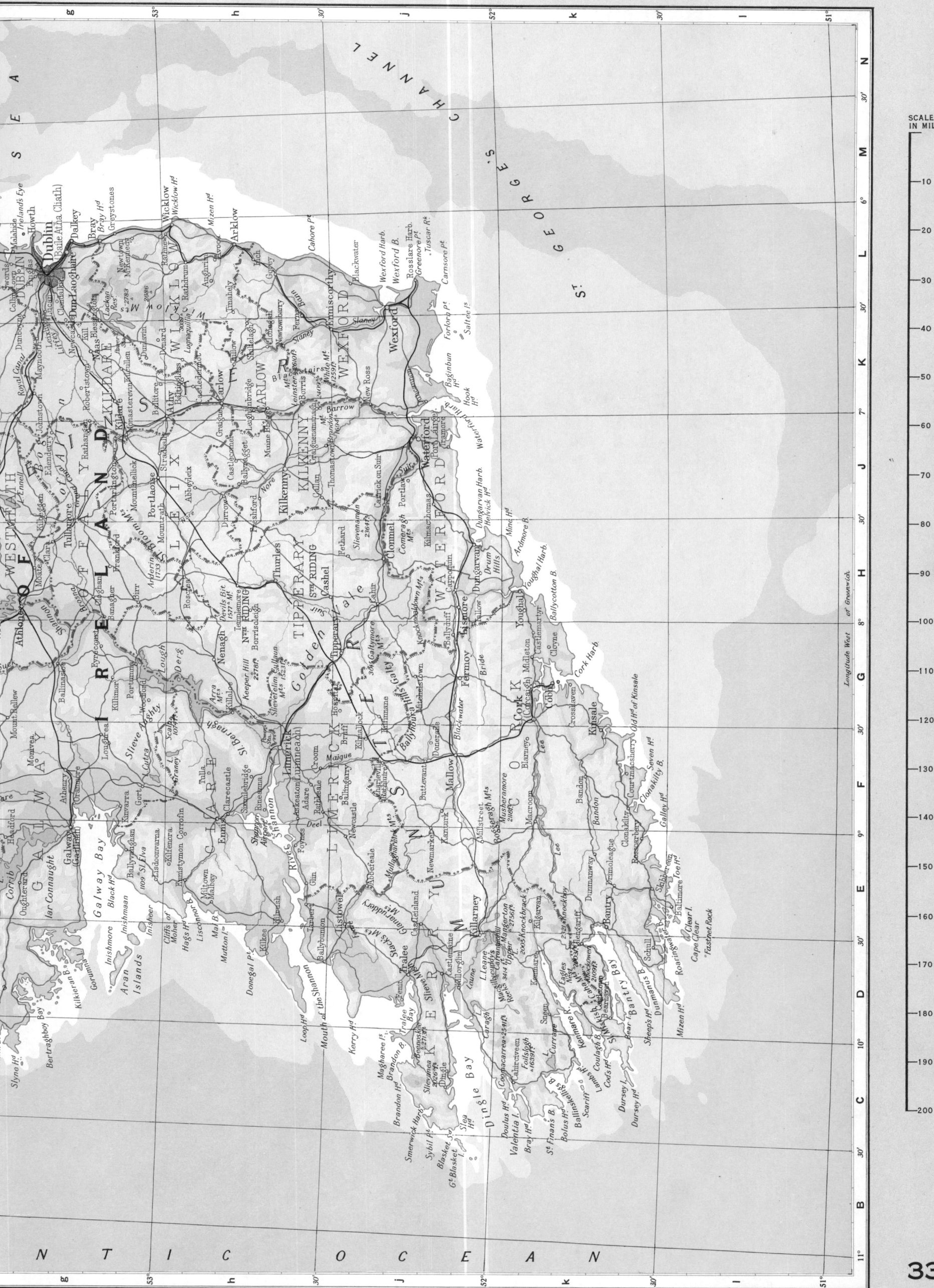

STATE BOUNDARY

COUNTY BOUNDARIES

SCALE: 1 INCH TO 20 MILES

SCALE IN MILES

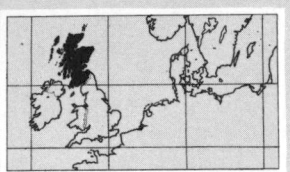

SCOTLAND

AREA: *30,405 sq. miles.* POPULATION: *5,190,800.*
CAPITAL: *Edinburgh (population: 468,765).*
Other principal towns with populations: GLASGOW
(979,798), ABERDEEN *(183,463).*

The map shows a narrow finger of land, mainly
upland, stretching northwards from the Cheviots.
In the north, the Highlands (Ben Nevis, 4,406
feet, is the highest peak in the British Isles)

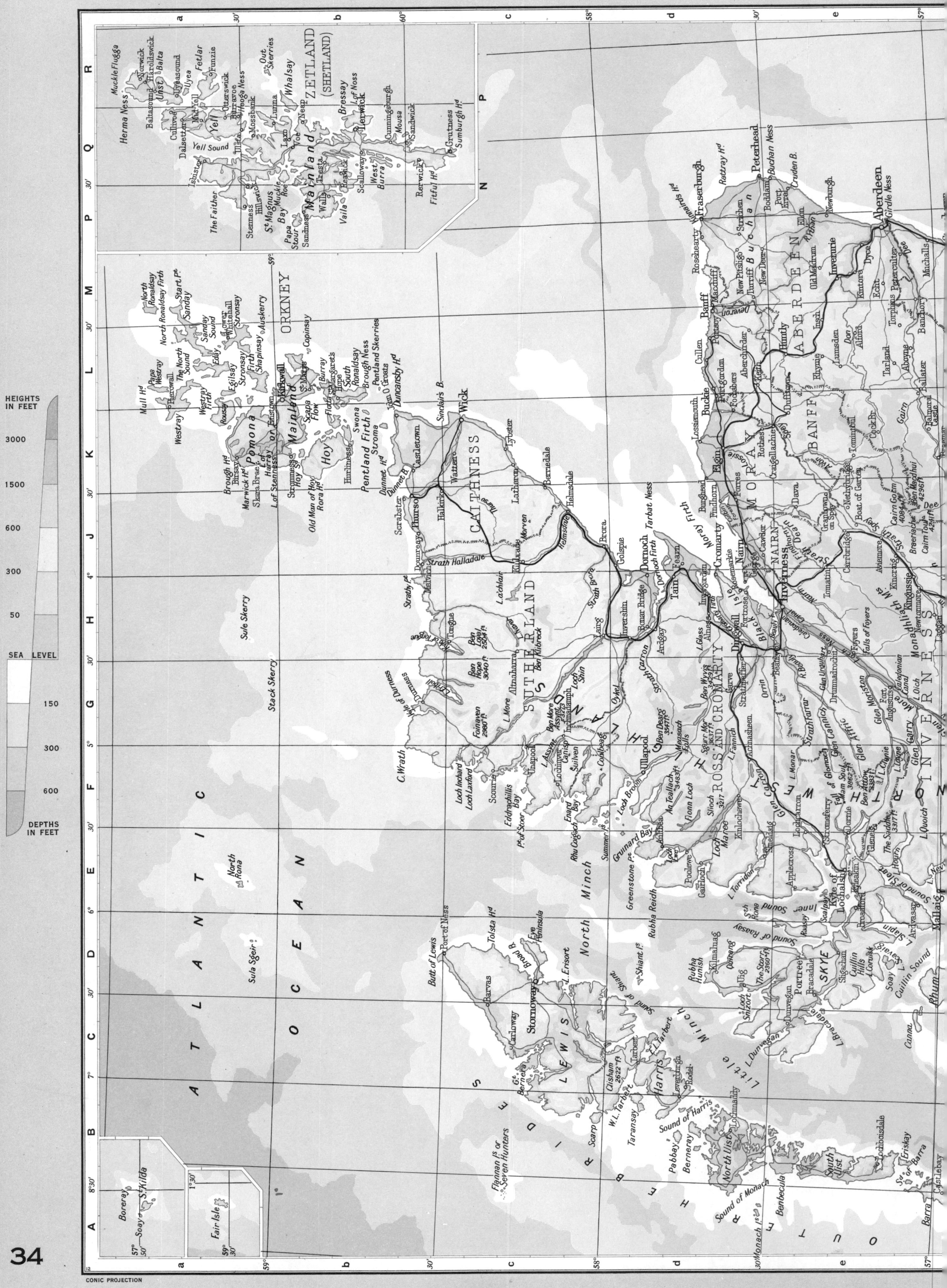

**HEIGHTS
IN FEET**

3000

1500

600

300

50

SEA LEVEL

150

300

600

**DEPTHS
IN FEET**

34

CONIC PROJECTION

SCALE: 1 INCH TO 20 MILES

MAIN ROADS

RAILWAYS

occupy nearly two-thirds of Scotland's total area. The Central Lowlands, where the Firth of Clyde reaches to within 30 miles of the Firth of Forth to which it is connected by canal, separate the Highlands from a third region, the Southern Uplands. The North West Highlands are separated from the rest by Lochs Linnhe, Lochy and Ness, which are connected by the Caledonian Canal to the Moray Firth to make another waterway stretching right across the country. The northern and western coasts are fringed by many islands and islets—to the north the Orkneys numbering 90, the Shetlands, 50 miles farther north, numbering about 100, and on the west the Hebrides, a group of more than 500.

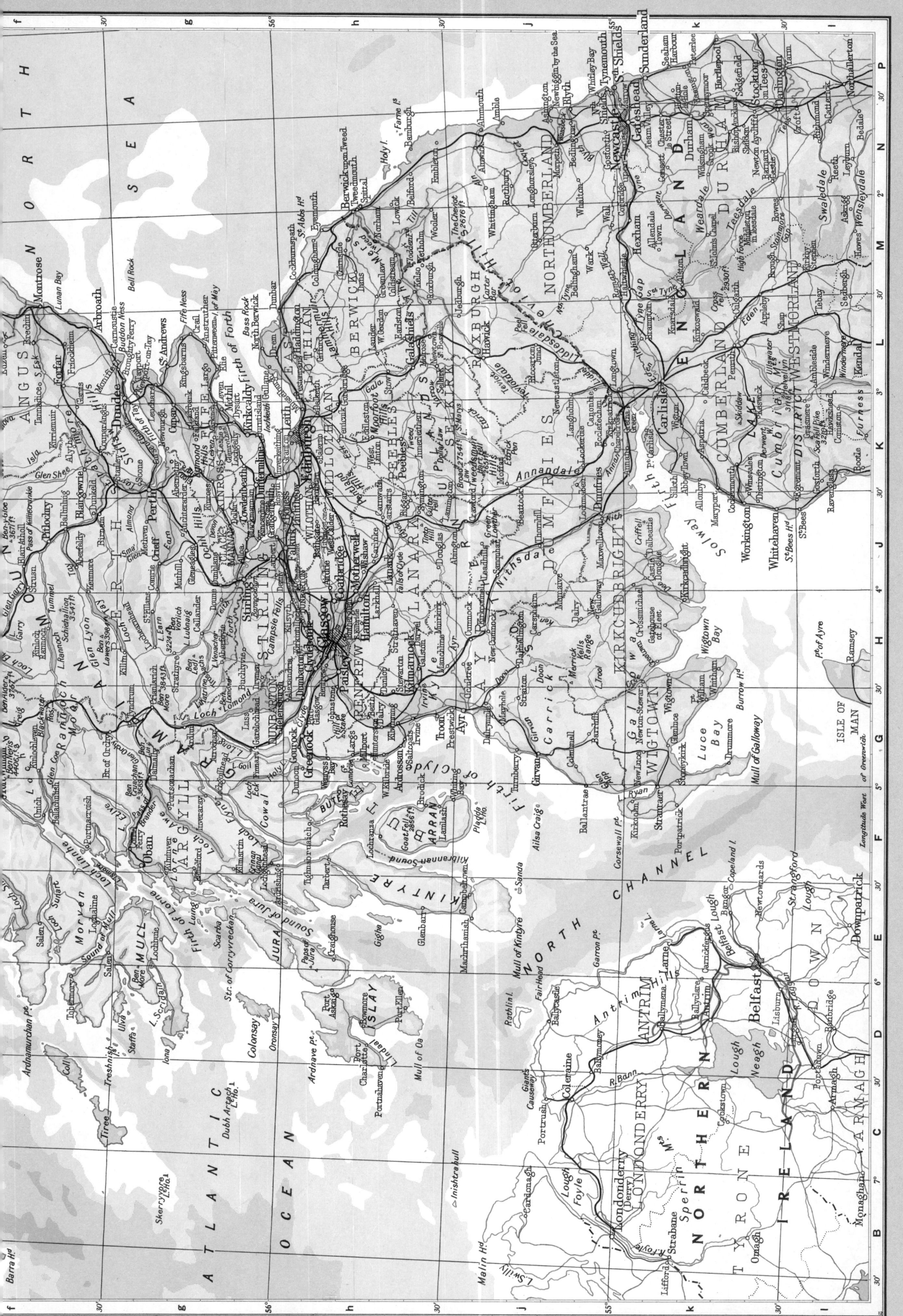

SCALE IN MILES

35

COUNTY BOUNDARIES

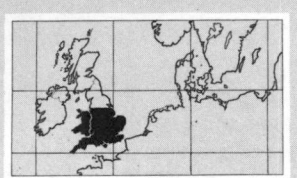

SOUTH ENGLAND AND WALES

Principal towns, with populations: LONDON
(Greater London Council Area): 7,913,600.
BIRMINGHAM: 1,101,440.   BRISTOL: 429,020.
NOTTINGHAM: 310,280.   CARDIFF: 259,700.

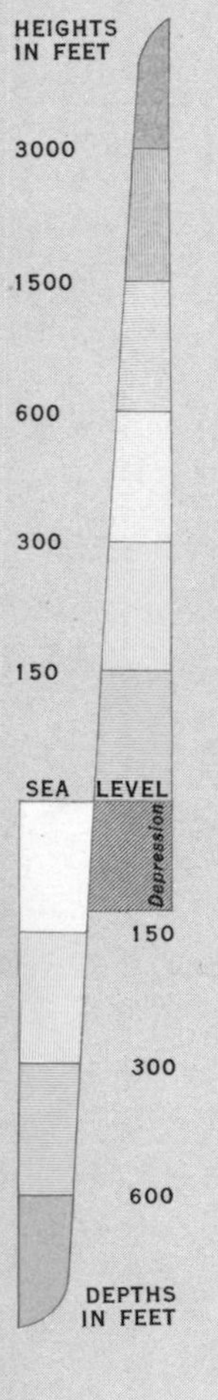

HEIGHTS
IN FEET

3000
1500
600
300
150
SEA LEVEL
Depression
150
300
600
DEPTHS
IN FEET

36

CONIC PROJECTION

12
3089

SCALE: 1 INCH TO 20 MILES

MAIN ROAD
RAILWAY

Peninsulas, such as that of Cornwall and Devon and the two arms of Wales, together with the great estuaries of the Severn, the Thames and the Wash, give this map its unmistakable shape. From the Welsh mountains (Snowdon, 3,560 feet, is the highest peak in England and Wales) the land slopes eastwards to the Fens of East Anglia, parts of which are below sea level. Fanning out from Salisbury Plain, in the south, are the lines of chalk hills that become the Chilterns, in Oxfordshire and Buckinghamshire, the North Downs, in Surrey and Kent, and the South Downs, in Sussex. Across the centre of the map, from south-west to north-east, runs the limestone belt of the Cotswolds.

SCALE IN MILES

COUNTY BOUNDARIES

SCALE: 1 INCH TO 20 MILES

© JOHN BARTHOLOMEW & SON LTD.

37

NORTH ENGLAND

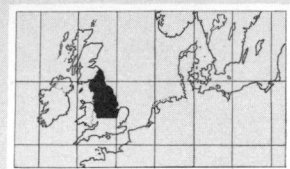

Principal towns, with populations: LIVERPOOL: 712,040. MANCHESTER: 625,250. LEEDS: 508,000. SHEFFIELD: 486,490. HULL: 298,000.

Prominent on this map are the Pennine Chain, and its two spurs forming the Lake District and the Cheviot Hills. From this central watershed flow the famous rivers of the north: the Tyne, Tees, Ouse and Trent to the east, and the Mersey to the west.

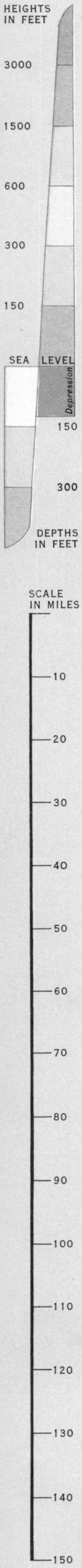

HEIGHTS IN FEET
3000
1500
600
300
150
SEA LEVEL
150
300
DEPTHS IN FEET

SCALE IN MILES
10
20
30
40
50
60
70
80
90
100
110
120
130
140
150

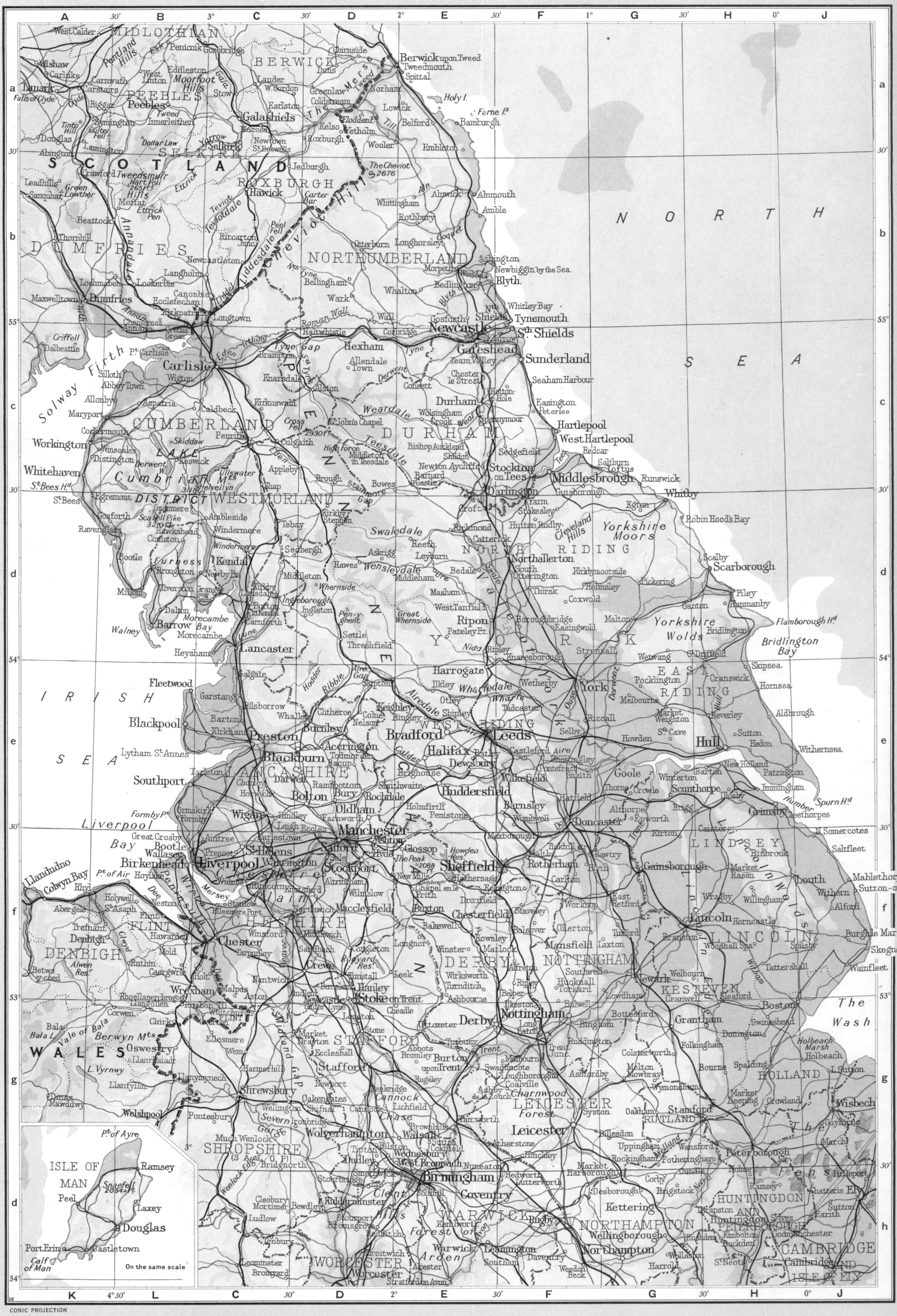

ISLE OF MAN
On the same scale

38

CONIC PROJECTION

SCALE: 1 INCH TO 20 MILES

MAIN ROADS
COUNTY BOUNDARIES
RAILWAYS

THE ARCTIC

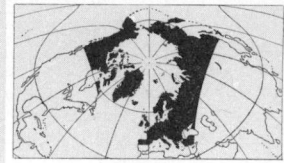

The Asian and North American continents almost meet at the narrow and shallow Bering Strait, only 45 miles across. Between them lies the Arctic Ocean, nearly enclosed and always covered with drifting ice. Another outstanding feature of this map is the high plateau of Greenland, covered with ice up to 11,000 feet thick, yet reaching down to the same latitude as Oslo and Leningrad.

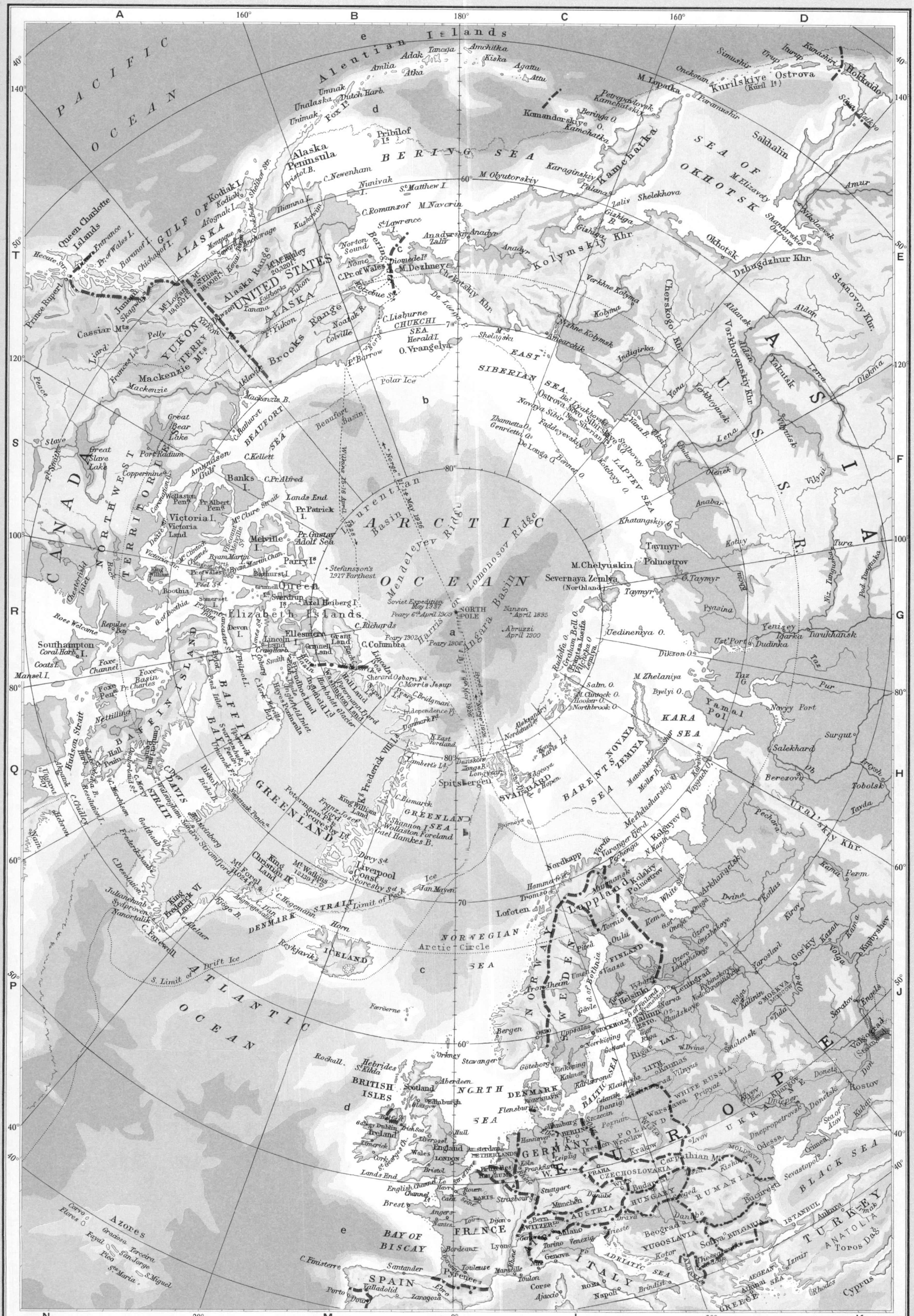

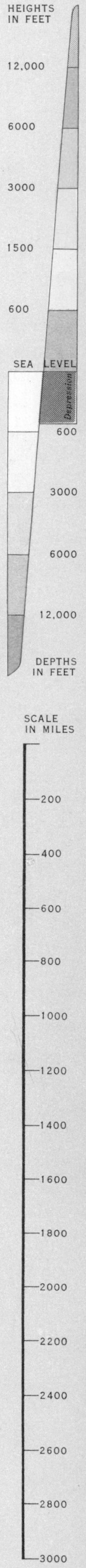

HEIGHTS IN FEET

12,000
6000
3000
1500
600
SEA LEVEL
Depression
600
3000
6000
12,000
DEPTHS IN FEET

SCALE IN MILES

200
400
600
800
1000
1200
1400
1600
1800
2000
2200
2400
2600
2800
3000

39

LAMBERT'S AZIMUTHAL EQUAL-AREA PROJECTION

INTERNATIONAL BOUNDARIES

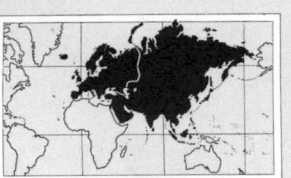

EURASIA

This vast land mass—the largest in the world—covers more than a quarter of the Earth's land surface and is inhabited by over three-quarters of its population. Across the whole area, from the Pyrénées to the backbone of W. Malaysia, runs an almost continuous belt of fold mountains, of which the highest, the Himalayas (Everest,

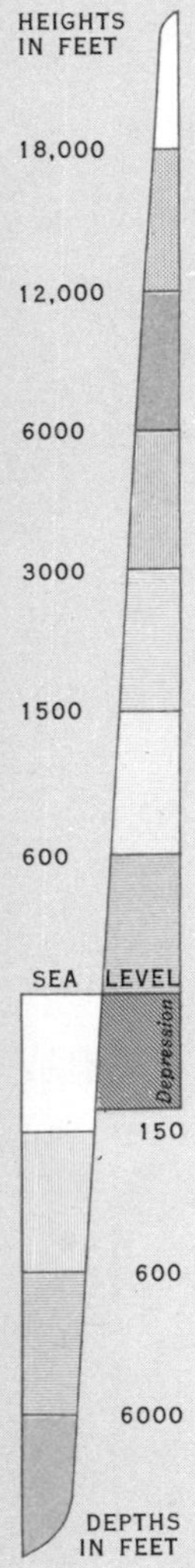

HEIGHTS
IN FEET

18,000

12,000

6000

3000

1500

600

SEA LEVEL

Depression

150

600

6000

DEPTHS
IN FEET

40

LAMBERT'S AZIMUTHAL EQUAL-AREA PROJECTION

SCALE: 1 INCH TO 474 MILES

INTERNATIONAL BOUNDARIES

STATE BOUNDARIES

29,028 feet), form a central branch. There is also an undersea range fringing the east as a chain of islands from the Aleutians south to the Philippines. Contrasting with the central highlands are the immense low-lying plains of northern Russia, while in between lies a great zone of desert stretching from Mongolia to Arabia. From the frozen tundra of the Arctic to the dense rain forests of W. Malaysia, there is every type of climate and soil, and for climatic reasons the population centres are mainly in the west, south and south-east. In India, for instance, the average population density is 392 per square mile; in Siberia it is less than five.

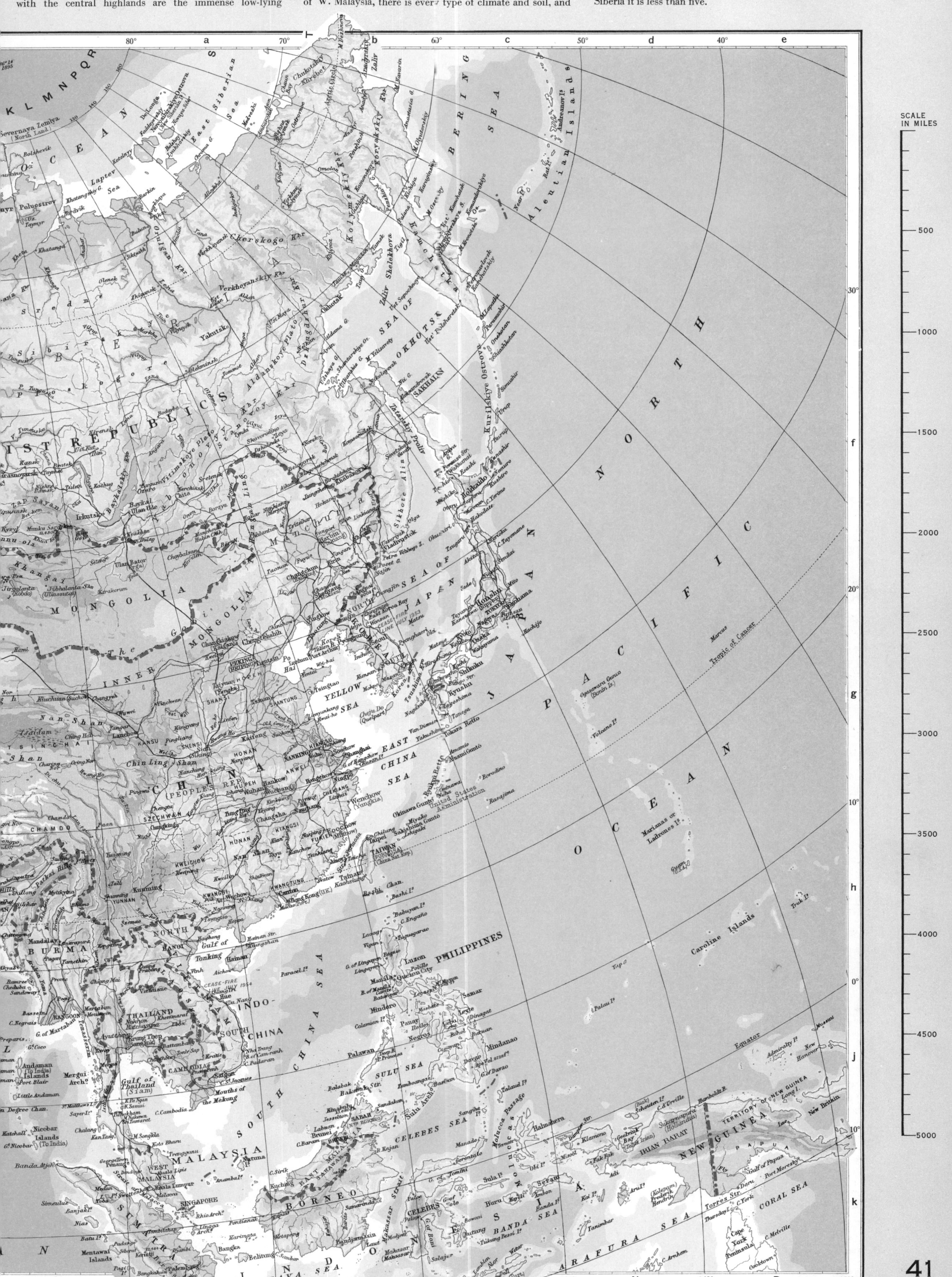

SCALE: 1 INCH TO 474 MILES

41

© JOHN BARTHOLOMEW & SON LTD.

EUROPE

Itself a peninsula of Asia, Europe is made up of smaller peninsulas such as Scandinavia, Iberia, Italy and Greece. Characteristic of these countries are north-south backbones of mountains, some of them offshoots of the great chain of fold mountains that winds across the entire continent from the Pyrénées to the Black Sea.

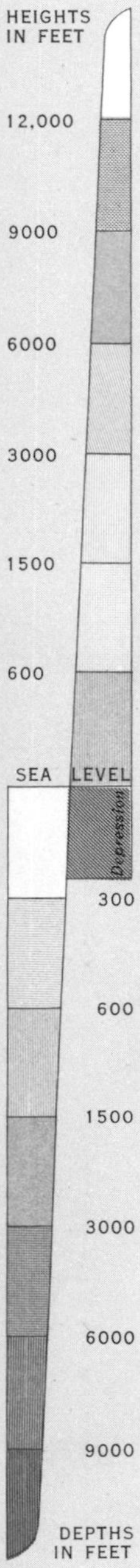

HEIGHTS
IN FEET

12,000
9000
6000
3000
1500
600
SEA LEVEL
Depression
300
600
1500
3000
6000
9000

DEPTHS
IN FEET

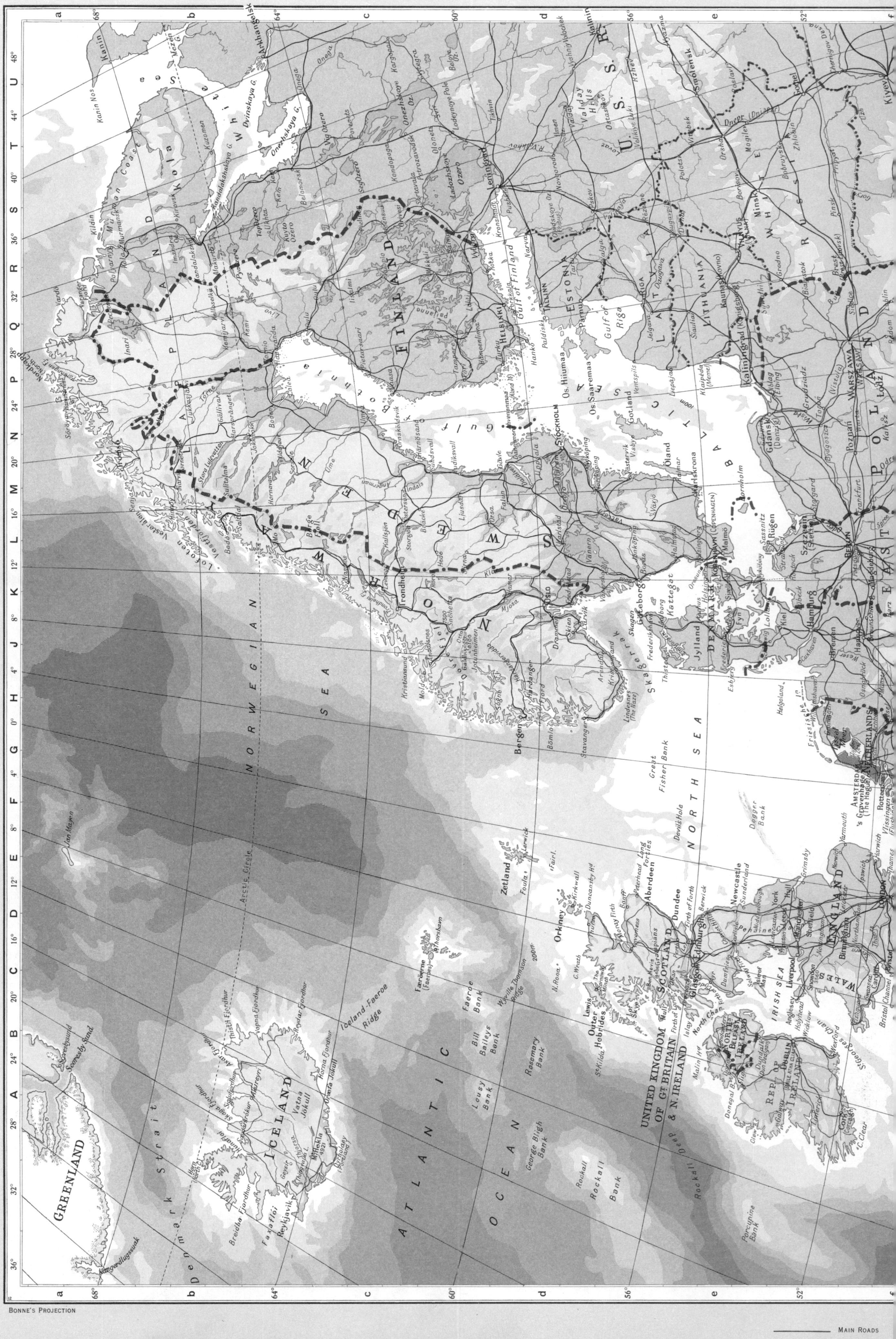

BONNE'S PROJECTION

SCALE: 1 INCH TO 158 MILES

MAIN ROADS
RAILWAYS

This east-west axis separates the other two major features of the map: the broad North European Plain stretching from Ireland to Russia, and the two basins of the Mediterranean, each as deep as the mountains are high.

This relatively small continent contains many striking geographical contrasts which are paralleled by the diversity of its peoples and cultures, among them the great Greek and Roman civilizations from which the whole world has

derived so much. The maritime outlook prevalent in the western areas of Europe led to the great explorations that took these people and their cultures to the farthest corners of the Earth.

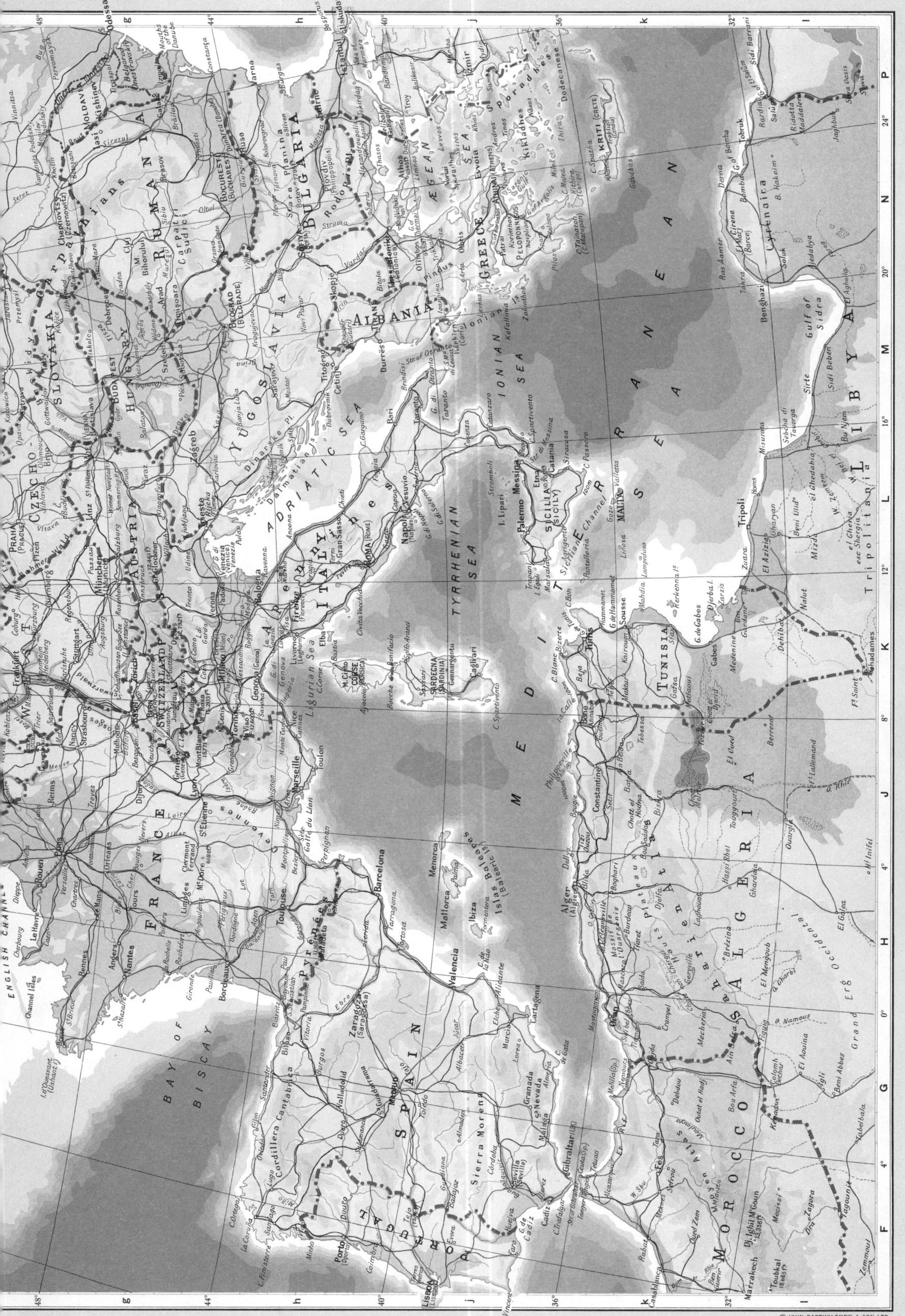

INTERNATIONAL BOUNDARIES

STATE BOUNDARIES

SCALE: 1 INCH TO 158 MILES

SCALE IN MILES

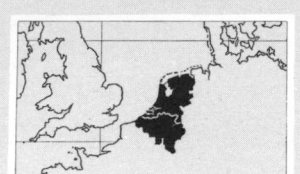

THE LOW COUNTRIES   BELGIUM, NETHERLANDS, LUXEMBOURG

BELGIUM AREA: *11,779 sq. miles.* POPULATION: *9,528,000.* CAPITAL: *Brussels.* CURRENCY: *100 centimes=1 franc.*

NETHERLANDS AREA: *12,978 sq. miles.* POPULATION: *12,455,000.* CAPITAL: *Amsterdam.* (GOVT. *The Hague.*) CURRENCY: *100 cents=1 guilder.*

LUXEMBOURG AREA: *998 sq. miles.* POPULATION: *335,000.* CAPITAL: *Luxembourg.* CURRENCY: *100 centimes=1 franc.*

HEIGHTS IN FEET

1500
600
300
60
SEA LEVEL
Depression
80
DEPTHS IN FEET

SCALE IN MILES

10
20
30
40
50
60
70
80
90
100
110
120
130
140
150

44

CONIC PROJECTION

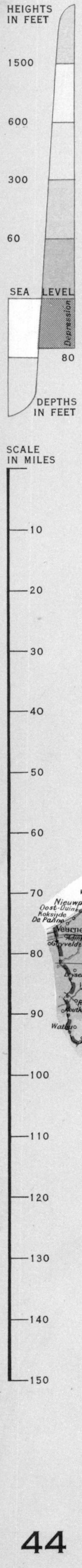

SCALE: 1 INCH TO 20 MILES

—————— INTERNATIONAL BOUNDARIES

------------ STATE BOUNDARIES

SWITZERLAND

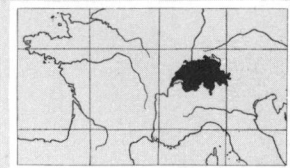

AREA: *15,941 sq. miles.* POPULATION: *5,945,000.*
CAPITAL: *Berne.* CURRENCY: *100 centimes=1
franc.* The Swiss Alps, rising to 15,203 feet

(Monte Rosa), cover more than half of Switzerland, making it the most mountainous country
in Europe. The country is divided into three

belts, running north-east to south-west, by the
broad valley of the Aare and the narrower one of
the Upper Rhein and Upper Rhône.

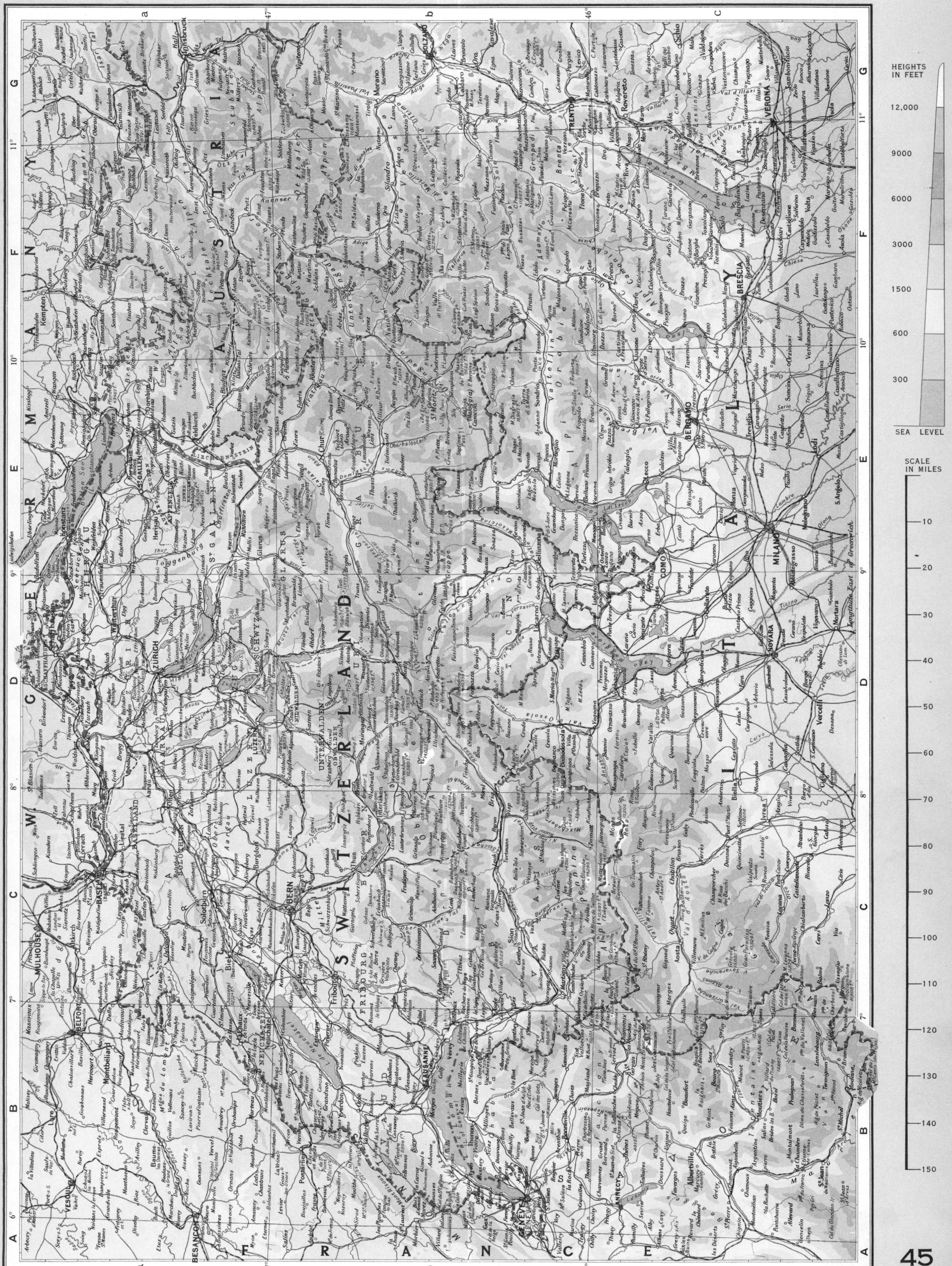

HEIGHTS
IN FEET

12,000

9000

6000

3000

1500

600

300

SEA LEVEL

SCALE
IN MILES

10
20
30
40
50
60
70
80
90
100
110
120
130
140
150

MAIN ROADS
RAILWAYS

CONIC PROJECTION

SCALE: 1 INCH TO 20 MILES

45

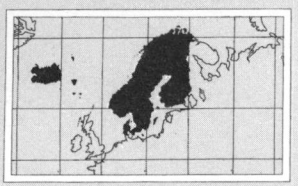

SCANDINAVIA AND BALTIC

NORWAY, SWEDEN, DENMARK, FINLAND, WITH ICELAND

NORWAY AREA: *125,198 sq. miles.* POPULATION: *3,753,000*
CAPITAL: *Oslo.* CURRENCY: *100 öre=1 krone.*
SWEDEN AREA *173,634 sq. miles.* POPULATION: *7,808,000.*
CAPITAL: *Stockholm.* CURRENCY: *100 öre=1 krona.*
From the backbone of mountains shared by Norway

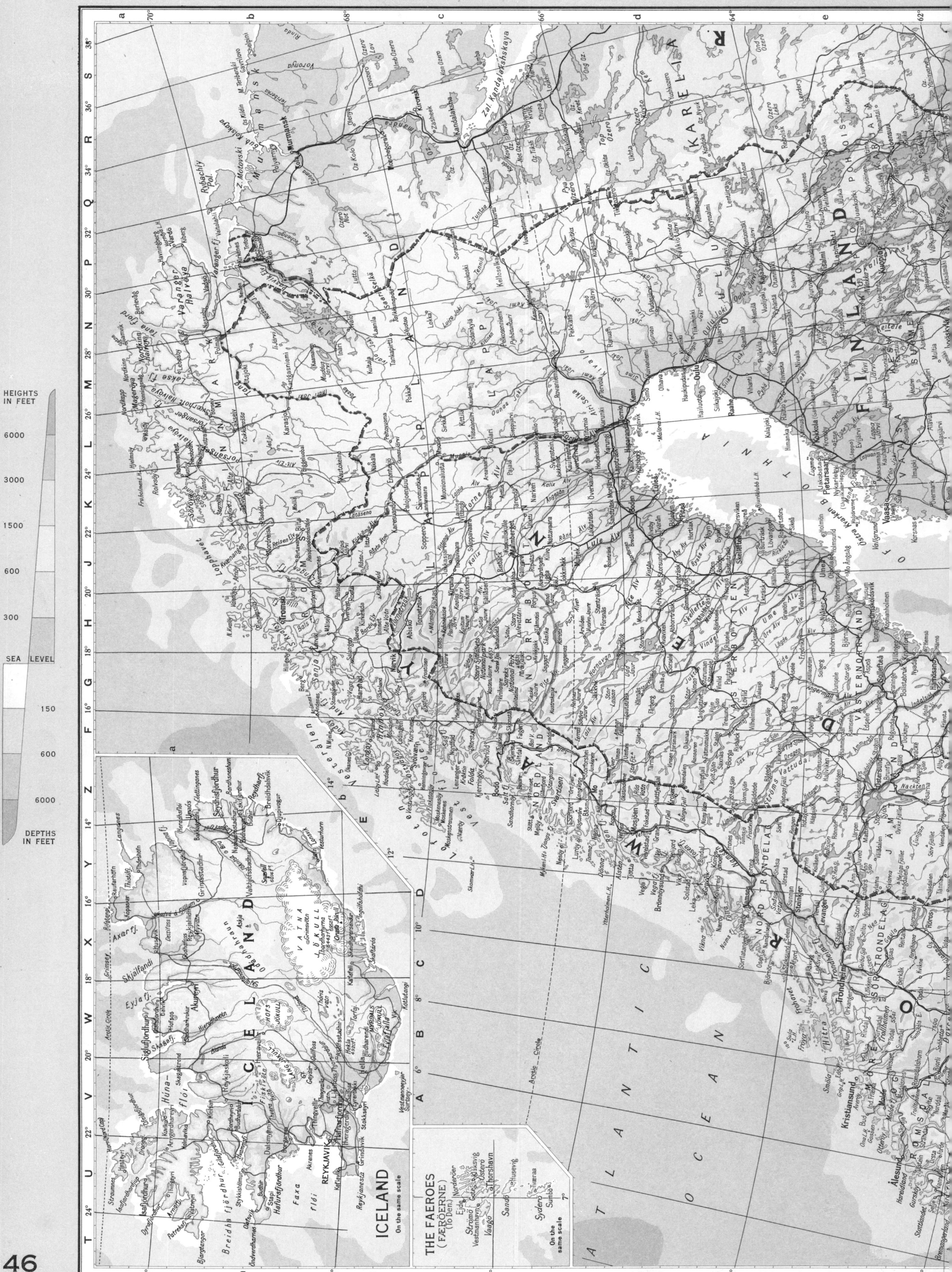

HEIGHTS
IN FEET

6000
3000
1500
600
300
SEA LEVEL
150
600
6000

DEPTHS
IN FEET

ICELAND
On the same scale

THE FAEROES
(FÆRÖERNE)
(To Den.)
On the same scale

CONIC PROJECTION

46

SCALE: 1 INCH TO 71 MILES

————— MAIN ROADS
————— RAILWAYS

and Sweden come rivers that feed the many lakes on both sides. Norway continues as a high, rugged plateau, falling abruptly to a coastline broken by fjords and islands. Sweden, low-lying in the south, is better suited to cultivation and settlement.

DENMARK AREA: *16,619 sq. miles.* POPULATION: *4,797,000.* CAPITAL: *Copenhagen.* CURRENCY: *100 øre=1 krone.* Smallest and lowest-lying of the Scandinavian countries, Denmark rarely rises more than 500 feet above sea level. Besides the peninsula of Jutland, it comprises the four main islands of Zealand, Fünen, Lolland and Falster.

FINLAND AREA: *130,119 sq. miles.* POPULATION: *4,639,000.* CAPITAL: *Helsinki.* CURRENCY: *100 pennis=1 markka.*

ICELAND AREA: *39,768 sq. miles.* POPULATION: *195,000.* CAPITAL: *Reykjavik.* CURRENCY: *100 aurar=1 króna.*

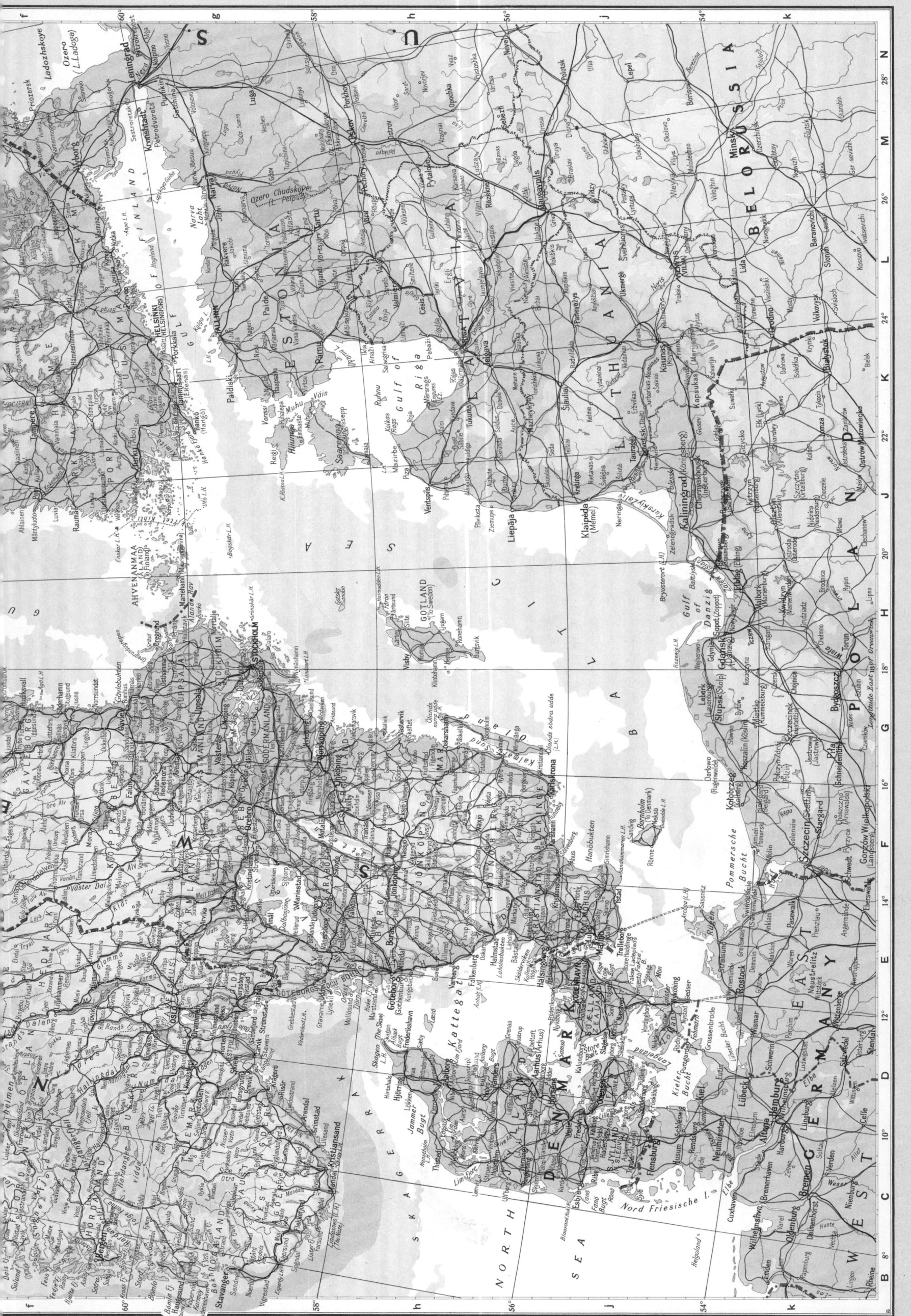

SCALE IN MILES

© JOHN BARTHOLOMEW & SON LTD.

47

SCALE: 1 INCH TO 71 MILES

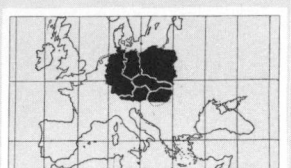

CENTRAL EUROPE

GERMANY, POLAND, CZECHOSLOVAKIA, AUSTRIA

GERMANY (Fed. Republic) AREA: 95,913 sq. miles. POPULATION: 59,676,000. CAPITAL: *Bonn.* CURRENCY: 100 Pfennige = 1 Deutsche Mark.
EAST GERMANY AREA: 41,634 sq. miles. POPULATION: 17,067,000. CAPITAL: *East Berlin.* CURRENCY: 100 Pfennige = 1 DM Ost.
Germany is highest in the south, where the Bavarian Alps form a bound-

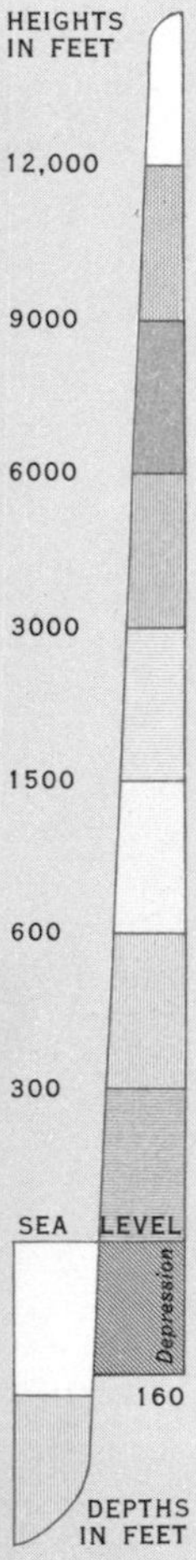

HEIGHTS IN FEET

12,000
9000
6000
3000
1500
600
300
SEA LEVEL
Depression
160
DEPTHS IN FEET

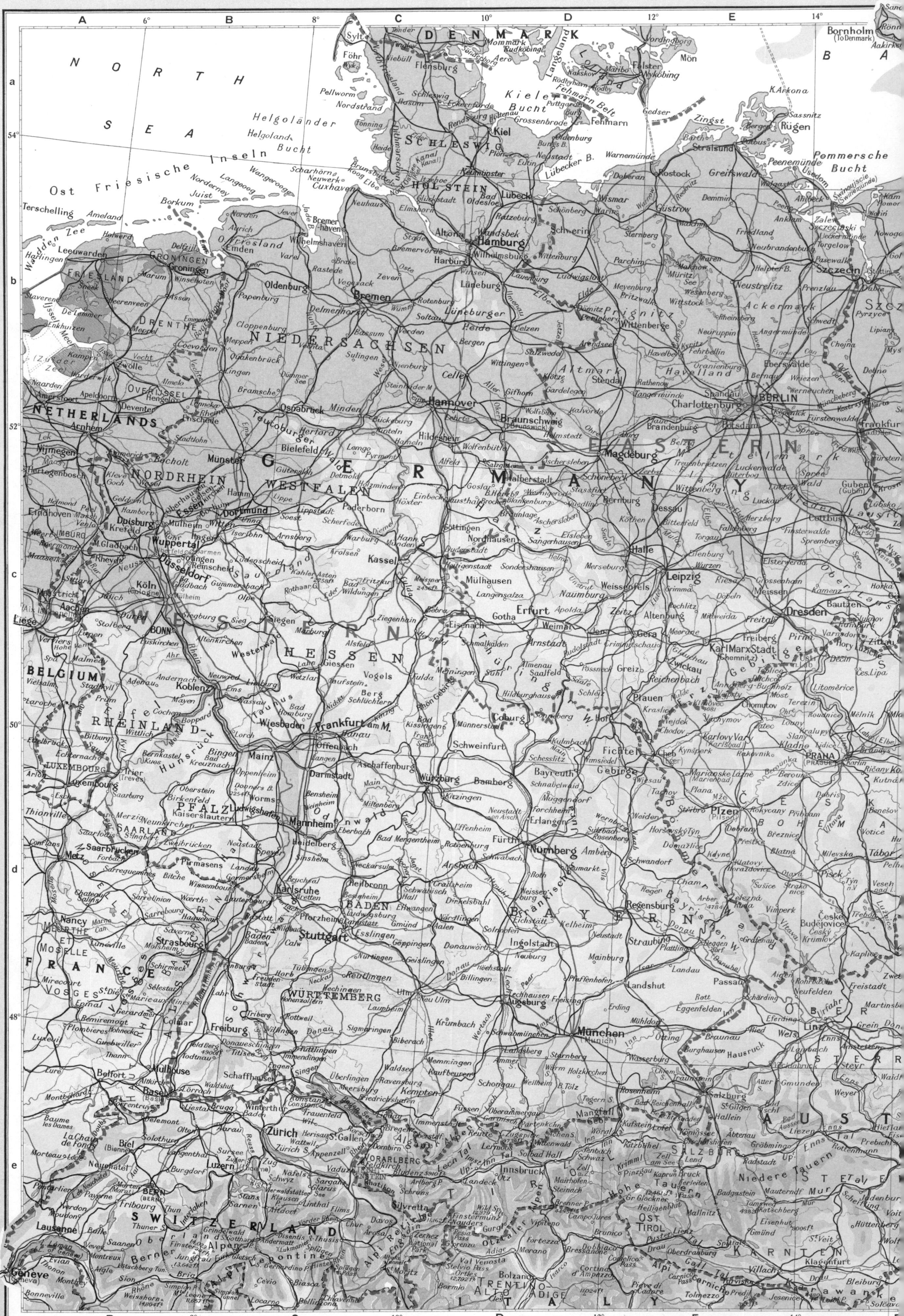

48

CONIC PROJECTION

SCALE: 1 INCH TO 47 MILES

MAIN ROADS
RAILWAYS

ary with Austria. Lower mountains in the centre give way to the North German Plain, now divided between East and West Germany. Except for the Danube, all important rivers—the Rhein, Ems, Weser, Elbe and Oder—follow this northwards slope, flowing into the Baltic or North Sea.

POLAND AREA: 120,664 sq. miles. POPULATION: 31,698,000. CAPITAL: Warsaw. CURRENCY: 100 groszy=1 zloty.
Except in the south, where it shares the Carpathians with Czechoslovakia, Poland is a vast plain connecting north Germany with the Russian steppes.

CZECHOSLOVAKIA AREA: 49,354 sq. miles. POPULATION: 14,240,000. CAPITAL: Prague. CURRENCY: 100 haler= 1 koruna.
AUSTRIA AREA: 32,374 sq. miles. POPULATION: 7,290,000. CAPITAL: Vienna. CURRENCY: 100 Groschen=1 Schilling.

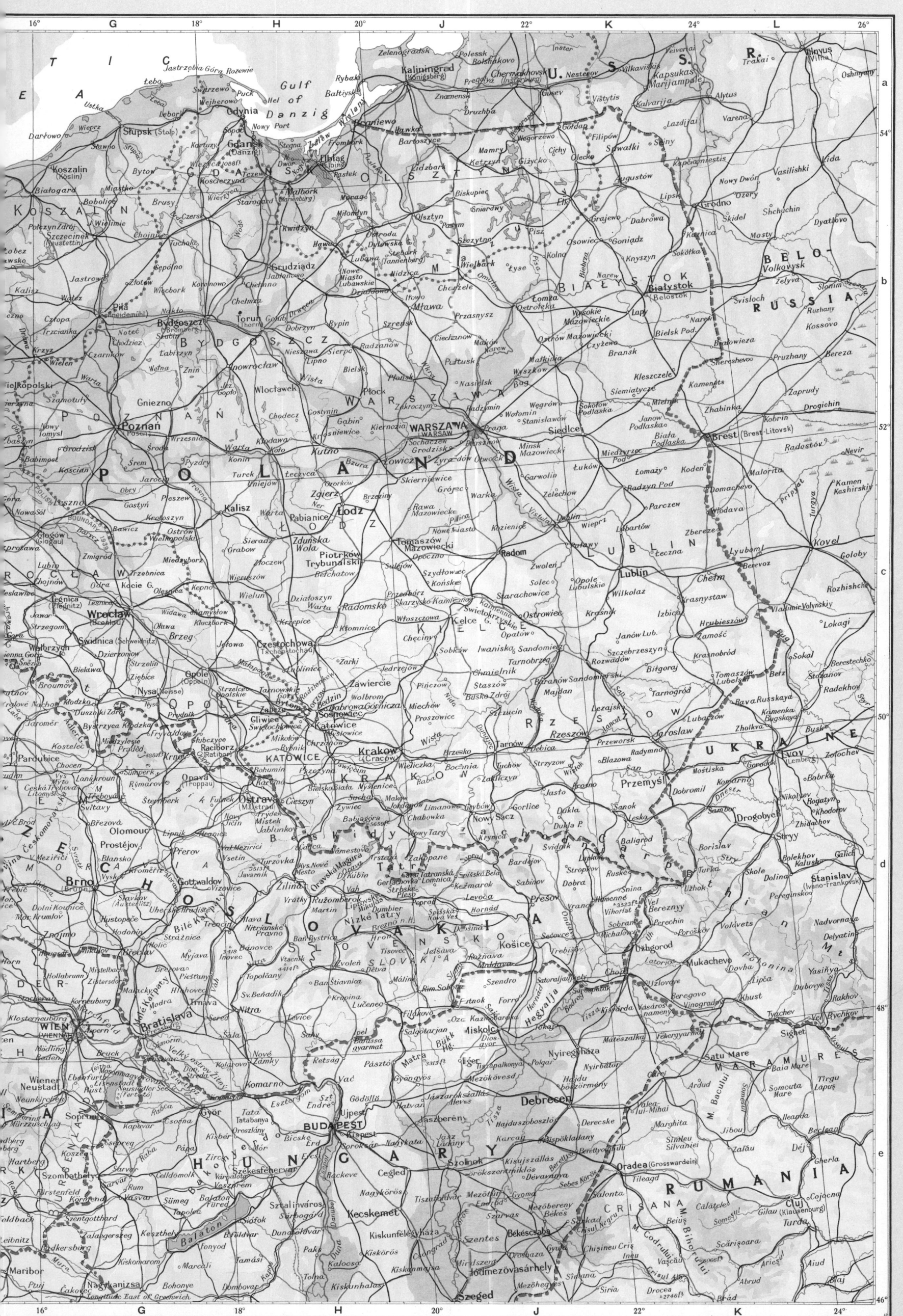

SCALE IN MILES

© JOHN BARTHOLOMEW & SON LTD.

INTERNATIONAL BOUNDARIES
STATE BOUNDARIES

SCALE: 1 INCH TO 47 MILES

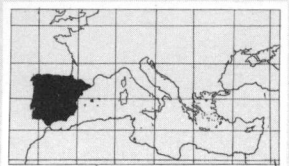

IBERIAN PENINSULA

SPAIN, PORTUGAL

SPAIN AREA: *194,883 sq. miles.* POPULATION: *31,871,000.* CAPITAL: *Madrid.*
CURRENCY: *100 céntimos = 1 peseta.*
PORTUGAL AREA: *35,453 sq. miles.* POPULATION: *9,218,000.* CAPITAL:
Lisbon. CURRENCY: *100 centavos = 1 escudo.* Roughly pentagonal in shape,

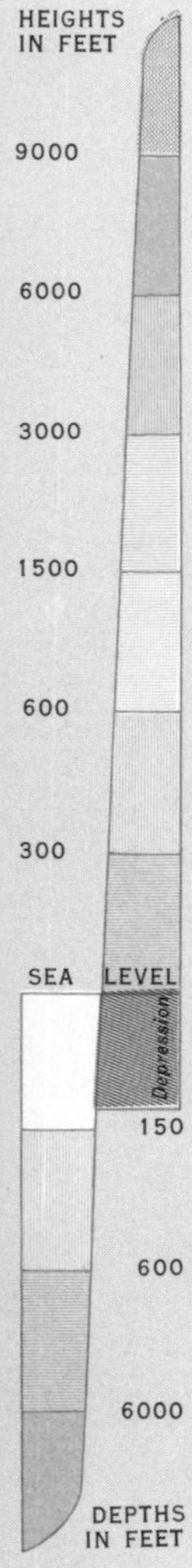

HEIGHTS
IN FEET

9000

6000

3000

1500

600

300

SEA LEVEL

150

600

6000

DEPTHS
IN FEET

ATLANTIC OCEAN

BAY OF BI

50

CONIC PROJECTION

SCALE: 1 INCH TO 47 MILES

MAIN ROADS

RAILWAYS

the Iberian peninsula is divided between Spain, Portugal and the small state of Andorra. Seven-eighths of it is bordered by sea, the remainder by the high wall of the Pyrénées, which separates it from France and the land mass of Europe. Southwards, only eight and a half miles away at its nearest point, lies the continent of Africa. More than half the peninsula is covered by the Meseta, a high central plateau which is surrounded and traversed by mountain ranges. The rivers, notably the Tagus, flow mainly westwards. The four main islands of the Balearic group form a province of Spain; the Canary Islands are another province.

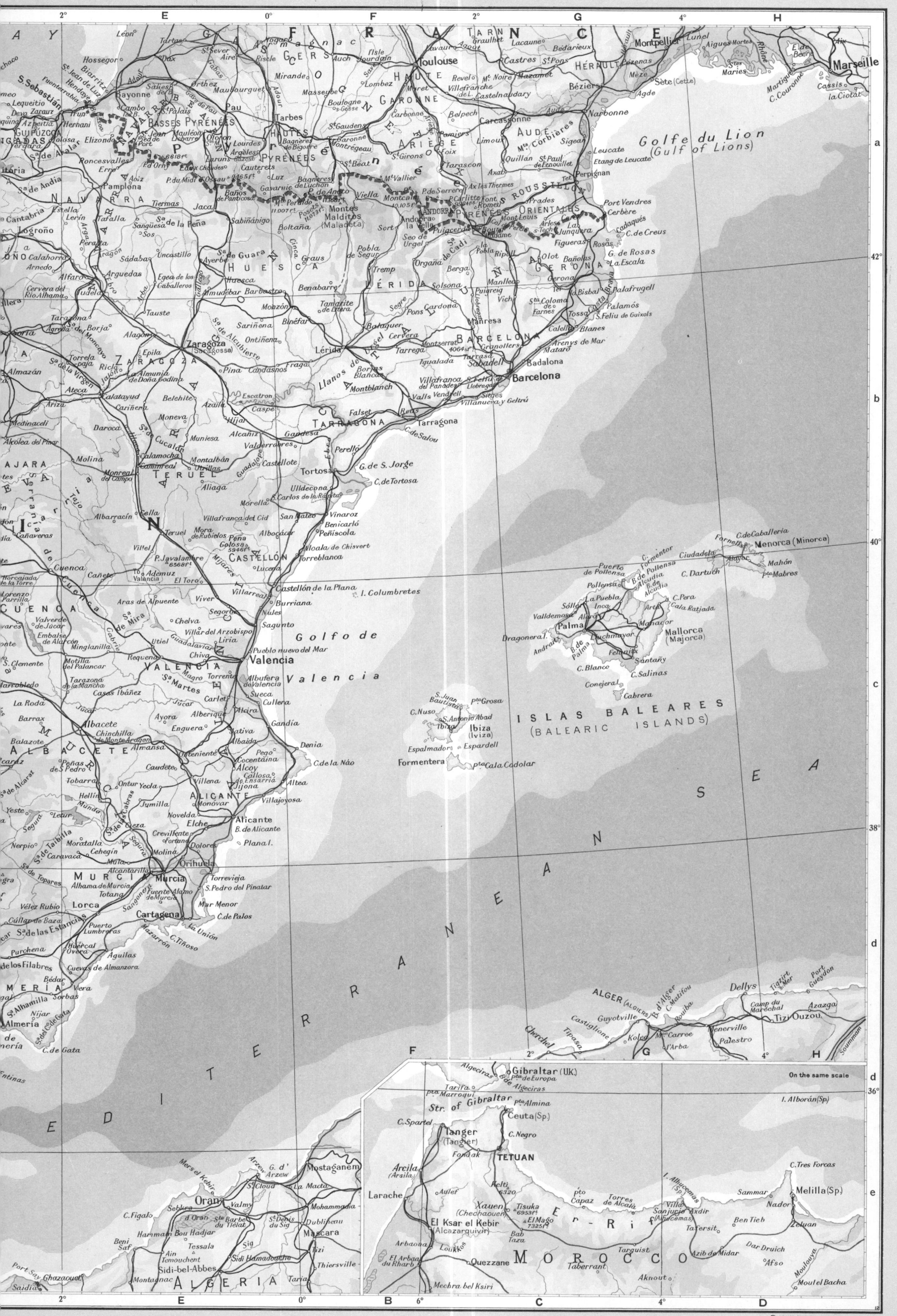

SCALE
IN MILES

INTERNATIONAL BOUNDARIES

STATE BOUNDARIES

51

SCALE: 1 INCH TO 47 MILES

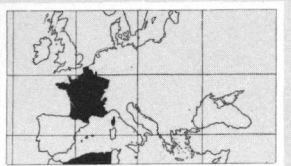

FRANCE

AND NORTHERN ALGERIA

AREA: *212,974 sq. miles.* POPULATION: *49,440,000.* CAPITAL: *Paris.* CURRENCY: *100 centimes=1 nouveau franc.* Around France are three seas, into which flow the four great French rivers: the Seine into the English Channel, the Loire and Garonne into the Atlantic, and the Rhône into

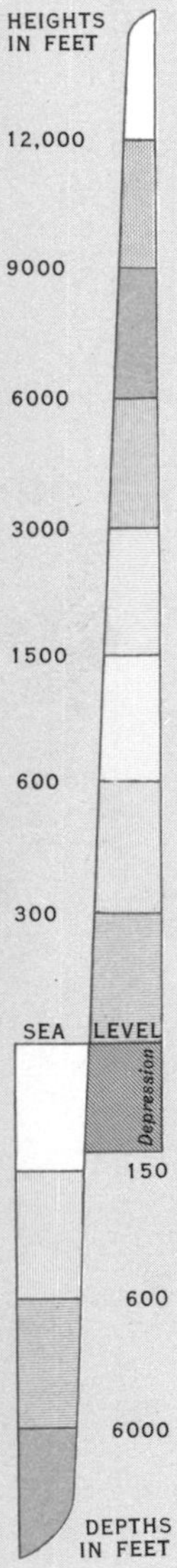

HEIGHTS IN FEET
12,000
9000
6000
3000
1500
600
300
SEA LEVEL
Depression
150
600
6000
DEPTHS IN FEET

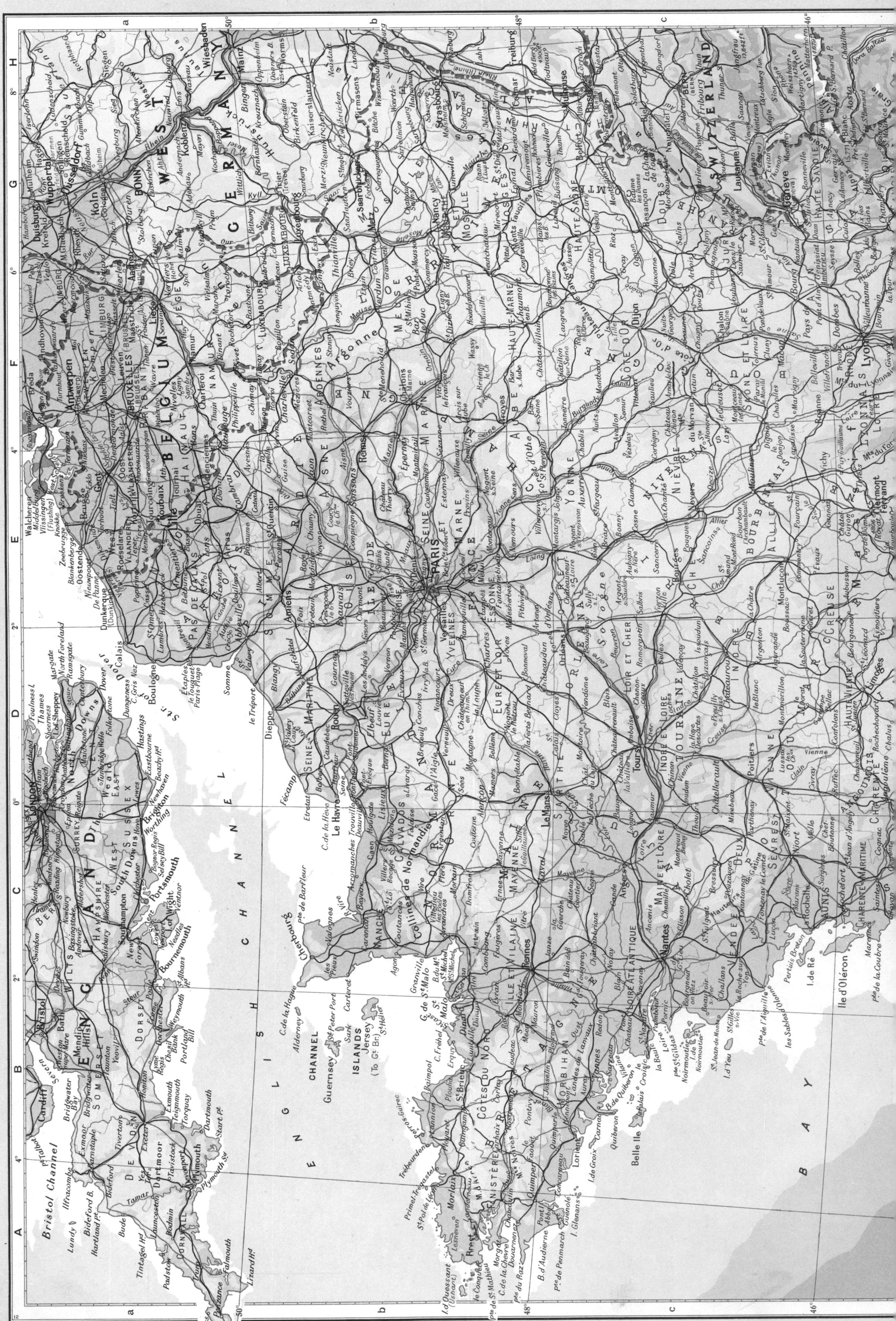

ENGLISH CHANNEL
PARIS
BELGIUM
WEST GERMANY
SWITZERLAND
CHANNEL ISLANDS
BAY

CONIC PROJECTION

SCALE: 1 INCH TO 47 MILES

MAIN ROADS

RAILWAYS

the Mediterranean. This maritime outlook gives the country its mild and even climate. A line drawn from Sedan, in the north-east, to Bayonne, in the south-west, divides the country roughly into its upland and lowland halves. The north-western half is mainly low-lying and includes the broad plains of Normandy and Brittany. On France's eastern borders rise the high mountains of the Vosges, the Jura and the Alps (Mont Blanc, 15,771 feet, is one of the highest peaks in Europe). Running southwards from the centre is the Massif Central, while the Pyrénées in the south-west form a natural barrier between France and Spain.

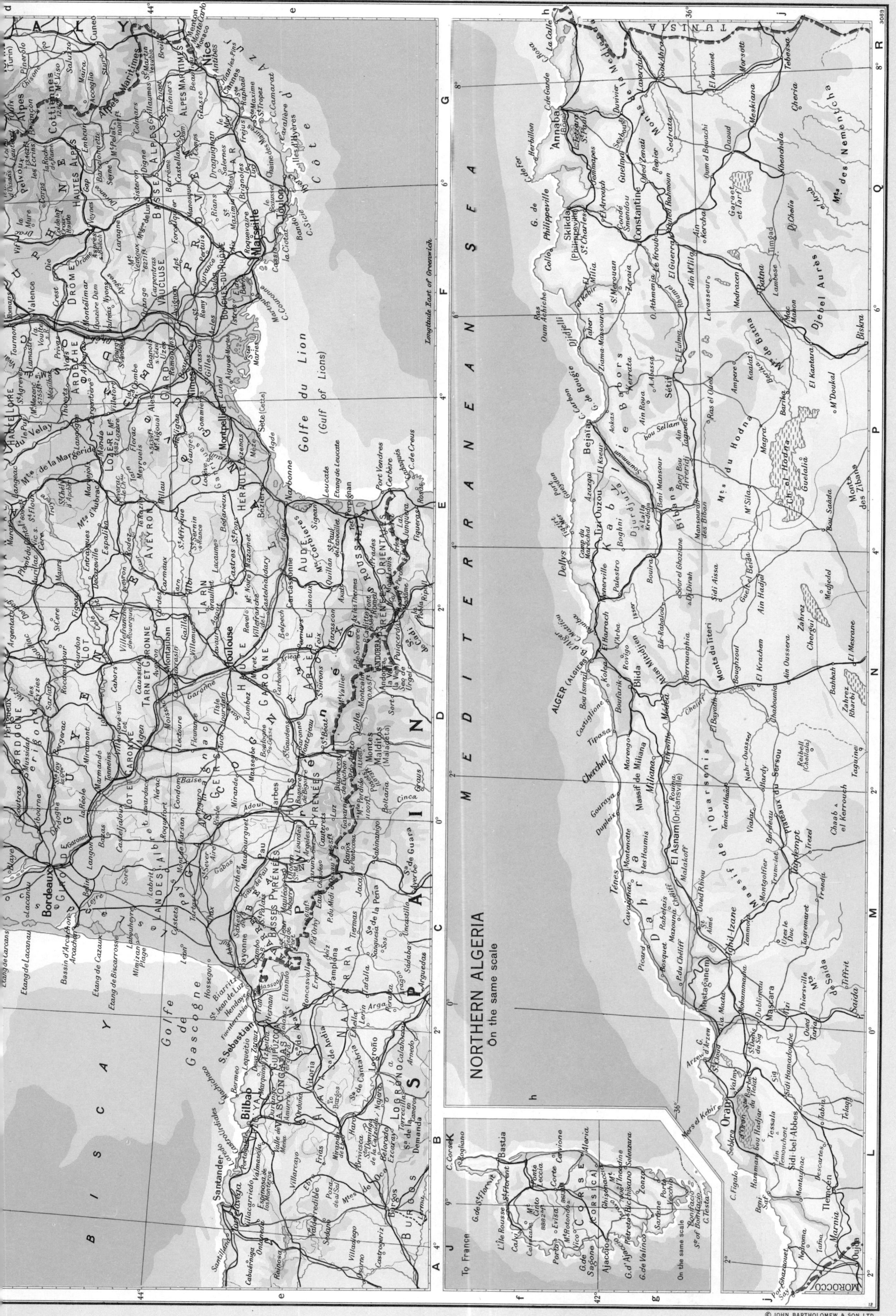

NORTHERN ALGERIA
On the same scale

© JOHN BARTHOLOMEW & SON LTD.

INTERNATIONAL BOUNDARIES
DEPARTMENT BOUNDARIES

SCALE: 1 INCH TO 47 MILES

SCALE
IN MILES

50
100
150
200
250
300
350
400
450
500

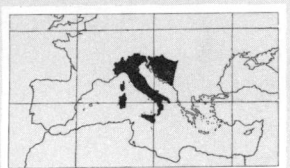

ITALY

AREA: *116,286 sq. miles.* POPULATION: *51,859,000.* CAPITAL: *Rome.* CURRENCY: *100 centesimi = 1 lira.*

Italy owes its boot-like shape to the Apennines which reach down the whole length of the country, culminating, across the Straits of Messina, in the island of Sicily. To the north the Alps encircle the peninsula like the head of a mushroom, shutting off Italy from the rest of Europe. The strange-shaped Dolomitic Alps (Dolomites) to the east form

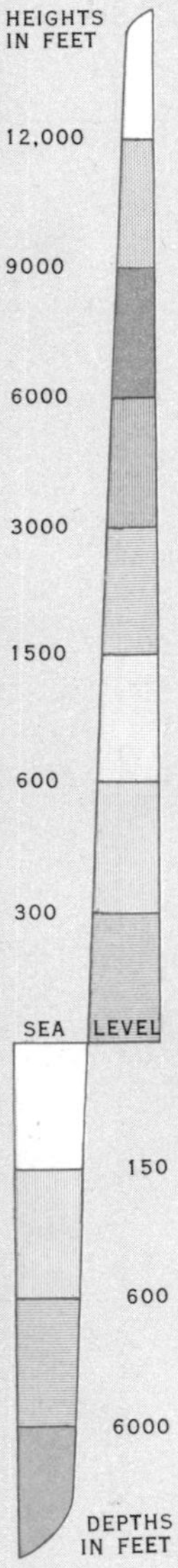

HEIGHTS
IN FEET

12,000
9000
6000
3000
1500
600
300
SEA LEVEL
150
600
6000

DEPTHS
IN FEET

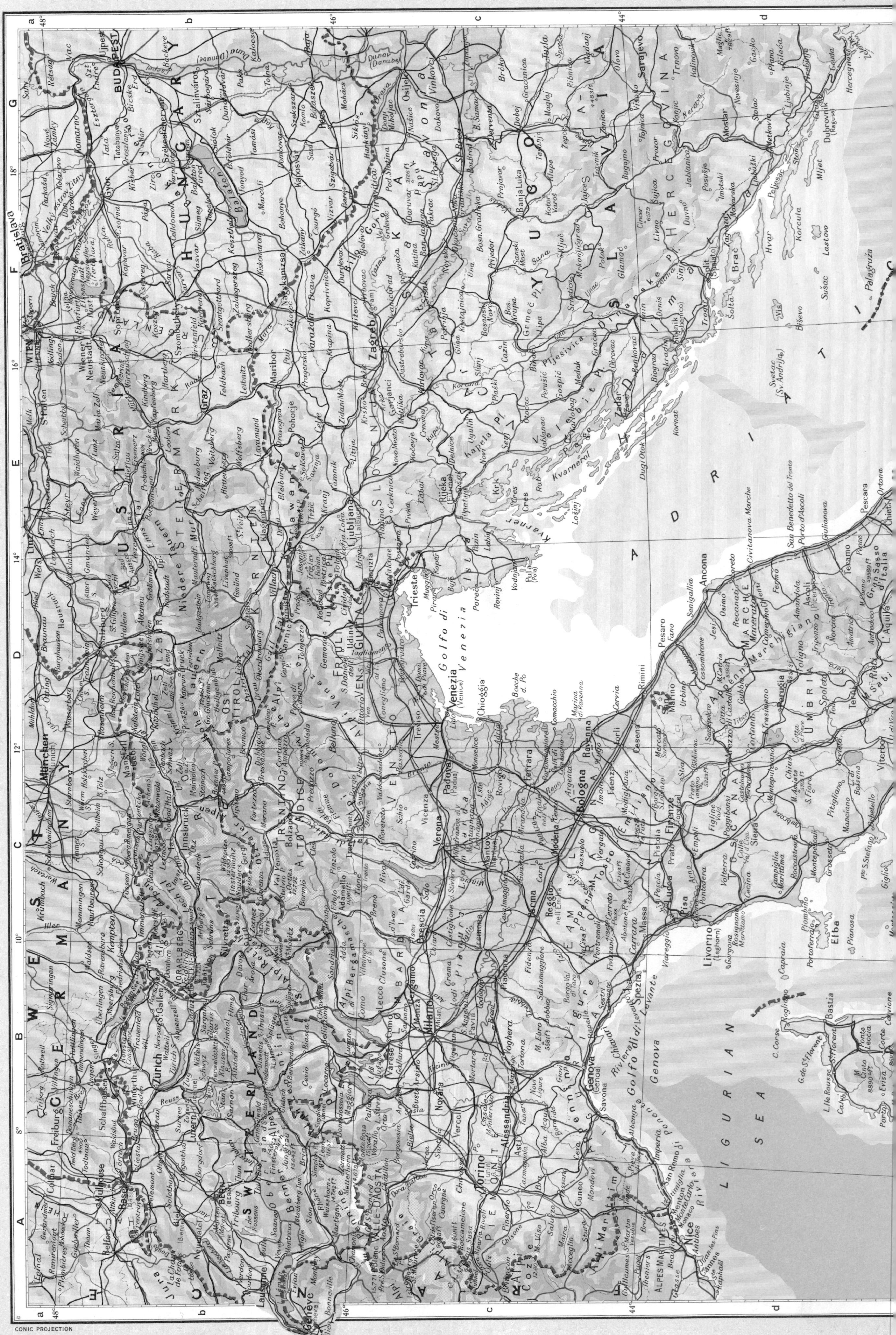

CONIC PROJECTION

SCALE: 1 INCH TO 47 MILES

MAIN ROADS
RAILWAYS

an important part of this mountain barrier which makes the country difficult to approach, and the names of the principal passes—the Simplon and St. Gotthard from Switzerland, and the Brenner from Austria—have become household words among travellers all over Europe.

Italy contains the only active volcanoes in Europe, notably Etna (the highest, 10,705 feet) in Sicily, and Vesuvius near Naples. Of the rivers, most of which are unnavigable, the longest is the Po (420 miles) which waters the fertile plain of Lombardy before entering the Adriatic through its delta between Venice and Ravenna. Other important rivers are the Tiber and the Arno.

SCALE: 1 INCH TO 47 MILES

SCALE IN MILES

© JOHN BARTHOLOMEW & SON LTD.

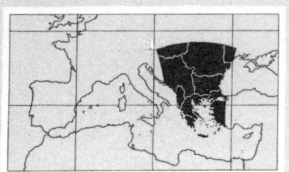

THE BALKANS
HUNGARY, RUMANIA, YUGOSLAVIA, BULGARIA, GREECE

HUNGARY AREA: 35,919 sq. miles. POPULATION: 10,179,000.
CAPITAL: *Budapest*. CURRENCY: 100 fillér = 1 forint.
RUMANIA AREA: 91,699 sq. miles. POPULATION: 19,143,000.
CAPITAL: *Bucharest*. CURRENCY: 100 bani = 1 leu.

HEIGHTS IN FEET

6000
3000
1500
600
300
SEA LEVEL
150
600
6000

56

CONIC PROJECTION

SCALE: 1 INCH TO 47 MILES

MAIN ROADS
RAILWAYS

YUGOSLAVIA AREA:98,766 sq.miles. POPULATION:19,756,000.
CAPITAL: *Belgrade.* CURRENCY: *100 paras=1 dinar.*
BULGARIA AREA: 42,796 sq. miles. POPULATION: 8,258,000.
CAPITAL: *Sofia.* CURRENCY: 100 stotinki=1 (new) lev.

GREECE AREA: 50,944 sq. miles. POPULATION: 8,612,000.
CAPITAL: *Athens.* CURRENCY: *100 lepta=1 drachma.*
The Balkan peninsula, with its broken coastline and
many offshore islands, is separated from the rest

of Europe by the river Danube (1,770 miles long and
western Europe's longest river) which flows eastwards from
Hungary and through the Iron Gate, a gorge between the
Carpathians and the barren Dinaric Alps in Yugoslavia.

SCALE
IN MILES

57

INTERNATIONAL BOUNDARIES
PROVINCIAL BOUNDARIES

SCALE: 1 INCH TO 47 MILES

© JOHN BARTHOLOMEW & SON LTD.

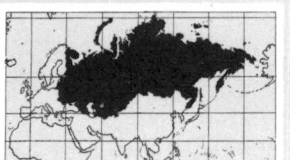

U.S.S.R.

AREA: *8,649,489 sq. miles.* POPULATION: *233,180,000.* CAPITAL: *Moscow.*
CURRENCY: *100 copecks=1 (new) rouble.*
The vast area of the U.S.S.R., straddling all Asia and half of Europe, shares
its immense boundaries with many countries in both continents. It is divided

HEIGHTS
IN FEET

20,000
12,000
10,000
6000
3000
1500
600

SEA LEVEL

150
600
6000

DEPTHS
IN FEET

58

CONIC PROJECTION

SCALE: 1 INCH TO 276 MILES

MAIN ROADS
RAILWAYS

structurally into three regions from west to east: two plains, separated by the Uralski Khrebet (which also form a useful dividing line between Asia and Europe) and a vast region of hazardous country ending in the remote peninsula of Kamchatka. On the north—south axis there are likewise three zones. The frozen tundra of the Arctic merges into forests and fertile plains, which end at the borders of the great desert belt stretching from Mongolia to the Caspian. In fact, the U.S.S.R. is hemmed in on three fronts by hot or cold deserts or mountains, so that easy access is found only on the western side, through Europe.

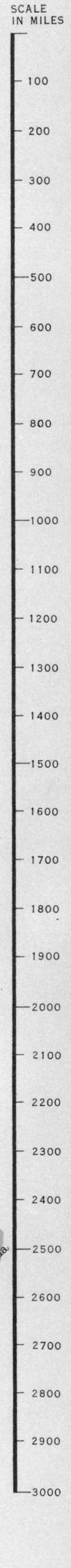

SCALE IN MILES

100 200 300 400 500 600 700 800 900 1000 1100 1200 1300 1400 1500 1600 1700 1800 1900 2000 2100 2200 2300 2400 2500 2600 2700 2800 2900 3000

59

© JOHN BARTHOLOMEW & SON LTD.

SCALE: 1 INCH TO 276 MILES

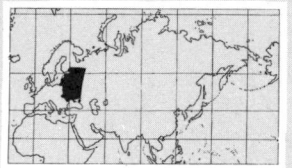

EUROPEAN RUSSIA

The area between the Baltic and the Black Sea is part of the enormous Russian Plain which stretches unbroken to the Central Russian uplands, before continuing eastwards. The comparatively low land in this district is shown up by the meandering rivers and the lakes and marshes of the Pripyat region. To the south, the mild undulations of the Ukrainian steppe interrupt the monotony of the northern plain.

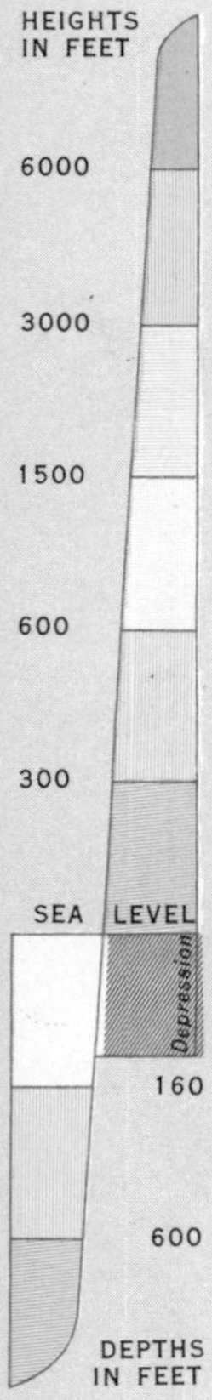

HEIGHTS
IN FEET

6000

3000

1500

600

300

SEA LEVEL

160

600

DEPTHS
IN FEET

60

CONIC PROJECTION

SCALE: 1 INCH TO 94 MILES

INTERNATIONAL BOUNDARIES
STATE BOUNDARIES

THE VOLGA BASIN

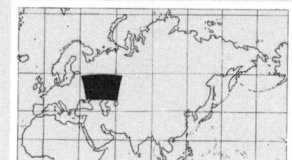

This map shows the highest and the lowest parts of European Russia, from the Urals, up to 5,500 feet high, to the northern end of the Caspian, 50 feet below sea level. The two main rivers are the Don, and the 2,400-mile-long Volga which flows through several immense artificial lakes, recently created. The huge, low-lying plain that circles the northern end of the Caspian is the largest area of inland drainage in the world.

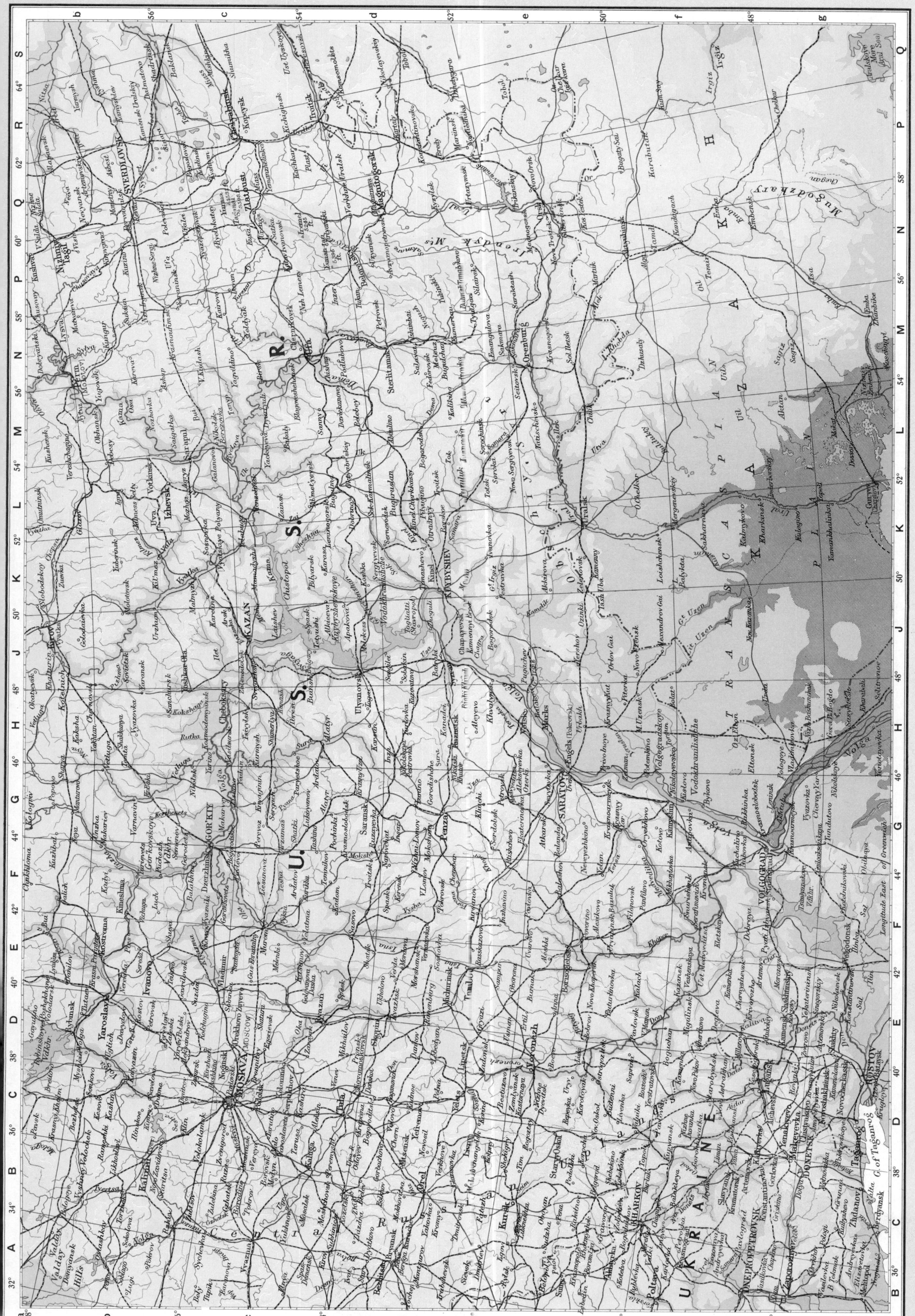

SCALE IN MILES

100
200
300
400
500
600
700
800
900
1000

CONIC PROJECTION

MAIN ROADS

RAILWAYS

SCALE: 1 INCH TO 94 MILES

THE FAR EAST

NORTH KOREA, SOUTH KOREA, PHILIPPINES, INDONESIA

NORTH KOREA AREA: *46,540 sq. miles.* POP: *12,100,000.*
CAPITAL: *Pyongyang.* CURRENCY: *100 jun=1 new won.*
SOUTH KOREA AREA: *38,004 sq. miles.* POPULATION:
29,086,000. CAP: *Seoul.* CURRENCY: *10 hwan=1 won.*

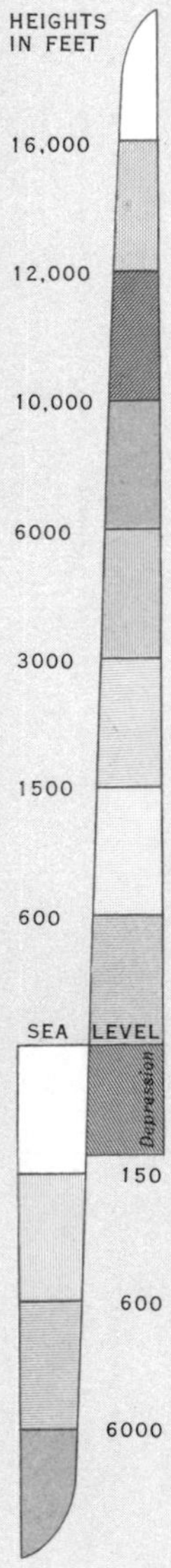

HEIGHTS
IN FEET

16,000
12,000
10,000
6000
3000
1500
600
SEA LEVEL
Depression
150
600
6000

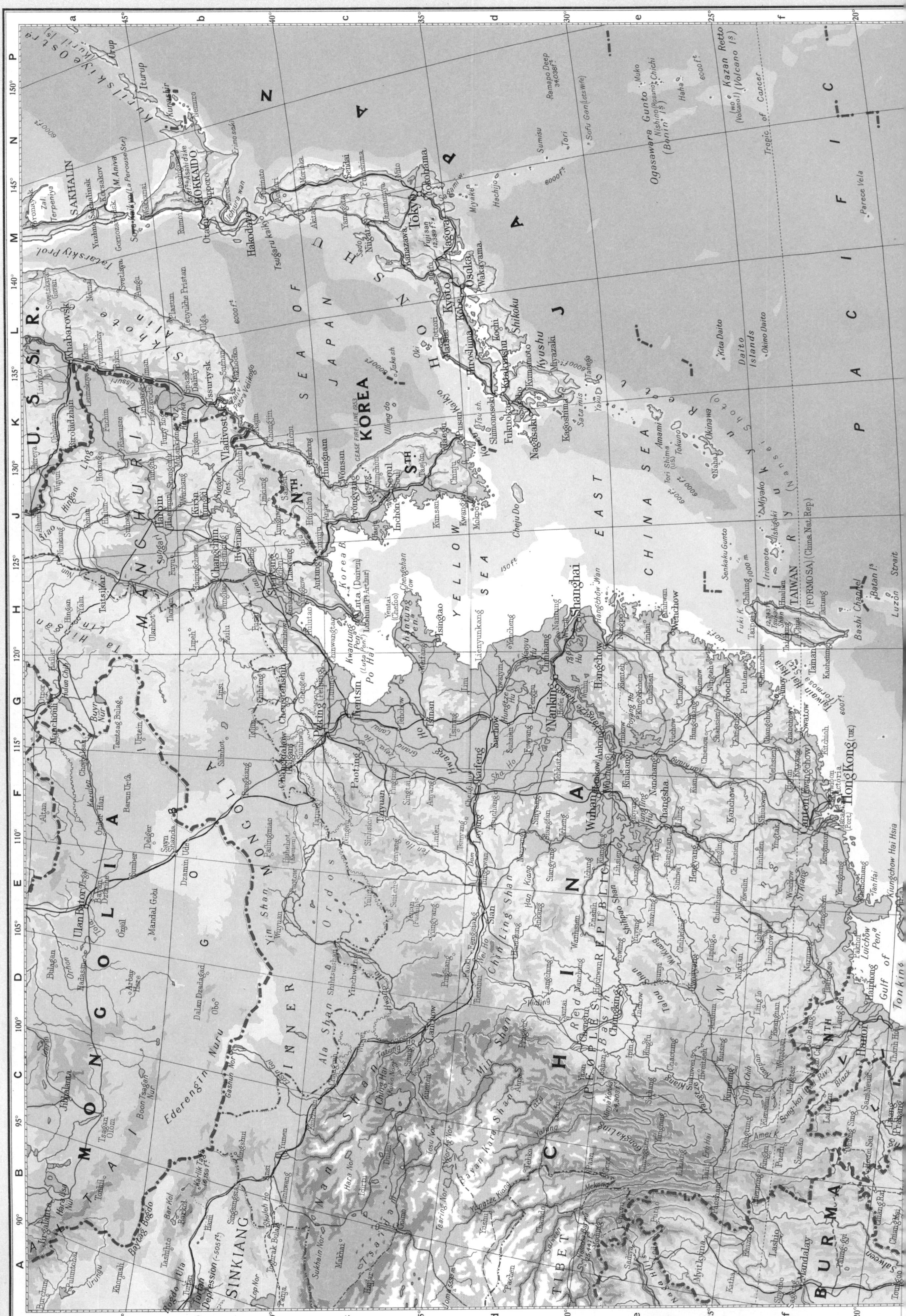

62

BONNE'S PROJECTION

SCALE: 1 INCH TO 237 MILES

MAIN ROADS
RAILWAYS

PHILIPPINES AREA: *115,830 sq. miles.* POP: *33,477,000.*
CAPITAL: *Manila.* CURRENCY: *100 centaros=1 peso.*
INDONESIA AREA: *735,488 sq. miles.* POP: *104,500,000.*
CAPITAL: *Djakarta.* CURRENCY: *100 sen=1 rupiah.*

From the high Tibetan plateau to the deep ocean bed off the Philippines is a drop of nearly 50,000 feet. The shallow seas of the Indonesian Archipelago and the mainly volcanic formation of the mountainous islands curving round West

Malaysia to New Guinea are a marked contrast to the Himalayan fold mountains. The Philippines, some 7,000 islands, form the apex of a triangle based on Indonesia and pointing north to the equally mountainous islands of Japan.

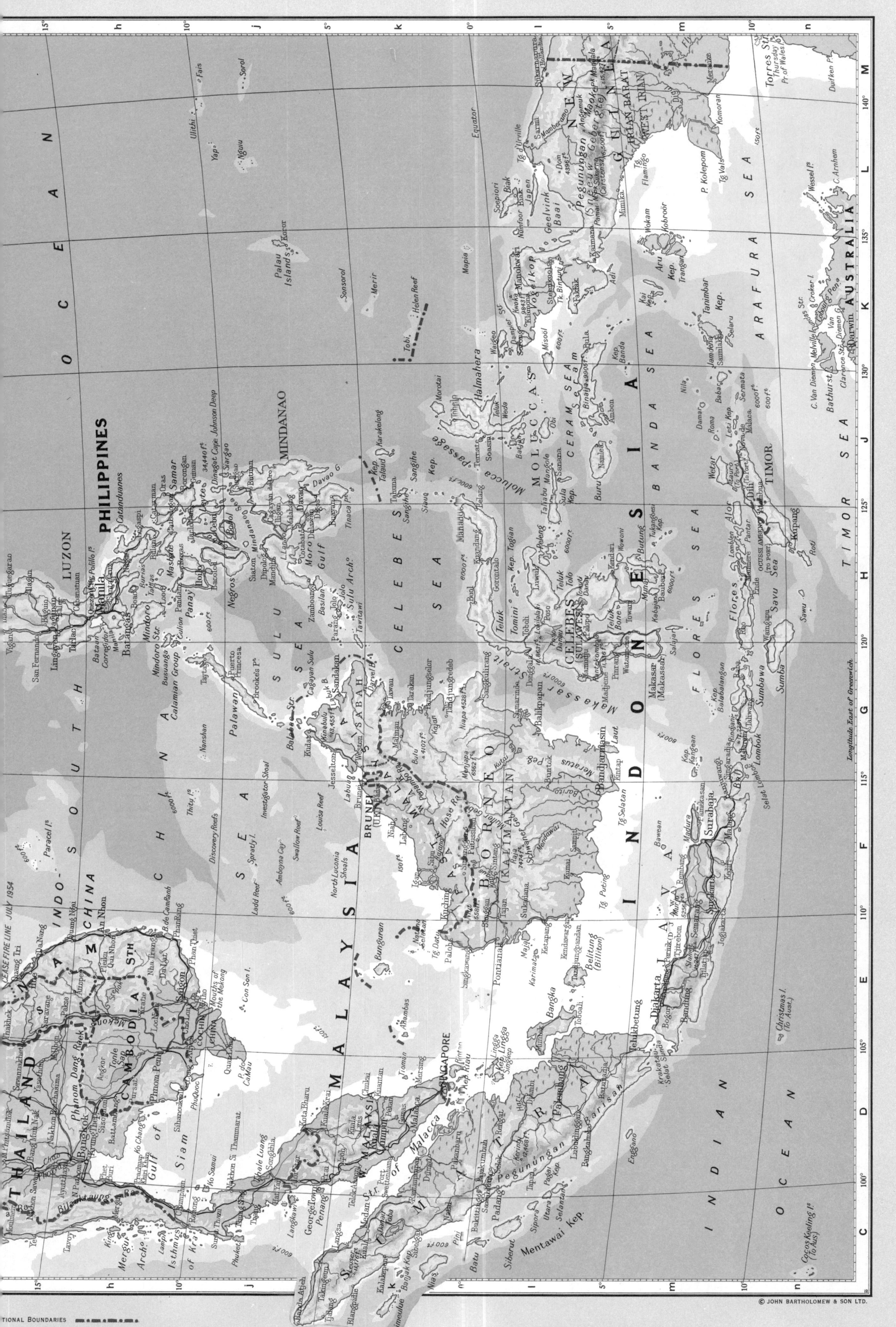

SCALE IN MILES

SCALE: 1 INCH TO 237 MILES

© JOHN BARTHOLOMEW & SON LTD.

63

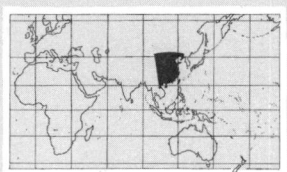

EAST CHINA

CHINA AREA: *3,691,502 sq. miles.* POPULATION: *700,000,000.* CAPITAL: *Peking.* CURRENCY: *100 fen=1 yuan.*

Though half covered by mountains, China has the largest population of any country in the world, and also the largest area of fertile land. The eastern half of the map shows a semi-circle of low-lying land dotted with lakes, testifying

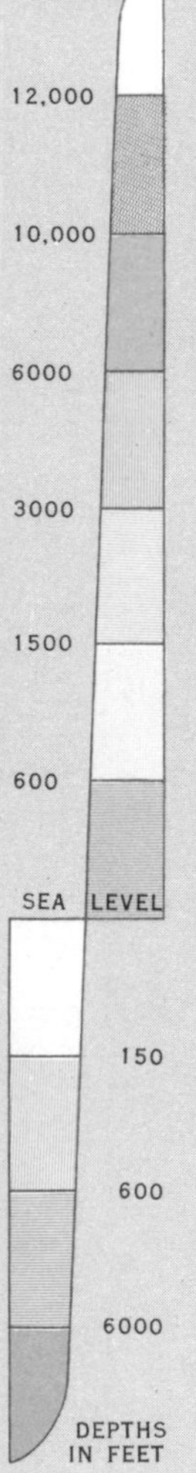

HEIGHTS IN FEET

12,000
10,000
6000
3000
1500
600
SEA LEVEL
150
600
6000

DEPTHS IN FEET

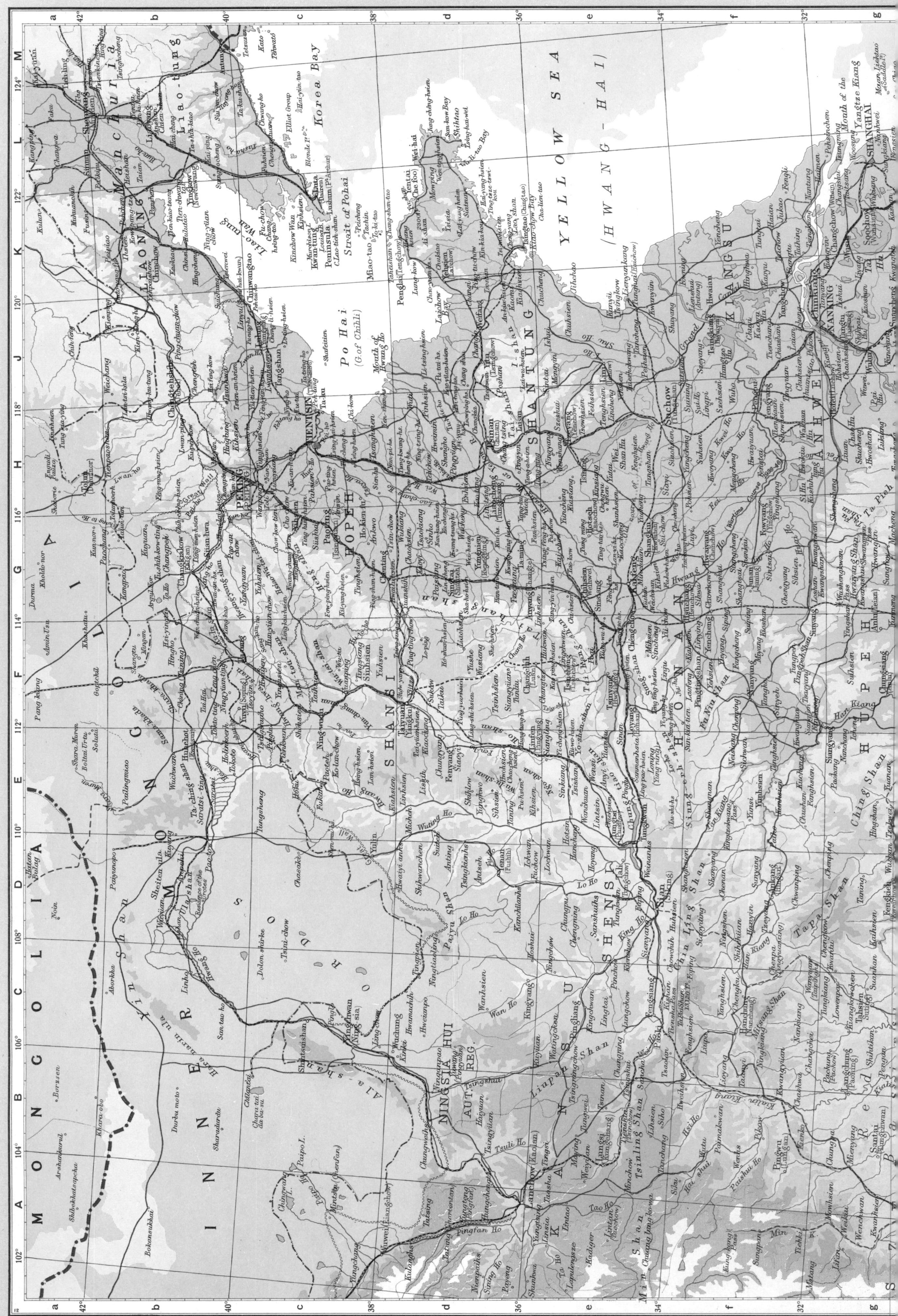

64

CONIC PROJECTION

SCALE: 1 INCH TO 94 MILES

———— MAIN ROADS
- - - - - - RAILWAYS

to inadequate river drainage. This area is backed by vast mountain ranges running north-east to Siberia, and cut up by mountainous tracts on a south-east axis reaching down to the coast of Chekiang. Each of the three main rivers, the Hwang Ho (Yellow River), the Yangtze Kiang and the Si Kiang, has a broad, well-watered valley, and together these valleys contain more than two-thirds of China's inhabitants. Sinkiang, the largest province, is mostly desert. Another desert, the Gobi, which separates northern China from Outer Mongolia, covers nearly one-third of China's total area. China's jagged south-eastern coastline contrasts sharply with the smoother coastline north of Shanghai.

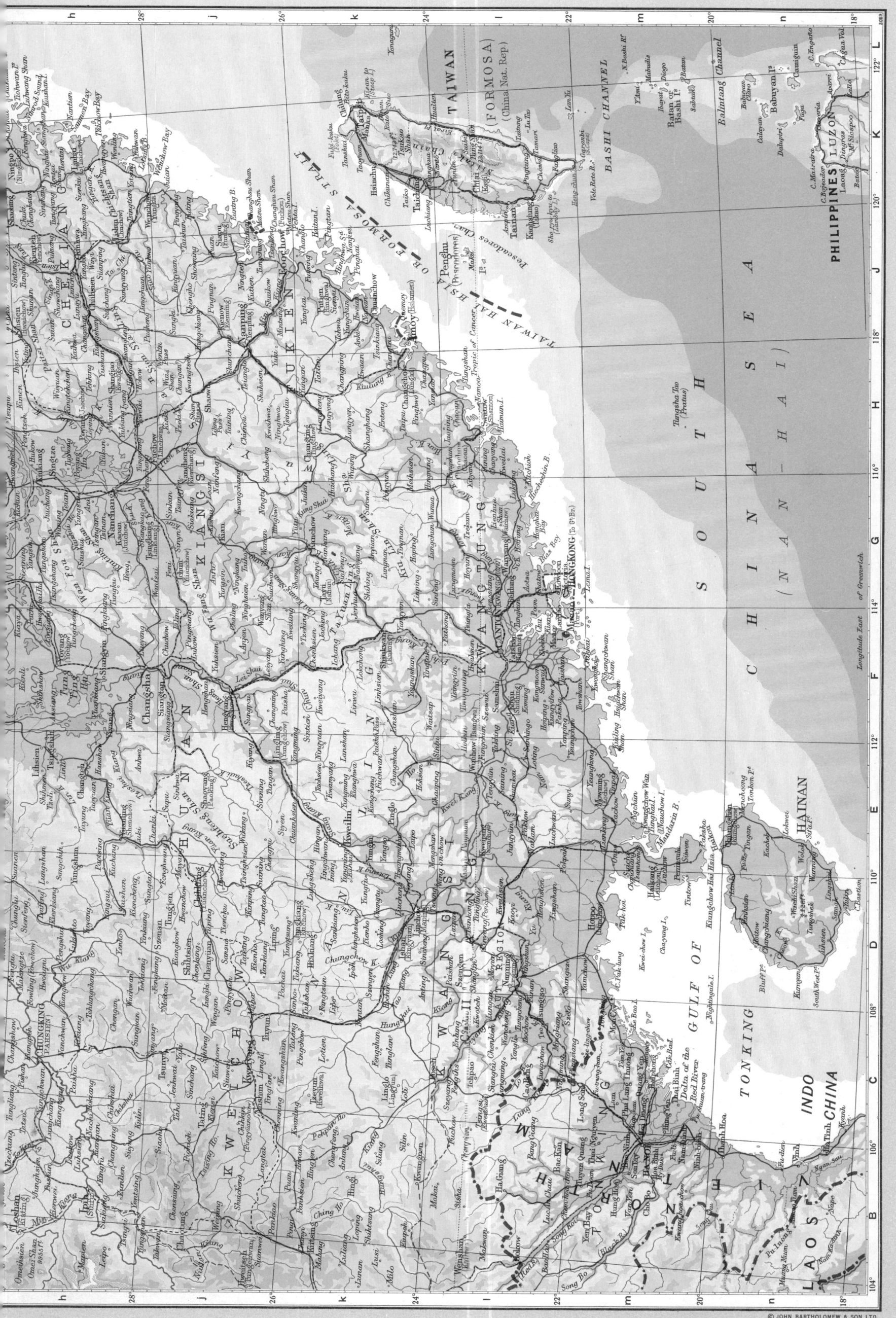

SCALE IN MILES

SCALE: 1 INCH TO 94 MILES

INTERNATIONAL BOUNDARIES

PROVINCIAL BOUNDARIES

JAPAN

AREA: *142,719 sq. miles.* **POPULATION:** *98,865,000.*
CAPITAL: *Tokyo.* **CURRENCY:** *100 sen=1 yen.*
Japan consists of a group of four large islands and many smaller ones, stretching from north to south over a thousand miles and separated from China by the shallow Sea of Japan. The main island is Honshu, which is approximately the same size as Great Britain. Off Japan's east coast the Pacific Ocean is almost at its deepest.

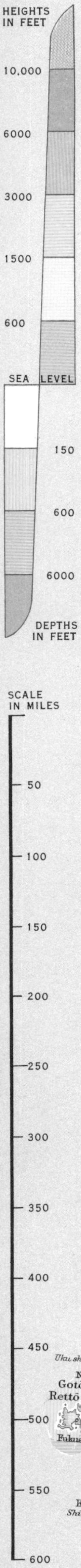

HEIGHTS
IN FEET

10,000
6000
3000
1500
600
SEA LEVEL
150
600
6000
DEPTHS
IN FEET

SCALE
IN MILES
50
100
150
200
250
300
350
400
450
500
550
600

66

CONIC PROJECTION

SCALE: 1 INCH TO 94 MILES

INTERNATIONAL BOUNDARIES
PROVINCIAL BOUNDARIES

SOUTH-EAST ASIA

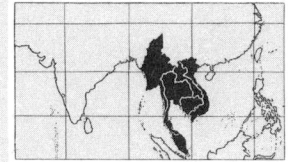

THAILAND AREA: *198,455 sq. miles.* POPULA-
TION: *10,500,000.* CAPITAL: *Bangkok.*
WEST MALAYSIA AREA: *50,690 sq. miles.*
POPULATION: *8,298,000.* CAPITAL: *Kuala Lumpur.*

NORTH VIETNAM AREA: *61,293 sq. miles.*
POPULATION: *19,000,000.* CAPITAL: *Hanoi.*
SOUTH VIETNAM AREA: *65,948 sq. miles.*
POPULATION: *16,543,000.* CAPITAL: *Saigon.*

LAOS AREA: *88,780 sq. miles.* POP: *2,635,000*
CAPITAL: *Luang Prabang.* (GOVT: *Vientiane.*)
CAMBODIA AREA: *69,900 sq. miles.* POPULA
TION: *6,250,000.* CAPITAL: *Phnom-Penh.*

HEIGHTS
IN FEET

18,000
12,000
6000
3000
1500
600
SEA LEVEL
150
600
6000

DEPTHS
IN FEET

SCALE
IN MILES

100
200
300
400
500
600
700
800
900
1000

67

CONIC PROJECTION

MAIN ROADS
RAILWAYS

SCALE: 1 INCH TO 158 MILES

3089

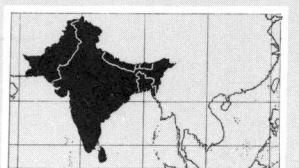

INDIA, PAKISTAN
CEYLON, BURMA

INDIA AREA: *1,229,215 sq. miles.* POP: (excluding Kashmir-Jammu, Sikkim):
433,000,000. CAPITAL: *Delhi.* CURRENCY: *100 naye paise= 1 rupee.*
PAKISTAN AREA: *365,528 sq. miles.* POP: (excl. Kashmir-Jammu, Gilgit, Baltistan):
105,044,000. CAP: *Rawalpindi (Islamabad under construct.).* CURRENCY: *100 paisas=1 r...*

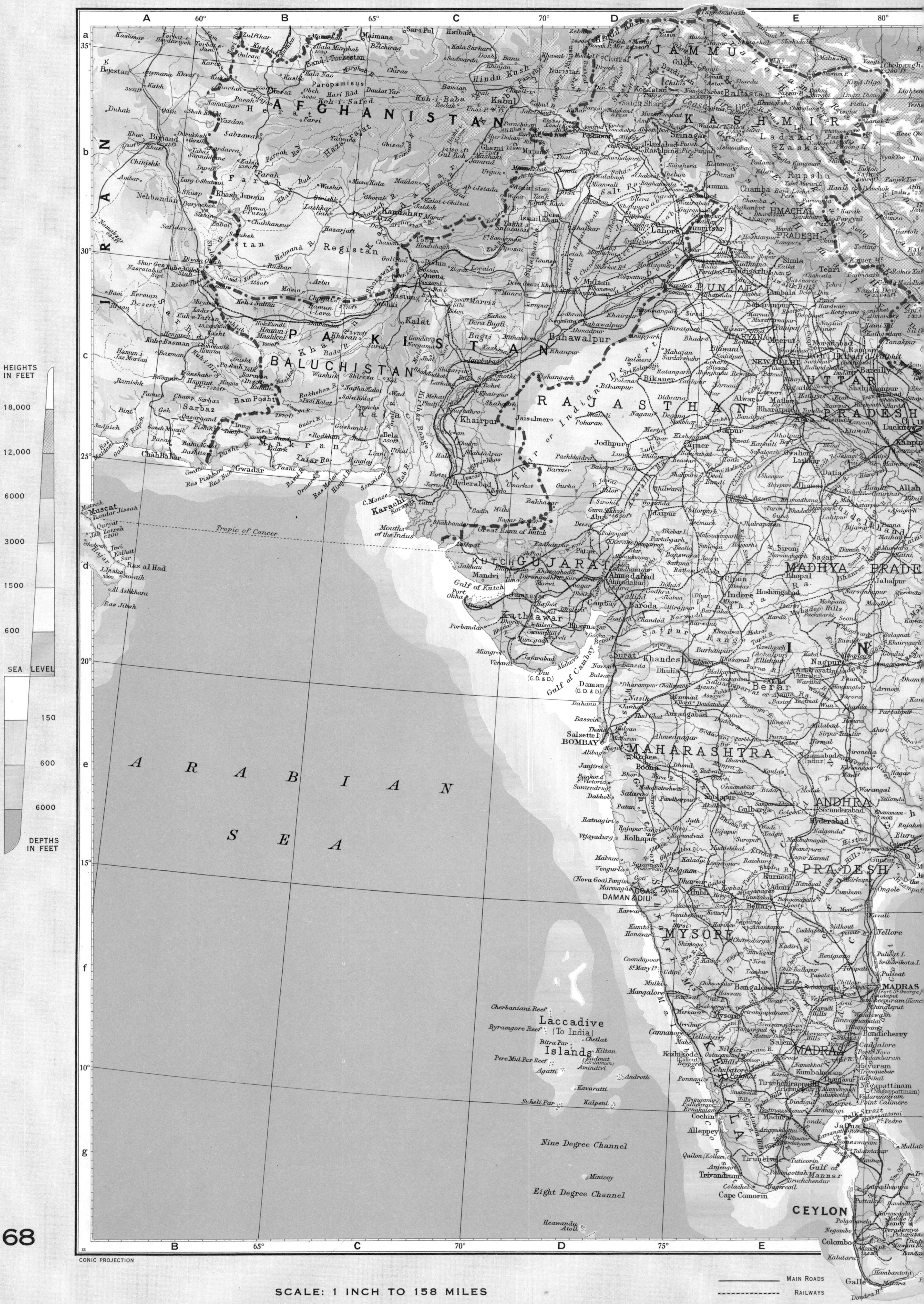

HEIGHTS
IN FEET

18,000

12,000

6000

3000

1500

600

SEA LEVEL

150

600

6000

DEPTHS
IN FEET

A 60° B 65° C 70° D E 80°

AFGHANISTAN

IRAN

PAKISTAN

BALUCHISTAN

JAMMU

KASHMIR

LADAKH

PUNJAB

RAJASTHAN

UTTAR PRADESH

HARYANA

HIMACHAL PRADESH

Tropic of Cancer

KUTCH GUJARAT

MADHYA PRADESH

ARABIAN

SEA

MAHARASHTRA

ANDHRA

PRADESH

DAMAN & DIU

MYSORE

Cherbaniani Reef
Byramgore Reef

Laccadive
(To India)

Islands

MADRAS

Nine Degree Channel

Eight Degree Channel

CEYLON

Colombo

68

CONIC PROJECTION

SCALE: 1 INCH TO 158 MILES

———— MAIN ROADS
---- RAILWAYS

CEYLON AREA: *25,332 sq. miles.* POPULATION: *11,500,000.*
CAPITAL: *Colombo.* CURRENCY: *100 cents=rupee.*
BURMA AREA: *261,789 sq. miles.* POPULATION: *25,246,000.*
CAPITAL: *Rangoon.* CURRENCY: *100 pyas=1 kyat.*

The Indian peninsula falls into three main regions: the Himalayas, the great plains of the Indus and the Ganges, and the Deccan plateau. The mountains to the north virtually seal off the peninsula from the rest of Asia. Along the coast from the Gulf of Cambay down to Cape Comorin, runs the long mountain range of the Western Ghats. The high mountains of Burma are separated by the valley of the Irrawaddy and Sittang rivers.

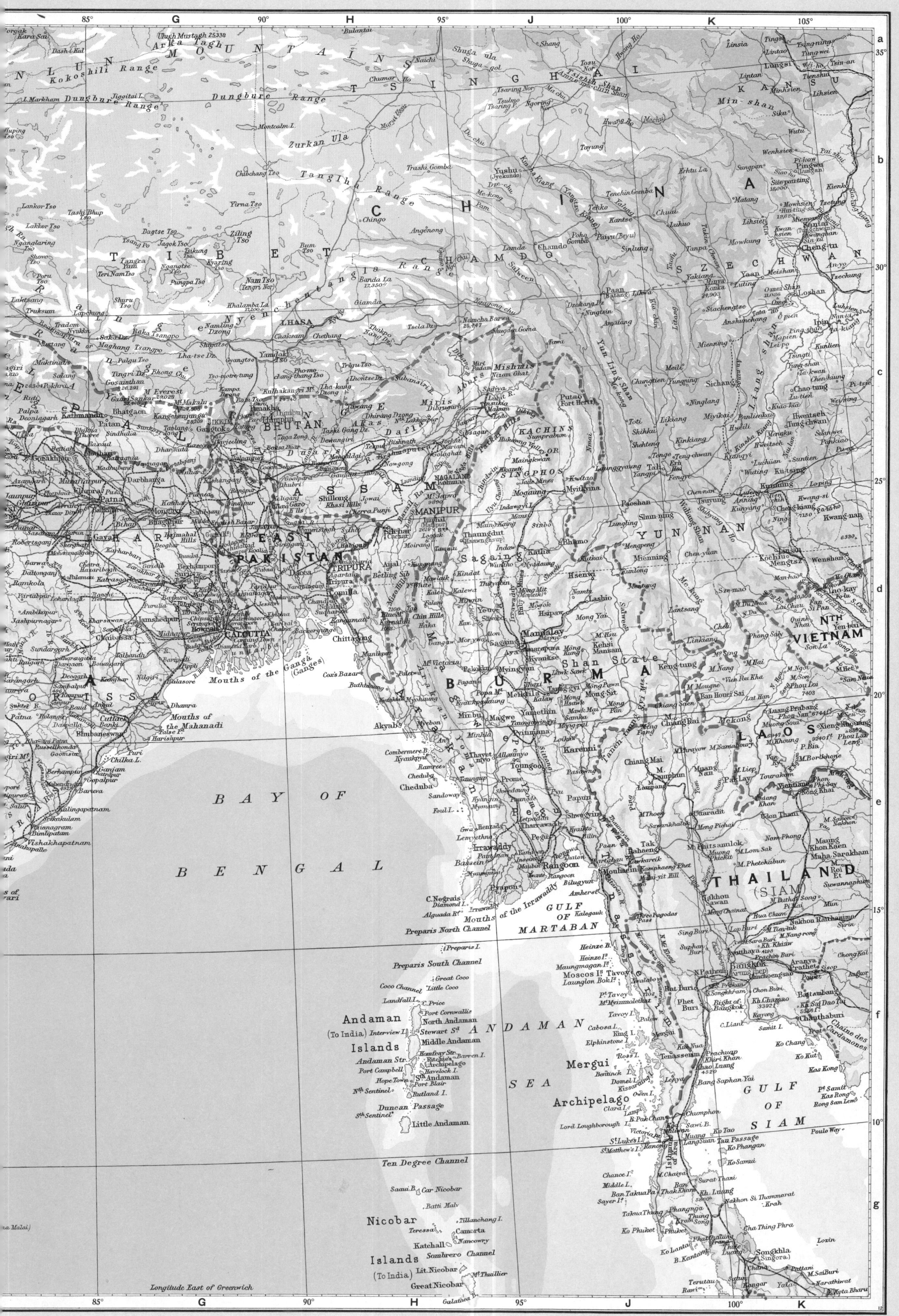

SCALE
IN MILES

© JOHN BARTHOLOMEW & SON LTD.

69

SCALE: 1 INCH TO 158 MILES

PUNJAB AND KASHMIR

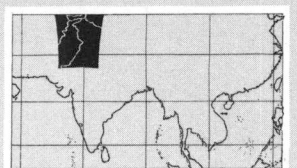

To the north-west of the Indian peninsula a region of contrasts ranges from the arid deserts of the lower Indus plain to the perpetual snows of the high Himalayas in Kashmir, part of the district known as the Roof of the World. The area is intersected by the erratic courses of the Indus and its tributaries, which rise close to the eastward-flowing Brahmaputra River, shown on the opposite map.

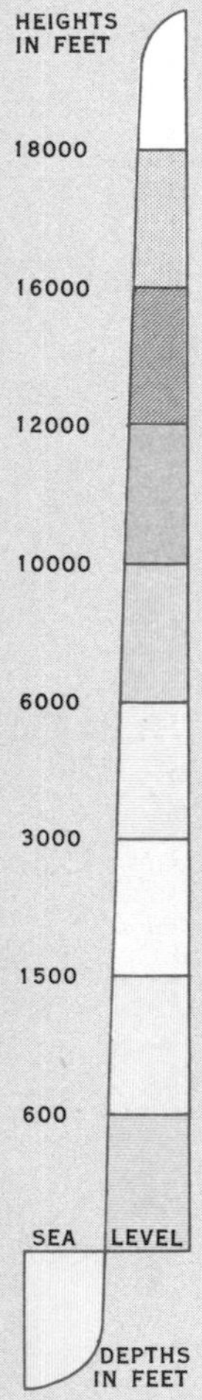

HEIGHTS
IN FEET

18000

16000

12000

10000

6000

3000

1500

600

SEA LEVEL

DEPTHS
IN FEET

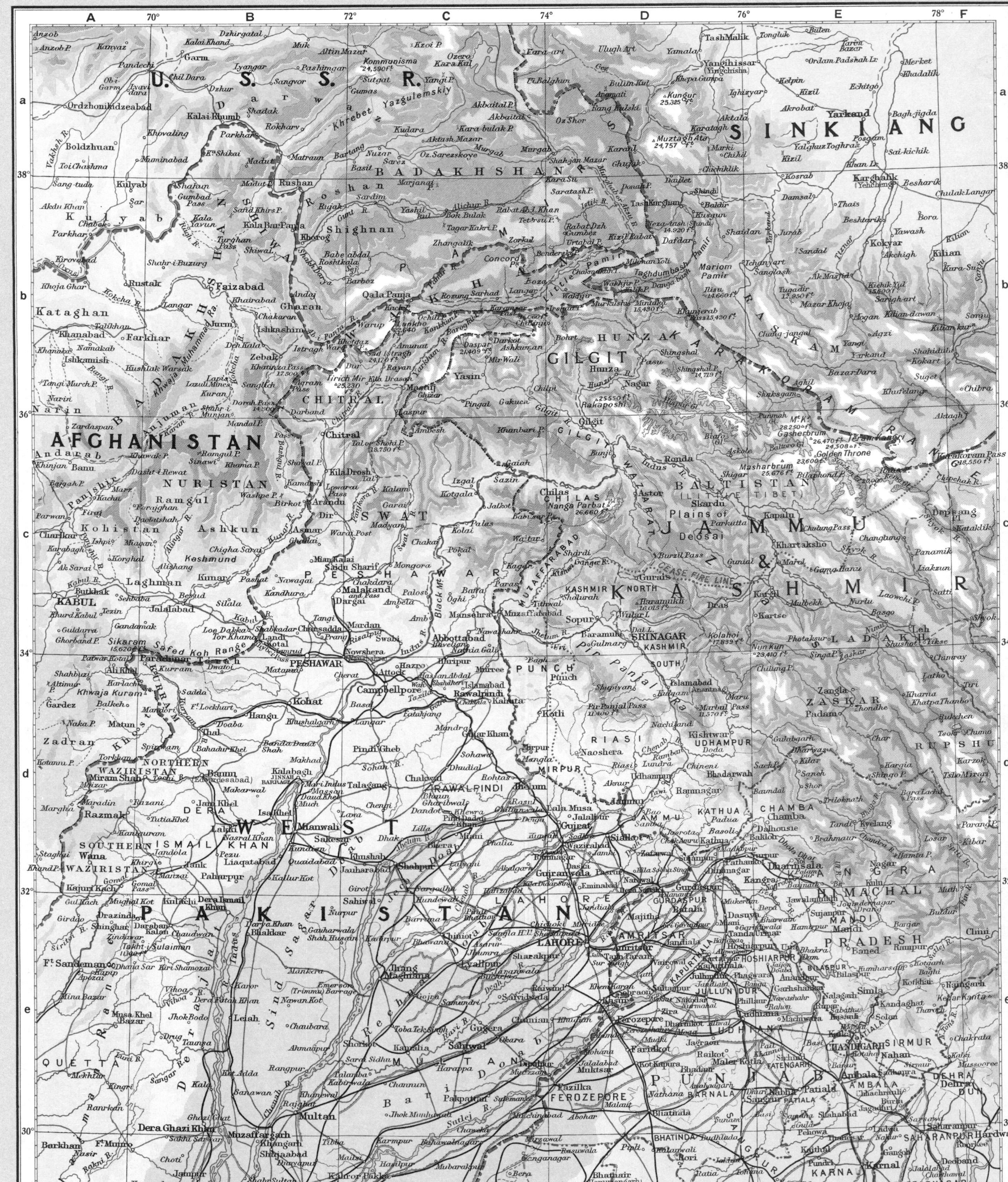

70

CONIC PROJECTION

SCALE: 1 INCH TO 63 MILES

INTERNATIONAL BOUNDARIES

STATE BOUNDARIES

PLAIN OF THE GANGES

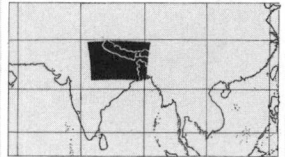

The Ganges valley is one of the most thickly populated regions in the world. The population is entirely dependent on the rivers that flow down from the north-west, across the plain, and through their many deltas into the Bay of Bengal. These rivers bring with them rich alluvial deposits and provide waters for irrigation. The largest river in the plain is revered throughout India as Mother Ganges.

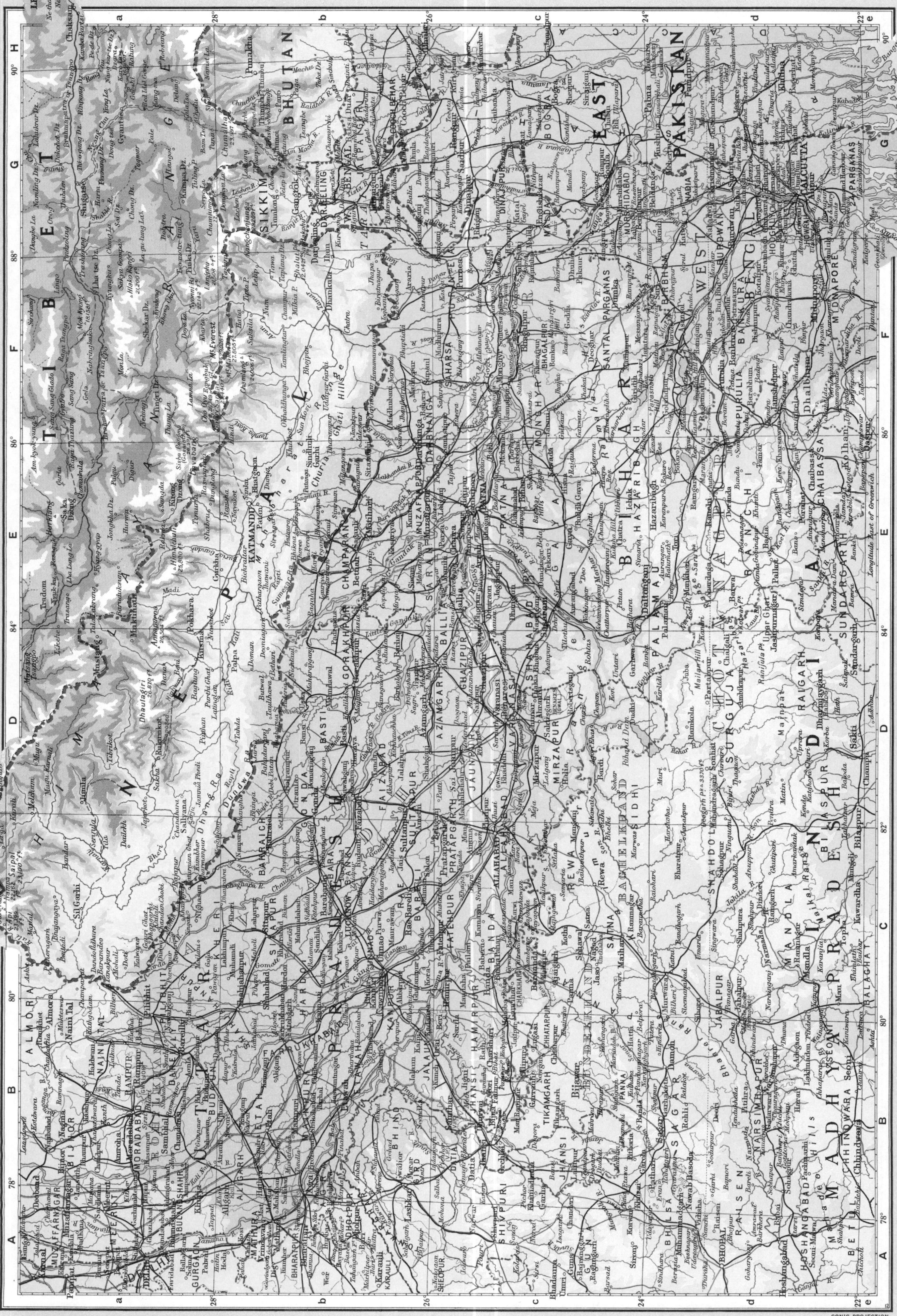

SCALE
IN MILES

50
100
150
200
250
300
350
400
450
500

MAIN ROADS _____
RAILWAYS _____

CONIC PROJECTION

SCALE: 1 INCH TO 63 MILES

71

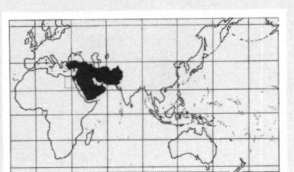

THE MIDDLE EAST
AND AFGHANISTAN

TURKEY AREA: 301,380 sq. miles. POPULATION: 32,901,000. CAPITAL: Ankara. CURRENCY: 100 piastres (kurus)=1 pound.
IRAQ AREA: 173,259 sq. miles. POPULATION: 8,338,000. CAPITAL: Baghdad. CURRENCY: 1,000 fils=1 dinar.

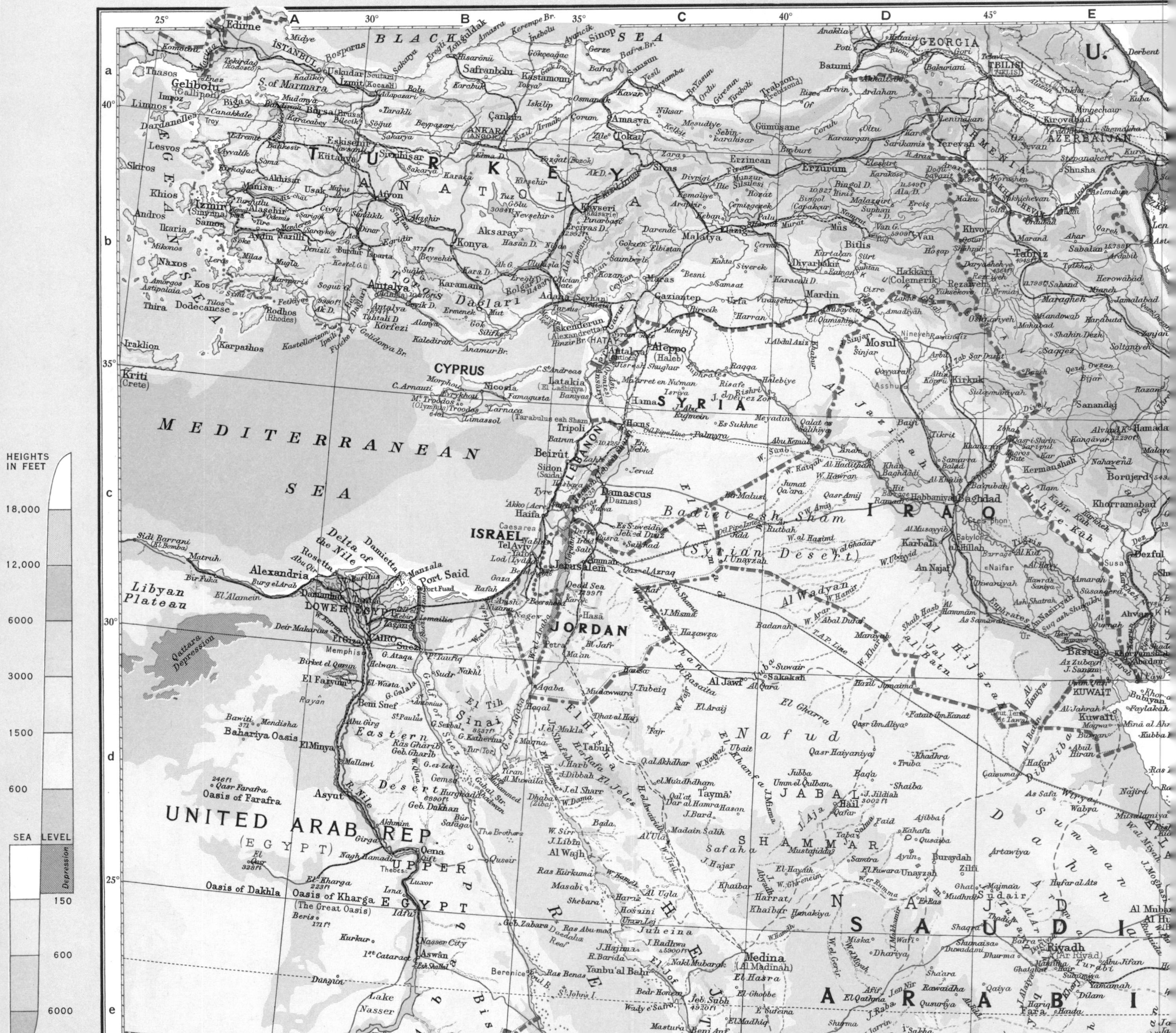

HEIGHTS IN FEET

18,000
12,000
6000
3000
1500
600
SEA LEVEL
Depression
150
600
6000

DEPTHS IN FEET

BLACK SEA
MEDITERRANEAN SEA
TURKEY
ANATOLIA
CYPRUS
SYRIA
LEBANON
ISRAEL
JORDAN
IRAQ
Baghdad
Damascus
Beirût
Jerusalem
Aleppo
Mosul
Kirkuk
Basra
KUWAIT
Kuwait
Syrian Desert
Badiet esh Sham
Nafud
JABAL SHAMMAR
NAJD
SAUDI ARABIA
Riyadh
Mecca
Medina
Jiddah
RED SEA
UNITED ARAB REP.
(EGYPT)
LOWER EGYPT
UPPER EGYPT
CAIRO
Alexandria
Port Said
Suez
Libyan Plateau
Qattara Depression
Oasis of Farafra
Oasis of Dakhla
Oasis of Kharga
(The Great Oasis)
Lake Nasser
Nubian Desert
Eastern Desert
Delta of the Nile
SUDAN
KORDOFAN
Khartoum
Omdurman
Berber
Atbara
ETHIOPIA
Asmara
Massawa
YEMEN
Sana
SOUTHERN
Aden
GEORGIA
U.
ISTANBUL
ANKARA
Ankara

MAIN ROADS
RAILWAYS

SCALE: 1 INCH TO 158 MILES

CONIC PROJECTION

72

IRAN (PERSIA) AREA: *636,293 sq. miles.* POPULATION: *25,780,000.* CAPITAL: *Tehran.* CURRENCY: *100 dinars=1 rial.*
AFGHANISTAN AREA: *250,000 sq. miles.* POP: *15,909,000,* CAPITAL: *Kabul.* CURRENCY: *100 puls=1 afghāni.*

SAUDI ARABIA AREA: *869,803 sq. miles.* POPULATION: *6,750,000.* CAPITALS: *Mecca and Riyadh.* CURRENCY: *20 qurush=1 rial.*
The map shows the fold mountain belt widening from the

Georgian Caucasus into the broad plateau of Persia, and narrowing at the heights of the Hindu Kush. The deep rift of the Jordan and the Dead Sea broadens into the Red Sea, and continues south as the Great Rift Valley of Africa.

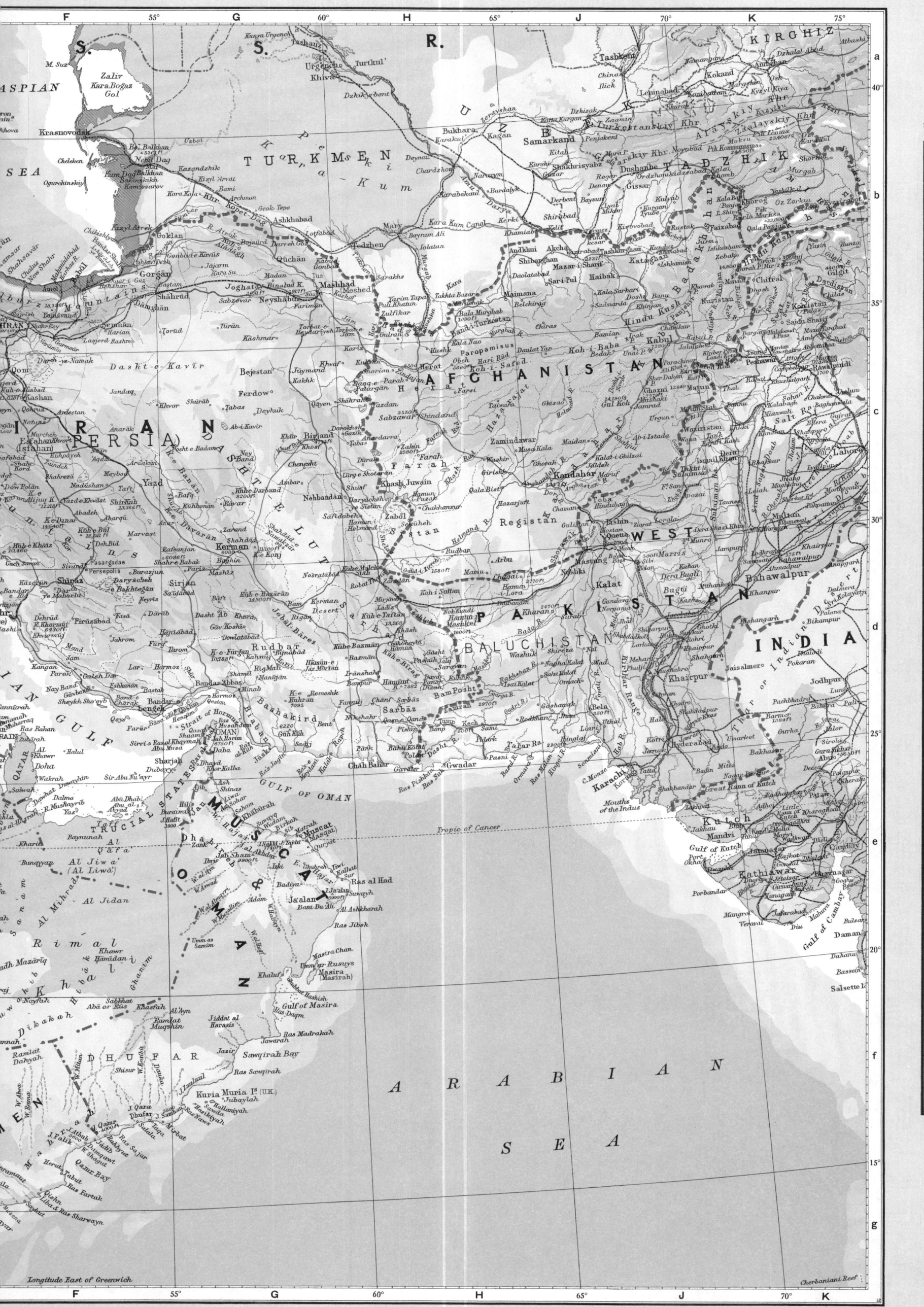

SCALE: 1 INCH TO 158 MILES

INTERNATIONAL BOUNDARIES
STATE BOUNDARIES

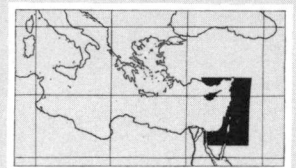

THE LEVANT AND JORDAN

SYRIA AREA: *71,210 sq. miles.*
POPULATION: *5,300,000.*
CAPITAL: *Damascus.*
CURRENCY: *100 piastres=1 pound.*

LEBANON AREA: *4,000 sq. miles.*
POPULATION: *2,405,000.*
CAPITAL: *Beirut.*
CURRENCY: *100 piastres=1 pound.*

ISRAEL AREA: *7,992 sq. miles.*
POPULATION: *2,629,000.*
CAPITAL: *Jerusalem.*
CURRENCY: *100 agorot=1 pound.*

JORDAN AREA: *37,737 sq. miles.*
POPULATION: *1,976,000.*
CAPITAL: *Amman.*
CURRENCY: *1,000 fils=1 dinar.*

HEIGHTS IN FEET

9000
6000
3000
1500
600
300
SEA LEVEL
Depression
150
600
6000

DEPTHS IN FEET

SCALE IN MILES
25
50
75
100
125
150
175
200
225
250

74

CONIC PROJECTION

SCALE: 1 INCH TO 39 MILES

— · —— · — INTERNATIONAL BOUNDARIES
· · · · · · · · · STATE BOUNDARIES
++++++++++ ARMISTICE LINE

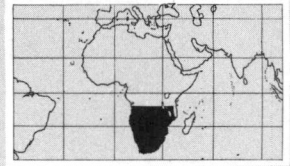

ZAMBIA	**RHODESIA**	**S. WEST AFRICA**	**MALAWI**	**REP. OF S. AFRICA**	**BOTSWANA**	**MOÇAMBIQUE**	
AREA: 288,130 sq. m.	AREA: 150,333 sq. m.	AREA: 325,608 sq. m.	AREA: 49,066 sq. m.	AREA: 471,818 sq. m.	AREA: 220,000 sq. m.	AREA: 302,227 sq. m.	
POP: 3,837,000.	POP: 4,400,000.	POP: 574,000.	POP: 4,042,000.	POP: 18,298,000.	POP: 580,000.	POP: 6,956,000.	
CAP: Lusaka.	CAP: Salisbury.	CAP: Windhoek.	CAP: Zomba.	CAPS: Pretoria, Cape Town.	CAP: Gaberones.	CAP: Lourenço Marques.	

HEIGHTS IN FEET

9000
6000
3000
1500
600
SEA LEVEL
150
600
6000
DEPTHS IN FEET

SCALE IN MILES

100
200
300
400
500
600
700
800
900
1000

On the same scale

TRISTAN DA CUNHA (U.K.)
Edinburgh
Inaccessible I.
Nightingale I.
Tristan I.

THE CAPE
1 INCH TO 13 MILES

WITWATERSRAND
1 INCH TO 16 MILES

Limit of Gold-bearing Area

Contours at 600-1000-2000-3000-4000 Feet

Contours at 500-6000 Feet

75

LAMBERT'S AZIMUTHAL EQUAL-AREA PROJECTION

MAIN ROADS ————
RAILWAYS ————

SCALE: 1 INCH TO 197 MILES

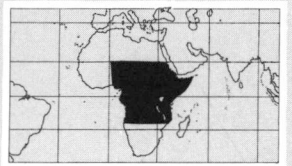

CENTRAL and EAST AFRICA

CONGO, KENYA, UGANDA, TANZANIA, ETHIOPIA, MADAGASCAR

ANGOLA AREA: *481,351 sq. miles.* POP: *5,154,000.* CAP: *Luanda.*

KENYA AREA: *224,960 sq. miles.* POP: *9,643,000.* CAP: *Nairobi.*

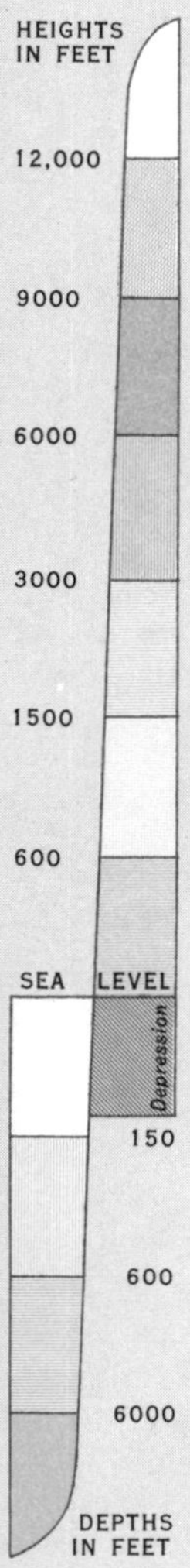

HEIGHTS IN FEET

12,000
9000
6000
3000
1500
600
SEA LEVEL
Depression
150
600
6000

DEPTHS IN FEET

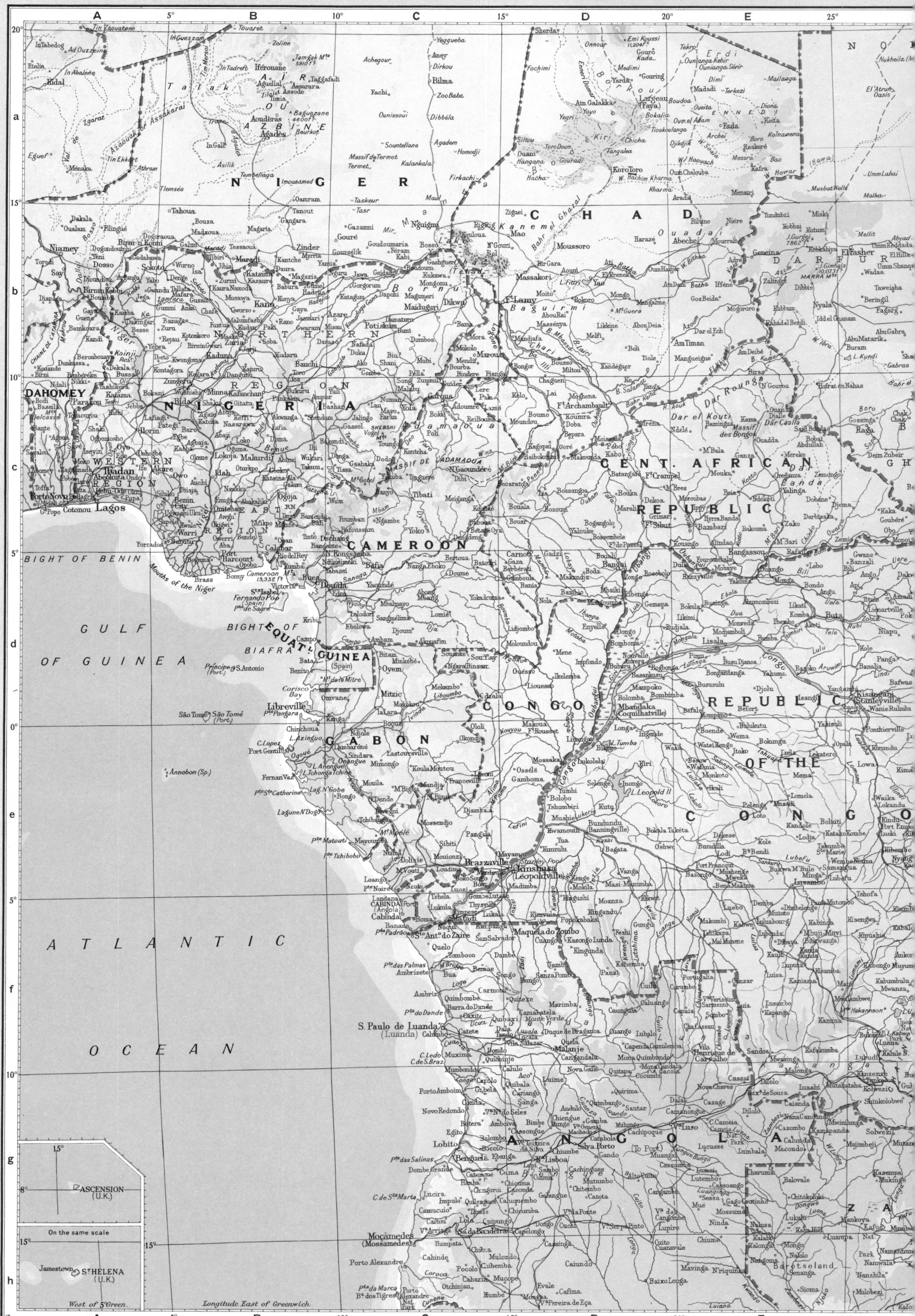

ASCENSION (U.K.)

On the same scale

Jamestown S.T HELENA (U.K.)

West of 5° Green.

Longitude East of Greenwich

76

LAMBERT'S AZIMUTHAL EQUAL-AREA PROJECTION

SCALE: 1 INCH TO 197 MILES

——— MAIN ROADS

– – – RAILWAYS

REP. OF THE CONGO AREA: 905,380 sq. miles. POP: (Africans only): 15,986,000. CAP: Kinshasa
CAMEROON REPUBLIC AREA: 183,568 sq. miles. POP: 5,229,000. CAP: Yaoundé.
UGANDA AREA: 93,981 sq. miles. POP: 7,740,000. CAPS: Kampala, Entebbe.
TANZANIA AREA: 362,720 sq. m. POP: 10,500,000. CAP: Dar es Salaam.
ETHIOPIA AREA: 471,776 sq. miles. POP: 23,000,000. CAP: Addis Ababa.
SOMALI REPUBLIC AREA: 246,200 sq. miles. POP: 2,500,000. CAP: Mogadiscio.
MALAGASY REP. AREA: 230,036 sq. miles. POP: 6,420,000. CAP: Tananarive.

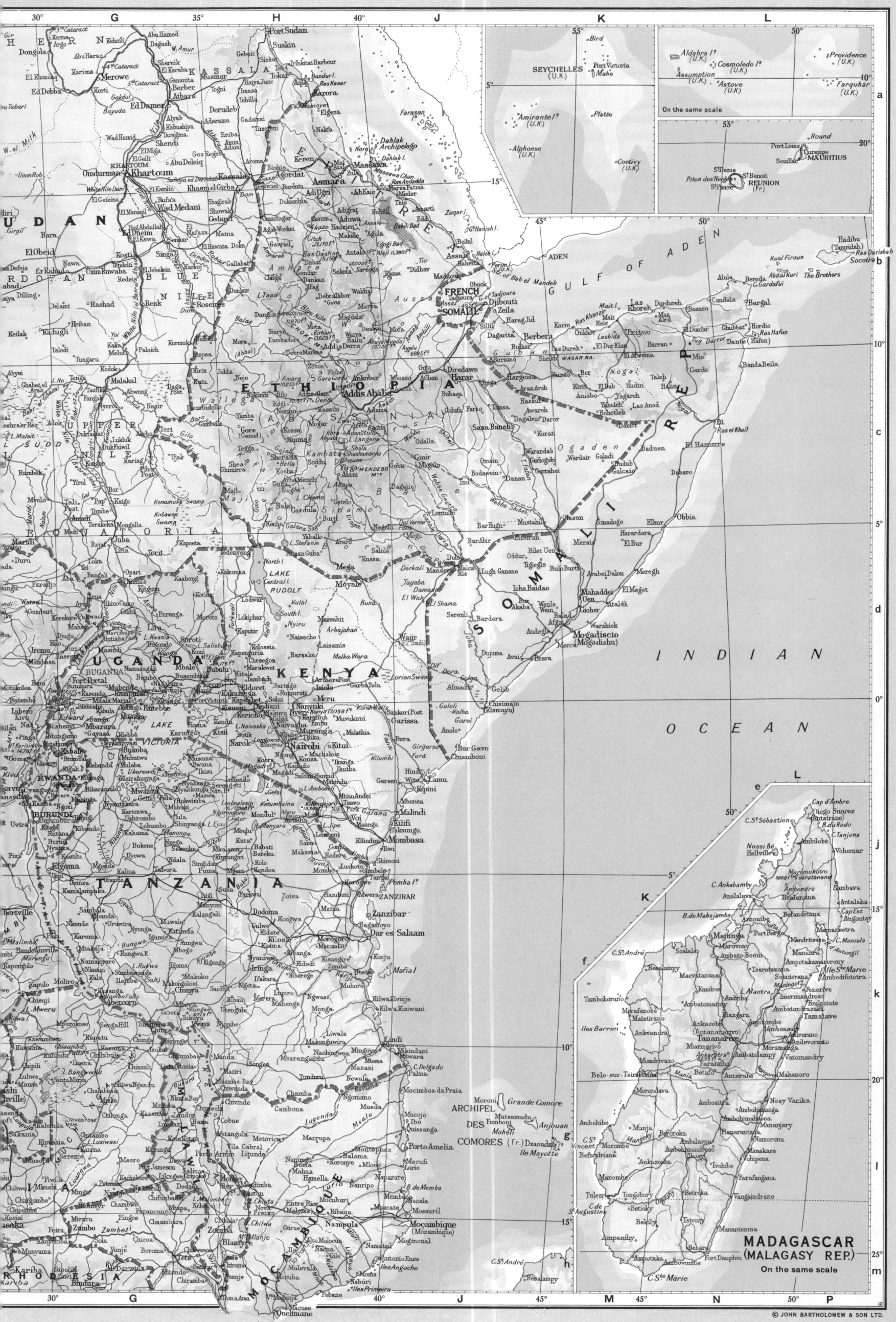

© JOHN BARTHOLOMEW & SON LTD.

SCALE: 1 INCH TO 197 MILES

INTERNATIONAL BOUNDARIES
STATE BOUNDARIES

77

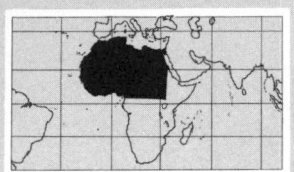

NORTH AND WEST AFRICA

MOROCCO, LIBYA, UNITED ARAB REP, SUDAN, GHANA, NIGERIA

MOROCCO AREA: 171,305 sq. miles. POP: 13,451,000. CAP: Rabat.
TUNISIA AREA: 63,380 sq. miles. POP: 4,458,000. CAP: Tunis.

HEIGHTS IN FEET

12,000
9000
6000
3000
1500
600
SEA LEVEL
Depression
150
600
6000
DEPTHS IN FEET

78

LAMBERT'S AZIMUTHAL EQUAL-AREA PROJECTION

SCALE: 1 INCH TO 197 MILES

MAIN ROADS
RAILWAYS

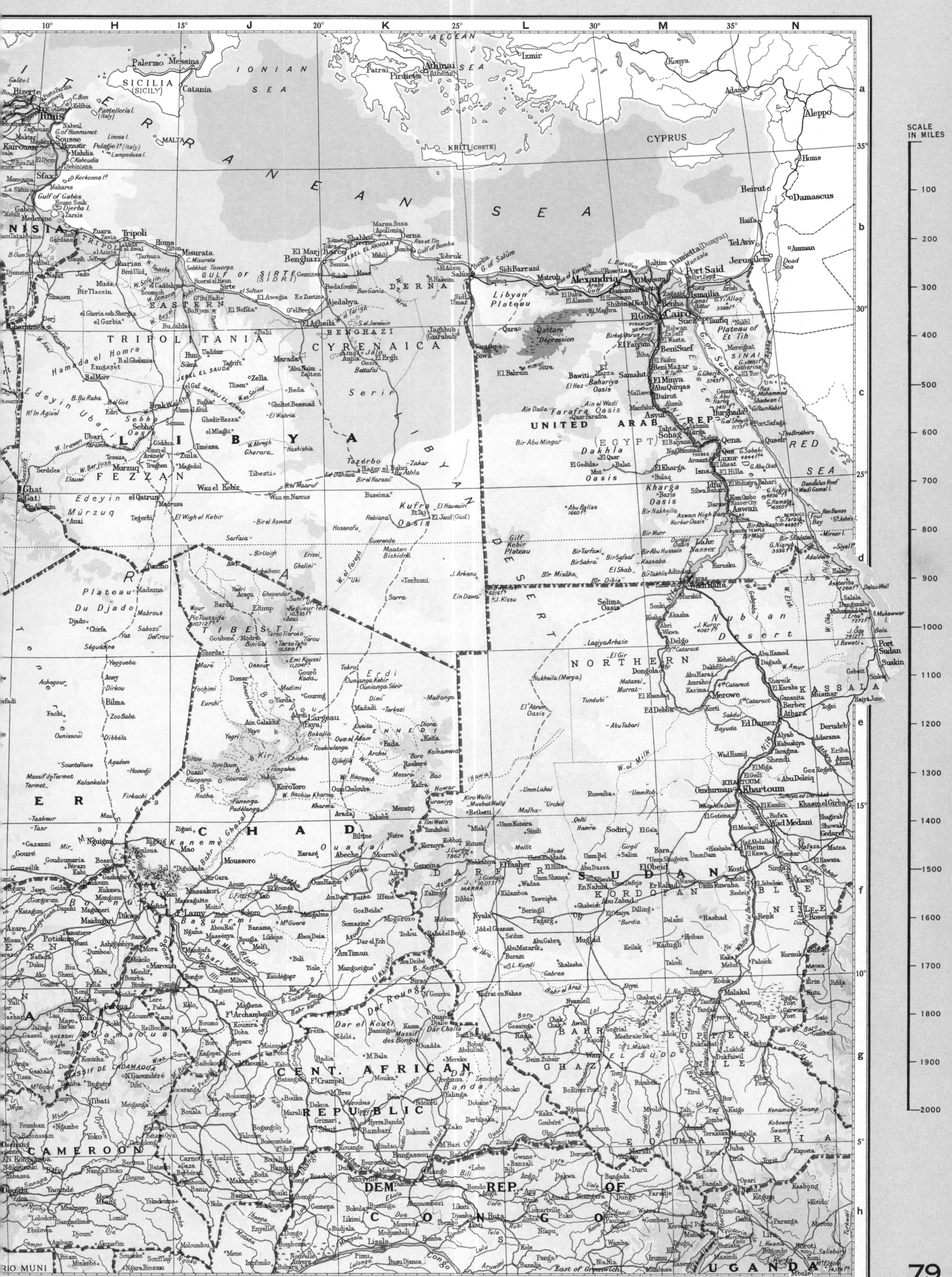

LIBYA AREA: 679,358 sq. miles. POP:
1,677,000. CAPS: Tripoli, Benghazi.
UNITED ARAB REP. AREA: 386,198
sq. m. POP. 30,147,000. CAP: Cairo.

SUDAN AREA: 967,500 sq. miles. POP:
13,940,000. CAP: Khartoum.
NIGERIA AREA: 356,668 sq. miles. POP
57,500,000. CAP: Lagos.

GHANA AREA: 92,100 sq. miles. POP:
7,945,000. CAP: Accra.
LIBERIA AREA: 43,000 sq. miles. POP:
1,090,000. CAP: Monrovia.

SIERRA LEONE AREA: 27,699 sq. mile.
POP: 2,403,000. CAP: Freetown.
ALGERIA AREA: 919,591 sq. miles.
POP: 12,102,000. CAP: Algiers.

79

© JOHN BARTHOLOMEW & SON LTD.

INTERNATIONAL BOUNDARIES
STATE BOUNDARIES

SCALE: 1 INCH TO 197 MILES

SCALE IN MILES

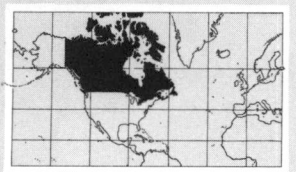

CANADA

AREA: *3,851,809 sq. miles*. POPULATION: *19,919,000*.
CAPITAL: *Ottawa*. CURRENCY: *100 cents=1 dollar*.
From the mountains of Alberta and British Columbia in the west, the land slopes down towards Hudson Bay in the north-east and then rises slightly again to the east in Quebec Province. Most of the rivers and vast lake areas (the inland water area of Canada is over 291,500 square miles) follow this north-east trend, the lakes

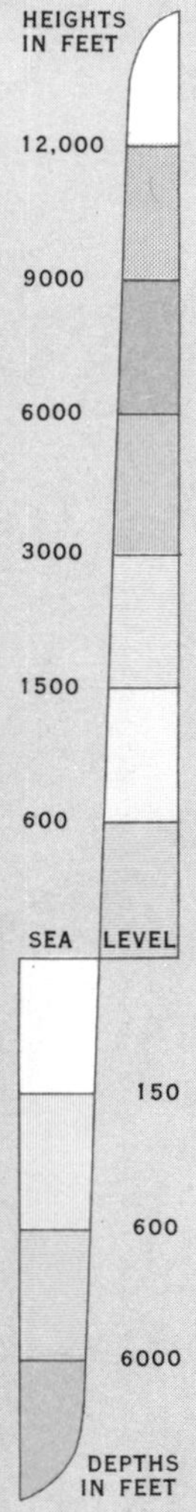

HEIGHTS
IN FEET

12,000
9000
6000
3000
1500
600

SEA LEVEL

150
600
6000

DEPTHS
IN FEET

80

CONIC PROJECTION

SCALE: 1 INCH TO 197 MILES

MAIN ROADS
RAILWAYS

themselves lying in deep depressions grooved out by the passage of the Ice Cap which once covered the whole country. The foothills of the Rocky Mountain system, of which the mountains of western Canada form part, reach down to the sea in the west, where the coast is fringed with many islands and inlets. To the east of the Rockies and towards the Hudson Bay lowlands stretch the Great Plains. A small area of the Yukon Territory and a large part of the North-West Territories and the archipelago to the north of them lie well within the Arctic Circle. The population of these northern lands is sparse. The most densely populated areas of Canada lie within 200 miles of the southern border.

SCALE IN MILES

81

INTERNATIONAL BOUNDARIES
PROVINCE BOUNDARIES

SCALE: 1 INCH TO 197 MILES

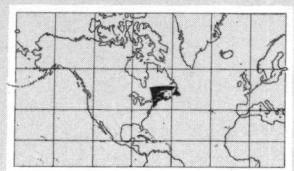

GULF OF ST. LAWRENCE

The Gulf of St. Lawrence and the St. Lawrence River have for long been of great importance as a means of access to Canada's interior. In April 1959 a 27-foot channel from Montreal to Lake Erie was opened, thus extending the old waterway (now the St. Lawrence Seaway) to a length of 2,342 miles and enabling ocean-going vessels to navigate from the Atlantic to Duluth at the western end of Lake Superior.

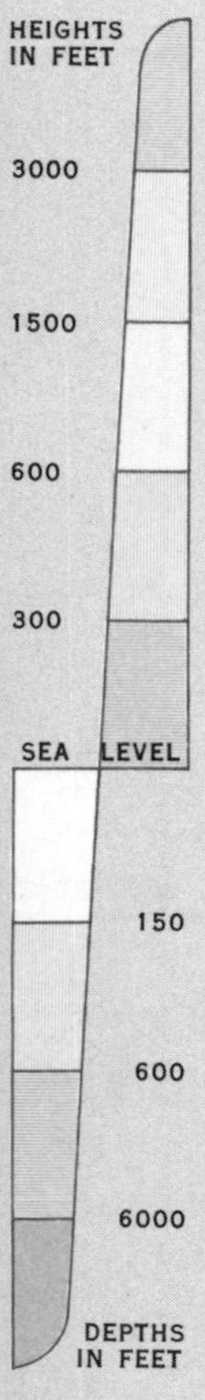

HEIGHTS
IN FEET

3000

1500

600

300

SEA LEVEL

150

600

6000

DEPTHS
IN FEET

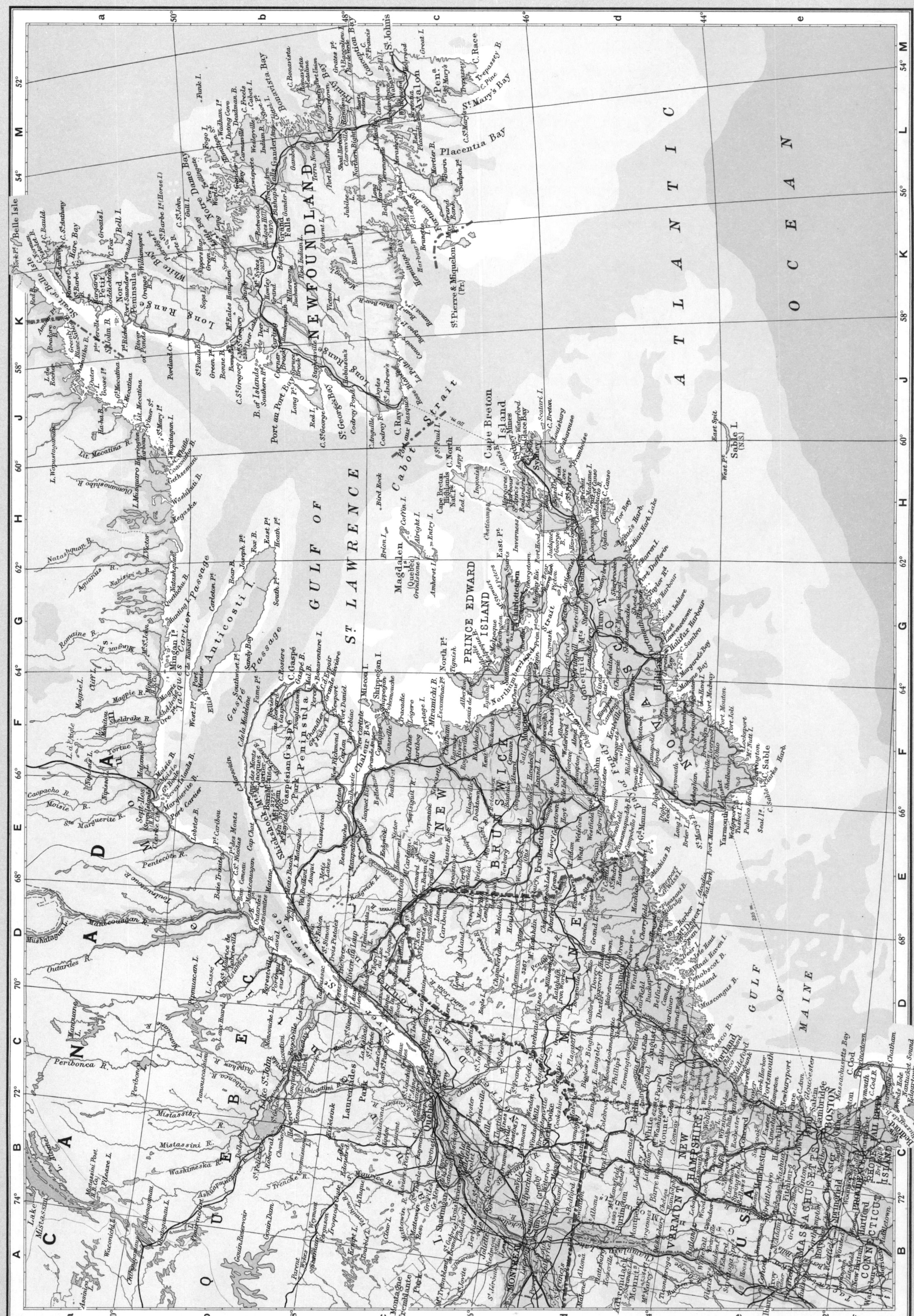

82

Bonne's Projection

SCALE: 1 INCH TO 79 MILES

INTERNATIONAL BOUNDARIES

PROVINCE AND STATE BOUNDARIES

These lakes, the greatest body of fresh water in the world, have a total area of approximately 95,000 square miles, and as a region of inland navigation they are unparalleled. Lake Michigan is entirely in the United States, while the other lakes are shared between the United States and Canada.

SCALE IN MILES

50
100
150
200
250
300
350
400
450
500
550
600
650
700
750
800

MAIN ROADS _____
RAILWAYS _____

SCALE: 1 INCH TO 79 MILES

BONNE'S PROJECTION

UNITED STATES OF AMERICA

AREA: *3,615,212 sq. miles.* POPULATION: *196,842,000.* CAPITAL: *Washington, D.C.* CURRENCY: *100 cents=1 dollar.* The United States can be divided into six

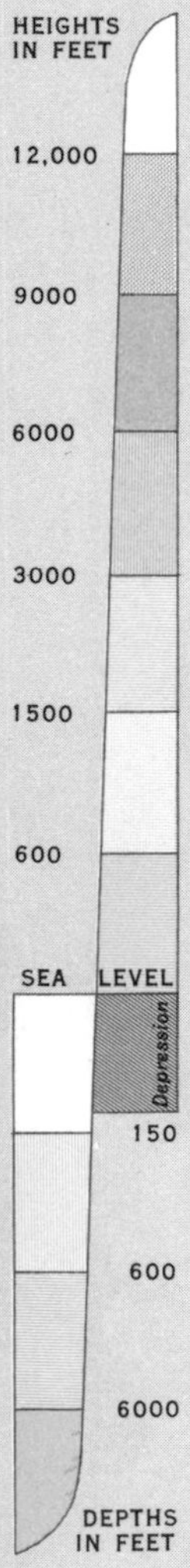

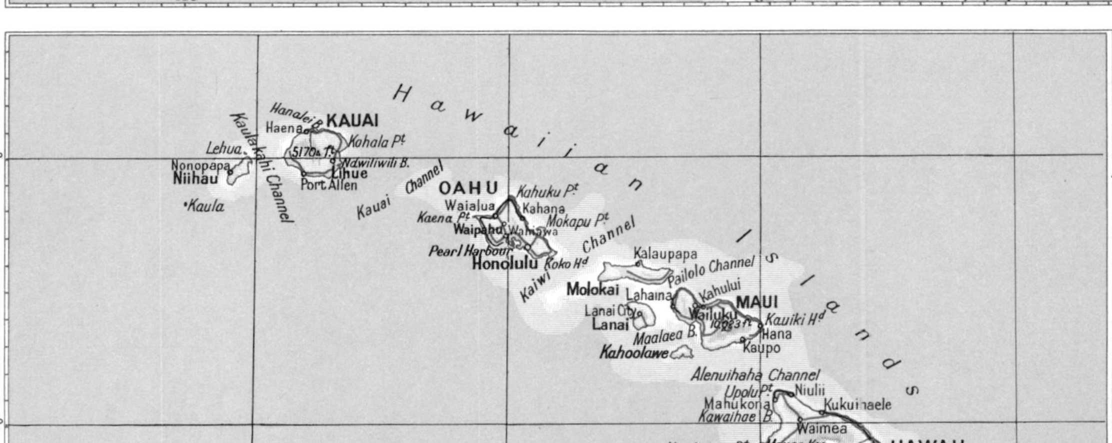

HEIGHTS IN FEET

12,000
9000
6000
3000
1500
600

SEA LEVEL
Depression

150
600
6000

DEPTHS IN FEET

P A C I F I C   O C E A N

HAWAII

SCALE : 1 INCH TO 98 MILES
0   50   100 Miles

SAN FRANCISCO
1 INCH TO 6 MILES

CONIC PROJECTION

84

SCALE: 1 INCH TO 197 MILES

MAIN ROADS
RAILWAYS

north–south sections. Reading the map from east to west, these are—a broad plain edging the Atlantic; the Appalachian Mountains; the Mississippi Basin; the Great Plains; the Rocky Mountains, and beyond, and along the Pacific coast, more mountains interspersed with fertile valleys. The state of Alaska, in the extreme north-west, is separated from the main body of the land by Western Canada. The northern part of the State lies within the Arctic Circle, and to the west it is separated from the U.S.S.R. by the Bering Strait. Hawaii consists of 20 islands (eight inhabited) in the North Pacific some 2,000 miles from San Francisco.

SCALE IN MILES

NEW YORK
1 INCH TO 6 MILES

ALASKA
SCALE: 1 INCH TO 394 MILES

INTERNATIONAL BOUNDARIES

STATE BOUNDARIES

© JOHN BARTHOLOMEW & SON LTD.

85

SCALE: 1 INCH TO 197 MILES

MIDDLE ATLANTIC STATES

The Atlantic seaboard in this north-east area of the United States is flanked by lowlands. The broken coastline is deeply penetrated by Chesa-peake, Delaware and Narragansett Bays. To the west and north of the lowlands lie the Appalachian, Catskill and Adirondack Mountains, while to the north-west is the Allegheny Plateau. To the south is Washington, in the District of Columbia, the seat of the U.S. Federal Government.

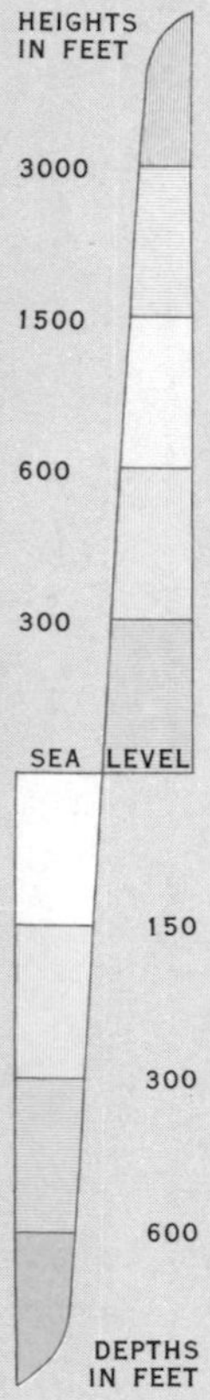

HEIGHTS
IN FEET

3000

1500

600

300

SEA LEVEL

150

300

600

DEPTHS
IN FEET

SCALE
IN MILES

25

50

75

100

125

150

175

200

225

250

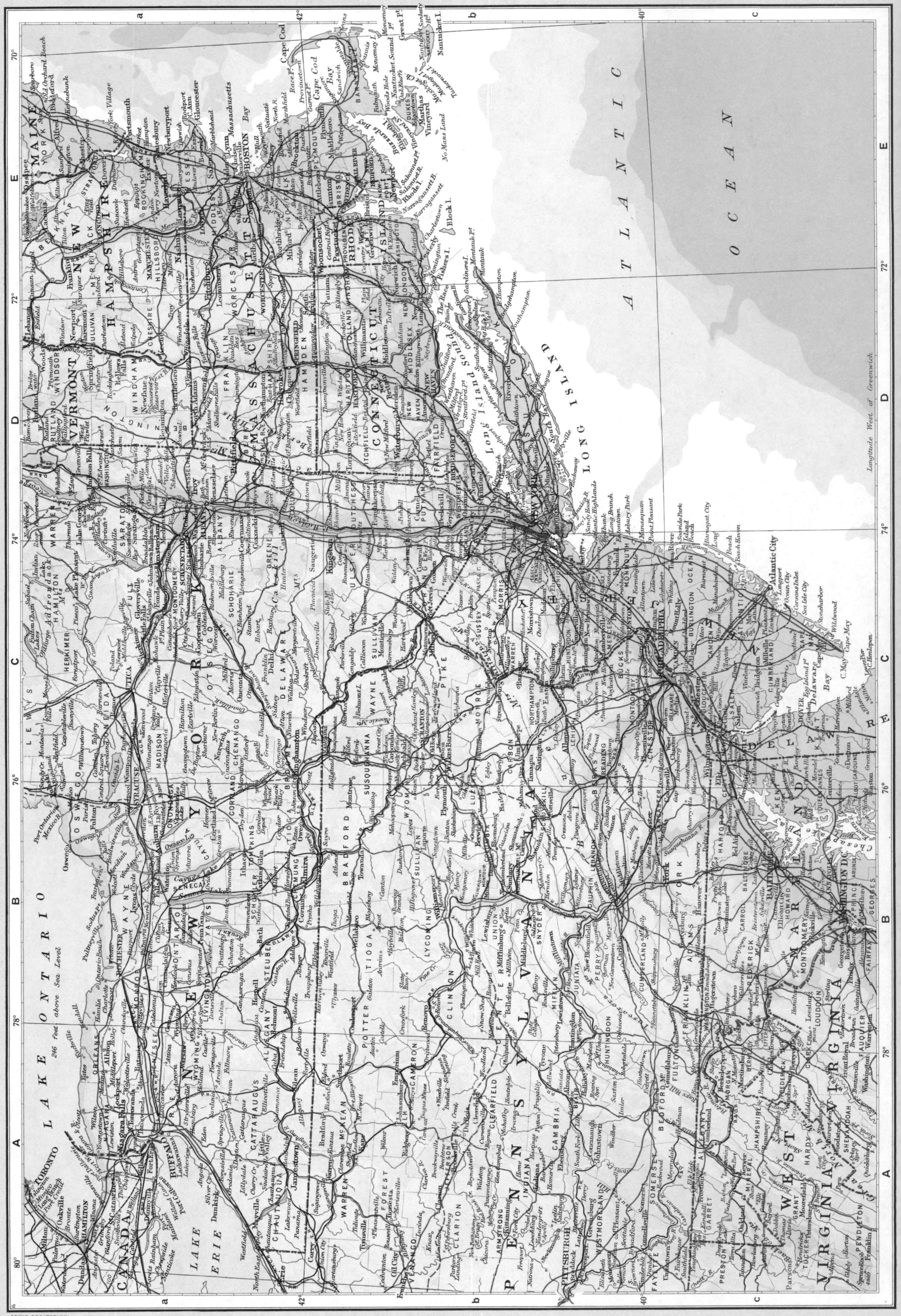

86

CONIC PROJECTION

SCALE: 1 INCH TO 39 MILES

MAIN ROADS
RAILWAYS

PACIFIC COAST

The map shows the States of Washington, Oregon, California and Nevada. The Coast Ranges on the west are separated by the Willamette Valley and the Central Valley of California from the Cascade Mountains and the Sierra Nevada. Beyond lies an extensive area of high basins, plateaux and ranges.

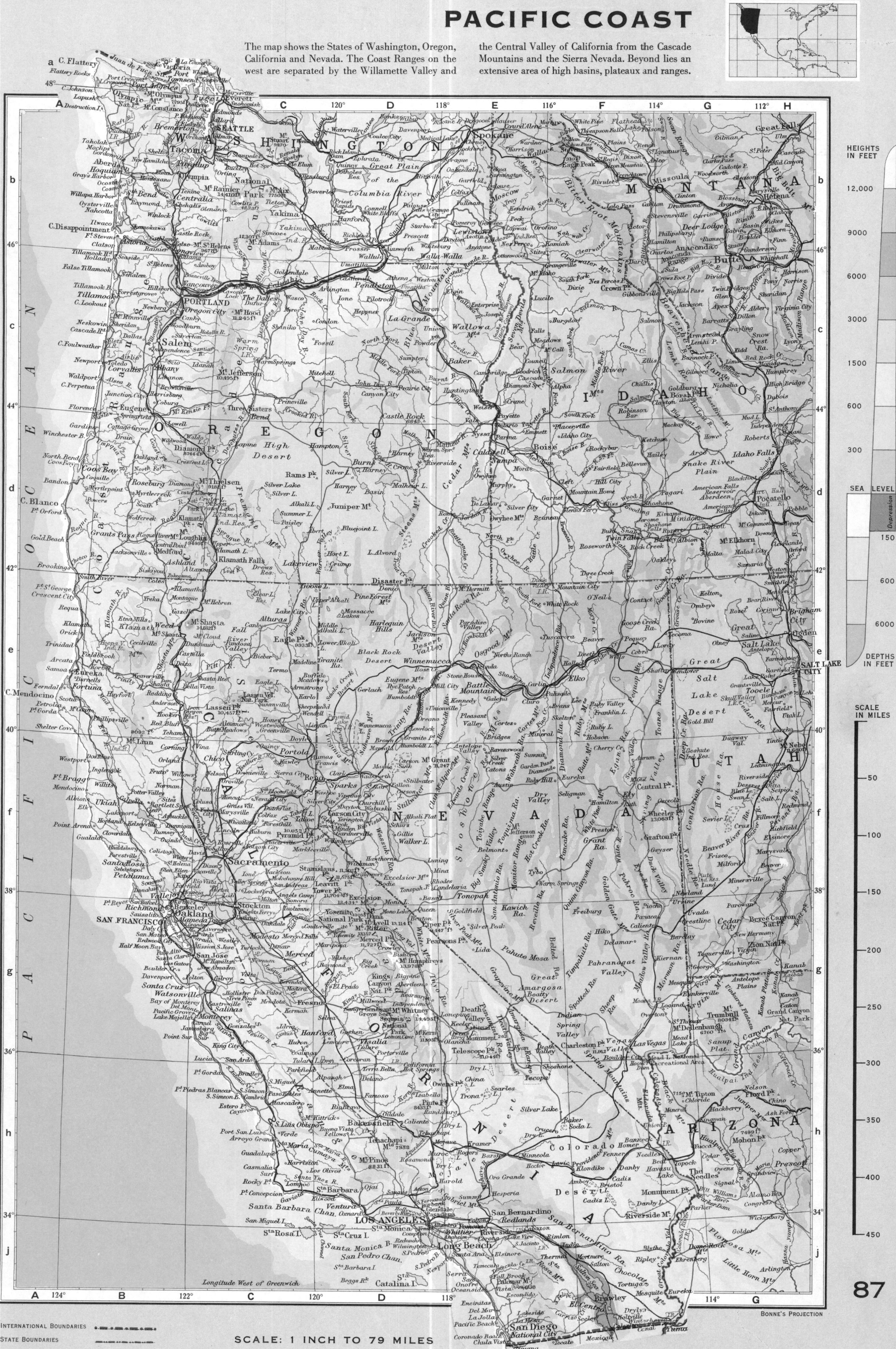

HEIGHTS IN FEET

12,000

9000

6000

3000

1500

600

300

SEA LEVEL

Depression

150

600

6000

DEPTHS IN FEET

SCALE IN MILES

50

100

150

200

250

300

350

400

450

87

Bonne's Projection

INTERNATIONAL BOUNDARIES
STATE BOUNDARIES

SCALE: 1 INCH TO 79 MILES

MEXICO GUATEMALA, HONDURAS, BRITISH HONDURAS, EL SALVADOR

MEXICO AREA: 761,600 sq. miles. POP: 44,145,000. CAP: Mexico City.
GUATEMALA AREA: 42,042 sq. miles. POP: 4,575,000. CAP: Guatemala City.
HONDURAS AREA: 43,277 sq. miles. POP: 2,363,000. CAP: Tegucigalpa.

BRITISH HONDURAS AREA: 8,867 sq. miles. POP: 109,000. CAP: Belize.
EL SALVADOR AREA: 8,260 sq. miles. POP: 3,037,000. CAP: San Salvador.

HEIGHTS IN FEET

12,000
9000
6000
3000
1500
600
SEA LEVEL
150
600
6000
DEPTHS IN FEET

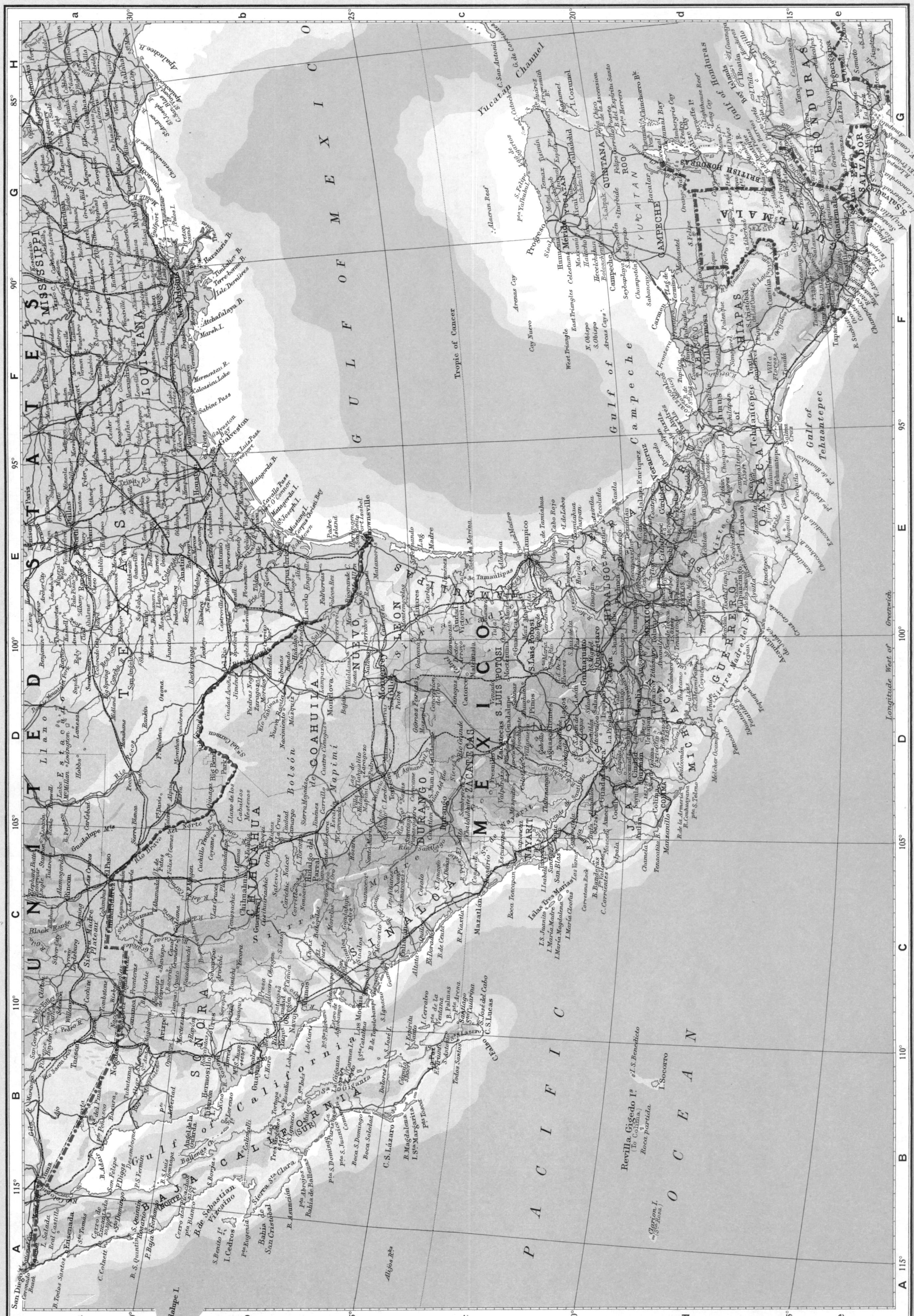

88

BONNE'S PROJECTION

SCALE: 1 INCH TO 158 MILES

INTERNATIONAL BOUNDARIES
STATE BOUNDARIES

WEST INDIES AND THE PANAMA CANAL — THE CARIBBEAN

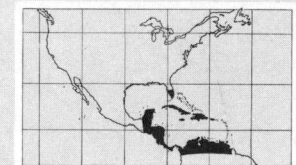

NICARAGUA AREA: 57,143 sq. miles. POPULATION: 1,655,000. CAP: *Managua.*
COSTA RICA AREA: 19,695 sq. miles. POPULATION: 1,486,000. CAP: *San José.*
PANAMA AREA: 28,575 sq. miles. POPULATION: 1,287,000. CAP: *Panama City.*

CUBA AREA: 44,218 sq. miles. POPULATION: 7,833,000. CAP: *Havana.*
JAMAICA AREA: 4,232 sq. miles. POPULATION: 1,839,000. CAP: *Kingston.*

CANAL ZONE
SCALE: 1 INCH TO 16 MILES
Canal ——— Railway ——
Contours are drawn at 300 and 600 Feet

SCALE IN MILES

MAIN ROADS ———
RAILWAYS ——————

Bonne's Projection

SCALE: 1 INCH TO 158 MILES

89

SOUTH AMERICA - NORTH

BRAZIL, PERU, ECUADOR, COLOMBIA, VENEZUELA

BRAZIL AREA: *3,286,170 sq. miles.* POPULATION: *84,679,000**.
CAPITAL: *Brasilia.*
BOLIVIA AREA: *424,163 sq. miles.* POPULATION: *3,748,000.*
CAPITAL: *La Paz.*

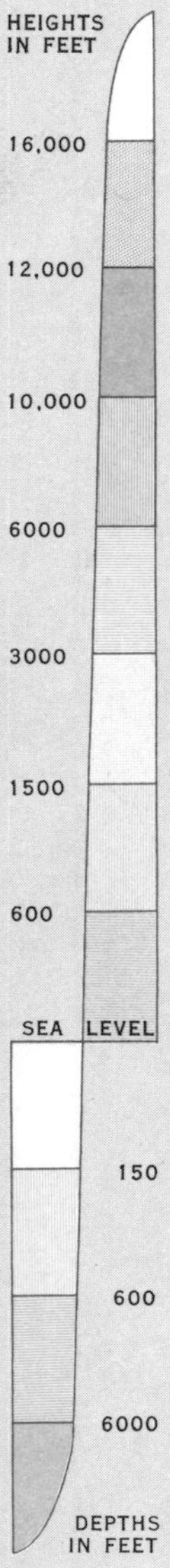

HEIGHTS IN FEET

16,000
12,000
10,000
6000
3000
1500
600
SEA LEVEL
150
600
6000

DEPTHS IN FEET

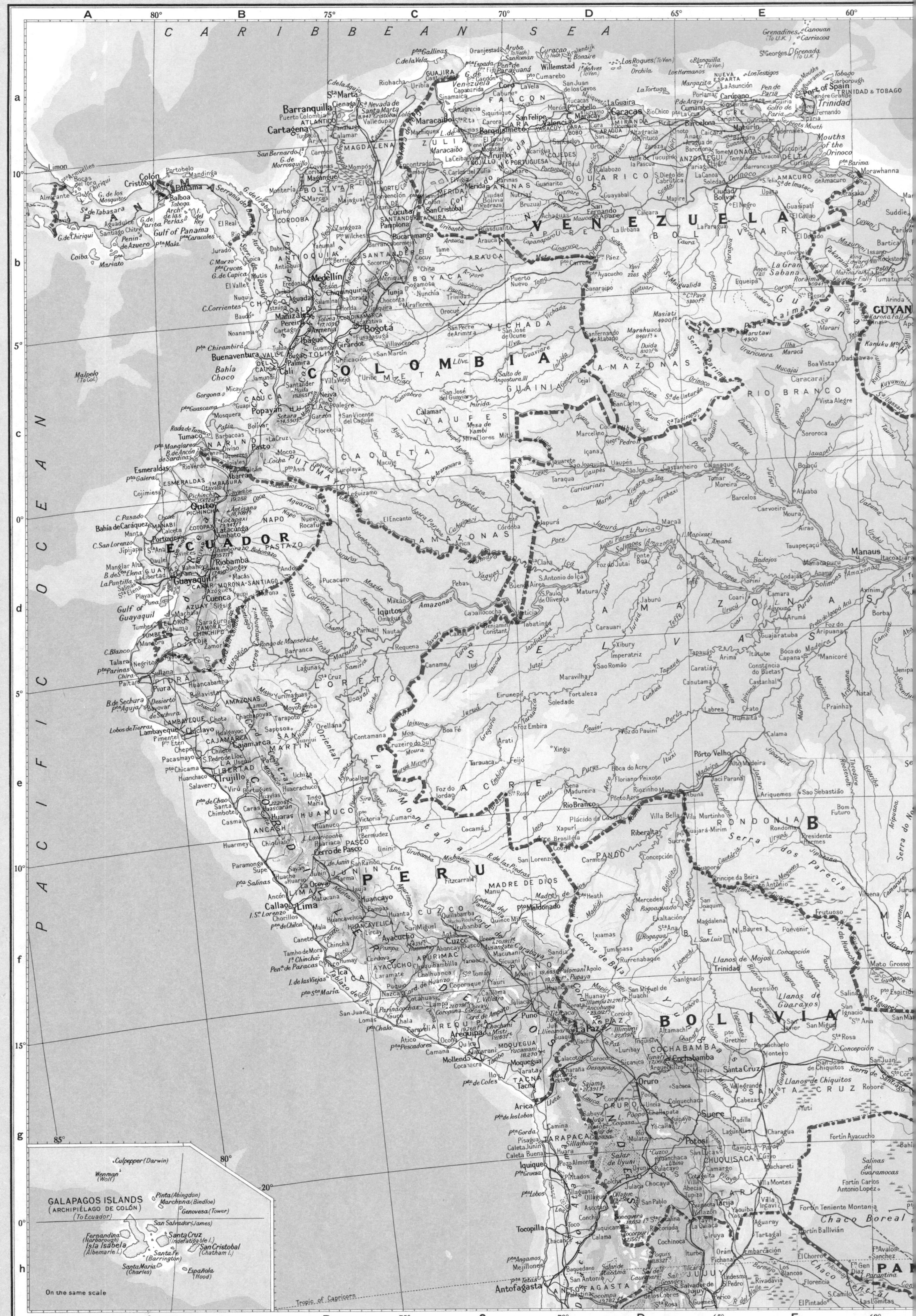

GALAPAGOS ISLANDS
(ARCHIPIÉLAGO DE COLÓN)
(To Ecuador)

On the same scale

90

LAMBERT'S AZIMUTHAL EQUAL-AREA PROJECTION

SCALE: 1 INCH TO 197 MILES

MAIN ROADS
RAILWAYS

PERU AREA: *496,222 sq. miles.* POP: *12,012,000*.* CAPITAL: *Lima.*
ECUADOR AREA: *104,506 sq. miles.* POPULATION: *5,326,000*.* CAP: *Quito.*

COLOMBIA AREA: *455,355 sq. miles.* POPULATION: *18,068,000.* CAPITAL: *Bogotá.*
VENEZUELA AREA: *352,143 sq. miles.* POPULATION: *9,030,000*.* CAP: *Caracas.*

GUYANA AREA: *83,000 sq. miles.* POPULATION: *665,000.* CAPITAL: *Georgetown.*
SURINAM AREA: *55,000 sq. miles.* POPULATION: *345,000.* CAPITAL: *Paramaribo.*

FRENCH GUIANA AREA: *35,100 sq. miles.* POPULATION: *37,000.* capital: *Cayenne.*

*Figure excludes Indian jungle population.

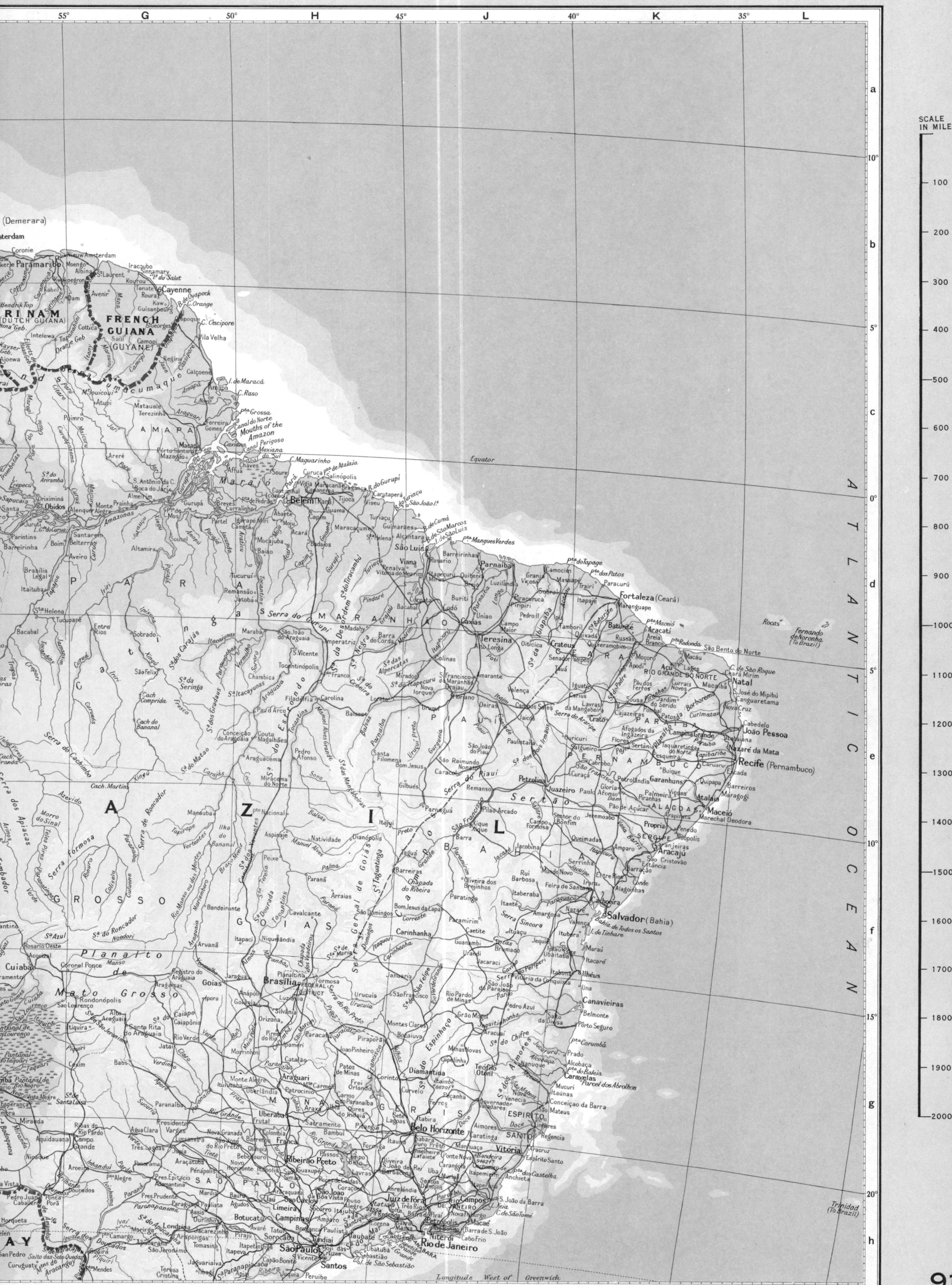

SCALE
IN MILES

100
200
300
400
500
600
700
800
900
1000
1100
1200
1300
1400
1500
1600
1700
1800
1900
2000

91

© JOHN BARTHOLOMEW & SON LTD.

ATIONAL BOUNDARIES

AND PROVINCIAL BOUNDARIES

SCALE: 1 INCH TO 197 MILES

SOUTH AMERICA-SOUTH
ARGENTINA, CHILE, PARAGUAY, URUGUAY

ARGENTINA AREA: 1,072,646 sq. miles. POPULATION: 22,691,000. CAPITAL: *Buenos Aires.*

CHILE AREA: 286,397 sq. miles. POPULATION: 8,591,000. CAPITAL: *Santiago.*

PARAGUAY AREA: 157,047 sq. miles. POPULATION: 2,094,000. CAPITAL: *Asunción.*

URUGUAY AREA: 72,172 sq. miles POPULATION: 2,749,000. CAPITAL: *Montevideo.*

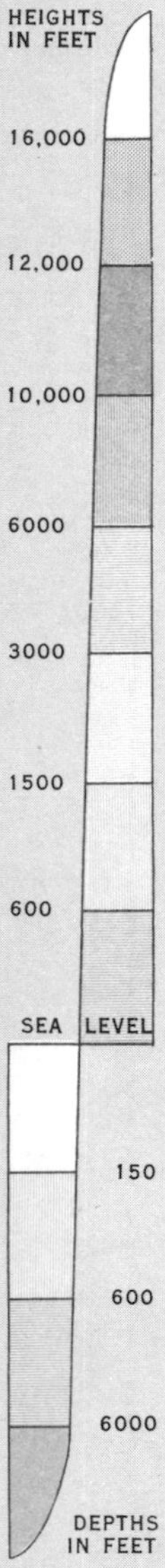

HEIGHTS IN FEET

16,000
12,000
10,000
6000
3000
1500
600

SEA LEVEL

150
600
6000

DEPTHS IN FEET

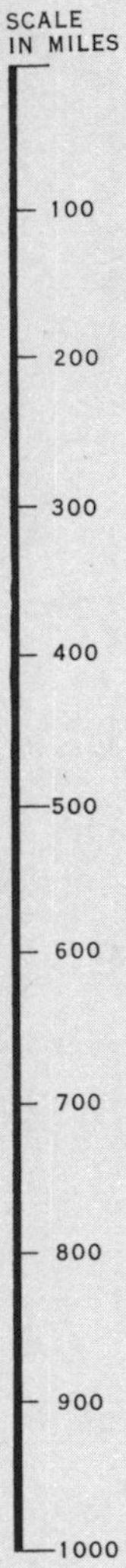

SCALE IN MILES

100
200
300
400
500
600
700
800
900
1000

92

LAMBERT'S AZIMUTHAL EQUAL-AREA PROJECTION

SCALE: 1 INCH TO 197 MILES

INTERNATIONAL BOUNDARIES — PROVINCIAL BOUNDARIES — MAIN ROADS — RAILWAYS

NEW ZEALAND

AREA: *103,736 sq. miles.* POP: *2,676,000.* CAPITAL: *Wellington.* CURRENCY: *100 cents=1 dollar.* New Zealand includes North Island and South Island, the considerably smaller Stewart Island to the south, and a number of minor islands. The main islands are mountainous with rich coastal plains. North Island has volcanic peaks and hot springs. South Island includes the Southern Alps (Mount Cook 12,349 ft.) and the Tasman Glacier.

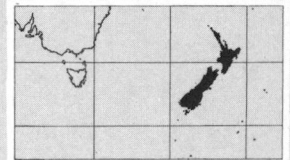

HEIGHTS IN FEET

6000
3000
1500
600
SEA LEVEL
150
600
6000

DEPTHS IN FEET

SCALE IN MILES

50
100
150
200
250
300
350
400
450
500

NORTH ISLAND

Three Kings I˚.
Spirits Bay
North Cape
C. Maria Van Diemen
North Cape
C. Reinga

Doubtless B.
Rangaunu B.

Mangonui
Ahipara B.
Kaitaia
Okaihau
Russell
C. Brett
Tauroa Pt.
Kawakawa
Kaikohe
Bay of Islands

Hokianga Har.
Rawene
Hikurangi
Donnellys Crossing
Kaihu
Whangarei
Hen & Chicken

Dargaville
Bream

Ruawai
Little Barrier I.
Great Barrier I.

Kaipara Har.
Kawau
C. Colville
Mercury Is. (Iles d' Haussez)

Helensville
Hauraki
Gulf
Waiheke
Mercury Bay
Takapuna
Coromandel
Devonport
Peninsula
CENTRAL
AUCKLAND
Onehunga
AUCKLAND
Manukau Har.
Papakura
Thames
Waiuku
Pukekohe
Mercer
Mayor I.
Tuakau
Paeroa
Waihi

Glen Afton
Morrinsville
White I.
C. Runaway
Hicks Bay
Huntly
Matakana I.
Ngaruawahia
Matamata
Tauranga Har.
East C.
HAMILTON
Cambridge
Te Puke
Raglan
Te Awamutu
Bay of
Plenty
Whakatane
Tuparoa
Kawhia
Te Aroha
Rotorua
Opotiki
Tokomaru Bay
Waitomo
Te Kuiti
Mangakino
Galatea
Talaga Bay
Awakino
Taupo
UREWERA
Patutahi
Gisborne

Ohura
Taumarunui
Murupara
Wairoa
NORTH
Tangiwai
TARANAKI BIGHT
Waikaremoana
Poverty Bay
New Plymouth
Waitara
Taihora
Mokau
Morere
Inglewood
Mt. Egmont
Stratford
TARANAKI
Frasertown
Kahutara Pt.
C. Egmont
Eltham
Toko
Napier
Mahia Peninsula
Opunake
Ohakune
Eskdale
HAWKE
Portland I.
SOUTH
Taihape
Hastings
TARANAKI BIGHT
Hawera
Hawke
Patea
C. Kidnappers
Bay
Havelock N.
Wanganui
Marton
WELLINGTON
Waipukurau
Waipawa
Danevirke
Ormondville
Feilding
Woodville
Palmerston N.
Pahiatua
Foxton
Levin
C. Turnagain
Herbertville
Otaki
Ekatahuna
Kapiti I.
Mauriceville
Masterton
Whakataki
Castlepoint
Paraparaumu
Carterton
Greytown
Petone
Hutt
Featherston
WELLINGTON
Martinborough
Lake Wairarapa
Palliser Bay
C. Palliser

SOUTH ISLAND

C. Farewell
Farewell Spit
C. Stephens
COOK STRAIT
Golden Bay
Separation Pt.
D'Urville I.
Rock Pt.
Takaka
Tasman Bay
Mt. Cobb
The Twins
Motueka
Karamea
Mt. Arthur
Nelson
Richmond
Blenheim
Karamea
Tuamarina
Bight
Seddonville
Renwick
Granity
Glenhope
Rai Valley
Westport
Picton
Havelock
MARLBOROUGH
C. Foulwind
Murchison
Seddon
C. Campbell
Buller
NELSON
Ward
Reefton
Springs Jn.
Wharanui
Inangahua Jn.
Springs
Runanga
Kaikoura
Greymouth
Brunner
Lewis Pass
Kaikoura
Hokitika
Kumara
Hanmer
Otira
Arthur's Pass
Waiau
Ross
Culverden
L. Sumner
Cheviot
Waikari
Waipara
Harihari
Rangiora
Pegasus Bay
SOUTH
Whataroa
Sefton
Kaiapoi
Franz Josef
Sheffield
Waimakariri
ISLAND
Oxford
Christchurch
WESTLAND
Mt. Tyndall
Darfield
Lyttelton
Mt. Cook
Hermitage
Methven
Banks Peninsula
Tasman
Little River
CANTERBURY
Akaroa
Mt. Sefton
L. Ellesmere
Haast
Swingbourne
Rakaia
Okuru
Springburn
Ashburton
Jackson Head
Tekapo
Tinwald
Cascade Pt.
Fairlie
Geraldine
L. Pukaki
Cave
Temuka
Awarua or
Big Bay
Canterbury
Bight
Pareora
Timaru
St. Andrews
Makikihi
Milford Sd.
Mt. Aspiring
Omarama
Waimate
George Sd.
Milford
Wanaka
L. Hawea
Waitaki
Morven
Caswell Sd.
Kinloch
Hawea Flat
Oamaru
Queenstown
Arrowtown
Kurow
Secretary I.
Te Anau
Cromwell
Ngapara
Hampden
Doubtful Sd.
L. Te Anau
Alexandra
Ranfurly
Herbert
Nelson
Manapouri
Wakatipu
Naseby
Kingston
OTAGO
Middlemarch
Palmerston
Breaksea Sd.
Manapouri
Roxburgh
Waikouaiti
Revolution I.
Lumsden
Dusky Sound
Athol
Ettrick
Millers Flat
Waihola
C. Providence
Dipton
Riversdale
Beaumont
Port Chalmers
Preservation Inlet
Orepuki
Waikaia
Clinton
Lawrence
Otago Peninsula
Puysegur Pt.
SOUTHLAND
Gore
Mataura
DUNEDIN
Te Waewae Bay
Winton
Edendale
Milton
Solander I.
Riverton
Wyndham
Balclutha
Owaka
Kaitangata
Codfish I.
Obata
Bluff
Tokanui
Invercargill
Tahakopa
Oban
Foveaux Strait
Patterson Inlet
STEWART
Shelter Pt.
Snares Is.
ISLAND
Southwest C.
Port Pegasus

Bounty Is.

TASMAN SEA

PACIFIC OCEAN

Longitude East of Greenwich

CONIC PROJECTION

SCALE: 1 INCH TO 79 MILES

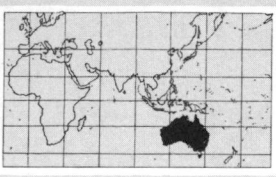

AUSTRALIA

AREA: *2,971,081 sq. miles.* POPULATION: *11,541,000* (excluding full-blooded aborigines). CAP: *Canberra.* Australia, the largest island in the world, comprises six States and two Territories. Although two-fifths of Australia lie within the Tropic of Capricorn, the general climate is more temperate than that of corresponding regions in other parts of the world. Despite its great deserts, the country has vast

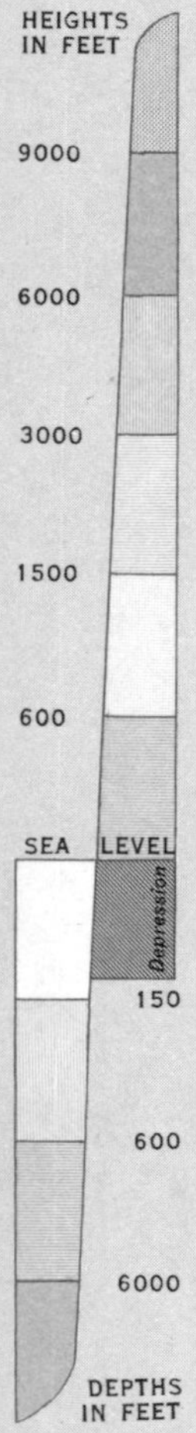

HEIGHTS IN FEET

9000
6000
3000
1500
600
SEA LEVEL
Depression

DEPTHS IN FEET

150
600
6000

BONNE'S PROJECTION

SCALE: 1 INCH TO 197 MILES

MAIN ROADS
ARTESIAN BASINS
RAILWAYS

Longitude East of Greenwich

acreages of fertile and well-watered land. Reading the map from east to west, one sees a narrow strip of fertile coastland, beyond which mountain ranges reach from Melbourne in the south right up to the Cape York Peninsula. These mountains, the Great Dividing Range, form a natural division between the coastal land and a fertile tableland, which is flanked on the west by an extensive inland plain. North of Spencer Gulf lies the Lake Eyre Basin, an inland drainage basin partly below sea level into which the rivers from the eastern plateau drain. Farther westwards, poorly watered plains give way to enormous deserts. Another strip of watered fertile land lies in the extreme south-west.

SCALE: 1 INCH TO 197 MILES

INTERNATIONAL BOUNDARIES
STATE BOUNDARIES

© JOHN BARTHOLOMEW & SON LTD.

INDIAN OCEAN

With an area of 28,350,000 square miles, the Indian Ocean is the third largest ocean in the world. It extends from the Indian Cape Comorin down to the Antarctic Continent, and in an east-west direction from Australia to Africa. A remarkable feature of this area is the central ridge of shallower water running down almost to the Antarctic Continent, somewhat similar to that in the Atlantic but with no counterpart in the Pacific.

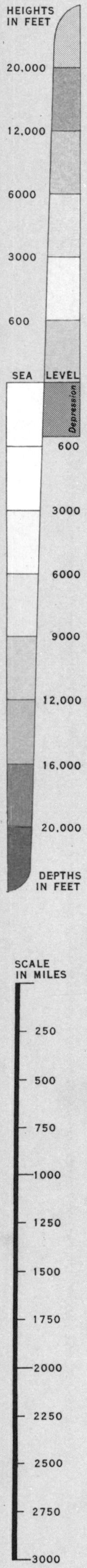

HEIGHTS
IN FEET

20,000
12,000
6000
3000
600
SEA LEVEL
Depression
600
3000
6000
9000
12,000
16,000
20,000
DEPTHS
IN FEET

SCALE
IN MILES

250
500
750
1000
1250
1500
1750
2000
2250
2500
2750
3000

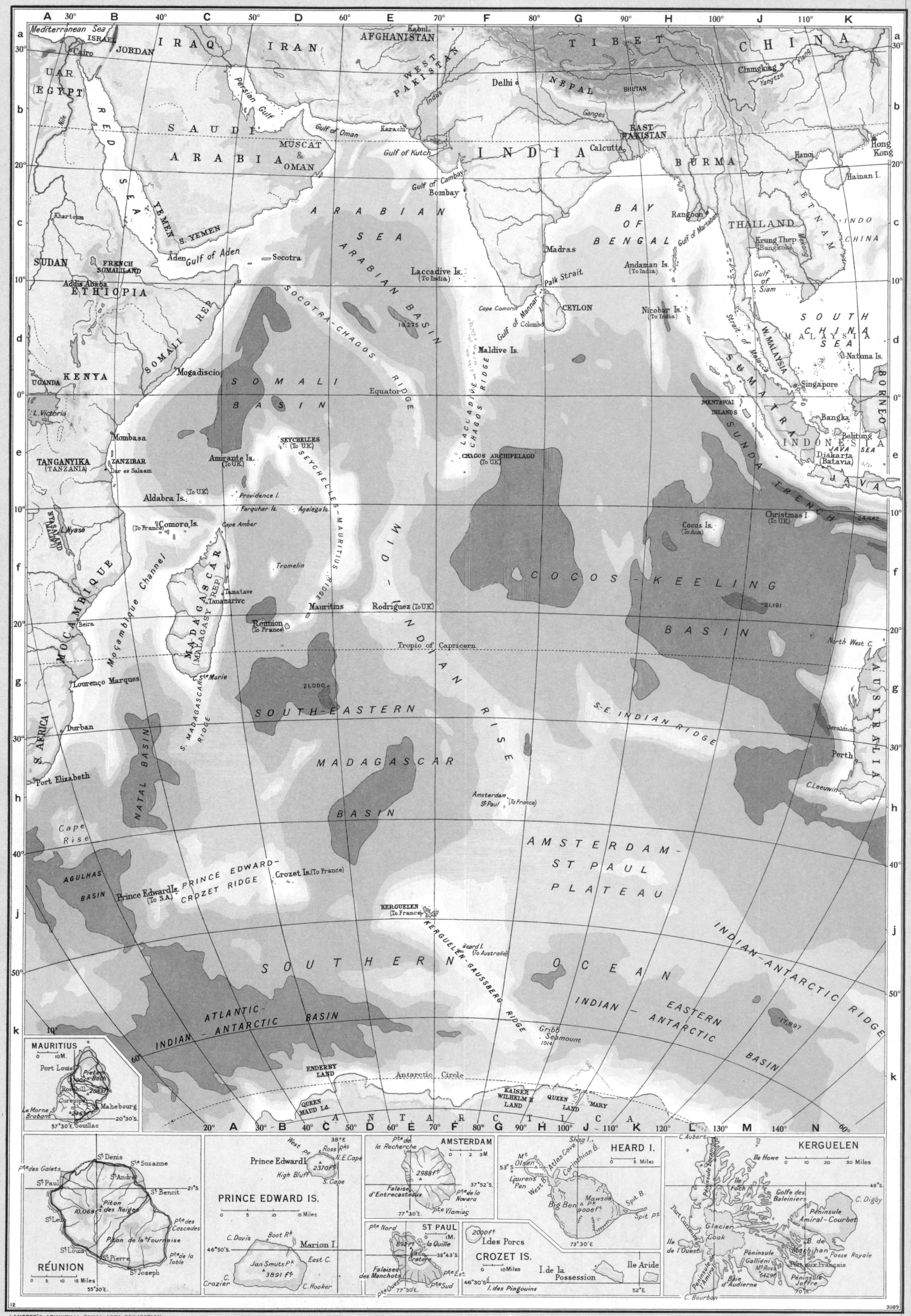

Mediterranean Sea
ISRAEL
JORDAN
IRAQ
IRAN
AFGHANISTAN
Kabul
TIBET
CHINA
Cairo
Chungking
Yangtze
U.A.R.
(EGYPT)
SAUDI
ARABIA
PAKISTAN
Delhi
NEPAL
BHUTAN
Hanoi
Hong Kong
Khartoum
YEMEN
S. YEMEN
MUSCAT & OMAN
Gulf of Oman
Karachi
Gulf of Kutch
INDIA
Calcutta
EAST PAKISTAN
BURMA
Hainan I.
RED SEA
SUDAN
Aden
Gulf of Aden
Socotra
Gulf of Cambay
Bombay
ARABIAN
SEA
Rangoon
THAILAND
INDO CHINA
FRENCH SOMALILAND
Addis Ababa
ETHIOPIA
ARABIAN BASIN
Laccadive Is.
(To India)
Cape Comorin
Gulf of Mannar
CEYLON
Madras
Andaman Is.
(To India)
Krung Thep
Bangkok
Gulf of Siam
UGANDA
KENYA
Mogadiscio
SOCOTRA-CHAGOS RIDGE
SOMALI BASIN
Maldive Is.
Palk Strait
Gulf of Colombo
Nicobar Is.
(To India)
SOUTH CHINA SEA
L. Victoria
TANGANYIKA
(TANZANIA)
ZANZIBAR
Dar es Salaam
Mombasa
SOMALI REP.
Equator
SEYCHELLES
(To UK)
Amirante Is.
CHAGOS ARCHIPELAGO
(To UK)
MENTAWAI ISLANDS
Singapore
SUMATRA
INDONESIA
BORNEO
Natuna Is.
Bangka
Belitung
NYASALAND
Nyasa
Aldabra Is.
(To UK)
Providence I.
Farquhar Is.
Agalega Is.
LACCADIVE-CHAGOS RIDGE
Cocos Is.
(To Aust)
Christmas I.
(To UK)
Djakarta
(Batavia)
JAVA SEA
JAVA
Comoro Is.
(To France)
Cape Amber
Tromelin
SEYCHELLES-MAURITIUS RIDGE
MID-
Mauritius
Rodriguez (To UK)
COCOS-KEELING
BASIN
SUNDA TRENCH
MOÇAMBIQUE
Mozambique Channel
MADAGASCAR
(MALAGASY REP.)
Tamatave
Tananarive
Réunion
(To France)
INDIAN
Tropic of Capricorn
North West C.
Beira
C. Ste Marie
MADAGASCAR RIDGE
SOUTH-EASTERN
RISE
S.E. INDIAN RIDGE
Geraldton
AUSTRALIA
Lourenço Marques
Durban
NATAL BASIN
MADAGASCAR
BASIN
Amsterdam
St Paul (To France)
AMSTERDAM-
ST PAUL
PLATEAU
Perth
C. Leeuwin
S. AFRICA
Port Elizabeth
Cape Rise
AGULHAS
BASIN
Prince Edward Is.
(To S.A.)
PRINCE EDWARD-
CROZET RIDGE
Crozet Is. (To France)
KERGUELEN
(To France)
Heard I.
(To Australia)
KERGUELEN-GAUSSBERG RIDGE
INDIAN-ANTARCTIC RIDGE
ATLANTIC-
INDIAN-
ANTARCTIC BASIN
SOUTHERN
OCEAN
INDIAN-
ANTARCTIC BASIN
EASTERN
Gribb Seamount
ENDERBY LAND
Antarctic Circle
QUEEN MAUD LD.
ANTARCTIC
KAISER WILHELM II LAND
QUEEN MARY LAND

MAURITIUS
Port Louis
Mahebourg
Le Morne Brabant
Souillac

RÉUNION
St Denis
St André
St Benoit
St Paul
Piton des Neiges
Piton de la Fournaise
St Louis
St Pierre
St Joseph

PRINCE EDWARD IS.
Prince Edward I.
Marion I.
Jan Smuts Pk
3891 ft

AMSTERDAM
ST PAUL
I. des Porcs

CROZET IS.
I. de la Possession
Ile Aride

HEARD I.
Big Ben

KERGUELEN
Ile Howe
Golfe des Baleiniers
Péninsule Amiral-Courbet
Glacier Cook

SCALE: 1 INCH TO 632 MILES

LAMBERT'S AZIMUTHAL EQUAL-AREA PROJECTION

96

ATLANTIC OCEAN

The Atlantic Ocean has an area of 31,839,306 square miles, and an average depth of 13,880 feet. It has the largest drainage area of all the oceans. Running southwards from Iceland to within a short distance of Antarctica is a well-defined central ridge, the curve of which follows the line of the African coast. Only the surface water on either side of this submarine barrier can cross it.

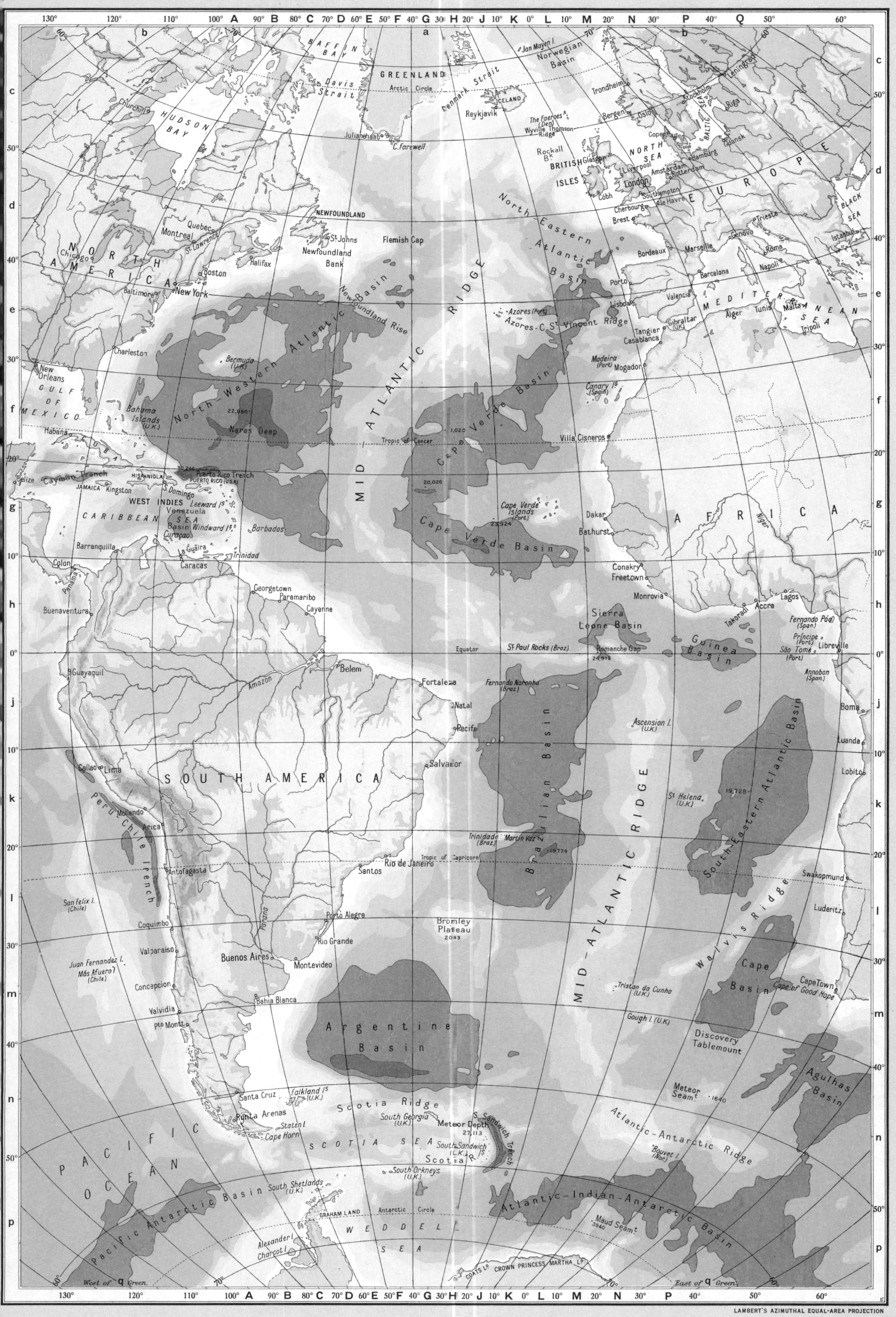

HEIGHTS IN FEET

12,000
6000
3000
600
SEA LEVEL
600
6000
9000
12,000
16,000
20,000

DEPTHS IN FEET

SCALE IN MILES

250
500
750
1000
1250
1500
1750
2000
2250
2500
2750
3000
3250
3500
3750
4000

BAFFIN BAY
GREENLAND
Davis Strait
Arctic Circle
Denmark Strait
Jan Mayen I.
Norwegian Basin
Norwegian Sea
ICELAND
Reykjavik
C. Farewell
Juliahehaab
Wyville Thomson Ridge
The Faeroes (Den)
Trondheim
Bergen
Oslo
Stockholm
Leningrad
Riga
Copenhagen
Gdansk
BALTIC SEA
BLACK SEA

NORTH AMERICA
Churchill
HUDSON BAY
Chicago
Montreal
Quebec
St Lawrence
NEWFOUNDLAND
St Johns
Newfoundland Bank
Flemish Cap
Halifax
Boston
New York
Baltimore
Charleston
New Orleans
GULF OF MEXICO
Habana
Bahama Islands (U.K.)
Belize
Cayman Trench
JAMAICA Kingston
HISPANIOLA
S Domingo
Puerto Rico Trench
PUERTO RICO (U.S.A)
WEST INDIES
Leeward Is.
Venezuela
Windward Is.
Barbados
Curaçao
CARIBBEAN SEA
Trinidad
La Guaira
Barranquilla
Caracas
Colon
Panama
Buenaventura
Guayaquil
Callao
Lima
Mollendo
Arica
Antofagasta
San Felix I. (Chile)
Coquimbo
Juan Fernandez I.
Más Afuera I. (Chile)
Valparaiso
Concepcion
Valdivia
Pto Montt
SOUTH AMERICA
Georgetown
Paramaribo
Cayenne
Amazon
Belem
Fortaleza
Natal
Recife
Salvador
Rio de Janeiro
Santos
Porto Alegre
Rio Grande
Buenos Aires
Montevideo
Bahia Blanca
Santa Cruz
Punta Arenas
Cape Horn
Staten I.

REYKJAVIK
Rockall B.
BRITISH ISLES
Glasgow
Liverpool
London
Southampton
Cobh
Cherbourg
Le Havre
Brest
NORTH SEA
Amsterdam
Rotterdam
Hamburg
EUROPE
Bordeaux
Marseille
Porto
Lisboa
MEDITERRANEAN SEA
Genova
Roma
Trieste
Barcelona
Valencia
Napoli
Istanbul
Tangier
Gibraltar
Casablanca
Alger
Tunis
Malta
Tripoli
Madeira (Port)
Mogador
Canary Is (Spain)
Villa Cisneros
AFRICA
Cape Verde Islands (Port)
Dakar
Bathurst
Conakry
Freetown
Monrovia
Takoradi
Accra
Lagos
Niger
Fernando Poó (Span)
Principe (Port)
Libreville
São Tomé (Port)
Annobon (Span)
Boma
Luanda
Lobito
Swakopmund
Luderitz
Cape Town
Cape of Good Hope

North Eastern Atlantic Basin
Azores (Port)
Azores-C St Vincent Ridge
MID ATLANTIC RIDGE
NEWFOUNDLAND RISE
North-Western Atlantic Basin
Bermuda (U.K.)
Nares Deep
22,960
Tropic of Cancer
Cape Verde Basin
1,020
20,026
Cape Verde Basin
23,924
Sierra Leone Basin
St Paul Rocks (Braz)
Romanche Gap
24,418
Equator
Guinea Basin
Fernando Noronha (Braz)
Ascension I. (U.K.)
Brazilian Basin
St Helena (U.K.)
19,728
Trinidade (Braz)
Martin Vaz
19,774
Tropic of Capricorn
South Eastern Atlantic Basin
Walvis Ridge
Bromley Plateau
2043
MID-ATLANTIC RIDGE
Tristan da Cunha (U.K.)
Cape Basin
Gough I. (U.K.)
Discovery Tablemount
Agulhas Basin
Meteor Seamt 1640
Argentine Basin
Falkland Is (U.K.)
Scotia Ridge
South Georgia (U.K.)
Meteor Depth 27,113
S. Sandwich Is.
South Sandwich Trench
SCOTIA SEA
Scotia R.
South Orkneys
Atlantic-Antarctic Ridge
Bouvet I. (Nor)
Meteor Seamt 3940

PACIFIC OCEAN
Pacific Antarctic Basin
South Shetlands (U.K.)
GRAHAM LAND
Alexander I.
Charcot I.
Antarctic Circle
WEDDELL SEA
Atlantic-Indian-Antarctic Basin
Maud Seamt 3940
COATS LD
CROWN PRINCESS MARTHA LD
West of q Green.
East of q Green.

PERU-CHILE TRENCH

97

LAMBERT'S AZIMUTHAL EQUAL-AREA PROJECTION

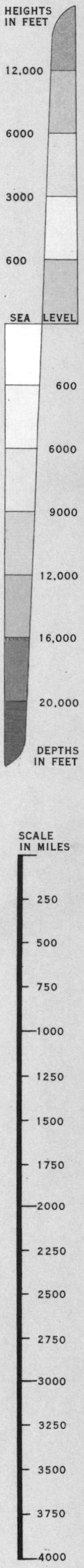

SCALE: 1 INCH TO 758 MILES

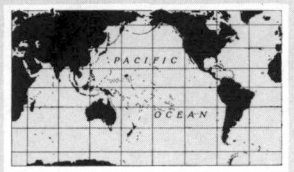

PACIFIC OCEAN

The Pacific, in area some 63,986,000 sq. miles, is the largest of the oceans. It is more than twice the size of the Atlantic, the next largest ocean, and occupies nearly half the Earth's surface. In the north it is almost landlocked, its only outlet to the Arctic Ocean being through the Bering Strait. It stretches 9,455 miles from this

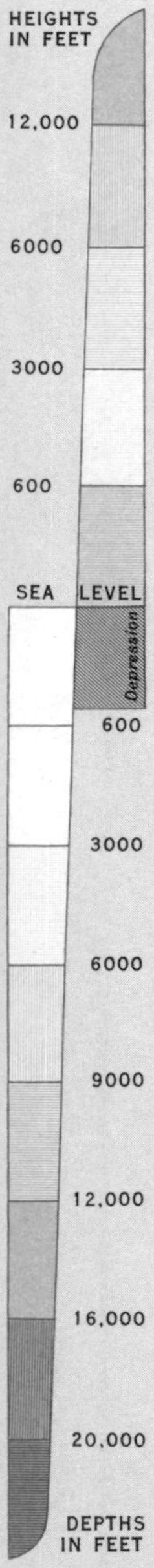

HEIGHTS IN FEET

12,000

6000

3000

600

SEA LEVEL

600

3000

6000

9000

12,000

16,000

20,000

DEPTHS IN FEET

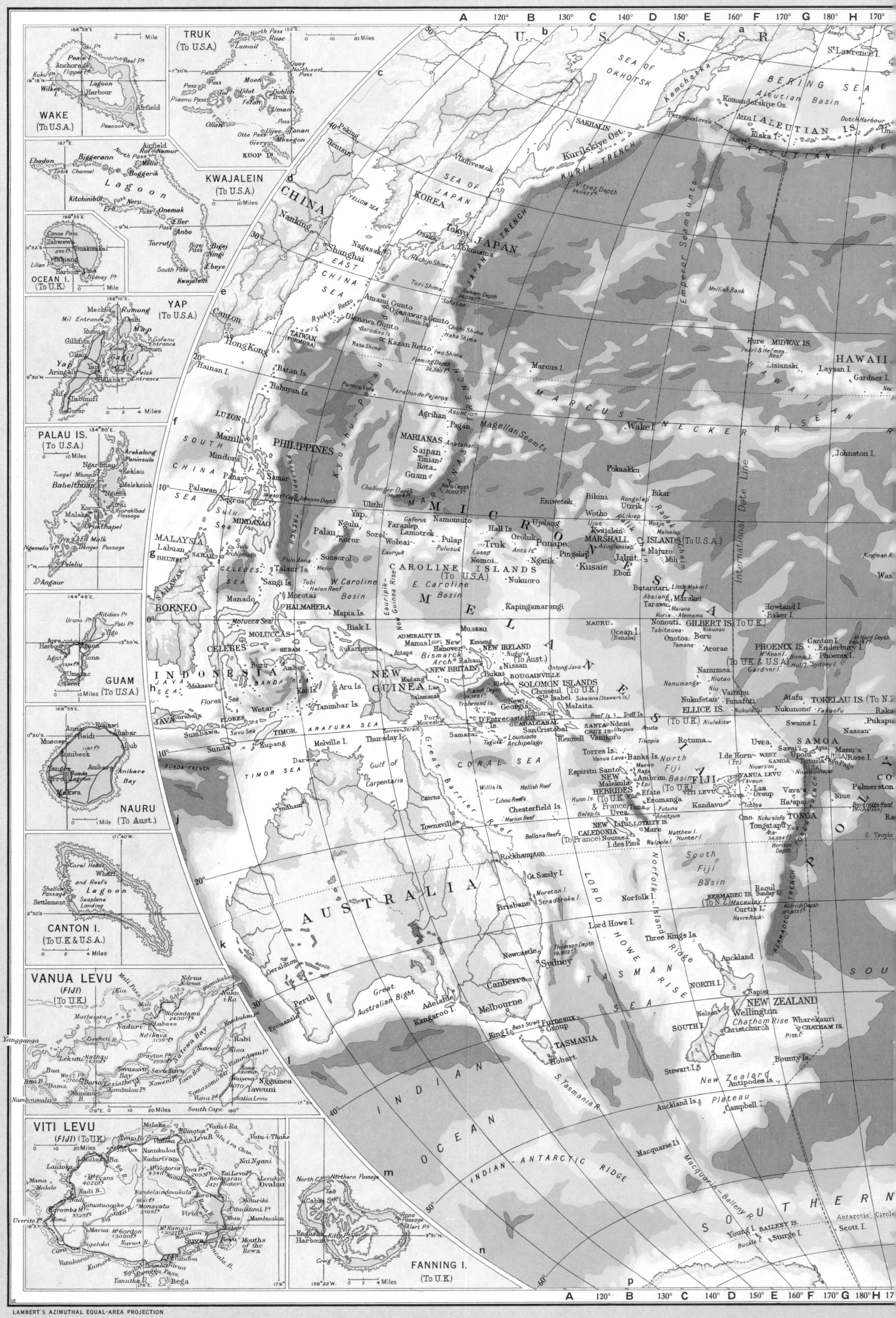

98

LAMBERT'S AZIMUTHAL EQUAL-AREA PROJECTION

SCALE: 1 INCH TO 711 MILES

strait to the Antarctic and at its broadest is 10,492 miles across. It has an average depth of about 14,000 feet, but in its deepest regions, which are off the Philippine Islands, a depth of 35,800 feet has been recorded. The islands of the Pacific fall into three main groups, Micronesia, Melanesia and Polynesia. Nearly all these islands are either volcanic or have a capping of coral over a submarine volcanic peak. The volcanic islands are very fertile and often mountainous, while the coral islands or atolls are mostly bare, desolate and low-lying. There are active volcanoes in the Solomon Islands, the New Hebrides and the Tonga group and Hawaii.

© JOHN BARTHOLOMEW & SON LTD.

SCALE: 1 INCH TO 711 MILES

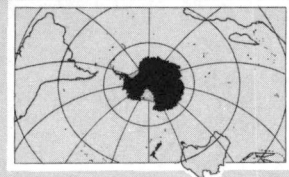

THE ANTARCTIC

The Antarctic comprises those seas and lands round the South Pole which lie within the Antarctic Circle at 66° 33′ S. It has a total area of about four and a half million square miles. The continent is uniquely isolated, and is covered by an ice cap thousands of feet thick. Much of the rock surface beneath the ice is below sea level. If the ice cap were to melt, the sea level all over the Earth would rise by two or three hundred feet.

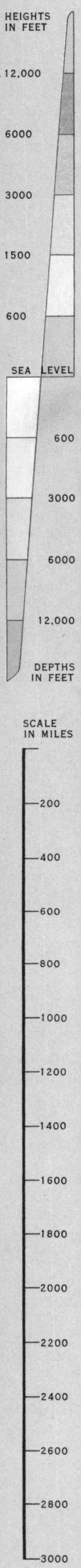

HEIGHTS
IN FEET

12,000
6000
3000
1500
600

SEA LEVEL

600
3000
6000
12,000

DEPTHS
IN FEET

SCALE
IN MILES

200
400
600
800
1000
1200
1400
1600
1800
2000
2200
2400
2600
2800
3000

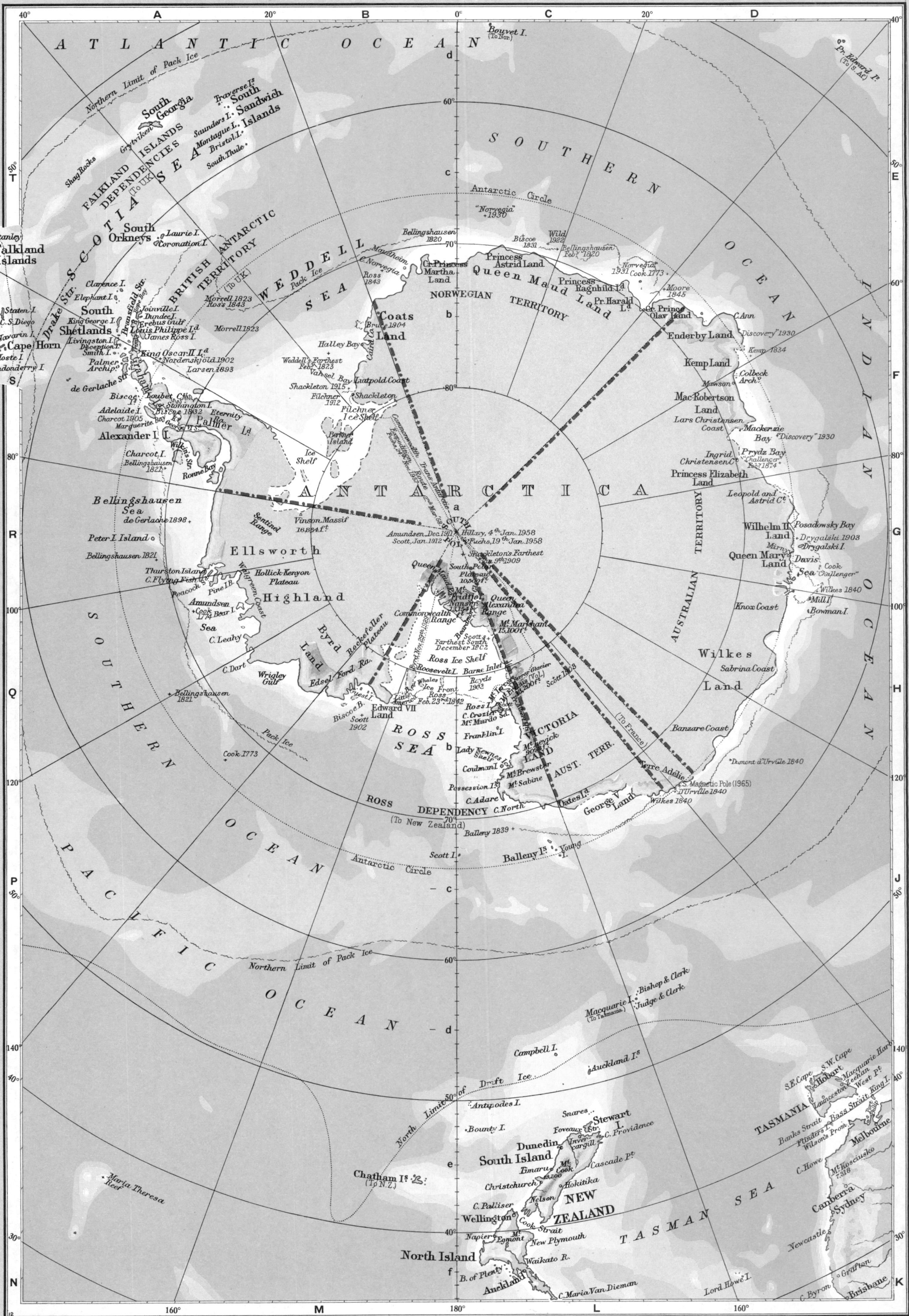

ATLANTIC OCEAN

SOUTHERN OCEAN

INDIAN OCEAN

PACIFIC OCEAN

SOUTHERN OCEAN

Northern Limit of Pack Ice

Bouvet I.
(To Nor.)

Pr. Edward I.
(To S. Af.)

Antarctic Circle

Traverse Is.
South Georgia
Grytviken
Shag Rocks
South Sandwich Islands
Saunders I.
Montague I.
Bristol I.
South Thule

FALKLAND ISLANDS DEPENDENCIES
To UK

SCOTIA SEA

WEDDELL SEA

Norvegia
1930

Bellingshausen
1820

Biscoe
1831

Wild
1922

Bellingshausen
Feb.1920

Norvegia
1931 Cook 1773

Moore
1845

Pr. Prince
Olav Land

C.Ann

Enderby Land

Discovery 1930

Kemp 1834

Kemp Land

Colbeck
Arch.

Mawson

MacRobertson Land

Mackenzie
Bay "Discovery" 1930

Lars Christensen
Coast

Pr. Harald
Ld.

Princess Ragnhild Ld.

Princess Astrid Land

C.Princess
Martha
Land

Queen Maud Land

NORWEGIAN TERRITORY

C.Norvegia

Moydholm

Ross
1843

Bruce 1904

Coats Land

Halley Bay

Weddell's Farthest
Feb.1823

Vahsel Bay
Shackleton 1915

Filchner
1912

Filchner Ice Shelf

Luitpold Coast

Shackleton
Ice Shelf

Berkner
Island

Ingrid
Christensen C.

Pryds Bay
Challenger
1874

Princess Elizabeth
Land

Leopold and
Astrid C.

Wilhelm II
Land

Posadowsky Bay

Drygalski 1903
Drygalski I.

Queen Mary
Land

Davis
Sea
Cook "Challenger"

Wilkes 1840

Mill I.
Bowman I.

Knox Coast

Wilkes Land

Sabrina Coast

Banzare Coast

Terre Adélie

Magnetic Pole (1965)
D'Urville 1840

Dumont d'Urville 1840

Wilkes 1840

George V Land

Oates Ld.

AUSTRALIAN TERRITORY

(To France)

South Orkneys
Laurie I.
Coronation I.

Clarence I.
Elephant I.

BRITISH ANTARCTIC TERRITORY
To UK

Joinville I.
Dundee I.
Louis Philippe Ld.
James Ross I.
Erebus Gulf

Morrell 1823
Ross 1843

Morrell 1823

Nordenskjöld 1902
Larsen 1893

King Oscar II Ld.

Bransfield Str.

South Shetlands
King George I.
Livingston I.
Smith I.
Deception I.
Palmer Archip.
de Gerlache Str.

Staten I.
C.S.Diego
Navarin I.
C.Horn
Hoste I.
Londonderry I.

Cape Horn

Falkland Islands

Stanley

Drake Str.

Biscoe
Loubet Cst.
Stonington I.
Adelaide I.
Biscoe 1832
Charcot 1905
Marguerite I.

Alexander I.

Charcot 1910
Bellingshausen
1821

Eternity

Palmer Ld.

Wilkins Str.

Ronne Bay

Ice Shelf

Bellingshausen Sea
de Gerlache 1898

Peter I Island

Bellingshausen 1821

Thurston Island
C.Flying Fish

Peacock
Cook 1774 Bear I.

Amundsen
Sea

C.Leahy

Sentinel Range

Vinson Massif
16864 Ft.

ANTARCTICA

Ellsworth Highland

Hollick-Kenyon
Plateau

Pine I.B.

Byrd
Land

Rockefeller
Plateau

Wrigley
Gulf

C.Dart

Edsel Ford Ra.

Edward VII
Land

Biscoe B.
Scott
1902

Whales B.
Little
America

Ross
Ice Front
Feb.23 1842

Cook 1773

Pack Ice

ROSS
DEPENDENCY

(To New Zealand)

C.North

Balleny 1839

Scott I.

Balleny Is.

Young

Antarctic Circle

Amundsen Dec.19 1911
Scott, Jan.1912

E. Hillary, 4th Jan.1958
Fuchs, 19th Jan.1958

SOUTH POLE

Shackleton's Farthest
9th 1909

Commonwealth
Trans-Antarctic
Expedition Route

Queen Maud Ra.

South Polar
Plateau
10500 Ft.

Nansen I.

Beardmore Glacier

Queen
Alexandra
Range

Mt.Markham
15,100 Ft.

Commonwealth
Range

Scott,
Farthest South
December 1902

Ross Ice Shelf

Roosevelt I.

Barne Inlet

Royds
1903

ROSS
SEA

Roosevelt I.

Ross I.
C.Crozier
Mt.Murdo Sd.
Franklin I.

Mt.Erebus
Mt.Terror

Mt.Melbourne

VICTORIA
LAND

Mt.Nevick
(Vol.)

Mt.Brewster

Possession I.

Mt.Sabine

C.Adare

AUST.TERR.

Lady Newnes Bay
Coulman I.

Northern Limit of Pack Ice

Draft Ice

North Limit of Draft Ice

Macquarie
(To Tasmania)

Bishop & Clerk
Judge & Clerk

Campbell I.

Auckland Is.

Antipodes I.

Snares

Bounty I.

Chatham Is.
(To N.Z.)

Maria Theresa
Reef

Foveaux Str.
C.Providence

Invercargill

Dunedin
South Island

Mt.Cook
Timaru

Christchurch

Cascade Pt.
Hokitika

Nelson

NEW ZEALAND

C.Palliser

Wellington

Napier
Mt.Egmont
New Plymouth

Cook Strait

North Island

B.of Plenty

Waikato R.

Auckland

C.Maria Van Dieman

Lord Howe I.

TASMANIA

S.E.Cape
S.W.Cape
Hobart
Launceston
Macquarie Harb.
West Pt.
Maatsuyker
Kelvin

Banks Strait
Flinders I.
Bass Strait
Wilsons Prom.

C.Howe

Mt.Kosciusko
7316

Melbourne

Canberra
Sydney

Newcastle

C.Byron
Grafton

Brisbane

TASMAN SEA

100

LAMBERT'S AZIMUTHAL EQUAL-AREA PROJECTION

SCALE: 1 INCH TO 474 MILES

INTERNATIONAL BOUNDARIES

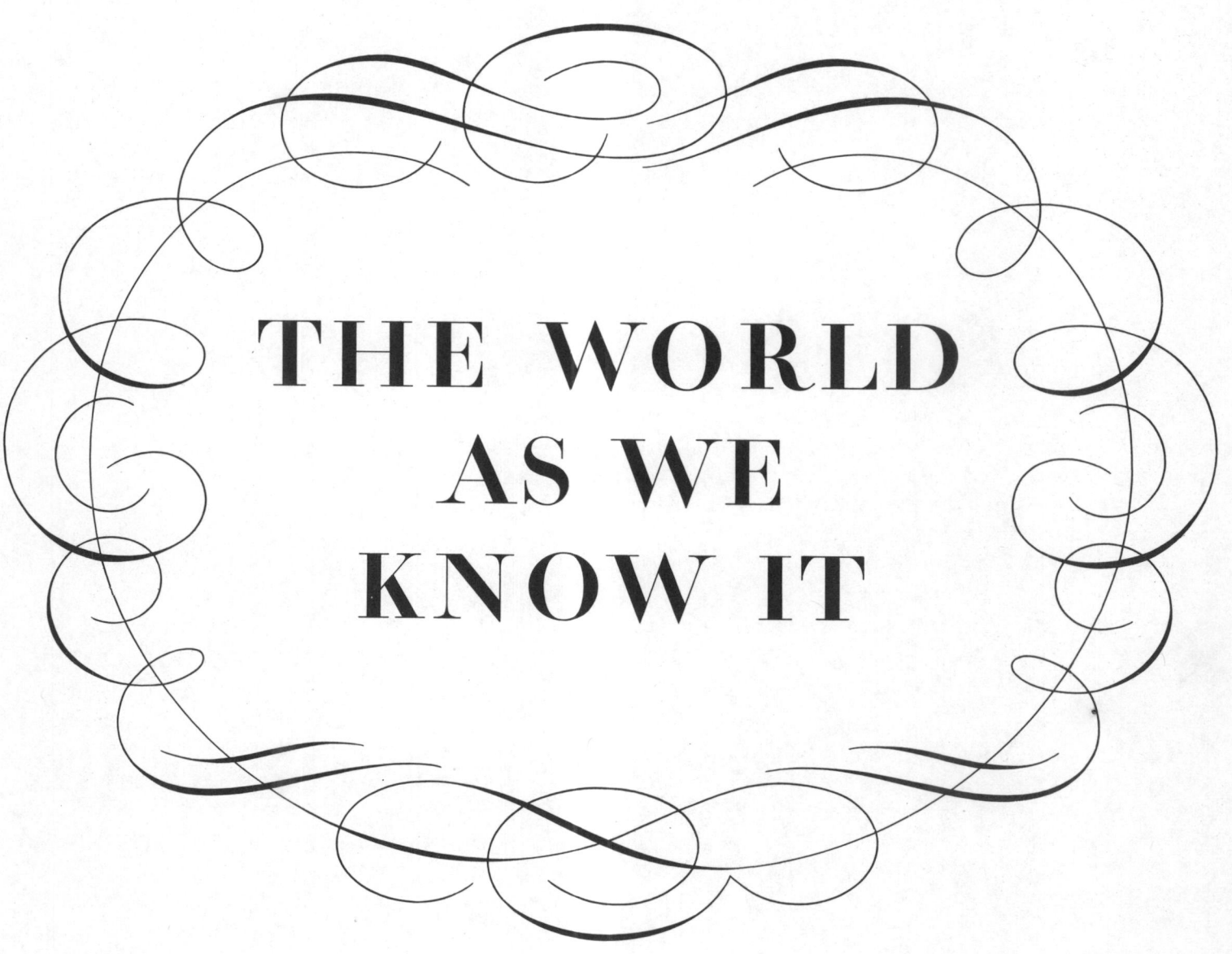

SECTION THREE

THE WORLD AS WE KNOW IT

CONTENTS

OUR PLACE AMONG THE GALAXIES

*As the stars of the heaven, and as the sand
which is upon the sea shore*—GENESIS 22

FOR centuries man believed the Earth to be the centre of Creation. The true picture is far more awe-inspiring. We live on a small planet revolving round a star of only average size which is itself revolving, with thousands of millions of other stars, in one galaxy among millions in a Universe that may well be boundless.

Scientific observation has as yet revealed no limits to the Universe and has so far probed only a fraction of it. Yet to travel to the frontiers of that observed fraction, even at 186,300 miles per second (the speed of light) would take 6,000 million years, about 20,000 times the total period that human life is estimated to have existed on Earth.

The different bodies and structures in the Universe, all of which appear to be receding from us, range from single galaxies to mammoth clusters containing over 500 galaxies.

Although the cluster of galaxies to which our galaxy belongs is comparatively small (it has only 25 members), our galaxy itself, the Milky Way System, ranks among the larger of the known stellar systems. Counting its almost 100,000 million stars (of which the Sun with its family of planets is one) at the rate of one star a second would take about 2,500 years.

Seen edge-on from outside, the Milky Way System looks like a fairly flat disk with a thick cloud of stars near and round its centre. Seen at right angles, it looks like a giant Catherine wheel in which two main arms spiral out from the centre. The Sun lies in one of these arms. It is so far away from the centre that it needs about 225 million years to complete one orbit round the "hub" of the Catherine wheel. Calculated on the basis of the Sun's estimated age, it can have made only about 30 complete circuits.

The stars forming the Milky Way are not evenly distributed, but thin out from the central plane of the galaxy and from its bulbous centre. The myriads of stars forming the centre are hidden from the Earth by vast formations of cosmic dust and

BOUNDLESS SKY

A barred spiral galaxy. The "bar" involves the nucleus and curves outwards to fofm trailing arms strongly indicative of rotation.

An elliptical galaxy. This shows no spiral structure and appears to be comparatively free from cosmic gas and dust.

A spiral galaxy, full view, with its central nucleus and trailing spiral arms. The whole vast complex of stars, dust and gas is rotating in a way that would tend to "wind up" the arms.

Our Solar System is somewhere here

A spiral galaxy seen edge-on. The central bulge or nucleus is a great swarm of millions of stars. The dark markings in the central plane are caused by clouds of obscuring cosmic dust

are not directly visible. If we look in the direction of the plane, however, from our position slightly outside it, we see the stars distributed in greater depth and number, so that they appear to merge into a single luminous band. This bright streak in the sky has been known for centuries as the Milky Way, a name now given to the whole of the system.

Surrounding the galaxy and forming part of it are compact swarms of stars known as globular star clusters. Beyond them again lie thousands of millions of other galaxies with a considerable range in size and structure. The nearest comparable in size to our own is the Great Galaxy in Andromeda (centre of left-hand page), just over two million "light-years" away, a distance that light, in travelling at 186,300 miles per second, would take just over two million years to cover.

As man probes deeper into the Universe, the number of galaxies seems to grow as immense as the space through which they hurtle.

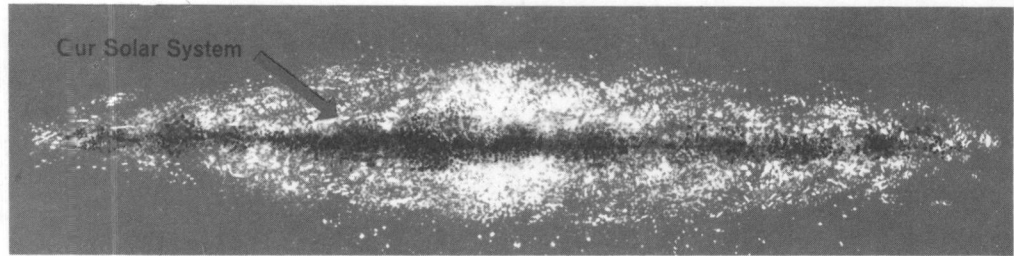

Our Solar System

The Milky Way, one of the millions of stellar galaxies in the Universe, is so vast that it would take a rocket, hurtling along its diameter at 100,000 miles per hour, 670 million years to make the journey from end to end. Travelling at the same speed across our solar system, from the Sun to its farthest dependent planet, Pluto, a rocket would take only four years and two months.

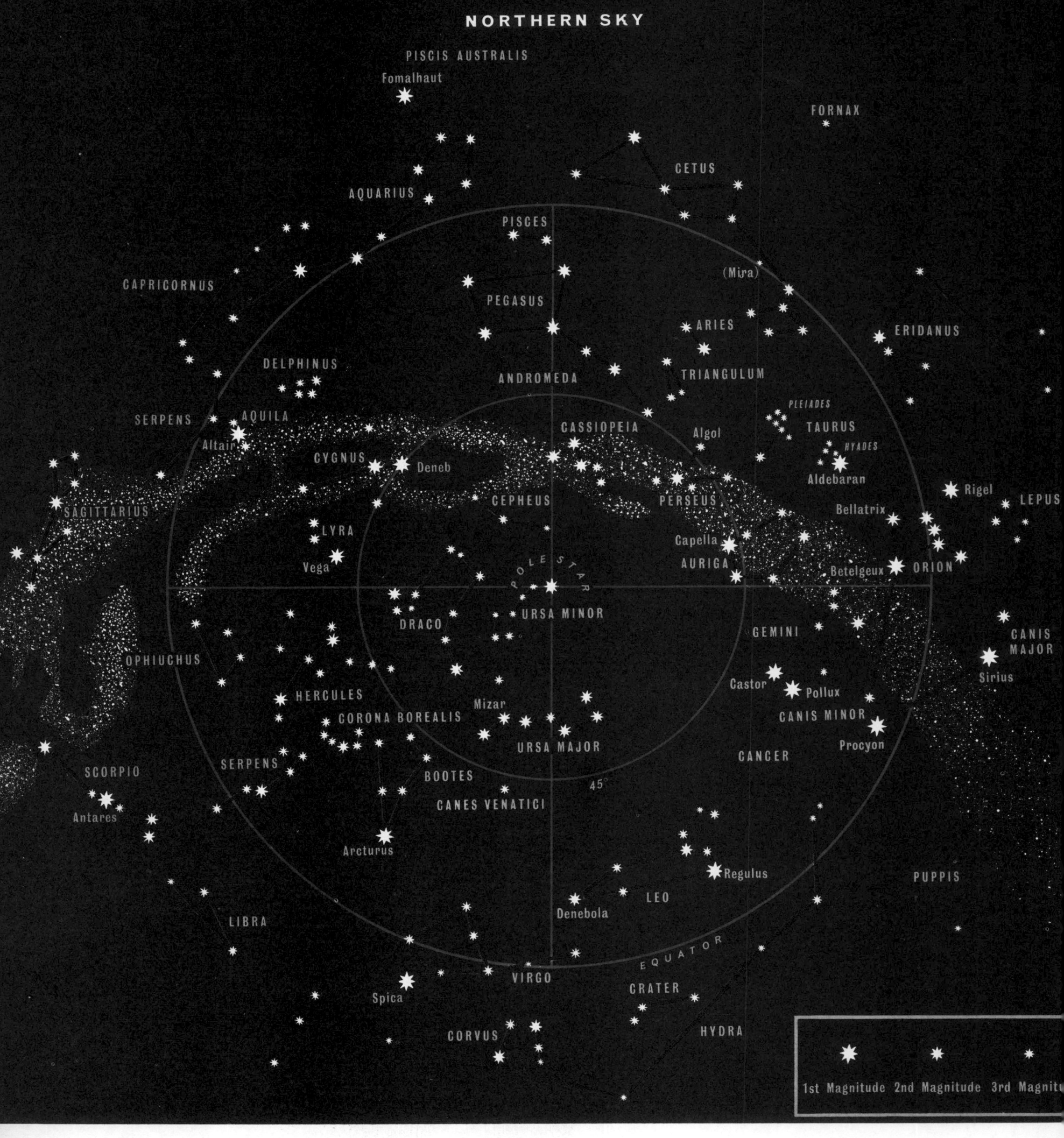

PISCIS AUSTRALIS
Fomalhaut

FORNAX

CETUS

AQUARIUS

PISCES

(Mira)

ARIES

ERIDANUS

CAPRICORNUS

PEGASUS

TRIANGULUM

DELPHINUS

ANDROMEDA

PLEIADES
TAURUS

SERPENS

AQUILA
Altair

CASSIOPEIA

Algol

HYADES
Aldebaran

CYGNUS
Deneb

CEPHEUS

PERSEUS

Rigel

LEPUS

SAGITTARIUS

Bellatrix

LYRA

Capella

Betelgeux
ORION

Vega

AURIGA

POLE STAR

DRACO

URSA MINOR

GEMINI

CANIS
MAJOR

OPHIUCHUS

Castor
Pollux

Sirius

HERCULES

Mizar

CANIS MINOR

CORONA BOREALIS

URSA MAJOR

CANCER

Procyon

SCORPIO

SERPENS

BOOTES

45°

Antares

CANES VENATICI

Regulus

LIBRA

LEO

PUPPIS

Denebola

Arcturus

EQUATOR

VIRGO

CRATER

Spica

HYDRA

CORVUS

1st Magnitude   2nd Magnitude   3rd Magnitu

THE STARS AROUND US

THE LIGHT FROM MANY STARS STARTED ITS JOURNEY LONG BEFORE MAN APPEARED ON EARTH

For one star differeth from another in glory — 1 CORINTHIANS 15

WHEN we look at the stars we are looking back deep into the past; for we see them, not as they are now, but often as they were hundreds of years ago. The light we receive from most of them began its great journey long before we were born, and from the more distant stars long before man appeared on Earth.

Even light from the Sun – a mere 93 million miles away – takes eight minutes to reach the Earth. From the nearest star, Proxima Centauri in the Southern Hemisphere, it takes more than four years. Since light, travelling at 186,300 miles a second, covers some six million million miles in a year, this means that the distance between the Earth and Proxima Centauri is about 26 million million miles.

But the vast distances in space need a unit of measurement larger than the mile. Astronomers use the "light-year," which is the distance travelled by light in one year. In these terms,

Proxima Centauri is four and one-third light-years away from the Earth. The distance from Earth to the bright star Altair is about 16 light-years, to Vega 26 light-years, to Deneb 1,500 light-years, while some of the stars of the Milky Way are so far distant that their light takes thousands of years to reach us. The stars are therefore placed at great distances in space, not only from the Earth, but also from one another.

The stars vary greatly in size. Though our Sun seems large to us, and could easily contain the Earth a million times over, it is no more than an average star in the rest of the heavens. Some stars, called super-giants, make the Sun seem a tiny dwarf. Betelgeux, for instance, could contain not only the Sun and the Earth's orbit round it, but the entire orbit of the planet Mars – an orbit of some 284 million miles in diameter. At the other end of the scale are stars that are only a few thousandths of the Sun's size.

Stars also vary considerably in actual brightness, and so are graded into different "magnitudes." The brightest stars belong to the first magnitude, those slightly less bright to the second, and so on until we reach the sixth magnitude which consists of stars just visible to the naked eye on a very clear night. A star of the first magnitude is 100 times brighter than a star of the sixth magnitude. Compared with some first-magnitude stars, the Sun's light is like that of a glow-worm shining beside a searchlight.

Thus the brighter stars in the sky – like Rigel and Regulus – are not necessarily the nearest to us. Several very faint stars are in fact nearer to Earth than most of the bright ones, though the brilliant Alpha Centauri, in the Southern Hemisphere, and Altair, in the Northern Hemisphere, are fairly close neighbours – as stars go.

From earliest times, men have grouped the stars under names

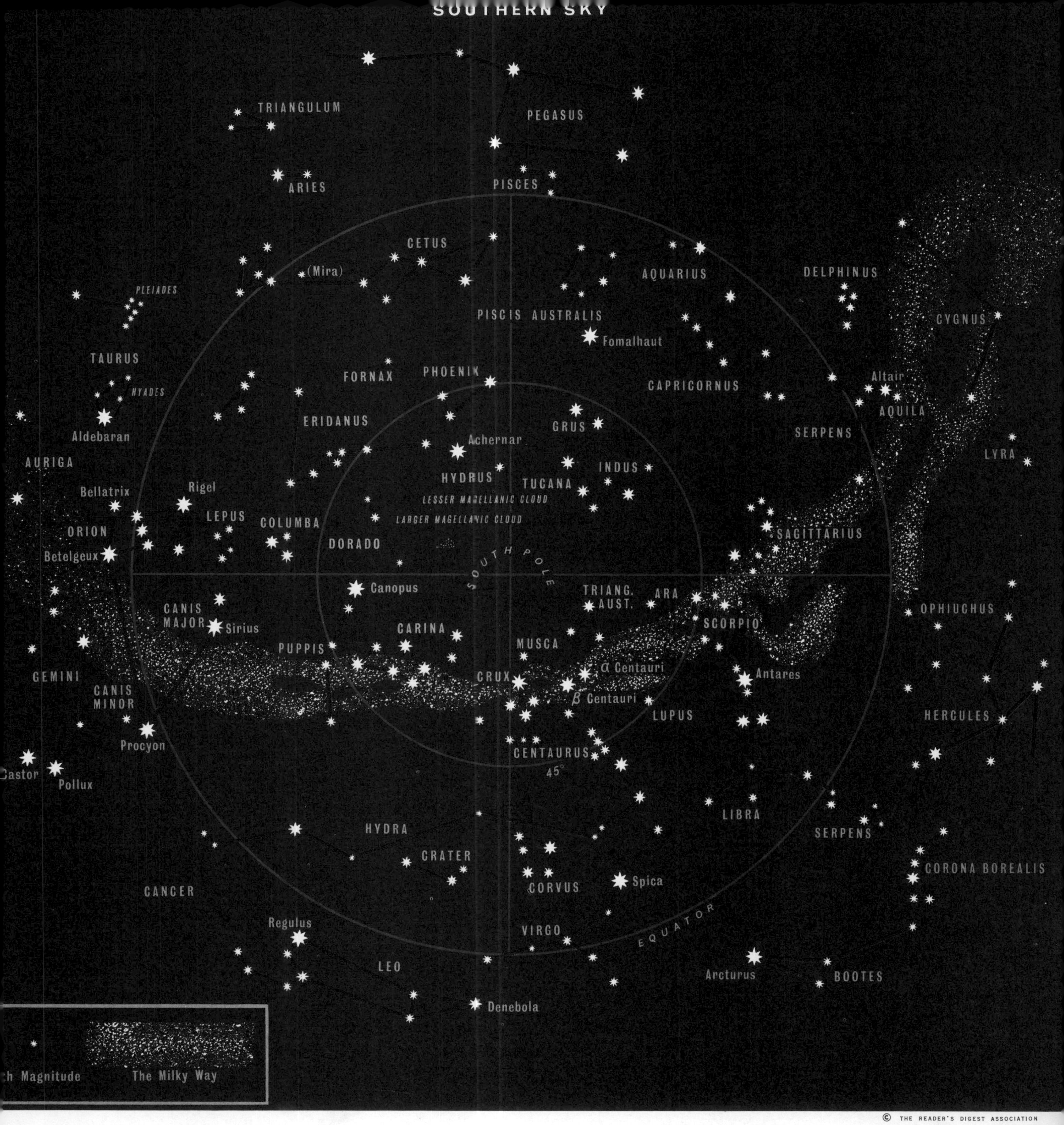

TRIANGULUM

PEGASUS

ARIES

PISCES

CETUS

(Mira)

AQUARIUS

DELPHINUS

PLEIADES

PISCIS AUSTRALIS

CYGNUS

Fomalhaut

TAURUS

FORNAX

PHOENIX

CAPRICORNUS

Altair

HYADES

ERIDANUS

Achernar

GRUS

AQUILA

Aldebaran

INDUS

SERPENS

AURIGA

HYDRUS

TUCANA

LYRA

Rigel

LESSER MAGELLANIC CLOUD

Bellatrix

LEPUS

COLUMBA

LARGER MAGELLANIC CLOUD

SAGITTARIUS

ORION

DORADO

Betelgeux

SOUTH POLE

OPHIUCHUS

Canopus

TRIANG.

CANIS

AUST.

ARA

MAJOR

CARINA

Sirius

MUSCA

SCORPIO

PUPPIS

α Centauri

Antares

CRUX

GEMINI

β Centauri

CANIS

LUPUS

MINOR

HERCULES

Procyon

CENTAURUS

45°

Castor

LIBRA

Pollux

HYDRA

SERPENS

CRATER

CORONA BOREALIS

CANCER

CORVUS

Spica

Regulus

VIRGO

EQUATOR

LEO

Denebola

Arcturus

BOOTES

Magnitude   The Milky Way

of animals and legendary heroes. A few of these constellation figures, as they are called, such as Orion and Corona Borealis (the Northern Crown), do look something like the figures they are supposed to represent, though most call for powerful feats of imagination. Among the brighter stars, however, some make definite patterns: five in Cygnus (the Swan) form a cross, and seven in Ursa Major (the Great Bear) suggest the Plough shape by which they are known.

The maps show the positions of the brightest stars in both Hemispheres. During one year, people living in the Northern Hemisphere can see all the stars on the left-hand map, but never those in the region of the Southern Cross, which are hidden by the Earth's bulk. Similarly, people living south of the Equator can see the stars on the right-hand map, but never the Plough or the North Pole Star. Only from the Equator would you eventually see almost every star in both Hemispheres.

Because the Earth rotates on its axis, the stars – like the Sun by day—*appear* to wheel from east to west across the sky. In the Northern Hemisphere, only Polaris, the Pole Star, seems to stand still because it is almost directly above the North Pole. Not only does it show the position of north, but its angular height above the northern horizon is roughly equal to the observer's latitude. Since the latitude of London is about 51½°N, the Pole Star, as seen from London, is about 51½° above the horizon.

The southern sky has no bright star like Polaris to mark the position of the south celestial pole. To find this position we must draw a line from the tip of the Southern Cross to the bright star Achernar: the point above the South Pole lies midway along this line and slightly to the right of it.

With the naked eye, we can see from 2,000 to 2,500 stars on a clear night. Binoculars will show thousands more, and a large telescope can reach out to thousands of millions of stars. Most of these lie in the bright girdle of the Milky Way, once thought to be the road along which the souls of the dead travelled to heaven.

Many "stars" turn out to be not just single objects, but clusters of two, three or even more stars. Some of these "double stars," as they are called, are two stars held close together by the force of gravitation. Others only appear to be together because one happens to be almost behind the other in our line of sight, though they may in fact be an immense distance apart.

Of the larger star clusters, one of the finest is the Pleiades in the northern sky. When you first count the members of this group you will probably manage only six or seven, but on very clear nights this number can be pushed up to twelve or fourteen. A pair of binoculars will show many more, though it needs a really large telescope to reveal the 200 and more stars in this cluster. All these stars are travelling together through space. They form a moving family of suns all of which, presumably, had a common origin.

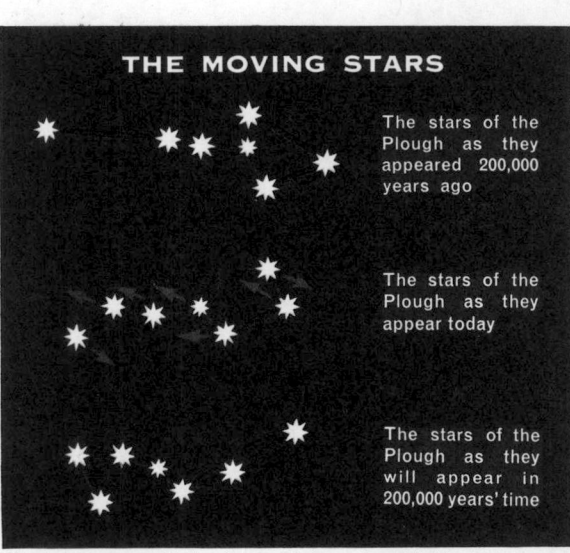

THE MOVING STARS

The stars of the Plough as they appeared 200,000 years ago

The stars of the Plough as they appear today

The stars of the Plough as they will appear in 200,000 years' time

The stars are never motionless in space, but move through it at tremendous speeds. The diagrams show the stars of the Plough as their positions are changing in relation to each other and as seen from the Earth. This motion is called the "proper motion" of the stars. It is not their motion in three-dimensional space, since we see only the two-dimensional aspect. As shown by the arrows, the five inner stars are travelling in approximately the same direction, forming a moving family of suns. The two outer stars, moving the opposite way, are not members of this group.

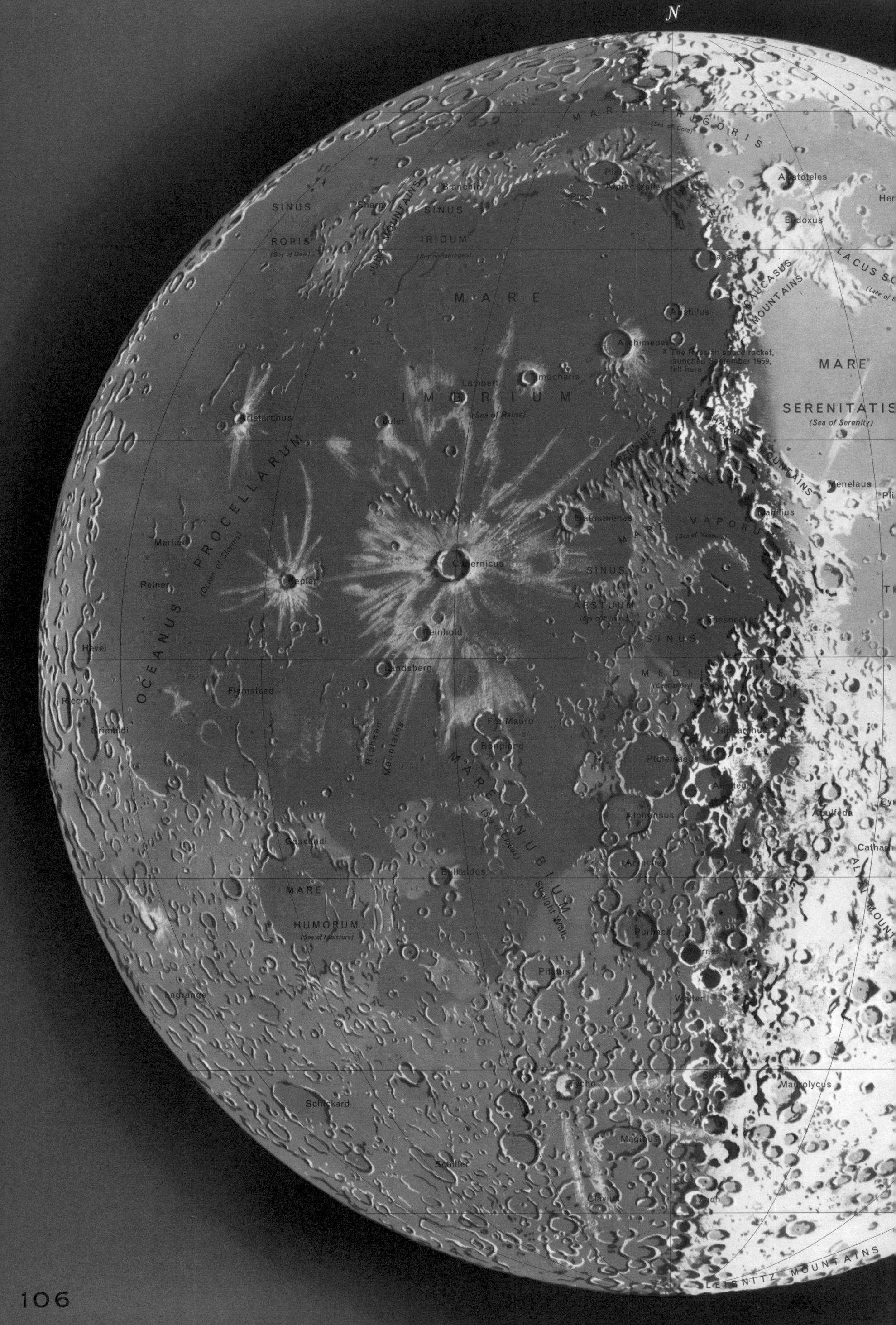

N

MARE FRIGORIS
(Sea of Cold)

Aristoteles

Her

Plato   Eudoxus

Alpine Valley

Bianchini   Cassini

SINUS   Sharp   SINUS
RORIS   IRIDUM
(Bay of Dew)   (Bay of Rainbows)

CAUCASUS   LACUS SO
MOUNTAINS   (Lake of t)

MARE   Aristillus

Archimedes   MARE
SERENITATIS
(Sea of Serenity)

x The Russian space rocket,
launched September 1959,
fell here

Lambert   Timocharis

I M B R I U M
(Sea of Rains)

Euler   APENNINES   Menelaus

Aristarchus   HAEMUS   Manilius
MOUNTAINS

Eratosthenes   MARE   VAPORU
(Sea of Vapours)

Marius   SINUS

Reiner   Kepler   Copernicus   AESTUUM
(Bay of Heats)

Reinhold   SINUS

Hevel   MEDII
(Central Bay)

Landsberg   Hipparchus

Riccioli   Ptolemaeus

Grimaldi   Flamsteed   Alphonsus   Abulfeda   Cy

Ripphaen   Fra Mauro   Arzachel   Cathan
Mountains
Bonpland

MARE   NUBIUM
(Sea of Clouds)

Gassendi   Bullialdus

Straight Wall

Purbach

MARE   Werner

HUMORUM
(Sea of Moisture)   Pitatus

Lagrange   Stofler   Maurolycus

Tycho

Schickard   Maginus

Schiller   Clavius   Zach

LEIBNITZ MOUNTAINS

THE MOON

EARTH'S SATELLITE

He appointed the Moon for seasons—PSALM 104

THE Moon is unique in our Solar system. Many planets have satellites, but these are small in relation to their mother planets. The Moon is the only satellite of a size comparable to its planet, Earth.

MAIN FEATURES. The large map shows the near side of the Moon; the far side is hidden because the Moon rotates only once each time it travels round the Earth. (Since the Moon spins so slowly, its "day" lasts about two weeks, and is followed by two weeks of night.) The features marked on the map are all visible through good binoculars. They are best seen, not at full Moon when the Sun shines directly on them making no shadows, but when they are near the "terminator", or irregular edge of the Moon, and the Sun is lower in the lunar sky.

To the naked eye the Moon seems to be made up of bright and darker patches. The bright parts are mountains and craters which catch the light of the Sun; the large darker areas are the low-lying plains. Once thought to be seas, these plains are still called by such names as Mare Imbrium (Sea of Rains) and Oceanus Procellarum (Ocean of Storms) though in fact the Moon is entirely without water.

The mountains on the Moon are broad rather than high. The highest range is probably the Leibnitz Mountains near the Moon's south pole, with an estimated height of well over 20,000 feet. In relation to the Moon's size they appear higher still; a corresponding mountain range on Earth would tower 14 miles into the sky.

The most striking features are the many thousands of craters, named after philosophers and men of science. Either volcanic or meteoritic in origin, they range in size from pits of a mile or less across to magnificent walled plains such as Clavius, which is some 150 miles in diameter. Two of the finest are Copernicus and Tycho, both over 50 miles across and with walls rising to heights above two miles. From these two craters, and some others, bright streaks radiate for thousands of miles across mountains and valleys. The origin of these bright streaks is unknown; they seem, however, to be surface deposits of some kind.

SIZE AND GRAVITY. With a diameter about one-quarter of the Earth's, the Moon has a surface area less than half that of the Atlantic Ocean, and the part we can see is about the size of North America. Its gravitational pull is correspondingly smaller, only about one-sixth of the Earth's.

A six-foot man who could jump six feet on the Earth would be able to clear about 18 feet on the Moon, and his descent would be much slower. A space ship would need a velocity of only some 5,000 m.p.h. to take off from the Moon, compared with 25,000 m.p.h. required to escape from the Earth's gravity.

EFFECTS OF NO ATMOSPHERE. The Moon is without atmosphere, its gravity being too weak to hold down gas in any quantity. To an Earth-dweller, this produces some startling effects. The edges of shadows on the Moon are razor-sharp, unsoftened by mists or similar products of the atmosphere. There is no erosion due to weather, and the Moon's features have therefore undergone little major change since they were formed. There is no sound, which is a vibration transmitted through the air. Nor is there any twilight: day comes instantly because there is no atmosphere to be lit up before the Sun comes over the horizon. With no atmosphere to protect it from the Sun by day or to imprison the heat by night, the Moon has great extremes of temperature. At the equator, the day-time temperature at the Moon's surface rises to 100° C., as high as that of boiling water, and at night the temperature sinks to at least −168°C., as low as that of liquid air. Under these conditions no life as we know it can exist.

Average distance from Earth	238,856 miles	Mass in terms of Earth	1:81
Diameter	2,160 miles *(Earth's diameter 7,920 miles)*	Sidereal Period	27·3 days *(approx.)* *(time taken to make one complete circuit of Earth)*
Density	3·3 times that of water *(Earth's density 5·5 times that of water)*	Synodic Period	29·5 days *(approx.)* *(interval between one new Moon and the next)*

THE FAR SIDE OF THE MOON

Chart of the reverse side of the Moon, compiled from photographic positions obtained by the U.S. Orbiter vehicles and the Soviet Zond-3. When this chart was made in the autumn of 1967 only a very small portion of the far side of the moon had not been photographed.

Near the edge of the chart appear some features which can be identified on the map of the visible hemisphere: Mare Marginis and Mare Smythii. Mare Orientalis is of special interest as it can just be seen from Earth as a foreshortened plain, but the far-side photographs have shown that it is of very complex structure, and it is of significance in studies of how the Moon's features were moulded. Two other interesting features are the dark-floored crater Tsiolkovskii and the dark patch of the Mare Moscoviae.

The names of features on the far side of the moon are under consideration by the International Astronomical Union.

Earth's atmosphere, the blanket of gases surrounding the planet, is the element that, more than any other, enables life to exist. Without its protective insulation, temperatures would swing from unbearable cold at night to unbearable heat during the day. Air is composed of nitrogen (78 per cent), oxygen (21 per cent), argon (nearly one per cent) and small amounts of other gases. No one knows how far above the earth the atmosphere extends, but it is probably at least 1,000 miles. The air is not a uniform mass but can be divided into layers, each with its own characteristics.

EXOSPHERE

The air here is so rarefied that its density is only one millionmillionth of that at ground level. Air particles move freely, some escaping into the near-vacuum of outer space.

(250 miles)

IONOSPHERE

In the ionosphere the air particles are electrically charged (ionized) by the Sun's ultra-violet radiation, and congregate in four main layers: D, E, F_1 and F_2. It is these layers which reflect radio waves back to the ground. The temperature increases rapidly from $-73°C$. at the D layer (at a height of about 45 miles) to perhaps as much as $1,600°C$. at 200 miles.

F2 Layer (155 miles)

The glowing Auroras (Northern and Southern Lights) are thought to be caused when jets of atomic matter, shot out from the Sun, are deflected by the Earth's magnetic field towards the North and South Poles. They occur at varying heights between 40 and 600 miles.

F1 Layer (90-150 miles)

It is mainly in the lower ionosphere that meteors from outer space burn up as they meet the increased air resistance. F_2 and F_1 (bottom) layers (known as the Appleton layer—although at night the F_1 layer is absent) reflect short radio waves. E layer reflects long radio waves. Also called the Heaviside layer, it is the lowest stable layer. D layer is unstable and unpredictable, and is usually present only in daytime.

Meteors generally burn out above this level.

CHEMOSPHERE

E Layer which extends about 30 miles above this line.
HYDROXYL ZONE where water vapour is broken up by sunlight into hydrogen atoms and molecules of one hydrogen and one oxygen atom (hydroxyl).

D Layer (45 miles)

The chemosphere is defined mainly by an accumulation of ozone gas at about 20 to 30 miles high. Ozone absorbs some of the Sun's ultra-violet rays and is the Earth's main line of defence against the Sun's harmful effects. The ozone belt is marked by very high temperatures compared with those around it.

STRATOSPHERE

Throughout the ten-mile-thick layer of stratosphere, the temperature varies little, and is usually about $-60°C$. At the lower boundary, the tropopause, the direct effects of Earth's weather are not usually felt, and it is here that jet airliners fly to get above the weather.

TROPOSPHERE

From the ground to the tropopause the temperature drops steadily from about $15°C$ at sea level (in temperate zones) to about $-56°C$. at seven miles (the average height of the troposphere) while the air thins out rapidly with increasing height. Air pressure at sea level is 14·7 lb. per square inch, but at six miles it is less than 4·9. The troposphere is the region of clouds and weather.

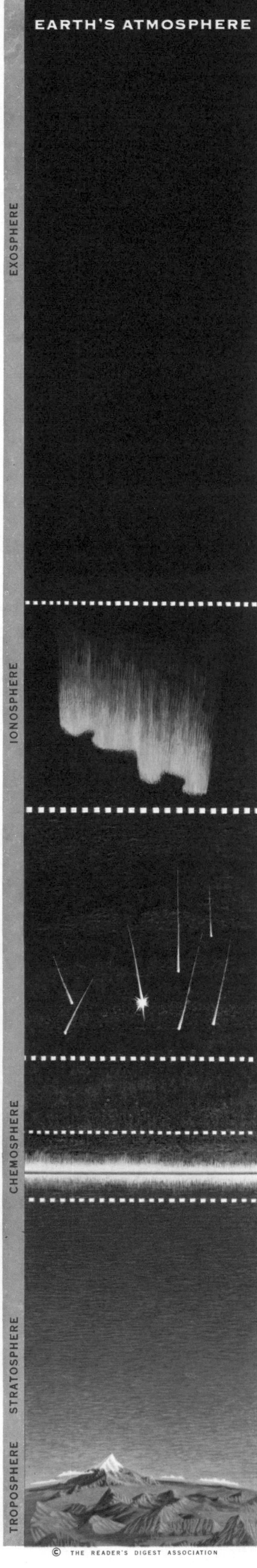

© THE READER'S DIGEST ASSOCIATION

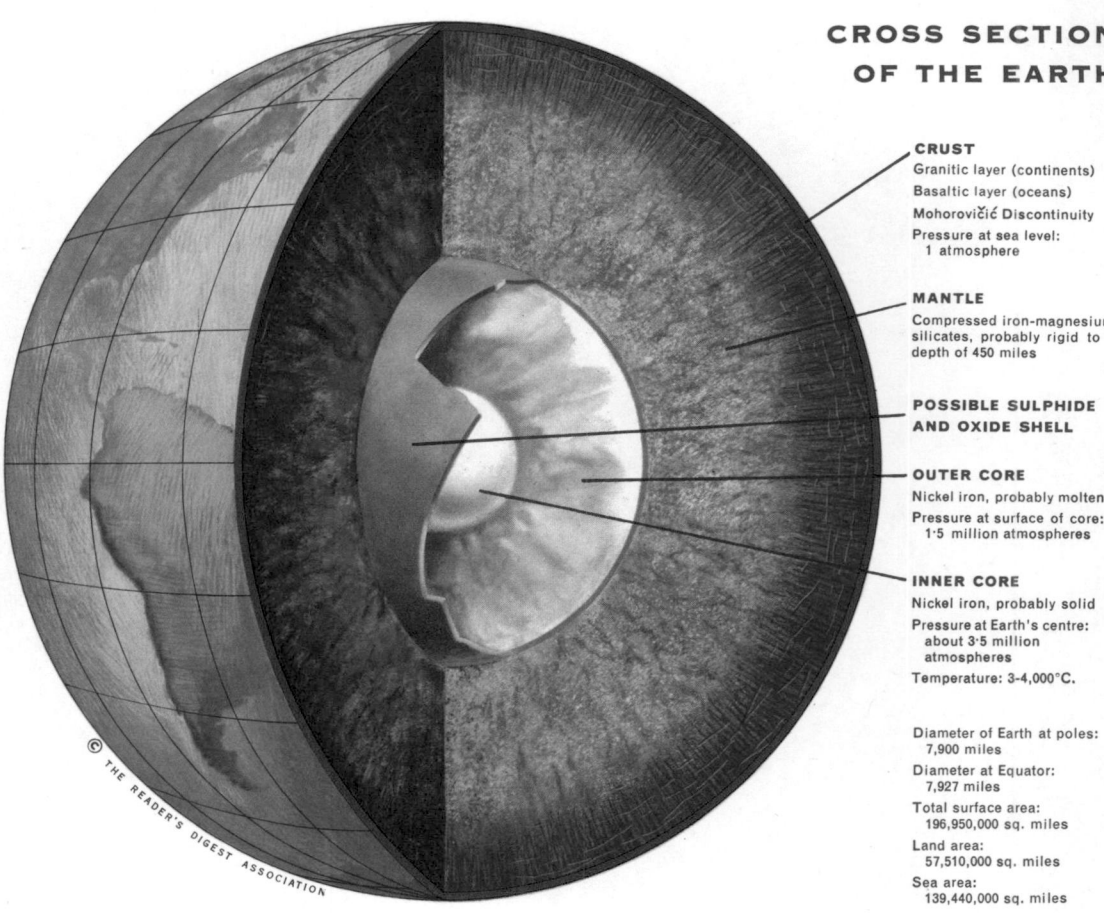

CROSS SECTION OF THE EARTH

CRUST
Granitic layer (continents)
Basaltic layer (oceans)
Mohorovičić Discontinuity
Pressure at sea level:
1 atmosphere

MANTLE
Compressed iron-magnesium silicates, probably rigid to a depth of 450 miles

POSSIBLE SULPHIDE AND OXIDE SHELL

OUTER CORE
Nickel iron, probably molten
Pressure at surface of core:
1·5 million atmospheres

INNER CORE
Nickel iron, probably solid
Pressure at Earth's centre:
about 3·5 million atmospheres
Temperature: 3-4,000°C.

Diameter of Earth at poles:
7,900 miles
Diameter at Equator:
7,927 miles
Total surface area:
196,950,000 sq. miles
Land area:
57,510,000 sq. miles
Sea area:
139,440,000 sq. miles

© THE READER'S DIGEST ASSOCIATION

THE EARTH'S STRUCTURE

Let the waters under the heaven be gathered together unto one place, and let the dry land appear — GENESIS 1

THE continental parts of the Earth's Crust are composed of many different kinds of rock which, as a whole, have the density and composition of granite. This granite layer is often called "sial" because of the predominance of *sil*ica and *al*umina in its composition. The granite layer, or "sial," floats on a denser layer, which has an average density and composition similar to that of the common black volcanic lava known as basalt. This so-called "basaltic" layer (termed "sima" because of its richness in *si*lica and *ma*gnesium) directly underlies the ocean floor, and here forms the thinnest part of the Earth's Crust. In continental areas the granitic and basaltic layers together reach an average thickness of between 20 and 25 miles. In oceanic areas, the basaltic layer alone averages a thickness of about three miles.

Knowledge that the Earth could not consist entirely of these surface rocks came first from the planet's weight, measured by its pull of gravity; for these materials are far too light to account for a total mass of 6,600 million million million tons. The density (weight per unit of volume) of rocks at the Earth's centre may in fact be as high as 16, compared with only 2·7 at the surface.

The best clues to what lies beneath the Earth's exterior are provided by records of earthquake shocks. Shock waves passing through the Earth are found to change their direction and speed at certain levels which are known as discontinuities. The first major discontinuity is at the base of the basaltic layer where the latter rests on the Mantle. This is named the Mohorovičić Discontinuity (Moho for short) after the Yugoslav scientist who discovered it. At this level a marked change in the velocity of earthquake waves takes place. This could indicate either an actual change in the chemical nature of the rocks or merely a change in their physical state; but precisely which we do not yet know.

The Mantle extends to a depth of 1,800 miles, where a second major discontinuity marks the beginning of the Outer Core. Although nothing is known directly about the rocks of the Earth's interior, it is widely accepted that the material near the inner edge of the Mantle is two to three times as heavy as the surface rocks.

The Outer Core, 1,310 miles thick, is probably formed of heavy metals (iron and nickel) in molten form; but because of the tremendous pressure, this fluid substance would be unlike any fluid we know on the Earth's surface. The next layer, the Inner Core, 850 miles thick, is believed to consist of the same materials as the Outer Core, but forced into a solid state by increased pressure—three million times greater at the centre of the Earth than at the surface. Temperature also increases sharply with descent into the Earth, until it may reach at least 4,000°C.

Some scientists believe that at the centre of the Earth there is a nucleus of high-density atoms, descended from the atoms that were the starting point of our solar system.

ROCKS AND THEIR ORIGINS

IGNEOUS — Basalt — Granite

SEDIMENTARY — Shale — Sandstone — Limestone

METAMORPHIC — Schist — Gneiss

IGNEOUS rocks are those that solidified directly from molten silicates, which geologists call magma. The Mantle obviously belongs to this category as do also the basaltic layer and much of the granitic layer. Igneous rocks include the fine-grained lavas, which have cooled quickly at the surface, and the coarse grained "plutonic" rocks which have cooled and crystallized slowly at depth.

Sedimentary rocks are formed when igneous rocks are eroded and laid down as sediment under the sea. Shale, which is mud layers compacted under great pressure, composes 80 per cent of these rocks. Others are sandstone —sand cemented into rock-form by other minerals—and limestone and chalk, which are in part the calcareous remains of countless marine creatures. Fossils are often found in the geologically younger sedimentary rocks.

Sedimentary and igneous rocks of all ages, which have been subjected to the intense pressures and heat in the roots of mountain chains, are now in a "metamorphosed" condition.

Because the older parts of the continents are crisscrossed with old eroded-down mountain chains these "metamorphic" rocks have a wide surface distribution. During metamorphism shales become schists, granite becomes gneiss, limestone becomes marble, and sandstone becomes quartzite. The changes involve re-crystallization, and the growth of new minerals from those composing the original rocks. The older metamorphic rocks are frequently rich in deposits of the base and precious metals.

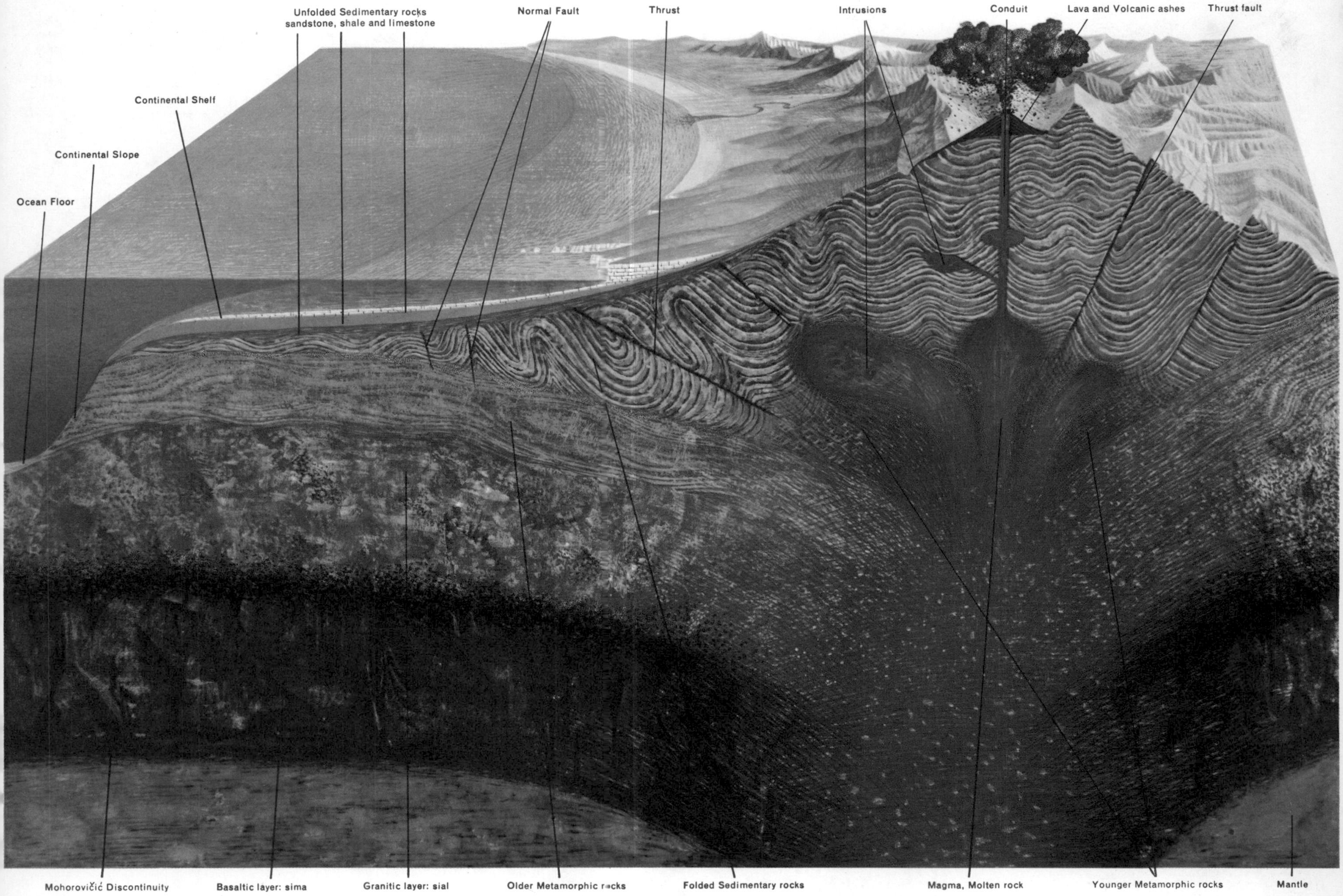

Ocean Floor — Continental Slope — Continental Shelf — Unfolded Sedimentary rocks sandstone, shale and limestone — Normal Fault — Thrust — Intrusions — Conduit — Lava and Volcanic ashes — Thrust fault

Mohorovičić Discontinuity — Basaltic layer: sima — Granitic layer: sial — Older Metamorphic rocks — Folded Sedimentary rocks — Magma, Molten rock — Younger Metamorphic rocks — Mantle

DIAGRAMMATIC SECTION THROUGH THE CRUST

IN the great jig-saw of rocks that form the Earth's surface, the pieces are slowly and endlessly being rearranged. These changes originate deep in the Earth's interior.

The constant movements in the depths of the Earth mount in intensity from time to time, culminating in orogenies, profound disturbances in the Earth's Crust which give rise to great mountain ranges. The early stage of an orogeny is, paradoxically, downwarping of the Crust and formation of a sea-filled basin in which great thicknesses of sediments accumulate. Later the sides of the basin move towards each other, and the bottom moves up; the sedimentary rocks caught in this "vice" are folded and slide over each other, piling up into a great mountain chain. The fractures along which the sliding takes place are called "thrusts" or "thrust-faults". Heat and pressure in the depths of the downwarp—the "roots" of the mountain range—metamorphose the sedimentary rocks and cause molten granitic rock to form. This rises under great pressure with molten basalt from the Mantle, either crystallizing on the way up to form "intrusions", or drilling an outlet in the Earth's surface to pour out as volcanic lava and ashes. When the folded rocks appear above the sea surface, the destructive action of wind, rain, frost and waves begins. Eventually the mountains succumb; layers of sediment are deposited in places over the eroded rocks, and a surface of low relief with meandering rivers is all that is left.

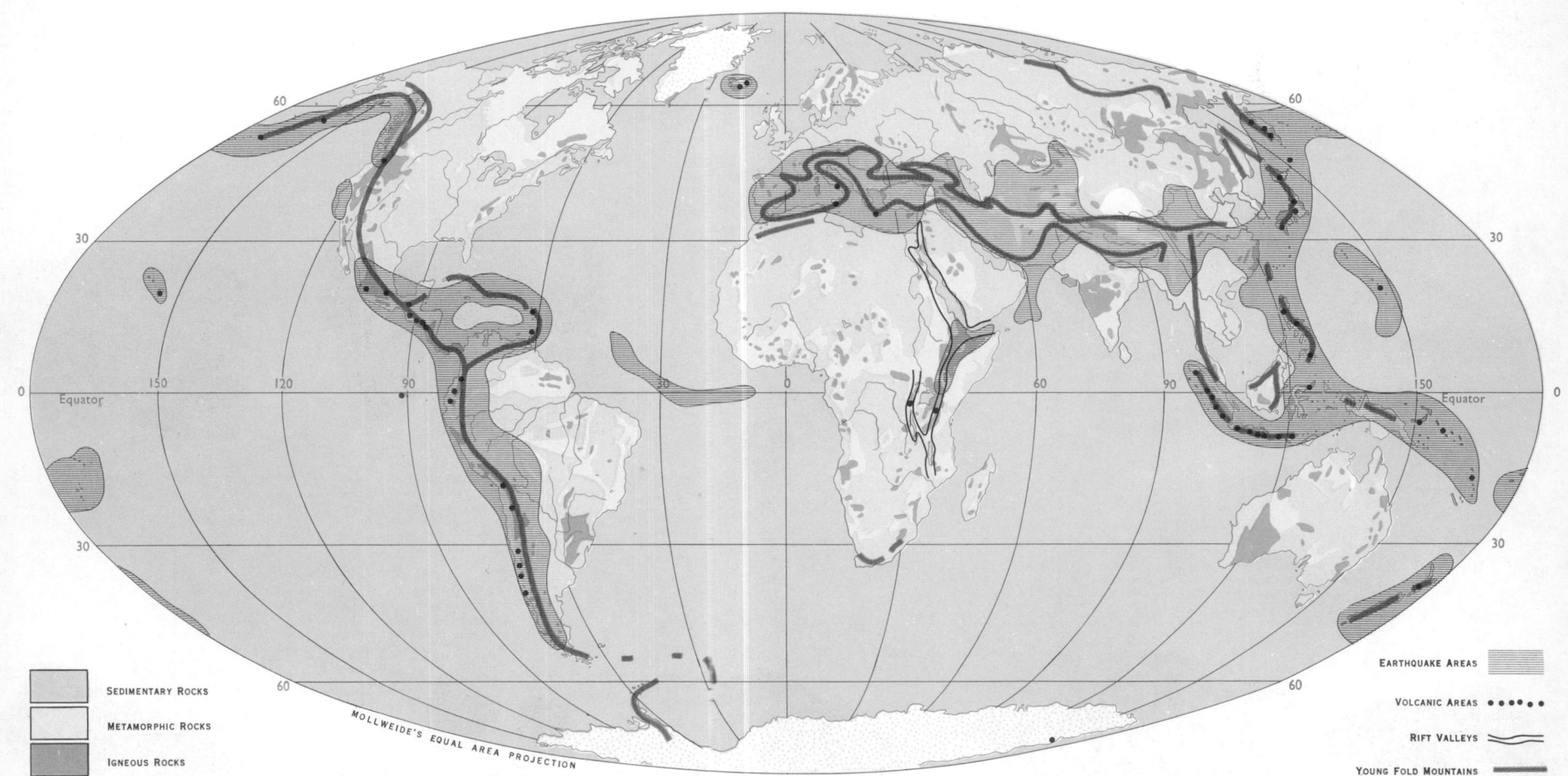

SEDIMENTARY ROCKS
METAMORPHIC ROCKS
IGNEOUS ROCKS

EARTHQUAKE AREAS
VOLCANIC AREAS
RIFT VALLEYS
YOUNG FOLD MOUNTAINS

MOLLWEIDE'S EQUAL AREA PROJECTION

THE ROCKS AND STRUCTURAL FEATURES OF THE EARTH'S CRUST

THE map shows only the rocks to be seen on the surface of the Earth. The predominance of sedimentary rock is illusory, as these rocks form a thin skin over much thicker layers of metamorphic and igneous rock. Earthquake activity and active volcanoes indicate that the Earth's Crust is still unstable. Earthquakes are sudden adjustments of parts of the Crust in response to pressures generated during mountain-building and volcanic activity. Volcanoes are of two sorts: quiet outflows through tension cracks which reach down to chambers of molten rock; and explosively drilled pipes, generally in regions of active or recent mountain-building, through which bursts highly pressurized, gas-charged magma, giving violent eruptions. Present-day earthquakes and volcanic belts follow the more recent belts of mountain-building—The Alps, Himalayas, Rockies and Andes. The "Ring of Fire" round the Pacific is noteworthy; so is the Great Rift Valley extending north—south from the Jordan Valley to the Zambesi, along which the ground has sunk between parallel faults, with consequent volcanic activity.

THE EARTH'S

MINERALS FROM THE

Surely there is a mine for silver, and a place for gold which they refine. Iron is taken out of the earth, and brass is molten out of stone — JOB 28

F ROM the prized flints of Stone-Age man to the uranium ores of the atomic scientist, minerals have contributed vitally to the growth of civilization. Man has long recognized their importance as the source of precious metals and precious stones, and of base metals such as copper, lead and zinc. Tomb paintings made in the Nile Valley nearly 5,000 years ago show craftsmen weighing malachite and precious metals, smelting mineral ores and carving emeralds into gems.

Rocks are made up of minerals, and minerals themselves are composed of one or more of the 90-odd natural elements in the Earth's Crust. While a few elements, such as gold, are found in the pure state, the majority occur in chemical combination with other elements. Thus oxides are produced when

GALENA
Sulphide and chief ore of lead. Leaden pans for holding plants were used in the Hanging Gardens of Babylon. Lead is used in storage batteries, paint pigments, ammunition, solder, type and bearing metal, and as a safety shield with radio-active material. *Missouri, U.S.A.*

FLUORITE (FLUORSPAR)
Calcium fluoride. Ornamental stone in Victorian times. Raw material for the production of hydrofluoric acid which is used in the aluminium, petroleum, steel and plastic industries; fluorite is used as a flux in steel-making and in the ceramic industry. *Illinois, U.S.A.*

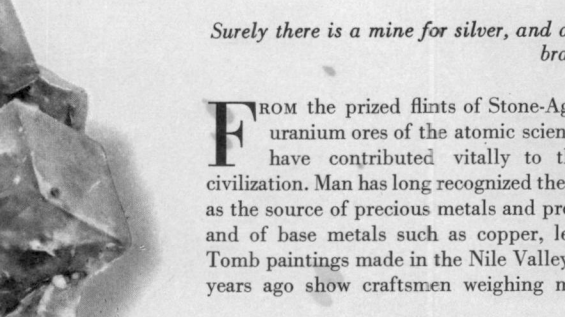

URANIUM MINERALS
Atomic energy developments are based on uranium. Uranium does not occur uncombined in nature but is present in over 150 minerals.

SPHALERITE
Sulphide and chief ore of zinc. Frequently occurs with galena. Zinc is used in die-castings, galvanizing steel, in brasses, dry battery cells; the oxide is used in rubber, paints, ceramics, cosmetics, etc. *Sullivan Mine, British Columbia*

ASBESTOS
A group of fire-resistant, fibrous silicate minerals. The long fibres can be spun into fabrics. The short fibres are mixed with cement to make asbestos board. *Quebec, Canada*

PITCHBLENDE
Uranium oxides with other components. The massive variety of uraninite, the most important ore. *Shinkolobwe, Katanga, Congo*

TORBERNITE
Hydrated copper-uranium phosphate. Green plates resemble a mica. *Cornwall*

CASSITERITE
Oxide and chief ore of tin. Alloyed with copper, it was the basis of Bronze Age implements. Used in tin-plating, solders, bronze, bearing and type metal, pewter, and die-casting. *W. Malaysia*

TOPAZ
Silicate of fluorine and aluminium. Used as gemstone and in refractories. *Ouro Preto, Brazil*

OLIVINE
Magnesium-iron silicate. A common rock-forming mineral. Used as a moulding sand. Peridot and chrysolite are gem varieties. *Zebirget, Egypt*

Sullivan Mine, British Columbia, *Sphalerite* Coal,
Minnesota, *Hematite* Quebec, *Asbestos*
U.S.A., *Garnet* Sudbury, Ontario, *Pentlandite*
Illinois, *Fluorite*
Missouri, *Galena* W. Virginia, *Coal* Air
Texas, *Sulphur*

Mexico, *Silver*
Jamaica, *Bauxite*

Colombia, *Emerald*

Equator

Brazil, *Quartz*

Minas Gerais, *Aquamarine*
Ouro Preto, *Topaz*

Oil

ALUMINA MINERALS
Although the most abundant metal in the Earth's Crust, aluminium does not occur in the free state, and commercial production did not start until the late 19th century. Alloys are used extensively in motor vehicles, aircraft, ships and domestic goods. Aluminium is used in electric transmission lines. Ruby and sapphire are gem varieties of corundum, a natural aluminium oxide.

CORUNDUM
Hardness only exceeded by diamond. Used as an abrasive in grinding optical glass. Mixed with magnetite and other minerals to form emery. *Transvaal, South Africa*

SAPPHIRE
Corundum gemstones of whatever colour are sapphires with the exception of red (ruby); commonly blue. *Ceylon*

RUBY
"Pigeon-blood" red variety. Large rubies are among the most precious of stones. *Mogok, Burma*

BAUXITE
Rock composed of aluminium hydroxides. Chief ore of aluminium; also used in making abrasives, refractories, chemicals, high-alumina cement, insulating materials, as a catalyst by the oil industry, and as a flux in steel manufacture. *Jamaica*

CINNABAR
Sulphide and chief ore of mercury (quick-silver). Mercury is used in the chemical, electrical and metal industries, and in scientific instruments, dental preparations, and detonators. *Almaden, Spain*

COPPER MINERALS
Copper and gold were the first metals used by man. Both occur in the free state and are easily worked. Copper is used extensively in the electrical industry, also in bronze, brass and other alloys. About 12 of the 165 known copper minerals are commercially important.

IRON MINERALS
Iron is industry's indispensable metal. Although iron minerals occur abundantly, pure iron is too soft for use, so man learnt to harden it by adding carbon. Thus the Iron Age followed the Bronze Age in Europe and W. Asia. A moderate amount of carbon produces steel, an excess produces cast-iron.

AZURITE
Hydrated copper carbonate. *Katanga, Congo*

CHALCOPYRITE
Copper-iron-sulphide. Crystals of chalcopyrite and quartz are shown. Most widespread and important ore of copper. *Zambia*

MALACHITE
Hydrated copper carbonate. An ornamental stone as well as a valuable ore. *Katanga, Congo*

MAGNETITE
Magnetic iron oxide. Crystals show octahedral form. Lodestone (leading-stone), a variety with magnetic polarity, was used in primitive compasses. *Kiruna, Sweden*

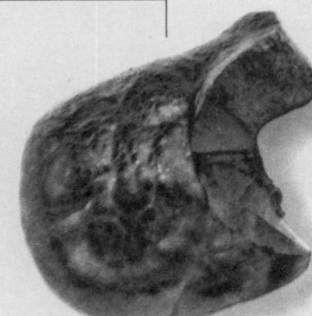

HEMATITE
Oxide of iron. The "kidney-ore" variety is shown. Used as an ornamental stone in signet rings, tie-pins and cuff links. *Minnesota, U.S.A.*

TREASURES

EARTH'S CRUST

metals combine with oxygen, and sulphides when metals combine with sulphur. Minerals are formed in various ways, for example, by crystallization from molten lava, rather as ice crystals form when water freezes, and by crystallization from vapours, as in the formation of sulphur crystals by the cooling of sulphur-bearing vapours round active volcanoes.

Some 2,000 minerals have been recorded so far, and, although new minerals are still being discovered, it is unlikely that any large deposit of a new mineral will be found in the accessible parts of the Earth's Crust. At depths below those of the present deepest mine, we may one day find new minerals that are stable at the high pressures and temperatures nearer the centre of the Earth. The advent of space travel opens up the possibility of the discovery of new minerals which would be stable on other planets where conditions are so different from our own.

This small selection of the Earth's minerals shows the variety of their natural forms and colours. Their more commercially important deposits and the locations of the world's oilfields are indicated on the map.

APATITE
Calcium phosphate. Chief constituent of phosphate-rock. Used in manufacture of fertilizers, cleansing products, smoke-bombs, pesticides, and phosphorus alloys.
Kola Peninsula, Russia

PENTLANDITE
Nickel-iron sulphide. Frequently occurs with chalcopyrite. Used extensively in stainless steels and other alloys; nickel is alloyed with copper to make Britain's "silver" coins and the U.S. five-cent "nickel". *Sudbury, Ontario*

BERYLLIUM MINERALS
Beryllium is unusually light and strong and has valuable metallurgical properties. Used in alloys with copper, nickel, and aluminium; also in X-ray tubes, and nuclear reactors. Beryl is the commercial source of beryllium; aquamarine and emerald are gemstone varieties with similar composition.

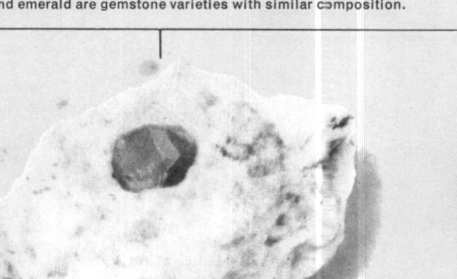

KAOLIN (CHINA CLAY)
Hydrated aluminium silicate. Used in paper, rubber, ceramics (notably porcelain and china), chemicals, cosmetics, insecticides and petroleum catalysts. *Cornwall*

AQUAMARINE
Sea-green variety.
Minas Gerais, Brazil

ZIRCON
Zirconium silicate. Besides being a gemstone, zircon in mineral form is used as foundry sand and in abrasives and ceramics. Zirconium metal is used in nuclear reactors, steel alloys, and in the chemical and electrical industries.

BERYL
Silicate of beryllium and aluminium. Can occur in large crystals up to 25 tons in weight. Gemstone if clear and transparent.
Mocambique

EMERALD
Grass-green, unflawed stones exceeding six carats command high prices. Ranks with diamond and ruby as the most precious stone. *Colombia*

CARBON MINERALS
Native crystalline carbon occurs as two important minerals: diamond and graphite. Coals consist largely of non-crystalline carbon of organic origin. Combination with hydrogen produces the natural hydrocarbons which constitute petroleums and bitumens.

(map)

Peninsula, *Apatite*
Magnetite

Urals, *Platinum*

Korea, *Graphite*

Zebirget, *Olivine*

Mogok, *Ruby*

Ceylon, *Sapphire*
West Malaysia, *Cassiterite*

Equator

Katanga,
ende, *Azurite, Malachite*
Zambia, *Chalcopyrite*

Mocambique, *Beryl*
Transvaal, *Corundum*
Kimberley, *Diamond*
The Rand, *Gold*

New South Wales, *Opal*

DIAMOND
Hardest known mineral and the most valuable gemstone. Crystallized deep down at high temperature and pressure, and brought to surface in volcanic "kimberlite" pipes. Photograph shows a diamond in kimberlite. Most diamonds are minute and imperfect, and are used in industry for cutting or as abrasives. *Kimberley, South Africa*

COAL
Bituminous coal showing banded structure. Besides being a fuel, coal is a source of coal gas, coke, tar, ammonia and many hydrocarbon chemicals. *United Kingdom*

GRAPHITE
One of the softest minerals. The "lead" in lead pencils. Used in foundry facings, steel-making, lubricants, refractory crucibles, electrical equipment, pigments and in atomic piles. *Korea*

SULPHUR (BRIMSTONE)
Native sulphur (illustrated), metallic sulphide ores, "sour" natural and refinery gas, and coal are all commercial sources of sulphur. Used in manufacture of sulphuric acid and many other chemicals, paper, rubber goods, steel, textiles. *Texas, U.S.A.*

GOLD
Man used gold for decoration from early times. It is hardened by alloying with copper, silver, palladium or nickel for use in jewellery, dentistry and scientific equipment. *The Rand, South Africa*

PLATINUM
Native platinum usually contains variable amounts of the other platinum-group metals—palladium, iridium, osmium, rhodium and ruthenium—some of which are employed to harden pure platinum in commercial applications. Platinum is used in anti-corrosive chemical ware, electrical components and laboratory instruments. Platinum and palladium are both used as catalysts, and in jewellery, dentistry and medicine. *Urals*

SILVER
Specimen of native silver with milky-white quartz. Silver sulphides are important ores commonly associated with lead, copper and zinc ores. Used in coinage, plate, jewellery and dentistry, and in the photographic, electrical and chemical industries. *Mexico*

SILICA MINERALS
Silicon does not occur uncombined, but its oxide, quartz, and the large group of silicates are the most important rock-forming minerals. Silicon is the most abundant element in the Earth's Crust after oxygen; it is used in electronic components and alloys, and for manufacturing silicones. Chalcedony is a crystalline variety of quartz intimately mixed with opal and other constituents. Flint is a common dark grey-brown variety of chalcedony; precious varieties are shown below.

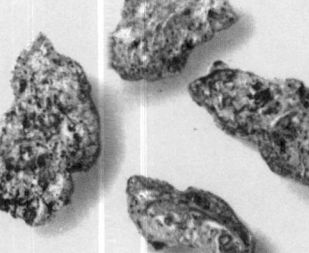

GARNET
Garnet is the name of a group of silicates. The photograph shows crystals in a metamorphic rock; garnet is also a semi-precious gemstone. The iron-aluminium garnet, almandine, is used as an abrasive. *U.S.A.*

OPAL
A hydrated non-crystalline form of silica (silicon dioxide) which shows a beautifully variegated play of colours or "fire". Gemstone. *New South Wales, Australia*

QUARTZ
One of the commonest minerals. High-grade quartz is used in crystal-controlled oscillator units (as in quartz-clocks) and other electronic instruments, also for optical purposes and in fused quartz ware. *Brazil*

VARIETIES OF CHALCEDONY

HALITE (ROCK SALT)
Sodium chloride. Man requires about 12 lb. of salt a year. Apart from its use in food-seasoning and preserving, salt is chiefly used by the chemical industry. *Cheshire*

ONYX
An agate with regular bands in sharply contrasted colours.

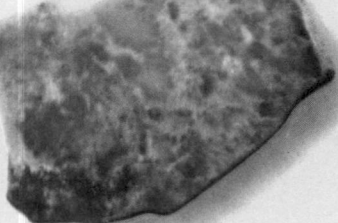

CHRYSOPRASE
Apple-green variety coloured by nickel oxide.

CARNELIAN
Reddish variety coloured by ferric oxide.

AGATE
Greyish variety in which irregular bands conform to shape of original cavity. Easily stained and used for umbrella handles, brooches, etc., also in laboratory equipment.

THE AGES OF THE EARTH

And the Earth was waste and void—GENESIS 1

Of the 4,500 million and more years of the Earth's existence only the last 600 million years can be traced with accuracy. Almost nothing is known of conditions during the first 1,000 million years, before the Earth's Crust consolidated. The historian, relying on archaeological discoveries and the written records of ancient civilizations, can reach back a mere 6,000 years into the past, but the geologist can reconstruct the story in considerable detail for 600 million years before the historian's record begins. The geologist's evidence lies in the rocks and in the fossilized relics of plants and animals that many of the rocks contain.

Although little is known of the 3,000 million years which elapsed after consolidation of the Earth's Crust, the earliest and most primitive forms of life—seaweeds and invertebrate marine creatures—must have been evolving for many millions of years before their fossilized remains were first abundantly preserved in the rocks formed about 600 million years ago. The earliest vertebrates—primitive types of fish-like animals—did not appear for another 100 million years. Land plants first established themselves little more than 400 million years ago, and amphibious animals about 350 million years ago. Mammals, of which man, through his brain, is the most advanced, date back a little less that 250 million years; man himself has emerged only within the last million years.

The course of evolution has not been smooth and unbroken; some plants and animals evolved only to die out millions of years later, never to reappear; others have persisted almost unchanged. Major disturbances of the Earth's Crust caused important changes in geography and climate, which in turn influenced the evolution and distribution of animal and plant life. These major disturbances separate the four *eras* of geological history: the Proterozoic (first life), the Palaeozoic (ancient life), the Mesozoic (middle life), and the Cainozoic (modern life).

Within each of the four eras there were crustal disturbances which again broke up the geological record, but to a lesser degree. The rocks formed during the *periods* of time between these disturbances are grouped together as distinct *systems*, most of which have been named after the places where the rocks were first studied; e.g. the county of Devon, and the Jura Mountains of central Europe.

Thus, the evidence deduced from rocks and fossils reveals not only the general pattern of evolution in plant and animal life, but the development of the world's oceans, continents, mountain ranges and rivers, as well as changes in climatic conditions. From geological research we know that lion, rhinoceros, elephant and hippopotamus once roamed over the country we now call Britain, and that the summit of Mount Everest—where marine fossils have been found—is composed of limestone which was originally formed under the sea.

GEOLOGY OF THE BRITISH ISLES

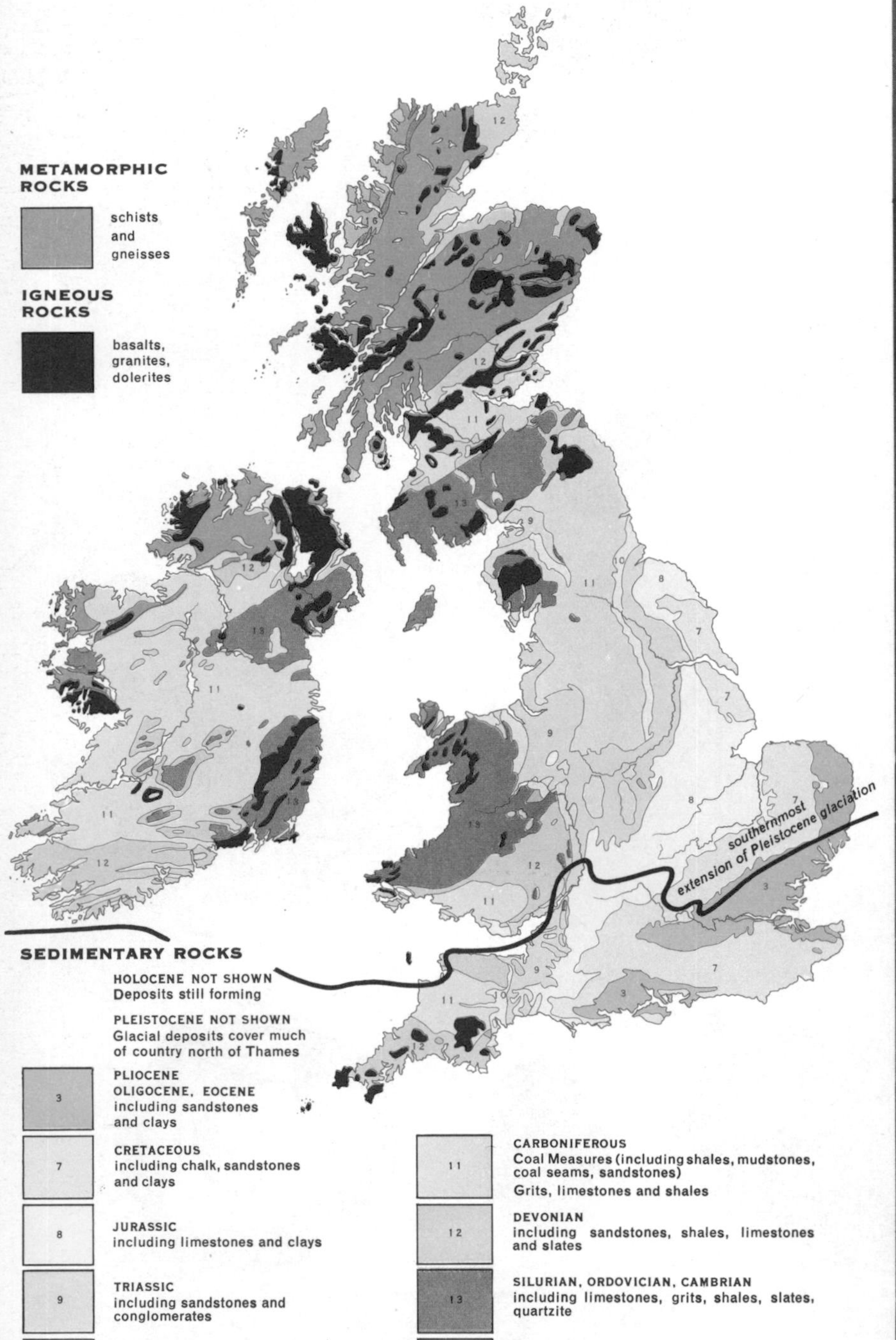

METAMORPHIC ROCKS
schists and gneisses
IGNEOUS ROCKS
basalts, granites, dolerites
southernmost extension of Pleistocene glaciation
SEDIMENTARY ROCKS
HOLOCENE NOT SHOWN Deposits still forming
PLEISTOCENE NOT SHOWN Glacial deposits cover much of country north of Thames
3 PLIOCENE OLIGOCENE, EOCENE including sandstones and clays
7 CRETACEOUS including chalk, sandstones and clays
8 JURASSIC including limestones and clays
9 TRIASSIC including sandstones and conglomerates
10 PERMIAN including limestones and sandstones
11 CARBONIFEROUS Coal Measures (including shales, mudstones, coal seams, sandstones) Grits, limestones and shales
12 DEVONIAN including sandstones, shales, limestones and slates
13 SILURIAN, ORDOVICIAN, CAMBRIAN including limestones, grits, shales, slates, quartzite
16 PRE-CAMBRIAN including grits, conglomerates, sandstones

	GEOLOGICAL DIVISIONS	GEOGRAPHICAL CONDITIONS
CAINOZOIC (MODERN LIFE)	**Holocene** started 10 thousand years ago	The ice continues to retreat, causing the sea level to rise further. Britain, joined to Europe during the glacial period, is cut off from the Continent. Landscape much as we see it today. Climatic conditions gradually become more equable. In North Africa and the Middle East, increasing dryness produces deserts.
	Pleistocene started about 2 million years ago *lasted c 2 million years*	Ice-sheets and glaciers cover most of Europe, America, Antarctica and the Himalayas. The ice melts periodically, thus raising the sea level, and the land masses of Europe and North America, which have been pressed down by the enormous weight of the ice, begin to rise. (Scandinavia today continues to rise at a rate of a centimetre a year.) Melting ice forms the Great Lakes of North America, the lakes of Switzerland and Northern Italy, and the lakes of Great Britain. The tremendous weight of retreating glaciers cuts out the fjords of Norway. Landscape begins to take on present-day form and appearance. A period of abnormal and extreme climatic changes.
	Pliocene started about 7 million years ago *lasted c 5 million years*	Continents and oceans begin to take on their present form. Land subsidence leads to formation of the North Sea, the Black and Caspian Seas, the Sea of Aral. Formation of mountain ranges continues, though on a reduced scale. Climatic conditions are much like today's, but with a broader temperate zone.
	Miocene started about 26 million years ago *lasted 19 million years*	Powerful Earth movements lead to a further retreat of the sea. The Mediterranean becomes virtually a land-locked ocean. The European and Asian land masses are finally joined together. Increased rainfall leads to intense erosion in some parts. Further powerful movements in the Earth's Crust complete formation of the Alps and lead to formation of the Himalayas. Much volcanic activity. Climates tend to become more varied: dry and arid in some regions, cool and wet in others.
	Oligocene started about 38 million years ago *lasted 12 million years*	Throughout this period the land mass grows at the expense of the sea. Extensive movements of the Earth's Crust in the Americas and in Europe. The Alps begin to form. Warm, temperate conditions continue, but parts of the land mass experience a cycle of cooler winters.
	Eocene and Palaeocene (combined) started about 65 million years ago *lasted c 27 million years*	The subsidence of much of Europe causes the seas to advance once again. Tropical vegetation, like that in present-day Malaya, flourishes in southern England. Mountain ranges which began to form in the Cretaceous period continue to grow. Volcanic activity leads to the formation of the Atlantic and Indian Oceans, and causes vast amounts of lava to be deposited in areas as far apart as the Arctic, Scotland and Ireland, and southern India. Tropical conditions are more widespread than today, but glaciers exist on high mountain ranges in western North America.
MESOZOIC (MIDDLE LIFE)	**Cretaceous** chalk started about 136 million years ago *lasted 71 million years*	Land areas bordering the sea consist of far-reaching swamps. The rivers flow slowly and form enormous deltas. Widespread deposits of chalk, now seen in Britain in the white cliffs of Dover and Dorset. Chalk formations also accumulate in North America, north-west Canada, Alaska and Mexico. Period of major mountain-building. The Rocky Mountains, the Andes, many European ranges and the Panama Ridge—giving rise to the Gulf Stream—begin to emerge. The climate continues to be mild, causing vegetation to grow abundantly as far north as Greenland, though parts of Australia appear to be covered by glaciers.
	Jurassic after Jura mountains in France and Switzerland started about 193 million years ago *lasted c 57 million years*	The seas advance again. Most land areas consist of forests or swampy plains with lakes and meandering rivers. The high mountains, already eroded by the arid climate of the previous period are reduced to low hills by the wet conditions. Much of Asia and Europe, including the neighbourhood of Britain, is invaded by the sea. A period marked by the formation of limestone, as in the Cotswolds, southern Germany, France and Switzerland. The climate is predominantly mild, becoming sub-tropical in some regions later in the period There is sufficient rainfall to support luxuriant vegetation.
	Triassic after three-fold mountain system in Germany started about 225 million years ago *lasted c 32 million years*	Deserts and shrub-covered mountains make up most of the Earth's land area. What is, today Britain is covered by warm, salt lakes surrounded by deserts. Formation of marl and sandstone deposits in the warm seas. Hot, dry conditions prevail almost everywhere. Climate becomes wetter towards the end of the period.
PALAEOZOIC (ANCIENT LIFE)	**Permian** After Russian province of Perm started about 280 million years ago *lasted 55 million years*	The British Isles form part of a semi-arid continent. Arms of the sea are cut off and turned into vast inland lakes by the warping of the Earth's Crust. The lakes start evaporating, a process that eventually leads to the formation of the world's chief potash deposits. A period of considerable Earth movements. Lofty mountains form in Europe, Asia and eastern U.S.A. (Appalachians). Contrasting climatic conditions. Mainly arid in Northern Hemisphere, with occasional warm and humid zones, but ice-age conditions cover much of the Southern Hemisphere.
	Carboniferous the coal age (Upper Pennsylvanian and Lower Mississippian) started about 345 million years ago *lasted 65 million years*	Clear, shallow seas widespread in early period; most of Europe and large parts of Russia unde water. Later, sea beds begin to rise, exposing great stretches of land. Other land areas sink producing brackish swamps over much of Europe and North America. Chief coal-forming period, particularly in Northern Hemisphere. Partly-rotted vegetation i forest swamps slowly accumulates as peat, and later forms coal. The land climate is extremely dry throughout most of the period, but in some regions it i warm and moist enough to encourage dense vegetation.
	Devonian after county of Devon where fossils of this period first found started about 395 million years ago *lasted 50 million years*	Land area increases at expense of sea. A period of extensive mountain-building and volcani activity. Pebbles, sand and mud, washed off the newly-made mountains, form the "Old Rec Sandstone" of north-west Europe. The shales and slates of Devon and Cornwall also date fron this period. Warm and semi-arid climate in north-west Europe and over a large part of North America with heavy seasonal rain. Equable conditions prevail elsewhere.
	Silurian after Celtic tribe, the Silures started about 435 million years ago *lasted c 40 million years*	The level of the seas tends to rise and fall periodically, causing regular changes in the lan areas. Rocks formed in this period have been found in Shropshire and Worcestershire, in th Baltic and in the region of the Niagara Falls. New mountain ranges are beginning to form. Less volcanic activity than in Ordovician times. Generally warm and equable climate, but exceptionally dry in certain areas.
	Ordovician after Celtic tribe, the Ordovices started about 500 million years ago *lasted c 65 million years*	The seas continue to advance and retreat. Many areas of the sea floor become dry land as th shallow seas deposit ever-increasing amounts of sand and mud, as in North America. Rocks of Ordovician period have been found not only in Wales but also in parts of Nort America and north-west Europe. Mountain-building in these regions. Volcanic eruptions on th floor of the sea, which covers central Wales during this period, creates huge volcanic bed out of which Snowdon is subsequently carved. The climate appears warm and even, with no marked climatic zones.
	Cambrian after Cambria, Roman name for Wales started about 570 million years ago *lasted 70 million years*	Shallow seas cover much of the Earth. The seas tend to advance on and retreat from the lan areas, some of which are probably little more than deserts. Cambrian rocks form in Wales, north-west Scotland and western England. Similar roc formations occur in Canada, and the U.S.A.—rocks from which the Grand Canyon is later carve form in this period. Considerable volcanic activity in Europe, but no evidence of importan mountain-building in this period. Climatic conditions are moderately warm and equable.
PROTEROZOIC	**Pre-Cambrian**	Beginning as a whirling globe of inter-stellar gas, the Earth passes through a liquid state an forms a solidified crust. Thick, steamy atmosphere surrounds the planet. As the Earth's surfac cools, water vapour condenses as rain to produce rivers and seas. The surface now forms a barre landscape of mountains, deserts, volcanoes and steaming lava fields. Many pre-Cambrian rocks have been so crushed and altered by heat and by pressure of sub sequent Earth movements that it is almost impossible to determine their original nature. The hot climate is broken up by a series of ice ages.

VEGETATION	LIFE IN THE SEA	LIFE ON LAND	EVOLUTION OF LIFE
th the retreat of the ice and e arrival of warmer summers, ests begin to spread all over rope. Tundra vegetation (mossy, arshy plains) is replaced by birch d pine, followed by hazel and en by oak and elder.	Marine life much as it is today.	Man learns to domesticate animals and cultivate plants.	
cceeding ice ages cause many nts in Europe to perish, leaving y hardier varieties—oak, willow, plar, elm, hawthorn. In America d Asia, vegetation seeking warmer mates encounters no sea or mount-barriers, and more plants survive.	Marine life much as it is today.	Ape-like creatures develop enough intelligence to make stone implements for cutting up animals they have killed, thus marking the transition to primitive man. Probably originating in Africa, primitive man spreads to Asia and Europe. Alternating ice ages and warm periods change the migration habits of other mammals. n one glacial period, reindeer and Arctic fox roam southern England. In the warmer period, hippopotamuses live in the Thames, lions range as far north as Yorkshire. True elephants, horses, oxen first appear.	
me plants of this period, such the maidenhair tree, die out in rope but survive in China and rth America.	Giant sharks become extinct, as did creatures that grew to a great size in other periods. Marine life, both plant and animal, becomes much as it is today. There are only marginal developments from this period onwards.	The number of mammal species declines, with the notable exception of the man-like apes, which continue to develop and thrive. These apes come to include not only the forest-dwellers, but the species known as Australopithecus which walks upright in open country and may be ancestral to man. Elephants also thrive, and roam as far afield as Suffolk and Norfolk.	
ld, damp climate in Europe and rth America stimulates development of deciduous woods — maple, k and poplar. Cedars and sequoias established on higher ground. e great plains of North America come covered with prairie grasses.	Bony fish continue to increase in variety. Sharks, particularly abundant during this period, grow to enormous sizes, measuring over 60 feet in length, and having teeth six inches long.	Proconsul, a primitive anthropoid ape living in central Africa, migrates to Asia and Europe. A gibbon-like ape, known as Pliopithecus, is common in the forests of southern Europe. Elephants, steadily increasing in size, spread from Africa into Europe, Asia and North America. Long-legged waterbirds, ducks and pelicans live in rivers and lakes. Primitive penguins, some as tall as man, live in Antarctica.	
a cooler climate affects some rts of the world, forests dwindle d grasslands spread, leading to an rease in grass-eating mammals.	A period in which new species of crabs, mussels and snails evolve.	The ancestors of modern cats, dogs and bears evolve. The number of plant-eating animals increases—small elephants with short trunks, and tusks in both upper and lower jaws, hoofed animals with odd numbers of toes, and giant rhinoceros. A tail-less, primitive ape, possibly related to the ancestors of man, appears.	
wering plants, including deciuous trees, become dominant. The rm climatic zone, which stretches ht up to Greenland, allows palms grow in the region of Bourne-uth, and Malayan-type jungles the region of London.	Marine reptiles have become extinct, but two groups of mammals—early whales and sea-cows—begin to adapt themselves to life in the sea. Most species of fish in the ocean take on the shape and forms we know today.	Many varieties of modern mammals come into existence—ancestors of the elephant, the rhinoceros, the horse, the pig, and cattle. Giant reptiles have disappeared, but crocodiles, turtles and land tortoises evolve, as do all groups of insects that we know today. Primitive monkeys and gibbons appear in Burma.	
mild climate with alternating sons—a feature of this period—courages the growth of deciduous es—fig, magnolia, poplar, plane. e parallel evolution of insects and ctar-bearing flowers encourages e spread of flowering plants.	Fish evolving in this period are closely related to the porbeagle sharks, rays and herrings of today. Marine life continues to be dominated by reptiles, giant turtles and mosasaurs—long, slender creatures resembling sea-serpents. Flying reptiles (pterosaurs) have a wing span of over 20 feet. (Their remains have been found in Yorkshire, Kent and Sussex.)	Giant reptiles, dinosaurs and pterosaurs, dominate life on land and in the air. Ichthyosaurs dominate life in the sea. Birds evolve into two types: one with well-developed wings, similar to modern birds, the other a sea-bird, almost wingless but with strongly developed legs for swimming. By the end of the period dinosaurs become extinct. Mammals remain inconspicuous throughout this period, but by its end placental mammals (whose young are nourished directly by the mother's blood until birth) have developed.	
nifers, cycads, ferns and tree-ns continue to flourish. Some ads have flower-like cones—the st step in the evolution of wers.	In the seas, the dominant animals are aquatic reptiles like ichthyosaurs. Rapid swimmers, they prey on fish and other marine creatures.	Reptiles increase in size and variety. Some take to the air; the first bird, Archaeopteryx, evolves feathers from scales, but retains many reptilian characteristics such as teeth, solid bones and a jointed tail. Pterosaurus develops wings made of skin stretched between body and fingers. Some reptiles, too large for survival on land (Diplodocus, length 84 feet, weight 35 tons), live in swamps and marshes. Mammals remain small and primitive, no bigger than rats, and live mostly in woodlands.	
id conditions in the Northern emisphere discourage the development of plant life at the ginning of the period. Later, tter conditions stimulate the wth of conifers, cycads and ns.	The first ichthyosaurs, carnivorous, fish-shaped reptiles, evolve in this period. So do flying fish and the first lobster-like creatures.	Reptiles continue to dominate life on land. The first mammals—warm-blooded creatures—evolve from the reptiles. Dinosaurs, no more than six inches long, are present for the first time. The first flies and termites appear.	
seasonal differences of climate d temperature develop, ever-een plants begin to decrease in mber, and deciduous plants, le to withstand periods of drought d frost, appear.	This period marks the end of the dominance by marine creatures, as animal and plant life on land increases.	Creatures capable of living on land increase in number and variety, ending the period of domination by marine creatures. As in the sea, however, animal life is predominantly reptilian. A great variety of insects begins to emerge.	
ant evergreen trees, reaching ights of over 100 feet flourish in e tropical swamp of the period ich knows no seasonal changes temperature.	Amphibious creatures continue to develop. Living in swamp-land on the edge of lakes, they are small, salamander-like animals to begin with, but reach sizes of up to 15 feet by the end of the period. Marine life, both plant and animal, abounds in many varieties.	The reptile becomes the first creature to breed on land. Certain species of insects develop wings.	
rth begins to look green, as nts with roots, stems and leaves lve. They range from small, herb-e growths to trees of 40 feet or re in height. By the end of the riod, various kinds of ferns, horse-s and seed-ferns have evolved.	Rapid evolution of vertebrate animals. Ancestors of all modern fish evolve. Primitive sharks, measuring up to 20 feet, appear. In consequence, this period has become known as the "Age of Fish." By the end of the period, the first amphibious animals have come into existence.	With land plants o feed on, the first invertebrate animals leave the sea and adapt themselves to life on land. They include millipedes, mites, spiders, and wingless insects.	
nts first adapt themselves to e on land, but are still leafless. ossil remains have been found in stralia.)	New species of vertebrate animals develop in the sea. Appearance of sea-scorpions, heavily armoured animals reaching nine feet in length. (Fossil remains of Jamoytius, a primitive vertebrate of this period, have been found in Lanarkshire.) Plant life becomes more varied in structure, and coral reefs develop on a large scale.	First plants appear on land.	
nt life confined to the sea.	All life still restricted to water, but first vertebrates appear. (Remains of ostracoderms—bony, armoured creatures—have been found in western U.S.A.) Plant life does not advance beyond seaweeds.	No life.	
nt life confined to the sea.	Life exists only in the seas. All the major groups of invertebrates evolve. Seaweeds, still the only plants, provide food for these animals: worms, jellyfish, starfish, sponges — and trilobites, the dominant and most advanced animals, of which there are more than 1,000 species, ranging in size from a pin-head to 18 inches. (All now extinct.)	No life.	
aweeds are the only form of getation.	Life originates in the warm seas at some time during this period. (How it originated is still a mystery.) It is very primitive, taking the form of seaweeds and mainly soft-bodied invertebrate animals.	No life.	

THE GREAT OCEANS

And the gathering together of the waters called he Seas—GENESIS 1

OUR world is awash with water. No other planet, as far as we know, has anything like a sea, but seven-tenths of the Earth is covered by great oceans, the Pacific alone having an area of more than 63 million square miles. The seas' average depth is 12,000 feet (two and a half miles) compared with an average land height of only 2,500 feet.

Beneath the surface there is no uniform mass of water, but a series of well-defined layers, each with its own characteristics, such as temperature, salt-content and marine life.

Coursing through these layers are fast currents, some of them hundreds of miles long and up to 100 miles wide. These currents not only affect the positions of fishing grounds, but may also influence the world's climate; for a change in the direction of a current can alter the weather far inland.

The sea bed is not merely land covered by water. It consists of a thin layer

The *continental shelves* are the threshold of the sea; submerged slabs of land, rather than the true ocean bed, with floors made of the same material as the adjacent land; the edge of this shelf is often nearly parallel to the coastline. They vary in width from a few miles to the 800 miles of the Russian Arctic and slope very gently to depths between 200 and 1,000 feet.

The *continental slopes* mark the edge of the continent. Sloping quickly to oceanic depths, they are the longest and highest escarpments known. Their average height is 12,000 feet, but some drop in unbroken slopes of 30,000 feet—a thousand feet higher than Mount Everest.

From the foot of the continental slopes the deep ocean basins reach out across half the surface of our planet. These basins, some two and a half miles down, are, in fact, ribbed with mountain ranges, pitted with deep valleys and floored by abyssal plains. The basins are carpeted with sediment, formed by the minute remains of creatures and rocks sifting down through the sea since time began. In places, the carpet is two miles thick—often built up at a rate of fractions of an inch in thousands of years. Scientists, lowering their instruments to the sea bed, take cores of the sediment, which they interpret like the rings in the trunk of a tree. One day they hope to sink a core right down to the hard rock beneath the sediment; they may then be able to trace the story of the oceans back to their very beginning.

Winding, steep-sided canyons cut across the edges of many continental slopes. Some may have been worn away by underwater currents; others, near the mouths of big rivers, were probably carved by slow erosion from the rivers when the sea was much shallower.

Challenger Deep is one of the deepest parts of the sea bed. Its floor lies 35,640 feet beneath the surface of the Pacific. There the water is perpetually near-freezing, yet forms of life are still to be found. The United States bathyscaphe *Trieste* touched bottom on 23rd January 1960 in Challenger Deep which is part of the Marianas Trench.

The volcanic island of Krakatoa completely disappeared in 1883 after the most explosive eruption ever recorded. When the volcano blew up, the sound was heard 3,000 miles away. Great tidal waves, which drowned tens of thousands of people, were felt even in the English Channel; and the volcanic dust tinged sunsets the world over for nearly a year. A thousand feet beneath the surface of Sunda Strait was a vast crater, all that remained of an island that had once stood 1,400 feet above the sea. In 1929, a new island suddenly emerged in the same place, it was named Anak Krakatoa—Child of Krakatoa.

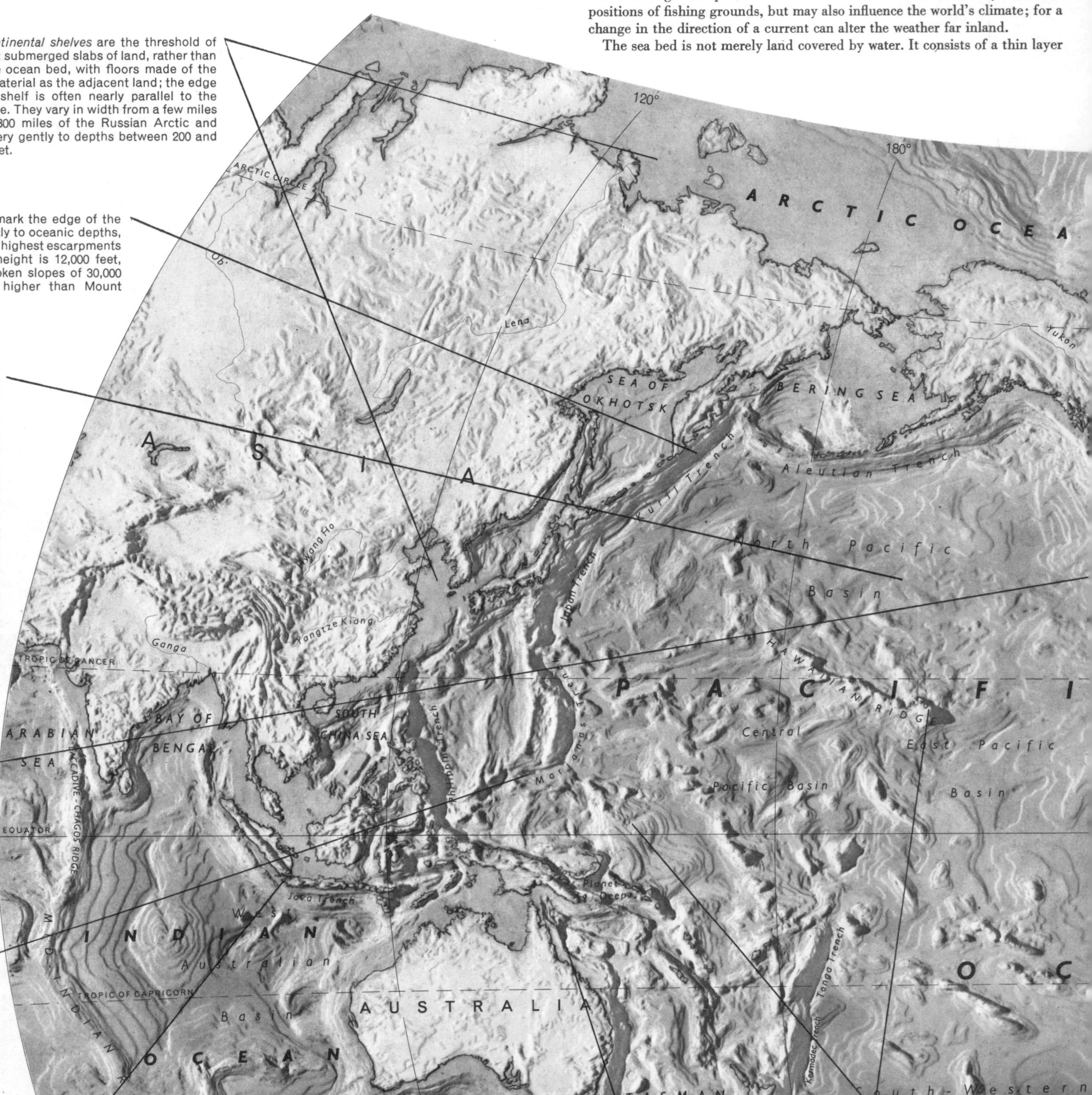

Most mid-ocean islands are volcanic, thrust up through the sea bed by violent eruptions. The Hawaiian volcano Mauna Kea is the highest mountain on Earth. It rises sheer from the sea bed to 31,000 feet, of which only 13,823 feet show above the surface.

Coral is formed of the skeletons of tiny marine animals—yet the coral islands are the largest structures built by any living creature. The Great Barrier Reef of Australia, 1,260 miles long and 500 feet thick, is a vast coral honeycomb where fish, plant and rock forms make the most exotic jungle in the world. The coral atolls that dot the Pacific are monuments to sunken islands—and to the tiny creatures that build them, keeping pace with each island's descent into the sea bed. When the depth of Eniwetok atoll was measured, it was found that countless generations of coral animals had piled the atoll 4,000 feet thick on the submerged stump of island.

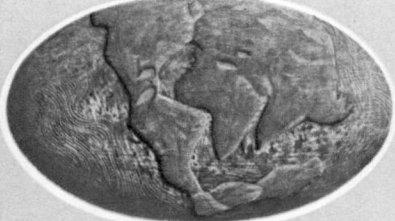

CONTINENTAL DRIFT

If the continents of the world are cut from a map, they can be made to fit together like the pieces of a jigsaw. Hence the theory that the Earth was originally one enormous continent, before it split up and the pieces drifted apart to their present positions. The theory, formulated earlier in this century, has recently won fresh scientific support. Magnetic measurements, showing which way rocks were facing when they were first formed, indicate that rocks all over the world were once differently orientated—in a pattern that seems to fit the theory of Continental Drift. Sandstones, some 200 million years old, found in Britain, suggest a Saharan climate; and the magnetic measurements indicate that Britain was then where the Sahara is now.

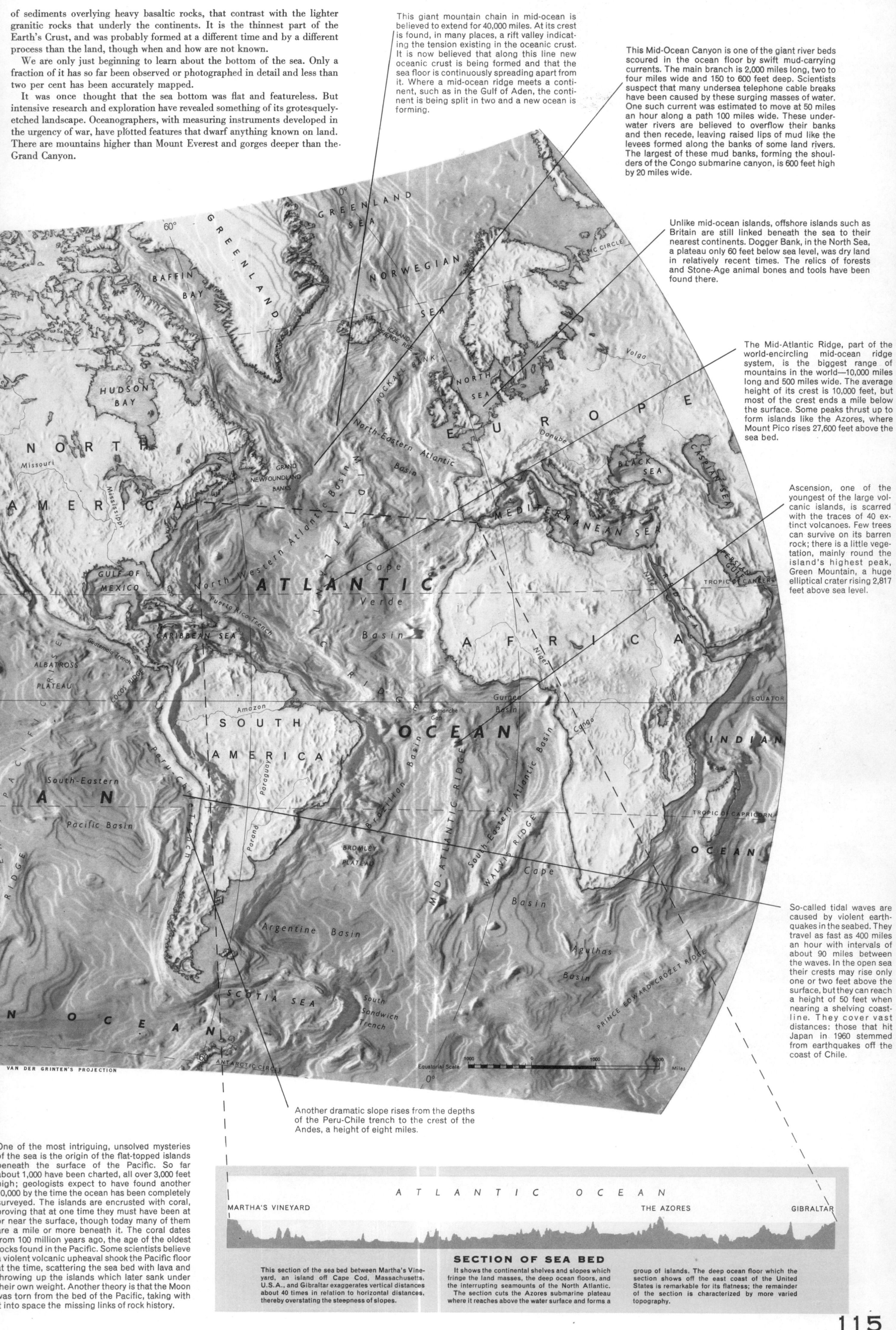

of sediments overlying heavy basaltic rocks, that contrast with the lighter granitic rocks that underlie the continents. It is the thinnest part of the Earth's Crust, and was probably formed at a different time and by a different process than the land, though when and how are not known.

We are only just beginning to learn about the bottom of the sea. Only a fraction of it has so far been observed or photographed in detail and less than two per cent has been accurately mapped.

It was once thought that the sea bottom was flat and featureless. But intensive research and exploration have revealed something of its grotesquely-etched landscape. Oceanographers, with measuring instruments developed in the urgency of war, have plotted features that dwarf anything known on land. There are mountains higher than Mount Everest and gorges deeper than the Grand Canyon.

This giant mountain chain in mid-ocean is believed to extend for 40,000 miles. At its crest is found, in many places, a rift valley indicating the tension existing in the oceanic crust. It is now believed that along this line new oceanic crust is being formed and that the sea floor is continuously spreading apart from it. Where a mid-ocean ridge meets a continent, such as in the Gulf of Aden, the continent is being split in two and a new ocean is forming.

This Mid-Ocean Canyon is one of the giant river beds scoured in the ocean floor by swift mud-carrying currents. The main branch is 2,000 miles long, two to four miles wide and 150 to 600 feet deep. Scientists suspect that many undersea telephone cable breaks have been caused by these surging masses of water. One such current was estimated to move at 50 miles an hour along a path 100 miles wide. These underwater rivers are believed to overflow their banks and then recede, leaving raised lips of mud like the levees formed along the banks of some land rivers. The largest of these mud banks, forming the shoulders of the Congo submarine canyon, is 600 feet high by 20 miles wide.

Unlike mid-ocean islands, offshore islands such as Britain are still linked beneath the sea to their nearest continents. Dogger Bank, in the North Sea, a plateau only 60 feet below sea level, was dry land in relatively recent times. The relics of forests and Stone-Age animal bones and tools have been found there.

The Mid-Atlantic Ridge, part of the world-encircling mid-ocean ridge system, is the biggest range of mountains in the world—10,000 miles long and 500 miles wide. The average height of its crest is 10,000 feet, but most of the crest ends a mile below the surface. Some peaks thrust up to form islands like the Azores, where Mount Pico rises 27,600 feet above the sea bed.

Ascension, one of the youngest of the large volcanic islands, is scarred with the traces of 40 extinct volcanoes. Few trees can survive on its barren rock; there is a little vegetation, mainly round the island's highest peak, Green Mountain, a huge elliptical crater rising 2,817 feet above sea level.

So-called tidal waves are caused by violent earthquakes in the seabed. They travel as fast as 400 miles an hour with intervals of about 90 miles between the waves. In the open sea their crests may rise only one or two feet above the surface, but they can reach a height of 50 feet when nearing a shelving coastline. They cover vast distances: those that hit Japan in 1960 stemmed from earthquakes off the coast of Chile.

Another dramatic slope rises from the depths of the Peru-Chile trench to the crest of the Andes, a height of eight miles.

One of the most intriguing, unsolved mysteries of the sea is the origin of the flat-topped islands beneath the surface of the Pacific. So far about 1,000 have been charted, all over 3,000 feet high; geologists expect to have found another 10,000 by the time the ocean has been completely surveyed. The islands are encrusted with coral, proving that at one time they must have been at or near the surface, though today many of them are a mile or more beneath it. The coral dates from 100 million years ago, the age of the oldest rocks found in the Pacific. Some scientists believe a violent volcanic upheaval shook the Pacific floor at the time, scattering the sea bed with lava and throwing up the islands which later sank under their own weight. Another theory is that the Moon was torn from the bed of the Pacific, taking with it into space the missing links of rock history.

VAN DER GRINTEN'S PROJECTION

SECTION OF SEA BED

This section of the sea bed between Martha's Vineyard, an island off Cape Cod, Massachusetts, U.S.A., and Gibraltar exaggerates vertical distances about 40 times in relation to horizontal distances, thereby overstating the steepness of slopes.

It shows the continental shelves and slopes which fringe the land masses, the deep ocean floors, and the interrupting seamounts of the North Atlantic. The section cuts the Azores submarine plateau where it reaches above the water surface and forms a group of islands. The deep ocean floor which the section shows off the east coast of the United States is remarkable for its flatness; the remainder of the section is characterized by more varied topography.

VERTICAL DISTRIBUTION OF CLOUDS

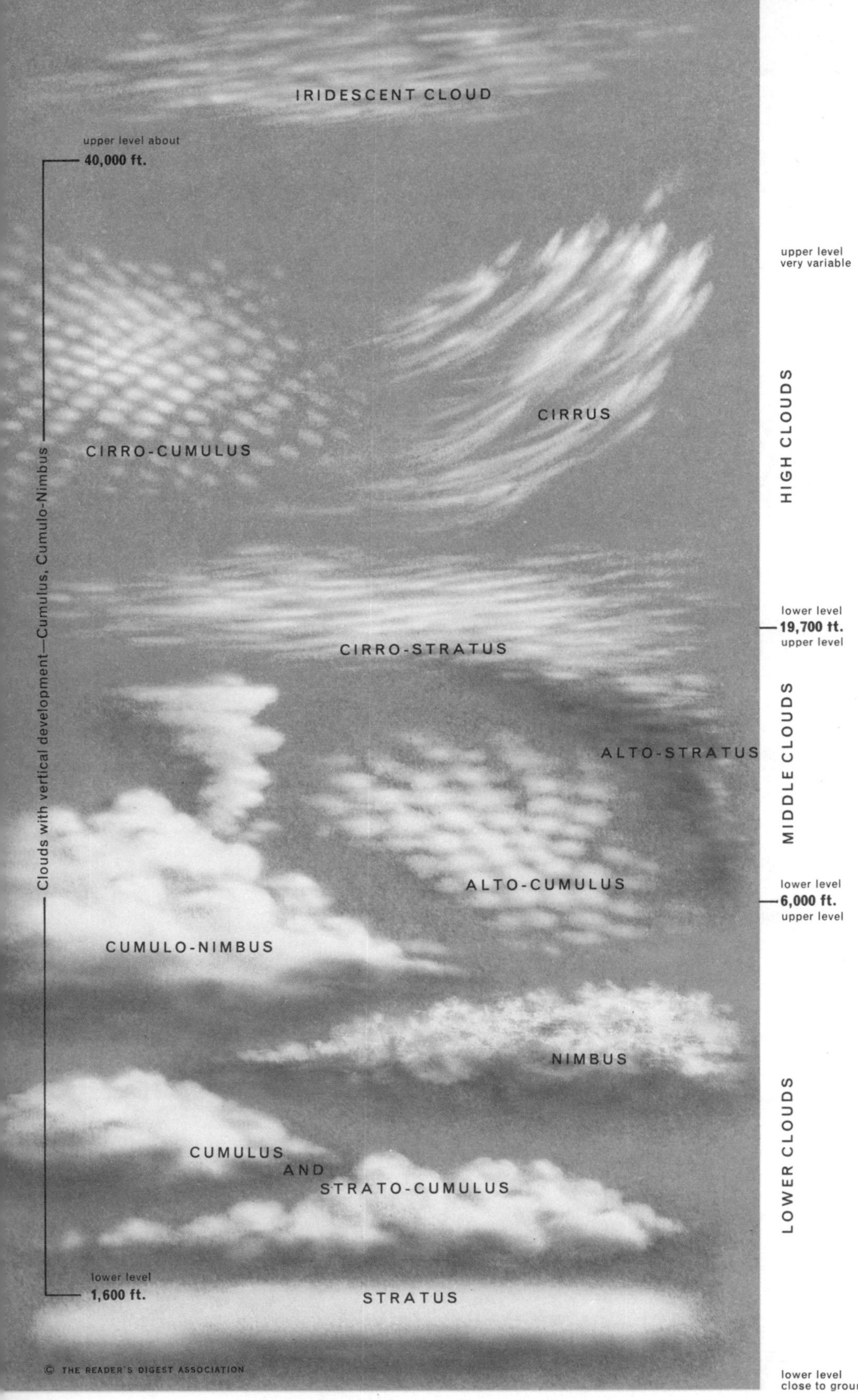

IRIDESCENT CLOUD

upper level about
40,000 ft.

CIRRUS

CIRRO-CUMULUS

HIGH CLOUDS

upper level
very variable

CIRRO-STRATUS

ALTO-STRATUS

MIDDLE CLOUDS

lower level
19,700 ft.
upper level

ALTO-CUMULUS

CUMULO-NIMBUS

lower level
6,000 ft.
upper level

NIMBUS

Clouds with vertical development—Cumulus, Cumulo-Nimbus

LOWER CLOUDS

CUMULUS
AND
STRATO-CUMULUS

lower level
1,600 ft.

STRATUS

lower level
close to ground

© THE READER'S DIGEST ASSOCIATION

Cumulus and cumulo-nimbus clouds may develop vertically and extend through
many thousands of feet of atmosphere across the high, middle and lower cloud belts.

AIR-PRESSURE: JANUARY

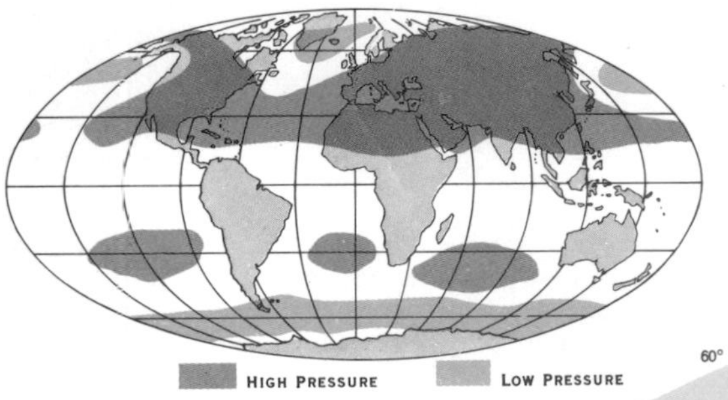

■ HIGH PRESSURE   ■ LOW PRESSURE

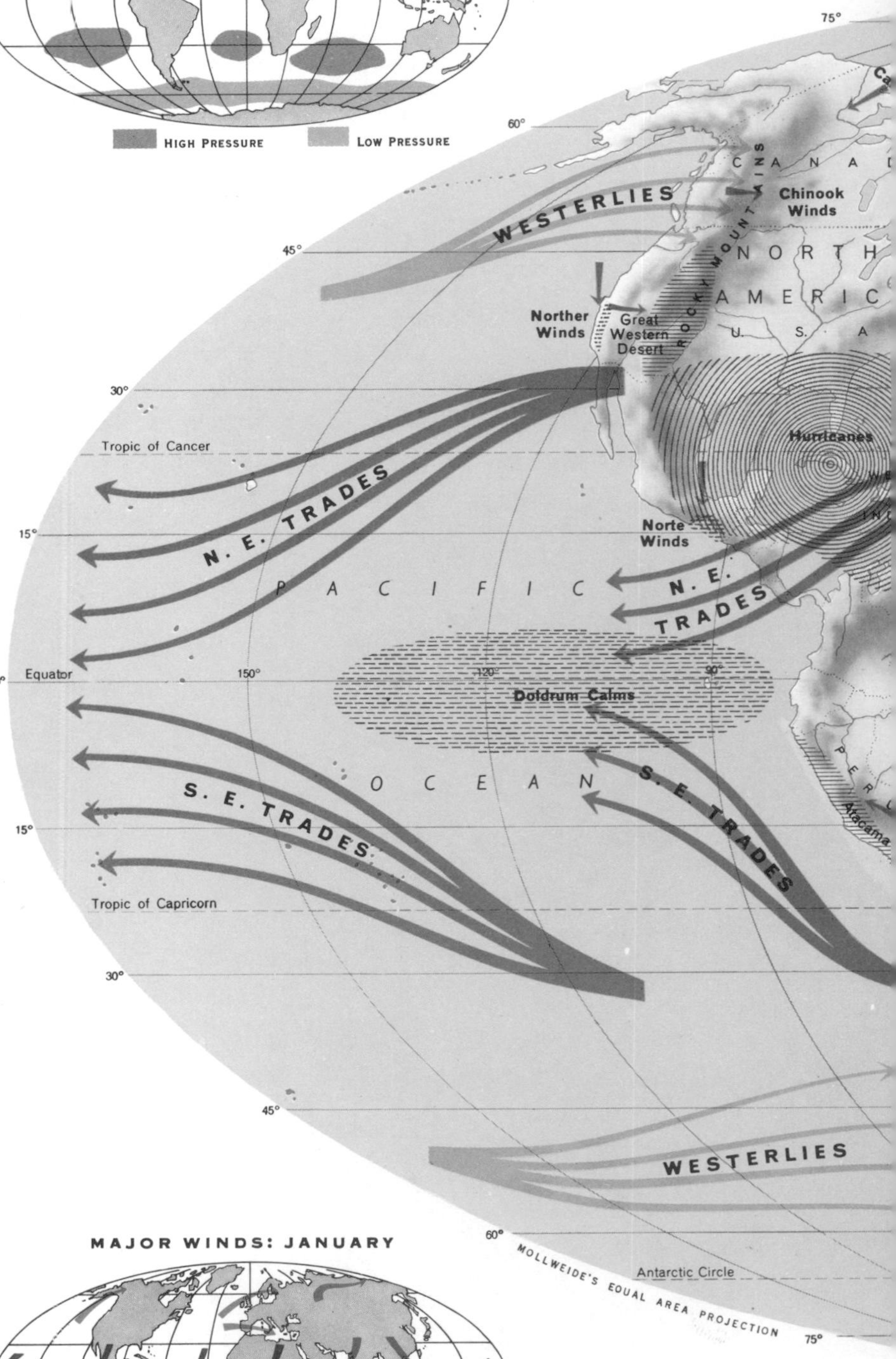

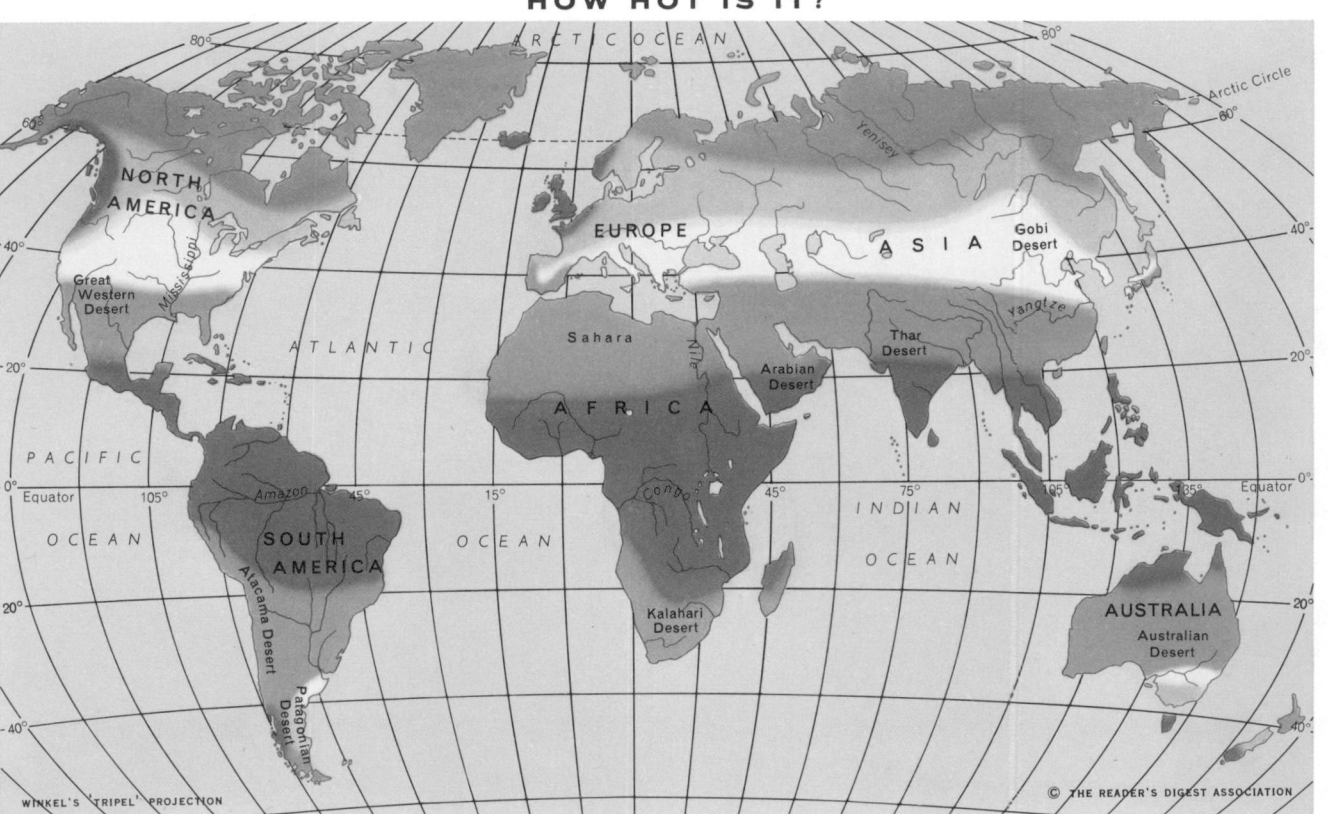

WESTERLIES   Chinook
Winds

NORTH
AMERICA
CANADA
U.S.A.

75°
60°
45°F.
30°
15°

Norther
Winds

Great
Western
Desert

Hurricanes

Tropic of Cancer

N. E. TRADES

Norte
Winds

N. E.
TRADES

P A C I F I C

Equator   150°   Doldrum Calms   O C E A N   S. E. TRADES

S. E. TRADES

Tropic of Capricorn

WESTERLIES

Antarctic Circle

MOLLWEIDE'S EQUAL AREA PROJECTION

MAJOR WINDS: JANUARY

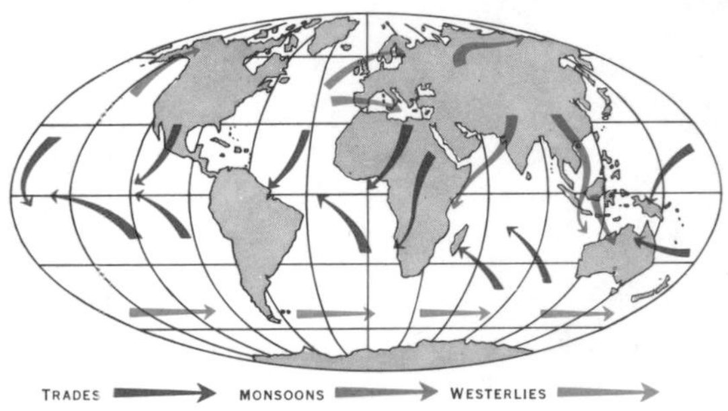

TRADES →   MONSOONS →   WESTERLIES →

HOW HOT IS IT?

ARCTIC OCEAN
Arctic Circle

NORTH
AMERICA

EUROPE

ASIA
Gobi
Desert

Great
Western
Desert

Mississippi
Yenisei

ATLANTIC

Sahara

Thar
Desert

Yangtze

Arabian
Desert

AFRICA

PACIFIC

Equator   105°   Amazon   15°   Nile   Congo   45°   75°   105°   135°   Equator

SOUTH
AMERICA

OCEAN

OCEAN

INDIAN

OCEAN

Atacama Desert

Kalahari
Desert

AUSTRALIA
Australian
Desert

Patagonian Desert

WINKEL'S 'TRIPEL' PROJECTION

© THE READER'S DIGEST ASSOCIATION

■	ALWAYS COLD
■	WARM SUMMER / COLD WINTER
□	HOT SUMMER / COLD WINTER
■	COOL SUMMER / MILD WINTER
■	HOT SUMMER / WARM WINTER
■	ALWAYS HOT

Almost all our heat comes from the Sun, and the
amount depends largely on how much of the Earth's
atmosphere the Sun's rays must penetrate. The closer
to vertical the Sun becomes, the lesser the amount of
atmosphere to be penetrated and the more heat we
receive, though clouds and the nature of the surface
affect it. The Sun's rays give little heat to the air.

Air is mainly warmed by contact with the Earth's surface. The sea warms more slowly and parts with its
heat more slowly, so that climates near oceans are

more equable than those in the centre of continents.

The heat of the Tropics is, to some extent, distributed
by ocean currents and winds. Thanks to the Gulf
Stream and prevailing south-westerly winds the British
Isles enjoy an average temperature of 50°F. Labrador,
on the same latitude, does not enjoy these physical
phenomena. It has an average temperature of 32°F.

Average temperatures fall as we rise above sea level
at about one degree Fahrenheit for every 300 feet in
Great Britain, so that high mountains are always cold.

PATTERNS

*But there went up a mist from the earth, which
watered the whole face of the ground*—GENESIS 2

THE climates of the World are mainly dependent
upon latitude. Within the Tropics the climate
remains fairly stable, but outside the Tropics
climates, due to the twice-yearly swing of the Sun
across the Equator, are seasonal. These swings of the
Sun have the effect of shifting the belts of high
pressure, as shown in the small pressure-maps.

Since the discovery of the barometer, we now know
that the atmosphere has weight: where the atmosphere has piled up to give high pressure it tends to
flow outwards on the surface of the Earth, just as
water would do, and so becomes a wind. The rotation
of the Earth causes winds to bend to the right in the
Northern Hemisphere, and to the left in the Southern
Hemisphere. In the North Atlantic, for example, the
winds flowing towards the Equator are north-easterly
and are known as the North East Trades, while the
winds flowing towards the North Pole are south-
westerly and are known as the Westerlies.

The flow of the major winds is shown diagrammatic-
ally on the large map; the shift in their flow from
summer to winter is shown on the small wind-maps.

When the land becomes heated during the summer
months, the air above tends to rise, and surface
winds blow in to take its place, so that often at the
coast there are land breezes at night, and sea breezes
by day. This is better seen on a larger scale in the
Monsoons, which blow inwards to the continent of
Asia in the summer, and less strongly and outwards
in the winter.

The major winds are not constant, since they are
affected and complicated by cyclonic depressions.

AIR-PRESSURE: JULY

HIGH PRESSURE   LOW PRESSURE

Main map — WHERE WILL IT BLOW?

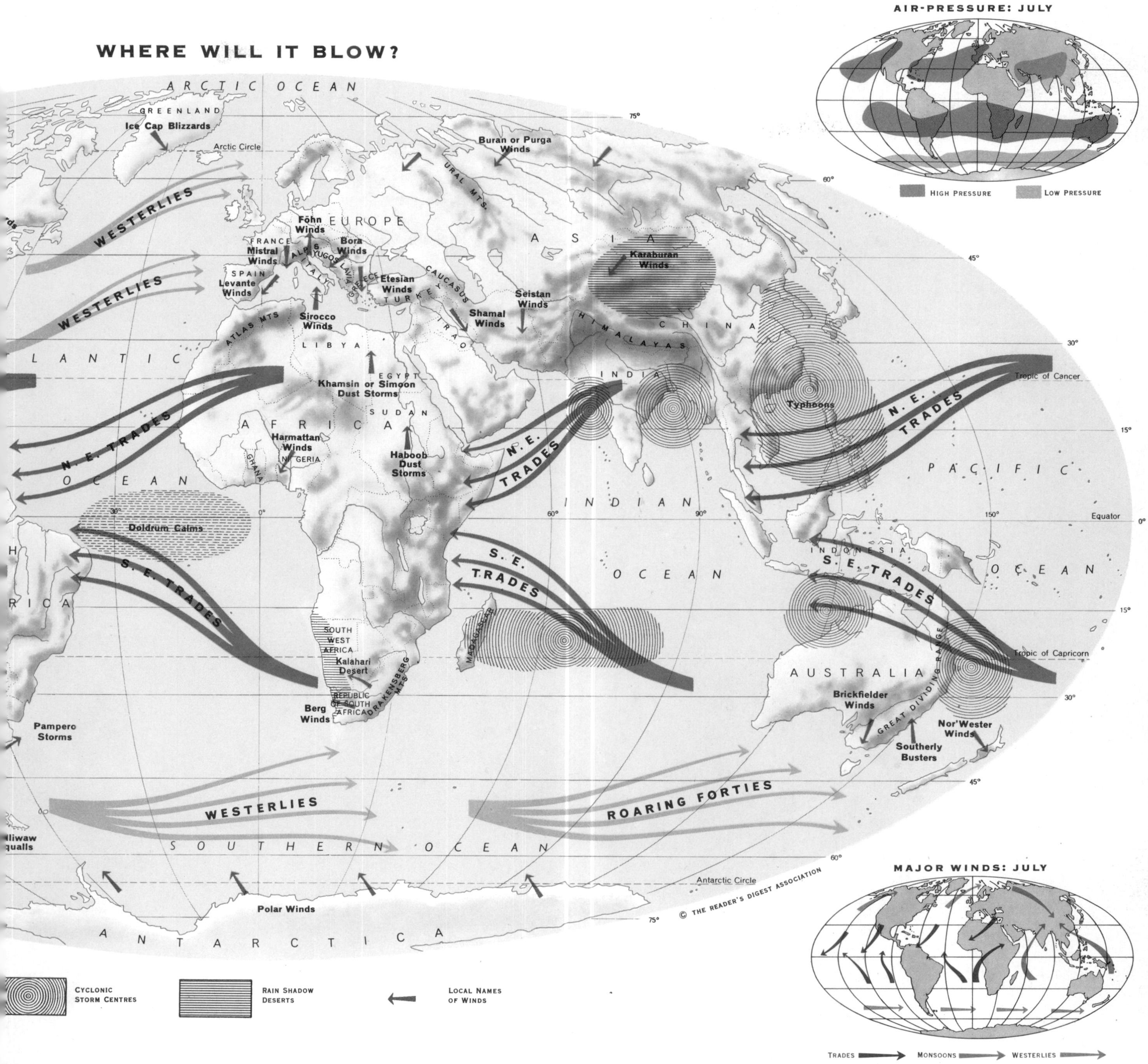

ARCTIC OCEAN

GREENLAND
Ice Cap Blizzards

Arctic Circle

Buran or Purga Winds

URAL MTS

WESTERLIES

WESTERLIES

EUROPE
Föhn Winds
FRANCE
Mistral Winds
Bora Winds
SPAIN
Levante Winds
ITALY
YUGOSLAVIA
GREECE
Etesian Winds
TURKEY
CAUCASUS
ASIA
Karaburan Winds
CHINA

Seistan Winds
Shamal Winds
IRAQ

ATLAS MTS
Sirocco Winds
LIBYA
EGYPT
Khamsin or Simoon Dust Storms

HIMALAYAS
INDIA

Typhoons
Tropic of Cancer

N.E. TRADES
PACIFIC

AFRICA
SUDAN
Harmattan Winds
NIGERIA
GHANA
Haboob Dust Storms

N.E. TRADES
N.E. TRADES

OCEAN
ATLANTIC

Doldrum Calms

INDIAN OCEAN
Equator
150°

S.E. TRADES
S.E. TRADES
INDONESIA
S.E. TRADES

AFRICA
MADAGASCAR
SOUTH WEST AFRICA
Kalahari Desert
REPUBLIC OF SOUTH AFRICA
DRAKENSBERG
Berg Winds

AUSTRALIA
Brickfielder Winds
GREAT DIVIDING RANGE
Nor'Wester Winds
Southerly Busters
Tropic of Capricorn

Pampero Storms

Williwaw Squalls

WESTERLIES
ROARING FORTIES

SOUTHERN OCEAN

Antarctic Circle

Polar Winds

ANTARCTICA

© THE READER'S DIGEST ASSOCIATION

Legend:
Cyclonic Storm Centres
Rain Shadow Deserts
Local Names of Winds

MAJOR WINDS: JULY

TRADES   MONSOONS   WESTERLIES

OF CLIMATE

The most constant winds are the South East Trades and the Westerlies in the higher latitudes of the Southern Hemisphere, where there is little land interference.

There are many local winds brought about by local conditions. Of those shown on the map, the Föhn of Switzerland and the Chinook of the Rockies in Canada are warm winds which blow down the mountains and melt the snows. A less pleasant warm wind is the Sirocco, which blows from North Africa across the Mediterranean to Northern Italy. The soft Etesian winds of the Aegean Sea are often mentioned in Greek literature. The cold Mistral, blowing down the Rhône Valley from the Alps, is an example of the unpleasant winds usually associated with high mountains adjacent to flat country. The vast Sahara Desert causes the Harmattan to bring dust to West Africa from November to March; but this wind, being dry, is a welcome change in West Africa's usually humid climate. The violent Pampero, blowing out to sea from Argentina, has long been known as a dangerous wind to sailing ships.

The Doldrums is a zone near the Equator where the rising of hot air creates calms and variable winds together with thunderstorms. In the days of sail, ships were often delayed in this area. A little farther away from the Equator there are occasional storms of great violence, known as typhoons in the East, as hurricanes in the Caribbean, and as tornadoes when they occur inland. These storms always follow a curved path, which can usually be forecast. All winds are slowed down by friction against the surface of the Earth, and produce eddies accompanied by rapid variations of air pressure. High up in the atmosphere winds are much more rapid, but much more steady.

HOW WET IS IT?

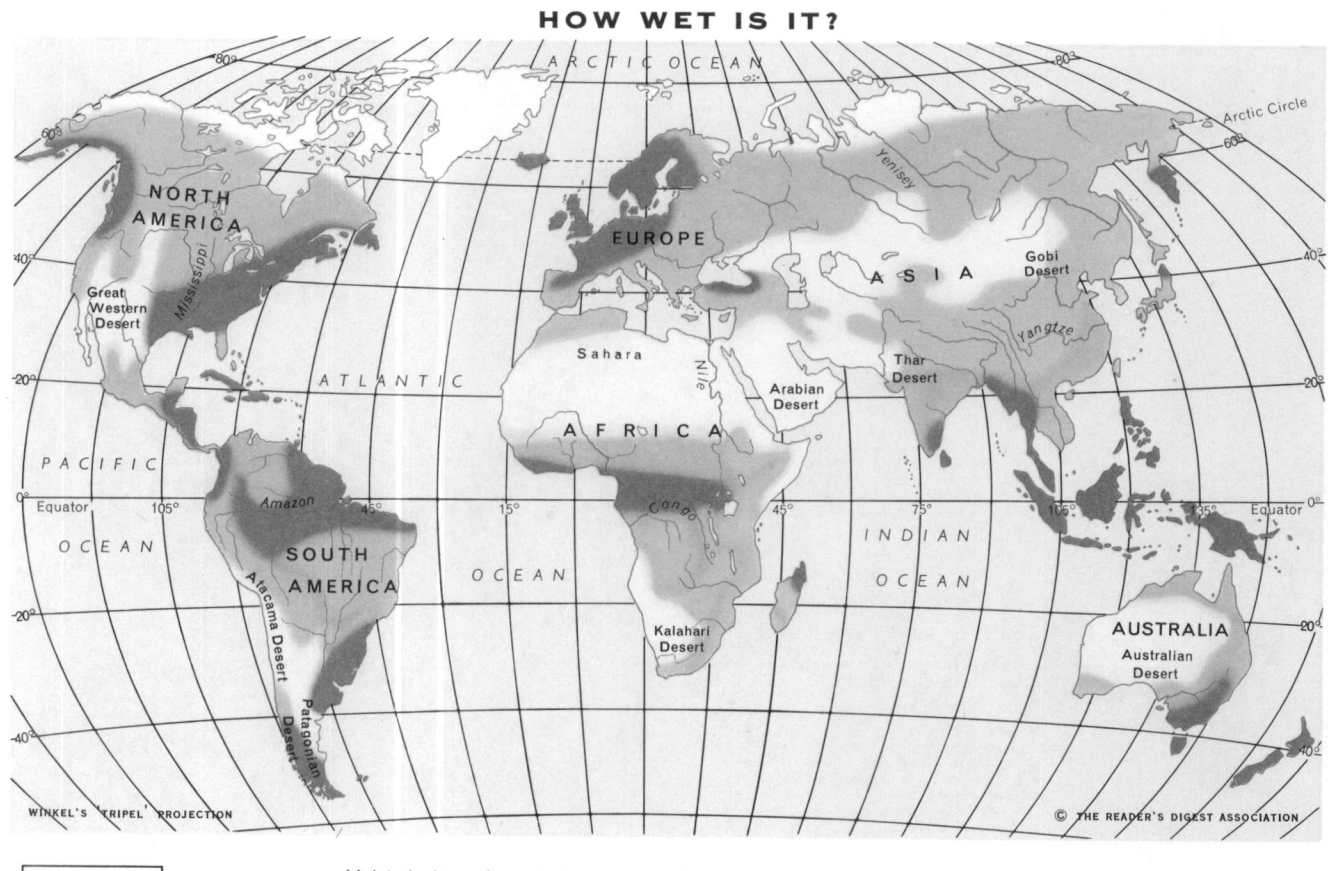

NORTH AMERICA
Great Western Desert
Mississippi
ATLANTIC
PACIFIC OCEAN
Equator
105°
SOUTH AMERICA
Amazon
Atacama Desert
Patagonian
WINKEL'S 'TRIPEL' PROJECTION

ARCTIC OCEAN
Arctic Circle
EUROPE
ASIA
Yenisey
Gobi Desert
Sahara
Nile
Arabian Desert
Thar Desert
Yangtze
AFRICA
Congo
INDIAN OCEAN
Kalahari Desert
AUSTRALIA
Australian Desert

© THE READER'S DIGEST ASSOCIATION

Legend:
Light Snow
Seldom Rainy
Light Seasonal Rain
Heavy Seasonal Rain
Rainfall in Every Month

Moist air rises when winds force it against a mountain or blow it over heavier, colder air. As the moist air rises it cools and condenses into minute drops of water, forming clouds. When the droplets in the clouds become too heavy to be sustained, they fall as rain.

Air is most likely to be moist over the sea and where temperatures are high. The wettest places of all are in the Tropics, where the sea air is blown against the windward slopes of high mountains. Rainfall belts move northwards and southwards following the ap-

parent movement of the Sun, so that some places, such as the Mediterranean, have most of their rain in the winter, while others, such as the Monsoon regions, have most in the summer.

The driest areas on Earth are where winds have blown for long distances over heated land. But a local dry area may be caused by a range of mountains extracting all the rain on its windward side, leaving what is called a rain-shadow on its leeward side. Such an area is the desert of Northern Chile.

117

FRONTIERS OF CULTIVATION

DEVELOPMENT OF THE NATURAL AND CULTIVATED AREAS OF THE WORLD

And the earth brought forth grass, herb yielding seed after its kind,
tree bearing fruit, wherein is the seed thereof, after its kind — GENESIS 1

Only about one-tenth of the world's land surface is at present under cultivation—little more than one acre per person.

The map shows the general distribution of vegetation—areas from which the natural vegetation has been cleared and the land cultivated for food and industrial crops such as fibres, cotton and rubber; areas where the natural vegetation is being utilized and developed; and areas which have remained in their natural state, with little or no vegetation.

In the areas of cultivation the maintenance of soil fertility is of the first importance. Bad husbandry, including the entire removal of trees, destroys the natural structure of the soil, with the result that it turns into dust, as in the great Dust Bowl of the United States, or into new man-made deserts, or is washed off unprotected slopes by rain, leaving behind bare unproductive subsoil, as in Yugoslavia and Greece.

The areas of *intensive* cultivation are those in which the optimum use is made of the soil. In Europe, the U.S.S.R., North America and parts of South America, South Africa and Austra- lasia, cultivation of all kinds on a commercial scale is carried on, mainly with the aid of machinery. But in South and East Asia, where land is scarce and therefore precious, and the crops must support some of the densest rural populations in the world, much of the work is done with simple hand tools. Yet, even so, two crops of paddy rice a year are obtained as well as other kinds of cereal.

In the areas of *secondary* cultivation farming with crude tools and by means of rudimentary techniques predominates. The crops are largely grown for home consumption, though in some cases enough foods, such as cacao, oil-palm and peanuts, are grown for sale in local markets.

The areas of *shifting* cultivation are to be found near and among the tropical rain forests. Here land is generally cleared

Ice Caps. Sparse growth of mosses and lichens in Antarctic regions; groups of dwarf willow, birch, mountain ash and alder in southern parts of Greenland, with mosses, saxifrage, Iceland poppy and other alpine plants among lichen-covered rocks.

Tundra. Subsoil permanently frozen, scanty vegetation of mosses and lichens; stunted bushes and trees (willow and Arctic birch) at the warmer margins. Warm, short summers thaw surface soil which produces rich growth of grass and flowering shrubs.

Coniferous Forest. Natural vegetation comprises coniferous trees with some decid- uous trees and evergreens. Coniferous for- ests provide vast supplies of soft timber. In northern Asia the forests are mainly in- accessible owing to spring flooding of the great rivers.

Mountains. Below snow line alpine flowers flourish and slopes provide pasture for sheep and cattle; coniferous forests abound in nor- thern latitudes though on mountain slopes of eastern Australia softwoods are found, and vegetation of the temperate regions of both hemispheres is found in central East Africa.

Grassland or Savannah. Areas richly covered by tall grass (sometimes tough, coarse and almost impenetrable), scattered trees or none at all, with undergrowth of herb- aceous flowering plants, some with edible fruits. Fine ranching country in Rhodesia, East Africa and Angola, and in middle lati- tudes grain now grows.

Scrubland. Semi-arid regions of coarse grassland with low-growing dry brush and dwarf shrubs; used for grazing in Australia and South America.

Desert and Semi-desert. There are few desert areas where nothing grows. After rain small patches of quick-growing plants may spring up to flourish for only a few weeks. Desert oases are fertile regions. General vegetation is low thorny bush; typical tree is the date palm.

Tropical Rain Forest. These hot, wet for- ests (or selvas) contain luxuriant vegetation and a variety of trees, mainly hardwood, with tall, unbranched boles topped by thick crowns of leaves which prevent sunlight from reaching the ground. Clearance of land may be followed by quick-growing rank grass, bamboo and weeds, but successfully cleared land is fertile.

indiscriminately for individual needs, and after being wastefully denuded of its fertility by primitive farming methods, is abandoned.

Where land in the tropical rain forests is successfully cleared and maintained, it is fertile and suitable for the cultivation on a commercial scale of such plantation crops as rubber, tobacco, sugar, tea, oil-palm and cacao.

The areas of coniferous forest provide the major part of the world's soft timber—spruce, pine, fir—and by means of intensive afforestation some forests are being maintained and developed. The world's major logging and timber-working industries are found in North America and Europe.

The mountain slopes and much of the grassland and scrubland areas provide grazing for cattle and sheep and may thus be naturally maintained. Tropical grassland areas, when fully developed, may provide a variety of crops, such as maize, millet, cotton, sugar and groundnuts, with grain predominating in the more temperate regions.

Even in the deserts there are large areas of oases where the land is extremely fertile, and not only food crops are grown but grazing is also provided. The desert soil is often fine alluvial dust which, when irrigated, is exceptionally fertile, as in the Nile Valley, the Indus Plains and Lower Colorado. Some oases may cover hundreds of square miles.

But the patterns of cultivation vary from country to country according to their economic and social development. In the highly developed countries relatively few workers are able to provide sufficient of the right kind of food for the entire community. In the United States, for instance, 4,500,000 people (about 6 per cent of the working population) are employed on cultivation. On the other hand, in India 145,000,000 people (70 per cent of the working population) employed on cultivation produce barely enough food both in quantity and quality for the whole population of that country.

As the result of great advances in agricultural science since the Second World War, the yields in some areas such as North America, Europe, Australia and New Zealand have risen rapidly. In the less developed regions, post-war increases in agricultural production have been achieved mainly by bringing new land into cultivation. But as yet these areas have scarcely begun to benefit from applying scientific and improved technical methods of farming, so that only one-fifth of the world's agricultural output is produced with the aid of machines.

The symbols on the map show the areas where scientific and improved technical methods are being applied to improve the quality and yield of crops, and to bring back into cultivation land that is infertile or semi-arid. Of these techniques, irrigation and water conservation are of the first importance. Irrigation is one of man's earliest known ways of making the earth productive. In Egypt, in about 3000 B.C., the first Pharaoh built an embankment to control the flood waters of the Nile, and cultivation in Egypt today still depends on irrigated land. In China, ancient irrigation systems, some built 2,000 years ago, are still in use. In Latin America, the proper use of water supplies has now brought large areas of land under cultivation.

Other techniques which are being applied include the breeding of improved, disease-and-pest-resistant varieties of seed; the building up of soil fertility through the use of legumes and crop rotation; the introduction of a more varied and nutritious diet and to lessen a country's economic dependence on a single crop; forest conservation and afforestation; the better use of organic wastes as manures and the increased application of artificial fertilizers; better methods of cultivation, improved tools and the increased use of farm machinery; the reclamation and settlement of new lands; the control of pests, such as the locust and the tsetse fly.

By these methods, added to his own traditional skills, man is making the earth more fertile and so extending the frontiers of cultivation.

Extensive multi-purpose projects—reclamation, irrigation, community settlement, etc.

Irrigation schemes—water conservation, dams, canals, etc.

New, improved and diversified varieties of crops

Dry farming techniques

Land clearance, development and reclamation schemes

Improvement of soil fertility through application of artificial and natural fertilizers, addition of trace elements and inclusion of legumes and improved grasses

Pest control schemes

Larger symbols indicate countrywide schemes

Intensive Cultivation. These regions are the great food and industrial-crop producing areas. They fall into two classes—mechanized farming on an extensive scale (as in North America) for both home consumption and export; and farming for home consumption only in some of the underdeveloped regions (as in the Middle and Far East).

Secondary Cultivation. Farming at a relatively primitive level, giving low yields, and primarily for local consumption.

Shifting Cultivation. Areas cleared in the rain forests and neighbouring bushlands by indiscriminate burning and farmed for several seasons until the soil fertility is exhausted. The process is then repeated elsewhere on new land.

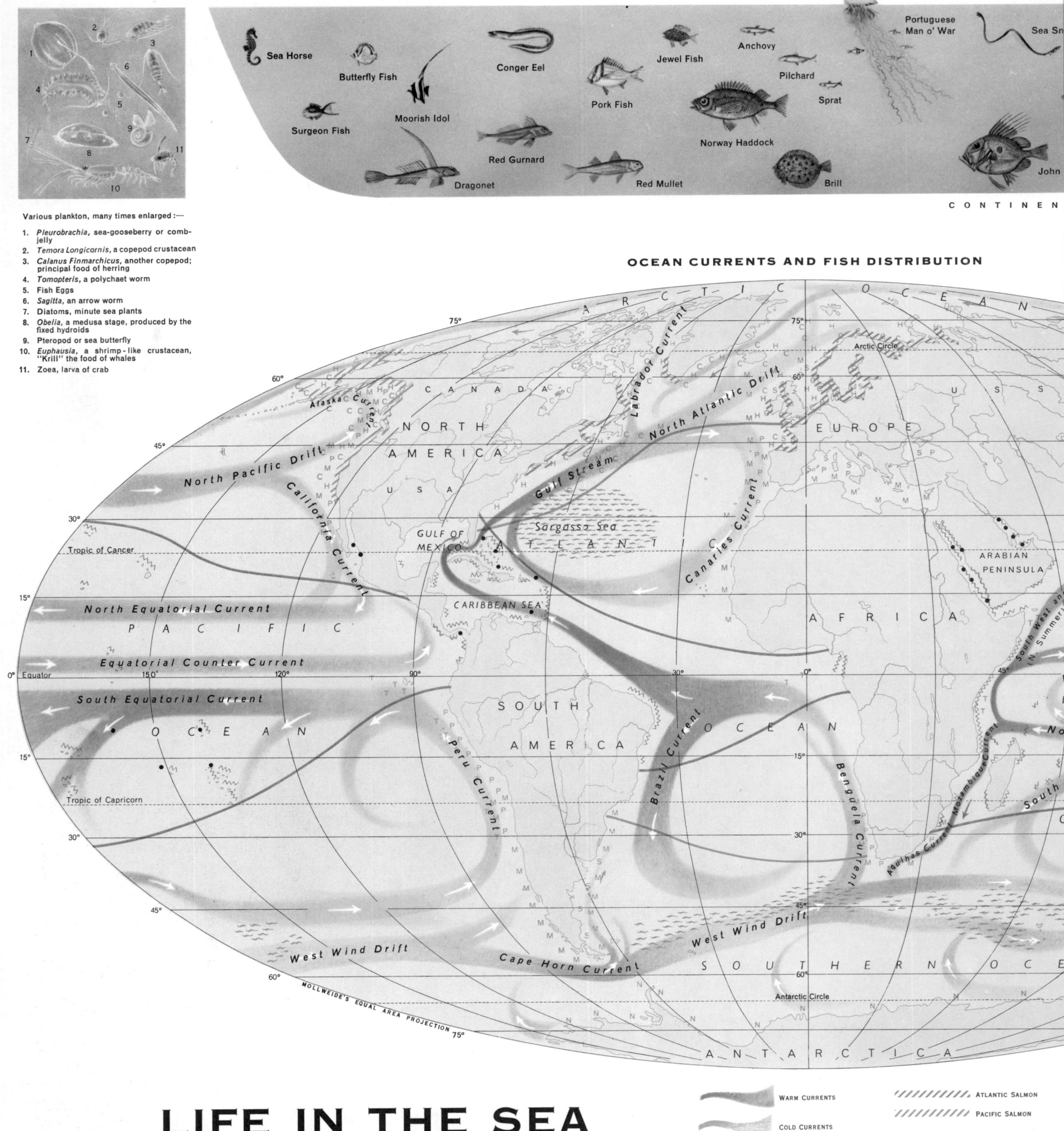

Various plankton, many times enlarged:—

1. *Pleurobrachia*, sea-gooseberry or comb-jelly
2. *Temora Longicornis*, a copepod crustacean
3. *Calanus Finmarchicus*, another copepod; principal food of herring
4. *Tomopteris*, a polychaet worm
5. Fish Eggs
6. *Sagitta*, an arrow worm
7. Diatoms, minute sea plants
8. *Obelia*, a medusa stage, produced by the fixed hydroids
9. Pteropod or sea butterfly
10. *Euphausia*, a shrimp-like crustacean, "Krill" the food of whales
11. Zoea, larva of crab

OCEAN CURRENTS AND FISH DISTRIBUTION

WARM CURRENTS	///////// ATLANTIC SALMON
COLD CURRENTS	///////// PACIFIC SALMON
FLOATING WEED	∿∿∿ CORAL REEFS
	•••••• PEARLS

LIFE IN THE SEA

And God said, Let the waters bring forth abundantly the moving creature that hath life—GENESIS 1

THE SEA, where life began, contains almost every main category of animal life—including mammals, the warm-blooded group to which man belongs. True fish are but a small section of the sea's community: whereas there are 15,000 known species of sea-fish, there are 60,000 known species of mollusc (the group which includes oysters, mussels, etc.).

In the sea, as on land, life depends largely on plants, and the plants of the ocean are almost as productive, acre for acre, as the plants on land. The pastures of the sea and the basis of its life cycle are countless myriads of free-floating, microscopic plants known as phytoplankton. These are the food of minute animals called zooplankton. Zooplankton are preyed upon by larger animal species, which themselves provide food for still bigger creatures. So continues a ruthless and never-ending cycle, for the plants in their turn are nourished by minerals derived in part from the decay of marine organisms.

Since most plants need sunlight for their survival, marine plants grow only within about 300 feet of the water's surface. A large part of sea life is, therefore, confined to this topmost layer, which is continually being refertilized by the action of the ocean currents.

The movement of currents, by which the oceans "plough" themselves, is caused by three main forces: the prevailing wind, the Earth's rotation and differences in the sea's density. Winds drive immense bodies of water before them, forming surface currents. At the same time, the Earth's rotation, which deflects moving things to the right in the Northern Hemisphere and to the left in the Southern Hemisphere, causes these ocean surface currents to move in a clockwise or anti-clockwise direction, as shown by the whirls on the map.

Where currents meet or diverge, where cold or salty water sinks beneath water that is less dense, or where coastal winds blow the surface water seawards, a circulation is set up which may penetrate to the ocean bottom. Surface water is then replaced by upwelling water rich in nutrient salts, which stimulate new growths of marine plants. Thus the herbivorous animal plankton thrives and the sea becomes fertile for fish. It is understandable that many of the world's great fisheries are found along the paths of ocean currents.

Beneath the sunlit 300-foot layer, life is sparser and creatures need special equipment for the fierce struggle for survival. Angler fish, with huge, expanding stomachs, can swallow creatures larger than themselves, and thus make one meal last a long time. Other fish, like *Gigantura*, have very sensitive tubular (telescopic) eyes that help them to see their prey in the near-darkness. Perhaps the most remarkable adaptation to life in the deep is that of certain deep-sea angler fish. Their reproduction depends on but one chance meeting in the barren depths, after which the female carries the male permanently with her. The male is much the smaller and is parasitic on his partner.

For the most part, however, the sea's species have not had to assume such specialized forms to cope with their environment. The oceans do not have the harsh seasonal and regional contrasts of land. Surface water temperature in any one region seldom varies more than a few degrees, and fish, whose bodies consist largely of fluid at the same temperature as their surroundings, do not, therefore, need any particular mechanism for keeping warm or cool. Again, the profusion of wings, limbs and other organs needed on land to overcome the burden of gravity is unnecessary for creatures whose element is the buoyant sea.

As few sea creatures have mechanisms, such as sweat glands, for adapting themselves to changing conditions, they are sensitive to the slightest variation in their surroundings. With some exceptions such as sharks and whales, which can range freely up and down the oceans, each species is confined to its own particular zone, where pressure, light, temperature and the quantity of salt in the water are more or less constant.

In this stable environment some creatures have remained unchanged throughout their entire history. The now-famous Coelacanth, one of a group of fish thought to have been extinct for 60 million years, has remained essentially like its relatives as they appear in fossils. It is considered the closest living relation of the long-extinct fish that is accepted as the ancestor of all land animals.

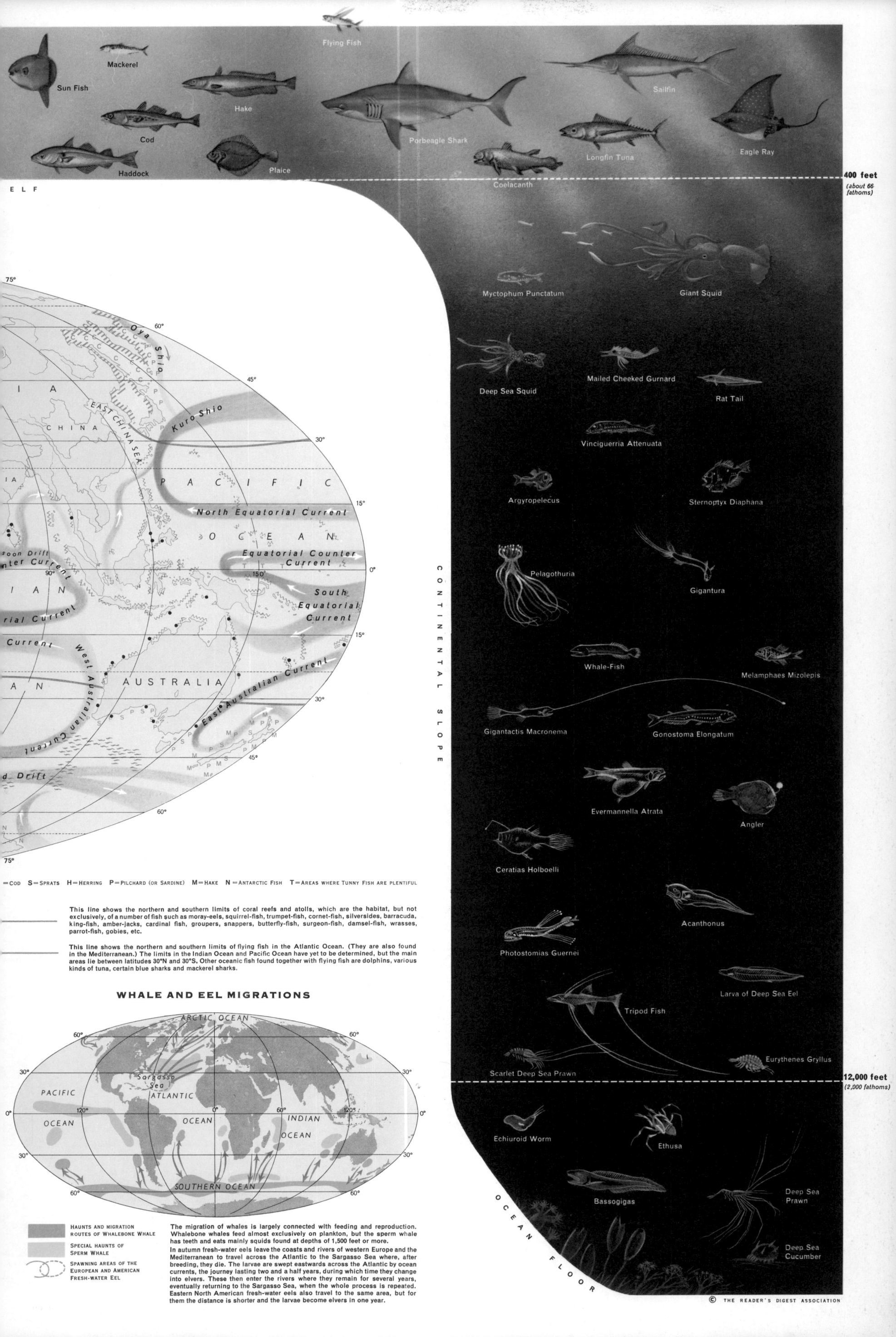

Sun Fish

Mackerel

Flying Fish

Hake

Cod

Haddock

Plaice

Porbeagle Shark

Sailfin

Longfin Tuna

Eagle Ray

Coelacanth

400 feet
(about 66 fathoms)

E L F

Myctophum Punctatum

Giant Squid

Deep Sea Squid

Mailed Cheeked Gurnard

Rat Tail

Vinciguerria Attenuata

Argyropelecus

Sternoptyx Diaphana

Pelagothuria

Gigantura

Whale-Fish

Melamphaes Mizolepis

Gigantactis Macronema

Gonostoma Elongatum

Evermannella Atrata

Angler

Ceratias Holboelli

Acanthonus

Photostomias Guernei

Larva of Deep Sea Eel

Tripod Fish

Eurythenes Gryllus

Scarlet Deep Sea Prawn

12,000 feet
(2,000 fathoms)

Echiuroid Worm

Ethusa

Bassogigas

Deep Sea Prawn

Deep Sea Cucumber

C O N T I N E N T A L S L O P E

O C E A N F L O O R

Oya Shio

East China Sea

Kuro Shio

CHINA

IA

IA

P A C I F I C

North Equatorial Current

O C E A N

Equatorial Counter Current

South Equatorial Current

Monsoon Drift

nter Current

I A N

rial Current

Current

West Australian Current

AUSTRALIA

East Australian Current

d Drift

75°

60°

45°

30°

15°

0°

15°

30°

45°

60°

75°

90°

150°

C=Cod S=Sprats H=Herring P=Pilchard (or Sardine) M=Hake N=Antarctic Fish T=Areas where Tunny Fish are plentiful

This line shows the northern and southern limits of coral reefs and atolls, which are the habitat, but not exclusively, of a number of fish such as moray-eels, squirrel-fish, trumpet-fish, cornet-fish, silversides, barracuda, king-fish, amber-jacks, cardinal fish, groupers, snappers, butterfly-fish, surgeon-fish, damsel-fish, wrasses, parrot-fish, gobies, etc.

This line shows the northern and southern limits of flying fish in the Atlantic Ocean. (They are also found in the Mediterranean.) The limits in the Indian Ocean and Pacific Ocean have yet to be determined, but the main areas lie between latitudes 30°N and 30°S. Other oceanic fish found together with flying fish are dolphins, various kinds of tuna, certain blue sharks and mackerel sharks.

WHALE AND EEL MIGRATIONS

ARCTIC OCEAN

PACIFIC OCEAN

Sargasso Sea

ATLANTIC OCEAN

INDIAN OCEAN

SOUTHERN OCEAN

60°

30°

0°

30°

60°

120°

0°

60°

120°

HAUNTS AND MIGRATION ROUTES OF WHALEBONE WHALE

SPECIAL HAUNTS OF SPERM WHALE

SPAWNING AREAS OF THE EUROPEAN AND AMERICAN FRESH-WATER EEL

The migration of whales is largely connected with feeding and reproduction. Whalebone whales feed almost exclusively on plankton, but the sperm whale has teeth and eats mainly squids found at depths of 1,500 feet or more.
In autumn fresh-water eels leave the coasts and rivers of western Europe and the Mediterranean to travel across the Atlantic to the Sargasso Sea where, after breeding, they die. The larvae are swept eastwards across the Atlantic by ocean currents, the journey lasting two and a half years, during which time they change into elvers. These then enter the rivers where they remain for several years, eventually returning to the Sargasso Sea, when the whole process is repeated. Eastern North American fresh-water eels also travel to the same area, but for them the distance is shorter and the larvae become elvers in one year.

BIRD MIGRATION

A MYSTERY OF ENDURANCE AND NAVIGATION

And let fowl fly above the earth in the open firmament of heaven — GENESIS 1

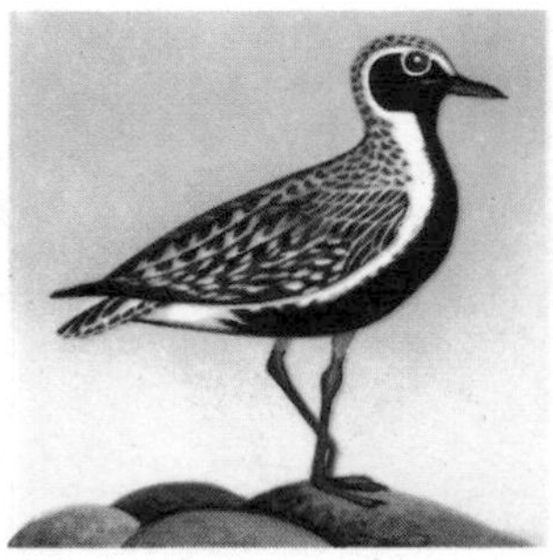
Golden Plover

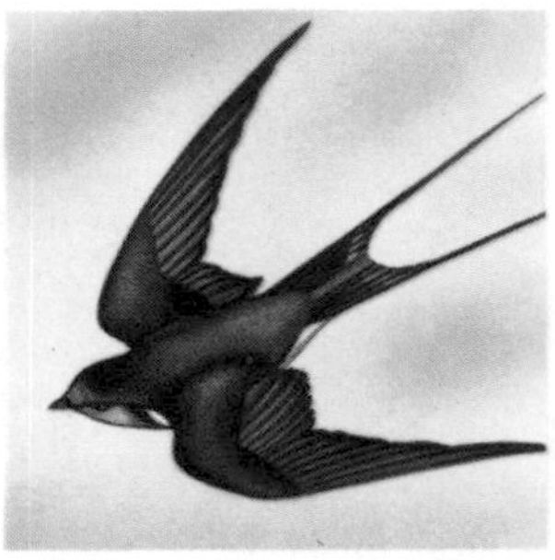
Swallow

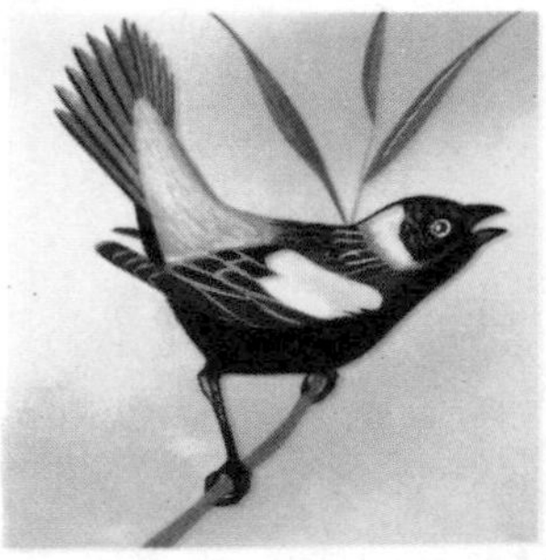
Bobolink

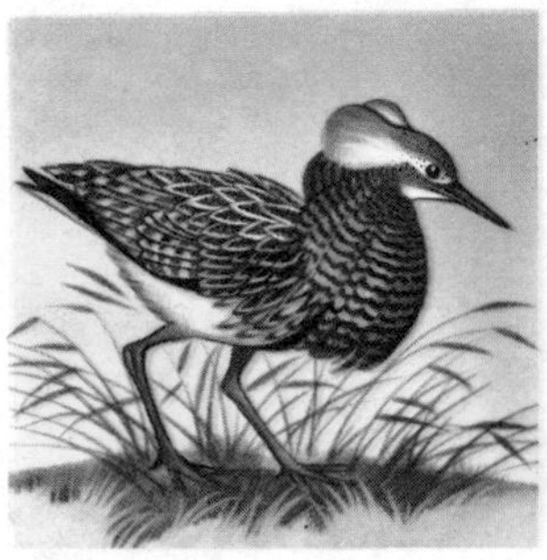
Ruff

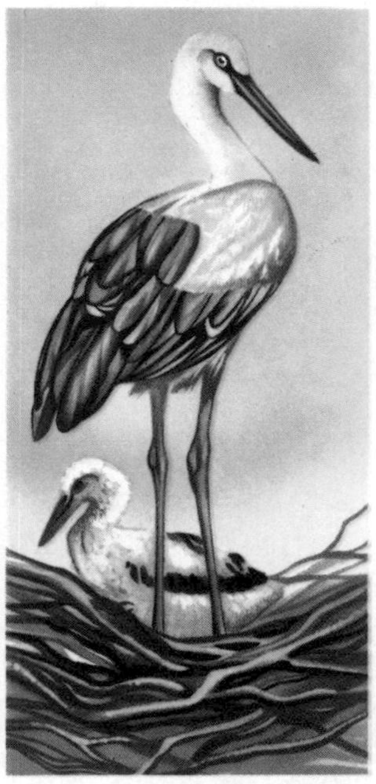
White Stork

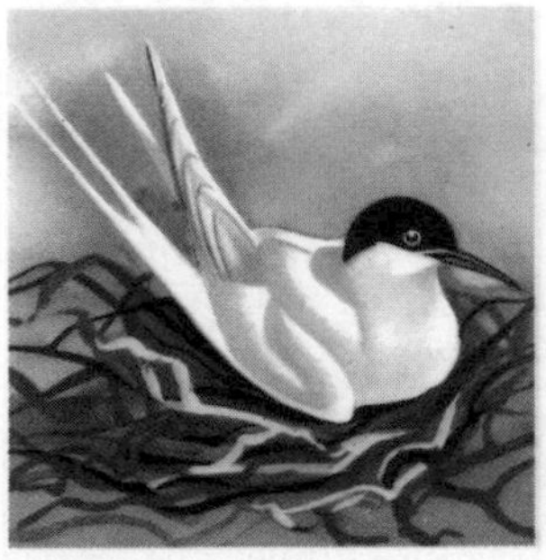
Arctic Tern

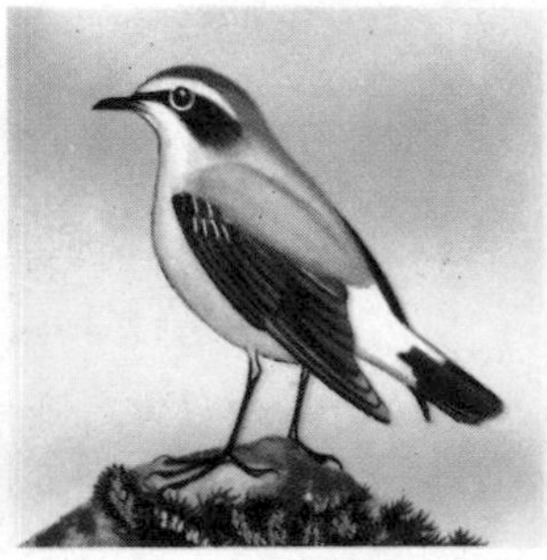
Greenland Wheatear

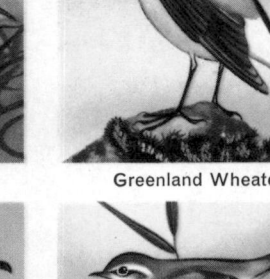

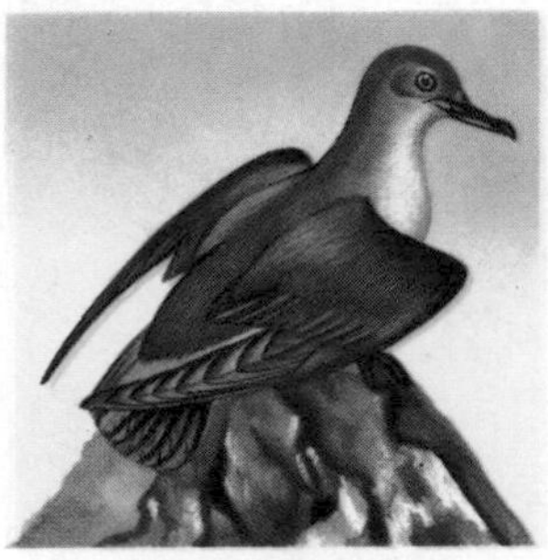
Sooty Shearwater

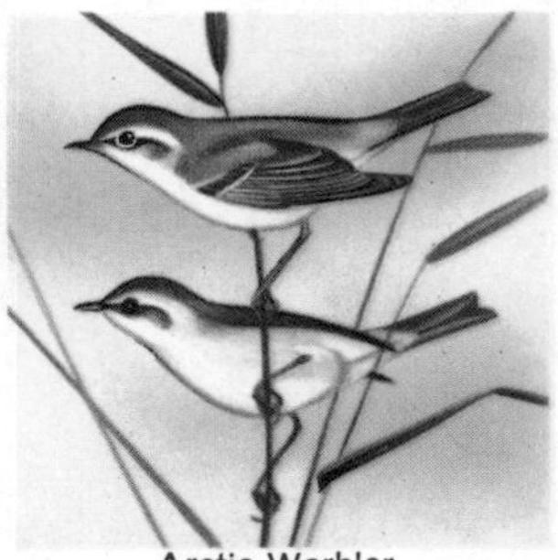
Arctic Warbler
Siberian Willow Warbler

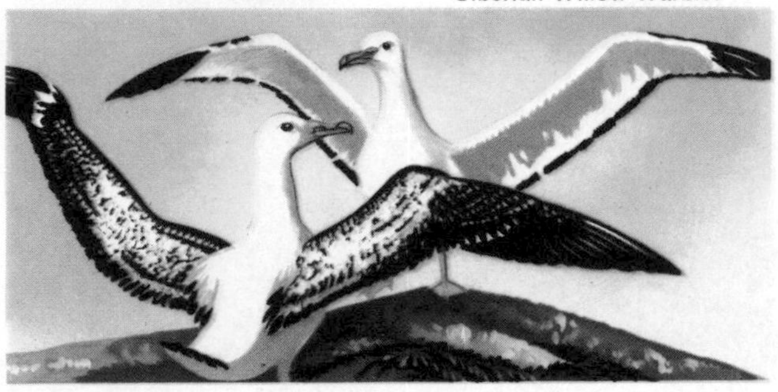
Wandering Albatross

THERE are well over 8,000 known and named species of birds, and a great many of them are migratory. Despite all dangers of storms, droughts, and of man himself, millions of birds undertake twice-yearly journeys that span whole continents and oceans.

The great northern land masses of the Northern Hemisphere support a huge breeding population, which migrates south for the winter. The land areas south of the Equator are too small to support a comparable breeding population of land birds. Instead, there are great ocean masses which support vast sea bird populations, millions of which move north during the southern winter. The northern summer day is longer than the 12-hour day at the Equator, and therefore gives more time for hunting—a critical factor for birds whose young may eat many times their own weight in food during the time they are in the nest. When breeding is over and the young ones reared, glandular changes within the body, probably caused by the lengthening nights of approaching winter, stimulate the migratory instinct, but the *actual* moment of departure is influenced by the local weather conditions and the physical readiness of the birds themselves.

Before migrating, birds lay in stores of energy in the form of internal fat deposits. Some species may even double their body weight and in this way are enabled to stay on the wing for at least 90 hours and perhaps as long as 120. Ornithologists believe that some of the Greenland Wheatears, only a little larger than the House Sparrow, fly direct from Greenland to the north coast of Spain, an overwater flight of nearly 2,000 miles, and that the Blackpoll Warbler, smaller than the House Sparrow, may fly directly from New England to Venezuela. After such a journey a bird may have halved its starting weight and so must rest while it accumulates fresh stores of fat.

MORE than any species, the Swallow is symbolic of this incredible and complicated migratory instinct. It breeds in Europe, Asia, North Africa and, as the Barn Swallow, in North America, and winters in the Southern Hemisphere. Flying by day, and feeding on the wing, European swallows show a preference for short sea crossings, such as the Strait of Gibraltar, passing south round the edge of the Sahara. In the spring the return journey is more direct: many swallows fly over the Sahara instead of round it, and cross the Mediterranean on a broad front.

Of all migrants, none travels farther than the Arctic Tern. After a short breeding season in the higher latitudes of the Northern Hemisphere (where long hours of summer daylight give ample time for feeding on the abundant supply of fish), some North American Arctic Terns cross the North Atlantic to join up with Arctic Terns from North-West Europe etc.; others pass down the western Atlantic, and Arctic Terns wearing rings fixed in Russia and Wales have been recovered in Australia. No other bird enjoys as much daylight during the year, but finding it involves an annual journey of about 22,000 miles.

Migratory birds often navigate with phenominal accuracy. The general direction of movements of some of them are indicated by the arrows on the map. The Pacific Golden Plover, which breeds in the extreme west of Alaska and in eastern Siberia, crosses the Pacific to make pinpoint arrivals on such small islands as Hawaii and Tonga. In one experiment, a Manx Shearwater, captured and ringed in Wales, was flown to Boston, U.S.A., and released. Twelve and a half days later it arrived home, having crossed 3,000 miles of ocean.

Shearwaters are great travellers, and many from Britain winter off the coasts of Brazil and Argentina; one has even reached South Australia. One incredible young bird completed the 5,000-mile journey to Brazil in less than three weeks of leaving the nest. The Great Shearwater is among the fewer species that migrates northwards. It breeds on the lonely island of Tristan da Cunha in the South Atlantic, and spends the summer in the North Atlantic, penetrating as far as the Davis Strait off Greenland. Its cousin, the Sooty Shearwater (known to sailors as the Mutton Bird), also migrates northwards from its breeding areas in the Falkland Islands and small islands off Cape Horn, Tasmania and New Zealand. One bird, ringed in New Zealand, was recovered in the Sea of Okhotsk, to the north of Japan.

WHILE winter quarters are generally nearer the Equator than summer ones, they are not always directly south. East Siberian Willow Warblers (song-birds so small that three of them together weigh only one ounce) undertake the immense journey to East Africa. The Arctic Warbler spends the summer as far west as Northern Norway and winters in south-east Asia and Indonesia—thus crossing at right angles the path of the East Siberian Willow Warbler. One species of Shrike nests in central Asia and winters in equatorial Africa—1,200 miles south, but 2,500 miles west.

The instinct to migrate brings together in huge flocks birds that are normally solitary. Even the most hospitable countryside cannot always provide sustenance for more than a few pairs of nesting birds per acre; and yet, with the onset of winter, birds collect in clouds that darken the northern skies. The Bobolink, or Rice Bird, is a solitary inhabitant of North American meadowlands. On the autumn migration flight, Bobolinks gather in immense flocks to invade the rice fields of the Carolinas and devastate the crops.

Size has little to do with the migration instinct. Tiny Humming Birds migrate 500 miles across the Gulf of Mexico. On the other hand, the Wandering Albatross, with a wing span of twelve feet, breeds on islands such as Tristan da Cunha, South Georgia, and Kerguelen, and spends the rest of the year soaring across the southern oceans, far from land. It is thought that these birds may circumnavigate the world several times between their breeding seasons.

The phenomenon of migration was known as long ago as Biblical times. The Book of Jeremiah notes the flight of White Storks, which leave the North European Plain in spectacular numbers and cross Israel and the Nile Valley. But, despite this long familiarity with migration, there is still much to be learned about it. How high do migrating birds fly? How do they navigate?

Radar has largely answered the altitude question: most migrations take place below 5,000 feet, but there are records of really small birds at 10,000, 15,000 and 20,000 feet.

Experiments with caged migrants suggest that they may use the sun and the stars as aids to navigation. Birds placed in a planetarium, beneath a replica of the night sky, turned at once in the direction of the southern winter quarters to which they were due to fly. Birds, it seems, are equipped with instincts that may surpass man's most elaborate instruments.

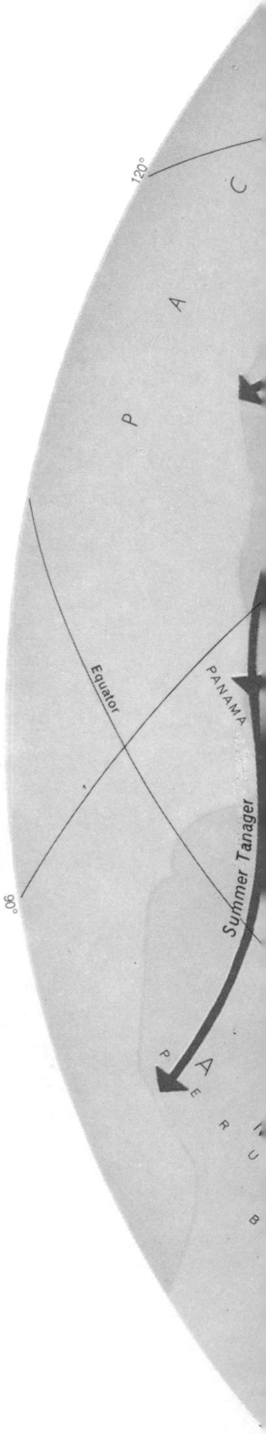

SPECIES	LENGTH IN INCHES	BREEDING AREA	WINTERING AREA	DISTANCE APART (APPROX.)
Arctic Skua (Parasitic Jaeger)	16½	Arctic America, Greenland, Arctic Europe, north Siberia	West Africa, Persian Gulf, Arabian Gulf, Australia, New Zealand, South America	4,000-8,000 miles
Arctic Tern	14-15	North Canada, Greenland, Iceland, north Europe	South and west African coasts, Antarctica	11,000 miles
Arctic Warbler	4¾	North and north-east Europe, north Siberia	South-east Asia	4,000-7,000 miles
Blackpoll Warbler	5–5½	Alaska, east to Northern Labrador and New England	Colombia, Venezuela to French Guiana	2,500–5,000 miles
Black and white Cuckoo	13	India	East and south-east Africa	3,500-4,500 miles
Blue-cheeked Bee-eater	11	North India, west China	East Africa	4,000-5,500 miles

SPECIES	LENGTH IN INCHES	BREEDING AREA	WINTERING AREA	DISTANCE APART (APPROX
Bobolink	6½-8	South-east Canada, north-east and mid-west U.S.A.	Bolivia, Paraguay, Brazil	5,000 miles
Buff-breasted Sandpiper	7½	Arctic Canada	Argentina and Uruguay	6,000-8,000 miles
East Siberian Willow Warbler	4½	North-east Siberia	East Africa	8,000 miles
Great Shearwater	17-18	Tristan da Cunha	North Atlantic	6,000-8,000 miles
Long-tailed Cuckoo	16½	New Zealand	Samoa and Fiji	2,000 miles
Manx Shearwater	14	British Isles, Brittany, Atlantic Islands, Mediterranean	North and South Atlantic	500-5,000 miles
Needle-tailed Swift	7½	East Siberia, Japan	Australia, Tasmania	6,000-8,000 miles

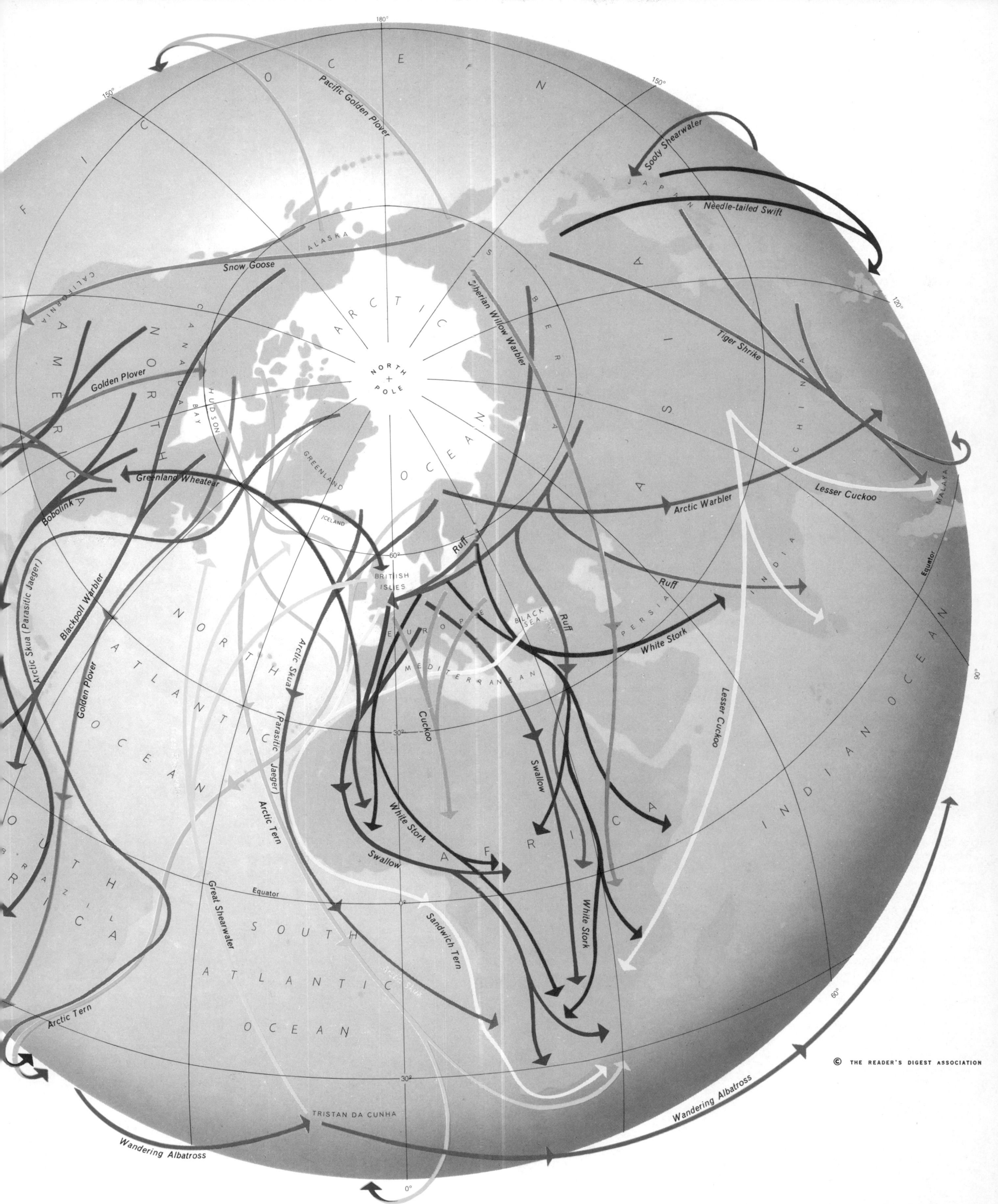

© THE READER'S DIGEST ASSOCIATION

SPECIES	LENGTH IN INCHES	BREEDING AREA	WINTERING AREA	DISTANCE APART (APPROX.)
Pacific Golden Plover	10-11	West Alaska, north-east Siberia	Hawaii, Tonga, Indonesia, Australia	6,000-8,000 miles
Pintail (New World)	22	North-west Alaska east to Hudson Bay, south to Iowa, N. Colorado, S. California	Middle and southern United States to West Indies and Panama, west to Hawaii	1,000-4,000 miles
Ruff	8½-12	North and west Europe, Siberia	West Europe, South Africa, Iraq, Persia, India, Ceylon	3,000-6,000 miles
Sandwich Tern	16	Shores of North Sea and west Mediterranean, Black Sea	West and South Africa	1,000-5,000 miles
Scarlet Grosbeak	5¾	North-east Europe	India, south-east Asia	3,000-6,000 miles
Shining Cuckoo	7¼	New Zealand	Solomon Islands	1,800 miles

SPECIES	LENGTH IN INCHES	BREEDING AREA	WINTERING AREA	DISTANCE APART (APPROX.)
Snow Goose	25-30	East Siberia, Alaska, north-west Canada	West U.S.A. especially California	2,000-3,000 miles
Sooty Shearwater	16	New Zealand, Falkland Is., Cape Horn	North Atlantic, north Pacific	6,000-9,000 miles
Summer Tanager	7-7½	North America, north to as far as the Great Lakes	Mexico southwards to Peru	1,000-4,000 miles
Swallow (European)	7-7½	Europe, north to about 68°	Central and South Africa	5,000-7,000 miles
Tiger Shrike	7	China, east Siberia, Japan	Malaya, Sumatra, Celebes, Borneo	3,000-4,000 miles
Wandering Albatross	44-53	Tristan da Cunha, Gough Island	Southern oceans, chiefly south of 40°S.	unknown
White Stork	40	Mid-Europe	Tropical and South Africa	4,000-7,000 miles

In all the areas of the world colonized by man, the domestication of certain mammals has invariably led to the extinction or near-extinction of the wilder species. The extent of man's advance has depended on the availability of pasture for animals which, through selective breeding, he adapted for his own purposes. Sheep, cattle, pigs, goats and horses (providing food, milk, clothing and transport) are of little interest zoologically but are vastly important economically. In areas with seasonal or scanty rainfall and sparse pasturage, domestic animals may be herded or ranched—a few to the square mile—over wide distances, and may be the primary factor in the regions' economy. In more favoured zones "mixed" farming is usual: animal husbandry and crop cultivation are practised in close conjunction with each other on the same farm unit. In either case wild animals are robbed of the territories best able to support them.

Map labels:

CANADA C. 10, S. 1, P. 5
U.S.A. C. 93, S. 31, P. 51
MEXICO C. 21, S. 6, P. 9
BRAZIL C. 69, S. 20, P. 44
URUGUAY C. 7, S. 23, P. 3
ARGENTINA C. 40, S. 47, P. 3
UNITED KINGDOM C. 11, S. 26, P. 6
FRANCE C. 18, S. 8, P. 8
SPAIN C. 3, S. 16, P. 6
W. GERMANY S. 1, C. 12, P. 15
POLAND C. 8, S. 4, P. 12
ITALY C. 9, S. 11, P. 4
YUGOSLAVIA C. 5, S. 11, P. 4
TURKEY C. 12, S. 29, P. 4
U.S.S.R. C. 67, S. 120, P. 44
IRAN C. 5, S. 17
CHINA C. 45, S. 53, P. 145
INDIA C. 159, S. 39, P. 5
PAKISTAN C. 24, S. 7, P. 5
SUDAN C. 9, S. 8
BRITISH E. AFRICA C. 16, S. 7, P. 1
REPUBLIC OF S. AFRICA C. 12, S. 38, P. 1
AUSTRALIA C. 17, S. 149, P. 1
NEW ZEALAND C. 6, S. 46, P. 1

C = CATTLE   S = SHEEP   P = PIGS   FIGURES IN MILLIONS

Legend:
HOME LIVESTOCK — LIVESTOCK BRED IN CONJUNCTION WITH OTHER FARMING PRACTICES
RANCH AND HERD LIVESTOCK

THE SPREAD OF MAMMALS

Let the Earth bring forth the living creature after its kind — GENESIS 1

FROM the time terrestrial animal life began, some 350 million years ago, the face of the Earth has undergone immense changes, and even in the relatively recent period since mammals evolved from reptiles, more reshaping of land has occurred. It was once possible for species from Southern Asia to spread by age-long migration through Europe and, by means of a land-bridge where the Bering Strait is now, to the Americas. But barriers to migrations, and new avenues for them, have been appearing and disappearing since the time creatures first had need to travel in search of food and warmth.

For the most important animals of the present day—the warm-blooded mammals, of which man himself is one—the Earth has set strict limits. The geological changes that decided the patterns of movement also brought about changes in environment, and these changes, allied to other natural causes, speeded up the evolution of mammals, especially on the African, Euro-Asian and North American continents. One result is that mammals can now be grouped in five main regions, each of which is bounded by natural barriers—mountains, deserts and seas.

The formation of the Sahara Desert created one of the barriers to migration, so that the mammals to the south of the desert, living in tropical or semi-tropical conditions, have evolved in quite a different way from the mammals to the north of it. In Australia, the most primitive species of mammals in the world have

survived, for, with the disappearance of any land connection with Asia some 135 million years ago, they became isolated, and more active and dominating mammals were prevented from reaching the area. The Himalayas, formed about 25 million years ago, stopped any large-scale interchange of species between northern Asia and the Oriental Region; and the Bering Strait, during the recent Pleistocene Period, effectively cut off the Americas from Europe and Asia.

Some mammals learned to hunt in the air, like bats, others to live in trees, like monkeys, some to burrow under the ground, like moles, and still others, such as whales, went back to the sea from which life first came. And all of them developed characteristics according to their surroundings; the whales, for instance, developed layers of blubber under the skin to insulate them from the cold of the oceans, and some of the whales, because of the buoyancy of the water, were able to grow to a huge bulk and so become the largest of all mammals.

A natural spread took some mammals to the cold north, and these became more hairy, like the polar bear and the musk-ox. On the other hand, in the tropics, the elephant and the hippopotamus became almost hairless.

There are nearly 5,000 species of mammals, in bewildering varieties of shape and form. Among them are the primates, headed by man, whose unique specialization is that he can fashion his environment to suit his own needs.

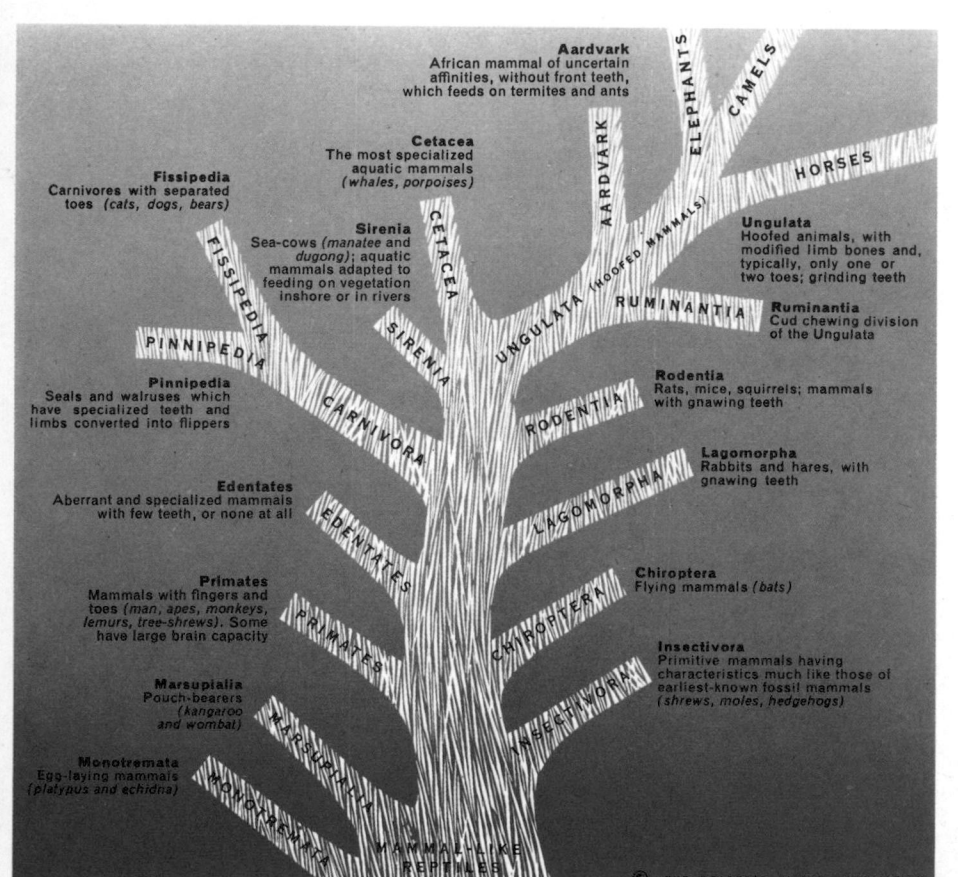

THE MAMMALIAN TREE

Aardvark
African mammal of uncertain affinities, without front teeth, which feeds on termites and ants

Cetacea
The most specialized aquatic mammals (whales, porpoises)

Fissipedia
Carnivores with separated toes (cats, dogs, bears)

Sirenia
Sea-cows (manatee and dugong); aquatic mammals adapted to feeding on vegetation inshore or in rivers

Pinnipedia
Seals and walruses which have specialized teeth and limbs converted into flippers

Ungulata
Hoofed animals, with modified limb bones and, typically, only one or two toes; grinding teeth

Ruminantia
Cud chewing division of the Ungulata

Rodentia
Rats, mice, squirrels; mammals with gnawing teeth

Edentates
Aberrant and specialized mammals with few teeth, or none at all

Lagomorpha
Rabbits and hares, with gnawing teeth

Primates
Mammals with fingers and toes (man, apes, monkeys, lemurs, tree-shrews). Some have large brain capacity

Chiroptera
Flying mammals (bats)

Marsupialia
Pouch-bearers (kangaroo and wombat)

Insectivora
Primitive mammals having characteristics much like those of earliest-known fossil mammals (shrews, moles, hedgehogs)

Monotremata
Egg-laying mammals (platypus and echidna)

MAMMAL-LIKE REPTILES

© THE READER'S DIGEST ASSOCIATION

The similarity between the marine animals on either side of the Central American isthmus suggests that here the sea, at one time, was unbroken. Wide rivers across the isthmus now form barriers to the migration of land animals, but the nine-banded armadillo, typical of the South American fauna, has continued to spread northwards, for while swimming it is able to gulp air to inflate its intestines, and thereby gain buoyancy for its heavy body.

CENTRAL AMERICAN ISTHMUS

NEOTROPICAL REGION

Nine-Banded Armadillo
Puma
Llama
Guanaco
South American Tapir

The **Neotropical** Region (South America) is characterized by marsupials (opossum and small, shrew-like pouch-bearers) and edentates (mammals with few teeth or none at all, such as sloths, anteaters and armadillos). These were probably the region's only mammals until later Tertiary times when others, notably llamas, jaguars, pumas, some fox-like wolves and a few deer, arrived from the north across the land-bridge of Central America. Peccaries take the place of pigs of other regions, and the monkeys, although similar to those of Africa and Asia, form a distinct sub-order.

As mammals evolve and change their characteristics to suit their environments, their bony structures are the features which modify most slowly. In classifying mammals, therefore, emphasis is always placed on the character of the teeth, skull and skeleton. Where these features have become specialized, the animals are graded according to the degree of their specializations. On this basis man and the other primates appear low down on the genealogical tree, while the camel, elephant and whale are at the top. Man's pre-eminence in the world is due to his greater brain capacity, his grasping hand and his ability to use speech; but his limbs with their five digits and his face are still anatomically primitive.

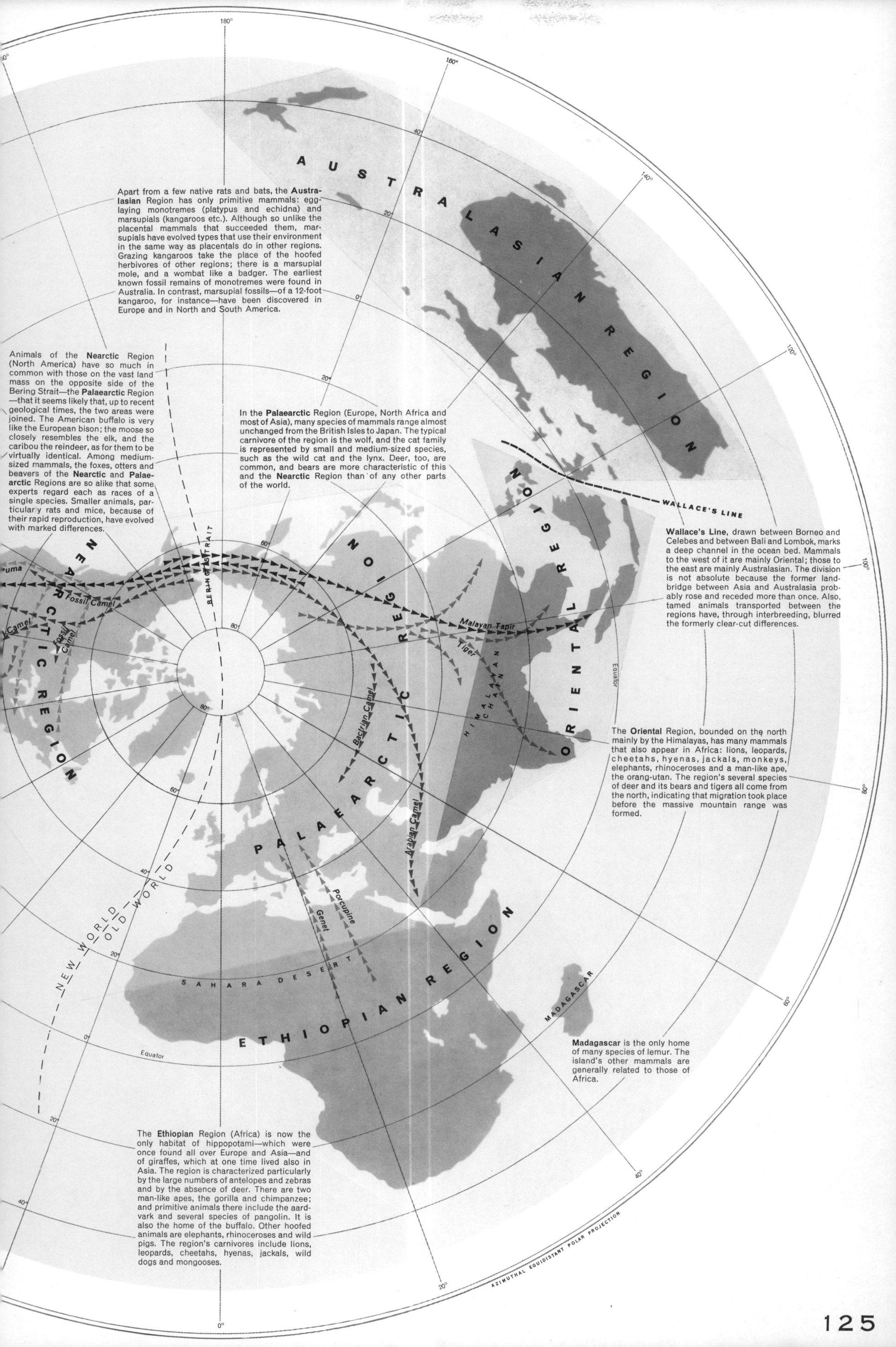

Apart from a few native rats and bats, the **Austra-lasian** Region has only primitive mammals: egg-laying monotremes (platypus and echidna) and marsupials (kangaroos etc.). Although so unlike the placental mammals that succeeded them, mar-supials have evolved types that use their environment in the same way as placentals do in other regions. Grazing kangaroos take the place of the hoofed herbivores of other regions; there is a marsupial mole, and a wombat like a badger. The earliest known fossil remains of monotremes were found in Australia. In contrast, marsupial fossils—of a 12-foot kangaroo, for instance—have been discovered in Europe and in North and South America.

Animals of the **Nearctic** Region (North America) have so much in common with those on the vast land mass on the opposite side of the Bering Strait—the **Palaearctic** Region —that it seems likely that, up to recent geological times, the two areas were joined. The American buffalo is very like the European bison; the moose so closely resembles the elk, and the caribou the reindeer, as for them to be virtually identical. Among medium-sized mammals, the foxes, otters and beavers of the **Nearctic** and **Palae-arctic** Regions are so alike that some experts regard each as races of a single species. Smaller animals, par-ticularly rats and mice, because of their rapid reproduction, have evolved with marked differences.

In the **Palaearctic** Region (Europe, North Africa and most of Asia), many species of mammals range almost unchanged from the British Isles to Japan. The typical carnivore of the region is the wolf, and the cat family is represented by small and medium-sized species, such as the wild cat and the lynx. Deer, too, are common, and bears are more characteristic of this and the **Nearctic** Region than of any other parts of the world.

Wallace's Line, drawn between Borneo and Celebes and between Bali and Lombok, marks a deep channel in the ocean bed. Mammals to the west of it are mainly Oriental; those to the east are mainly Australasian. The division is not absolute because the former land-bridge between Asia and Australasia prob-ably rose and receded more than once. Also, tamed animals transported between the regions have, through interbreeding, blurred the formerly clear-cut differences.

The **Oriental** Region, bounded on the north mainly by the Himalayas, has many mammals that also appear in Africa: lions, leopards, cheetahs, hyenas, jackals, monkeys, elephants, rhinoceroses and a man-like ape, the orang-utan. The region's several species of deer and its bears and tigers all come from the north, indicating that migration took place before the massive mountain range was formed.

Madagascar is the only home of many species of lemur. The island's other mammals are generally related to those of Africa.

The **Ethiopian** Region (Africa) is now the only habitat of hippopotami—which were once found all over Europe and Asia—and of giraffes, which at one time lived also in Asia. The region is characterized particularly by the large numbers of antelopes and zebras and by the absence of deer. There are two man-like apes, the gorilla and chimpanzee; and primitive animals there include the aard-vark and several species of pangolin. It is also the home of the buffalo. Other hoofed animals are elephants, rhinoceroses and wild pigs. The region's carnivores include lions, leopards, cheetahs, hyenas, jackals, wild dogs and mongooses.

THE EVOLUTION OF MAN

When men began to multiply on the face of the earth—GENESIS 6

WE may learn something about early man in two different ways: by comparing the biology of man with that of other animals and so determining the degree of their relationship (taxonomy); and by looking at fossils and so determining their age and development (palaeontology).

By comparing man with other living creatures we know that he is a primate, having a large brain, a grasping hand with nails instead of claws, and eyesight which has been developed at the expense of his sense of smell. Primates include tree-shrews, lemurs, monkeys and apes. Within this group man shows the greatest resemblance to apes, not only in his posture and means of locomotion, but in the development and co-ordination of his brain and hands, and in the biochemistry of his blood. Man has, however, been distinguished from other primates, both living and fossil, by his ability to make and use tools.

The comparison of living forms enables us to estimate the affinities of fossils, even from their fragmentary remains; and by studying the tools and animal remains found with fossil men, we can discover something of their way of life and the environment in which they lived.

In the study of the modern races of man reference is made to inherited differences in anatomy, morphology and biochemistry. A race can be defined by using as many sorting criteria as can be seen or measured, such as colouring, hair and eye form, and blood groups; but other criteria, such as stature and weight, which are closely related to nutrition, are of little help. Blood groups appear to be relatively stable criteria, and show marked differences in frequency in different populations. For example, though blood Group B is common among specialized Mongoloids, it is rare among South American Indians—an unspecialized Mongoloid group.

But any individual racial group is continually in a process of change through natural selection and intermarriage with neighbouring groups or migrants, so that a "pure" race does not exist.

The evolution of man and the present distribution of the races are shown on the accompanying maps and charts.

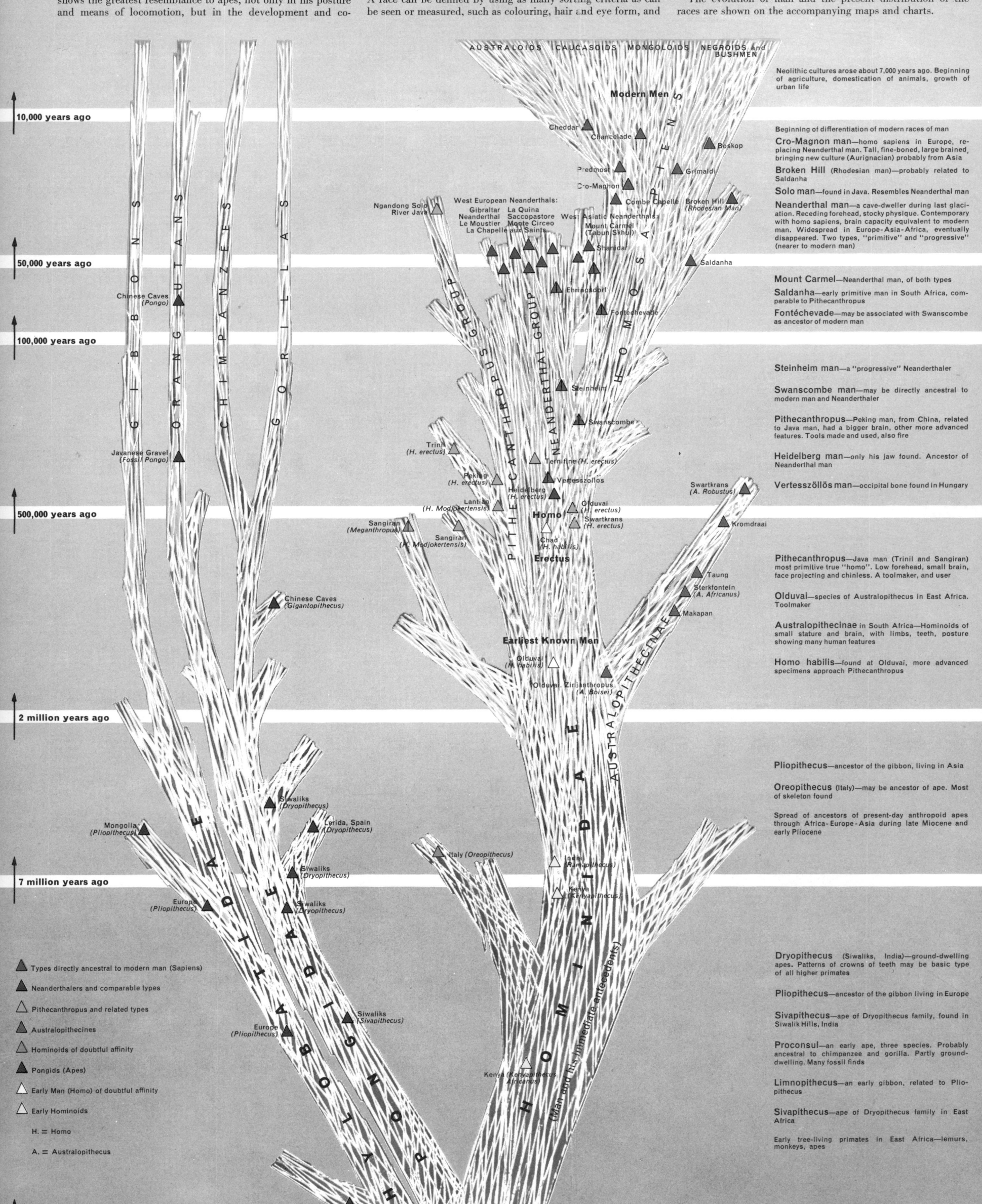

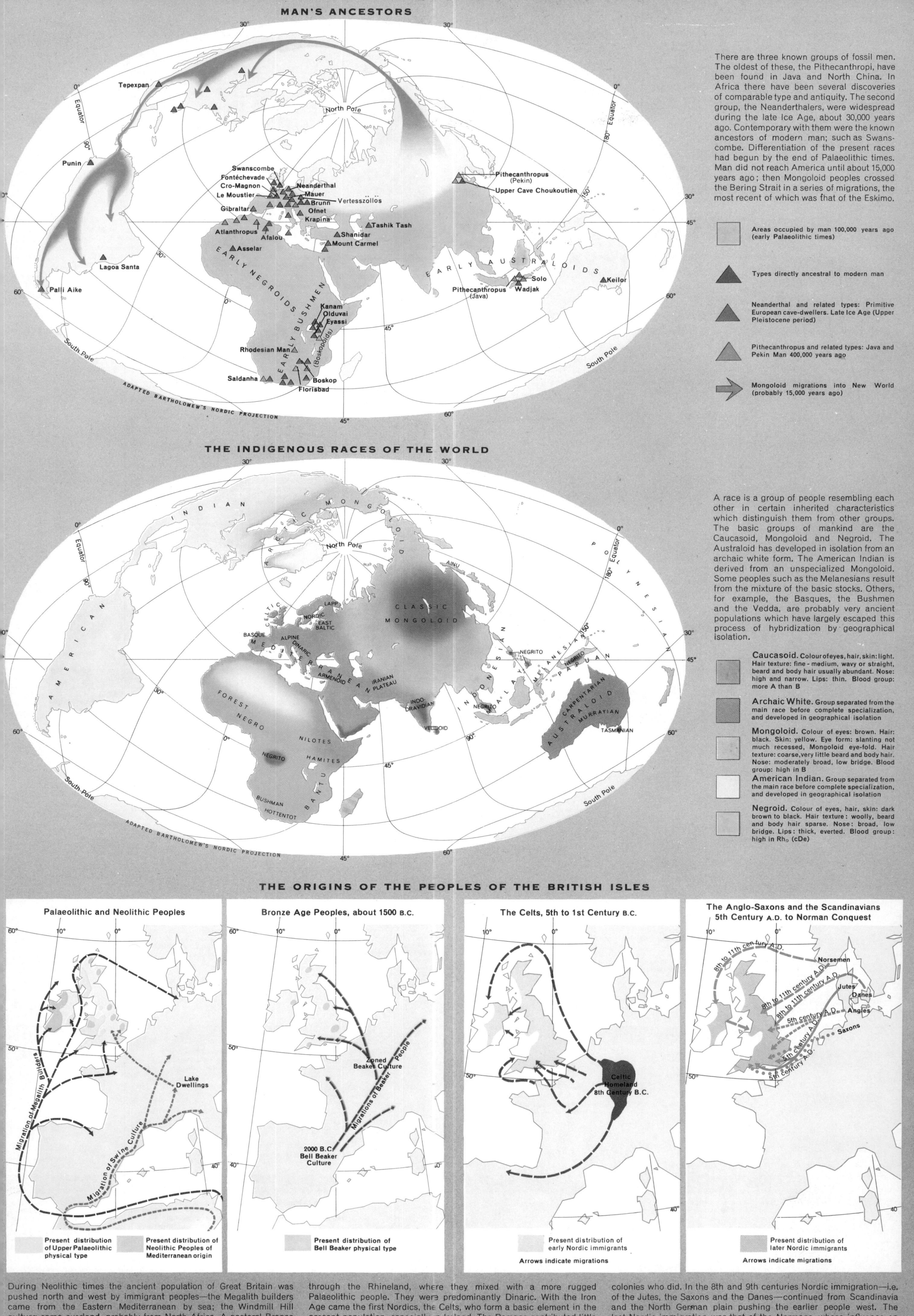

MAN'S ANCESTORS

There are three known groups of fossil men. The oldest of these, the Pithecanthropi, have been found in Java and North China. In Africa there have been several discoveries of comparable type and antiquity. The second group, the Neanderthalers, were widespread during the late Ice Age, about 30,000 years ago. Contemporary with them were the known ancestors of modern man; such as Swanscombe. Differentiation of the present races had begun by the end of Palaeolithic times. Man did not reach America until about 15,000 years ago; then Mongoloid peoples crossed the Bering Strait in a series of migrations, the most recent of which was that of the Eskimo.

Areas occupied by man 100,000 years ago (early Palaeolithic times)

Types directly ancestral to modern man

Neanderthal and related types: Primitive European cave-dwellers. Late Ice Age (Upper Pleistocene period)

Pithecanthropus and related types: Java and Pekin Man 400,000 years ago

Mongoloid migrations into New World (probably 15,000 years ago)

Map labels: Tepexpan, Punin, Lagoa Santa, Palli Aike, Swanscombe, Fontéchevade, Cro-Magnon, Le Moustier, Gibraltar, Atlanthropus, Afalou, Asseler, Saldanha, Neanderthal, Mauer, Ofnet, Krapina, Brunn, Vertesszollos, Tashik Tash, Shanidar, Mount Carmel, Kanam, Olduvai, Eyassi, (Boskop(ss)), Rhodesian Man, Boskop, Florisbad, Pithecanthropus (Pekin), Upper Cave Choukoutien, Pithecanthropus (Java), Solo, Wadjak, Keilor

EARLY NEGROIDS, EARLY BUSHMEN, EARLY AUSTRALOIDS, North Pole, South Pole, Equator

ADAPTED BARTHOLOMEW'S NORDIC PROJECTION

THE INDIGENOUS RACES OF THE WORLD

A race is a group of people resembling each other in certain inherited characteristics which distinguish them from other groups. The basic groups of mankind are the Caucasoid, Mongoloid and Negroid. The Australoid has developed in isolation from an archaic white form. The American Indian is derived from an unspecialized Mongoloid. Some peoples such as the Melanesians result from the mixture of the basic stocks. Others, for example, the Basques, the Bushmen and the Vedda, are probably very ancient populations which have largely escaped this process of hybridization by geographical isolation.

Caucasoid. Colour of eyes, hair, skin: light. Hair texture: fine - medium, wavy or straight, beard and body hair usually abundant. Nose: high and narrow. Lips: thin. Blood group: more A than B

Archaic White. Group separated from the main race before complete specialization, and developed in geographical isolation

Mongoloid. Colour of eyes: brown. Hair: black. Skin: yellow. Eye form: slanting not much recessed, Mongoloid eye-fold. Hair texture: coarse, very little beard and body hair. Nose: moderately broad, low bridge. Blood group: high in B

American Indian. Group separated from the main race before complete specialization, and developed in geographical isolation

Negroid. Colour of eyes, hair, skin: dark brown to black. Hair texture: woolly, beard and body hair sparse. Nose: broad, low bridge. Lips: thick, everted. Blood group: high in Rh₀ (cDe)

Map labels: ARCTIC MONGOLOID, CLASSIC MONGOLOID, CELTIC, NORDIC, LAPP, EAST BALTIC, ALPINE, DINARIC, ARMENOID, BASQUE, MEDITERRANEAN, IRANIAN PLATEAU, INDO DRAVIDIAN, VEDDOID, NEGRITO, INDONESIAN, MALAYAN, MELANESIAN, PAPUAN, POLYNESIA, AINU, AMERICAN, INDIAN, FOREST NEGRO, NILOTES, HAMITES, BANTU, BUSHMAN, HOTTENTOT, NEGRITO, CARPENTARIAN AUSTRALOID, MURRAYIAN, TASMANIAN, North Pole, South Pole

ADAPTED BARTHOLOMEW'S NORDIC PROJECTION

THE ORIGINS OF THE PEOPLES OF THE BRITISH ISLES

Palaeolithic and Neolithic Peoples
Migration of Megalith Builders
Migration of Swine Culture
Lake Dwellings

Present distribution of Upper Palaeolithic physical type

Present distribution of Neolithic Peoples of Mediterranean origin

Bronze Age Peoples, about 1500 B.C.
Zoned Beaker Culture
Migrations of Beaker People
2000 B.C. Bell Beaker Culture

Present distribution of Bell Beaker physical type

The Celts, 5th to 1st Century B.C.
Celtic Homeland 8th Century B.C.

Present distribution of early Nordic immigrants
Arrows indicate migrations

The Anglo-Saxons and the Scandinavians 5th Century A.D. to Norman Conquest
8th to 11th century A.D.
Norsemen
Jutes
Danes
Angles
Saxons
5th century A.D.

Present distribution of later Nordic immigrants
Arrows indicate migrations

During Neolithic times the ancient population of Great Britain was pushed north and west by immigrant peoples—the Megalith builders came from the Eastern Mediterranean by sea; the Windmill Hill culture came overland, probably from North Africa. A pastoral Bronze Age people, making characteristic drinking beakers, came from Spain through the Rhineland, where they mixed with a more rugged Palaeolithic people. They were predominantly Dinaric. With the Iron Age came the first Nordics, the Celts, who form a basic element in the present population, especially in Ireland. The Romans contributed little to British racial types but their Mediterranean mercenaries founded colonies who did. In the 8th and 9th centuries Nordic immigration—i.e. of the Jutes, the Saxons and the Danes—continued from Scandinavia and the North German plain pushing the earlier people west. The last Nordic immigration was that of the Normans, whose influence on the physical type in Britain was mainly confined to the ruling classes.

EGYPT AND BABYLONIA 2000-1500 B.C.

R. Danube
BLACK SEA
MEDITERRANEAN SEA
ASIA MINOR
MESOPOTAMIA
PHOENICIA
PALESTINE
Babylon
Ur
LOWER EGYPT
Gizeh
Memphis
UPPER EGYPT
Thebes
ARABIA
RED SEA
PERSIAN GULF
ARABIAN SEA
R. Nile
R. Tigris
R. Euphrates
Syr Darya
Amu Darya
CASPIAN SEA
R. Volga
R. Dnepr

HELLENISTIC EMPIRE ABOUT 300 B.C.

R. Rhine
R. Danube
R. Dnepr
R. Volga
BLACK SEA
CASPIAN SEA
MEDITERRANEAN SEA
MACEDONIA
Corinth
Athens
Sparta
LYDIA
ASSYRIA
Antioch
PARTHIA
Seleucia
PERSIA
BABYLONIA
Jerusalem
Alexandria
EGYPT
Persepolis
PERSIAN GULF
RED SEA
ARABIAN SEA
R. Nile
R. Indus
Syr Darya
Amu Darya

ROMAN EMPIRE A.D. 180

Hadrian's Wall
BRITAIN
Roman Wall
GAUL
R. Rhine
R. Danube
R. Dnepr
R. Volga
BLACK SEA
CASPIAN SEA
Rome
SPAIN
Carthage
GREECE
MEDITERRANEAN SEA
R. Tigris
R. Euphrates
PERSIAN GULF
R. Nile
RED SEA
Syr Darya
Amu Darya

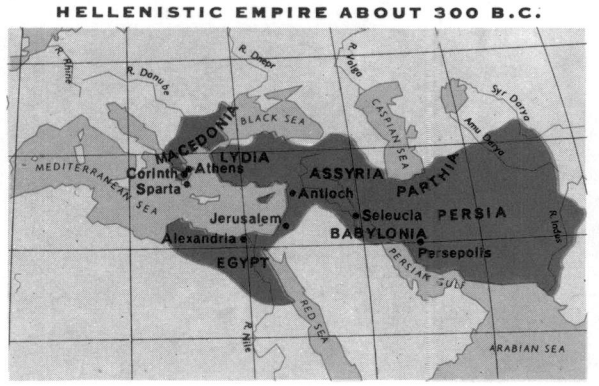

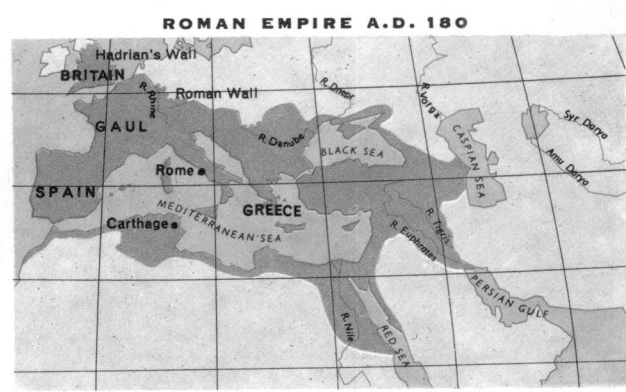

THE GROWTH OF CIVILIZATIONS

A TIME CHART OF MAN'S PROGRESS THROUGH THE AGES

Almost all the great civilizations originated in river valleys, were nourished by trade, and came to maturity in cities. The conditions of life in the cities provided the intellectual stimulus in which philosophers and scientists could study the meaning of the Universe and the nature of matter; artists and writers could express the ideals and aspirations of their people through the medium of architecture, literature, painting and music.

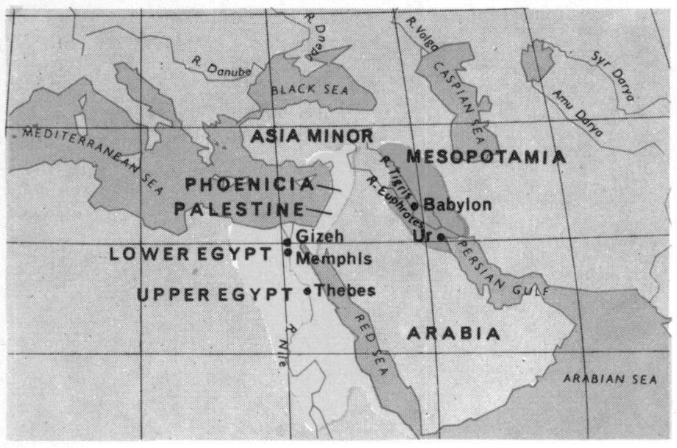

The course of civilization can be traced in the five main geographical areas shown below. The progress of a civilization is marked by man's increasing control over Nature through applied mathematics and science, the evolution of writing, legal codes, and political and religious organizations. Political development usually began with the formation of city states, some of which expanded into empires or federations, but all have proved to be transient. Religions first exerted local, then national influence; and some spread beyond their countries of origin.

NEAR EAST

The union of the peoples of the Upper and Lower Nile some 5,000 years ago heralded the first major civilization in history. During its development, mathematics made possible the building of the Gizeh Pyramids; hieroglyphs were turned into alphabetic writing on stone and papyrus reed; and medicine was born. About 1500 B.C. the Egyptian Empire extended as far as Syria, but slowly declined after its failure to subdue the Hittites and Assyrians. A most vigorous civilization then developed in the fertile valleys of Mesopotamia. Here the Babylonians and Assyrians had adopted the cuneiform writing, the mathematical discoveries and the technical advances of the Sumerians—the first to found city states in the Tigris and Euphrates valleys. The Babylonian and Assyrian Empires spread east and west until they were checked by the rise of the Persians.

The Persian Empire extended from the Indus Valley to the Mediterranean, and embraced Zoroastrianism. Meanwhile the Hebrews, after long migrations and exile in Egypt, settled in the "Promised Land" of Palestine. Their contribution was primarily religious, and paved the way for both Christianity and Islam.

After nearly a thousand years of Greek and Roman domination, another civilization was born in the Near East when, in the 7th century A.D., Arab rule and Islam spread as far as Persia and Spain. The Arabs preserved the knowledge of ancient science, philosophy and geography, translated Ptolemy, Euclid and Aristotle, and introduced into Europe the use of numerals and paper-making. Islam seemed seriously threatened when the Arabs were ousted from Spain and were defeated by the Turks in the Near East. The Turks, in taking over the Arab Empire, became Muslims, and the predominance of Islam continued. After being repelled in Central Europe, the Ottoman Empire began its slow decline. A revival of nationalism among the Arabs led to the foundation of the Arab League.

EUROPE

Western civilization originated in the Aegean, but received its real character from the cultures of Greece, Rome and Jerusalem. The Arabs and the Christian Church had preserved different aspects of these cultures, and, in their development, carried them farther. The Greeks, entering the Aegean from the north, built city states which, though constantly at odds with one another, shared a common cultural development, used the alphabet brought to them by trading Phoenicians, and provided the starting points for most of our own ideas and ideals.

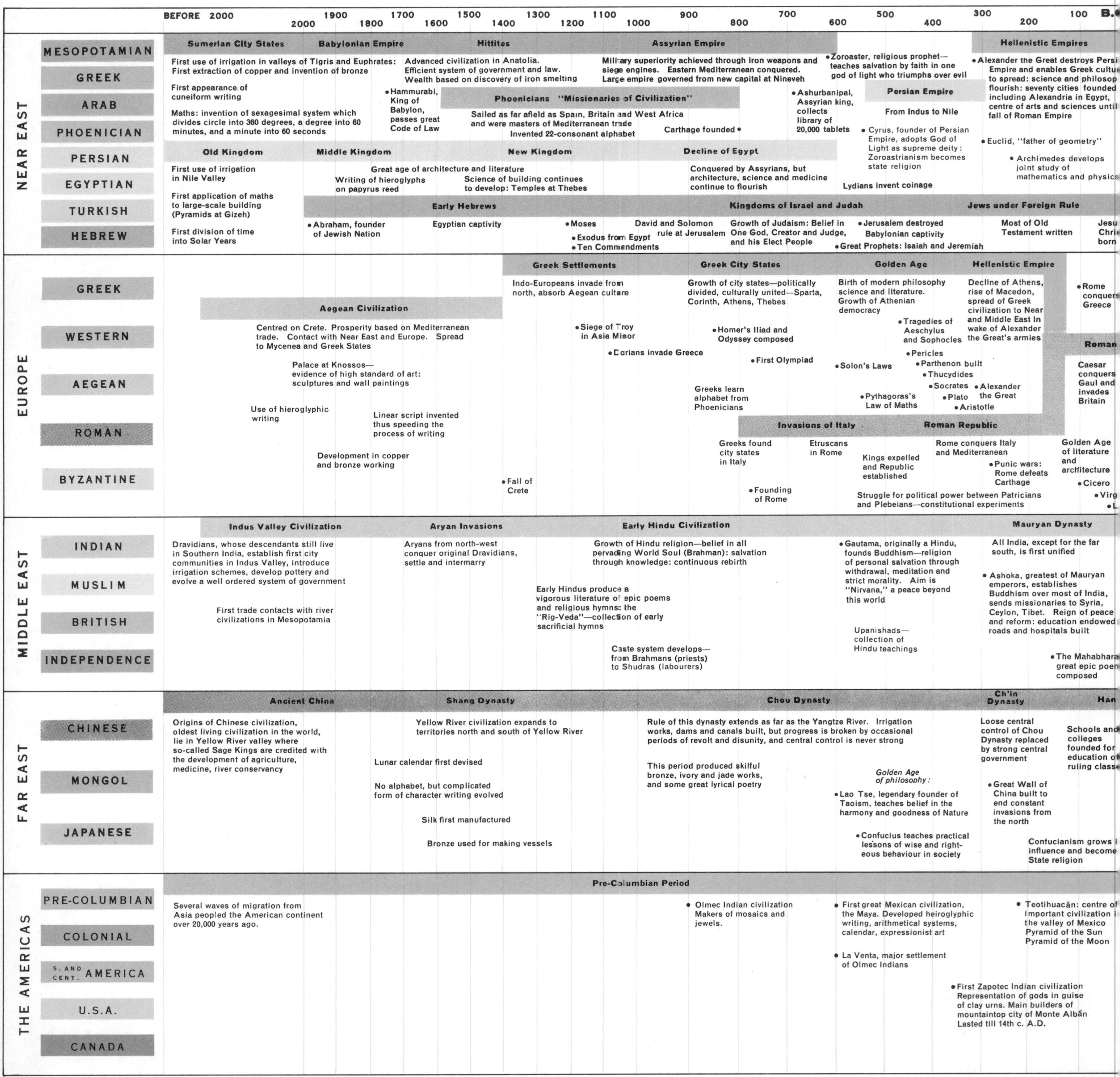

BEFORE 2000
2000
1900
1800
1700
1600
1500
1400
1300
1200
1100
1000
900
800
700
600
500
400
300
200
100
B.C.
NEAR EAST
MESOPOTAMIAN
GREEK
ARAB
PHOENICIAN
PERSIAN
EGYPTIAN
TURKISH
HEBREW
Sumerian City States
Babylonian Empire
Hittites
Assyrian Empire
Hellenistic Empires
First use of irrigation in valleys of Tigris and Euphrates: First extraction of copper and invention of bronze
Advanced civilization in Anatolia. Efficient system of government and law. Wealth based on discovery of iron smelting
Military superiority achieved through iron weapons and siege engines. Eastern Mediterranean conquered. Large empire governed from new capital at Nineveh
Zoroaster, religious prophet—teaches salvation by faith in one god of light who triumphs over evil
Alexander the Great destroys Persi... Empire and enables Greek cultu... to spread: science and philosop... flourish: seventy cities founded including Alexandria in Egypt, centre of arts and sciences until fall of Roman Empire
First appearance of cuneiform writing
Hammurabi, King of Babylon, passes great Code of Law
Phoenicians "Missionaries of Civilization"
Ashurbanipal, Assyrian king, collects library of 20,000 tablets
Persian Empire
Maths: invention of sexagesimal system which divides circle into 360 degrees, a degree into 60 minutes, and a minute into 60 seconds
Sailed as far afield as Spain, Britain and West Africa and were masters of Mediterranean trade
Invented 22-consonant alphabet
Carthage founded
From Indus to Nile
Cyrus, founder of Persian Empire, adopts God of Light as supreme deity: Zoroastrianism becomes state religion
Euclid, "father of geometry"
Old Kingdom
Middle Kingdom
New Kingdom
Decline of Egypt
Archimedes develops joint study of mathematics and physics
First use of irrigation in Nile Valley
Great age of architecture and literature
Writing of hieroglyphs on papyrus reed
Science of building continues to develop: Temples at Thebes
Conquered by Assyrians, but architecture, science and medicine continue to flourish
Lydians invent coinage
First application of maths to large-scale building (Pyramids at Gizeh)
Early Hebrews
Kingdoms of Israel and Judah
Jews under Foreign Rule
First division of time into Solar Years
Abraham, founder of Jewish Nation
Egyptian captivity
Moses
Exodus from Egypt
Ten Commandments
David and Solomon rule at Jerusalem
Growth of Judaism: Belief in One God, Creator and Judge, and his Elect People
Jerusalem destroyed
Babylonian captivity
Great Prophets: Isaiah and Jeremiah
Most of Old Testament written
Jesu... Chris... born
EUROPE
GREEK
WESTERN
AEGEAN
ROMAN
BYZANTINE
Greek Settlements
Greek City States
Golden Age
Hellenistic Empire
Indo-Europeans invade from north, absorb Aegean culture
Growth of city states—politically divided, culturally united—Sparta, Corinth, Athens, Thebes
Birth of modern philosophy science and literature. Growth of Athenian democracy
Decline of Athens, rise of Macedon, spread of Greek civilization to Near and Middle East in wake of Alexander the Great's armies
Rome conquers Greece
Aegean Civilization
Centred on Crete. Prosperity based on Mediterranean trade. Contact with Near East and Europe. Spread to Mycenea and Greek States
Siege of Troy in Asia Minor
Homer's Iliad and Odyssey composed
Tragedies of Aeschylus and Sophocles
Roman
Dorians invade Greece
First Olympiad
Pericles
Palace at Knossos—evidence of high standard of art: sculptures and wall paintings
Solon's Laws
Parthenon built
Thucydides
Socrates
Alexander the Great
Plato
Aristotle
Caesar conquers Gaul and invades Britain
Greeks learn alphabet from Phoenicians
Pythagoras's Law of Maths
Use of hieroglyphic writing
Linear script invented thus speeding the process of writing
Invasions of Italy
Roman Republic
Greeks found city states in Italy
Etruscans in Rome
Kings expelled and Republic established
Rome conquers Italy and Mediterranean
Punic wars: Rome defeats Carthage
Golden Age of literature and architecture
Cicero
Virg...
Development in copper and bronze working
Fall of Crete
Founding of Rome
Struggle for political power between Patricians and Plebeians—constitutional experiments
MIDDLE EAST
INDIAN
MUSLIM
BRITISH
INDEPENDENCE
Indus Valley Civilization
Aryan Invasions
Early Hindu Civilization
Mauryan Dynasty
Dravidians, whose descendants still live in Southern India, establish first city communities in Indus Valley, introduce irrigation schemes, develop pottery and evolve a well ordered system of government
Aryans from north-west conquer original Dravidians, settle and intermarry
Growth of Hindu religion—belief in all pervading World Soul (Brahman): salvation through knowledge: continuous rebirth
Gautama, originally a Hindu, founds Buddhism—religion of personal salvation through withdrawal, meditation and strict morality. Aim is "Nirvana," a peace beyond this world
All India, except for the far south, is first unified
Ashoka, greatest of Mauryan emperors, establishes Buddhism over most of India, sends missionaries to Syria, Ceylon, Tibet. Reign of peace and reform: education endowed roads and hospitals built
Early Hindus produce a vigorous literature of epic poems and religious hymns: the "Rig-Veda"—collection of early sacrificial hymns
First trade contacts with river civilizations in Mesopotamia
Upanishads—collection of Hindu teachings
Caste system develops—from Brahmans (priests) to Shudras (labourers)
The Mahabhara... great epic poem composed
FAR EAST
CHINESE
MONGOL
JAPANESE
Ancient China
Shang Dynasty
Chou Dynasty
Ch'in Dynasty
Han
Origins of Chinese civilization, oldest living civilization in the world, lie in Yellow River valley where so-called Sage Kings are credited with the development of agriculture, medicine, river conservancy
Yellow River civilization expands to territories north and south of Yellow River
Rule of this dynasty extends as far as the Yangtze River. Irrigation works, dams and canals built, but progress is broken by occasional periods of revolt and disunity, and central control is never strong
Loose central control of Chou Dynasty replaced by strong central government
Schools and colleges founded for education of ruling classes
Lunar calendar first devised
This period produced skilful bronze, ivory and jade works, and some great lyrical poetry
Golden Age of philosophy:
No alphabet, but complicated form of character writing evolved
Lao Tse, legendary founder of Taoism, teaches belief in the harmony and goodness of Nature
Great Wall of China built to end constant invasions from the north
Silk first manufactured
Confucius teaches practical lessons of wise and righteous behaviour in society
Confucianism grows in influence and becomes State religion
Bronze used for making vessels
THE AMERICAS
PRE-COLUMBIAN
COLONIAL
S. AND CENT. AMERICA
U.S.A.
CANADA
Pre-Columbian Period
Several waves of migration from Asia peopled the American continent over 20,000 years ago.
Olmec Indian civilization Makers of mosaics and jewels.
First great Mexican civilization, the Maya. Developed heiroglyphic writing, arithmetical systems, calendar, expressionist art
Teotihuacán: centre of important civilization in the valley of Mexico Pyramid of the Sun Pyramid of the Moon
La Venta, major settlement of Olmec Indians
First Zapotec Indian civilization Representation of gods in guise of clay urns. Main builders of mountaintop city of Monte Albán Lasted till 14th c. A.D.

ARAB EMPIRE A.D. 732

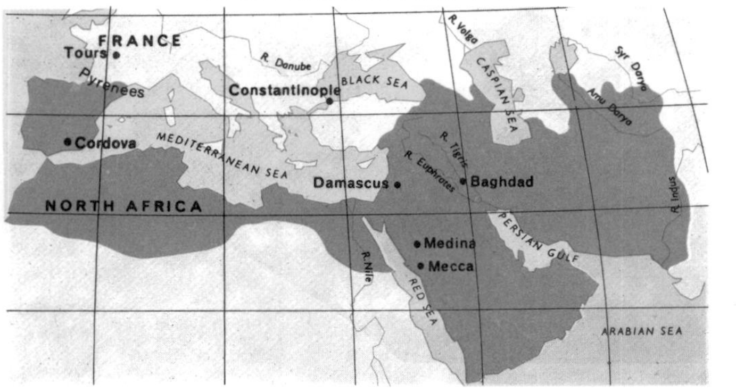

INDIA AND CHINA A.D. 300-900

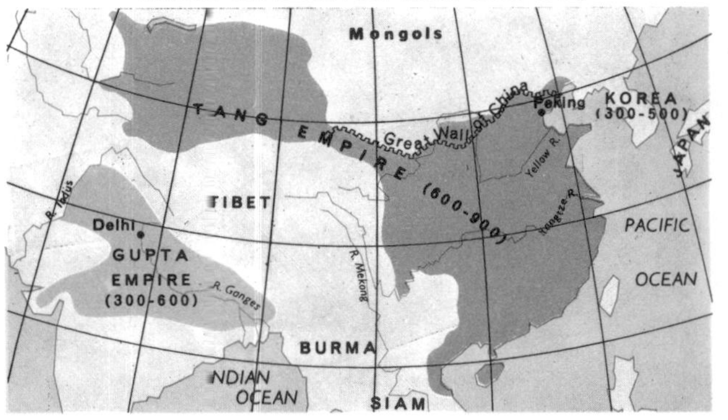

Alexander the Great's victories over the Persian Empire carried Greek culture to the Near and Middle East. But it was spread still farther by the Romans, who conquered Greece and became masters of the Mediterranean and much of Europe. The Romans excelled as administrators. They created an enlightened and impartial system of law, an international language, imposing architecture, and a network of roads. The Roman Empire was divided into East and West in the 4th century A.D., but although the Western Empire disintegrated in the following century, the Eastern or Byzantine Empire, with Constantinople as its capital, resisted the onslaught of the Arabs and the Turks for nearly ten centuries, and spread its religion and culture to Bulgaria and Russia.

Meanwhile Christianity penetrated central Europe, the Church becoming responsible for the preservation of knowledge inherited from the past. The rebirth of classical learning during the Renaissance started a scientific and artistic revolution. Protestantism broke the religious supremacy of the Church of Rome. New lands were discovered, and European ideas spread to many parts of the world. The 19th century saw a great industrial revolution, brought about by the advance of science and technology and an unprecedented growth in population.

MIDDLE EAST—INDIA

Indian history is a record of constant invasions from the north-west, which brought contacts with foreign civilizations and an influx of alien races and religions. Until recently, political unity has never lasted long. The formative influences on Indian thought, art and society have been religious. India has produced many outstanding spiritual leaders from Buddha to Gandhi.

The ancient city civilization of the Indus Valley was destroyed by Aryan invaders, who intermingled with the original inhabitants and evolved the Hindu religion. In the 6th century B.C. Buddhism branched off from the main stream of Hinduism but made little impact until the 3rd century B.C., when Asoka, the greatest of the emperors of the Mauryan dynasty, patronized it, encouraged its adoption by the people and sent Buddhist missionaries to Burma and Ceylon. After Asoka's death came a revival of Hinduism in India. Buddhism rapidly lost its hold there, but spread to China, where it was widely accepted.

Hindu culture saw its golden age under the Gupta dynasty in the 3rd century A.D., when mathematics, astronomy, scholarship and architecture made great forward strides.

In the 10th century A.D., waves of Muhammadan invaders settled in India, and so initiated the long rivalry between Hindu and Muslim. In the 16th century new invaders, the Moguls, established Muhammadan rule over most of India. They produced great architecture, such as the Taj Mahal, and gave India many able and enlightened rulers. By the beginning of the 18th century the Mogul Empire had declined, and European powers were fighting one another for supremacy in the Indian sub-continent. Britain emerged from this struggle, to rule until 1947, when India and Pakistan became autonomous nations.

FAR EAST—CHINA

For centuries China was, geographically, almost inaccessible, and consequently its civilization developed in relative isolation. It absorbed its many invaders, and adapted their ideas to its own traditional culture.

The Chinese, the oldest living civilization, was more than once further advanced and more vigorous than other civilizations. It was practical and humanist, rather than religious. Originating in the Yellow River Valley, it spread north and south, reaching its first golden age in the 6th and 5th centuries B.C. under the Chou Dynasty. In this period the somewhat legendary Lao Tse founded Taoism. Later, under the same dynasty, Confucius taught a more active way of wise and righteous living through knowledge and adherence to a strict moral code. Confucianism was developed by Mencius, and became the official state religion under the Han Dynasty 2,000 years ago. The Han Emperors were the first rulers in the world to use a Civil Service (Mandarin class), entry into which was by competitive examination. Their reforms were made possible by the work of their predecessors, the Ch'in Dynasty, who imposed a large measure of central control for the first time, and built the Great Wall for protection against invasion from the north.

Buddhism spread from India to China during the 1st century A.D. It made an immediate appeal to the Chinese who, in turn, passed its teaching on to Korea and Japan.

After a period of disorder, and invasion by the Huns and Tartars, Chinese culture and scholarship flowered again, under the Tang and Sung Dynasties. Mongol invasions interrupted this golden age, but Kublai Khan, grandson of Ghengis Khan and the most enlightened and progressive of the Mongol Emperors, encouraged contact with the outside world. Under the Ming Dynasty, which drove out the Mongol Dynasty, the richness and variety of Chinese life became the envy of foreign traders, travellers and missionaries. But their successors, the Manchus, made a deliberate attempt to isolate China. This led to internal stagnation and, after the "Boxer Rebellion" in 1900, ended in the collapse of Imperial China. Sun-Yat-Sen proclaimed a republic in 1912, and after nearly forty years of almost continual civil strife and of war with Japan, the communists won control in 1949.

THE AMERICAS

No great early Indian civilization is known in North America. In Central and South America many Indian civilizations succeeded one another, as shown in the chart. All were notable for their architecture and art. The last of them, the Aztec and the Inca, were overthrown in the early 16th century by the Spaniards, who then divided the country between themselves and the Portuguese and imposed the Roman Catholic religion on the Indians. From the end of the 15th century North America and parts of South America were gradually colonized by other Europeans, who took with them their own civilization. From subsequent wars and revolutions, Canada, the United States, and the countries of Central and South America emerged as they are today.

A.D. 100 · 200 · 300 · 400 · 500 · 600 · 700 · 800 · 900 · 1000 · 1100 · 1200 · 1300 · 1400 · 1500 · 1600 · 1700 · 1800 · 1900

Roman Palestine · **Neo-Persian Empire** · **Arab-Muslim Civilization in Near East and Spain** · **Ottoman Empire** · **Arab Nationalism Modern Palestine** · **Modern Turkey**

- Roman supremacy over Near East
- • Fall of Jerusalem and dispersal of the Jews
- New Testament written
- • Galen. Greek doctor leading medical authority till the 16th century
- • Claudius Ptolemy, of Alexandria, constructs first map on assumption that world is spherical in shape
- Monasticism originates in Near East and spreads to Europe
- Sassanians rule from Indus to Mediterranean. Zoroastrianism revived as state religion
- • Chosroes I successfully defies Roman Empire and rules over a highly developed society until conquered by the Arabs: grants toleration for Christians
- • Muhammad at Mecca
- • Qurân edited
- Islam, influenced by Judaism, teaches, "There is no god but Allah, and Muhammad is His Prophet." Brotherhood of all Muslims: Caliphs extend militant Islam to Indus and Pyrenees but are checked in France and at Constantinople
- Arab civilization at Baghdad, Damascus and Cordova. Knowledge of ancient cultures preserved
- Study of mathematics, astronomy, alchemy and geography flourishes
- Paper and block printing introduced from China
- Islam invades India, brings back Indian numerals to Near East and Europe
- • Averroes: commentaries on Plato and Aristotle
- • Avicenna: philosopher, one of the world's greatest teachers of medicine
- • Batuta: traveller and explorer, stimulates study of geography
- Turks, a Central Asian warrior race, embrace Islam, take over Arab Empire, rule from Belgrade to Persian Gulf, block Western trade with Far East
- • Seljuk Turks capture Baghdad, fight Crusaders for possession of Holy Land
- • Arabs expelled from Spain
- • Constantinople captured from Greeks
- • Suleiman the Magnificent—his reign marks height of Ottoman Empire's power
- • Battle of Lepanto breaks Turkish sea-power in Mediterranean
- Islam continues to dominate Near East but wanes in Europe
- • Last unsuccessful siege of Vienna marks Islam's final attempt to conquer Europe
- Series of Balkan revolts lead to break-up of Empire
- From Morocco to Persia—Western influence grows, then declines
- • Arab League founded
- • Foundation of new state of Israel
- • Turkish Republic founded by Kemal Atatürk

Early Christian Era · **Empire** · **Decline and Fall** · **Dark Ages** · **High Middle Ages** · **Eastern Roman Empire Byzantine Civilization** · **Renaissance and Reformation** · **Age of Reason, Industrialism and Socialism**

- Despite persecution Christianity steadily grows
- Travels of St. Paul
- "Pax Romana" from Spain to Persia. Creation of advanced system of law and administration
- Augustus, first Emperor
- • Marcus Aurelius
- Spread of Greco-Roman culture throughout Roman Empire. Romans surpass Greeks in architectural achievements
- • Colosseum built
- Gradual military and economic decline in Western part of Empire
- • Division into Western and Eastern Empires
- • Constantine recognizes Christianity
- • St. Augustine writes "City of God"
- *Missions:* • St. Patrick, Ireland • St. Columba, Scotland • St. Augustine, England • St. Boniface, Germany
- Greek culture, Roman government. Greek Orthodox Church breaks with Roman Papacy. Byzantine Empire defends East against Turks, and its religion and culture penetrate into Russia and Balkans
- • Justinian codifies Roman Law and builds St. Sophia
- Art and architecture of great brilliance—use of mosaics
- • Separation of Western and Eastern Churches
- Fall of Constantinople •
- Civilization rests on concept of "Christendom" and the unity of Europe—Holy Roman Empire. Pope and Emperor contest leadership. The Church serves as guardian of culture. Outlook spiritual rather than material
- • Revival of idea of one unified Empire by Charlemagne
- Growth of monastic orders and foundation of numerous monasteries: Benedictines and Cistercians
- Crusades
- *Friars:* Franciscans and Dominicans
- *Gothic Cathedrals:* • Chartres • Rheims
- *Foundation of Universities:* • Bologna • Paris • Oxford
- • Giotto • Dante • Chaucer
- Intellectual and artistic revolution. Revived interest in classical knowledge stimulates progress in art, literature, science and philosophy
- • First printing press
- Luther and Calvin break away from the Church of Rome
- • Erasmus
- • van Eyck • Brunelleschi • Michelangelo
- *Expansion of Europe:* • Columbus in West Indies • Vasco da Gama in Africa and India • Cortez in Mexico • Cook in Pacific • Puritans in North America
- Scientific discoveries transform man's understanding of Universe and undermine religious creeds. Industrial revolution causes urbanization, creates new wealth and gives West political and economic hegemony. Political power and education no longer confined to upper classes.
- • William Harvey, physician, discovers circulation of blood
- • Galileo's telescope and laws of motion
- • Newton's law of gravity
- • Darwin's law of Evolution
- • Faraday, chemist and pioneer of electro-magnetism
- • Steel first made by Bessemer
- • Watt's steam engine
- • Einstein's Theory of Relativity
- • Nuclear fission
- Exploration of Space begins
- *Philosophers:* • Descartes • Locke • Kant • Rousseau • Marx
- • French Revolution
- • Freud's psychology
- • Russian Revolution
- Classicism and Romanticism in the Arts
- Painting: • Rembrandt • Hogarth • Goya • Turner • v. Gogh — Modern Art: • Picasso
- Literature: • Shakespeare • Voltaire • Goethe • Balzac • Tolstoy • J. Joyce
- Music: • Bach • Beethoven • Chopin • Verdi • Stravinsky

Independent States · **Gupta Dynasty** · **Rival States** · **Mohammedan Invasions and Settlements** · **Mogul Empire** · **British Rule** · **Independence**

- Mauryan Empire crumbles under foreign invaders who import Greek and Persian influences. In its place arise a number of short-lived kingdoms
- Hinduism asserts itself as a unifying factor in this period of political disunity
- Buddhism reaches China
- This dynasty once again unifies much of India and marks golden age of Hindu literature, art and science
- Sanskrit becomes universal literary language
- Astronomy: Theory of rotation of earth discovered by Hindus
- Architecture: shrines, temples and caves
- Maths—decimal system and use of zero evolved, later brought to Europe by Arabs
- • Kalidasa—poet and dramatist
- Gupta Empire breaks up under impact of Hun and early Arab invasions into a number of Hindu kingdoms
- Buddhism progressively disappears from India, its country of origin, but is dominant in the religion and culture of Burma, Siam, Java and Ceylon
- Militant Muslim invaders overrun Hindu kingdoms and for first time settle in India, thus beginning the bitter Muslim-Hindu rivalry. Hinduism in turn becomes more militant
- Muslim rule spreads over most of north India and the Deccan
- • First Muslim dynasty established at Delhi
- Muslim architecture introduced
- Mogul rulers (Muslim) unite most of India, restore law and order
- • Babur founds Mogul empire
- • Akbar seeks toleration for all religions. Encourages trade, arts and sciences. Most brilliant period in Muslim India
- • Jesuits welcomed
- • Taj Mahal built
- Rivalry between Portuguese, Dutch, French and British traders
- • Britain defeats France in Seven Years War: influence of East India Company supreme
- • Indian Mutiny
- India under British Crown, law and order strengthened, roads and railways built, currency unified
- Gandhi leads independence movement through passive resistance
- • Former Indian Empire attains independence as India and Pakistan

Dynasty · **Dark Ages** · **Tang Dynasty** · **Sung Dynasty** · **Mongols** · **Ming Dynasty** · **Manchu Dynasty** · **Republic**

- Policy of strengthening central control continues. Hans are first to create a permanent Civil Service (Mandarin class)
- Buddhism comes from India
- First use of paper
- Period of disorder
- Hun and Tartar invasions and disappearance of central control
- Rapid spread of Buddhism
- Central control and a high degree of unity re-established Golden Age of learning, science and art. Traders and scholars make contact with India and Arab countries
- • Academy of Letters founded
- Block printing, magnetic compass, gunpowder invented
- Manufacture of porcelain perfected
- Landscape, animal, flower and bird painting thrives
- • Imperial Academy of Painting founded
- Neo-Confucianism of Chu Hsi
- China becomes part of Mongol Empire. Kublai Khan encourages trade with outside world. Fails to conquer Japan and Java
- • Kublai Khan visited by Marco Polo
- Mings drive out Mongols, restore Confucianism and Mandarin class
- Renaissance of scholarship and painting
- • Ming Code of Law
- • Jesuit missionaries
- The Manchus from Manchuria oust the Mings and found a new dynasty. They extend Chinese overlordship to Korea, Mongolia, Indo-China and attempt to exclude foreigners from China
- European powers seek to open up China
- • The anti-European Boxer Rising fails
- • Revolution of Sun-Yat-Sen. Collapse of Manchus and end of Imperial China
- • Communist Revolution

Japanese

- Japan remains a closed community until 5th century A.D.; its earlier history is legendary
- Buddhism is introduced from China via Korea, and with it Chinese writing
- Chinese culture penetrates into Japan and exists side by side with ancient Japanese feudal and religious customs
- Painting, architecture and landscape gardening flourish
- • Christianity introduced by Francis Xavier
- Christianity exterminated, relations with outside world severed
- • Com. Perry, U.S. Navy, forces Japan to reopen communication with outside world
- Japan becomes modern, industrial state

Pre-Columbian Period · **Colonial Period** · **South and Central America** · **U.S.A.** · **Canada**

- • Period of authentic artistic splendour. Elaborate geometricism Purely religious inspiration
- • Tiahuanaco Indian civilization in Bolivia
- • Height of Mayan civilization at Chichen Itzá, Yucatán. Knowledge of arithmetic, astronomy and farming grows
- • Toltec Indians take over Teotihuacán. Building of superb cities such as Tula. Temple of the Plumed Serpent
- Aztec Indian civilization. Military people who, under Montezuma in early 16th c. dominated Mexico
- • Incas rule from Colombia to N.Chile. Efficient political system. Temple of the Sun at Cuzco
- • Columbus in W. Indies
- • Cabot in Labrador and N. America
- • Portuguese in Brazil
- • Cortez in Mexico
- • Pizarro in Peru
- • Slave Trade begins
- • English in Newfoundland and Virginia
- • Pilgrim Fathers
- • Cartier to St. Lawrence
- • French in Canada
- • Independence generally throughout 19th c.
- • Washington President
- • Monroe Doctrine
- • B. Franklin
- • Boston Tea Party
- E. A. Poe
- • Declaration of Independence
- Morse
- • Lincoln frees slaves: Civil War
- Literature: Mark Twain, Emerson, Thoreau, Longfellow, Walt Whitman
- • Stock Exchange collapses. Roosevelt New Deal
- • First satellite and astronauts
- Kennedy assassinated
- Battle of Quebec
- • Treaty of Paris
- • Upper and Lower Canada formed
- • Canada united
- • Dominion established
- • St. Lawrence Seaway opened

RELIGIONS—
THEIR ORIGINS AND ADHERENTS

In him we live, and move, and have our being — ACTS 17

RELIGION knows neither frontiers nor geographical barriers. With the exception of tribal religions which, though differing from one another in form and ritual, all seek to explain the mystery of life by insisting that Nature is animated by spirits, most religions have, for one reason or another, spread beyond the lands of their origins.

JUDAISM, which dates back to Moses in the 13th century B.C., when even the most advanced societies still worshipped a multiplicity of gods, is uncompromisingly monotheistic. After its

clash with Imperial Rome and the destruction of Jerusalem in A.D. 70 and 135, the Jews were expelled from the Holy Land, and a Jewish state was not again established in Palestine until 1948—almost 2,000 years later—although the majority of adherents of Judaism remain scattered throughout the world.

HINDUISM, the age-old religion of India, which honours many gods and goddesses—all of whom, however, are regarded as manifestations of the one divine spirit, Brahman—introduced into religious thinking the concept that spiritual peace and happiness can be attained only through physical and mental discipline (*yoga*—yoke). Its rigid caste divisions have been the target of innumerable reformers—among them men like Gandhi, Tagore and Bhave.

BUDDHISM, an offshoot of Hinduism, was founded by Gautama (563-483 B.C.) in North India and insists on rigid moral and

spiritual discipline in order to attain Nirvana, a condition where *karma* (deeds) have perished, the cycle of rebirth on earth has ceased, and supreme peace is attained. It spread widely throughout Asia, developing many local variations of philosophy, form and practice. In Japan, ZEN (meditation) Buddhism teaches enlightenment, while elsewhere many Buddhist teachers hold that salvation for all is possible only through the grace of Buddhas and *Bodhisattvas* (Beings of Enlightenment).

In China, from the 1st century A.D. onwards, Buddhism became mingled with the already established religions of CONFUCIANISM and TAOISM. Confucius' philosophy, which was of little influence in his own lifetime (551-479 B.C.), had been elaborated by subsequent generations of scholars both to provide a moral basis for the political structure of Imperial China and to embrace the hallowed forms of ancestor worship which

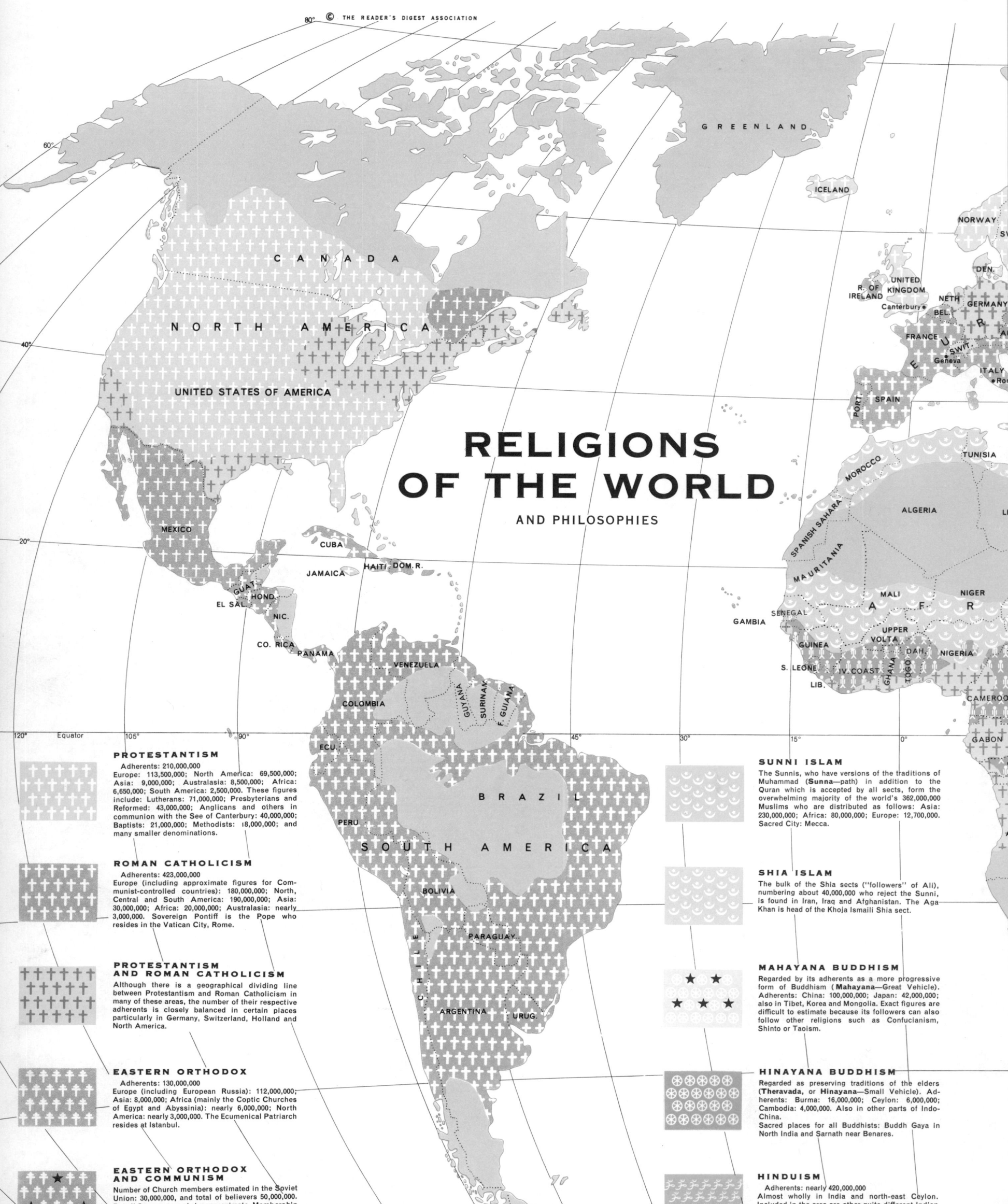

RELIGIONS OF THE WORLD
AND PHILOSOPHIES

PROTESTANTISM
Adherents: 210,000,000
Europe: 113,500,000; North America: 69,500,000; Asia: 9,000,000; Australasia: 8,500,000; Africa: 6,650,000; South America: 2,500,000. These figures include: Lutherans: 71,000,000; Presbyterians and Reformed: 43,000,000; Anglicans and others in communion with the See of Canterbury: 40,000,000; Baptists: 21,000,000; Methodists: 18,000,000; and many smaller denominations.

ROMAN CATHOLICISM
Adherents: 423,000,000
Europe (including approximate figures for Communist-controlled countries): 180,000,000; North, Central and South America: 190,000,000; Asia: 30,000,000; Africa: 20,000,000; Australasia: nearly 3,000,000. Sovereign Pontiff is the Pope who resides in the Vatican City, Rome.

PROTESTANTISM AND ROMAN CATHOLICISM
Although there is a geographical dividing line between Protestantism and Roman Catholicism in many of these areas, the number of their respective adherents is closely balanced in certain places particularly in Germany, Switzerland, Holland and North America.

EASTERN ORTHODOX
Adherents: 130,000,000
Europe (including European Russia): 112,000,000; Asia: 8,000,000; Africa (mainly the Coptic Churches of Egypt and Abyssinia): nearly 6,000,000; North America: nearly 3,000,000. The Ecumenical Patriarch resides at Istanbul.

EASTERN ORTHODOX AND COMMUNISM
Number of Church members estimated in the Soviet Union: 30,000,000, and total of believers 50,000,000. But all figures can only be approximate. Membership of Communist Party—the only party permitted—in the Soviet Union: 9,000,000. Membership is gained by election.

SUNNI ISLAM
The Sunnis, who have versions of the traditions of Muhammad (**Sunna**—path) in addition to the Quran which is accepted by all sects, form the overwhelming majority of the world's 362,000,000 Muslims who are distributed as follows: Asia: 230,000,000; Africa: 80,000,000; Europe: 12,700,000. Sacred City: Mecca.

SHIA ISLAM
The bulk of the Shia sects ("followers" of Ali), numbering about 40,000,000 who reject the Sunni, is found in Iran, Iraq and Afghanistan. The Aga Khan is head of the Khoja Ismaili Shia sect.

MAHAYANA BUDDHISM
Regarded by its adherents as a more progressive form of Buddhism (**Mahayana**—Great Vehicle). Adherents: China: 100,000,000; Japan: 42,000,000; also in Tibet, Korea and Mongolia. Exact figures are difficult to estimate because its followers can also follow other religions such as Confucianism, Shinto or Taoism.

HINAYANA BUDDHISM
Regarded as preserving traditions of the elders (**Theravada**, or **Hinayana**—Small Vehicle). Adherents: Burma: 16,000,000; Ceylon: 6,000,000; Cambodia: 4,000,000. Also in other parts of Indo-China.
Sacred places for all Buddhists: Buddh Gaya in North India and Sarnath near Benares.

HINDUISM
Adherents: nearly 420,000,000
Almost wholly in India and north-east Ceylon. Included in the area are other quite different Indian religions—Muslims: 54,000,000; Sikhs: 9,000,000; Jains: 2,300,000; Parsis: 112,000. Sacred Places: Benares, Amritsar, Mt. Abu, Bombay.

130

have always been practised in China: Taoism, based on the teachings of Lao Tse in the 6th century B.C., taught a quietist religion of living in the way (*tao*) of nature.

In Japan, from the 6th century A.D. onwards, Buddhism became mingled with the ancient religion of SHINTO, a nature worship of a multiplicity of deities honoured at shrines like that of Amaterasu, the Sun Goddess, at Ise, and many Japanese still attend the places of worship of both faiths.

One of the most active proselytizing faiths in the history of religion, ISLAM, was carried across Asia and Africa; it swept round the southern shores of the Mediterranean, crossed the Straits of Gibraltar into Spain and even penetrated into France after the death of its founder, Muhammad (A.D. 570-632). Almost a thousand years later, Islamic power penetrated far into Central Europe up to the walls of Vienna, and when the tide eventually

receded, it left behind, particularly in the Balkans, innumerable islands of Muslim communities.

The religion with the largest number of adherents and the most pronounced missionary zeal in the world today is CHRISTIANITY. It was founded in the 1st century A.D. by Jesus of Nazareth, who was accepted as the Christ, the Messiah or Anointed One, by his disciples who were then called Christians. His Crucifixion in Jerusalem and his Resurrection furnished the main articles of faith and the Symbol of the Cross.

Christianity spread quickly through the Roman Empire, where it became the official religion in the 4th century A.D., with the Pope in Rome—the successor of St. Peter, Christ's chief disciple—widely recognized as the supreme authority in a rapidly emerging Church hierarchy. The Eastern Church, which began in the Holy Land before there were any Christians in

Rome, rejected papal authority in the 11th century A.D.; and the Eastern Orthodox Church—comprising the historical patriarchal sees of Jerusalem, Antioch, Alexandria and Constantinople, to which was later added the patriarchate of Moscow (the largest today)—continued as a federation of mutually independent churches, standing in full communion with one another and united as equals. The ancient Armenian Jacobite, Syrian, Indian, and Coptic Abyssinian and Egyptian Churches are known, however, as the Separated Churches of the East.

A further rupture in Christian unity came in the 16th century with the Reformation movements of Protestantism, and Protestantism itself is now divided into many denominations. But the settlement of new continents has carried Christianity in one form or another to almost all parts of the world, and strong movements for Christian reunion are now in force.

WINKEL'S 'TRIPEL' PROJECTION

CHINESE RELIGIONS AND COMMUNISM

Confucianism and Taoism: Adherents: about 300,000,000 mainly in China and Asian countries on its borders. Sacred City: Peking.
Buddhism: adherents: 100,000,000. Exact figures unascertainable because many Chinese follow all three religions.
Communism: party membership (no other party permitted): about 14,000,000. Membership granted as an honour. Party militantly anti-religious.

SHINTO AND BUDDHISM

Shinto: adherents: 40,000,000 almost exclusively in Japan. Sacred places: Shrine of Amaterasu the Sun Goddess, at Ise.
Buddhism: adherents in Japan: 42,000,000. Exact figures unascertainable because many Japanese follow both faiths.

TRIBAL RELIGIONS

Practised by about 100,000,000. Mainly in Africa, and also among Australian Aborigines, North, South and Central American Indians and primitive communities in Burma, India, Mongolia, Siberia and Indonesia.

JUDAISM

Adherents: 12,000,000
Israel: nearly 2,000,000; U.S.A.: 5,600,000; U.S.S.R.: nearly 3,000,000; Europe (excluding European Russia): 1,250,000 (between five and six million Jews perished during the Second World War); Asia: nearly 2,000,000. Sacred City: Jerusalem.

TOO THINLY POPULATED

No large places of worship although there may be missionary activity in areas where there are tribal religions.

MOVEMENTS OF THE HEBREWS IN OLD TESTAMENT TIMES

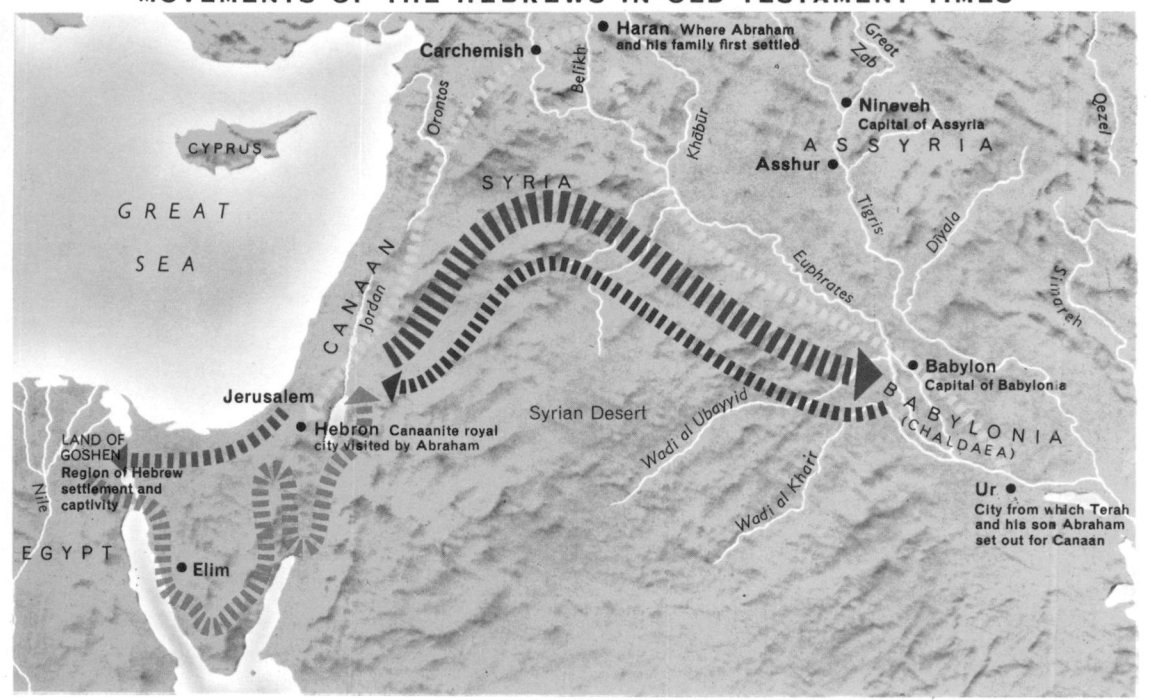

`c. 2000 B.C.` Abraham, from Ur of the Chaldaeans, enters the land of Canaan in answer to God's call	`c. 1220 B.C.` (?) Exodus from Egypt of Hebrew clans under Moses and the wanderings in the wilderness
18th cent. B.C. Increased Semitic migration into Egypt. Establishment of Hyksos rule	597 B.C. Beginning of Jewish exile in Babylon
	After 539 B.C. Return of many Jews to the Holy Land after liberation by Cyrus

INVASIONS OF THE HOLY LAND

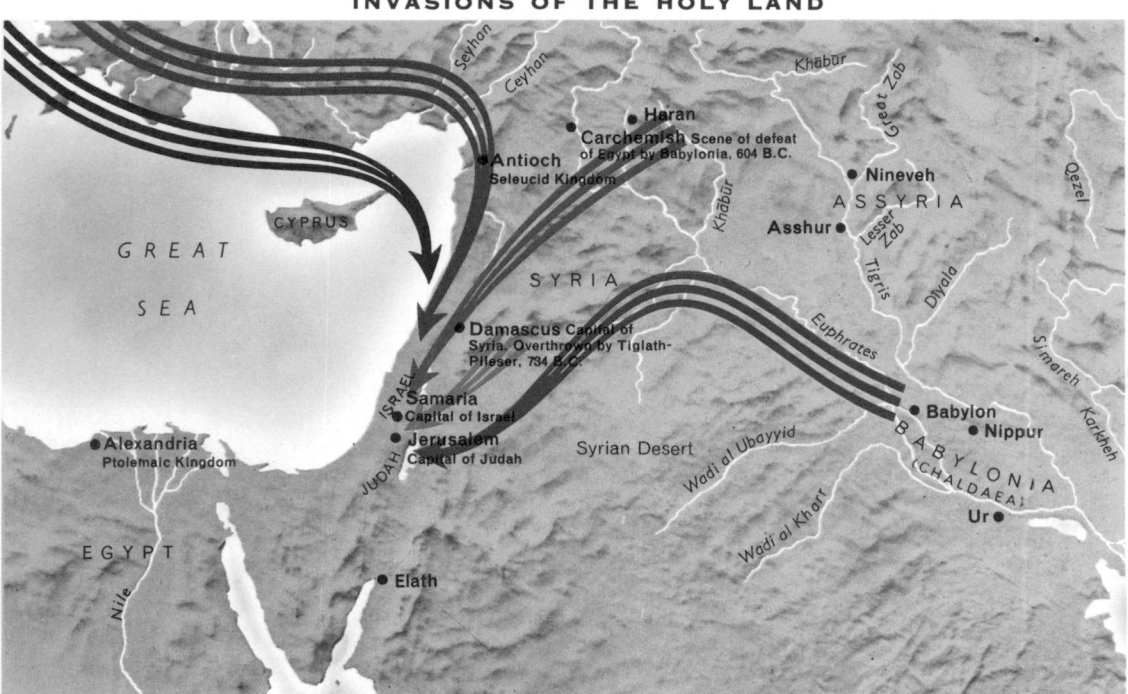

842 B.C. Israel engaged in disastrous war with Syria	597 B.C. Siege of Jerusalem by Nebuchadrezzar and first deportation of Jews to Babylon. 586 B.C. Fall of Jerusalem and second deportation
Assyrian invasions under Tiglath-Pileser III (745 B.C.), Sargon II (fall of Samaria, 721 B.C.), and Sennacherib (701 B.C. Siege of Jerusalem)	198 B.C. Palestine falls to the Seleucidae. Rebellion of Jews under Judas Maccabaeus. 166 B.C., against: Antiochus IV of Antioch
	63 B.C. Pompey occupies Jerusalem. Thereafter Palestine becomes part of Roman province of Syria

THE JOURNEYS OF SAINT PAUL

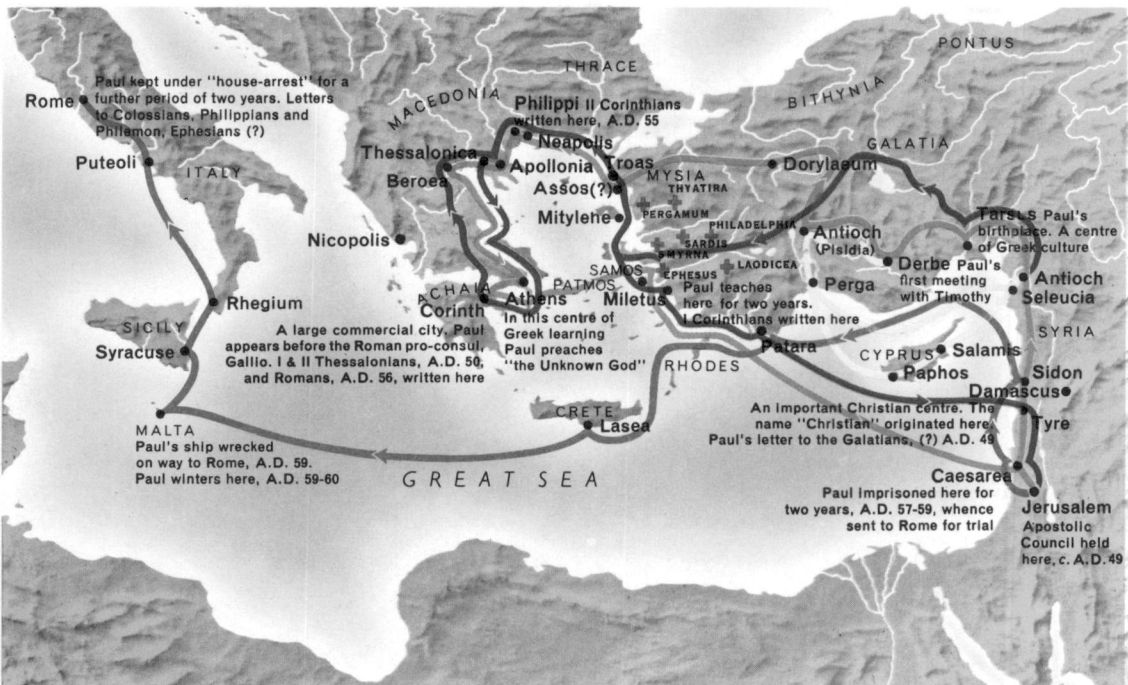

The first missionary journey to Cyprus and southern Asia Minor. Paul is accompanied by Barnabas and John Mark as far as Perga in Pamphylia. Paul's method was to address the local Jews first, whose reaction was invariably hostile. Thereupon he would turn to the Gentiles	The third missionary journey took Paul through Asia Minor and Greece again. He remained two years at Ephesus, finally going up to Jerusalem in A.D. 56
	Paul's journey to Rome, where he was kept in confinement in his own house for two more years. But the apostle seems finally to have been acquitted
The second missionary journey with Silas through Asia Minor and Greece. This seems to have lasted some years, and included a two years stay at Corinth	 The seven churches of Asia Minor

BIBLE LANDS

And ye shall be my witnesses both in Jerusalem, and in all Judaea and Samaria, and unto the uttermost part of the earth —ACTS 1

THE OLD TESTAMENT

THE Old Testament relates the history of the Hebrew people during some 2,000 years. Their story begins with the migration from the city of Ur, in ancient Chaldaea, of a band of Semites led by Abraham in response to a divine call. Abraham, with his family, settled for a time at Haran in northern Syria, but later, about 2000 B.C., moved south into Canaan. Hebrew clans subsequently entered Egypt, and remained there for an unknown period.

The Exodus from Egypt under the leadership of Moses and the wanderings in the wilderness subsequently led them to the Promised Land—"a land flowing with milk and honey." Here eventually they united to form a nation under King Saul and his successors, David and Solomon; but with the division of the kingdom which followed Solomon's death they found themselves surrounded by powerful and hostile neighbours. In this precarious situation the prophets sought to teach the people that only religious purity, social righteousness and political neutrality would save them from extinction. Nevertheless a series of foreign invasions culminated in the destruction of Jerusalem in 586 B.C., when a large part of the nation was carried off in captivity to Babylon.

In 539 B.C. Babylon itself was captured by the Persian King Cyrus, who gave permission to the exiled Jews to return to their native land. A small number did so, and began to rebuild the Temple and with it the national life.

But the days of political independence were over. Persian rule gave way to Greek, and when Antiochus IV attempted to unite the heterogeneous elements of his realm on the basis of a common Hellenistic culture and religion, the Jews rebelled under the intrepid and not unsuccessful leadership of Judas Maccabaeus. The priest-kingdom of his descendents, however, succumbed in 63 B.C. to yet another foreign invader—Pompey and his Roman legions.

The troubled history and prolonged sufferings of the Jewish people convinced them, in the end, that their sole hope lay in God, who, in his own good time, they believed, would intervene in the course of world events by sending a Messianic king under whom they would at last find deliverance.

THE NEW TESTAMENT

The New Testament covers a period of some 60 years, beginning with the birth of Jesus in Bethlehem, the true date of which is probably about 4 B.C. Apart from the nativity stories and a single incident in Jesus' youth, the Gospels deal with a period of no more than three years, from the opening of His public ministry in Galilee to His death in Jerusalem at the hands of the Romans. The events leading up to the crucifixion and Christ's subsequent resurrection "on the third day" are recorded in detail, for these constituted the essence of the earliest Christian preaching and teaching.

From the moment of the descent of the Holy Spirit at the time of the Jewish feast of Pentecost, Jesus' followers set about the dangerous work of proclaiming the Christian message and baptizing converts—at first Jews, but later also Gentiles—into the "New Israel," the Church. In this work, Saul of Tarsus—St. Paul—himself a converted Pharisee, took the lead.

Paul's own mission was to the Gentile world, and his many journeys took him through Asia Minor to Greece and eventually to Rome itself. Of his death the New Testament makes no mention, but tradition awards him the martyr's crown.

In spite of persecution by the Romans and much public hostility, Christianity spread to Africa, Spain and Gaul in the first century A.D., and ultimately became the faith of the Roman Emperor.

PLAN OF JERUSALEM

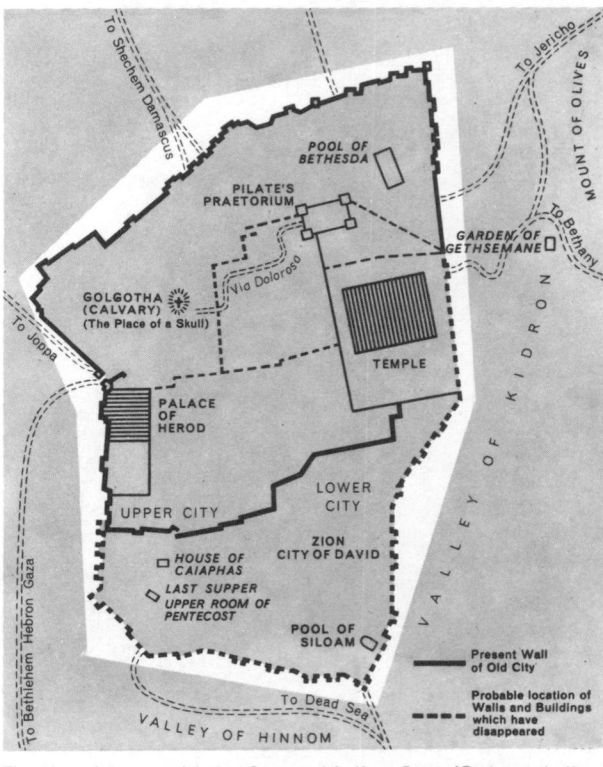

The sitings of the scene of the Last Supper and the Upper Room of Pentecost, the House of Caiaphas, the Way of the Cross (Via Dolorosa) and the Garden of Gethsemane are traditional only.

PALESTINE
IN THE TIME
OF JESUS

MT. HERMON

I T U R A E A

Caesarea Philippi Scene of Peter's
confession of faith, in recognition of
which Jesus promised him "the keys of
the Kingdom of Heaven".

Tyre

P
H
O
E
N
I
C
I
A

G R E A T

Ptolemais Formerly Acco.
Renamed by Ptolemy Philadelphus

Chorazin
A town cursed by Jesus
for its unbelief

Beth-saida Home of
Andrew, Peter and Philip

Capernaum
Here Jesus performed
many miracles and preached
in the synagogue

LAKE OF
GENNESARET
(Sea of Galilee)

S
Y
R
O
-

G A L I L E E

Tiberias
Founded by Herod
Antipas A.D. 17-22

Hippos

S E A

Cana
Scene of Jesus'
first recorded miracle

MT. CARMEL

MT.
TABOR

Abila

Nazareth
Home of Joseph and Mary

Gadara

Dora

Nain Here Jesus brought
to life the widow's son

Plain
of
Esdraelon

Megiddo

D E C A P O L I S

(Mediterranean Sea)

Scythopolis

Caesarea
Important centre of early
Christianity. Built by Herod

Pella Thither Christians
said to have fled before
the siege of Jerusalem

P
l
a
i
n

o
f

S
h
a
r
o
n

Aenon
(nr. Salim)
John the Baptist
baptized here

Gerasa

Sebaste (Samaria)
Rebuilt by Herod the Great

S A M A R I A

P

MT. GERIZIM
Site of Samaritan temple
destroyed by John Hyrcanus,
128 B.C.

Sychar
Jacob's Well

E

Antipatris

Alexandrium

Jordan

R

Joppa

Arimathea Home of Joseph,
a member of the Sanhedrin

A

Lydda

Ephraim

Philadelphia

E

Jamnia

Jericho Scene of healing by Jesus
of blind Bartimaeus. Mentioned also
in Parable of Good Samaritan

A

Emmaus
Scene of appearance
of the Risen Christ

Bethany
(or Bethabara)
Where John baptized

Azotus

Jerusalem
Capital of Judaea
Sacked by Romans,
A.D. 70

Bethany
Home of Lazarus and his
sisters, Martha and Mary

Kh. Qumran
Essene centre
MS. scrolls
discovered near
here. A.D. 1947

Ashkelon

Bethlehem
Birthplace of Jesus

Herodium

J U D A E A

S
A
L
T

S
E
A

Hebron

Machaerus Fortress built by
Herod. Scene, according to
Josephus, of the Baptist's beheading

(Dead Sea)

Beer-sheba

I D U M A E A

133

THE GREAT EXPLORATIONS

As cold waters to a thirsty soul,
so is good news from a far country—PROVERBS 25

ONLY a small proportion of the world remains to be explored, for man has always been a wanderer and a searcher for new things.

As early as 700 B.C. Phoenician and Carthaginian traders were seeking fresh lands in the Mediterranean and beyond for their merchandise. About 470 B.C. Hanno, the Carthaginian, sailed with a large fleet as far as Sierra Leone, bringing back tales of gorillas and of a "land of fire". (This was probably on account of the grass fires lighted before the rains in many parts of Africa.)

In 330 B.C. the Greek, Pytheas, sailed round Britain and into the North Sea, but more important than his journey for those who were to come after him was his discovery of a means of calculating latitude.

The most important exploration of this period was made by Alexander the Great in the years 330–323 B.C., when, accompanied by land surveyors and scribes to record details of the countries through which he passed, he marched his armies through Persia to India, and, like a true explorer, returned by a different route.

In the Second and First Centuries B.C. the Romans, in the expansion of their Empire, penetrated up the Nile, as far north as the Baltic, and westwards across Europe.

Westward exploration was extended by the Norsemen, first by their discovery of Iceland about A.D. 867, then Greenland in A.D. 982, and finally by their reaching the mainland of North America about four years later.

At about the same time the Arabs were voyaging far afield in the Indian Ocean, ranging from Spain to China, and as far south as Madagascar. Their greatest traveller was Ibn Batuta, who visited every Moslem country in a remarkable series of journeys that lasted almost thirty years. Buddhist missionaries, passing to and fro from India to China across the deserts of Takla-Makan and Gobi, had come across what came to be known as the Jade Route, along which for centuries traders carried jade from the Himalayas to China in exchange for silk.

In the same period envoys were sent by the Pope to the Great Khan of the Mongol Empire, and thus opened up the way for the Polos, father and son—Venetian jewel merchants and the most famous land travellers of the age—who journeyed twice across Asia.

Meanwhile, ship-building and navigation in Europe had considerably advanced and more extended voyages were possible. By A.D. 1487 the Portuguese had coasted down Africa, and in that year the Cape of Good Hope was rounded by Bartholomew Diaz. Thus opened the Great Age of Discovery, and in thirty years all the unknown oceans were crossed—Columbus reaching America in 1492, Vasco da Gama reaching India in 1498, and Magellan sailing across the Pacific and round the whole world in 1521.

Following on the heels of Columbus, the Portuguese spread down through Brazil, and the Spaniards endeavoured to cross the continent that lay between them and the riches of the East. In A.D. 1513 Balboa crossed the Isthmus of Panama, and a few years later Cortez conquered Mexico, and by 1540 the Spaniards had reached the Gulf of California. The English and the French gained footings in North America, and, with the Dutch, began to seek a North-West Passage in the Arctic as a route to China. By A.D. 1650 the existence of all the continents except Antarctica had been proved.

THEN followed the Age of Scientific Discovery, when expeditions by land and sea had exploration for knowledge as their aim. The greatest leader of such an expedition was Captain Cook who, in only three great voyages, explored Australia and New Zealand, circumnavigated Antarctica, and sailed through the Bering Strait. Exploration by land was slower, and it was not until the Nineteenth Century that English and American expeditions crossed North America, and South America was fully penetrated.

Africa was the last major continent to be crossed. Serious exploration was begun in 1795 by Mungo Park in West Africa, and thirty years later the Lander brothers found the mouth of the River Niger. In 1849, David Livingstone, who usually travelled alone and was perhaps the greatest land explorer ever known, began his journeys in Southern and Central Africa: his work was continued after his death by his friend, Stanley.

Major interest was then centred round the north and south Polar regions. In 1909 the American, Peary, was the first to reach the North Pole, and in 1958 the American submarine *Nautilus* travelled *beneath* it. In 1911 the Norwegian, Amundsen, was the first to reach the South Pole, followed a month later by the Englishman, Scott; and in 1955–58, Sir Vivian Fuchs led a British Commonwealth expedition which crossed the Antarctic continent from the Weddell Sea to the Ross Sea.

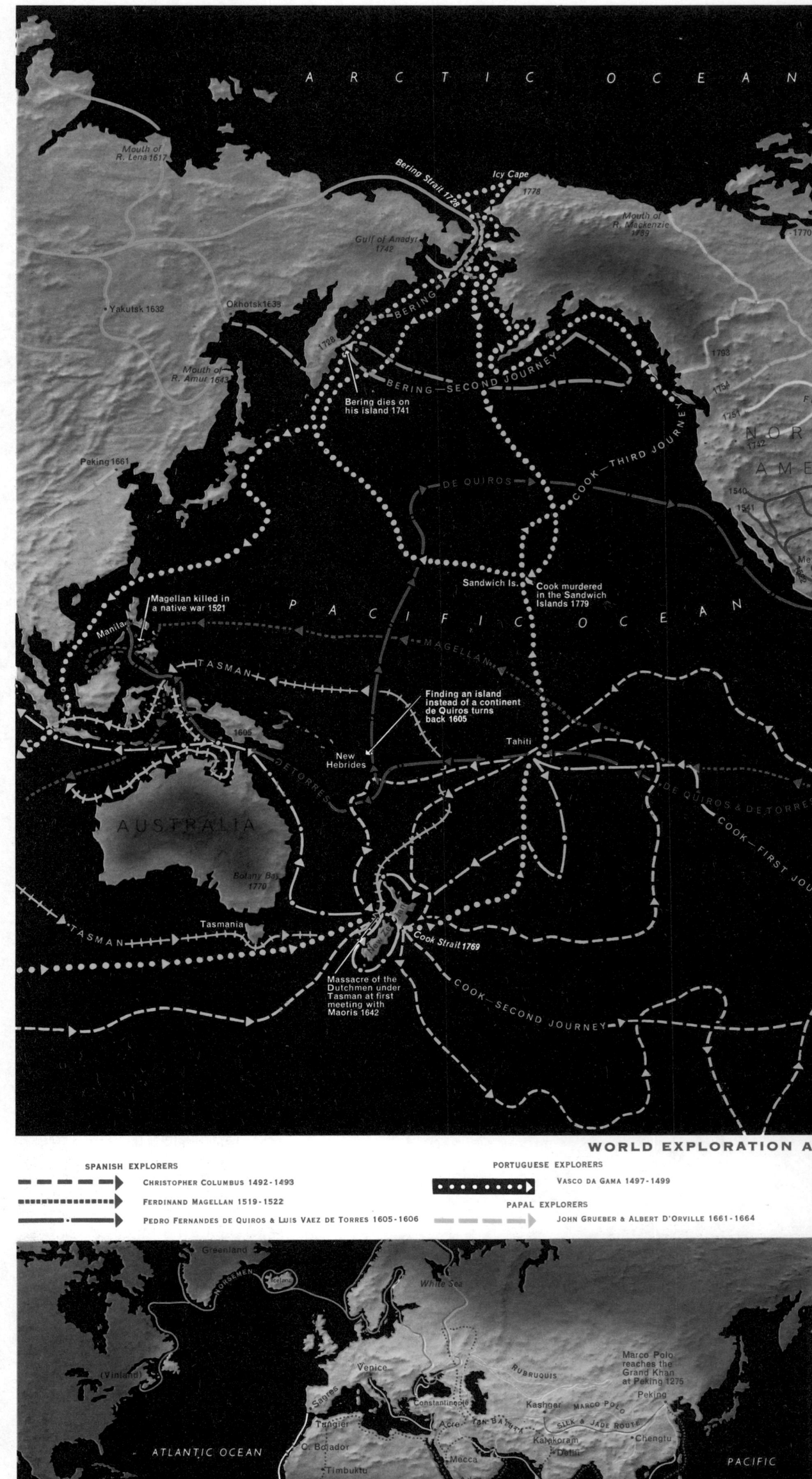

WORLD EXPLORATION A[...]

THE WORLD AS KNOWN IN 1490

DISCOVERY BETWEEN 1492 AND 1780

(Top map labels)

Baffin Bay 1616 · NORTH ATLANTIC OCEAN · First landfall of Columbus 1492 · Cuba · Cartagena 1532 · Bogota 1538 · Quito 1533 · To El Dorado · Guayaquil 1535 · Mouth of R. Amazon 1541 · SOUTH AMERICA · Callao 1615 · Cuzco 1533 · Potosi 1545 · Asunción 1537 · Buenos Aires 1542 · Valdivia 1552 · Port St. Julian · Mutiny among Magellan's men and desertion at Port St. Julian 1520 · SOUTH ATLANTIC OCEAN · Strait · Magellan · Cape Horn · SOUTHERN OCEAN

DUTCH AND ENGLISH EXPLORERS · Gulf of St. Lawrence 1534 · COLUMBUS

EUROPE · Moscow · Amsterdam 1594 · Lisbon · Huelva · Cadiz · to Rome 1664 · BARENTZ · Barentz dies after being the first to winter far North 1597 · White Sea · GROEBER & D'ORVILLE

RUSSIAN EXPLORERS · Chelyuskin 1742 · Mouth of R. Lena 1617 · Mouth of R. Yenisey 1610 · Mouth of R. Ob 1577 · Tobolsk 1587 · Tomsk 1604 · Yakutsk 1632 · Okhotsk 1638 · Krasnoyarsk 1628 · Mouth of R. Amur 1643 · ASIA · Peking 1661 · Lahore · Agra 1609 · Lhasa 1661 · Groeber and D'Orville first Europeans to visit Lhasa

AFRICA · C. Bojador · Vasco da Gama reaches Calicut 1498 · Mombasa 1498 · INDIAN OCEAN · Manila · VASCO DA GAMA · MAGELLAN · From England · To England · Mouth of Great Fish R. 1487 · Cape of Good Hope · To England · AUSTRALIA · Botany Bay 1770 · COOK—FIRST JOURNEY · TASMAN—SECOND JOURNEY · TORRES · TASMAN · Tasmania · COOK—THIRD JOURNEY · COOK—SECOND JOURNEY · Cook is first man to cross the Antarctic Circle 1773

© THE READER'S DIGEST ASSOCIATION

Legend

ENGLISH EXPLORERS	DUTCH EXPLORERS
JAMES COOK—FIRST JOURNEY 1768-1771	WILLIAM BARENTZ 1594-1597
JAMES COOK—SECOND JOURNEY 1772-1775	ABEL TASMAN 1642-1644
JAMES COOK—THIRD JOURNEY 1776-1780	

DUTCH & ENGLISH EXPLORERS	RUSSIAN EXPLORERS
	VITUS BERING—FIRST JOURNEY 1728-1729
FRENCH EXPLORERS	VITUS BERING—SECOND JOURNEY 1741

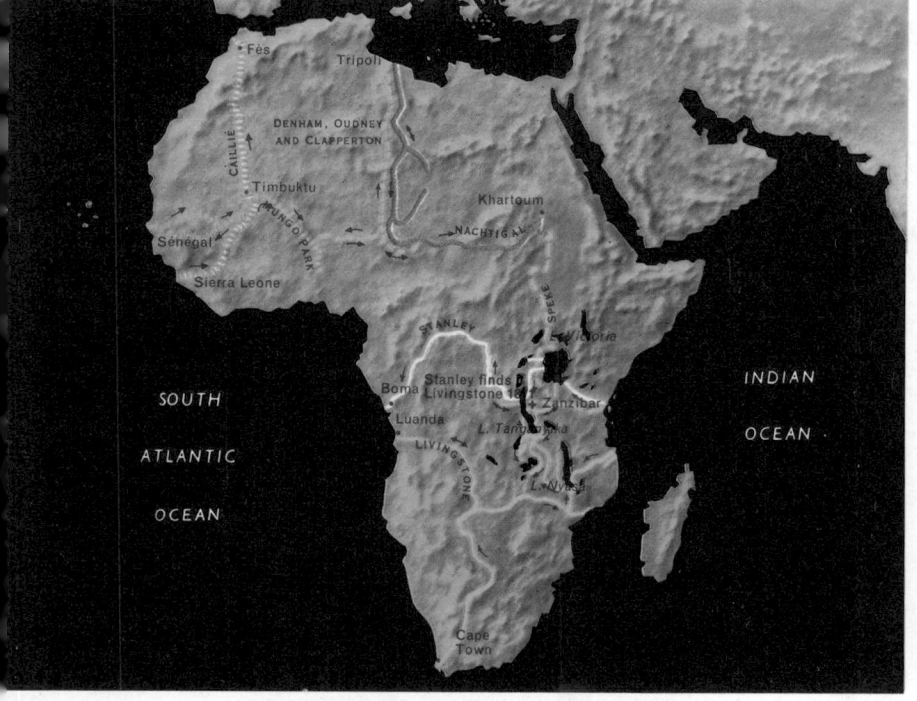

THE OPENING UP OF AFRICA

(Map labels) Fès · Tripoli · DENHAM, OUDNEY AND CLAPPERTON · CAILLÉ · Timbuktu · Khartoum · NACHTIGAL · Senegal · Sierra Leone · MUNGO PARK · STANLEY · Stanley finds Livingstone · Boma · Luanda · Zanzibar · L. Tanganyika · LIVINGSTONE · SOUTH ATLANTIC OCEAN · INDIAN OCEAN · Cape Town

MUNGO PARK 1795-1797; 1805-1806	RENÉ CAILLIÉ 1827-1828	SPEKE WITH BURTON 1857-1859 SPEKE WITH GRANT 1860-1863
DENHAM, OUDNEY AND CLAPPERTON 1822-1824	LIVINGSTONE 1849-1856; 1858-1864; 1866-1873	NACHTIGAL 1869-1874
		STANLEY 1874-1877

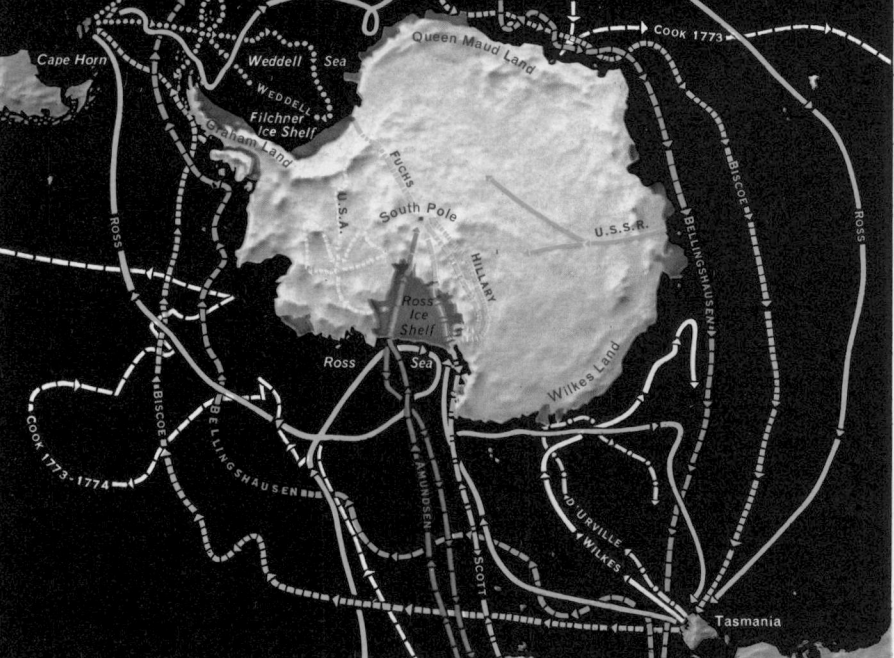

EXPLORATION OF ANTARCTICA

(Map labels) Cape Horn · Weddell Sea · Queen Maud Land · Cook 1773 · WEDDELL · Filchner Ice Shelf · Graham Land · ROSS · U.S.A. · South Pole · Fuchs · Hillary · U.S.S.R. · BELLINGSHAUSEN · BISCOE · Ross Ice Shelf · Ross Sea · Wilkes Land · COOK 1773-1774 · BELLINGSHAUSEN · DUMONT D'URVILLE · WILKES · SCOTT · AMUNDSEN · Tasmania

BELLINGSHAUSEN 1819-1822	WILKES 1840	FUCHS 1955-1958
BISCOE 1831-1832	ROSS 1840-1843	HILLARY 1957-1958
WEDDELL 1822-1823	AMUNDSEN 1911-1912	U.S.A. 1957-1960
DUMONT D'URVILLE 1840	SCOTT 1910-1913	U.S.S.R. 1957-1960

135

Oceania 32 million	Africa 768 million	Central and S. America 638 million	N. America 354 million	U.S.S.R. 353 million	Europe 527 million

2000

2,000 Million   1,000 Million

1950

WORLD POPULATION

And God said unto them, Be fruitful, and multiply — GENESIS 1

In the middle of the 1800's the world's population was estimated to be 1,000 million; by the mid 1920's, less than a century later, the population had doubled; and in 1963 it had reached 3,000 million. After carefully considering the rates of birth, maternal and infant mortality, and the expectation of life in every country, the United Nations forecast that by A.D. 2000 the figure will have increased to over 6,000 million and that it may reach nearly 7,000 million. The phenomenal expansion is shown on the chart in the centre of these pages. The total population in 1966 of the four groups listed in the table below right is 3,296,335,000. It can be seen that while the populations of the Western Hemisphere and Australasia have steadily increased since 1900, the populations of Africa and Asia (with the exception of the U.S.S.R., China and Japan) show a much more rapid expansion. Improved food production and increasing medical knowledge are largely responsible for the expansion in these areas.

MIGRATIONS SINCE A.D. 1650

© THE READER'S DIGEST ASSOCIATION

1900

1850

1800

Movements of populations occur mainly for political, religious and economic reasons. The more important migrations of the past three hundred years are shown.

Europeans to U.S.A. During the 17th century about 500,000 people emigrated from Great Britain to settle in New England (*Mayflower* 1620), Virginia and Maryland (though some settled in the West Indies, mostly in Barbados), to be followed in the 18th century by three times that number (mainly Irish and Scots). In the 19th century the number further increased, and was added to by German, Austro-Hungarian and Italian immigrants. From 1900 to 1920 a total of 14,500,000 from many countries were admitted (1,042,000 in 1907—a peak for any one year). In the next 30 years only 5,500,000 were admitted, but during the years 1951-9 the rate of immigration increased to a total of 2,250,000. In the following six years the number of immigrants from Europe alone was 750,000.

Europeans to Canada During the 17th century Quebec Province was settled by the French, but later the majority of immigrants came from Great Britain. Until 1900 settlement was slow, but from 1900 to 1920 about 2,250,000 people entered the country, followed by 1,500,000 in the next 30 years. Thereafter immigration greatly increased, over 2,000,000 Europeans settling in Canada in 1951-67.

Europeans to South America South America has always mainly attracted the Spanish, Portuguese and Italians, Argentina and Brazil being their principal goals. Immigration was slow until the 1890's, but reached its peak before 1914. Between 1900 and 1920 about 3,000,000 people settled in Argentina, and about 1,500,000 in Brazil.

The Slave Trade Traffic in slaves from West Africa began in the 16th century, reaching its peak in the late 18th and early 19th centuries. About 20,000,000 slaves were taken mainly to the tobacco, sugar and coffee plantations of the Caribbean and Brazil. Many of them moved on to the cotton fields of the southern states of what is now the U.S.A.

Europeans to Australia and New Zealand The first white people settled in Australia in 1788, but immigration was slow until the period of the Gold Rush between 1850 and 1860. After 1860 it slowed down again until the turn of the century. Between 1901 and 1920 about 400,000 emigrated to Australia, mostly from the United Kingdom, but in the twenty years from 1945 over 2,500,000 settled in Australia, about half of whom were British. Emigration to New Zealand has followed much the same pattern, but on a smaller scale.

French to Algeria French traders became established in Algeria in the 16th century. In 1842 the country became a French colony, although Algiers had been captured in 1830. By 1848 government-sponsored settlers totalled 40,000, and in 1881 northern Algeria became a province of France. Settlement continued until the unrest preceeding independence in 1963; then about four-fifths of the French population left for metropolitan France.

Europeans to Central and East Africa Few Europeans settled in Rhodesia before the discovery of the diamond deposits in 1880, development of which began in 1889 when Cecil Rhodes financed the trek to Salisbury. By 1960 nearly 300,000 had settled in Zambia and Rhodesia. East Africa was largely settled through official encouragement from 1906 onwards.

Dutch in South Africa The first Europeans to settle in the Cape were the Dutch in 1652. Emigrants from the British Isles did not arrive in any numbers until the late 18th century. In 1836 Dutch farmers (Boers) began their revolt against British rule in Cape Colony and made the Great Trek across the Orange River, to found the Orange Free State and the Transvaal. During the next ten years probably 14,000 Boers moved northwards. In the early 20th century there were mass movements of Africans (mostly from Moçambique, Basutoland, Bechuanaland and Nyasaland) to the Transvaal, especially to industrial Johannesburg.

Chinese to Other Parts of Asia From the middle of the 19th century the Chinese migrated in large numbers, mainly to Malaya, Indonesia, Burma and Ceylon. In 1948 there were 9,500,000 abroad, mostly in Asia, though over 200,000 were in the U.S.A. In the 1920's there were mass movements to Manchuria, Mongolia and Asiatic Russia.

Internal Migration in the U.S.S.R. Since 1918 great movements of European Russians to the east of the Urals have taken place. The Second World War accelerated industrial growth beyond the Urals, and a feature of the recent Five Year Plans has been the movement to and the settling of people in Kazakhstan and farther east.

Indians to Malaya and Africa In the mid 19th century Indians migrated to Ceylon, Burma and Malaya, Mauritius, Natal, East Africa and the West Indies. These migrations have continued on a small scale in the 20th century.

Migration between India and Pakistan After the 1947 partition of the former Indian Empire into India (Hindu majority) and Pakistan (Moslem majority) large religious minorities were left on either side of the border. Between 1947 and 1949 about 10,000,000 people were resettled.

Internal Migration in the U.S.A. From the end of the 18th century, when pioneers started the movement westwards, migration to the west has continued, as well as movement from the Atlantic seaboard to the south. In the fifteen years 1950-65 the population of California increased 75 per cent and that of Florida by over 100 per cent compared with a 23 per cent increase in the remainder of the U.S.A. Many negroes have moved north from the southern states; Puerto Ricans have settled in cities in the eastern states.

Jewish Migration Intermittent migrations of Jews from many countries into Palestine took place after the First World War, but since the formation of the State of Israel in 1948 many European Jews have been admitted. In 1949 over 239,000 settled in Israel, to be followed in the next fifteen years by nearly 900,000.

Internal Migration in Europe The Second World War left millions of displaced persons in Central Europe, who came mainly from Poland, Russia, the Baltic States, Hungary and the Balkans. Although the problem of resettlement was largely solved by 1951, it was not ended until the early 1960's.

Commonwealth to Great Britain In the 1950's increasing numbers of West Indians were attracted to Great Britain by better prospects of employment than at home. In the ten years 1951-60 the total number of immigrants was 175,000. In each of the three years following the Commonwealth Immigration Act, 1962, an average of 11,500 West Indians and 28,000 Indians and Pakistanis settled in Britain.

1750

1700

1650

. 2000: 6,130 million

China
1,045 million

Rest of Asia
2,413 million

| 1,000 | Million | | 2,000 | Million | | 3,000 | Million | 2000 |

1950

1900

1850

1800

1750

1700

1650

The Netherlands, with 960 people to the square mile, is the most densely populated country in the world. In Europe, England follows with 895 people to the square mile and Belgium with 809. Taiwan with 921 and South Korea with 765 head the list in Asia; Nigeria with 162 heads the list in Africa; and Puerto Rico with 776 people to the square mile is the most densely populated area in the Caribbean. Australia is over twenty-eight times as large, but less than a sixth as densely populated as New Zealand; the United States of America, with an area slightly less than that of Canada, has almost ten times Canada's population.

WORLD POPULATION A.D. 1650-2000

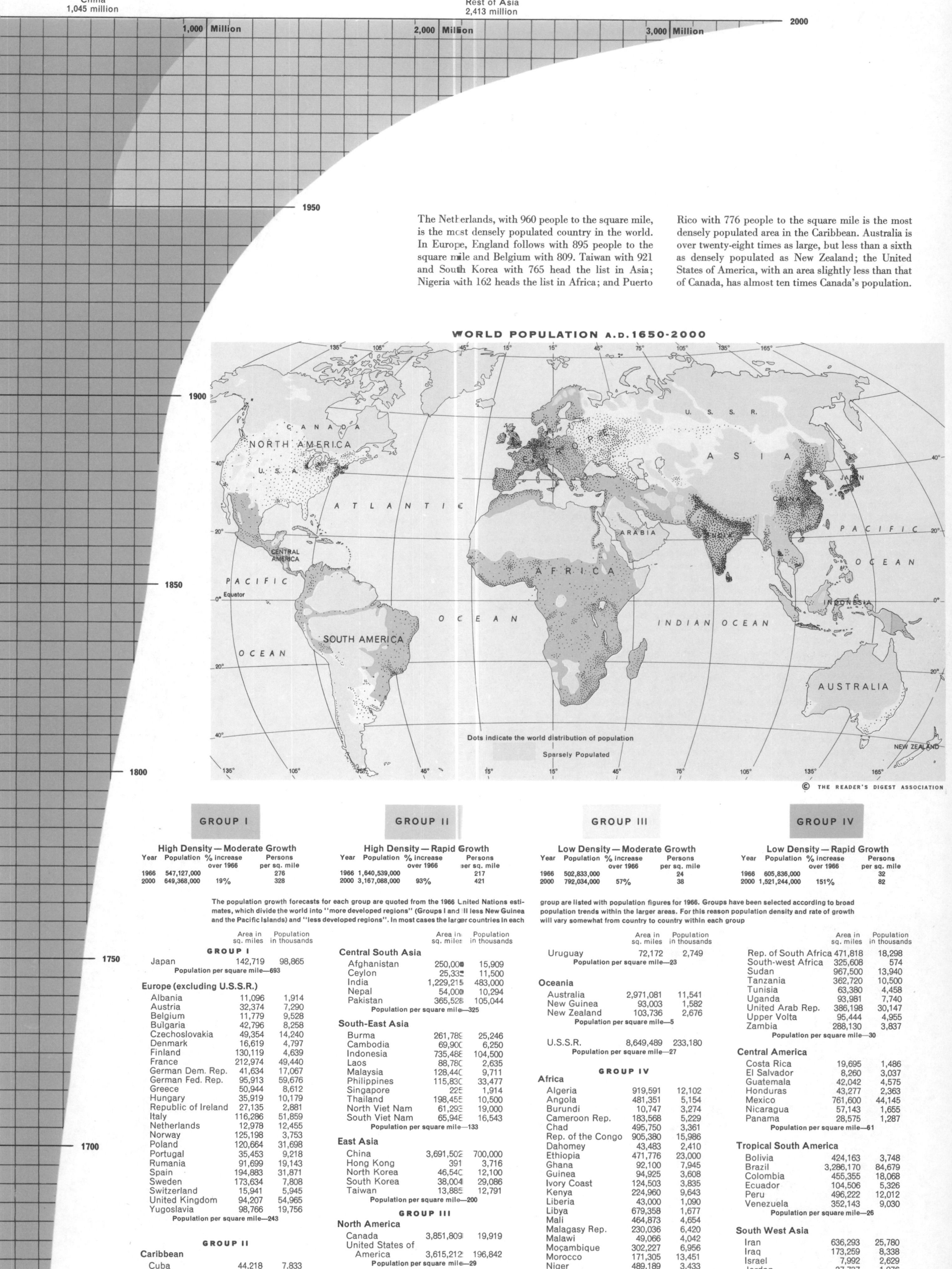

Dots indicate the world distribution of population

Sparsely Populated

© THE READER'S DIGEST ASSOCIATION

GROUP I	GROUP II	GROUP III	GROUP IV
High Density — Moderate Growth	**High Density — Rapid Growth**	**Low Density — Moderate Growth**	**Low Density — Rapid Growth**

Year	Population	% increase over 1966	Persons per sq. mile
1966	547,127,000		276
2000	649,368,000	19%	328

Year	Population	% increase over 1966	Persons per sq. mile
1966	1,640,539,000		217
2000	3,167,088,000	93%	421

Year	Population	% increase over 1966	Persons per sq. mile
1966	502,034,000		24
2000	792,034,000	57%	38

Year	Population	% increase over 1966	Persons per sq. mile
1966	605,836,000		32
2000	1,521,244,000	151%	82

The population growth forecasts for each group are quoted from the 1966 United Nations estimates, which divide the world into "more developed regions" (Groups I and II less New Guinea and the Pacific Islands) and "less developed regions". In most cases the larger countries in each group are listed with population figures for 1966. Groups have been selected according to broad population trends within the larger areas. For this reason population density and rate of growth will vary somewhat from country to country within each group

	Area in sq. miles	Population in thousands
GROUP I		
Japan	142,719	98,865
Population per square mile—693		
Europe (excluding U.S.S.R.)		
Albania	11,096	1,914
Austria	32,374	7,290
Belgium	11,779	9,528
Bulgaria	42,796	8,258
Czechoslovakia	49,354	14,240
Denmark	16,619	4,797
Finland	130,119	4,639
France	212,974	49,440
German Dem. Rep.	41,634	17,067
German Fed. Rep.	95,913	59,676
Greece	50,944	8,612
Hungary	35,919	10,179
Republic of Ireland	27,135	2,881
Italy	116,286	51,859
Netherlands	12,978	12,455
Norway	125,198	3,753
Poland	120,664	31,698
Portugal	35,453	9,218
Rumania	91,699	19,143
Spain	194,883	31,871
Sweden	173,634	7,808
Switzerland	15,941	5,945
United Kingdom	94,207	54,965
Yugoslavia	98,766	19,756
Population per square mile—243		
GROUP II		
Caribbean		
Cuba	44,218	7,833
Dominican Republic	18,816	3,750
Haiti	10,714	4,485
Jamaica	4,232	1,839
Puerto Rico	3,435	2,668
Trinidad and Tobago	1,980	1,000
Population per square mile—259		

	Area in sq. miles	Population in thousands
Central South Asia		
Afghanistan	250,000	15,909
Ceylon	25,332	11,500
India	1,229,215	483,000
Nepal	54,000	10,294
Pakistan	365,528	105,044
Population per square mile—325		
South-East Asia		
Burma	261,789	25,246
Cambodia	69,900	6,250
Indonesia	735,488	104,500
Laos	88,780	2,635
Malaysia	128,440	9,711
Philippines	115,830	33,477
Singapore	225	1,914
Thailand	198,455	10,500
North Viet Nam	61,293	19,000
South Viet Nam	65,948	16,543
Population per square mile—133		
East Asia		
China	3,691,502	700,000
Hong Kong	391	3,716
North Korea	46,540	12,100
South Korea	38,004	29,086
Taiwan	13,885	12,791
Population per square mile—200		
GROUP III		
North America		
Canada	3,851,809	19,919
United States of America	3,615,212	196,842
Population per square mile—29		
Temperate South America		
Argentina	1,072,646	22,691
Chile	286,397	8,591
Paraguay	157,047	2,094

	Area in sq. miles	Population in thousands
Uruguay	72,172	2,749
Population per square mile—23		
Oceania		
Australia	2,971,081	11,541
New Guinea	93,003	1,582
New Zealand	103,736	2,676
Population per square mile—5		
U.S.S.R.	8,649,489	233,180
Population per square mile—27		
GROUP IV		
Africa		
Algeria	919,591	12,102
Angola	481,351	5,154
Burundi	10,747	3,274
Cameroon Rep.	183,568	5,229
Chad	495,750	3,361
Rep. of the Congo	905,380	15,986
Dahomey	43,483	2,410
Ethiopia	471,776	23,000
Ghana	92,100	7,945
Guinea	94,925	3,608
Ivory Coast	124,503	3,835
Kenya	224,960	9,643
Liberia	43,000	1,090
Libya	679,358	1,677
Mali	464,873	4,654
Malagasy Rep.	230,036	6,420
Malawi	49,066	4,042
Moçambique	302,227	6,956
Morocco	171,305	13,451
Niger	489,189	3,433
Nigeria	356,668	57,500
Rhodesia	150,333	4,400
Rwanda	10,169	3,110
Senegal	75,750	3,490
Sierra Leone	27,699	2,403
Somali Rep.	246,200	2,500

	Area in sq. miles	Population in thousands
Rep. of South Africa	471,818	18,298
South-west Africa	325,608	574
Sudan	967,500	13,940
Tanzania	362,720	10,500
Tunisia	63,380	4,458
Uganda	93,981	7,740
United Arab Rep.	386,198	30,147
Upper Volta	95,444	4,955
Zambia	288,130	3,837
Population per square mile—30		
Central America		
Costa Rica	19,695	1,486
El Salvador	8,260	3,037
Guatemala	42,042	4,575
Honduras	43,277	2,363
Mexico	761,600	44,145
Nicaragua	57,143	1,655
Panama	28,575	1,287
Population per square mile—61		
Tropical South America		
Bolivia	424,163	3,748
Brazil	3,286,170	84,679
Colombia	455,355	18,068
Ecuador	104,506	5,326
Peru	496,222	12,012
Venezuela	352,143	9,030
Population per square mile—26		
South West Asia		
Iran	636,293	25,780
Iraq	173,259	8,338
Israel	7,992	2,629
Jordan	37,737	1,976
Lebanon	4,000	2,405
Saudi Arabia	869,803	6,750
Syria	71,210	5,300
Turkey	301,380	32,901
Yemen	75,391	4,925
Population per square mile—42		

WHAT THE WORLD IS EATING

There is nothing better for a man than that he should eat and drink — ECCLESIASTES 2

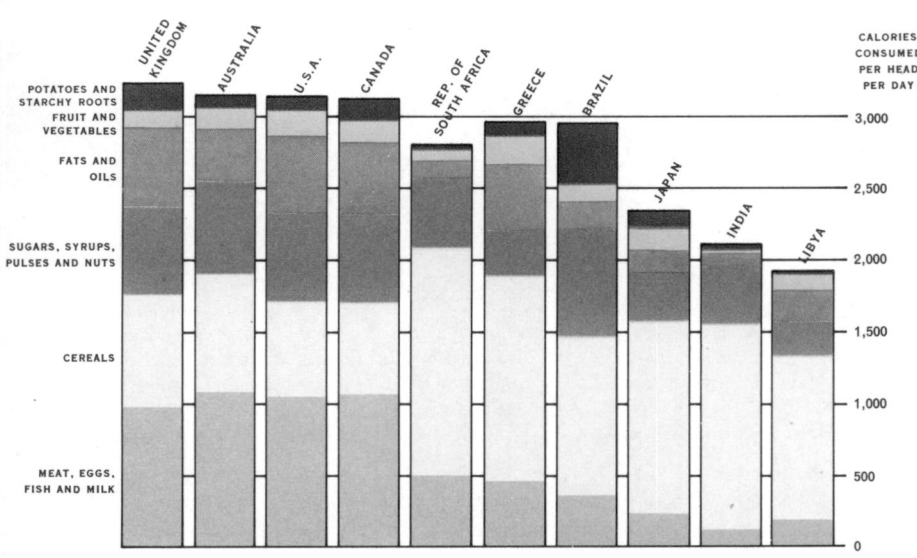

POTATOES AND STARCHY ROOTS
FRUIT AND VEGETABLES
FATS AND OILS
SUGARS, SYRUPS, PULSES AND NUTS
CEREALS
MEAT, EGGS, FISH AND MILK

(UNITED KINGDOM, AUSTRALIA, U.S.A., CANADA, REP. OF SOUTH AFRICA, GREECE, BRAZIL, JAPAN, INDIA, LIBYA)

CALORIES CONSUMED PER HEAD PER DAY — 3,000 / 2,500 / 2,000 / 1,500 / 1,000 / 500 / 0

EVERY day the world has to find food for more than 3,000 million human beings, and this number is steadily increasing.

We need sufficient food to give us energy (carbohydrates) and to provide the materials from which our bodies can be built and maintained (proteins), but to ensure good health our diet must include foods which provide vitamins and minerals as well.

Carbohydrates are obtained chiefly from cereals (wheat, maize, rye, oats, barley, rice, sorghums and millets), from roots and tubers (potatoes, sweet potatoes, yams and cassava), and from sugar. Proteins are obtained from meat and fish, from pulses (dry beans, peas, broad beans, lentils and chick-peas), and from nuts, oil-seeds and oil-containing fruit. Vitamins and minerals are obtained from fresh fruit and vegetables. But milk, closely followed by eggs, is a complete food in itself.

For the calculation of food values, our food consumption is measured in terms of calories. A well-balanced daily diet may contain as many as 2,000 to 3,000 calories.

Many of the well-developed countries of Western Europe, North and South America, Australia and New Zealand are able to produce or purchase enough food to ensure that a well-balanced diet is available to all their people. But in many underdeveloped countries primitive methods of cultivation still exist so that the amount of food produced is scarcely enough to meet the minimum requirements of the community. A daily diet of 2,000 calories or less, composed mainly of carbohydrates with only a small proportion of the vital and expensive proteins, is the typical diet of millions of people in these areas—a diet deficient in quantity and quality, resulting in the serious undernourishment of two-thirds of the world's population.

Shortages of food, in terms of quantity and quality, are not the only causes of malnutrition. Religious taboos, local customs and prejudices, ignorance of elementary hygiene and of the value of certain local foodstuffs often deny whole communities an adequate and health-giving diet. In some parts of the world, through ignorance of simple sterilization methods, mothers refuse to give their babies fresh milk because of its bad effect on them in the unsterilized state. In Uganda, tribal people value milk so little that they prefer to live on millet and root crops. In many parts of Africa cattle and goats are regarded as a measure of wealth, so that meat is rarely consumed.

Much is being done today by education, by the spread of scientific and technical knowledge, by advancing industrialization and by a proper distribution of surplus foodstuffs, to improve and increase food supplies for the rapidly growing population of the world.

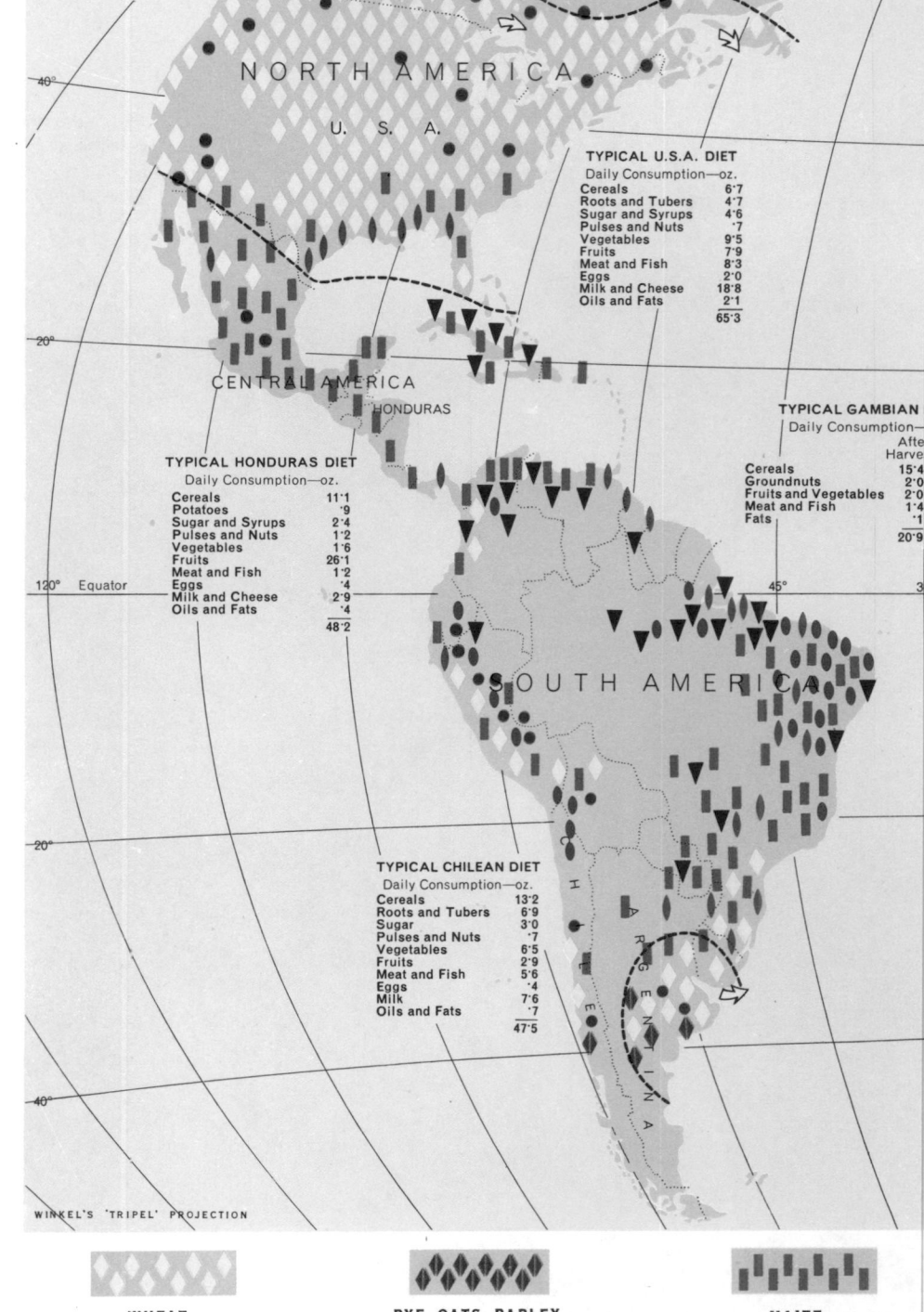

TYPICAL U.S.A. DIET
Daily Consumption—oz.
Cereals	6·7
Roots and Tubers	4·7
Sugar and Syrups	4·6
Pulses and Nuts	·7
Vegetables	9·5
Fruits	7·9
Meat and Fish	8·3
Eggs	2·0
Milk and Cheese	18·8
Oils and Fats	2·1
	65·3

TYPICAL HONDURAS DIET
Daily Consumption—oz.
Cereals	11·1
Potatoes	·9
Sugar and Syrups	2·4
Pulses and Nuts	1·2
Vegetables	1·6
Fruits	26·1
Meat and Fish	1·2
Eggs	·4
Milk and Cheese	2·9
Oils and Fats	·4
	48·2

TYPICAL GAMBIAN DIET
Daily Consumption—oz.
After Harvest
Cereals	15·4
Groundnuts	2·0
Fruits and Vegetables	2·0
Meat and Fish	1·4
Fats	·1
	20·9

TYPICAL CHILEAN DIET
Daily Consumption—oz.
Cereals	13·2
Roots and Tubers	6·9
Sugar	3·0
Pulses and Nuts	·7
Vegetables	6·5
Fruits	2·9
Meat and Fish	5·6
Eggs	·4
Milk	7·6
Oils and Fats	·7
	47·5

WINKEL'S 'TRIPEL' PROJECTION

COMPARISON OF POPULATION AND AGRICULTURAL PRODUCTION

(Bar chart — PERCENTAGE OF WORLD'S TOTAL, 0–45)
NORTH AMERICA / EUROPE (INC. U.S.S.R.) / FAR EAST (EXC. MAINLAND CHINA) / LATIN AMERICA / AFRICA / NEAR EAST / OCEANIA
Agricultural Production / Population

WHEAT

WHEAT, of which there are about 650 varieties, is the most important and widely grown of all cereal crops, and is chiefly milled into flour. Wheat products are rich in carbohydrates; the whole grain contains also proteins, fats, minerals and vitamins. It is therefore a major energy food, and highly nutritious. The hard varieties are used mainly for bread, the soft for cakes, biscuits, pastry. One hard species, durum, is manufactured into spaghetti, macaroni, semolina, etc. Flat (unleavened) bread is eaten in much of Africa and Asia. In India wheat is combined with fat and made into pancake-like wafers called *chappatis*. A small part of the world's wheat production is processed into malt, dextrose and alcohol.

RYE, OATS, BARLEY

RYE is mainly produced in the poorer soils and wetter areas of the northern temperate regions, and is consumed largely in central and eastern European countries as "black" bread, which is very nutritious and more warmth-giving than other varieties of bread. OATS are hardy and also flourish in poorer soils. They have a high protein, fat and vitamin B content, and are principally used for breakfast foods, cakes, biscuits, etc. BARLEY thrives in most temperate climates and even under subarctic and subtropical conditions. It is chiefly grown in Europe for the manufacture of beer, though in parts of Scotland and Scandinavia it is made into barley bread. It is the staple food grain of North Africa and parts of Asia, where it is eaten as flatbread, porridge and pearl barley.

MAIZE

MAIZE (Indian corn), one of the most widely distributed food crops, although of great nutritive value, is not as nutritious as wheat. Sometimes the cob is roasted whole, but generally the grain is ground into meal and eaten as porridge, such as the "stirabout" of Ireland, or in cake form, such as the "johnny-cakes" of the U.S.A. It is eaten as a basic food in Mexico and in some parts of South America as *tortilla*, a flat pancake, often in conjunction with soups or fruit or vegetables such as sweet potatoes. In North America it is harvested early and eaten as "sweet corn". In northern Italy it is eaten as "polenta". Corn-flour is prepared from maize by a process of washing. Maize is used industrially as corn-starch, corn-oil and alcohol.

PRODUCTION OF MEAT AND FISH

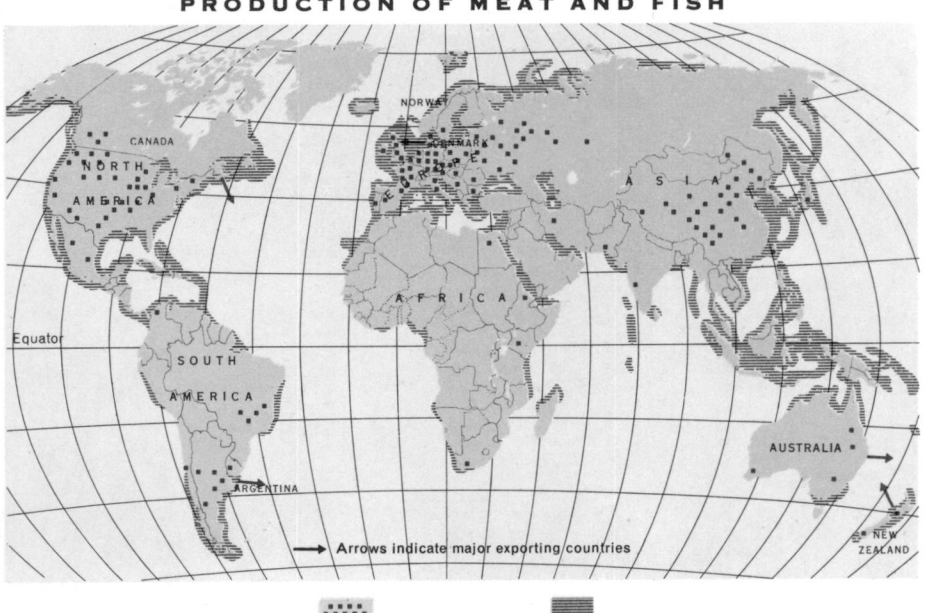

Arrows indicate major exporting countries

MEAT / FISH

PRODUCTION OF VEGETABLE OILS

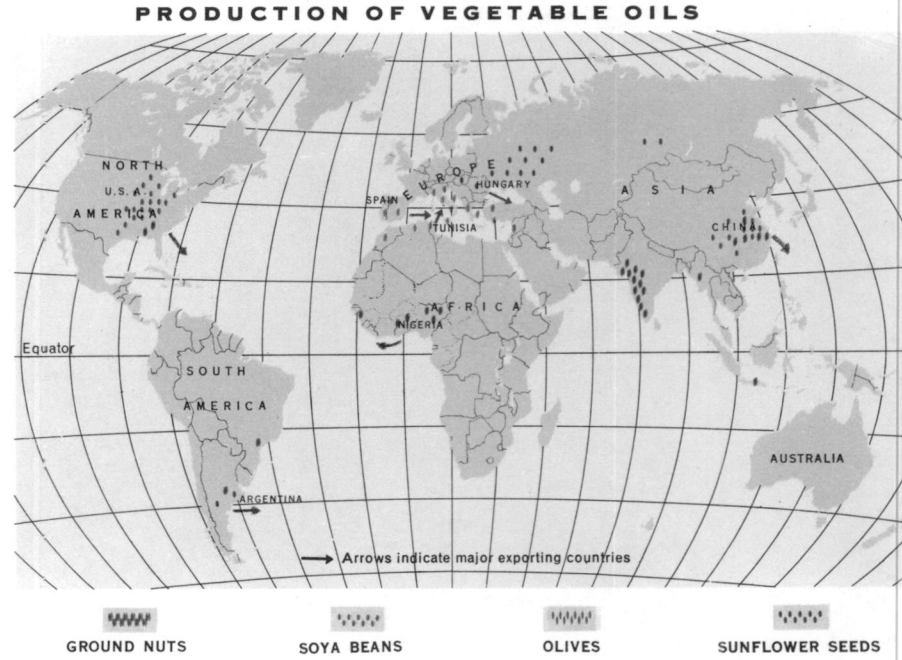

Arrows indicate major exporting countries

GROUND NUTS / SOYA BEANS / OLIVES / SUNFLOWER SEEDS

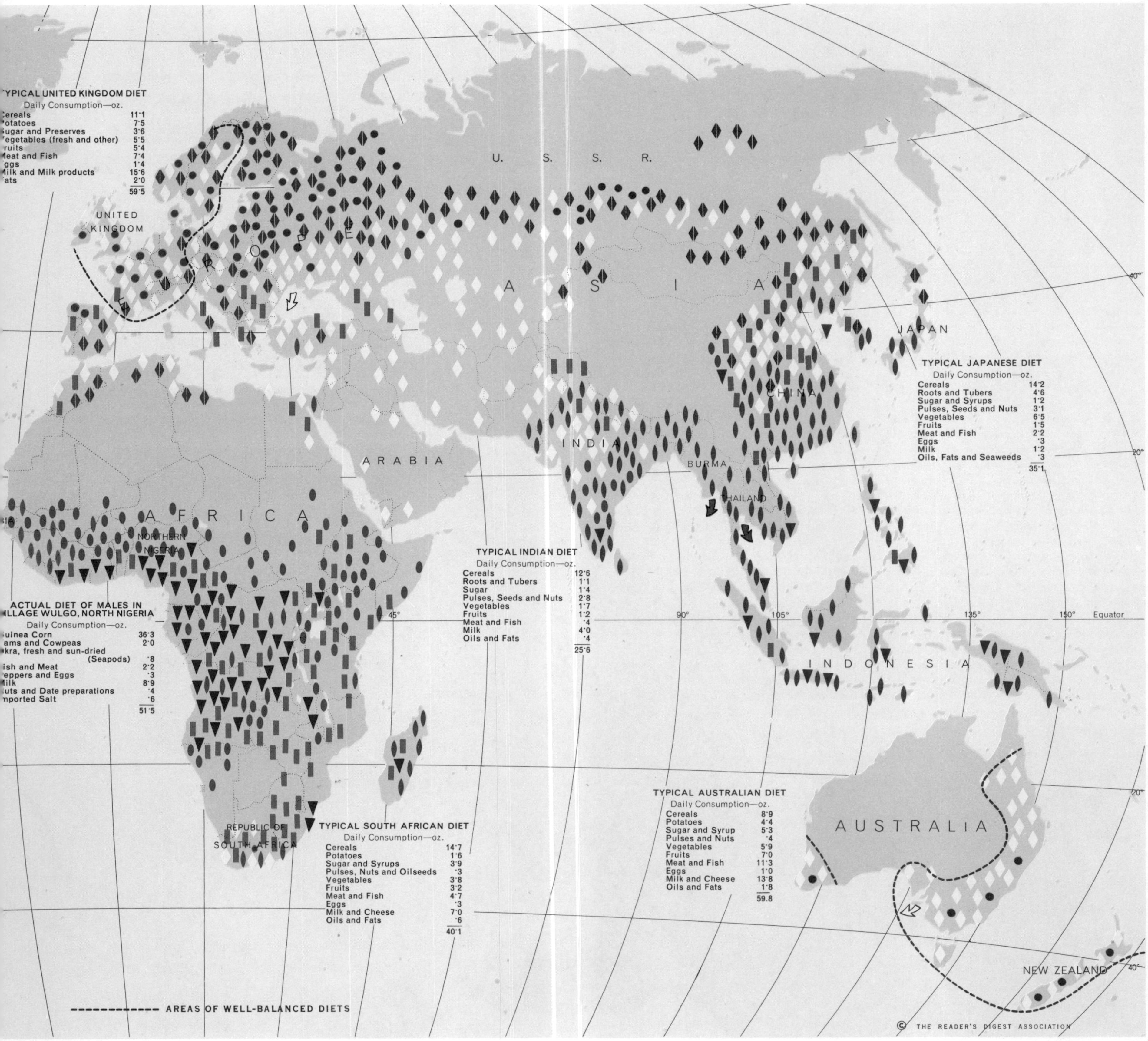

TYPICAL UNITED KINGDOM DIET
Daily Consumption—oz.
Cereals 11·1
Potatoes 7·5
Sugar and Preserves 3·6
Vegetables (fresh and other) 5·5
Fruits 5·4
Meat and Fish 7·4
Eggs 1·4
Milk and Milk products 15·6
Fats 2·0
59·5
U. S. S. R.
UNITED KINGDOM
E U R O P E
A S I A
JAPAN
TYPICAL JAPANESE DIET
Daily Consumption—oz.
Cereals 14·2
Roots and Tubers 4·6
Sugar and Syrups 1·2
Pulses, Seeds and Nuts 3·1
Vegetables 6·5
Fruits 1·5
Meat and Fish 2·2
Eggs ·3
Milk 1·2
Oils, Fats and Seaweeds ·3
35·1
CHINA
INDIA
ARABIA
BURMA
THAILAND
A F R I C A
NORTHERN NIGERIA
TYPICAL INDIAN DIET
Daily Consumption—oz.
Cereals 12·6
Roots and Tubers 1·1
Sugar 1·4
Pulses, Seeds and Nuts 2·8
Vegetables 1·7
Fruits 1·2
Meat and Fish ·4
Milk 4·0
Oils and Fats ·4
25·6
ACTUAL DIET OF MALES IN VILLAGE WULGO, NORTH NIGERIA
Daily Consumption—oz.
Guinea Corn 36·3
Yams and Cowpeas 2·0
Okra, fresh and sun-dried (Seapods) ·8
Fish and Meat 2·2
Peppers and Eggs ·3
Milk 8·9
Nuts and Date preparations ·4
Imported Salt ·6
51·5
45°
90°
105°
135°
150°
Equator
40°
20°
I N D O N E S I A
TYPICAL AUSTRALIAN DIET
Daily Consumption—oz.
Cereals 8·9
Potatoes 4·4
Sugar and Syrup 5·3
Pulses and Nuts ·4
Vegetables 5·9
Fruits 7·0
Meat and Fish 11·3
Eggs 1·0
Milk and Cheese 13·8
Oils and Fats 1·8
59.8
AUSTRALIA
NEW ZEALAND
REPUBLIC OF SOUTH AFRICA
TYPICAL SOUTH AFRICAN DIET
Daily Consumption—oz.
Cereals 14·7
Potatoes 1·6
Sugar and Syrups 3·9
Pulses, Nuts and Oilseeds ·3
Vegetables 3·8
Fruits 3·2
Meat and Fish 4·7
Eggs ·3
Milk and Cheese 7·0
Oils and Fats ·6
40·1
AREAS OF WELL-BALANCED DIETS
© THE READER'S DIGEST ASSOCIATION

MILLETS AND SORGHUMS

MILLETS and **SORGHUMS** include a number of grain crops that respond to primitive methods of cultivation, and can withstand the drought and poor soil of some of the drier parts of the Tropics. The ear contains small round seeds which are pounded into flour, which is eaten as a gruel or porridge with a seasoned stew of vegetables, but rarely with meat. In West Africa it is made into balls of doughy paste (couscous). These balls, fried in palm or shea-nut oil are known as "beignets" or "galettes" and sold in the streets. In Northern China, millets and sorghums, as well as wheat, form the staple food. When grain is abundant, considerable quantities are brewed into beer; *pombe*, made from millet, is widely drunk in Africa. A variety of millet (prosbo)—eaten mainly as a thick porridge—is a staple food in the U.S.S.R.

RICE

There are more than 2,500 varieties of rice, more than 1,000 of them in India alone. Rice has a high energy value, though it is relatively poor nutritively. It yields more food per acre than any other grain and is widely grown and widely eaten in China, India, Japan, Burma, etc. It forms a major part of the food in these countries, where, on the whole, the diet is largely deficient in animal proteins. Among the higher income groups, the rice is always accompanied by meat and vegetables. It is commonly eaten with curry, which varies from the hot curries of India, Pakistan and Ceylon to the more subtle flavours of Malaysia and Indonesia. In China a favourite combination is with pork. The removal of its outer husk (polishing) deprives rice of much of its goodness. *Sake*, a popular and potent drink in Japan, *Arrak* in Java and *Chemshu* in China are all brewed from rice.

POTATOES

POTATOES, of which there are some 2,000 varieties, are grown in almost every country in the world, though they succeed best in the cooler regions. They contain carbohydrates, proteins, vitamins and mineral salts and are, therefore, a most valuable energy food. Among the white races they form an important part of every diet, and in some parts of Europe they are the staple food. They are generally eaten as a vegetable, but are also turned into flour and used for making bread, pastry and dumplings. Potatoes are also processed into starch and dextrose, and since the middle of the 19th century have replaced grain as a source of alcohol for commercial uses, particularly in Germany. Sweet potatoes are botanically quite different from ordinary potatoes and must be considered a tropical crop, although they have a similar food value.

TROPICAL ROOT CROPS, BANANAS

Three of the principal root crops are **CASSAVA** (manioc), **YAMS** and **SWEET POTATOES**. They are grown mainly in west and central Africa, the Malay Archipelago, and Latin America. The root of *sweet* cassava can be cooked and eaten directly, but the root of *bitter* cassava must be soaked in water for a few days before cooking, to extract the prussic acid. The cooked cassava is usually pounded into flour or meal and eaten as a porridge, often accompanied by yams or other vegetables. Sweet potatoes (called yams in America) grow better in drier areas, with less than 50 inches of rain. Although not root crops, **BANANAS** and **PLANTAINS** form a staple food in many tropical countries. Bananas are eaten raw and also cooked as a vegetable. Plantains are similar to bananas but contain less sugar and are usually eaten cooked. All these crops are low in protein.

EXPORTS

The arrows indicate those places from which the world's chief food cereals, wheat (yellow) and rice (brown) are exported. About 20 per cent of all the wheat produced is exported. Argentina exports one-third of her wheat production, mainly to Brazil, Peru and western Europe; Australia exports two-thirds and Canada one half, principally to Britain, China and Japan; the U.S.A. exports about half her production, mainly to India, Pakistan and Japan. The U.S.S.R. is an important exporter, but in bad harvest years she also becomes a large importer. In most years Britain is the world's largest single importer of wheat. Only about five per cent of the world's production of rice enters international trade, most of which is confined to south and south-east Asia—Burma and Thailand being the major exporters and Japan the largest importer.

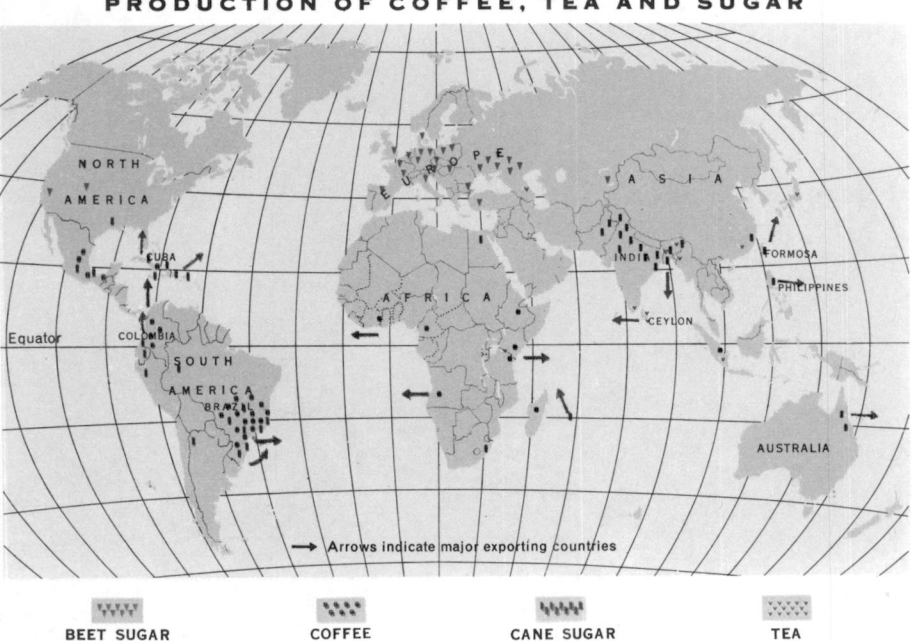

PRODUCTION OF COFFEE, TEA AND SUGAR

NORTH AMERICA
EUROPE
A S I A
CUBA
INDIA
FORMOSA
PHILIPPINES
A F R I C A
CEYLON
Equator
COLOMBIA
SOUTH AMERICA
BRAZIL
AUSTRALIA
Arrows indicate major exporting countries

BEET SUGAR | COFFEE | CANE SUGAR | TEA

PRODUCTION OF FRUIT

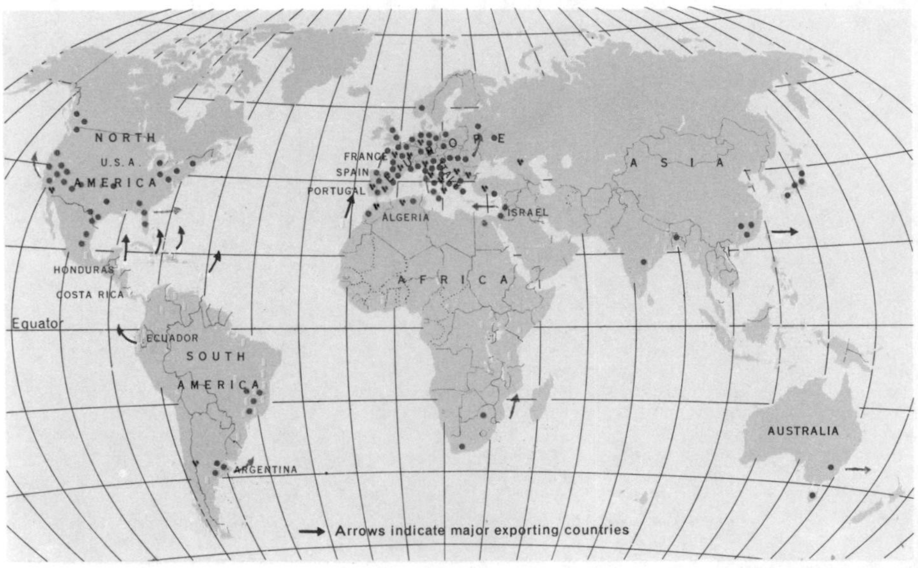

NORTH
U.S.A.
AMERICA
FRANCE
SPAIN
PORTUGAL
EUROPE
ALGERIA
ISRAEL
A S I A
HONDURAS
COSTA RICA
A F R I C A
Equator
ECUADOR
SOUTH AMERICA
ARGENTINA
AUSTRALIA
Arrows indicate major exporting countries

APPLES, PEARS AND PLUMS | BANANAS | CITRUS FRUITS | GRAPES

WORLD HEALTH

I pray that in all things thou mayest prosper and be in health —3 JOHN

HEALTH may be defined as the balanced relationship of the mind, the body and the external environment. The maps on these pages are concerned with certain significant aspects of health which are related primarily to the effects of environment, diet and climate.

Types of diseases vary with latitude and with the standard of living of the community. In the more advanced communities the major health problems are cancer, diseases of the heart and circulation, and nervous and mental disorders, most of which are associated with middle and old age.

In tropical and near-tropical climates, where many of the under-developed countries are situated, infectious diseases account for the majority of deaths. The underlying causes can be found in poor hygiene and sanitation, in over-crowding and in dietary deficiencies. The very young are the most affected, and mortality in infancy and early childhood is high.

The sharp distinction which exists between the health of the peoples in advanced and under-developed countries can be seen in their expectation of life at birth, which is much lower in the under-developed countries.

It is in the under-developed regions that the population is generally increasing most rapidly, and where malnutrition and malaria are the world's most urgent health problems. The low standard of living results in inadequate supplies of food and, in particular,

insufficient amounts of protein in the diet, which lead to deficiency diseases such as kwashiorkor, beriberi, pellagra, etc., and to the spread of infectious and parasitic diseases such as malaria, yellow fever, tuberculosis, cholera and bilharziasis.

Under the guidance of the United Nations Agencies (the World Health Organization, the Food and Agriculture Organization and the United Nations Children's Fund) these problems are being approached from many directions; in extending the production and consumption of cheap protein-rich foods; in the control of disease carriers such as the mosquito; in the development of preventive and curative medicine; and in improved sanitation and hygiene.

Government health organizations, often working in association with the United Nations Agencies, are actively concerned with these and many associated problems, such as the resistance to antibiotics and insecticides which some microbes, viruses, and insect and animal vectors have developed. Research into the use of new methods of prevention and control of the infectious diseases is being carried on. Mass campaigns for the eradication of yaws and smallpox and the control of leprosy and trachoma are in progress, and an international campaign against malaria is well advanced. The whole movement is towards the complete physical and mental well-being of man in every part of the world.

EXPECTANCY OF LIFE AT BIRTH

	YEARS
DENMARK	1936-1940 / 1963-1964
ITALY	1930-1932 / 1960-1962
NETHERLANDS	1931-1940 / 1961-1965
POLAND	1931-1942 / 1960-1961
SWEDEN	1931-1940 / 1961-1965
UNITED KINGDOM	1930-1932 / 1963-1965
ARGENTINA	1914 / 1959-1961
BRAZIL	1939-1941 / 1949-1951
MEXICO	1930 / 1956
AUSTRALIA	1932-1934 / 1960-1962
UNITED STATES OF AMERICA	1939-1941 / 1965
CANADA	1940-1942 / 1960-1962
REPUBLIC OF SOUTH AFRICA	1935-1937 / 1950-1952
CEYLON	1945-1947 / 1962
INDIA	1921-1931 / 1951-1960
PHILIPPINES	1938 / 1946-1949
JAPAN	1935-1936 / 1965
ISRAEL	1949 / 1965
CONGO (AFRICAN POPULATION)	1950-1952 / 1960-1966
SPAIN	1950 / 1960

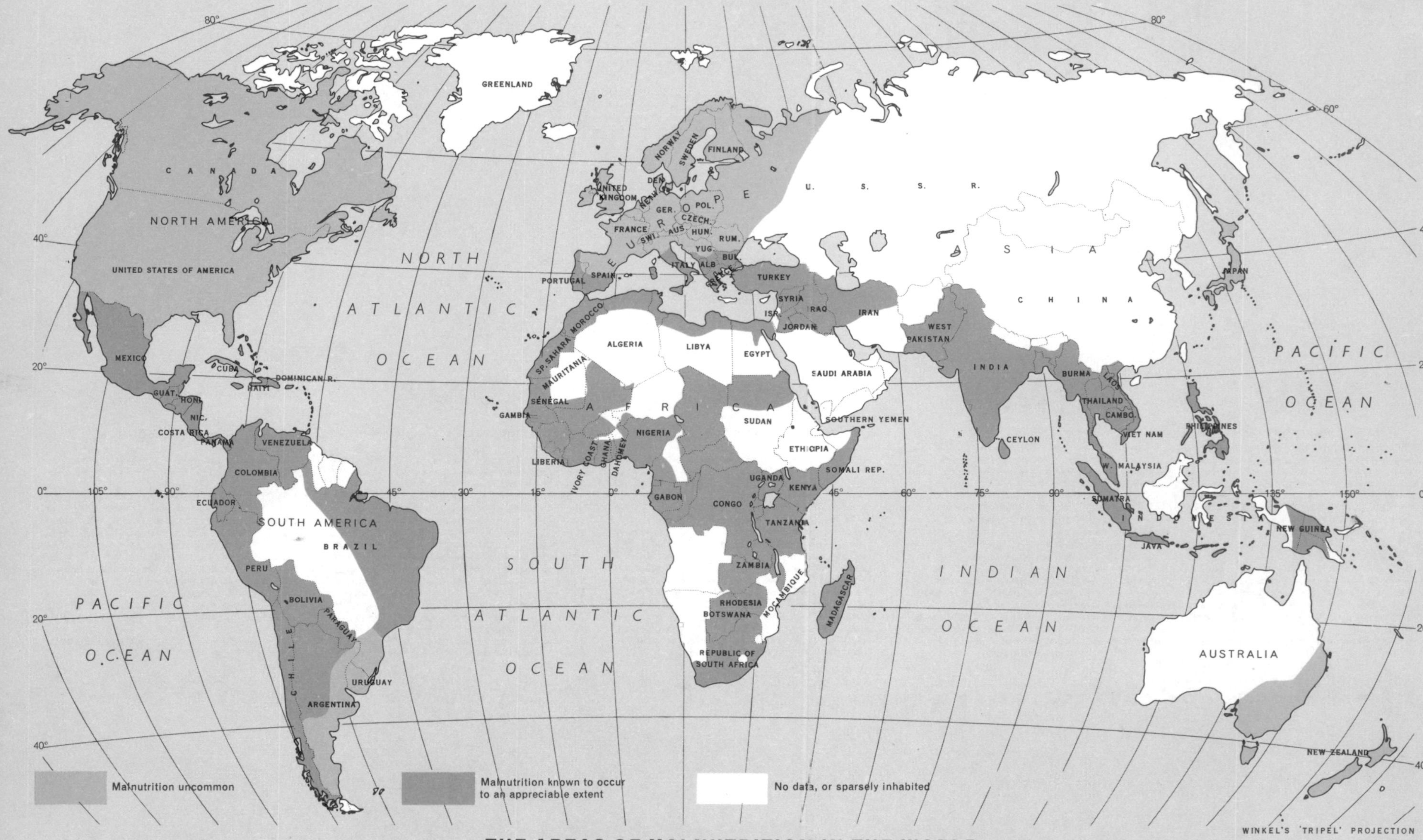

THE AREAS OF MALNUTRITION IN THE WORLD

Malnutrition uncommon   Malnutrition known to occur to an appreciable extent   No data, or sparsely inhabited

WINKEL'S 'TRIPEL' PROJECTION

The map shows roughly the areas where ill-health and disease due to diet deficiency are most common and serious. Under-nutrition and malnutrition occur where the food requirements of a population are greater than its capacity for obtaining them from its own land by agriculture or from the lands of other nations by trade, that is, in countries where the birth rate is high and industrial development is low. A satisfactory diet must supply enough calories and also fulfil the body's requirements for proteins, fats, minerals and vitamins. Proteins are of special importance. The amount of animal protein in a diet often gives a rough idea of its nutritive value and an indication of the general standard of living of the population concerned. In areas of malnutrition protein supplies are much lower than in a well-fed country, such as Great Britain. In many of these areas the population is expanding rapidly and includes large numbers of young children. A sufficient quantity of protein is particularly necessary during the early years of life when the body is growing most quickly. Protein deficiency is, therefore, one of the most serious of nutritional problems.

The chart compares the birth weights and rate of increase in

weight in well-nourished and malnourished infants and young children. During the early months of life a child can obtain the calories and nutrients it needs from its mother's milk, but in the period following weaning, from 6 months to 4 years, "critical" years when a good diet is particularly essential, a child in areas of malnutrition must usually subsist on his share of the meagre diet, mainly cereals and starchy roots, on which his family depends.

The high death rates in this age group, for example 1 in 11 live births in India and 1 in 17 in Mexico, as compared with 1 in 322 in Britain, are largely due to deficiencies in diet; kwashiorkor is prevalent in areas of protein deficiency, and other deficiency conditions are found in association with poor cereal diets. The common infectious diseases, such as measles and dysentery, are more likely to be fatal in children suffering from malnutrition.

While malnutrition is most prevalent in young children and expectant and nursing mothers, other groups also suffer. An insufficient and unbalanced diet impairs the health of people of all ages and thus affects their working capacity, with the result that the progress of entire communities may be retarded.

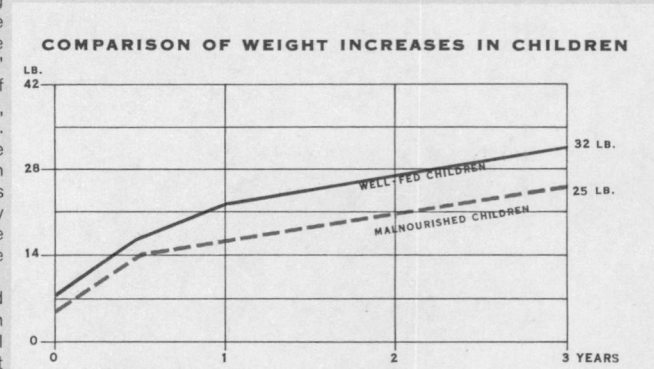

COMPARISON OF WEIGHT INCREASES IN CHILDREN

WELL-FED CHILDREN — 32 LB.
MALNOURISHED CHILDREN — 25 LB.

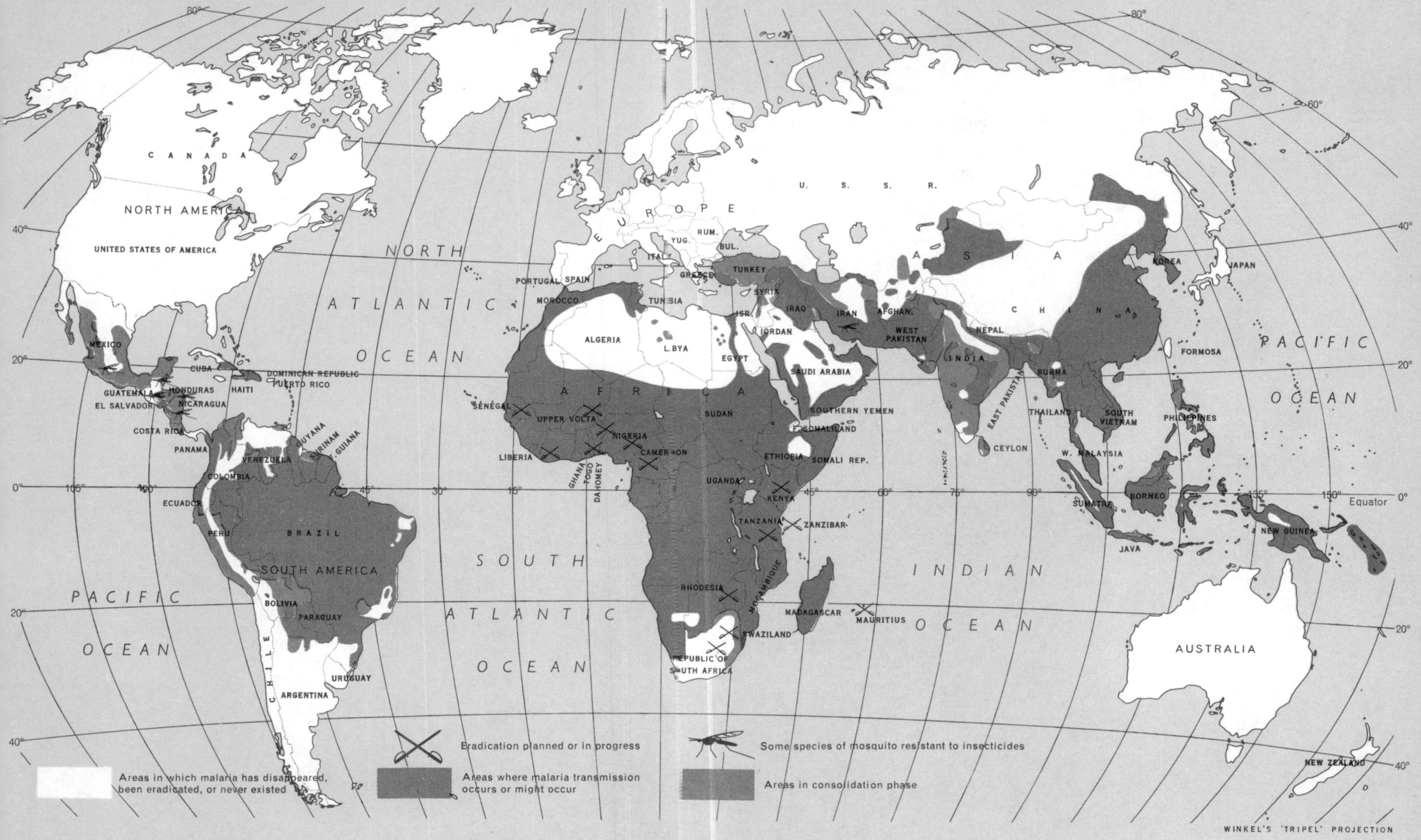
CANADA
NORTH AMERICA
UNITED STATES OF AMERICA
NORTH ATLANTIC OCEAN
EUROPE
U.S.S.R.
ASIA
CHINA
AFRICA
SOUTH AMERICA
BRAZIL
SOUTH ATLANTIC OCEAN
INDIAN OCEAN
PACIFIC OCEAN
AUSTRALIA
NEW ZEALAND
Equator
Areas in which malaria has disappeared, been eradicated, or never existed
Eradication planned or in progress
Areas where malaria transmission occurs or might occur
Some species of mosquito resistant to insecticides
Areas in consolidation phase
WINKEL'S 'TRIPEL' PROJECTION

MALARIA AND THE PROGRESS OF ERADICATION

Malaria is a constant threat to half the world's population. It is man's greatest single health problem. It kills one person in five, striking first at a country's most precious possession, its children. In tropical Africa alone, one in ten of all under-fours dies from its direct effects and many thousands more from its indirect effects, for malaria weakens the organism and makes it more susceptible to other diseases. Bilharziasis, cholera, leprosy, yaws, yellow fever and tuberculosis take a heavy toll of life in tropical countries, but none is as widespread, or as costly in its effects, as malaria.

Malaria stunts man's physical and mental growth, bringing chronic ill-health to millions; it impedes the economic and social progress of a country. Hundreds of millions of working days are lost each year through the sickness it causes; vast tracts of fertile land in Africa, Asia, South and Central America, have been abandoned or left uncultivated because of its ravages.

For centuries the only effective remedy against malaria was quinine. But in 1939, armed with the knowledge accumulated since the discovery in 1880 of the cause of malaria and its communication from one person to another through *Anopheles* mosquito bites, scientists concentrated on eliminating the mosquito. D.D.T. and other insecticides sprayed on the inside walls of dwellings, where the mosquitos rest after biting, killed the insects and remained active for as long as six months after initial sprayings. By this simple method it was possible to protect the population for as little as two to three shillings per head per year. In 1948 the World Health Organization launched a series of spraying campaigns designed to control malaria. Anti-malaria drugs, developed in the 1930's and found to be dramatically effective, particularly in the Second World War, were also used, but were more difficult to administer because of the widespread dispersal of the population in malarious areas. The number of people protected by World Health Organization campaigns increased from less than a million in 1949 to one hundred million in 1966.

In 1951 the mosquito counter-attacked. D.D.T. insecticides were becoming less effective, and in Greece the mosquito was developing a resistance to them. It became vital to interrupt the transmission of malaria and eradicate the disease before this sporadic resistance spread farther and made spraying campaigns ineffective. A world-wide campaign for the total eradication of malaria was launched.

Our map shows the progress of this campaign. By the end of 1966, of the 1,592 million people exposed to malaria, nearly 619 million were freed from its threat, 335 million were being protected by active eradication programmes, and a further 273 million will be protected within a few years. Greece, once the most malaria-ridden country in Europe, reduced its cases from one million in 1938 to very few in 1966. More than twenty countries have completely or virtually eliminated this disease, and a number of others have dramatically lowered their death rates at all ages.

Great progress has been made, but many millions of people still go unprotected. The attack on the mosquito becomes increasingly urgent as more and more species develop resistance to insecticides. Already 24 *Anopheles* species—half of them serious malaria carriers—are known to be immune to modern insecticides, including the most resistant species of all, *Anopheles gambiae*, which threatens over 90 per cent of the population of tropical Africa.

The total eradication of malaria is vital. Unless it is pursued energetically, the disease which has plagued man for thousands of years will spread anew throughout the world.

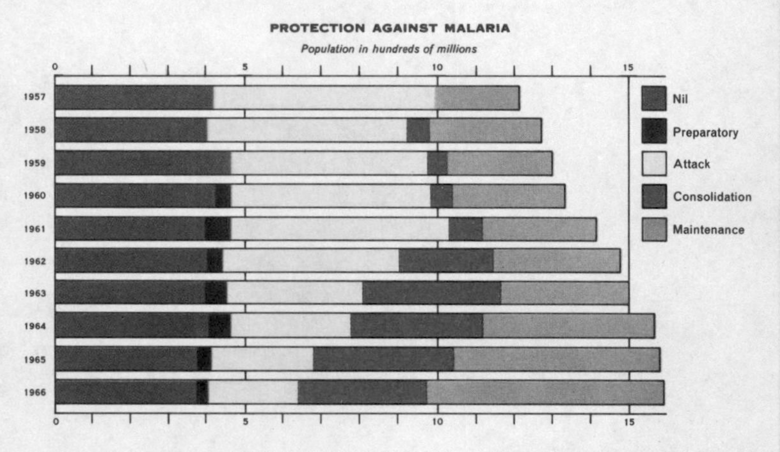
PROTECTION AGAINST MALARIA
Population in hundreds of millions
0
5
10
15
1957
1958
1959
1960
1961
1962
1963
1964
1965
1966
Nil
Preparatory
Attack
Consolidation
Maintenance

The above chart shows changes in the distribution of population in the originally malarious areas of the world (W.H.O. regions) by phase of malaria eradication between 1957 and 1966

HEALTH IN BRITAIN

Preventive, social and clinical medicine are now playing an increasingly vital part in the improvement of health.

A little over a century ago infectious diseases—cholera, diphtheria, smallpox, typhoid and tuberculosis—accounted for more than half the deaths in Britain. Childbirth was often dangerous; many babies did not survive infancy; men, women and even children (those over ten years old) worked a sixty-hour week in the factories and mines; and malnutrition, insanitary living conditions and lack of public hygiene measures so encouraged the spread of sickness and disease that man's expectancy of life at birth was less than fifty years.

Higher standards in living conditions, the discovery of sulphonamides and of antibiotics such as penicillin, and the introduction of vaccination and immunization have now drastically reduced the death rate from the infectious diseases. Not one person died of diphtheria in 1965 compared with nearly 10,000 a century ago. For every million of population only 39 died of pulmonary tuberculosis compared with 3,330 per million in 1859. The conquest and control of these and other diseases, and the greatly improved health of the community have come about not only by dramatic advances in medical science, but also by the development of preventive and social medicine. Better food, housing and sanitation; maternity clinics, child welfare and school health services, mass X-ray and industrial medicine; improvement in the hours and conditions of work; a new approach to the mentally ill and mentally disabled; all have contributed to the health and well-being of the nation. The striking reduction in the infant mortality rate from 147 per 1,000 live births in 1859 to 22 per 1,000 in 1965, the increase in the weight and height of schoolchildren, and the increase in life expectancy at one year of 21 years for men and 26 years for women, are indications of the better health of the people.

The major health problems are now mainly associated with the older age groups. Bronchitis causes nearly 30,000 deaths and the loss of 27 million working days a year, and the effects of rheumatic diseases cause the loss of a further 27 million working days. There has been a marked increase in the degenerative diseases, particularly cancer of the lung and diseases of the heart and circulation. These, and the various forms of arthritis, fall heaviest on people aged over fifty.

The increase in the figures for degenerative diseases is partly because medical science has learned to diagnose them more effectively, and partly because the population as a whole is living longer. But just as the infectious diseases are being conquered, so too it is hoped to overcome the degenerative disorders. Already early diagnosis of some forms of cancer has doubled and even trebled the rate of cure.

As medical science enables more and more people to live out the natural lifespan of threescore years and ten, and consequently to extend their working lives, the provision of special jobs for the older men and women to suit their slower reactions and declining manual dexterity, and of homes and hospital accommodation for the aged, are an especially important function of the country's Health Service.

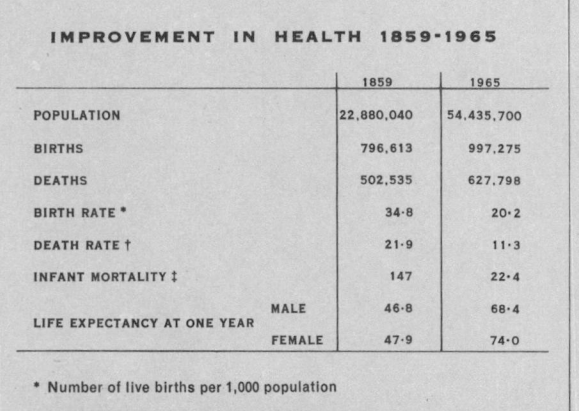

IMPROVEMENT IN HEALTH 1859-1965

		1859	1965
POPULATION		22,880,040	54,435,700
BIRTHS		796,613	997,275
DEATHS		502,535	627,798
BIRTH RATE *		34·8	20·2
DEATH RATE †		21·9	11·3
INFANT MORTALITY ‡		147	22·4
LIFE EXPECTANCY AT ONE YEAR	MALE	46·8	68·4
	FEMALE	47·9	74·0

* Number of live births per 1,000 population

† Number of deaths per 1,000 population

‡ Number of deaths of infants under 1 yr. per 1,000 live births

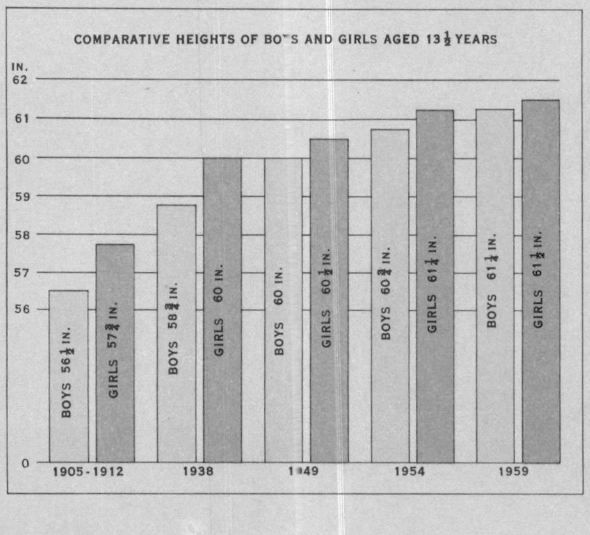
COMPARATIVE HEIGHTS OF BOYS AND GIRLS AGED 13½ YEARS
IN.
62
61
60
59
58
57
56
0
BOYS 56½ IN.
GIRLS 57¾ IN.
BOYS 58¾ IN.
GIRLS 60 IN.
BOYS 60 IN.
GIRLS 60½ IN.
BOYS 60¾ IN.
GIRLS 61¼ IN.
BOYS 61¼ IN.
GIRLS 61½ IN.
1905-1912
1938
1954
1959

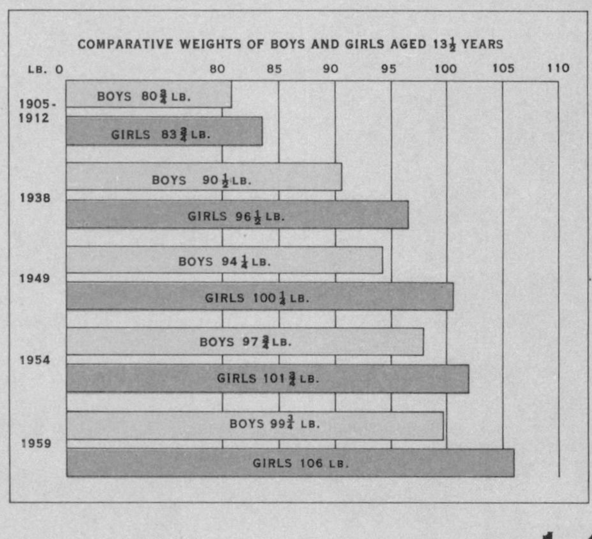
COMPARATIVE WEIGHTS OF BOYS AND GIRLS AGED 13½ YEARS
LB. 0
80
85
90
95
100
105
110
1905-1912
BOYS 80¾ LB.
GIRLS 83¾ LB.
1938
BOYS 90½ LB.
GIRLS 96½ LB.
1949
BOYS 94¼ LB.
GIRLS 100¼ LB.
1954
BOYS 97¾ LB.
GIRLS 101¾ LB.
1959
BOYS 99¾ LB.
GIRLS 106 LB.

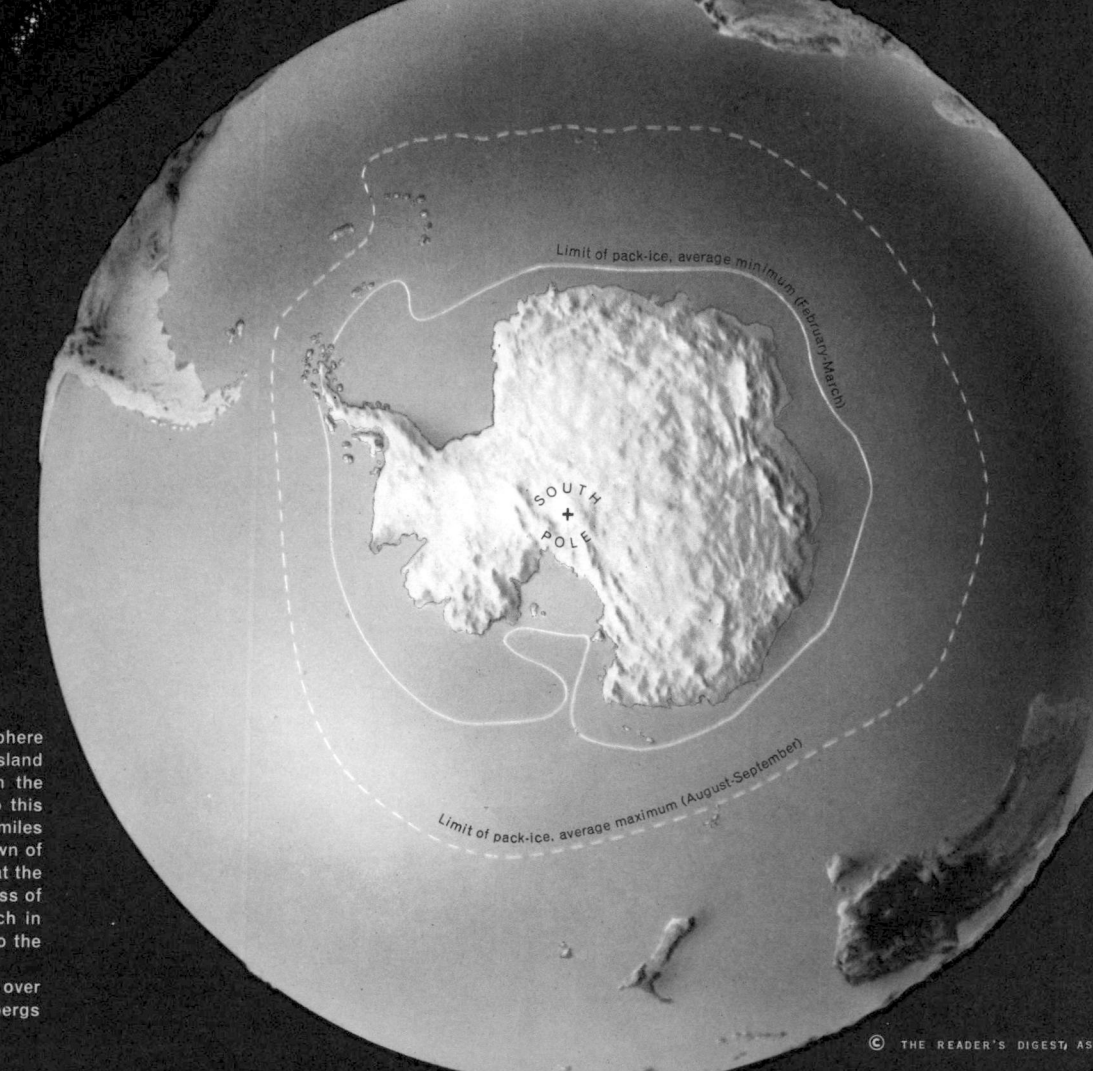

THE MASS OF LAND

In full summer, from a point above central eastern Europe, the whole range of the Earth's surface structure can be seen. To the north a great plain stretches from the North Sea across Europe into Siberia, and finally merges into the close-packed ice-floes of the Arctic. To the south an immense desert barrier sweeps from the shores of the Atlantic in a giant scimitar curve across the north of Africa, Arabia, Turkestan, and to the Gobi. Except for the Chinese borderlands, this desert barrier has been dominated for a thousand years by the Muslim religion, so that both Europe and Christianity were shut off from the immemorial East until the Portuguese found a sea-way round Africa—an ocean ring-road round the Middle East. In Asia the mountains broaden out from the Caucasus to form the great wall of the mighty Himalayas with the Tibetan plateau behind them; and farther south lie the hot and densely populated lands of southern Asia.

In winter a view from the same point would reveal a dramatically unbroken sheet of snow stretching from the northern plain of Poland to the Pacific, demonstrating how the cold intensifies as the land recedes from the maritime western edges and reaches into the heart of the continent.

AROUND

And God saw every thing that he had made—GENESIS

These are views of the world as no man has eve
seen it—a world exposed as a tangle of wild grandeur
as a blanket of water; as a globe roofed in ice; as
illusions of light and shadow. Earth-bound man

WHERE MEN LIGHTEN THE DARKNESS

At night the populated areas of the world prick out patterns of light, clustered thickly where population is densest.

From a point directly above London we see a half-world in which live nine out of every ten of the people of the Earth. The lights of western Europe form a bright galaxy, for this region contains 85 towns with populations of 200,000 or over. Across the Atlantic, in the eastern United States, glow the lights of 40 towns of similar size. To the east are the bright clusters in Pakistan and India, in China, Japan and Indonesia—the homes of more than 1,200 million people.

Elsewhere are smaller concentrations of light—in California, on the banks of the Nile, round the coasts of the continents—almost every-where except in the polar seas. Great black patches can be seen where unilluminated night broods over the circle of frozen northlands and over vast deserts and mountain ranges.

A CONTINENT OF ICE

Seen from a point directly over the South Pole, the Southern Hemisphere seems to be dominated by the shining ice cap that covers an island larger than the continent of Europe. In almost every direction the horizon is sea, although the tips of three continents extend into this half-world. Cape Horn, at the tip of South America, is 2,350 miles from the South Pole; Buenos Aires, the most southerly large town of South America, is 3,800 miles from it; the Cape of Good Hope, at the tip of Africa, with the port of Cape Town and the broadening mass of South Africa beyond, lies a similar distance away; Christchurch in New Zealand and Hobart in Tasmania, the largest towns near to the Pole, are 3,200 miles distant from it.

In this half-world there are only 25 towns with populations over 200,000. The stormy southern seas are deserted except for the icebergs which calve off the ice cap to drift far out into the ocean.

Limit of pack-ice, average minimum (February-March)

SOUTH + POLE

Limit of pack-ice, average maximum (August-September)

THE WATER PLANET

Tahiti is at the centre of this half-world—a half-world that is almost all water. The Pacific, largest of all oceans, shows its vast expanse. To the east and south of Tahiti are thousands of square miles of ocean without a single island or reef. In the western Pacific groups of tiny islands gleam white in the sunlight; far to the north Hawaii stands out as a solitary stepping stone on the 6,200 mile hop from North America to Asia. Solid land masses are far away, only just appearing on the horizon. To the south-west is Australia—with Sydney, a mere 3,801 miles from the island of Tahiti. The vast semicircle of the Americas serrates the opposite skyline; Vancouver is 4,888 miles away, Panama 5,180, Cape Horn 4,950. China and Japan lie out of sight. Tokyo is 5,893 miles from Tahiti.

Compare this hemisphere with the one to its left. There, millions of people live in the heart of Asia, and may be as far as three thousand miles from the open sea. Here, in the water hemisphere, live only a few hundred thousand people, thousands of miles from any sizeable land.

HE WORLD

nows the broad truths of geography only from the
g-saw of the details he can see. Here the jig-saw
as been completed; the world is seen in perspective.
Hold these pages 18 inches from your eyes. Each
alf-world will reveal the Earth just the size you
ould see it were you 25,000 miles out in space.

NORTH
+
POLE

DAWN ADVANCES

Part of the world is in shadow: it is at a stage between "new Earth" and "full Earth."

Dawn, advancing at the rate of 15 degrees longitude every hour, is just reaching the Americas. The first rays of the rising sun break from the east on the hills of Nova Scotia and Brazil, while the glaciers of Greenland are already in full daylight. It is nine in London and breakfast is over, four in the morning in New York, an hour after midnight in San Francisco, and noon in Baghdad.

Only at the equinoxes in March and September does every place in the world have an equal number of hours of darkness and light. In June the tilt of the Earth's axis brings full daylight all round the clock to the North Pole. It is then midsummer in the Northern Hemisphere and midwinter in the Southern.

THE ROOF OF THE WORLD

The North Pole, with its monotonous waste of broken ice, is the hub of this crowded view. The floating ice of the North Pole merges into the surrounding land masses. Round the Arctic lies the expanse of frozen northlands of Russia and Canada. Below comes the belt of coniferous forest which rings the world from the Atlantic Ocean to the Pacific, and, jumping the 50-mile gap between Siberia and North America, sweeps on again round the globe from the Pacific Ocean to the Atlantic. Below the forest region, great towns describe another circle round the globe—Leningrad 2,070 miles from the North Pole, Glasgow 2,360, Quebec 3,000 and Edmonton 2,520. Along this ring of towns the transcontinental railways, the trunk roads, the busiest air-routes make a web of communications that is continued across the oceans by ships and planes navigating on "great circle" routes. Far on the horizon lies the belt of desert and mountain between temperate and tropical lands.

FACTS ABOUT THE EARTH

Estimated age of the Earth . . at least 4,500 million years
Superficial area . . . . . . 196,950,000 sq. miles
Land surface . . . . . . 57,510,000 sq. miles
Water surface (71% of total area) . 139,440,000 sq. miles
Equatorial circumference . . . . 24,902 miles
Meridional circumference . . . . 24,860 miles
Volume of the Earth . . . 260,000,000,000 cubic miles
Mass, or weight . . . 6,586,542,500,000,000,000,000 tons

It is estimated that the Earth attracts 14·9 tons of cosmic dust annually.
Highest point of the Earth's land surface—
Mount Everest . . . . 29,028 feet
Lowest point of the Earth's land surface—
Shores of the Dead Sea, Israel-Jordan 1,299 feet below sea level
Greatest ocean depth—Marianas Trench, off the Philippines . . . . 36,198 feet below sea level

The Earth makes one complete revolution round the Sun every 365 days, 5 hours, 48 minutes and 46 seconds.

The Earth makes one complete rotation on its axis in 23 hours and 56 minutes.

The Earth revolves in its orbit round the Sun at a speed of 66,600 miles per hour.

The Earth rotates on its axis at an equatorial speed of more than 1,000 miles per hour.

CONTINENTS

	Area square miles	Mean Elevation feet	Highest Elevation feet	Lowest Elevation feet	Highest Recorded Temperature	Lowest Recorded Temperature
AFRICA	11,693,000	1,900	Mt. Kilimanjaro, Tanzania 19,340	Lake Assal, Fr. Somaliland 492 below sea level	Al Aziziyah, Libya 136·4°F	Semrir, Morocco —11·4°F
ANTARCTICA	5,150,000	6,000	Vinson Massif 16,864	Sea level	Hope Bay, Graham Land 59·4°F	Nr. Vostok —126·9°F
ASIA	16,943,000	3,000	Mt. Everest, Nepal–Tibet 29,028	Dead Sea, Israel–Jordan 1,299 below sea level	Jacobabad, Pakistan 127·1°F	Verkhoyansk, Siberia —89·9°F
AUSTRALIA	2,967,909	1,000	Mt. Kosciusko, N. S. Wales 7,316	Lake Eyre, South Australia 52 below sea level	Cloncurry, Queensland 127·5°F	Charlotte Pass, N. S. Wales —8·0°F
EUROPE*	4,053,300	980	Mt. El'brus, U.S.S.R. 18,482	Caspian Sea, U.S.S.R. 92 below sea level	Seville, Spain 124·0°F	Ust'-Shchugor, U.S.S.R. —67·0°F
NORTH AMERICA	9,365,000	2,000	Mt. McKinley, Alaska 20,320	Death Valley, California 282 below sea level	Death Valley, California 133·9°F	Snag, Yukon —81·0°F
SOUTH AMERICA	6,880,000	1,800	Mt. Aconcagua, Argentina 22,834	Salinas Grandes, Argentina 131 below sea level	Rivadavia, Argentina 120·0°F	Sarmiento, Argentina —27·4°F

* Including U.S.S.R. west of Ural'skiy Khrebet.

HIGHEST MOUNTAINS OF THE WORLD

	feet		feet		feet		feet
Everest, Nepal-Tibet	29,028	Nanda Devi, India	25,645	Muztagh Ata, Sinkiang	24,757	Mercedario, Argentina	22,211
K2 (Godwin Austen), Kashmir-Sinkiang	28,250	Rakaposhi, Kashmir	25,550	Kommunisma, (Pik), U.S.S.R.	24,590	Huascarán, Peru	22,205
Kangchenjunga, Nepal-India	28,209	Lamet, India-Tibet	25,447	Pobedy, (Pik), U.S.S.R.-Sinkiang	24,407	Llullaillaco, Argentina-Chile	22,057
Makalu, Tibet-Nepal	27,805	Namcha Barwa, Tibet	25,447	Chomolhari, Bhutan-Tibet	23,997	Kailas, Tibet	22,028
Dhaulagiri, Nepal	26,810	Gurla Mandhata, Tibet	25,355	Lenina, (Pik), U.S.S.R.	23,406	Yerupaja, Peru	21,759
Nanga Parbat, Kashmir	26,660	Ulugh Muztagh, Tibet	25,338	Aconcagua, Argentina	22,834	Ancohuma, Bolivia	21,490
Annapurna, Nepal	26,504	Kungur, Sinkiang	25,325	Illimani, Bolivia	22,579	Sajama, Bolivia	21,390
Gasherbrum, Kashmir	26,470	Tirich Mir, Pakistan	25,230	Ojos del Salado, Chile-Argentina	22,539	Illampu, Bolivia	21,276
Gosainthan, Tibet	26,291	Amne Machin, China	25,000	Bonete, Argentina	22,546	Coropuna, Peru	21,079
		Minya Konka, China	24,903	Tupungato, Chile	22,310	Chimborazo, Ecuador	20,577

The total number of active volcanoes is 485, and the most violent eruption on record is that of Krakatoa (Indonesia) in 1833

PRINCIPAL OCEANS AND SEAS OF THE WORLD

	Area sq. miles	Average Depth in feet	Greatest Depth in feet		Area sq. miles	Average Depth in feet	Greatest Depth in feet		Area sq. miles	Average Depth in feet	Greatest Depth in feet
Pacific Ocean	63,986,000	14,040	36,198	Bering Sea	878,000	1,665	13,422	Hudson Bay	472,000	440	1,500
Atlantic Ocean	31,530,000	12,880	30,143	Caribbean Sea	750,000	8,400	23,750	Japan, Sea of	405,000	4,835	10,200
Indian Ocean	28,350,000	13,000	22,968	Gulf of Mexico	700,000	4,700	12,426	North Sea	221,000	180	1,998
Arctic Ocean	5,541,600	4,200	17,850	Okhotsk, Sea of	582,000	3,000	12,621	Red Sea	178,000	1,490	7,254
Mediterranean Sea	1,145,000	4,500	14,435	East China Sea	480,000	610	10,500	Black Sea	168,500	4,300	7,362
South China Sea	895,000	5,400	16,456	Yellow Sea	480,000	160	348	Baltic Sea	158,000	221	1,300

LONGEST RIVERS OF THE WORLD

	miles		miles		miles		miles
Nile, Africa	4,090	Hwang Ho (Yellow), China	2,700	Volga, U.S.S.R.	2,290	Purus, South America	1,850
Amazon, South America	4,050	Lena, U.S.S.R.	2,645	Madeira, South America	2,100	Brahmaputra, Asia	1,800
Mississippi—Missouri, U.S.A.	3,760	Mackenzie, Canada	2,635	Paraná, South America	2,050	Orinoco, South America	1,800
Irtysh, U.S.S.R.	3,200	Mekong, Asia	2,600	Indus, Asia	1,980	São Francisco, S. America	1,800
Yangtze, China	3,100	Niger, Africa	2,600	Yukon, Alaska	1,979	Danube, Europe	1,770
Amur, Asia	2,900	Yenisey, U.S.S.R.	2,360	St. Lawrence, Canada	1,945	Salween, Burma—China	1,750
Congo, Africa	2,718	Murray—Darling, Australia	2,310	Rio Grande, U.S.A.	1,885	Euphrates, Asia	1,700

PRINCIPAL LAKES OF THE WORLD

	sq. miles		sq. miles		sq. miles		sq. miles
Caspian Sea, U.S.S.R.–Iran (salt)	170,000	Tanganyika, East Central Africa	12,700	Ontario, U.S.A.–Canada	7,540	Athabasca, Canada	3,058
Superior, U.S.A.–Canada	31,820	Great Bear, Canada	11,660	Balkhash, U.S.S.R.	7,050	Nicaragua, Nicaragua	3,000
Victoria, East Central Africa	26,200	Baykal, U.S.S.R.	11,580	Ladoga, U.S.S.R.	7,000	Reindeer, Canada	2,440
Aral, U.S.S.R. (salt)	24,400	Great Slave, Canada	11,170	Onega, U.S.S.R.	3,800	Torrens, Australia (salt)	2,400
Huron, U.S.A.–Canada	23,010	Erie, U.S.A.–Canada	9,940	Eyre, Australia (salt)	3,700	Koko Nor, China (salt)	2,300
Michigan, U.S.A.	22,400	Winnipeg, Canada	9,398	Rudolf, Kenya (salt)	3,500	Issyk-Kul', U.S.S.R.	2,276
Nyasa, East Central Africa	14,200	Chad, North Central Africa	8,000	Titicaca, Peru–Bolivia	3,200	Vänern, Sweden	2,150

SECTION FOUR

INDEX

PART ONE—THE BRITISH ISLES

PAGES 30-38

LIST OF COUNTIES AND ABBREVIATIONS

Counties in England

Bedford	Beds.
Berkshire	Berks.
Buckingham	Bucks.
Cambridge and Isle of Ely	Cambs.
Cheshire	Ches.
Cornwall	Corn.
Cumberland	Cumb.
Derby	—
Devon	—
Dorset	—
Durham	—
Essex	—
Gloucester	Glos.
Greater London Council Area	London
Hampshire	Hants.
Hereford	Herefs.
Hertford	Herts.
Huntingdon and Peterborough	Hunts.
Kent	—
Lancashire	Lancs.
Leicester	Leics.
Lincoln	Lincs.
Norfolk	Norf.
Northamptonshire	Northants.
Northumberland	N'land.
Nottinghamshire	Notts.
Oxford	Oxon.
Rutland	Rutl.
Shropshire (Salop)	Shrops.
Somerset	Som.
Staffordshire	Staffs.
Suffolk	Suff.
Surrey	—
Sussex	—
Warwick	Warks.
Westmorland	W'land.
Wiltshire	Wilts.
Worcestershire	Worcs.
Yorkshire	Yorks.
Monmouth	Mon.

Counties in Wales

Anglesey	Angl.
Brecknock	Brecon.
Caernarvon	Caern.
Cardigan	Card.
Carmarthen	Carm.
Denbigh	Denb.
Flint	—
Glamorgan	Glam.
Merioneth	Mer.
Montgomery	Mont.
Pembroke	Pemb.
Radnor	Rad.

Counties in Scotland

Aberdeen	A'deen.
Angus	—
Argyll	—
Ayr	—
Banff	—
Berwick	Ber.
Bute	—
Caithness	Caith.
Clackmannan	Clack.
Dumfries	Dumf.
Dunbarton	Dunb.
East Lothian	E. Loth.
Fife	—
Inverness	I'ness.
Kincardine	Kinc.
Kinross	—
Kirkcudbright	Kirkcud.
Lanark	—
Midlothian	M'loth.
Moray	—
Nairn	—
Orkney	—
Peebles	Peebl.
Perth	—
Renfrew	Renf.
Ross and Cromarty	Ross.
Roxburgh	Rox.
Selkirk	Selk.
Shetland	Shet.
Stirling	Stir.
Sutherland	Suth.
West Lothian	W. Loth.
Wigtown	Wig.

Counties in N. Ireland

Antrim	Ant.
Armagh	Arm.
Down	—
Fermanagh	Ferm.
Londonderry	Lond.
Tyrone	—

Counties in the Republic of Ireland (Eire)

Carlow	Leix	Waterford
Cavan	Limerick	Westmeath
Clare	Longford	Wexford
Cork	Louth	Wicklow
Donegal	Mayo	
Dublin	Meath	
Galway	Monaghan	
Kerry	Offaly	
Kildare	Roscommon	
Kilkenny	Sligo	
Leitrim	Tipperary	

Abbreviations

B.	Bay
C.	Cape
Co.	County
Dist.	District
Div.	Division
E.	East
Eng.	England
Gt.	Great
Hd.	Head
I.	Island
Ire.	Ireland
L.	Lake
Lt. Ho.	Light House
Mt.	Mountain
N.	North
Oc.	Ocean
Pk.	Peak
Prov.	Province
Pt.	Point
Res.	Reservoir
Scot.	Scotland
S.	South
Sd.	Sound
Str.	Strait
W.	West

Abbe **Broa**

A

Abbeyfeale, Limerick, Eire 33 Ej
Abbeyleix, Leix, Eire 33 Jh
Abbey Town, Cumb., Eng. 38 Bc
Abbots Bromley, Staffs., England 37 Lc
Abbotsbury, Dorset, Eng. 36 Jg
Aberaeron, Wales 36 Fd
Aberchirder, Banff, Scot. 34 Ld
Aberdare, Glam., Wales 36 He
Aberdeen and co., Scot. 34 Me
Aberdovey, Mer., Wales 36 Fc
Aberfeldy, Perth, Scotland 35 Jf
Aberfoyle, Perth, Scotland 35 Hg
Abergavenny, Mon. 36 He
Abergele, Denbigh, Wales 36 Gb
Abernethy, Perth, Scotland 35 Kg
Aberthaw, Glam., Wales 36 Hf
Abertillery, Mon. 36 He
Aberystwyth, Card., Wales 36 Fd
Abingdon, Berks., England 37 Me
Abington, Lanark, Scotland 35 Jh
Aboyne, Aberdeen, Scotland 34 Le
Accrington, Lancs., Eng. 38 De
Achill, Mayo, Eire 32 Df
Achill Hd. and I., Mayo, Eire 32 Cf
Achnasheen, Ross., Scot. 34 Fd
Aclare, Sligo, Eire 32 Fe
Adare, Limerick, Eire 33 Fh
Ailsa Craig, I., Ayr, Scot. 35 Fj
Aintree, Lancs., England 38 Cf
Air, Pt. of, Flint, Wales 36 Hb
Airdrie, Lanark, Scotland 35 Jh
Aire Gap, Yorks., England 38 De
Aire, R., Yorks., England 38 Ee
Airedale, Yorks., England 38 Ee
Alcester, Warwick, Eng. 37 Ld
Aldbrough, Yorks., England 38 He
Aldeburgh, Suffolk, Eng. 37 Td
Alderney, I., Channel Is. 37 Kk
Aldershot, Hants., England 37 Nf
Alexandria, Dumb., Scot. 35 Gh
Alford, Aberdeen, Scotland 34 Le
Alford, Lincs., England 38 Jf
Alfreton, Derby, England 38 Ff
Allen, L., Leitrim, Eire 32 Ge
Allen, Bog of, Offaly, etc., Eire 33 Jg
Allendale Town, N'land., Eng. 38 Dc
Alloa, Clackmannan, Scot. 35 Jg
Allonby, Cumberland, Eng. 38 Bc
Almond, R., Perth, Scotland 35 Jg
Aln, R., N'land., Eng. 38 Eb
Alness, Ross., Scot. 34 Hd
Alnmouth, N'land., Eng. 38 Eb
Alnwick, N'land., Eng. 38 Eb
Alston, Cumberland, Eng. 38 Dc
Althorpe, Lincs., England 38 Ge
Altnaharra, Suth., Scot. 34 Hc
Alton, Hants., England 37 Nf
Altrincham, Cheshire, Eng. 38 Df
Alwen, Res., Denb., Wales 36 Gb
Alyth, Perth, Scotland 35 Kf
Amble, N'land., Eng. 38 Eb
Ambleside, W'land., Eng. 38 Cd
Amersham, Bucks., England 37 Ne
Amesbury, Wilts., England 37 Lf
Amlwch, Anglesey, Wales 36 Fb
Ammanford, Carm., Wales 36 Ge
Ampthill, Bedford, England 37 Pd
Andover, Hants., England 37 Mf
Anglesey, co. and I., Wales 36 Fb
Angus, co., Scotland 35 Lf
Annan, Dumfries, Scotland 35 Kk
Annan, R., Dumfries, Scot. 35 Kj
Annandale, Dumfries, Scot. 35 Kj
Anstruther, Fife, Scotland 35 Lg
An Teallach, mt., Ross and Cromarty, Scotland 34 Fd
Antrim and co., N. Ireland 32 Ld
Antrim Hills, Antrim, N. Ire. 32 Lc
An Uaimh, Meath, Eire 32 Kf
Appleby, W'land., Eng. 38 Dc
Applecross, Ross., Scot. 34 Ee
Appledore, Devon, England 36 Ff
Aran I., Donegal, Eire 32 Fc
Aran Is., Galway, Eire 33 Dg
Aran Mawddwy, mt., Merioneth, Wales 36 Gc
Arbroath, Angus, Scotland 35 Lf
Ardara, Donegal, Eire 32 Gd
Ardee, Louth, Eire 32 Kf
Arden, Forest of, Warwick, England 37 Ld
Arderin, pk., Offaly-Leix, Eire 33 Hg
Ardgay, Ross., Scot. 34 Hd
Ardglass, Down, N. Ireland 32 Me
Ardlui, Dunbarton, Scotland 35 Gg
Ardmore B., Waterford, Eire 33 Hk
Ardnamurchan Pt., Argyll, Scotland 35 Df
Ardnave Pt., Islay, Scotland 35 Dh
Ardrishaig, Argyll, Scotland 35 Fg
Ardrossan, Ayr, Scotland 35 Gh
Ards Pen., Down, N. Ire. 32 Md
Ardvasar, Skye, Scotland 34 Ee
Argyll, co., Scotland 35 Fg
Arisaig, and Sd. of, I'ness., Scotland 35 Ef
Arkaig, L., Inverness, Scot. 34 Ff
Arklow, Wicklow, Eire 33 Lh
Armagh and co., N. Ire. 32 Ke
Arra Mts., Tipperary, Eire 33 Gh
Arran, I., Bute, Scotland 35 Fh
Arrochar, Dunbarton, Scot. 35 Gg
Arrow, L., Sligo, Eire 32 Ge
Arun, R., Sussex, England 37 Nf
Arundel, Sussex, England 37 Ng
Ascot, Berks., England 37 Nf
Ashbourne, Derby, England 38 Ef
Ashburton, Devon, England 36 Gg
Ashby-de-la-Zouch, Leicester, England 37 Lc
Ashdown Forest, Sussex, England 37 Qf
Ashford, Kent, England 37 Rf
Ashfordby, Leicester, Eng. 37 Nc
Ashington, Northumberland, England 38 Eb
Ashton, Lancs., England 38 Df
Askeaton, Limerick, Eire 33 Fh
Askrigg, Yorks., England 38 Dd
Aspatria, Cumberland, Eng. 38 Bc
Assynt, L., Sutherland, Scot. 34 Fc
Aston, Cheshire, England 38 Cf
Athboy, Meath, Eire 32 Kf
Athenry, Galway, Eire 33 Fg
Atherstone, Warwick, Eng. 37 Lc
Athleague, Roscommon, Eire 33 Gf
Athlone, Westmeath, Eire 33 Gg
Athy, Kildare, Eire 33 Kh
Attleborough, Nor., Eng. 37 Sc
Auchterarder, Perth, Scot. 35 Jg
Audlem, Cheshire, England 38 Df
Aughnacloy, Tyrone, N. Ire. 32 Ke
Aughrim, Wicklow, Eire 33 Lh
Aultbea, Ross., Scot. 34 Ed
Auskerry, I., Orkney, Scot. 34 La
Aviemore, Inverness, Scot. 34 Je
Avoca, Wicklow, Eire 33 Lh
Avon, R., Banff, Scotland 34 Ke
Avon, R., Hants., England 37 Lg
Avon, R., Warwick-Worcester, England 37 Ld
Avon, R., Wilts., etc., England 37 Kf
Avonmouth, Glos., Eng. 36 Je
Axbridge, Somerset, Eng. 36 Jf
Axminster, Devon, England 36 Jg
Aycliffe, Durham, England 38 Ec
Aylesbury, Bucks., England 37 Ne
Aylsham, Norfolk, England 37 Sc
Ayr and co., Scotland 35 Gj
Ayr, R., Ayr, Scotland 35 Hh
Ayre, Pt. of, Isle of Man 38 Ld

B

Bacup, Lancs., England 38 De
Badenoch, dist., I'ness., Scot. 34 Hf
Baginbun Hd., Wexford, Eire 33 Kj
Bagshot, Surrey, England 37 Nf
Baile Atha Cliath, see Dublin
Bailieborough, Cavan, Eire 32 Kf
Bakewell, Derby, England 37 Lb
Bala and L., Mer., Wales 36 Gc
Bala, Vale of, Mer., Wales 36 Gc
Balbriggan, Dublin, Eire 32 Lf
Baldock, Herts., England 37 Pe
Balerno, Midlothian, Scot. 35 Kh
Ballachulish, Argyll, Scot. 35 Ff
Ballaghaderreen, Roscommon, Eire 32 Ff
Ballantrae, Ayr, Scotland 35 Fj
Ballater, Aberdeen, Scotland 34 Ke
Ballina, Mayo, Eire 32 Ee
Ballinasloe, Galway, Eire 33 Gg
Ballindine, Mayo, Eire 32 Ff
Ballingarry, Limerick, Eire 33 Fj
Ballinluig, Perth, Scotland 35 Jf
Ballinrobe, Mayo, Eire 32 Ef
Ballinskelligs B., Kerry, Eire 33 Ck
Ballitore, Kildare, Eire 33 Kg
Ballybofey, Donegal, Eire 32 Hd
Ballybunion, Kerry, Eire 33 Dh
Ballycastle, Antrim, N. Ire. 32 Lc
Ballycastle, Mayo, Eire 32 Ee
Ballyclare, Antrim, N. Ire. 32 Md
Ballyconnell, Cavan, Eire 32 He
Ballycotton B., Cork, Eire 33 Hk
Ballyduff, Waterford, Eire 33 Gj
Ballygar, Galway, Eire 33 Gf
Ballygawley, Tyrone, N. Ire. 32 Je
Ballyhaise, Cavan, Eire 32 Je
Ballyhaunis, Mayo, Eire 32 Ff
Ballyhoura Hills, Cork, etc., Eire 33 Fj
Ballyjamesduff, Cavan, Eire 32 Jf
Ballymahon, Longford, Eire 33 Hf
Ballymena, Antrim, N. Ire. 32 Ld
Ballymoney, Antrim, N. Ire. 32 Kc
Ballymote, Sligo, Eire 32 Fe
Ballynahinch, Down, N. Ire. 32 Me
Ballyquintin Pt., Down, N. Ireland 32 Ne
Ballyragget, Kilkenny, Eire 33 Jh
Ballyshannon, Donegal, Eire 32 Gd
Ballyvaughan, Clare, Eire 33 Eg
Balmoral Castle, Aberdeen, Scotland 34 Ke
Balta, I., Shetland, Scotland 34 Ra
Baltasound, Shetland, Scot. 34 Ra
Baltimore, Cork, Eire 33 El
Baltinglass, Wicklow, Eire 33 Kh
Bamburgh, N'land., Eng. 38 Ea
Bampton, Devon, England 36 Hg
Bampton, Oxford, England 37 Le
Banagher, Offaly, Eire 33 Hg
Banavie, Inverness, Scotland 35 Ff
Banbridge, Down, N. Ire. 32 Le
Banchory, Kincardine, Scotland 34 Le
Bandon and R., Cork, Eire 33 Fk
Banff, Banff, Scotland 34 Ld
Banff, co., Scotland 34 Ke
Bangor, Caernarvon, Wales 36 Fb
Bangor, Down, N. Ireland 32 Md
Bann, R., N. Ireland 32 Ld
Bann, R., Wicklow, Eire 33 Lh
Bannockburn, Stirling, Scot. 35 Jg
Bantry, Cork, Eire 33 Ek
Bantry B., Cork, Eire 33 Dk
Bardsey, I., Caernarvon, Wales 36 Ec
Bargoed, Glamorgan, Wales 36 He
Barham, Kent, England 37 Sf
Barmouth, Mer., Wales 36 Fc
Barnard Castle, Durham, England 38 Ec
Barnet, London, England 37 Pe
Barnsley, Yorks., England 38 Fe
Barnstaple, Devon, England 36 Ff
Barra, I., Outer Hebrides, Scotland 34 Ae
Barra Hd., Outer Hebrides, Scotland 35 Af
Barra, Sd. of, Outer Hebrides, Scotland 34 Be
Barrhill, Ayr, Scotland 35 Gj
Barrow, Lancs., England 38 Bd
Barrow, R., Carlow, Eire 33 Kj
Barry, Glamorgan, Wales 36 Hf
Barton, Lancs., England 38 Ce
Barton, Lincs., England 38 He
Barvas, Lewis, Scotland 34 Cc
Basildon, Essex, England 37 Qe
Basingstoke, Hants., Eng. 37 Mf
Bass Rock, E. Lothian, Scot. 35 Lg
Bath, Somerset, England 36 Kf
Bathgate, W. Lothian, Scot. 35 Jh
Batley, Yorks., England 38 Ee
Battle, Sussex, England 37 Qg
Bawtry, Notts., England 38 Ff
Beachy Hd., Sussex, England 37 Qg
Beaconsfield, Bucks., Eng. 37 Ne
Beaminster, Dorset, England 36 Jg
Bear I., Cork, Eire 33 Dk
Bearhaven, Cork, Eire 33 Dk
Beaulieu, Hants., England 37 Mg
Beauly, Inverness, Scotland 34 He
Beauly Firth, I'ness., Scot. 34 He
Beauly, R., Inverness, Scot. 34 Ge
Beaumaris, Anglesey, Wales 36 Fb
Beccles, Suffolk, England 37 Td
Bedale, Yorks., England 38 Ed
Beddgelert, Caern., Wales 36 Fb
Bedford and co., England 37 Pd
Bedlington, N'land., Eng. 38 Eb
Bedworth, Warwick, Eng. 37 Md
Beenoskee, mt., Kerry, Eire 33 Cj
Beith, Ayr, Scotland 35 Gh
Belcoo, Fermanagh, N. Ire. 32 He
Belfast, Antrim, N. Ireland 32 Md
Belfast L., N. Ireland 32 Md
Belford, N'land., Eng. 38 Ea
Bell Rock, North Sea, Scot. 35 Mg
Bellingham, N'land., Eng. 38 Db
Belmullet, Mayo, Eire 32 Ce
Belper, Derby, England 38 Ff
Belturbet, Cavan, Eire 32 Je
Ben Alder, mt., I'ness., Scot. 35 Hf
Ben Attow, mt., Ross., Scot. 34 Fe
Benbane Hd., Antrim, N. Ireland 32 Lc
Benbecula, I., Outer Hebrides, Scotland 34 Be
Benbulbin, pk., Sligo, Eire 32 Ge
Benbury, mt. Mayo, Eire 32 Df
Ben Cruachan, mt., Argyll, Scotland 35 Fg
Ben Dearg, mt., Perth, Scot. 35 Jf
Ben Dearg, mt., Ross., Scot. 34 Gd
Ben Hope, mt., Suth., Scot. 34 Gc
Ben Klibreck, mt., Suth., Scotland 34 Hc
Ben Lawers, mt., Perth, Scotland 35 Hf
Ben Ledi, mt., Perth, Scot. 35 Hg
Ben Lomond, mt., Stirl., Scotland 35 Gg
Ben Loyal, mt., Sutherland 34 Hc
Ben Lui, mt., Argyll, Scot. 35 Gg
Ben Macdhui, mt., A'deen., Scotland 34 Je
Ben More, mt., Mull, Scot. 35 Dg
Ben More, mt., Perth, Scot. 35 Gg
Ben More, mt., Suth., Scot. 34 Gc
Ben Nevis, mt., I'ness., Scotland 35 Gf
Ben Vorlich, mt., Perth, Scotland 35 Hg
Benwee Hd., Mayo, Eire 32 De
Ben Wyvis, mt., Ross., Scot. 34 Gd
Ben-y-Gloe, mt., Perth, Scotland 35 Jf
Bere Regis, Dorset, Eng. 37 Kg
Berkeley, Gloucester, Eng. 36 Ke
Berkhamsted, Herts., Eng. 37 Ne
Berkshire (Berks.), co., Eng. 37 Mf
Bernera, Great, I., Lewis, Scotland 34 Cc
Berneray, I., Outer Hebrides, Scotland 34 Bd
Berriedale, Caithness, Scot. 34 Jc
Bertraghboy B., Galway, Eire 33 Dg
Berwick, co., Scotland 35 Lh
Berwick-upon-Tweed, Northumberland, Eng. 38 Ea
Berwyn Mts., Denbigh, etc., Wales 36 Hc
Bethesda, Caern., Wales 36 Fb
Betws-y-Coed, Caern., Wales 36 Gb
Beverley, Yorks., England 38 He
Bewdley, Worcs., Eng. 36 Kd
Bexhill, Sussex, England 37 Qg
Bicester, Oxford, England 37 Me
Bideford and B., Devon, England 36 Ff
Bigbury B., Devon, England 36 Gh
Biggar, Lanark, Scotland 35 Jh
Biggleswade, Bedford, Eng. 37 Pd
Billericay, Essex, England 37 Qe
Billesdon, Leicester, Eng. 37 Nc
Bilsborrow, Lancs., Eng. 38 Ce
Bilston, Staffs., England 37 Kc
Binbrook, Lincs., England 38 Hf
Bingham, Notts., England 38 Gg
Bingley, Yorks., England 38 Ee
Birkenhead, Cheshire, Eng. 38 Bf
Birmingham, Warwick, Eng. 37 Ld
Birnam, Perth, Scotland 35 Jf
Birr, Offaly, Eire 33 Hg
Birsay, Orkney, Scotland 34 Ka
Bishop Auckland, Durham, England 38 Ec
Bishop Rock Lt. Ho., Scilly Is., England 36 Bj
Bishops Castle, Shrops., Eng. 36 Jd
Bishops Stortford, Herts., England 37 Qe
Bishops Waltham, Hants., England 37 Mg
Black Hd., Clare, Eire 33 Eg
Black Mt., Carmarthen, Wales 36 Ge
Black Mts., Brecknock, Wales 36 He
Blackburn, Lancs., England 38 De
Blackdown Hills, Devon-Somerset, England 36 Hg
Black Isle, dist., Ross., Scot. 34 Hd
Blackmoor, Dorset, Eng. 36 Jg
Blackpool, Lancs., Eng. 38 Be
Black Rock, Mayo, Eire 31 Af
Blacksod B., Mayo, Eire 32 Ce
Blackstairs, Carlow-Wexford, Eire 33 Kh
Blackwater, Essex, England 37 Re
Blackwater, Wexford, Eire 33 Lj
Blackwater Res., Inverness, Scotland 35 Gf
Blackwater, R., Cork, Eire 33 Fj
Blackwater, R., Meath, Eire 32 Kf
Blackwater, R., N. Ireland 32 Ke
Blaenavon, Mon. 36 He
Blagdon, Somerset, England 36 Jf
Blair Atholl, Perth, Scot. 35 Jf
Blairgowrie, Perth, Scot. 35 Kf
Blakeney, Gloucester, Eng. 36 Je
Blakeney, Norfolk, England 37 Sc
Blandford, Dorset, England 37 Kg
Blarney, Cork, Eire 33 Fk
Blasket I., Gt., Kerry, Eire 33 Bj
Blasket Sd., Kerry, Eire 33 Bj
Blessington, Wicklow, Eire 33 Lg
Bletchley, Bucks., England 37 Ne
Bloody Foreland, Donegal, Eire 32 Gc
Blue Stack Mts., Donegal, Eire 32 Gd
Blyth and R., N'land., Eng. 38 Eb
Blyth, Notts., England 38 Ff
Boat of Garten, Inverness, Scotland 34 Je
Boddam, Aberdeen, Scot. 34 Ne
Boderg, L., Roscommon, Eire 32 Gf
Bodmin, Cornwall, England 36 Eh
Bodmin Moors, Corn., Eng. 36 Eg
Bofin, L., Roscommon, Eire 32 Gf
Boggeragh Mts., Cork, Eire 33 F
Bognor Regis, Sussex, Eng. 37 Ng
Bolsover, Derby, England 38 Ff
Bolton, Lancs., England 38 De
Bolus Hd., Kerry, Eire 33 Ck
Bonar Bridge, Suth., Scot. 34 Hd
Bo'ness, W. Lothian, Scot. 35 Jg
Bootle, Cumberland, Eng. 38 Bd
Bootle, Lancs., England 38 Bf
Boreray, I., St. Kilda, Scot. 34 Aa
Boroughbridge, Yorks, England 38 Fd
Borris, Carlow, Eire 33 Kh
Borrisoleigh, Tipperary, Eire 33 Hh
Boscastle, Cornwall, Eng. 36 Eg
Boston, Lincs., England 38 Hg
Botley, Hants., England 37 Mg
Bottesford, Leicester, Eng. 38 Gg
Bourne, Lincs., England 38 Hg
Bournemouth, Hants., England 37 Lg
Bovey Tracey, Devon, Eng. 36 Gg
Bow, Devon, England 36 Gg
Bowes, Yorks., England 38 Dc
Bowmore, Islay, Scotland 35 Dh
Boyle, Roscommon, Eire 32 Gf
Boyne R., Meath, etc., Eire 32 Lf
Bracadale, Skye, Scotland 34 De
Bracadale, L., Skye, Scot. 34 Ce
Brackley, Northants., Eng. 37 Md
Bracknell, Berks., Eng. 37 Nf
Bradford, Wilts., England 37 Kf
Bradford, Yorks., England 38 Ee
Bradninch, Devon, Eng. 36 Hg
Bradwell, Essex, England 37 Re
Bradworthy, Devon, Eng. 36 Fg
Braemar, Aberdeen, Scot. 34 Kf
Braeriach, mt., Aberdeen, Scotland 34 Je
Braintree, Essex, England 37 Re
Brampton, Cumberland, England 38 Cc
Brander, Pass of, Argyll, Scotland 35 Fg
Brandon, Suffolk, England 33 Rd
Brandon B., Kerry, Eire 33 Cj
Brandon Hd., Kerry, Eire 33 Cj
Brandon, mt., Kilkenny, Eire 33 Kj
Branston, Lincs., England 38 Gf
Braunton, Devon, England 36 Ff
Bray Hd., Kerry, Eire 33 Ck
Bray and Hd., Wicklow, Eire 33 Lg
Brechin, Angus, Scotland 35 Lf
Brecknock, co., Wales 36 Ge
Brecon, Brecknock, Wales 36 He
Brecon Beacons, Mts., Brecknock, Wales 36 He
Brendon Hills, Som., Eng. 36 Hf
Brentford, London, England 37 Pf
Brentwood, Essex, Eng. 37 Qe
Bressay, I., Shetland, Scot. 34 Qb
Bride, R., Cork, etc., Eire 33 Gj
Bridgend, Glamorgan, Wales 36 Gf
Bridge of Orchy, Argyll, Scotland 35 Gf
Bridgnorth, Shropshire, England 36 Kc
Bridgwater, Somerset, Eng. 36 Jf
Bridgwater B., Somerset, England 36 Hf
Bridlington and B., Yorks., England 38 Hd
Bridport, Dorset, England 36 Jg
Brigg, Lincs., England 38 He
Brighouse, Yorks., England 38 Ee
Brightlingsea, Essex, Eng. 37 Se
Brighton, Sussex, England 37 Pg
Brigstock, Northants., England 37 Nd
Brill, Bucks., England 37 Me
Bristol, Somerset-Gloucester, England 36 Jf
Bristol Channel, England-Wales 36 Ff
Briton Ferry, Glam., Wales 36 Ge
Brixham, Devon, England 36 Hh
Broad B., Lewis, Scotland 34 Dc
Broadford, Skye, Scotland 34 Ee
Broad Haven, Mayo, Eire 32 De
Broad Law, hill, Peebles, Scotland 35 Kj
Broadstairs, Kent, England 37 Sf

Brodick, *Arran, Scotland* 35 Fh
Bromley, *London, England* 37 Qf
Bromsgrove, *Worcester, England* 37 Kd
Bromyard, *Hereford, Eng.* 36 Jd
Broom, L., *Ross., Scot.* 34 Fd
Brora, *Sutherland, Scotland* 34 Jc
Brosna, R., *Offaly, etc., Eire* 33 Hg
Brough, *Cumberland, Eng.* 38 Dc
Brough Hd., *Orkney, Scot.* 34 Ka
Brough Ness, *Orkney, Scot.* 34 Lb
Broughton, *Lancs., Eng.* 38 Bd
Broughty Ferry, *Angus, Scotland* 35 Lg
Brownhills, *Staffs, Eng.* 37 Lc
Broxburn, *W. Lothian, Scotland* 35 Kh
Bruff, *Limerick, Eire* 33 Fj
Bruton, *Somerset, England* 36 Kf
Brynamman, *Carm., Wales* 36 Ge
Brynmawr, *Brecknock, Wales* 36 He
Buchan, dist., *A'deen., Scot.* 34 Md
Buchan Deep, *North Sea* 30 Gc
Buchan Ness, *A'deen., Scotland* 34 Ne
Buchlyvie, *Stirling, Scot.* 35 Hg
Buckden, *Huntingdon, Eng.* 37 Pd
Buckie, *Banff, Scotland* 34 Ld
Buckingham and co., *Eng.* 37 Nd
Buddon Ness, *Angus, Scot.* 35 Lg
Bude, *Cornwall, England* 36 Eg
Budleigh Salterton, *Devon, England* 36 Hg
Builth Wells, *Brecknock, Wales* 36 Hd
Bull Rock, *Kerry, Eire* 31 Aj
Bulwell, *Notts., England* 38 Ff
Buncrana, *Donegal, Eire* 32 Jc
Bundoran, *Donegal, Eire* 32 Ge
Bungay, *Norfolk, England* 37 Sd
Buntingford, *Herts., Eng.* 37 Pe
Bure, R., *Norfolk, England* 37 Sc
Bures, *Essex, England* 37 Re
Burford, *Oxford, England* 37 Le
Burgess Hill, *Sussex, Eng.* 37 Pg
Burghead, *Moray, Scotland* 34 Kd
Burgh-le-Marsh, *Lincs., England* 38 Jf
Burnham, *Essex, England* 37 Re
Burnham, *Somerset, Eng.* 36 Hf
Burnham Market, *Norfolk, England* 37 Rc
Burnley, *Lancs., England* 38 De
Burntisland, *Fife, Scotland* 35 Kg
Burravoe, *Shetland, Scot.* 34 Qa
Burray, I., *Orkney, Scot.* 34 Lb
Burrow Hd., *Wigtown, Scotland* 35 Hk
Burry Inlet, *Carmarthen-Glamorgan, Wales* 36 Fe
Burry Port, *Carm., Wales* 36 Fe
Burslem, *Staffs., England* 37 Kb
Burton-in-Kendal, *Westmorland, England* 38 Cd
Burton Port, *Donegal, Eire* 32 Gd
Burton-upon-Trent, *Staffs., England* 37 Lc
Bury, *Lancs., England* 38 De
Bury St. Edmunds, *Suffolk, England* 37 Rd
Bushmills, *Antrim, N. Ireland* 32 Kc
Bute, co., *Scotland* 35 Fh
Bute, I., *Bute, Scotland* 35 Fh
Buttevant, *Cork, Eire* 33 Fj
Buxton, *Derby, England* 38 Ef

C

Cader Idris, mt., *Merioneth, Wales* 36 Gc
Caergwrle, *Flint, Wales* 36 Hb
Caerleon, *Mon.* 36 Je
Caernarvon and co., *Wales* 36 Fb
Caernarvon B., *Caern., Wales* 36 Eb
Caerphilly, *Glam., Wales* 36 He
Caersws, *Mont., Wales* 36 Hc
Caha Mts., *Cork-Kerry, Eire* 33 Dk
Cahir, *Tipperary, Eire* 33 Hj
Cahirciveen, *Kerry, Eire* 33 Ck
Cahore Pt., *Wicklow, Eire* 33 Lh
Cairn Gorm, mt., *Inverness, Scotland* 34 Je
Cairngorms, mts., *Inverness, etc., Scotland* 30 Ec
Cairn Toul, mt., *Aberdeen, Scotland* 34 Je
Caister, *Norfolk, England* 37 Tc
Caistor, *Lincs., England* 38 He
Caithness, co., *Scotland* 34 Jc
Caldbeck, *Cumb., Eng.* 38 Bc
Calder R., *Yorks., England* 38 Ee
Caledonian Canal, *Inverness, Scotland* 34 He
Calf of Man, I., *Isle of Man* 38 Kd
Callan, *Kilkenny, Eire* 33 Jh
Callander, *Perth, Scotland* 35 Hg
Callington, *Cornwall, Eng.* 36 Fh
Calne, *Wilts., England* 37 Kf
Camborne, *Cornwall, Eng.* 36 Dh
Cambrian Mts., *Wales* 36 Ge
Cambridge and Isle of Ely, co., *Eng.* 37 Pc
Camelford, *Cornwall, Eng.* 36 Eg
Campbeltown, *Argyll, Scot.* 35 Ej
Campsie Fells, *Stirl., Scot.* 35 Hg
Canisp, mt., *Suth., Scot.* 34 Fc
Canna, I., *Inverness, Scot.* 34 Ce
Cannock, *Staffs., England* 37 Kc
Cannock Chase, *Staffs., England* 37 Kc
Canonbie, *Dumfries, Scot.* 35 Lj
Canterbury, *Kent, Eng.* 37 Sf
Capel, *Surrey, England* 37 Pf
Cappoquin, *Waterford, Eire* 33 Hj
Caragh, L., *Kerry, Eire* 33 Dj
Cardiff, *Glamorgan, Wales* 36 Hf
Cardigan, *Cardigan, Wales* 36 Ed
Cardigan, co., *Wales* 36 Fd
Cardigan B., *Merioneth-Cardigan, Wales* 36 Ec
Carlingford and L., *Louth, Eire* 32 Le
Carlisle, *Cumberland, Eng.* 38 Bc
Carlow and co., *Eire* 33 Kh
Carloway, *Lewis, Scotland* 34 Cc
Carlton, *Notts., England* 38 Ff
Carluke, *Lanark, Scotland* 35 Jh
Carmarthen and co., *Wales* 36 Fe
Carmarthen B., *Carmarthen, etc., Wales* 36 Fe
Carndonagh, *Donegal, Eire* 32 Jc
Carnforth, *Lancs., Eng.* 38 Cd
Carno, *Montgomery, Wales* 36 Gc
Carnoustie, *Angus, Scot.* 35 Lf
Carnsore Pt., *Wexford, Eire* 33 Lj
Carnwath, *Lanark, Scot.* 35 Jh
Carra, L., *Mayo, Eire* 32 Ef
Carrantuohill, mt., *Kerry, Eire* 33 Dk
Carrbridge, *Inverness, Scot.* 34 Je
Carrick, dist., *Ayr., Scot.* 35 Gj
Carrickfergus, *Antrim, N. Ireland* 32 Md
Carrickmacross, *Monaghan, Eire* 32 Kf
Carrick-on-Shannon, *Leitrim, Eire* 32 Gf
Carrick-on-Suir, *Tipperary, Eire* 33 Jj
Carrowmore L., *Mayo, Eire* 32 De
Carse of Gowrie, *Perth, Scotland* 35 Kg
Carsphairn, *Kirkcud., Scot.* 35 Hj
Carstairs, *Lanark, Scotland* 35 Jh
Carter Bar, *Scot.-Eng.* 35 Mj
Cashel, *Tipperary, Eire* 33 Hh
Castlebar, *Mayo, Eire* 32 Ef
Castlebay, *Barra, Scotland* 34 Bf
Castlebellingham, *Louth, Eire* 32 Lf
Castleblayney, *Monaghan, Eire* 32 Ke
Castle Cary, *Somerset, Eng.* 36 Jf
Castlecomer, *Kilkenny, Eire* 33 Jh
Castlederg, *Tyrone, N. Ire.* 32 Hd
Castledermot, *Kildare, Eire* 33 Kh
Castle Douglas, *Kirkcudbright, Scot.* 35 Jk
Castleford, *Yorks., Eng.* 38 Fe
Castleisland, *Kerry, Eire* 33 Ej
Castlemaine, *Kerry, Eire* 33 Dj
Castlemartyr, *Cork, Eire* 33 Gk
Castlepollard, *Westmeath, Eire* 32 Jf
Castlerea, *Roscommon, Eire* 32 Gf
Castletown, *Caith., Scot.* 34 Kb
Castletown, *Cork, Eire* 33 Dk
Castletown, *Isle of Man* 38 Kd
Castlewellan, *Down, N. Ireland* 32 Me
Catterick, *Yorks., Eng.* 38 Ed
Cavan and co., *Eire* 32 Jf
Cawdor, *Nairn, Scotland* 34 Jd
Ceanannus Mór, *Meath, Eire* 32 Ki
Cemaes, *Anglesey, Wales* 36 Fb
Cerne Abbas, *Dorset England* 36 Kg
Channel Is., *English Channel* 37 Jk
Chapel-en-le-Frith, *Derby, England* 38 Ef
Chard, *Somerset, England* 36 Jg
Chardstock, *Devon, Eng.* 36 Hg
Charing, *Kent, England* 37 Rf
Charlbury, *Oxford, Eng.* 37 Le
Charlestown, *Mayo, Eire* 32 Ff
Charleville, *Cork, Eire* 33 Fj
Charnwood Forest, *Leicester, England* 37 Mc
Chatham, *Kent, England* 37 Rf
Chatteris, *Cambridge, Eng.* 37 Qd
Chawton, *Hants., England* 37 Nf
Cheadle, *Staffs., England* 37 Lc
Cheddar, *Somerset, Eng.* 36 Jf
Chelmer, R., *Essex, Eng.* 37 Qe
Chelmsford, *Essex, Eng.* 37 Qe
Cheltenham, *Gloucester, England* 37 Ke
Chepstow, *Mon.* 36 Je
Chertsey, *Surrey, England* 37 Nf
Cherwell, R., *Oxford, etc., England* 37 Me
Chesham, *Bucks., England* 37 Ne
Cheshire, co., *England* 38 Cf
Cheshire Plain, *Cheshire-Lancs., Eng.* 38 Cf
Chesil Bank, *Dorset, Eng.* 36 Jg
Chester, *Cheshire, England* 38 Cf
Chesterfield, *Derby, Eng.* 38 Ff
Chester-le-Street, *Durham, England* 38 Ec
Cheviot, The, pk., *Northumberland, Eng.* 38 Db
Cheviot Hills, *Eng.-Scot.* 38 Db
Chichester, *Sussex, Eng.* 37 Ng
Chigwell, *Essex, England* 37 Qe
Chilbolton, *Hants., Eng.* 37 Mf
Chilham, *Kent, England* 37 Rf
Chiltern Hills, *England* 37 Ne
Chippenham, *Wilts., Eng.* 37 Kf
Chipping Campden, *Gloucester, England* 37 Ld
Chipping Norton, *Oxford, England* 37 Le
Chipping Sodbury, *Gloucester, England* 36 Ke
Chirk, *Denbigh, Wales* 36 Hc
Chirnside, *Berwick, Scot.* 35 Mh
Chiseldon, *Wilts., Eng.* 37 Lf
Cholsey, *Berks., England* 37 Me
Chorley, *Lancs., England* 38 Ce
Christchurch, *Hants., Eng.* 37 Lg
Chudleigh, *Devon, England* 36 Gg
Chulmleigh, *Devon, Eng.* 36 Gg
Church Stretton, *Shropshire, England* 36 Jc
Cinderford, *Glos., Eng.* 36 Ke
Cirencester, *Glos., Eng.* 37 Le
Clackmannan and co., *Scot.* 35 Jg
Clacton-on-Sea, *Essex, England* 37 Se
Clara, *Offaly, Eire* 33 Hg
Clare, *Suffolk, England* 37 Rd
Clare, co., *Eire* 33 Eh
Clare I., *Mayo, Eire* 32 Cf
Clare, R., *Galway, Eire* 33 Fg
Clarecastle, *Clare, Eire* 33 Fh
Claremorris, *Mayo, Eire* 32 Ff
Claydon, *Suffolk, England* 37 Sd
Clear, C. and I., *Cork, Eire* 33 El
Cleddau, R., *Pemb., Wales* 36 Ee
Cleethorpes, *Lincs., Eng.* 38 He
Clent Hills, *Worcester-Warwick, England* 37 Kd
Cleobury Mortimer, *Shropshire, England* 36 Jd
Clevedon, *Somerset, Eng.* 36 Jf
Cleveland Hills, *Yorks., England* 38 Fd
Clew B., *Mayo, Eire* 32 Df
Clifden, *Galway, Eire* 33 Cg
Cliffe, *Kent, England* 37 Rf
Clisham, mt., *Harris, Scot.* 34 Cd
Clitheroe, *Lancs., England* 38 De
Cloghan, *Offaly, Eire* 33 Hg
Clogher, *Tyrone, N. Ire.* 32 Je
Clogher Hd., *Louth, Eire* 32 Lf
Clonakilty, *Cork, Eire* 33 Fk
Clonakilty B., *Cork, Eire* 33 Fk
Clondalkin, *Dublin, Eire* 33 Lg
Clonegall, *Carlow, Eire* 33 Kh
Clones, *Monaghan, Eire* 32 Je
Clonmel, *Tipperary, Eire* 33 Hj
Clova, *Angus, Scotland* 35 Kf
Clovelly, *Devon, England* 36 Fg
Cloyne, *Cork, Eire* 33 Gk
Clun, *Shropshire, England* 36 Hd
Clun Forest, *Radnor, etc., Wales* 36 Hd
Clunie, L., *I'ness., etc., Scot.* 34 Fe
Clwyd, R., *Denbigh, etc., Wales* 36 Hb
Clyde, Falls of, *Lanark, Scotland* 35 Jh
Clyde, Firth of, *Scotland* 35 Gh
Clyde, R., *Scotland* 35 Gh
Clydebank, *Dunbarton, Scotland* 35 Hh
Coalville, *Leicester, Eng.* 37 Mc
Coatbridge, *Lanark, Scot.* 35 Hh
Cóbh, *Cork, Eire* 33 Gk
Cock Bridge, *A'deen., Scot.* 34 Ke
Cockburnspath, *Berwick, Scotland* 35 Mh
Cockermouth, *Cumb., Eng.* 38 Bc
Cod's Hd., *Cork, Eire* 33 Ck
Colchester, *Essex, England* 37 Re
Coldingham, *Berwick, Scot.* 35 Mh
Coldstream, *Berwick, Scot.* 35 Mh
Coleraine, *Londonderry, N. Ireland* 32 Kc
Coll, I., *Argyll, Scotland* 35 Cf
Collinstown, *Dublin, Eire* 33 Lg
Collooney, *Sligo, Eire* 32 Fe
Colmonell, *Ayr, Scotland* 35 Gj
Colne, *Lancs., England* 38 De
Colne, R., *Essex, England* 37 Re
Colonsay, I., *Argyll, Scot.* 35 Dg
Colsterworth, *Lincs., Eng.* 38 Gg
Colwyn B., *Denbigh, Wales* 36 Gb
Colyton, *Devon, England* 36 Hg
Comber, *Down, N. Ireland* 32 Md
Comeragh Mts., *Waterford, Eire* 33 Hj
Comrie, *Perth, Scotland* 35 Jg
Cong, *Mayo, Eire* 33 Ef
Congleton, *Cheshire, Eng.* 38 Df
Coniston, *Lancs., England* 38 Bd
Conn, L., *Mayo, Eire* 32 Ee
Connacht, prov., *Eire* 31 Ag
Connel Ferry, *Argyll, Scotland* 35 Fg
Connemara, *Galway, Eire* 33 Cf
Consett, *Durham, England* 38 Ec
Conway, *Caern., Wales* 36 Gb
Conwil Elvet, *Carm., Wales* 36 Fe
Cookham, *Berks., England* 37 Ne
Cookstown, *Tyrone, N. Ire.* 32 Kd
Coomacarrea, mt., *Kerry, Eire* 33 Ck
Cootehill, *Cavan, Eire* 32 Je
Copeland I., *Down, N. Ire.* 35 Ek
Copinsay, I., *Orkney, Scot.* 34 Lb
Coquet, R., *N'land., Eng.* 38 Eb
Corbridge, *N'land., Eng.* 38 Dc
Corby, *Northants., England* 37 Nd
Corcaigh, see Cork
Cork and co., *Eire* 33 Gk
Cork Harbour, *Cork, Eire* 33 Gk
Cornwall, co., *England* 36 Eh
Cornwall, C., *Cornwall, England* 36 Ch
Corrib, L., *Galway, Eire* 33 Eg
Corrofin, *Clare, Eire* 33 Eh
Corryvreckan, Str. of, *Argyll, Scotland* 35 Eg
Corsewall Pt., *Wigtown, Scotland* 35 Fj
Corsham, *Wilts., England* 37 Kf
Coruisk, L., *Skye, Scotland* 34 De
Corwen, *Merioneth, Wales* 36 Hc
Cotswold Hills, *Glos., England* 37 Ke
Coulagh B., *Cork, Eire* 33 Ck
Coulbeag, mt., *Ross., Scot.* 34 Fc
Coupar Angus, *Perth, Scot.* 35 Kf
Courtmacsherry, *Cork, Eire* 33 Fk
Coventry, *Warwick, Eng.* 37 Ld
Cowal, dist., *Argyll, Scot.* 35 Fg
Cowbridge, *Glam., Wales* 36 Hf
Cowdenbeath, *Fife, Scot.* 35 Kg
Cowes, *I. of Wight, Eng.* 37 Mg
Cowley, *Oxford, England* 37 Me
Coxwold, *Yorks., England* 38 Fd
Craigellachie, *Banff, Scot.* 34 Ke
Craighouse, *Jura, Scotland* 35 Eh
Crail, *Fife, Scotland* 35 Lg
Cranborne, *Dorset, Eng.* 37 Lg
Cranbrook, *Kent, England* 37 Rf
Cranleigh, *Surrey, England* 37 Nf
Cranswick, *Yorks., Eng.* 38 He
Cranwell, *Lincs., England* 38 Hf
Craven Arms, *Shrops., Eng.* 36 Jd
Crawford, *Lanark, Scotland* 35 Jj
Crawley, *Sussex, England* 37 Pf
Creag Meagaidh, mt., *Inverness, Scotland* 34 Gf
Crediton, *Devon, England* 36 Gg
Cree, R., *Kirkcud., Scot.* 35 Hk
Creetown, *Kirkcud., Scot.* 35 Hk
Crewe, *Cheshire, England* 38 Df
Crewkerne, *Somerset, Eng.* 36 Jg
Crianlarich, *Perth, Scot.* 35 Gg
Criccieth, *Caern., Wales* 36 Fc
Crickhowell, *Brecknock, Wales* 36 He
Cricklade, *Wilts., England* 37 Le
Crieff, *Perth, Scotland* 35 Jg
Criffell, mt., *Kirkcud., Scot.* 35 Jk
Crinan Canal, *Argyll, Scot.* 35 Fg
Croagh Patrick, mt., *Mayo, Eire* 32 Df
Croft, *Yorks., England* 38 Ed
Cromarty, *Ross., Scot.* 34 Jd
Cromarty Firth, *Ross and Cromarty, Scotland* 34 Hd
Cromer, *Norfolk, England* 37 Sc
Crook, *Durham, England* 38 Ec
Croom, *Limerick, Eire* 33 Fh
Cross Fell, *Cumberland, England* 38 Dc
Crosshaven, *Cork, Eire* 33 Gk
Crossmichael, *Kirkcudbright, Scot.* 35 Jk
Crossmolina, *Mayo, Eire* 32 Ee
Crowland, *Lincs., England* 38 Hg
Crowle, *Lincs., England* 38 Ge
Croydon, *London, England* 37 Pf
Cruden B., *Aberdeen, Scot.* 34 Ne
Crumlin, *Antrim, N. Ire.* 32 Ld
Crymmych Arms, *Pembroke, Wales* 36 Ee
Cuckfield, *Sussex, England* 37 Pf
Cuilcagh, mt., *Fermanagh, N. Ireland* 32 He
Cuillin Hills, *Skye, Scotland* 34 De
Cuillin Sd., *Skye, Scotland* 34 De
Culgaith, *Cumberland, Eng.* 38 Cc
Cullaun, pk., *Limerick, Eire* 33 Gh
Cullen, *Banff, Scotland* 34 Ld
Cullivoe, *Shetland, Scotland* 34 Qa
Cullompton, *Devon, Eng.* 36 Hg
Culter Fell, *Scotland* 35 Jh
Cumberland, co., *England* 38 Bc
Cumbrian mts., *Cumberland, etc., Eng.* 38 Bc
Cumnock, *Ayr, Scotland* 35 Hj
Cunningsburgh, *Shetland, Scotland* 34 Qb
Cupar, *Fife, Scotland* 35 Kg
Currane, L., *Kerry, Eire* 33 Ck
Curraun, *Mayo, Eire* 32 Df
Curraun Pen., *Mayo, Eire* 32 Df
Cushendall, *Antrim, N. Ire.* 32 Lc
Cushendun, *Antrim, N. Ire.* 32 Lc
Cutra, L., *Galway, Eire* 33 Fg
Cwmbran, *Mon.* 36 He

D

Dagenham, *London, England* 37 Qe
Dalbeattie, *Kirkcud., Scot.* 35 Jk
Dalkeith, *Midlothian, Scot.* 35 Kh
Dalkey, *Dublin, Eire* 33 Lg
Dalmally, *Argyll, Scotland* 35 Gg
Dalmellington, *Ayr, Scot.* 35 Hj
Dalry, *Ayr, Scotland* 35 Gh
Dalry, *Kirkcudbright, Scot.* 35 HJ
Dalrymple, *Ayr, Scotland* 35 Gj
Dalsetter, *Shetland, Scot.* 34 Qa
Dalton, *Lancs., England* 38 Bd
Dalwhinnie, *I'ness., Scot.* 34 Hf
Darlington, *Durham, Eng.* 38 Ec
Dart, R., *Devon, England* 36 Gg
Dartford, *Kent, England* 37 Qf
Dartmoor, *Devon, England* 36 Gg
Dartmouth, *Devon, Eng.* 36 Gh
Dartry Mts., *Leitrim-Sligo, Eire* 32 Ge
Darvel, *Ayr, Scotland* 35 Hh
Darwen, *Lancs., England* 38 De
Dava, *Moray, Scotland* 34 Je
Daventry, *Northants, Eng.* 37 Md
Dawlish, *Devon, England* 36 Hg
Deal, *Kent, England* 37 Sf
Dean, Forest of, *Gloucester, England* 36 Je
Debenham, *Suffolk, Eng.* 37 Sd
Deddington, *Oxford, Eng.* 37 Le
Dee, R., *Aberdeen, Scot.* 34 Me
Dee, R., *Denb., etc., Wales* 36 Hb
Dee, R., *Kirkcud., Scot.* 35 Jk
Deel, R., *Limerick, Eire* 33 Fh
Denbigh and co., *Wales* 36 Hb
Denny, *Stirling, Scotland* 35 Jg
Deptford, *Wilts., England* 37 Lf
Derby, *Derby, England* 38 Eg
Derby, co., *England* 38 Ef
Derg, L., *Donegal, Eire* 32 Hd
Derg, L., *Tipperary, etc., Eire* 33 Gh
Derg, R., *Donegal, etc., Eire-N. Ireland* 32 Hd
Derravaragh, L., *Westmeath, Eire* 32 Jf
Derry, see Londonderry
Derryveagh mts., *Donegal, Eire* 32 Gd
Derwent, R., *N'land., Eng.* 38 Dc
Derwent, R., *Yorks., Eng.* 38 Ge
Derwent Water, *Cumberland, England* 38 Bc
Desborough, *Northants, England* 37 Nd
Deveron, R., *Banff, Scot.* 34 Ld
Devil's Bit mt., *Tipperary, Eire* 33 Hh
Devil's Bridge, *Cardigan, Wales* 36 Gd
Devil's Elbow, *Aberdeen, Scotland* 35 Kf
Devil's Hole, *North Sea* 30 Hd
Devizes, *Wilts., England* 37 Lf
Devon, co., *England* 36 Gg
Devon, R., *Perth, etc., Scotland* 35 Jg
Devonport, *Devon, England* 36 Fh
Dewsbury, *Yorks., England* 38 Ee
Dinas Mawddwy, *Mer., Wales* 36 Gc
Dingle and B., *Kerry, Eire* 33 Cj
Dingwall, *Ross, Scotland* 34 Hd
Diss, *Norfolk, England* 37 Sd
Distington, *Cumb., Eng.* 38 Ac
Docking, *Norfolk, England* 37 Rc
Dodman Pt., *Corn., Eng.* 36 Eh
Dolgellau, *Wales* 36 Gc
Dollar, *Clack., Scotland* 35 Jg
Dollar Law, *Peebles, Scot.* 35 Kh
Don, R., *Aberdeen, Scot.* 34 Le
Don, R., *Yorks., etc., Eng.* 38 Fe
Donaghadee, *Down, N. Ireland* 32 Md
Donard, *Wicklow, Eire* 33 Kg
Doncaster, *Yorks., Eng.* 38 Fe
Donegal and co., *Eire* 32 Gd
Donegal B., *Donegal-Sligo, Eire* 32 Fd
Donegal Pt., *Clare, Eire* 33 Dh
Doneraile, *Cork, Eire* 33 Fj
Donington, *Lincs., Eng.* 38 Hg
Doon, L. and R., *Ayr, Scot.* 35 Hj
Dorchester, *Dorset, Eng.* 36 Kg
Dorking, *Surrey, England* 37 Pf
Dorking Gap, *Surrey, Eng.* 37 Pf
Dornie, *Ross, Scotland* 34 Fe
Dornoch, *Sutherland, Scot.* 34 Hd
Dornoch Firth, *Suth., etc., Scotland* 34 Hd
Dorset, co., *England* 36 Jg
Douglas, *Isle of Man* 38 Ld
Douglas, *Lanark, Scotland* 35 Jh
Doulus Hd., *Kerry, Eire* 33 Ck
Doune, *Perth, Scotland* 35 Hg
Dounreay, *Caith., Scot.* 34 Jb
Dover, *Kent, England* 37 Sf
Dover, Strait of, *England-France* 37 Sg
Dovercourt, *Essex, Eng.* 37 Se
Dowlais, *Glam., Wales* 36 He
Down, co., *N. Ireland* 32 Le
Downham Market, *Norfolk, England* 37 Qc
Downpatrick, *Down, N. Ireland* 32 Me
Downpatrick Hd., *Mayo, Eire* 32 Ee
Downton, *Wilts., England* 37 Lg
Dowsing Lightship, *North Sea* 31 Hg
Drem, *E. Lothian, Scot.* 35 Lg
Drimoleague, *Cork, Eire* 33 Ek
Drogheda, *Louth, Eire* 32 Lf
Drogheda B., *Louth-Meath, Eire* 32 Lf
Droitwich, *Worcs., Eng.* 37 Kd
Dromara, *Down, N. Ire.* 32 Me
Dromod, *Leitrim, Eire* 32 Hf
Dromore, *Down, N. Ire.* 32 Le
Dromore, *Sligo, Eire* 32 Fe
Dromore, *Tyrone, N. Ire.* 32 Jd
Dronfield, *Derby, England* 38 Ef
Drum Hills, *Waterford, Eire* 33 Hj
Drumlish, *Longford, Eire* 32 Hf
Drummore, *Wig., Scotland* 35 Gk
Drumnadrochit, *Inverness, Scotland* 34 He
Drumochter Pass, *Perth, Scotland* 35 Hf
Drumshambo, *Leitrim, Eire* 32 Ge
Drymen, *Stirling, Scot.* 35 Hg
Dubh Artach Lt. Ho., *Atlantic Oc.* 35 Cg
Dublin and co., *Eire* 33 Lg
Dudgeon Lightship, *North Sea* 31 Hg
Dudley, *Worcs., England* 37 Kc
Dufftown, *Banff, Scotland* 34 Ke
Dulverton, *Somerset, Eng.* 36 Gf
Dumbarton, *Dunb., Scot.* 35 Gh
Dumfries and co., *Dumf., Scotland* 35 Jj
Dunany Pt., *Louth, Eire* 32 Lf
Dunbarton, co., *Scotland* 35 Gg
Dunblane, *Perth, Scotland* 35 Jg
Dunboyne, *Meath, Eire* 33 Lg
Duncannon, *Wexford, Eire* 33 Kj
Duncansby Hd., *Caithness, Scotland* 34 Kb
Dundalk, *Louth, Eire* 32 Le
Dundalk B., *Louth, Eire* 32 Lf
Dun Dealgan, see Dundalk
Dundee, *Angus, Scotland* 35 Lg
Dundrum and B., *Down, N. Ireland* 32 Me
Dunfanaghy, *Donegal, Eire* 32 Hc
Dunfermline, *Fife, Scot.* 35 Kg
Dungannon, *Tyrone, N. Ire.* 32 Kd
Dungarvan and Harb., *Waterford, Eire* 33 Hj
Dungeness, *Kent, England* 37 Rg
Dungiven, *Londonderry, N. Ireland* 32 Kd
Dungloe, *Donegal, Eire* 32 Gd
Dunkeld, *Perth, Scotland* 35 Jf
Dunkery Beacon, *Somerset, England* 36 Gf
Dunlaoghaire, *Dublin, Eire* 33 Lg
Dunlavin, *Wicklow, Eire* 33 Kg
Dunlop, *Ayr, Scotland* 35 Gh
Dunmanus B., *Cork, Eire* 33 Dk
Dunmanway, *Cork, Eire* 33 Ek
Dunmore, *Galway, Eire* 32 Ff
Dunmow, Great, *Essex, England* 37 Qe
Dunnet B., *Caithness, Scot.* 34 Kb
Dunnet Hd., *Caith., Scot.* 34 Kb
Dunoon, *Argyll, Scotland* 35 Gh
Duns, *Berwick, Scotland* 35 Mh
Dunstable, *Bedford, Eng.* 37 Ne
Dunster, *Somerset, Eng.* 36 Hf
Dunvegan, *Skye, Scotland* 34 Ce
Dunvegan, L., *Skye, Scot.* 34 Cd
Durham and co., *England* 38 Ec
Durness, and Kyle of, *Sutherland, Scotland* 34 Gb
Durrow, *Leix, Eire* 33 Jh
Dursey I., and Hd., *Cork, Eire* 33 Ck
Dursley, *Gloucester, Eng.* 36 Ke
Durston, *Somerset, Eng.* 36 Hf
Dyce, *Aberdeen, Scotland* 34 Me
Dyfi, R., *Mont., Wales* 36 Gc
Dymchurch, *Kent, England* 37 Sf
Dysart, *Fife, Scotland* 35 Kg

E

Eagle, I., *Mayo, Eire* 32 Ce
Eagles Nest, mt., *Kerry, Eire* 33 Dk
Ealing, *London, England* 37 Pe
Eardisley, *Hereford, Eng.* 36 Jd
Earith, *Hunts., England* 37 Qd
Earlestown, *Lancs., England* 38 Cf
Earls Colne, *Essex, Eng.* 37 Re
Earlston, *Berwick, Scot.* 35 Lh
Earn, L., *Perth, Scotland* 35 Hg
Earn, R., *Perth, Scotland* 35 Jg
Easington, *Durham, Eng.* 38 Fc
Easingwold, *Yorks., Eng.* 38 Fd
Eask, L., *Donegal, Eire* 32 Gd
Eastbourne, *Sussex, Eng.* 37 Qg
East Dereham, *Norf., Eng.* 37 Rc
East Grinstead, *Sussex, England* 37 Pf
East Harling, *Norf., Eng.* 37 Rd
East Kilbride, *Lanark, Scot.* 35 Hh
Eastleigh, *Hants., England* 37 Mg
East Looe, *Cornwall, Eng.* 36 Fh
East Lothian, co., *Scotland* 35 Lh
East Retford, *Notts., Eng.* 38 Gf
East Riding, div., *Yorks., England* 38 Ge
Eastry, *Kent, England* 37 Sf
East Suffolk, div., *Suffolk, England* 37 Sd
East Sussex, div., *Sussex, England* 37 Qg
Ebbw Vale, *Mon.* 36 He
Ecclefechan, *Dumf., Scot.* 35 Kj
Eccles, *Lancs., England* 38 Df
Eccleshall, *Staffs., England* 38 Dg
Echt, *Aberdeen, Scotland* 34 Me
Eck, L., *Argyll, Scotland* 35 Gg
Eckington, *Derby, England* 38 Ef
Eday, I., *Orkney, Scotland* 34 La
Eddleston, *Peebles, Scot.* 35 Kh
Eddrachillis B., *Sutherland, Scotland* 34 Fc
Eddystone Lt. Ho., *Corn., England* 36 Fh
Eden, R., *Cumb., England* 38 Cc
Edenbridge, *Kent, England* 37 Pf
Edenderry, *Offaly, Eire* 33 Jg
Edge Hill, *Warwick, Eng.* 37 Ld
Edgeworthstown. See Mostrim
Edgware, *London, England* 37 Pe
Edinburgh, *M'loth., Scot.* 35 Kh
Edzell, *Angus, Scotland* 35 Lf
Egilsay, *Orkney, Scotland* 34 La
Egremont, *Cumb., England* 38 Bd
Egton, *Yorks., England* 38 Gd
Eigg, I., *Inverness, Scotland* 35 Df
Eil, L., *Inverness, Scotland* 35 Ff
Eire. See Ireland, Republic of
Elgin, *Moray, Scotland* 34 Kd
Elham, *Kent, England* 37 Sf
Elie, *Fife, Scotland* 35 Lg
Ellesmere, *Shrops., Eng.* 36 Jc
Ellesmere Port, *Cheshire, England* 38 Cf
Ellon, *Aberdeen, Scotland* 34 Me
Elphin, *Roscommon, Eire* 32 Gf
Ely, *Cambridge, England* 37 Qd
Embleton, *N'land., Eng.* 38 Ea
Emsworth, *Hants., England* 37 Ng
Enard B., *Ross, Scotland* 34 Fc
Enfield, *London, England* 37 Pe
Ennell, L., *Westmeath, Eire* 33 Jg
Ennis, *Clare, Eire* 33 Fh
Enniscorthy, *Wexford, Eire* 33 Kh
Enniscrone, *Sligo, Eire* 32 Ee
Enniskillen, *Fermanagh, N. Ireland* 32 He
Ennistyion, *Clare, Eire* 33 Eh
Epping, *Essex, England* 37 Qe
Epping Forest, *Essex, Eng.* 37 Qe
Epsom, *Surrey, England* 37 Pf
Epworth, *Lincs., England* 38 Ge
Eriboll, L., *Suth., Scotland* 34 Gb
Ericht, L., *Perth etc., Scot.* 35 Hf
Eriskay, I., *S. Uist, Scot.* 34 Be
Erne, L., *Fermanagh, N. Ire.* 32 He
Erne, L., Upper, *Fermanagh, N. Ireland* 32 He
Erne, R., *Donegal, Eire* 32 Ge
Errigal, mt., *Donegal, Eire* 32 Gc
Erris, Hd., *Mayo, Eire* 32 Ce
Esk, R., *M'loth., Scotland* 35 Kh
Esk, N. and S., Rs., *Angus, etc., Scotland* 35 Lf
Essex, co., *England* 37 Qe
Etive, L., *Argyll, Scotland* 35 Fg
Eton, *Bucks., England* 37 Nf
Ettrick, R., *Selkirk, Scot.* 35 Kj
Ettrick Pen., hill, *Dumfries, Scotland* 35 Kj
Evesham, *Worcester, Eng.* 37 Ld
Evesham, Vale of, *Warwick-Worcester, England* 37 Ld
Ewe, L., *Ross, Scotland* 34 Ed
Exe, R., *Devon-Somerset, England* 36 Gg
Exeter, *Devon, England* 36 Gg
Exminster, *Devon, England* 36 Hg
Exmoor, *Somerset, England* 36 Gf
Exmouth, *Devon, England* 36 Hg
Exton, *Somerset, England* 36 Gf
Eye, *Suffolk, England* 37 Sd
Eye Pen., *Lewis, Scotland* 34 Dc
Eyemouth, *Berwick, Scot.* 35 Mh
Eyrecourt, *Galway, Eire* 33 Gg

F

Fair Hd., *Antrim, N. Ire.* 32 Lc
Fair Isle, *Scotland* 30 Fa
Fairford, *Gloucester, Eng.* 37 Le
Faither, The, *Shet., Scot.* 34 Pa
Fakenham, *Norfolk, Eng.* 37 Rc
Falkirk, *Stirling, Scotland* 35 Jh
Falkland, *Fife, Scotland* 35 Kg
Falmouth and B., *Cornwall, England* 36 Dh
Fanad Hd., *Donegal, Eire* 32 Hc
Fannich, L., *Ross, Scotland* 34 Fd
Fareham, *Hants., England* 37 Mg
Faringdon, *Berks., England* 37 Le
Farnborough, *Hants., Eng.* 37 Nf
Farnborough, *London, Eng.* 37 Qf
Farne Deep, *North Sea* 30 Ge
Farne Is., *N'land., England* 38 Ea
Farnham, *Surrey, England* 37 Nf
Farnworth, *Lancs., England* 38 De
Fastnet Rock, *Cork, Eire* 33 Dl
Faversham, *Kent, England* 37 Rf
Fawley, *Hants., England* 37 Mg
Feale, R., *Kerry, Eire* 33 Dj
Fearn, *Ross, Scotland* 34 Jd
Feeagh, L., *Mayo, Eire* 32 Df
Felixstowe, *Suffolk, Eng.* 37 Se
Fenit, *Kerry, Eire* 33 Dj
Fenny Stratford, *Bucks., England* 37 Nd
Fens, The, dist., *England* 37 Pd
Fermanagh, co., *N. Ireland* 32 He
Fermoy, *Cork, Eire* 33 Gj
Fernhurst, *Sussex, England* 37 Nf
Ferns, *Wexford, Eire* 33 Lh
Fethard, *Tipperary, Eire* 33 Hj
Fetlar, I., *Shetland, Scot.* 34 Ra
Ffestiniog, *Mer., Wales* 36 Gc
Fife, co., *Scotland* 35 Kg
Fife Ness, *Fife, Scotland* 35 Lg
Filey, *Yorks., England* 38 Hd
Findhorn, *Moray, Scotland* 34 Jd
Findhorn, R., *Nairn, etc., Scotland* 34 Je
Findon, *Sussex, England* 37 Pg
Finglas, *Dublin, Eire* 33 Lg
Finn, R., *Donegal, Eire* 32 Hd
Finnart, *Dunbarton, Scot.* 35 Gg
Finstown, *Orkney, Scotland* 34 Ka
Fintona, *Tyrone, N. Ireland* 32 Je
Fionn L., *Ross, Scotland* 34 Fd
Fishguard, *Pemb., Wales* 36 Ee
Fishguard B., *Pemb., Wales* 36 Ed
Fitful Hd., *Shetland, Scot.* 34 Qc
Fivemiletown, *Tyrone, N. Ireland* 32 Je
Flamborough Hd., *Yorks., England* 38 Hd
Flannan Is., *Scotland* 34 Ac
Fleet, *Hants., England* 37 Nf
Fleetwood, *Lancs., Eng.* 38 Be
Flint and co., *Wales* 36 Hb
Flodden Field, *N'land., England* 38 Da
Flotta, I., *Orkney, Scotland* 34 Kb
Fochabers, *Moray, Scotland* 34 Kd
Foilslogh, pk., *Kerry, Eire* 33 Ck

Foinaven, mt., Suth., Scot. 34 Gc
Folkestone, Kent, England 37 Sf
Folkingham, Lincs., Eng. 38 Gg
Fordingbridge, Hants., England 37 Lg
Foreland Pt., Devon, Eng. 36 Gf
Forest of Atholl, Perth, Scotland 35 Hf
Forfar, Angus, Scotland 35 Lf
Forlorn Pt., Wexford, Eire 33 Kj
Formby and Pt., Lancs., England 38 Be
Forres, Moray, Scotland 34 Jd
Fort Augustus, I'ness, Scot. 34 Ge
Fort George, I'ness., Scot. 34 Hd
Forth, Firth of, Scotland 35 Lg
Forth, R., Scotland 35 Hg
Fortrose, Ross, Scotland 34 Hd
Fort William, I'ness., Scot. 35 Ff
Fotheringhay, Northants, England 37 Nc
Foula, I., Shetland, Scotland 30 Ha
Foulness I., Essex, England 37 Re
Foulsham, Norfolk, England 37 Rc
Fovant, Wilts., England 37 Kf
Fowey, Cornwall, England 36 Eh
Foxford, Mayo, Eire 32 Ef
Foyers and Falls of, I'ness, Scotland 34 He
Foyle, L., Eire-N. Ireland 32 Jc
Foyle, R., Londonderry, etc., Eire-N. Ireland 32 Jd
Foynes, Limerick, Eire 33 Eh
Framlingham, Suffolk, Eng. 37 Sd
Frankford, Offaly, Eire 33 Hg
Fraserburgh, A'deen, Scot. 34 Nd
Frenchpark, Roscommon, Eire 32 Gf
Freshford, Kilkenny, Eire 33 Jh
Frinton-on-Sea, Essex, Eng. 37 Se
Frockheim, Angus, Scot. 35 Lf
Frome, Somerset, England 36 Kf
Frome, R., Dorset, Eng. 37 Kg
Funzie, Shetland, Scotland 34 Ra
Furness, dist., Lancs., Eng. 38 Bd
Fyne, L., Argyll, Scotland 35 Fg

G

Gaerwen, Anglesey, Wales 36 Fb
Gaillimh, see Galway
Gainsborough, Lincs., Eng. 38 Gf
Gairloch, Ross, Scotland 34 Ed
Gairlochy, I'ness, Scotland 34 Ff
Gairn, R., A'deen, Scot. 34 Ke
Gala, R., M'loth., etc., Scot. 35 Lh
Galashiels, Selkirk, Scotland 35 Lh
Galgate, Lancs., England 38 Ce
Galley Hd., Cork, Eire 33 Fk
Galloway, dist., Scotland 35 Gk
Galloway, Mull of, Wigtown, Scotland 35 Gk
Galston, Ayr, Scotland 35 Hh
Galtee mts., Limerick, etc., Eire 33 Gj
Galtymore, mt., Limerick, etc., Eire 33 Gj
Galway and co., Eire 33 Eg
Galway B., Clare-Galway, Eire 33 Eg
Ganton, Yorks., England 38 Gd
Gara, L., Sligo, Eire 32 Gf
Garelochhead, Dunbarton, Scotland 35 Gg
Garron Pt., Antrim, N. Ire. 32 Mc
Garry, L., Perth, Scotland 35 Hf
Garth, Brecknock, Wales 36 Hd
Garstang, Lancs., England 38 Ce
Garvagh, Londonderry, N. Ireland 32 Kd
Garve, Ross, Scotland 34 Gd
Gatehouse-of-Fleet, Kircudbright, Scotland 35 Hk
Gateshead, Durham, Eng. 38 Ec
Giant's Causeway, Antrim, N. Ireland 32 Kc
Gifford, E. Lothian, Scot. 35 Lh
Gigha, I., Argyll, Scotland 35 Eh
Gill, L., Sligo, Eire 32 Ge
Gillingham, Dorset, Eng. 37 Kf
Gillingham, Kent, England 37 Rf
Girdle Ness, A'deen, Scot. 34 Me
Girvan and R., Ayr, Scot. 35 Gj
Glamis, Angus, Scotland 35 Kf
Glamorgan, co., Wales 36 Ge
Glanaruddery mts., Kerry, Eire 33 Ej
Glasgow, Lanark, Scotland 35 Hh
Glas Maol, mt., Angus, Scotland 35 Kf
Glass L., Ross, Scotland 34 Hd
Glastonbury, Som., Eng. 36 Jf
Glen Affric, I'ness, Scot. 34 Ge
Glen App, Ayr, Scotland 35 Gj
Glenarm, Antrim, N. Ire. 32 Md
Glenbarr, Argyll, Scotland 35 Eh
Glen Cannich, I'ness, Scot. 34 Ge
Glen Carron, I'ness, Scot. 34 Fe
Glen Clova, Angus, Scot. 35 Kf
Glencoe, Argyll, Scotland 35 Gf
Glendowan mts., Donegal, Eire 32 Gd
Gleneagles, Perth, Scotland 35 Jg
Glenelg, I'ness, Scotland 34 Ee
Glen Farg, Perth, Scotland 35 Kg
Glenfinnan, I'ness, Scotland 35 Ff
Glengad Hd., Donegal, Eire 32 Jc
Glengariff, Cork, Eire 33 Dk
Glen Garry, I'ness, Scot. 34 Ge
Glen Garry, Perth, Scot. 35 Hf
Glenluce, Wigtown, Scot. 35 Gk
Glen Lyon, Perth, Scotland 35 Hf
Glen More, I'ness, Scotland 34 Hf
Glen Moriston, I'ness, Scot. 34 Ge
Glenamaddy, Galway, Eire 32 Ff
Glen Orchy, Argyll, Scot. 35 Gg
Glenrothes, Fife, Scotland 35 Kg
Glen Shee, Perth, Scotland 35 Kf
Glen Spean, I'ness, Scot. 35 Gf
Glenties, Donegal, Eire 32 Gd
Glen Urquhart, Inverness, Scotland 34 Ge
Glin, Limerick, Eire 33 Eh
Glomach, Fall of, Ross, Scotland 34 Fe
Glossop, Derby, England 38 Ef
Gloucester and co., Eng. 37 Ke
Glyndebourne, Sussex, England 37 Qg
Goat Fell, mt., Arran, Scot. 35 Fh
Godalming, Surrey, Eng. 37 Nf
Godmanchester, Hunts., England 37 Pd
Godshill, I. of Wight, Eng. 37 Mg
Gog Magog Hills, Cambs.-Suffolk, England 37 Qd
Goil, L., Argyll-Dunbarton, Scotland 35 Gg
Golden Vale, Tipperary-Limerick, Eire 33 Gh
Golspie, Sutherland, Scot. 34 Jd
Goodwin Sands, North Sea 37 Tf
Goole, Yorks., England 38 Ge
Gorebridge, M'loth., Scot. 35 Kh
Gorey, Jersey, Channel Is. 37 Kl
Gorey, Wexford, Eire 33 Lh
Goring, Oxford, England 37 Me
Gorleston, Suffolk, England 37 Tc
Gort, Galway, Eire 33 Fg
Gorumna I., Galway, Eire 33 Dg
Gosforth, Cumb., England 38 Bd
Gosforth, N'land, England 38 Eb
Gosport, Hants., England 37 Mg
Gourock, Renfrew, Scot. 35 Gh
Gower, pen., Glam., Wales 36 Fe
Gowna, L., Longford, Eire 32 Hf
Gowrie, Carse of, Perth, Scotland 35 Kg
Graigue, Leix, Eire 33 Kh
Graiguenamanagh, Kilkenny, Eire 33 Jh
Grain, Kent, England 37 Rf
Grampian mts., Scotland 35 Gg
Grampound, Corn., Eng. 36 Eh
Granard, Longford, Eire 32 Jf
Grand Canal, Eire 33 Jg
Graney, L., Clare, Eire 33 Fh
Grangemouth, Stirl., Scot. 35 Jg
Grange-over-Sands, Lancs., England 38 Cd
Grantham, Lincs., England 38 Gg
Granton, M'loth., Scotland 35 Kh
Grantown-on-Spey, Moray, Scotland 34 Je
Grasmere, W'land., Eng. 38 Bd
Gravesend, Kent, England 37 Qf
Grays, Essex, England 37 Qf
Great Blasket I., Kerry, Eire 33 Bj
Great Crosby, Lancs., Eng. 38 Bf
Great Cumbrae, I., Bute, Scotland 35 Gh
Great Driffield, Yorks., England 38 Hd
Great Dunmow, Essex, England 37 Qe
Great Malvern, Worcester, England 36 Kd
Great Ormes Hd., Caern., Wales 36 Gb
Great Rowsley, Derby, Eng. 38 Ef
Great Torrington, Devon, England 36 Fg
Great Yarmouth, Norfolk, England 37 Tc
Gt. Whernside, mt., Yorks, England 38 Ed
Greenlaw, Berwick, Scot. 35 Mh
Green Lowther, hill, Lanark, Scotland 35 Jj
Greenock, Renfrew, Scot. 35 Gh
Greenore, Louth, Eire 32 Le
Greenore Pt., Wexford, Eire 33 Lj
Greenstone Pt., Ross, Scotland 34 Ed
Greenwich, London, Eng. 37 Qf
Gretna Green, Dumfries, Scotland 35 Kk
Greystones, Wicklow, Eire 33 Lg
Grimsby, Lincs., Eng. 38 He
Gruinard B., Ross, Scotland 34 Ed
Grutness, Shetland, Scot. 34 Qc
Guernsey, I., Channel Is. 37 Jk
Guildford, Surrey, England 37 Nf
Guisborough, Yorks., Eng. 38 Fc
Gullane, E. Lothian, Scot. 35 Lg
Gunnislake, Cornwall, Eng. 36 Ff
Guyhirne, Camb., England 37 Qc
Gweebarra B., Donegal, Eire 32 Gd

H

Haddington, E. Lothian, Scotland 35 Lh
Hadleigh, Suffolk, England 37 Rd
Hags Hd., Clare, Eire 33 Eh
Hailsham, Sussex, England 37 Qg
Halesworth, Suffolk, Eng. 37 Sd
Halifax, Yorks., England 38 Ee
Halkirk, Caithness, Scot. 34 Jb
Halstead, Essex, England 37 Re
Haltwhistle, N'land., Eng. 38 Dc
Hamilton, Lanark, Scotland 35 Hh
Hampshire (Hants.), co., England 37 Mf
Handley, Dorset, England 37 Kg
Hanley, Staffs., England 37 Kb
Hard Deep, Channel Is. 31 Ak
Harlech, Merioneth, Wales 36 Fc
Harleston, Norfolk, Eng. 37 Sd
Harlow, Essex, England 37 Qe
Harmerhill, Shrops., Eng. 36 Jc
Haroldswick, Shet., Scot. 34 Ra
Harpenden, Herts., Eng. 37 Pe
Harray, L. of, Orkney, Scot. 34 Ka
Harris, Outer Hebrides, Scotland 34 Cd
Harris, Sd. of, Outer Hebrides, Scotland 34 Bd
Harrogate, Yorks., England 38 Ee
Harrold, Bedford, England 37 Nd
Harrow, London, England 37 Pe
Hart Fell, hill, Dumfries, Scotland 35 Kj
Hartland, Devon, England 36 Fg
Hartland Pt., Devon, Eng. 36 Ef
Hartlepool, Durham, Eng. 38 Fc
Harwell, Berks., England 37 Me
Harwich, Essex, England 37 Se
Haslemere, Surrey, Eng. 37 Nf
Hastings, Sussex, England 37 Rg
Hatfield, Herts., England 37 Pe
Hatfield, Yorks., England 38 Fe
Hatherleigh, Devon, Eng. 36 Fg
Hathersage, Derby, Eng. 38 Ef
Havant, Hants., England 37 Mg
Haverfordwest, Pembroke, Wales 36 Ee
Haverhill, Suffolk, England 37 Qd
Hawarden, Flint, Wales 36 Hb
Hawes, Yorks., England 38 Dd
Hawick, Roxburgh, Scotland 35 Lj
Hawkhurst, Kent, England 37 Rf
Hawkshead, Lancs., Eng. 38 Bd
Hayle, Cornwall, England 36 Dh
Hayling I., Hants., Eng. 37 Ng
Hay-on-Wye, Brecknock, Wales 36 Hd
Headcorn, Kent, England 37 Rf
Headford, Galway, Eire 33 Eg
Heathfield, Sussex, Eng. 37 Qg
Hebrides, Outer, Is., Scot. 34 Ae
Hedon, Yorks., England 38 He
Helensburgh, Dunb., Scot. 35 Gg
Helmdon, Northants., Eng. 37 Md
Helmsdale and R., Suth., Scotland 34 Jc
Helmsley, Yorks., England 38 Fd
Helston, Cornwall, Eng. 36 Dh
Helvellyn, mt., Cumb., Eng. 38 Cc
Helvick Hd., Waterford, Eire 33 Hj
Hemel Hempstead, Herts., England 37 Pe
Henley-on-Thames, Oxford, England 37 Me
Heoga Ness, Shet., Scot. 34 Qb
Hereford and co., England 36 Jd
Herma Ness, Shet., Scot. 34 Ra
Herne Bay, Kent, Eng. 37 Rf
Herstmonceux, Sussex, England 37 Qg
Hertford, Herts., England 37 Pe
Hertford (Herts), co., Eng. 37 Pe
Hetton-le-Hole, Durham, England 38 Fc
Hexham, N'land, England 38 Dc
Heysham, Lancs., England 38 Cd
Heytesbury, Wilts., Eng. 37 Kf
High Force, Durham, Eng. 38 Dc
HighWycombe, Bucks., England 37 Ne
Hillswick, Shetland, Scot. 34 Pb
Hinckley, Leicester, Eng. 37 Mc
Hindley, Lancs., England 38 Ce
Hindon, Wilts., England 37 Kf
Hingham, Norfolk, England 37 Rc
Hitchin, Herts., England 37 Pe
Hodder, R., Yorks., Eng. 38 De
Hoddesdon, Herts., Eng. 37 Qe
Holbeach and Marsh, Lincs., England 38 Jg
Holland, div., Lincs., Eng. 38 Hg
Holme, Huntingdon, Eng. 37 Pd
Holmfirth, Yorks., England 38 Ee
Holsworthy, Devon, Eng. 36 Fg
Holt, Denbigh, Wales 36 Jb
Holt, Norfolk, England 37 Sc
Holy I., Anglesey, Wales 36 Eb
Holy I., N'land., England 38 Ea
Holyhead, Anglesey, Wales 36 Eb
Holywell, Flint, Wales 36 Hb
Holywood, Down, N. Ire. 32 Md
Honiton, Devon, England 36 Hg
Hook Hd., Wexford, Eire 33 Kj
Horley, Surrey, England 37 Pf
Horn Hd., Donegal, Eire 32 Gc
Horncastle, Lincs., England 38 Hf
Horndean, Hants., England 37 Mg
Hornsea, Yorks., England 38 He
Horsham, Norfolk, Eng. 37 Sc
Horsham, Sussex, England 37 Pf
Horwich, Lancs., England 38 Ce
Hospital, Limerick, Eire 33 Gj
Hounslow, London, Eng. 37 Pf
Hourn, L., Inverness, Scot. 34 Ee
Hove, Sussex, England 37 Pg
Howden, Yorks., England 38 Ge
Howden Res., Derby-Yorks., England 38 Ef
Howth, Dublin, Eire 33 Lg
Howth Hd., Dublin, Eire 36 Bb
Hoy I., Orkney, Scotland 34 Kb
Hoy Sd., Orkney, Scotland 34 Kb
Hoylake, Cheshire, England 38 Bf
Hucknall Torkard, Notts., England 38 Ff
Huddersfield, Yorks., Eng. 38 Ee
Hugh Town, Scilly Is., Eng. 36 Bj
Hull and R., Yorks., Eng. 38 He
Humber, R., Lincs.-Yorks., England 38 He
Hungerford, Berks., Eng. 37 Lf
Hunmanby, Yorks., Eng. 38 Hd
Hunstanton, Norfolk, Eng. 37 Qc
Huntingdon, England 37 Pd
Huntingdon and Peterborough, co., Eng. 37 Pd
Huntly, Aberdeen, Scotland 34 Le
Hurliness, Orkney, Scot. 34 Kb
Hutton Rudby, Yorks., Eng. 38 Fd
Hyde, Cheshire, England 38 Df
Hythe, Hants., England 37 Mg
Hythe, Kent, England 37 Rf

Iar Connaught, Galway, Eire 33 Eg
Ilchester, Somerset, Eng. 36 Jg
Ilford, London, England 37 Qe
Ilfracombe, Devon, England 36 Ff
Ilkeston, Derby, England 38 Fg
Ilkley, Yorks., England 38 Ee
Ilminster, Somerset, Eng. 36 Jg
Immingham, Lincs., Eng. 38 He
Inch, Wexford, Eire 33 Lh
Inchard, L., Suth., Scotland 34 Fc
Inchkeith, I., Fife, Scotland 35 Kg
Inchnadamph, Suth., Scot. 34 Gc
Indaal, L., Islay, Scotland 35 Dh
Ingatestone, Essex, England 37 Qe
Ingleborough, mt., Yorks., England 38 Dd
Ingleton, Yorks., England 38 Dd
Inishark, I., Galway, Eire 32 Cf
Inishbofin, I., Donegal, Eire 32 Gc
Inishbofin, I., Galway, Eire 32 Cf
Inisheer, I., Aran Is., Eire 33 Dg
Inishkea, I., Mayo, Eire 32 Ce
Inishmaan, I., Aran Is., Eire 33 Dg
Inishmore, I., Aran Is., Eire 33 Dg
Inishmurray, I., Sligo, Eire 32 Fe
Inishowen, Donegal, Eire 32 Jc
Inishowen Hd., Donegal, Eire 32 Kc
Inishtrahull, I., Donegal, Eire 32 Jc
Inishtrahull Sd., Donegal, Eire 32 Jc
Inishturk, I., Mayo, Eire 32 Cf
Inner Sd., I'ness, Scotland 34 Ee
Innerleithen, Peebles, Scot. 35 Kh
Inny R., Longford, etc., Eire 32 Hf
Insch, Aberdeen, Scotland 34 Le
Inveraray, Argyll, Scotland 35 Fg
Inverbervie, Kinc., Scot. 35 Mf
Invergordon, Ross, Scot. 34 Hd
Inverkeithing, Fife, Scot. 35 Kg
Inverness, Inverness, Scot. 34 He
Inverness, co., Scotland 34 Fe
Invershin, Suth., Scotland 34 Hd
Inverurie, Aberdeen, Scot. 34 Me
Iona, I., Argyll, Scotland 35 Dg
Ipswich, Suffolk, England 37 Sd
Ireland, Republic of, W. Europe 32–33
Ireland's Eye, I., Dublin, Eire 33 Lg
Irish Sea, Gt. Britain-Ire. 31 Dg
Ironbridge, Shrops., Eng. 36 Kc
Irthing, R., Cumb., Eng. 38 Cc
Irvine and R., Ayr, Scot. 35 Gh
Irvinestown, Fermanagh, N. Ireland 32 He
Isbister, Shetland, Scotland 34 Qa
Isla, R., Angus, Scotland 35 Kf
Island Magee, Antrim, N. Ireland 32 Md
Islay, I., Argyll, Scotland 35 Dh
Isle of Ely, div., Cambridge, England 37 Pc
Isle of Man 31 Ef
Isle of Wight, Hants., Eng. 37 Mg
Itchen, R., Hants., England 37 Mg
Ivybridge, Devon, England 36 Gh

J

Jarrow, Durham, England 38 Fc
Jedburgh, Roxburgh, Scot. 35 Lj
Jersey, I., Channel Is. 37 Kl
John o' Groats, Caithness, Scotland 34 Kb
Johnstone, Renfrew, Scot. 35 Gh
Johnstown, Kildare, Eire 33 Kg
Jones Bank, Atlantic Oc. 31 Bl
Joyce's Country, Galway, Eire 33 Df
Julianstown, Meath, Eire 32 Lf
Jura and Sd. of, Argyll, Scotland 35 Eg

K

Kanturk, Cork, Eire 33 Fj
Katrine, L., Perth, Scotland 35 Gg
Keady, Armagh, N. Ireland 32 Ke
Keeper Hill, Tipperary, Eire 33 Gh
Keighley, Yorks., England 38 Ee
Keith, Banff, Scotland 34 Ld
Kells, see Ceanannus Mor
Kells Range, Kirkcudbright, Scotland 35 Hj
Kelso, Roxburgh, Scotland 35 Mh
Kelvedon, Essex, England 37 Re
Ken, R., Kircud., Scotland 35 Hj
Kendal, W'land, England 38 Cd
Kenilworth, Warwick, Eng. 37 Ld
Kenmare, Kerry, Eire 33 Dk
Kenmare R., Kerry-Cork, Eire 33 Ck
Kenmore, Perth, Scotland 35 Jf
Kennet, R., Berks.-Wilts., England 37 Lf
Kennet, Vale of, Berks., England 37 Mf
Kent, co., England 37 Rf
Kent, Vale of, Kent, Eng. 37 Qf
Kentford, Suffolk, England 37 Qd
Kerry, co., Eire 33 Cj
Kerry Hd., Kerry, Eire 33 Dj
Kesteven, div., Lincs., Eng. 38 Gf
Keswick, Cumb., England 38 Bc
Kettering, Northants., Eng. 37 Nd
Key, L., Roscommon, Eire 32 Ge
Keynsham, Somerset, Eng. 36 Jf
Kidderminster, Worcester, England 37 Kd
Kidwelly, Carm., Wales 36 Fe
Kilbeggan, Westmeath, Eire 33 Jg
Kilbrannan Sd., Scotland 35 Fj
Kilcoole, Wicklow, Eire 36 Bb
Kilcullen, Kildare, Eire 33 Kg
Kildare, co., Eire 33 Kg
Kilfenora, Clare, Eire 33 Eh
Kilfinnane, Limerick, Eire 33 Gj
Kilgarvan, Kerry, Eire 33 Ek
Kilkee, Clare, Eire 33 Dh
Kilkeel, Down, N. Ireland 32 Me
Kilkenny and co., Eire 33 Jh
Kilkieran B., Galway, Eire 33 Dg
Kill, Kildare, Eire 33 Kg
Killala and B., Mayo, Eire 32 Ee
Killaloe, Tipperary, Eire 33 Gh
Killarney, Kerry, Eire 33 Dj
Killarney, Upper L., Kerry, Eire 33 Dk
Killary Harb., Galway, Eire 32 Df
Killeshandra, Cavan, Eire 32 He
Killiecrankie, Perth, Scot. 35 Jf
Killimor, Galway, Eire 33 Gg
Killin, Perth, Scotland 35 Hg
Killorglin, Kerry, Eire 33 Dj
Killybegs, Donegal, Eire 32 Gd
Killyleagh, Down, N. Ire. 32 Me
Kilmacthomas, Waterford, Eire 33 Jj
Kilmallock, Limerick, Eire 33 Fj
Kilmaluag, Skye, Scotland 34 Dd
Kilmarnock, Ayr, Scotland 35 Hh
Kilmartin, Argyll, Scotland 35 Fg
Kilmelfort, Argyll, Scotland 35 Ff
Kilninver, Argyll, Scotland 35 Fg
Kilrea, Londonderry, N. Ire. 32 Kd
Kilrush, Clare, Eire 33 Eh
Kilsyth, Stirling, Scotland 35 Hh
Kiltamagh, Mayo, Eire 32 Ff
Kilwinning, Ayr, Scotland 35 Gh
Kimbolton, Hunts., Eng. 37 Pd
Kinbrace, Suth., Scotland 34 Jc
Kincardine, co., Scotland 34 Lf
Kincardine-on-Forth, Fife, Scotland 35 Jg
Kincraig, I'ness, Scotland 34 Je
Kineton, Warwick, England 37 Md
Kingsbarns, Fife, Scotland 35 Lg
Kingsbridge, Devon, Eng. 36 Gh
Kingsclere, Hants., Eng. 37 Mf
King's Court, Cavan, Eire 32 Kf
King's Lynn, Norfolk, Eng. 37 Qc
Kingston-on-Thames, London, England 37 Pf
Kingswear, Devon, England 36 Gh
Kington, Hereford, Eng. 36 Hd
Kingussie, I'ness, Scotland 34 He
Kinlochewe, Ross, Scotland 34 Fd
Kinlochleven, I'ness, Scot. 35 Gf
Kinloch Rannoch, Perth, Scotland 35 Hf
Kinnairds Hd., A'deen, Scot. 34 Nd
Kinross and co., Scotland 35 Kg
Kinsale, Cork, Eire 33 Fk
Kintore, A'deen, Scotland 34 Me
Kintyre, dist., Argyll, Scot. 35 Eh
Kintyre, Mull of, Argyll, Scotland 35 Ej
Kinvarra, Galway, Eire 33 Fg
Kirkby, W'land, England 38 Cd
Kirkbymoorside, Yorks., England 38 Gd
Kirkby Stephen, W'land., England 38 Dd
Kirkcaldy, Fife, Scotland 35 Kg
Kirkcolm, Wigtown, Scot. 35 Fk
Kirkconnel, Dumf., Scot. 35 Hj
Kirkcudbright, Kirkcud., Scotland 35 Hk
Kirkcudbright, co., Scot. 35 Hj
Kirkham, Lancs., England 38 Ce
Kirkintilloch, Dunb., Scot. 35 Hh
Kirkoswald, Cumb., Eng. 38 Cc
Kirkpatrick, Dumf., Scot. 35 Kj
Kirkwall, Orkney, Scotland 34 Lb
Kirriemuir, Angus, Scot. 35 Kf
Kirton, Lincs., England 38 Gf
Knaresborough, Yorks., England 38 Fd
Knarsdale, N'land, Eng. 38 Cc
Knighton, Radnor, Wales 36 Hd
Knockboy, mt., Cork-Kerry, Eire 33 Ek
Knockbrack, mt., Kerry, Eire 33 Dk
Knocklayd, mt., Antrim, N. Ireland 32 Lc
Knockmealdown mts., Tipperary, etc., Eire 33 Gj
Knockowen, mt., Cork, Eire 33 Dk
Knottingley, Yorks., Eng. 38 Fe
Knutsford, Cheshire, Eng. 38 Df
Kyle, dist., Ayr, Scotland 35 Gh
Kyleakin, Skye, Scotland 34 Ee
Kyle of Lochalsh, Ross, Scotland 34 Ee

L

Labadie Bank, Atlantic Oc. 31 Bk
Ladybank, Fife, Scotland 35 Kg
Lagan, R., Antrim-Down, N. Ireland 32 Le
Laggan, Inverness, Scotland 34 He
Laggan, L., Inverness, Scot. 34 Hf
Lairg, Sutherland, Scotland 34 Hc
Lake District, Cumb., etc., England 38 Bc
Lambay I., Dublin, Eire 33 Mg
Lambourn, Berks., England 37 Mf
Lamb's Hd., Kerry, Eire 33 Ck
Lamington, Lanark, Scot. 35 Jh
Lamlash, Arran, Scotland 35 Fh
Lammermuir Hills, E. Loth., Scotland 35 Lh
Lampeter, Cardigan, Wales 36 Fd
Lanark, Lanark, Scotland 35 Jh
Lanark, co., Scotland 35 Jh
Lancashire (Lancs), co., England 38 Ce
Lancaster, Lancs., England 38 Cd
Land's End, Corn., Eng. 36 Ch
Langholm, Dumf., Scotland 35 Lj
Langport, Somerset, Eng. 36 Jf
Laoighis, co., Eire, see Leix
Laois, co., see Leix, Eire
Lapford, Devon, England 36 Gg
Larbert, Stirling, Scotland 35 Jg
Largo, Fife, Scotland 35 Lg
Largs, Ayr, Scotland 35 Gh
Larkhall, Lanark, Scotland 35 Jh
Larne, Antrim, N. Ireland 32 Md
Larne L., Antrim, N. Ire. 32 Md
Latheron, Caithness, Scot. 34 Kc
Lauder, Berwick, Scotland 35 Lh
Laugharne, Carm., Wales 36 Fe
Launceston, Cornwall, Eng. 36 Fg
Laune, R., Kerry, Eire 33 Dj
Laurencekirk, Kincardine, Scotland 35 Mf
Laxey, Isle of Man 38 Ld
Laxford, L., Suth., Scotland 34 Fc
Laxo, Shetland, Scotland 34 Qb
Laxton, Notts., England 38 Gf
Lea, R., Herts., etc., Eng. 37 Qe
Leadhills, Lanark, Scotland 35 Jj
Leagrave, Bedford, England 37 Ne
Leamington, Warks., Eng. 37 Ld
Leane, L., Kerry, Eire 33 Dj
Leatherhead, Surrey, Eng. 37 Nf
Lechlade, Gloucester, Eng. 37 Le
Ledbury, Hereford, Eng. 36 Kd
Lee, R., Cork, Eire 33 Fk
Leeds, Yorks., England 38 Ee
Leek, Staffs., England 37 Kb
Leicester and co., England 37 Mc
Leigh, Lancs., England 38 Ce
Leighlinbridge, Carlow, Eire 33 Kh
Leighton Buzzard, Bedford, England 37 Ne
Leinster, prov., Eire 31 Bg
Leinster, mt., Carlow, Eire 33 Kh
Leiston, Suffolk, England 37 Td
Leith, M'loth, Scotland 35 Kh
Leith Hill, Surrey, England 37 Pf
Leitrim, co., Eire 32 Ge
Leix, co., Eire 33 Hh
Leixlip, Kildare, Eire 33 Lg
Leominster, Hereford, England 36 Jd
Lerwick, Shetland, Scotland 34 Qb
Leslie, Fife, Scotland 35 Kg
Letchworth, Herts., Eng. 37 Pe
Letterfrack, Galway, Eire 33 Df
Letterkenny, Donegal, Eire 32 Hg
Leuchars, Fife, Scotland 35 Lg
Leven, Fife, Scotland 35 Kg
Leven, L., Kinross, Scotland 35 Kg
Leverburgh, Harris, Scot. 34 Bg
Lewes, Sussex, England 37 Pd
Lewis, I., Scotland 34 Cc
Lewis, Butt of, Lewis, Scot. 34 Db
Leyburn, Yorks., England 38 Ed
Lichfield, Staffs., England 37 Lc
Liddel, R., Rox., etc., Scot. 35 Lj
Liddesdale, Roxburgh, Scot. 35 Lj
Liffey, R., Dublin-Kildare, Eire 33 Kg
Lifford, Donegal, Eire 32 Jd
Lifton, Devon, England 36 Fg
Limavady, Londonderry, N. Ireland 32 Kc
Limerick and co., Eire 33 Fh
Lincoln, Lincs., England 38 Gf
Lincoln (Lincs), co., Eng. 38 Hf
Lincoln Edge, Lincs., Eng. 38 Gf
Lincoln Wolds, Lincs., Eng. 38 Hf
Lindsey, div., Lincs., Eng. 38 Hf
Linlithgow, W. Loth., Scot. 35 Jh
Linnhe, L., Argyll, Scotland 35 Ff
Linn of Dee, A'deen, Scot. 34 Jf
Lisburn, Antrim, N. Ire. 32 Ld
Lisconnor B., Clare, Eire 33 Eh
Lisdoonvarna, Clare, Eire 33 Eg
Liskeard, Cornwall, Eng. 36 Fh
Lismore, Waterford, Eire 33 Hj
Lismore, I., Argyll, Scot. 35 Ff
Lisnaskea, Fermanagh, N. Ireland 32 Je
Listowel, Kerry, Eire 33 Ej
Litcham, Norfolk, England 37 Rc
Litchfield, Hants., England 37 Lf
Little Halibut Bank, North Sea 30 Gb
Littlehampton, Sussex, England 37 Ng
Little Ouse R., Norfolk, etc. England 37 Qd
Little Petherick, Cornwall, England 36 Eg
Littleport, Cambs., Eng. 37 Qd
Little Walsingham, Norfolk, England 37 Rc
Liverpool, Lancs., England 38 Cf
Liverpool B., Lancs., etc., England 38 Be
Lizard and Pt., Cornwall, England 36 Dj
Llandaff, Glam., Wales 36 Hf
Llandilo, Carm., Wales 36 Ge
Llandovery, Carm., Wales 36 Ge
Llandrindod Wells, Radnor, Wales 36 Hd
Llandudno, Caern., Wales 36 Gb
Llandyssul, Card., Wales 36 Fd
Llanelli, Carmarthen, Wales 36 Fe
Llanerchymedd, Anglesey, Wales 36 Fb
Llanfair Caereinion, Mont., Wales 36 Hc
Llanfyllin, Mont., Wales 36 Hc
Llangadock, Carm., Wales 36 Ge
Llangefni, Anglesey, Wales 36 Fb
Llangerniew, Denb., Wales 36 Gb
Llangollen, Denb., Wales 36 Hc
Llanidloes, Mont., Wales 36 Gd
Llanllyfni, Caern., Wales 36 Fb
Llanrhaiadn, Denb., Wales 36 Hc
Llanrhystyd, Card., Wales 36 Fd
Llanrwst, Denb., Wales 36 Gb
Llantrisant, Glam., Wales 36 He
Llanwrtyd Wells, Brecon., Wales 36 Gd
Llanymynech, Shrops., Eng. 36 Hc
Lleyn Pen., Caern., Wales 36 Ec
Llwyngwril, Mer., Wales 36 Fc
Lochaber, dist., Inverness, Scotland 35 Gf
Loch a' chlair, Suth., Scot. 34 Hc
Lochaline, Argyll, Scotland 35 Ef
Lochboisdale, S. Uist., Scotland 34 Be
Lochbuie, Mull, Scotland 35 Eg
Lochcarron, Ross, Scotland 34 Ee
Lochearnhead, Perth, Scot. 35 Hg
Lochgelly, Fife, Scotland 35 Kg
Lochgoilhead, Argyll, Scot. 35 Gg
Lochinver, Suth., Scotland 34 Fc
Lochmaben, Dumf., Scot. 35 Kj
Lochmaddy, N. Uist., Scot. 34 Bd
Lochnagar, mt., Aberdeen, Scotland 34 Kf
Lochranza, Arran, Scotland 35 Fh
Lochy, L., Inverness, Scot. 34 Gf
Lockerbie, Dumf., Scotland 35 Kj
Loddon, Norfolk, England 37 Sc
Loftus, Yorks., England 38 Gc
Lomond Hills, Fife, Scot. 35 Kg
Lomond, L., Dunb.-Stirl., Scotland 35 Gg
London, England 37 Pf
Londonderry and co., N. Ireland 32 Jc
Long, L., Argyll, Scotland 35 Gg
Long Compton, Warwick, England 37 Ld
Long Eaton, Derby, Eng. 38 Fg
Longford and co., Eire 32 Hf
Long Forties, North Sea 30 Gc
Longhorsley, N'land, Eng. 38 Eb
Long Melford, Suff., Eng. 37 Rd
Longnor, Staffs., England 37 Lb
Longships Lt. Ho., Corn., England 36 Ch
Long Stratton, Norf., Eng. 37 Sc
Long Sutton, Lincs., Eng. 38 Jg
Longton, Staffs., England 37 Kc
Longtown, Cumb., Eng. 38 Cb
Lonsdale, W'land, England 38 Cd
Looe, E. and W., Cornwall, England 36 Fh
Loop Hd., Clare, Eire 33 Dh
Lorn, Firth of, Scotland 35 Ef
Lorne, dist., Argyll, Scot. 35 Fg
Lossie, R., Moray, Scotland 34 Kd
Lossiemouth, Moray, Scot. 34 Kd
Lostwithiel, Corn., Eng. 36 Eh
Loughborough, Leic., Eng. 37 Mc
Loughor, Glam., Wales 36 Fe
Loughrea, Galway, Eire 33 Fg
Louth, Lincs., England 38 Hf
Louth and co., Eire 32 Kf
Lowdham, Notts., England 38 Gf
Lower Whitehall, Orkney, Scotland 34 La
Lowestoft, Suffolk, Eng. 37 Td
Lowick, N'land, England 38 Ea
Loyne, L., I'ness, etc., Scot. 34 Fe
Lubnaig, L., Perth, Scot. 35 Hg
Lucan, Dublin, Eire 33 Lg
Luce B., Wigtown, Scotland 35 Gk
Ludgershall, Wilts., Eng. 37 Lf
Ludlow, Shrops., England 36 Jd
Lugnaquilla, mt., Wicklow, Eire 33 Lh
Luimneach, see Limerick
Luing, I., Argyll, Scotland 35 Eg
Lumsden, A'deen, Scotland 34 Le
Lunan B., Kinc., Scotland 35 Mf
Lundy, I., Devon, England 36 Ef
Lune, R., Lancs., etc., Eng. 38 Cd
Lunna, Shetland, Scotland 34 Qb
Lurgan, Armagh, N. Ireland 32 Le
Luss, Dunbarton, Scotland 35 Gg

Luton, Bedford, England 37 Pe
Lutterworth, Leics., Eng. 37 Md
Lybster, Caith., Scotland 34 Kc
Lydd, Kent, England 37 Rg
Lydford, Devon, England 36 Fg
Lydney, Glos., England 36 Je
Lye, Worcester, England 37 Kd
Lyme B., Devon-Dorset, England 36 Jg
Lyme Regis, Dorset, Eng. 36 Jg
Lymington, Hants., Eng. 37 Lg
Lyndhurst, Hants., England 37 Lg
Lynton, Devon, England 36 Gf
Lytham St. Annes, Lancs., England 38 Be

M

Maamturk mts., Galway, Eire 33 Df
Mablethorpe, Lincs., Eng. 38 Jf
Macclesfield, Ches., Eng. 38 Df
Macduff, Banff, Scotland 34 Md
Macgillycuddy's Reeks, mts., Kerry, Eire 33 Dk
Machrihanish, Argyll, Scot. 35 Ej
Machynlleth, Mont., Wales 36 Gc
Macroom, Cork, Eire 33 Fk
Magee, I., Antrim, N. Ire. 32 Md
Magharee Is., Kerry, Eire 33 Cj
Maghera, Londonderry, N. Ireland 32 Kd
Magherafelt, Londonderry, N. Ireland 32 Kd
Magilligan Pt., Londonderry, N. Ireland 32 Kc
Maidenhead, Berks., Eng. 37 Ne
Maiden Newton, Dorset, England 36 Jg
Maidstone, Kent, England 37 Qf
Maigue, R., Limerick, Eire 33 Fj
Main, R., Antrim, N. Ire. 32 Ld
Mainland, Orkney, Scotland 34 Kb
Mainland, Shet., Scotland 34 Pb
Mal B., Clare, Eire 33 Eh
Malahide, Dublin, Eire 33 Lg
Maldon, Essex, England 37 Re
Malin Hd., Donegal, Eire 32 Jc
Malinmore, Donegal, Eire 32 Fd
Mallaig, I'ness, Scotland 34 Ee
Mallow, Cork, Eire 33 Fj
Malmesbury, Wilts., Eng. 37 Ke
Malpas, Cheshire, England 38 Cf
Maltby, Yorks., England 38 Ff
Malton, Yorks., England 38 Gd
Malvern Hills, Hereford-Worcester, England 36 Kd
Mam Soul, mt., Ross, Scot. 34 Fe
Manchester, Lancs., Eng. 38 Df
Mangerton, mt., Kerry, Eire 33 Ek
Mannin B., Galway, Eire 33 Cg
Manningtree, Essex, Eng. 37 Se
Manor Hamilton, Leitrim, Eire 32 Ge
Mansfield, Notts., England 38 Ff
Marazion, Cornwall, Eng. 36 Dh
March, Cambs., England 37 Qc
Marden, Hereford, England 36 Jd
Maree L., Ross, Scotland 34 Ed
Margam, Glam., Wales 36 Ge
Margate, Kent, England 37 Sf
Market Deeping, Lincs., England 38 Hg
Market Drayton, Shrops., England 36 Kc
Market Harborough, Leics., England 37 Nd
Markethill, Armagh, N. Ire. 32 Ke
Market Rasen, Lincs., Eng. 38 Hf
Market Weighton, Yorks., England 38 Ge
Markinch, Fife, Scotland 35 Kg
Marlborough, Wilts., Eng. 37 Lf
Marlow, Bucks., England 37 Ne
Marshfield, Glos., England 36 Kf
Martock, Somerset, Eng. 36 Jg
Marwick Hd., Orkney, Scot. 34 Ka
Maryport, Cumb., England 38 Bc
Masham, Yorks., England 38 Ed
Mask, L., Mayo, Eire 32 Ef
Mathry, Pembroke, Wales 36 De
Matlock, Derby, England 38 Ef
Mauchline, Ayr, Scotland 35 Hh
Maumakeogh, mt., Mayo, Eire 32 Ee
Maxwelltown, Dumf., Scot. 35 Jj
May, I. of, Fife, Scotland 35 Lg
Maybole, Ayr, Scotland 35 Gj
Maynooth, Kildare, Eire 33 Kg
Mayo, co., Eire 32 Ef
Mearns, Kinc., Scotland 35 Lf
Measach Falls, Ross, Scot. 34 Fd
Meath, co., Eire 32 Kf
Medway, R., Kent, England 37 Rf
Melbourne, Derby, Eng. 38 Fg
Melbourne, Yorks., Eng. 38 Ge
Melksham, Wilts., England 37 Kf
Melrose, Roxburgh, Scot. 35 Lh
Melton Constable, Norfolk, England 37 Sc
Melton Mowbray, Leicester, England 37 Nc
Melvich, Suth., Scotland 34 Jb
Melvin, L., Leitrim, etc., Eire-N. Ireland 32 Ge
Menai Bridge, Anglesey, Wales 36 Fb
Menai Str., Angl.-Caern., Wales 36 Fb
Mendip Hills, Somerset, England 36 Jf
Mere, Wilts., England 37 Kf
Merioneth, co., Wales 36 Fc
Merrick, mt., Kirkcud., Scotland 35 Hj
Merse, The, dist., Berwick, Scotland 35 Mh
Mersey, R., Ches.-Lancs., England 38 Cf
Merthyr Tydfil, Glam., Wales 36 He
Merton, Devon, England 36 Fg
Methil, Fife, Scotland 35 Kg
Methven, Perth, Scotland 35 Jg
Mevagissey, Corn., England 36 Eh
Mexborough, Yorks., Eng. 38 Ff
Middleham, Yorks., Eng. 38 Ed
Middlesbrough, Yorks., England 38 Fc
Middleton, W'land, Eng. 38 Cd
Middleton-in-Teesdale, Durham, England 38 Dc
Middlewich, Cheshire, Eng. 38 Df
Midhurst, Sussex, England 37 Ng
Midland Gap, Shrops., Eng. 36 Jc
Midleton, Cork, Eire 33 Gk
Midlothian, co., Scotland 35 Kh
Mid Yell, Shetland, Scot. 34 Qa
Milborne Port, Somerset, England 36 Kg
Mildenhall, Suffolk, Eng. 37 Rd
Milford, Donegal, Eire 32 Hc
Milford Haven, Pembroke, Wales 36 De
Millom, Cumb., England 38 Bd
Millport, Bute, Scotland 35 Gh
Millstreet, Cork, Eire 33 Ej
Miltown Malbay, Clare, Eire 33 Eh
Minch, Little, Scotland 34 Cd
Minch, North, Scotland 34 Dc
Mine Hd., Waterford, Eire 33 Hk
Minehead, Somerset, Eng. 36 Hf
Mitchelstown, Cork, Eire 33 Gj
Mizen Hd., Cork, Eire 33 Dl
Mizen Hd., Wicklow, Eire 33 Lh
Moate, Westmeath, Eire 33 Hg
Moffat, Dumfries, Scotland 35 Kj
Moher, Cliffs of, Clare, Eire 33 Eh
Mohill, Leitrim, Eire 32 Hf
Mold, Flint, Wales 36 Hb
Mole, R., Surrey, England 37 Pf
Monach Is., Outer Hebrides, Scotland 34 Ad
Monach, Sd. of, N. Uist, Scotland 34 Ad
Monadhliath mts., I'ness, Scotland 34 He
Monaghan and co., Eire 32 Ke
Monar, L., Ross, Scotland 34 Ee
Monasterevin, Leix, Eire 33 Jg
Moniaive, Dumf., Scotland 35 Jj
Monifieth, Angus, Scotland 35 Lg
Monivea, Galway, Eire 33 Fg
Monmouth and co. 36 Je
Montgomery and co., Wales 36 Hc
Montrose, Angus, Scotland 35 Mf
Moorfoot Hills, Peebles, etc. Scotland 35 Kh
Morar, L., I'ness, Scotland 34 Ef
Moray, co., Scotland 34 Jd
Moray Firth, Scotland 34 Jd
More, L., Suth., Scotland 34 Gc
Morecambe, Lancs., Eng. 38 Cd
Morecambe B., Lancs., England 38 Cd
Moreton, Glos., England 37 Le
Moreton Hampstead, Devon, England 36 Gg
Morpeth, N'land, England 38 Eb
Morriston, Glam., Wales 36 Ge
Morte Pt., Devon, England 36 Ff
Morven, Argyll, Scotland 35 Ef
Morven, mt., Caith., Scot. 34 Jc
Mossbank, Shet., Scotland 34 Qb
Mostrim, Longford, Eire 32 Hf
Motherwell, Lanark, Scot. 35 Jh
Mountain Ash, Glam., Wales 36 Ge
Mount Bellew, Galway, Eire 33 Gg
Mountmellick, Leix, Eire 33 Jg
Mountrath, Leix, Eire 33 Jg
Mounts B., Corn., England 36 Dh
Mourne Mts., Down, N. Ire. 32 Le
Mourne, R., Tyrone, N. Ire. 32 Jd
Mousa, I., Shet., Scotland 34 Qb
Moville, Donegal, Eire 32 Jc
Moy, R., Mayo-Sligo, Eire 32 Ef
Muchalls, Kinc., Scotland 34 Me
Much Wenlock, Shrops., England 36 Jc
Muck I., I'ness, Scotland 35 Df
Muckish, mt., Donegal, Eire 32 Hc
Muckle Flugga, I., Shetland, Scotland 34 Ra
Muckle Roe, I., Shetland, Scotland 34 Qb
Muckros Hd., Donegal, Eire 32 Fd
Muine Bheag, Carlow, Eire 33 Kh
Muirkirk, Ayr, Scotland 35 Hh
Mull Hd., Orkney, Scotland 34 La
Mull, I., Argyll, Scotland 35 Eg
Mull, Sd. of, Argyll, Scot. 35 Ef
Mullaghareirk mts., Limerick, etc., Eire 33 Ej
Mullingar, Westmeath, Eire 33 Jf
Mulroy B., Donegal, Eire 32 Hc
Mumbles, Glam., Wales 36 Fe
Mundesley, Norfolk, Eng. 37 Sc
Munster, prov., Eire 31 Ah
Murrisk, mts., Mayo, Eire 32 Df
Musheramore, mt., Cork, Eire 33 Fk
Musselburgh, M'loth, Scot. 35 Kh
Muthill, Perth, Scotland 35 Jg
Mutton I., Clare, Eire 33 Dh
Mweelrea, mt., Mayo, Eire 32 Df
Mynydd Bach, mts., Card., etc., Wales 36 Gd
Mynydd Eppynt, mts., Brecknock, Wales 36 Gd

N

Naas, Kildare, Eire 33 Kg
Nailsworth, Glos., England 37 Ke
Nairn, Nairn, Scotland 34 Jd
Nairn, co., Scotland 34 Je
Nairn, R., I'ness, etc., Scot. 34 He
Nantwich, Cheshire, Eng. 38 Cf
Narberth, Pemb., Wales 36 Ee
Nash Pt., Glam., Wales 36 Gf
Navan, Meath, Eire 32 Kf
Naver, L., Suth., Scotland 34 Hc
Nayland, Suffolk, England 37 Re
Naze, The, Essex, England 37 Se
Neagh, L., N. Ireland 32 Ld
Neap, Shetland, Scotland 34 Qb
Neath, Glamorgan, Wales 36 Ge
Needham Market, Suffolk, England 37 Sd
Needles, The, I. of Wight, England 37 Lg
Nelson, Lancs., England 38 De
Nene, R., Northants, etc., England 37 Nd
Nenagh, Tipperary, Eire 33 Gh
Nephin, mt., Mayo, Eire 32 Ee
Nephin Beg, mt., Mayo, Eire 32 De
Ness, L., I'ness, Scotland 34 He
Neston, Cheshire, England 38 Bf
Nethybridge, I'ness, Scot. 34 Je
Nevin, Caernarvon, Wales 36 Ec
Nevis, L., I'ness, Scotland 34 Ee
New Alresford, Hants., England 37 Mf
Newark, Notts., England 38 Gf
Newbiggin-by-the-Sea, Northumberland, Eng. 38 Eb
New Bridge, Mon. 36 He
Newbridge on Wye, Radn., Wales 36 Hd
Newburgh, A'deen, Scot. 34 Me
Newburgh, Fife, Scotland 35 Kg
Newbury, Berks., England 37 Mf
Newby Bridge, Lancs., England 38 Cd
Newcastle, Down, N. Ire. 32 Me
Newcastle, Dublin, Eire 33 Lg
Newcastle, Limerick, Eire 33 Ej
Newcastle, N'land, Eng. 38 Ec
Newcastle Emlyn, Carm., Wales 36 Fd
Newcastleton, Rox., Scot. 35 Lj
Newcastle-under-Lyme, Staffs., England 37 Kb
New Cumnock, Ayr, Scot. 35 Hj
New Deer, A'deen, Scot. 34 Md
Newent, Glos., England 36 Ke
New Forest, Hants., Eng. 37 Lg
New Galloway, Kircud., Scotland 35 Hj
Newhaven, Sussex, Eng. 37 Qg
New Holland, Lincs., Eng. 38 He
New Luce, Wigtown, Scot. 35 Gk
Newlyn East, Corn., Eng. 36 Dh
Newmarket, Cork, Eire 33 Ej
Newmarket, Suffolk, Eng. 37 Qd
New Mills, Derby, England 38 Ef
Newnham, Glos., England 36 Ke
New Pitsligo, A'deen, Scot. 34 Md
Newport, Essex, England 37 Qe
Newport, I. of Wight, Eng. 37 Mg
Newport, Mayo, Eire 32 Df
Newport, Mon. 36 He
Newport, Pemb., Wales 36 Ed
Newport, Shropshire, Eng. 36 Kc
Newport-on-Tay, Fife, Scotland 35 Lg
Newport Pagnell, Bucks., England 37 Nd
New Quay, Card., Wales 36 Ed
Newquay, Corn., England 36 Dh
New Radnor, Radnor, Wales 36 Hd
New Romney, Kent, Eng. 37 Rg
New Ross, Wexford, Eire 33 Kj
Newry, Down, N. Ireland 32 Le
Newry Canal, Armagh-Down, N. Ireland 32 Le
Newton Abbot, Devon, England 36 Gg
Newtonmore, I'ness, Scot. 34 He
Newton Stewart, Wig., Scotland 35 Hk
Newtown, Mont., Wales 36 Hc
Newtownards, Down, N. Ire. 32 Md
Newtownbarry, Wexford, Eire 33 Kh
Newtown Butler, Fermanagh, N. Ireland 32 Je
Newtown Hamilton, Armagh, N. Ireland 32 Ke
Newtown Mt. Kennedy, Wicklow, Eire 33 Lg
Newtown Stewart, Tyrone, N. Ireland 32 Jd
Nidd, R., Yorks., England 38 Ec
Nith, R., Dumfries, Scot. 35 Jj
Nithsdale, Dumfries, Scot. 35 Ji
Nobber, Meath, Eire 32 Kf
Nore, Lt. Ho., Thames, England 31 Hj
Nore, R., Leix, etc., Eire 33 Jh
Norfolk, co., England 37 Rc
Norfolk Broads, Norfolk, England 37 Sc
Norfolk Edge, hills, Norfolk, England 37 Rc
Norham, N'land, England 38 Da
North Channel, N. Ireland-Scotland 30 Df
North Downs, Kent, Eng. 37 Qf
North Foreland, Kent, England 37 Sf
North Sea, Europe 30 Gc
North Sd., The, Orkney, Scotland 34 La
Northallerton, Yorks., Eng. 38 Fd
Northampton and co., England 37 Nd
North Berwick, E. Loth., Scotland 35 Lg
Northern Ireland, Gt. Brit. 31 Cf
Northiam, Sussex, England 37 Rg
Northleach, Glos., England 37 Le
North Riding, Yorks., Eng. 38 Fd
North Rona, I., Scotland 34 Ea
North Ronaldsay Firth, Orkney, Scotland 34 Ma
North Ronaldsay, I., Orkney, Scotland 34 Ma
North Shields, N'land, England 38 Fb
North Somercotes, Lincs., England 38 Jf
North Uist, I., Outer Hebrides, Scotland 34 Bd
Northumberland, co., Eng. 38 Db
North Walsham, Norfolk, England 37 Sc
North West Highlands, Scotland 34 Fe
Northwich, Ches., England 38 Df
Northwold, Norfolk, Eng. 37 Rc
Norwich, Norfolk, England 37 Sc
Norwick, Shet., Scotland 34 Ra
Noss, I. of, Shet., Scotland 34 Rb
Nottingham, Notts., Eng. 38 Fg
Nottingham (Notts), co., England 38 Ff
Nuneaton, Warwick, Eng. 37 Mc
Nutts Corner, Antrim, N. Ireland 32 Ld
Nymphe Bank, St. George's Channel 31 Cj

O

Oa, Mull of, Islay, Scot. 35 Dh
Oakengates, Shrops., Eng. 36 Kc
Oakham, Rutland, England 37 Nc
Oban, Argyll, Scotland 35 Fg
Ochil Hills, Perth, Scot. 35 Jg
Ochiltree, Ayr, Scotland 35 Hj
Offaly, co., Eire 33 Hg
Oich, L., Inverness, Scot. 34 Ge
Okehampton, Devon, Eng. 36 Gg
Old Hd. of Kinsale, Cork, Eire 33 Fk
Oldcastle, Meath, Eire 32 Jf
Oldham, Lancs., England 38 De
Old Meldrum, Aberdeen, Scotland 34 Me
Ollerton, Notts., England 38 Ff
Olney, Bucks., England 37 Nd
Omagh, Tyrone, N. Ire. 32 Jd
Omey I., Galway, Eire 33 Cf
Ongar, Essex, England 37 Qe
Onich, Inverness, Scotland 35 Ff
Oranmore, Galway, Eire 33 Fg
Orford, Suffolk, England 37 Td
Orkney, Is. and co., Scot. 34 Kb
Ormskirk, Lancs., England 38 Ce
Oronsay, I., Argyll, Scot. 35 Dg
Orrin, R., Ross, Scotland 34 Gd
Oswestry, Shrops., Eng. 36 Hc
Otley, Yorks., England 38 Ee
Otterburn, N'land, Eng. 38 Db
Otterswick, Shet., Scot. 34 Qa
Ottery, R., Corn.-Devon, England 36 Fg
Ottery St. Mary, Devon, England 36 Hg
Oughterard, Galway, Eire 33 Eg
Oundle, Northants, Eng. 37 Pd
Ouse, R., Norfolk, etc., England 37 Qc
Ouse, R., Yorks., England 38 Fe
Outer Hebrides, Is., Scot. 34 Ae
Out Skerries, Shet., Scot. 34 Rb
Overton, Flint, Wales 36 Jc
Owel, L., Westmeath, Eire 33 Jf
Owemore R., Mayo, Eire 32 De
Ox mts., Mayo-Sligo, Eire 32 Fe
Oxford and co., England 37 Me
Oykel, R., Suth., Scotland 34 Gd

P

Pabbay, I., Outer Hebrides, Scotland 34 Bd
Padstow, Cornwall, Eng. 36 Eg
Paignton, Devon, England 36 Gh
Paisley, Renfrew, Scotland 35 Hh
Pangbourne, Berks., Eng. 37 Mf
Papa Stour, I., Shet., Scot. 34 Pb
Papa Westray, I., Orkney, Scotland 34 La
Paps of Jura, mts., Jura, Scotland 35 Eh
Parracombe, Devon, Eng. 36 Gf
Parrett R., Somerset, Eng. 36 Jf
Partry mts., Mayo, Eire 32 Ef
Pateley Bridge, Yorks., England 38 Ed
Patrington, Yorks., Eng. 38 He
Peak, The, mt., Derby, England 38 Ef
Peebles and co., Scotland 35 Kh
Peel, Isle of Man 38 Kd
Peel Fell, mt., Rox., Scot. 35 Lj
Pembridge, Hereford, Eng. 36 Jd
Pembroke and co., Wales 36 Ee
Pembroke Docks, Pemb., Wales 36 Ee
Penarth, Glam., Wales 36 Hf
Pencader, Carm., Wales 36 Fe
Penicuik, M'loth., Scotland 35 Kh
Penistone, Yorks., England 38 Ee
Penkilan Hd., Caernarvon, Wales 36 Ec
Penkridge, Staffs., Eng. 37 Kc
Pennine Chain, England 38 Cc
Penrith, Cumb., England 38 Cc
Penryn, Cornwall, England 36 Dh
Pentland Firth, Scotland 34 Kb
Pentland Hills, M'loth. etc., Scotland 35 Kh
Pentland Skerries, Orkney, Scotland 34 Lb
Pen-y-ghent, mt., Yorks., England 38 Dd
Penzance, Cornwall, Eng. 36 Ch
Perranporth, Corn., Eng. 36 Dh
Pershore, Worcester, Eng. 37 Kd
Perth, Perth, Scotland 35 Kg
Perth, co., Scotland 35 Hg
Peterborough, Hunts., England 37 Pc
Peterculter, A'deen, Scot. 34 Me
Peterhead, A'deen, Scot. 34 Nd
Peterlee, Durham, England 38 Fc
Petersfield, Hants., Eng. 37 Nf
Peterstow, Hereford, Eng. 36 Je
Petworth, Sussex, England 37 Ng
Pettigo, Donegal, Eire 32 Hd
Pewsey and Vale of, Wilts., England 37 Lf
Pickering, Yorks., England 38 Gd
Pierowall, Orkney, Scotland 34 La
Pitlochry, Perth, Scotland 35 Jf
Pittenweem, Fife, Scotland 35 Lg
Pladda Lt. Ho., Arran, Scot. 35 Fj
Plymouth, Devon, England 36 Fh
Plymouth Sound, Cornwall-Devon, England 36 Fh
Plynlimon, mt., Cardigan, Wales 36 Gd
Pocklington, Yorks., Eng. 38 Ge
Polegate, Sussex, England 37 Qg
Pollaphuca Res., Wicklow, Eire 33 Lg
Polperro, Cornwall, Eng. 36 Fh
Pomeroy, Tyrone, N. Ire. 32 Kd
Pomona, Orkney, Scotland 34 Ka
Pontardawe, Glam., Wales 36 Ge
Pontefract, Yorks., England 38 Fe
Pontesbury, Shrops., Eng. 36 Jc
Pontrilas, Hereford, Eng. 36 Je
Pontypool, Mon. 36 He
Pontypridd, Glam., Wales 36 He
Poole, Dorset, England 37 Lg
Poolewe, Ross, Scotland 34 Ed
Porlock, Somerset, England 36 Gf
Portadown, Armagh, N. Ireland 32 Le
Portaferry, Down, N. Ire. 32 Me
Portarlington, Leix, Eire 33 Jg
Port Askaig, Islay, Scotland 35 Dh
Port Carlisle, Cumb., Eng. 38 Bc
Port Charlotte, Islay, Scot. 35 Dh
Port Dinorwic, Caern., Wales 36 Fb
Port Ellen, Islay, Scotland 35 Dh
Port Erin, Isle of Man 38 Kd
Port Errol, A'deen, Scot. 34 Ne
Port Eynon, Glam., Wales 36 Fe
Port Glasgow, Renf., Scot. 35 Gh
Portglenone, Antrim, N. Ireland 32 Ld
Portgordon, Banff, Scot. 34 Kd
Porthcawl, Glam., Wales 36 Gf
Porth Neigwl, Caernarvon, Wales 36 Ec
Port Isaac, Cornwall, Eng. 36 Eg
Portishead, Somerset, Eng. 36 Jf
Port Lairge, see Waterford
Portland Bill, Dorset, Eng. 36 Kg
Portland Harbour, Dorset, England 36 Kg
Portland Isle, Dorset, Eng. 36 Kg
Portlaoise, Leix, Eire 33 Jg
Portlaw, Waterford, Eire 33 Jj
Portmadoc, Caern., Wales 36 Fc
Portnacroish, Argyll, Scot. 35 Ff
Portnahaven, Islay, Scot. 35 Ch
Port of Ness, Lewis, Scot. 34 Dc
Portpatrick, Wig., Scot. 35 Fk
Portree, Skye, Scotland 34 De
Portrush, Londonderry, N. Ireland 32 Kc
Portsalon, Donegal, Eire 32 Hc
Portsmouth, Hants., Eng. 37 Mg
Portsonachan, Argyll, Scot. 35 Fg
Portsoy, Banff, Scotland 34 Ld
Port Talbot, Glam., Wales 36 Ge
Portumna, Galway, Eire 33 Gg
Port William, Wig., Scot. 35 Gk
Potton, Bedford, England 37 Pd
Prawle Pt., Devon, Eng. 36 Gh
Prescot, Lancs., England 38 Cf
Presteigne, Radnor, Wales 36 Jd
Preston, Lancs., England 38 Ce
Prestonpans, E. Loth., Scot. 35 Lh
Prestwick, Ayr, Scotland 35 Gh
Princetown, Devon, Eng. 36 Gg
Pumpsaint, Carm., Wales 36 Gd
Purbeck Downs, Dorset, England 36 Jg
Purley, London, England 37 Pf
Pwllheli, Caern., Wales 6 Fc

Q

Quantock Hills, Somerset, England 36 Hf
Quirang, mt., Skye, Scot. 34 Dd
Quoich, L., I'ness, Scotland 34 Fe

R

Raasay, I. and Sd., Skye, Scotland 34 De
Radnor, co., Wales 36 Hd
Radnor Forest, Radnor, Wales 36 Hd
Radstock, Somerset, Eng. 36 Kf
Ramelton, Donegal, Eire 32 Hc
Ramor, L., Cavan, Eire 32 Jf
Ramsbottom, Lancs., Eng. 38 De
Ramsey, Hunts., England 37 Pd
Ramsey, Isle of Man 38 Ld
Ramsey I., Pemb., Wales 36 De
Ramsgate, Kent, England 37 Sf
Randalstown, Antrim, N. Ireland 32 Ld
Rannoch, L., Perth, Scot. 35 Hf
Rannoch, Moor, Argyll-Perth, Scotland 35 Gf
Raphoe, Donegal, Eire 32 Hd
Rathangan, Kildare, Eire 33 Jg
Rathdrum, Wicklow, Eire 33 Lh
Rathfriland, Down, N. Ire. 32 Le
Rathkeale, Limerick, Eire 33 Fh
Rathlin I., Antrim, N. Ire. 32 Lc
Rathluire, see Charleville
Rathnew, Wicklow, Eire 33 Lh
Rattray Hd., A'deen, Scot. 34 Nd
Ravenglass, Cumb., Eng. 38 Bd
Rayleigh, Essex, England 37 Re
Reading, Berks., England 37 Nf
Reawick, Shetland, Scotland 34 Qb
Redcar, Yorks., England 38 Fc
Redditch, Worcs., England 37 Ld
Redhill, Surrey, England 37 Pf
Redruth, Cornwall, England 36 Dh
Ree, L., Roscommon, Eire 33 Gf
Reedham, Norfolk, England 37 Sc
Reeth, Yorks., England 38 Ed
Reigate, Surrey, England 37 Pf
Renfrew and co., Renfrew, Scotland 35 Gh
Rerwick, Shetland, Scot. 34 Qc
Rhayader, Radnor, Wales 36 Hd
Rhondda, Glam., Wales 36 He
Rhosllanerchrugog, Denb., Wales 36 Hb
Rhu Coigach, Ross, Scot. 34 Fc
Rhum, I., I'ness, Scotland 34 De
Rhyl, Flint, Wales 36 Hb
Rhynie, Aberdeen, Scotland 34 Le
Ribble, R., Lancs.-Yorks., England 38 De
Riccall, Yorks., England 38 Fe
Riccarton Junction, Rox., Scotland 35 Lj
Richborough, Kent, Eng. 37 Sf
Richmond, London, Eng. 37 Pf
Richmond, Yorks., England 38 Ed
Rickmansworth, Herts., England 37 Pe
Ridgewell, Essex, England 37 Rd
Rineanna, Clare, Eire 33 Fh
Ringmer, Sussex, England 37 Qg
Ringwood, Hants., Eng. 37 Lg
Ripley, Derby, England 38 Ff
Ripley, Yorks., England 38 Ed
Ripon, Yorks., England 38 Ed
Risca, Mon. 36 He
Roade, Northants, England 37 Nd
Roag, L., Lewis, Scotland 30 Cb
Roaringwater B., Cork, Eire 33 Ek
Robe, R., Mayo, Eire 32 Ef
Robertstown, Kildare, Eire 33 Kg
Robin Hood's Bay, Yorks, England 38 Gd
Rochdale, Lancs., England 38 De
Rochester, Kent, England 37 Rf
Rochford, Essex, England 37 Re
Rockingham, Northants., England 37 Nc
Rodel, Harris, Scotland 34 Cd
Roman Wall, N'land, Eng. 38 Db
Romford, London, England 37 Qe
Romney Marsh, Kent, Eng. 37 Rf
Romsey, Hants., England 37 Lg
Roosky, Leitrim, Eire 32 Hf
Rora Hd., Orkney, Scotland 34 Kb
Roscommon and co., Eire 32 Gf
Roscrea, Tipperary, Eire 33 Hh
Rosehearty, A'deen, Scot. 34 Md
Rosemarkie, Ross, Scotland 34 Hd
Rosemary Bank, Atlantic Oc. 30 Aa
Ross, Hereford, England 36 Je
Rossan Pt., Donegal, Eire 32 Fd
Ross & Cromarty, co., Scot. 34 Fd
Rosscarbery, Cork, Eire 33 Ek
Rosslare Harb., Wexford, Eire 33 Lj
Rosslea, Fermanagh, N. Ire. 32 Je
Rosyth, Fife, Scotland 35 Kg
Rothbury, N'land, England 38 Eb
Rother, R., Kent-Sussex, England 37 Rf
Rotherham, Yorks., Eng. 38 Ff
Rothes, Moray, Scotland 34 Kd
Rothesay, Bute, Scotland 35 Fh
Rousay, I., Orkney, Scot. 34 Ka
Roxburgh, Rox., Scotland 35 Mh
Roxburgh, co., Scotland 35 Lj
Royal Canal, Eire 33 Kg
Royston, Herts., Eng. 37 Pd
Ruabon, Denbigh, Wales 36 Hc
Rubha Hunish, Skye, Scot. 34 Dd
Rubha Reidh, Ross, Scot. 34 Ed
Ruddington, Notts., Eng. 38 Fg
Rudyard Res., Staffs., Eng. 37 Kb
Rugby, Warwick, England 37 Md
Rugeley, Staffs., England 37 Lc
Rum, see Rhum
Runcorn, Ches., England 38 Cf
Runswick, Yorks., England 38 Gc
Rush, Dublin, Eire 33 Lf
Rushden, Northants., Eng. 37 Nd
Rutherglen, Lanark, Scot. 35 Hh
Ruthin, Denbigh, Wales 36 Hb
Rutland, co., England 37 Nc
Ryan, L., Wigtown, Scot. 35 Fk
Ryde, I. of Wight, England 37 Mg
Rye, Sussex, England 37 Rg

S

Saddle, The, mt., Ross, Scotland 34 Fe
Saffron Walden, Essex, England 37 Qd
St. Abbs Hd., Berwick, Scotland 35 Mh
St. Agnes, Cornwall, Eng. 36 Dh
St. Agnes, I., Scilly Is., Eng. 36 Bj
St. Albans, Herts., Eng. 37 Pe
St. Alban's Hd., Dorset, England 37 Kg
St. Andrews, Fife, Scotland 35 Lg
St. Anne, Alderney, Channel Is. 37 Kk
St. Asaph, Flint, Wales 36 Hb
St. Aubin, Jersey, Channel Is. 37 Kl
St. Austell and B., Corn., England 36 Eh
St. Bees, Cumb., England 38 Ad
St. Bees Hd., Cumb., Eng. 38 Ac
St. Blazey, Corn., England 36 Eh
St. Bride's B., Pembroke, Wales 36 De
St. Catherines Pt., I. of Wight, England 37 Mg
St. Clears, Carm., Wales 36 Fe
St. Columb, Corn., Eng. 36 Eh
St. Davids, Pemb., Wales 36 De
St. David's Hd., Pembroke, Wales 36 De
St. Day, Cornwall, England 36 Dh
St. Dogmells, Pemb., Wales 36 Ed
Saintfield, Down, N. Ire. 32 Me
St. Fillans, Perth, Scotland 35 Hg
St. Finan's B., Kerry, Eire 33 Ck
St. George's Channel, Eire-Wales 31 Cj
St. Germans, Corn., Eng. 36 Fh
St. Gowans Hd., Pemb., Wales 36 Ee
St. Helens, Lancs., England 38 Cf
St. Helier, Jersey, Channel Is. 37 Kl
St. Ives, Huntingdon, Eng. 37 Pd
St. Ives and B., Corn., England 36 Dh
St. John's Pt., Donegal, Eire 32 Gd
St. Johns Pt., Down, N. Ireland 32 Me
St. John's Chapel, Durham, England 38 Dc
St. Just, Cornwall, England 36 Ch
St. Kilda, Is., Scotland 30 Bc
St. Leonards, Sussex, Eng. 37 Rg
St. Magnus B., Shet., Scot. 34 Pb
St. Margaret's Hope, Orkney, Scotland 34 Lb
St. Martin's I., Scilly Is., England 36 Bj
St. Mary's, Orkney, Scot. 34 Lb
St. Mary's, I., Scilly Is., Eng. 36 Bj
St. Mary's L., Selkirk, Scot. 35 Kj
St. Neots, Hunts., England 37 Pd
St. Peter Port, Guernsey, Channel Is. 37 Jl
St. Sampson, Guernsey, Channel Is. 37 Jl
St. Teath, Cornwall, Eng. 36 Eg
Salcombe, Devon, England 36 Gh
Sale, Cheshire, England 38 Df
Salen, Argyll, Scotland 35 Ef
Salford, Lancs., England 38 Df
Salisbury, Wilts., England 37 Lf
Salisbury Plain, Wilts., England 37 Kf
Salop, co., see Shropshire
Saltash, Cornwall, England 36 Fh
Saltburn, Yorks., England 38 Gc
Saltcoats, Ayr, Scotland 35 Gh
Saltee Is., Wexford, Eire 33 Kj
Saltfleet, Lincs., England 38 Jf
Sanda, I., Argyll, Scotland 35 Ej
Sanday, I., Orkney, Scot. 34 Ma
Sanday Sd., Orkney, Scot. 34 La
Sandbach, Ches., England 38 Df
Sandgate, Kent, England 37 Sf
Sandness, Shetland, Scot. 34 Pb
Sandown, I. of Wight, Eng. 37 Mg
Sandringham, Norf., Eng. 37 Rc
Sandwich, Kent, England 37 Sf
Sandwick, Shetland, Scot. 34 Qc
Sandy, Bedford, England 37 Pd

PART TWO—WORLD INDEX

PAGES 39-100

LIST OF ABBREVIATIONS

Afghan. Afghanistan
Afr. Africa
Ala. Alabama
Alta. Alberta
Alg. Algeria
Antarc. Antarctica
Arabia. Saudi-Arabia
Arch. Archipelago
Argent. Argentina
Ariz. Arizona
Ark. Arkansas
Aust. Australia
Aut. Autonomous
B. Bay, Bahia, Baie, Bucht
Baluch. Baluchistan
B.C. British Columbia
Belg., Belgium, Belgian
Bol. Bolivia
Br. British
Bulg. Bulgaria
C. Cape, Cabo, Cap
Cal. California
Can. Canal
Car. Carolina
Cel. Celebes
Cent. Central
Chan. Channel
Co. County
Col. Colony
Colo. Colorado
Colomb. Colombia
Conn. Connecticut
Cord. Cordillera
Cr. Creek
Czech. Czechoslovakia
Del. Delaware
Den. Denmark
Dep. Department
Des. Desert
Dist. District
Div. Division
Dom. Dominicana
E. East, Eastern
Ecua. Ecuador
E.I. East Indies
Eiln. Eilanden
Eire Republic of Ireland
Eng. England
Erit. Eritrea
Ethio. Ethiopia
Fd. Fjord
Fla. Florida
Fr. French, France
G. Gulf, Golfe, Golfo, Guba
Ga. Georgia
Geb. Gebirge (Mountains)
Ger. Germany
G.F. Goldfield
Grp. Group
Gt. Great
Guat. Guatemala
Harb. Harbour
Hd. Head
Hisp. Hispaniola
Hond. Honduras
Hung. Hungary
I., Is. Island, Islands, Île, Îles
Ia. Iowa
Ida. Idaho
Ill. Illinois
Ind. Indiana
Indon. Indonesia
It. Italian, Italy
Iv. Cst. Ivory Coast
Jeb. Jebel (Mountain)
Kan. Kansas
Kazakh. Kazakhskaya S.S.R.
Kep. Kepulauan (Islands)
Kirgiz. Kirgizskaya S.S.R.
Ky, Kentucky
L. Lake, Loch, Lough, Lago, Lac, Lagoon, Lagoa
La. Louisiana
Ld. Land
Leb. Lebanon
Lit. Little
Lith. Lithuania
Lr. Lower
Madag. Madagascar
Man. Manitoba
Mass. Massachusetts
Maur. Mauritania
Md. Maryland
Me. Maine
Mex. Mexico
Mich. Michigan
Minn. Minnesota
Miss. Mississippi
Mo. Missouri
Mong. Mongolia
Mont. Montana
Moçamb. Moçambique
Mt., Mte. Mount, Mont, Monte
N. North, Northern, New
Nat. National
N.B. New Brunswick
N.C. North Carolina
N. Dak. North Dakota
Neb. Nebraska
Nev. Nevada
Nfd. Newfoundland
N.H. New Hampshire
Nic. Nicaragua
N. Ire. Northern Ireland
N.J. New Jersey
N. Mex. New Mexico
N.S. Nova Scotia
N.S.W. New South Wales
N.-W. Terr. North-West Territories
N.Y. New York
N.Z. New Zealand
O. Ohio
O., Os., Ostrov (Island)
Ova., Ostrova (Islands)
Oc. Ocean
O.F.S. Orange Free State
Okla. Oklahoma
Ont. Ontario
Ore. Oregon
Oz. Ozero (Lake)
Pa. Pennsylvania
Pac. Pacific
Pak. Pakistan
Pan. Panama
Para. Paraguay
P.E.I. Prince Edward Island
Pen. Peninsula
Phil. Philippines
Pk. Peak, Park
Plat. Plateau
Pol. Poluostrov (Peninsula)
Port. Portuguese, Portugal
Princip. Principality
Prot. Protectorate
Prov. Province
P. Point, Pointe
Pta. Punta (Point)
Pto. Puerto
Qnsld. Queensland
Que. Quebec
R. River, Rio, Rivière
Ra. Range
Rep. Republic
Res. Reservoir
Rhod. Rhodesia
R.I. Rhode Island
Rum. Rumania
Russ. Russia
S. South, Southern
Sa. Serra, Sierra
Sard. Sardinia
Sask. Saskatchewan
S.C. South Carolina
Scot. Scotland
Sd. Sound
S. Dak. South Dakota
S. San, Santo
Set. Settlement
Sol. Solomon
Som. Somaliland
Sp. Spanish, Spain
S.S.R. Soviet Socialist Republic
St., Ste., Sta. Saint, Sainte, Santa
Str. Strait
Swed. Sweden
Switz. Switzerland
Tan. Tanzania
Tenn. Tennessee
Terr. Territory
Tex. Texas
Trans. Transvaal
Ukr. Ukraine
Up. Upper
U.S.A. United States of America
U.S.S.R. Union of Soviet Socialist Republics
Ut. Utah
Uzbek. Uzbekskaya S.S.R.
Va. Virginia
Val. Valley
Vdkhr. Vodokhranilishche (Reservoir)
Venez. Venezuela
Vict. Victoria
Vol. Volcano
Vt. Vermont
W. West, Western
Wash. Washington
W.I. West Indies
Wis. Wisconsin
Wyo. Wyoming
Yugosl. Yugoslavia

Aachen, *Germany* 48 Ac
Aalborg, *Denmark* 47 Dh
Aalen, *Germany* 48 Dd
Aaelstrup, *Denmark* 47 Ch
Aalsmeer, *Netherlands* 44 Cb
Aalst. See Alost
Aalten, *Netherlands* 44 Ec
Aarau, *Switzerland* 45 Da
Aarberg, *Switzerland* 45 Ca
Aarburg, *Switzerland* 45 Ca
Aardenburg, *Netherlands* 44 Bc
Aare, R., *Switzerland* 45 Ca
Aargau, canton, *Switzerland* 45 Da
Aarhus, *Denmark* 47 Dh
Aars, *Denmark* 47 Ch
Aarschot, *Belgium* 44 Cd
Aba, *Congo* 77 Gd
Abacaxis R., *Brazil* 90 Fe
Abaco I., Gt., *Bahama Is.* 89 Da
Abaco I., Lit., *Bahama Is* 89 Da
Abadan, *Persia* 72 Ec
Abadeh, *Persia* 73 Fc
Abaete, *Brazil* 91 Hd
Abajo Pk., *Utah* 84 Ed
Abakan, *Russia* 59 Jc
Abal Dufaf, *Arabia* 72 Dc
Abancay, *Peru* 90 Cf
Abarqu, *Persia* 73 Fc
Abashiri & B., *Japan* 66 Jb
Abau, *Papua* 95 Jb
Abaya L., *Ethiopia* 77 Hc
Abbeville, *France* 52 Da
Abbottabad, *W. Pakistan* 70 Cc
Abdul Aziz, Jebel, *Syria* 72 Db
Abdulino, *Russia* 61 Ld
Abeche, *Chad* 79 Kf
Abeele, *Belgium* 44 Ad
Abelessa, *Algeria* 78 Fd
Abengourou, *Ivory Coast* 78 Eg
Abeokuta, *Nigeria* 78 Fg
Aberaeron, *Wales* 36 Fd
Aberdare, *Wales* 31 Ej
Aberdeen, *S. Dakota* 85 Gb
Aberdeen, *Washington* 87 Ab
Aberdeen & co., *Scotland* 30 Fc
Aberdeen L., *N.-W. Terr.* 80 Ld
Aberfeldy, *Scotland* 30 Ed
Aberfoyle, *Scotland* 30 Ed
Abergavenny, *Britain* 31 Ej
Aberystwyth, *Wales* 31 Eh
Abha, *Arabia* 72 Df
Abidjan, *Ivory Coast* 78 Eg
Ab-i-Istada L., *Afghanistan* 73 Jc
Abilene, *Texas* 84 Ge
Abingdon, *Virginia* 85 Kd
Abington, *Massachusetts* 86 Ea
Abisko, *Sweden* 46 Hb
Abitibi L., *Ontario* 81 Qg
Abitibi R., *Ontario* 81 Qg
Abomey, *Dahomey* 78 Fg
Abrantes, *Portugal* 50 Ac
Abrets, les, *France* 52 Fd
Abrud, *Rumania* 56 Da
Abruzzi, dep., *It.* 54 Dd
Abtehau, *Austria* 48 Ee
Abu, *India* 68 Dd
Abu al Abyad, *Trucial States* 73 Fe
Abu Arish, *Arabia* 72 Df
Abu Bahr, *Arabia* 72 Ee
Abu Deleiq, *Sudan* 79 Me
Abu Dhabi, *Trucial States* 73 Fe
Abu ed Duhur, *Syria* 74 Fb
Abu el Jurdhan, *Jordan* 74 Dg
Abu Jifan, *Arabia* 72 Ee
Abu Kemal, *Syria* 72 Dc
Abumombozi, *Congo* 76 Ed
Abunã, *Brazil* 90 De
Abu Qurqas, *Egypt* 79 Mc
Abuta, *Japan* 66 Gc
Abuya Myeda, Mt., *Ethiopia* 77 Hb
Abu Zabad, *Sudan* 79 Lf
Abyei, *Sudan* 79 Lg
Abyy, *Russia* 59 Pb
Åbyn, *Sweden* 46 Jd
Acajutla, *Salvador* 89 Bd
Acambaro, *Mexico* 88 Dc
Acaponeta, *Mexico* 88 Cc
Acapulco, *Mexico* 88 Dd
Acara & R., *Brazil* 91 Hd
Acarigua, *Venezuela* 90 Db
Acatlan, *Mexico* 88 Ed
Accra, *Ghana* 78 Eg
Achaguas, *Venezuela* 90 Db
Achao, *Chile* 92 Bf
Achill I., *Eire* 31 Ag
Achinsk, *Russia* 59 Jc
Achray, *Ontario* 83 Hc
Acklins, I., *Bahamas Is.* 89 Eb
Aconcagua, Mt., *Argentina* 92 Cd
Açores, Is., *Atlantic Ocean* 78 Ba
Acorizal, *Brazil* 91 Fg
Acoyapa, *Nicaragua* 89 Bd
Acre, *Israel* 74 De
Actaeon Grp., *Tuamotu Arch.* 99 Mk
Acton Vale, *Quebec* 83 Kc
Açu & R., *Brazil* 91 Ke
Ada, *Oklahoma* 84 Ge
Adair, C., *N.-W. Territories* 81 Sb
Adak, I., *Aleutian Is.* 85 Vm
Adalia. See Antalya
Adam, *Muscat & Oman* 73 Ge
Adama, *Ethiopia* 77 Hc
Adamello, Mt., *Italy* 54 Cb
Adams, *New York* 83 Hd
Adam's Bridge, *India-Ceylon* 68 Eg
Adams, Mt., *Washington* 87 Cb
Adam's Pk., *Ceylon* 68 Fg
Adana, *Turkey* 72 Cb
Adapazari, *Turkey* 72 Ba
Adare, *Eire* 31 Bh
Adare, C., *Antarctica* 100 Lb
Adavale, *Qnsld.* 95 He
Addis Ababa, *Ethiopia* 77 Hc
Addis Derra, *Ethiopia* 77 Hb
Addison, *New York* 86 Ba
Adelaer, C., *Greenland* 39 Pc
Adelaide, *Cape Province* 75 Df
Adelaide, *S. Australia* 95 Gf
Adelaide, I., *Antarctica* 100 Sc
Adelaide Pen., *N.-W. Terr.* 80 Mc
Adelaide River, *N. Terr. Aust.* 94 Fb
Adelboden, *Switzerland* 45 Cb
Ademuz, *Spain* 51 Eb
Aden, *S. Yemen* 72 Eg
Aden, col. & prot. See Southern Yemen
Aden, G. of, *Africa-Arabia* 40 Dg
Adh Dhahiriya, *Jordan* 74 Cf
Adhoi, *India* 68 Dd
Adhra, *Syria* 74 Ed
Adi, I., *W. Irian* 63 Kl
Adi Kaie, *Eritrea* 77 Hb
Adilabad, *India* 68 Ee
Adirondack Mts., *New York* 83 Jc
Adi Ugri, *Eritrea* 77 Hb
Admiralty G., *W. Australia* 94 Eb
Admiralty Is., *Pacific Ocean* 98 Dh
Adolfo Alsina, *Argentina* 92 De
Adoni, *India* 68 Ee
Adoumre, *Cameroon* 79 Hg
Adour R., *France* 53 Ce
Adra, *Spain* 50 Dd
Adraj, *Arabia* 73 Fe
Adrano, *Sicily* 55 Eg
Adrar, *Algeria* 78 Ec
Adria, *Italy* 54 Dc
Adrian, *Michigan* 83 De
Adriatic Sea, *Italy* 54 Ed
Aduwa, *Ethiopia* 77 Hb
Aegean Sea, *Greece* 57 Ee
Aeltre, *Belgium* 44 Bc
Æröskøbing, *Denmark* 47 Dj
Aesch, *Switzerland* 45 Ca
Afferden, *Netherlands* 44 Ec
Affua, *Brazil* 91 Gd
Afghanistan, *Asia* 73 Hc
Afif, *Arabia* 72 De
Afogados de Ingazeira, *Brazil* 91 Ke
Afognak I., *Alaska* 85 Xm
Afrin, *Syria* 74 Ea
Afula, *Israel* 74 De
Afyon, *Turkey* 72 Bb
Agab Workei, *Ethiopia* 77 Hb
Agadès, *Niger* 78 Ge
Agadir, *Morocco* 78 Db
Agartala, *India* 69 Hd
Agattu, I., *Aleutian Is.* 85 Um
Agawa, *Ontario* 83 Db
Agde, *France* 53 Ee
Agen, *France* 53 Dd
Agiabampo, *Mexico* 88 Cb
Agira, *Sicily* 55 Eg
Agnebilekrou, *Ivory Coast* 78 Eg
Agno, *Switzerland* 45 Dc
Agordat, *Eritrea* 77 Ha
Agra, *India* 71 Bb
Agram. See Zagreb
Agrigento, *Sicily* 55 Dg
Agrihan, I., *Mariana Is.* 98 Df
Agrinion, *Greece* 57 Ce
Agropoli, *Italy* 55 Ee
Agua Clara, *Brazil* 91 Gh
Aguadas, *Colombia* 90 Bb
Aguadilla, *Puerto Rico* 89 Fc
Aguadulce, *Panama* 89 Ce
Agua Prieta, *Mexico* 83 Ca
Aguaray, *Argentina* 92 Db
Aguascalientes, *Mexico* 88 Dc
Agudo, *Spain* 50 Cc
Agudos, *Brazil* 91 Hh
Aguilar, *Spain* 50 Cd
Aguilar de Campos, *Spain* 50 Ca
Aguilas, *Spain* 51 Ed
Aguirre, B., *Argentina* 92 Cj
Agulhas C., *Cape Province* 75 Cf
Agusta, *W. Australia* 94 Cf
Ahar, *Persia* 72 Eb
Ahmadnagar, *India* 68 De
Ahmadpur, *W. Pakistan* 70 Bf
Ahmedabad, *India* 68 Dd
Ahraura, *India* 71 Dc
Ahuachapan, *Salvador* 89 Ad
Ahualulco, *Mexico* 88 Dc
Ahus, *Sweden* 47 Fj
Ahvaz, *Persia* 72 Ec
Ahvenanmaa, *Finland* 47 Hf
Ahwar, *S. Yemen* 72 Eg
Aigle, *Switzerland* 45 Cb
Aihunkiu, *China* 62 Ja
Aijal, *India* 69 Hd
Aikawa, *Japan* 66 Fe
Aileron, *N. Terr., Aust.* 95 Fd
Aim, *Russia* 59 Nc
Aimores, *Brazil* 91 Jg
Ain, dep., *France* 52 Fc
Ain Galakka, *Chad* 78 Je
Ain Safra, *Mauritania* 78 Ce
Ain Sefra, *Algeria* 78 Eb
Aire, *France* 53 Ce
Aire, R., *England* 31 Gg
Airolo, *Switzerland* 45 Db
Aishihik L., *Yukon* 80 Dd
Aisne, dep., *France* 52 Eb
Aiun, El, *Sp. W. Africa* 78 Cc
Aix, *France* 53 Fe
Aix, Mt., *Washington* 87 Cb
Aix-la-Chapelle. See Aachen
Aiyina I., *Greece.* 57 Df
Aiyion, *Greece* 57 Ce
Aizpute, *Latvia* 47 Jh
Ajaccio & G. d', *Corsica* 55 Ba
Ajaigarh, *India* 71 Cc
Ajanta, *India* 68 Ed
Ajanta Ra. See Sahiadriparvat
Ajib, *Muscat & Oman* 73 Ge
Ajibba, *Arabia* 72 Dd
Ajigasawa, *Japan* 66 Gd
Ajlun, *Jordan* 74 De
Ajmer, *India* 68 Dc
Ajoewa, *Surinam* 91 Fc
Akalkot, *India* 68 Ee
Akan Nat. Park, *Japan* 66 Hc
Akanthou, *Cyprus* 74 Bb
Akaoka, *Japan* 66 Ch
Akarnania & Aitolia, *Greece* 57 Ce
Akaroa, *New Zealand* 93 De
Akashi, *Japan* 66 Dg
Akbarpur, *India* 71 Cb
Akcha, *Afghanistan* 73 Jb
Akhdhar, Jeb., *Muscat & Oman* 73 Ge
Akhisar, *Turkey* 72 Ab
Akhterin, *Syria* 74 Fa
Akhtopol, *Bulgaria* 56 Fc
Akhtyrka, *Ukraine* 60 Jf
Akimiski I., *N.-W. Terr.* 81 Qf
Akita, *Japan* 66 Ge
Akkrum, *Netherlands* 44 Da
Aklavik, *N.-W. Territories* 80 Dc
Akmolinsk, *Kazakh.* 58 Gc
Ako, *Nigeria* 76 Cb
Akola, *India* 68 Ed
Akpatok I., *N.-W. Terr.* 81 Td
Akra, Jebel el, *Turkey* 74 Db
Akron, *Ohio* 83 Fe
Akrotiri Pen., *Crete* 57 Eg
Aksaray, *Turkey* 72 Bb
Aksehir, *Turkey* 72 Bb
Aksha, *Russia* 59 Lc
Äksi, *Estonia* 47 Mg
Akti, *Greece* 57 Ed
Aktyubinsk, *Kazakh.* 58 Ec
Akure, *Nigeria* 73 Gg
Akureyri, *Iceland* 46 Wm
Akyab, *Burma* 69 Hd
Akzhal, *Kazakh.* 58 Hd
Alabama, state, *U.S.A.* 85 Je
Alabama R., *Alabama* 85 Je
Alaejos, *Spain* 50 Cb
Alagoas, *Brazil* 91 Ke
Alagoinhas, *Brazil* 91 Kf
Alagón, *Spain* 51 Eb
Alapur, *India* 71 Bb
Al'ayn, *Muscat & Oman* 73 Gf
Alaysky Khrebet, *Kirgiz.* 58 Ge
Alaja, *Syria* 74 Db
Alajuela, *Costa Rica* 89 Cd
Alam, *Ethiopia* 77 Hc
Alameda, *California* 87 Bg
Alameda, *Saskatchewan* 80 Lg
Alamogordo, *New Mexico* 84 Ee
Alamos, *Mexico* 88 Cb
Alamosa, *Colorado* 84 Ed
Åland. See Ahvenanmaa
Ålans Hav, *Swed.-Fin.* 47 Hg
Alapayevsk, *Russia* 61 Qb
Alasehir, *Turkey* 72 Ab
Ala Shan, *China* 62 Dc
Al Ashkharah, *Muscat & Oman* 73 Ge
Alaska, state, *U.S.A.* 85 Xl
Alaska, G. of, *Alaska* 85 Ym
Alaska Highway, *Alaska* 80 Cd
Alaska Pen, *Alaska* 85 Xm
Alaska Ra., *Alaska* 85 Xl
Alatyr, *Russia* 61 Hc
Alavus, *Finland* 46 Ke
Alazeyskoye Plat., *Russia* 59 Pb
Albacete, *Spain* 51 Ec
Alba de Tormes, *Spain* 50 Cb
Albaida, *Spain* 51 Ec
Alba Iulia, *Rumania* 56 Da
Albanel L., *Quebec* 82 Ba
Albania, *S. Europe* 56 Cd
Albany, *Georgia* 85 Ke
Albany, *New York* 83 Kd
Albany, *Oregon* 87 Bc
Albany, *W. Australia* 94 Cf
Albany R., *Ontario* 81 Qf
Albarracin, *Spain* 51 Eb
Albergaria a-Velha, *Port.* 50 Ab
Alberique, *Spain* 51 Ec
Albert, *New Brunswick* 82 Fd
Albert L., *Congo* 77 Gd
Albert Nat. Pk., *Congo* 77 Fe
Alberta, prov., *Canada* 80 Hf
Alberta Mt., *Alberta* 80 Hf
Albert Edward Mt., *Papua* 95 Ja
Albert Lea, *Minnesota* 85 Hc
Alberton, *Prince Edward I.* 82 Fe
Albertville, *Congo* 77 Ff
Albertville, *France* 52 Gd
Albi, *France* 53 Ee
Albina, *Surinam* 91 Gb
Albion, *Michigan* 83 Dd
Albion, *New York* 86 Aa
Albocácer, *Spain* 51 Eb
Albufeira, *Portugal* 50 Ad
Albuñol, *Spain* 50 Dd
Albuquerque, *New Mexico* 84 Ed
Alburquerque, *Spain* 50 Bc
Albury, *New South Wales* 95 Jg
Alcacer do Sal, *Portugal* 50 Ac
Alcalá de Chisvert, *Spain* 51 Fb
Alcalá de Henares, *Spain* 50 Db
Alcamo, *Sicily* 55 Dg
Alcañices, *Spain* 50 Bb
Alcañiz, *Spain* 51 Eb
Alcántara, *Brazil* 91 Jd
Alcántara, *Spain* 50 Bc
Alcantarilla, *Spain* 51 Ed
Alcaraz, *Spain* 51 Dc
Alcatraz, I., *San Francisco* 84
Alcázar de San Juan, *Spain* 50 Dc
Alchevsk, *Ukraine* 60 Lg
Alcira, *Spain* 51 Ec
Alcobaça, *Portugal* 50 Ac
Alcolea del Pinar, *Spain* 51 Db
Alcoutim, *Portugal* 50 Bd
Alcoy, *Spain* 51 Ec
Alcuhemas, *Morocco* 78 Ea
Aldabra Is., *Indian Ocean* 77 Ka
Aldama, *Chihuahua, Mexico* 88 Cb
Aldama, *Tamaulipas, Mexico* 88 Ec
Aldan & R., *Russia* 59 Mc
Aldeburgh, *England* 31 Jh
Alderney, I., *Channel Is.* 31 Ak
Aldershot, *England* 31 Gj
Al Dola, *S. Yemen* 72 Eg
Alegrete, *Brazil* 92 Ec
Aleih, *Lebanon* 74 Dd
Aleksandrov, *Russia* 60 Lc
Aleksandrovsk Sakhalinskiy, *Russia* 59 Pc
Aleksandry, Zemlya, *Arctic Ocean* 58 Da
Alekseyevka, *Russia* 61 Hd
Alekseyevka, *Kazakh.* 58 Gc
Alençon, *France* 52 Db
Alenquer, *Portugal* 50 Ac
Alenquer, *Brazil* 91 Gd
Aleppo, *Syria* 74 Fa
Ales, *France* 53 Fd
Aleshki, *Russia* 61 Ee
Alessandria, *Italy* 54 Bc
Ålesund, *Norway* 46 Be
Aletschhorn, Mt., *Switz.* 45 Cb
Aleutian Is., *Bering Sea* 85 Um
Alexander Arch., *Alaska* 85 Zm
Alexander I, I., *Antarctica* 100 Sc
Alexandra, *New Zealand* 93 Bf
Alexandretta. See Iskenderun
Alexandria, *Egypt* 79 Lb
Alexandria, *Louisiana* 85 He
Alexandria, *Ontario* 83 Jc
Alexandria, *Virginia* 86 Bc
Alexandrina, L., *S. Aust.* 95 Gg
Alexandroúpolis, *Greece* 57 Ed
Alexikovo, *Russia* 61 Fe
Aleysk, *Russia* 58 Hc
Alfaro, *Spain* 51 Ea
Ali Fāw, *Iraq* 72 Ed
Alfred, *Maine* 86 Ea
Aga, *Kazakh.* 58 Ed
Ålgård, *Norway* 47 Ag
Algarrobo del Aguila, *Argent.* 92 Ce
Algauer Alpen, *Austria, etc.* 48 De
Algeciras, *Spain* 50 Cd
Alger (Algiers), *Algeria* 53 Nf
Algeria, *N.-W. Africa* 78 Eb
Al Ghail, *Yemen* 72 Ef
Alghero, *Sardinia* 55 Be
Algo B., *Cape Province* 75 Df
Algoma, *Ontario* 83 Eb
Algoma, *Wisconsin* 83 Cc
Algonquin Park, *Ontario* 83 Gc
Alguada Reef, *Burma* 69 He
Alhama de Granada, *Spain* 50 Dd
Al Hasa, *Arabia* 72 Ed
Al Hauta, *S. Yemen* 72 Ef
Al Hayy, *Iraq* 72 Ec
Alhucemas, I., *Spain* 50 De
Alia, *Sicily* 55 Dg
Aliaga, *Spain* 51 Eb
Alibag, *India* 68 De
Alicante, *Spain* 51 Ec
Alice Springs, *N. Terr., Aust.* 95 Fd
Alicudi, I., *Italy* 55 Ef
Aliganj, *India* 71 Bb
Aligarh, *India* 70 Fg
Ali Khel, *Afghanistan* 73 Jc
Alimnia, I., *Greece* 57 Ff
Aling Kangri, *Tibet* 68 Fb
Alingsås, *Sweden* 47 Eh
Alipur, *India* 71 Gd
Alipur, *India* 71 Gb
Alipur, *W. Pakistan* 70 Bf
Alipura, *India* 71 Bc
Alirajpur, *India* 68 Dd
Alivérion, *Greece* 57 Ee
Al Jawf, *Arabia* 72 Cd
Al Jesab, *Arabia* 72 Ef
Aljustrel, *Portugal* 50 Ad
Alken, *Belgium* 44 Dd
Alkmar, *Netherlands* 44 Cb
Al Kut, *Iraq* 72 Ec
Allahabad, *India* 71 Cc
Allanmyo, *Burma* 69 Je
Allariz, *Spain* 50 Ba
Allaykha, *Russia* 59 Pa
Alle, *Belgium* 44 Ce
Allegan, *Michigan* 83 Dd
Alleghany Mts., *U.S.A.* 85 Kd
Allegheny R., *N.Y.*, etc. 86 Aa
Allen L., *Eire* 31 Bf
Allenby Bridge, *Jordan* 74 Df
Allentown, *Pennsylvania* 86 Cb
Alleppey, *India* 68 Eg
Alliance, *Ohio* 83 Fe
Allier, dep., *France* 52 Ec
Allier, R., *France* 52 Ed
Alliston, *Ontario* 83 Gc
Alloa, *Scotland* 30 Ed
All Pines, *Brit. Honduras* 89 Bc
Al Luhaygah, *Yemen* 72 Df
Allumette I., *Quebec* 83 Hc
Alma, *Michigan* 83 Dd
Alma, *New Brunswick* 82 Fd
Alma Ata, *Kazakh.* 58 Gd
Almadén, *Spain* 50 Cc
Almagro, *Spain* 50 Dc
Almansa, *Spain* 51 Ec
Almazán, *Spain* 51 Db
Almeirim, *Brazil* 91 Gd
Almeirim, *Portugal* 50 Ac
Almelo, *Netherlands* 44 Eb
Almeria & Gulf, *Spain* 51 Dd
Almirante, *Panama* 89 Ce
Almirópótamos, *Greece* 57 Ee
Almirós, *Greece* 57 De
Almodôvar, *Portugal* 50 Bd
Almodóvar, *Spain* 50 Cc
Almonte, *Ontario* 83 Hc
Almora, *India* 71 Ba
Almorox, *Spain* 50 Cb
Almudébar, *Spain* 51 Ea
Almunia de Doña Godina, la, *Spain* 51 Eb

Babar, I., Indonesia 63 Jm
Babati, Tanzania 77 He
Bab el Mandeb, Red Sea 77 Jb
Babenna, Syria 74 Eb
Babine L., Brit. Columbia 80 Fe
Babōl, Persia 73 Fb
Babura, Nigeria 76 Bb
Babuyan Is., Philippines 62 Hg
Babylon, Iraq 72 Dc
Bacabal, Brazil 91 Fe
Bacadehuachi, Mexico 88 Cb
Bacalar, Mexico 88 Gd
Bacău, Rumania 56 Fa
Bacerac, Mexico 88 Ca
Back R., N.-W. Territories 80 Mc
Backa Topola, Yugoslavia 56 Bb
Backbone Mts., W. Va.-Md. 86 Ac
Bäckefors, Sweden 47 Eg
Backergunge, East Pakistan 69 Hd
Bac Lieu, S. Vietnam 67 De
Bac-Ninh, N. Vietnam 67 Db
Bacoachic, Mexico 88 Ca
Bacolod, Philippines 63 Hh
Bada, Arabia 72 Cd
Badajos, Brazil 91 Hd
Badajoz, Spain 50 Bc
Badalona, Spain 51 Gb
Badarma, Russia 59 Kc
Badas, Brunei 63 Fk
Bad Axe, Michigan 83 Ed
Baden, Germany 48 Cd
Baden, Switzerland 45 Da
Baden-Baden, Germany 48 Cd
Badia, Arabia 72 Ee
Badin, W. Pakistan 68 Cd
Badiya, Muscat & Oman 73 Ge
Bad Kissingen, Germany 48 Dc
Bad Lands, Nebraska, etc. 84 Fc
Badon, Senegal 78 Cf
Badrinath, India 68 Eb
Baduen, Somalia 77 Kc
Badulla, Ceylon 68 Fg
Baelen, Belgium 44 Dc
Baena, Spain 50 Cd
Baetas, Brazil 90 Ee
Baffin B., N.-W. Territories 81 Tb
Baffin I., N.-W. Territories 81 Sc
Bafia, Cameroon 79 Hh
Bafoulabé, Mali 78 Cf
Baf'q, Persia 73 Gc
Bafra, Turkey 72 Ca
Bafra Br., Turkey 72 Ca
Baft, Persia 73 Gd
Bafwasende, Congo 76 Fd
Bagata, Congo 76 De
Bage, Brazil 92 Fd
Bagerhat, E. Pakistan 71 Gd
Baghdad, Iraq 72 Dc
Baghin, Persia 73 Gc
Baghpat, India 70 Ef
Bagnara Calabra, Italy 55 Ef
Bagnols-sur-Céze, France 53 Fd
Bagotville, Quebec 82 Cb
Bagra Kote, India 71 Gb
Baguio, Philippines 63 Hg
Bahaar-i-Gaz, Persia 73 Fb
Bahadurgarh, India 70 Ef
Bahama I., Grand, Bahama Is. 89 Da
Bahama Is., West Indies 89 Db
Bahawalpur, W. Pakistan 70 Bf
Baheri, India 71 Ba
Bahia. See Salvador
Bahia Blanca, Argentina 92 De
Bahia de Caráquez, Ecuador 90 Ad
Bahia Laura, Argentina 92 Cg
Bahia Negra, Paraguay 92 Eb
Bahraich, India 71 Cb
Bahrain I., Persian Gulf 73 Fd
Bahret el Ateibe, Syria 74 Ed
Bahret el Hijane, Syria 74 Ed
Bahret Homs, Syria 74 Ec
Bahu Kalat, Persia 73 Hd
Baiao, Brazil 91 Hd
Baibokoum, Chad 79 Jg
Baie St Paul, Quebec 83 Lb
Baiji, Iraq 72 Dc
Baile Atha Cliath (Dublin), Eire 31 Cg
Bailen, Spain 50 Dc
Baillie, N.-W. Territories 80 Fb
Baimak Tanalykovo, Russia 61 Nd
Bairnsdale, Victoria 95 Jg
Baital Faqih, Yemen 72 Dg
Baixo Longa, Angola 75 Bc
Baja, Hungary 56 Ba
Baja California, state, Mexico 88 Bb
Baján, Mexico 88 Db
Bajmok, Yugoslavia 56 Bb
Bakal, Russia 60 Hj
Bakaly, Russia 61 Lc
Bakel, Senegal 78 Cf
Baker, Oregon 87 Ec
Baker I., Pacific Ocean 98 Hg
Baker L., N.-W. Territories 80 Md
Baker, Mt., Washington 84 Bb
Bakersfield, California 87 Dh
Bakhasar, India 68 Dd
Baklansk, Russia 61 Sc
Bakloh, India 70 Dd
Bako, Ethiopia 77 Hc
Bakonyerdo, Hungary 49 Ge
Baksa Duar, India 71 Gb
Baku, Azerbaidzhan 58 Dd
Bala, Wales 31 Eh
Balabac Str., Philippines 63 Gj
Balagnat, India 68 Fd
Balakhta, Russia 59 Jc
Balaklava, Russia 60 Hj
Balama, Moçambique 77 Hg
Bala Murghab, Afghanistan 73 Hb
Balancan, Mexico 88 Fd
Balaquer, Spain 51 Fb
Balashov, Russia 61 Fe
Balasore, India 69 Gd
Balat, Egypt 79 Lc
Balaton, L., Hungary 49 Ge
Balazote, Spain 51 Dc
Balboa, Panama 89 De
Balbriggan, Eire 31 Cg
Balcarce, Argentina 92 Ee
Balchik, Bulgaria 56 Gc
Balclutha, New Zealand 93 Bg
Baldwin, Michigan 83 Dd
Baldwinsville, New York 86 Ba
Baldy Pk., Arizona 84 Ee
Baleares, Is., Medit. Sea 51 Gc
Balearic Is. See Baleares
Baler, Philippines 63 Hg
Balestrand, Norway 47 Bf
Baley, Russia 59 Lc
Bali, I., Indonesia 63 Fm
Balikesir, Turkey 72 Ab
Balikpapan, Borneo 63 Gl
Balk, Netherlands 44 Db
Balkans, The, Europe 56
Balkhash & Oz., Kazakh. 58 Gd
Ballabgarh, India 70 Ef
Ballachulish, Scotland 30 Dd
Balladonia, W. Aust. 94 Df
Ballaghaderreen, Eire 31 Bg
Ballantrae, Scotland 30 De
Ballarat, Victoria 95 Hg
Ballater, Scotland 30 Ec
Ballé, Mali 78 De
Ballenas, B. de, Mexico 88 Bb
Ballenas Channel, Mexico 88 Bb
Balleny Is., Antarctica 100 Lc
Ballia, India 71 Ec
Ballina, Eire 31 Af
Ballinasloe, Eire 31 Bg
Ballinrobe, Eire 31 Ag
Ballinskelligs B., Eire 31 Aj
Ballston Spa, New York 86 Da
Ballycastle, N. Ireland 30 Ce
Ballymahon, Eire 31 Bg
Ballymena, N. Ireland 31 Cf
Ballymoney, N. Ireland 30 Ce
Ballyshannon, Eire 31 Bf
Balombo, Angola 76 Cg
Balotra, India 68 Dc
Balrampur, India 71 Db
Balranald, New S. Wales 95 Hf
Balsaa, Brazil 91 He
Balsam, L., Ontario 83 Gc
Balta, Ukraine 60 Fh
Baltanás, Spain 50 Cb
Baltasar Brum, Uruguay 92 Ed
Baltic Sea, N.-W. Europe 47
Baltim, Egypt 79 Mb
Baltimore, Eire 31 Aj
Baltimore, Maryland 83 Hf
Baltistan, Kashmir 70 Dc
Baltiysk, Russia 47 Hj
Baluchistan, W. Pakistan 68 Bc
Balurghat, India 71 Gc
Bam, Persia 73 Gd
Bama, Nigeria 79 Hf
Bamako, Mali 78 Df
Bambari, Cent. Afr. Rep. 79 Kg
Bamberg, Germany 48 Dd
Bambui, Brazil 91 Hh
Bamenda, Nigeria 79 Gg
Bamfield, Michigan 83 Ec
Bamian, Afghanistan 73 Jc
Bampton, England 31 Ek
Bampur, Persia 73 Hd
Bam Tso, Tibet 69 Gc
Banaras, India 71 Dc
Banat, Rumania 56 Cb
Banayyan, Arabia 73 Fe
Banbury, England 31 Gh
Banchory, Scotland 30 Fc
Bancroft, Ontario 83 Hc
Banda, India 71 Cc
Banda Sea, Indonesia 63 Jm
Banda Beila, Somalia 77 Lc
Bandar Abbas, Persia 73 Gd
Bandarawela, Ceylon 68 Fg
Bandar-e Deylam, Persia 73 Fc
Bandar-e Lengeh, Persia 73 Fd
Bandar-e Pahlavi, Persia 72 Eb
Bandar-e Rig, Persia 73 Fd
Bandar-e Shapur, Persia 72 Ec
Bandar Shah, Persia 73 Fb
Bandera, Argentina 92 Dc
Banderas, B., Mexico 88 Cc
Bandiagara, Mali 78 Ef
Bandikui, India 68 Ec
Band-i-Qir, Persia 72 Ec
Bandirma, Turkey 72 Aa
Bandjarmasin, Borneo 63 Fl
Bandol, France 53 Fe
Bandon, Eire 31 Bj
Bandung, Java 63 Em
Baned, India 70 Ee
Baneh, Persia 72 Eb
Baneš, Cuba 89 Db
Bañeza, La, Spain 50 Ca
Banff & co., Scotland 30 Fc
Banff & Park, Alberta 80 Hf
Bangada, Congo 76 Fd
Bangalore, India 68 Ef
Bangassou, Cent. Afr. Rep. 79 Kh
Bangka, I., Indonesia 63 El
Bangkok, Siam 63 Dh
Bangkok, Bight of, Siam 67 Cd
Bang Mun Nak, Siam 63 Dg
Bangor, Maine 82 Dd
Bangor, N. Ireland 31 Df
Bangor, Pennsylvania 86 Cb
Bangor, Wales 31 Eg
Bang Saphan Yia, Siam 67 Bd
Bangui, Cent. Afr. Rep. 79 Jh
Bangweulu L., Zambia 77 Gg
Ban Houei Sai, Laos 67 Cb
Bania, Cent. Afr. Rep. 76 Dd
Bani Bu 'Ali, Muscat & Oman 73 Ge
Banica, Rep. Dominicana 89 Ec
Baniyas, Syria 74 Db
Baniyas, Syria 74 Dd
Banjak Kep., Indonesia 63 Ck
Banja Luka, Yugoslavia 54 Fc
Ban Jarunga, Yugoslavia 54 Fc
Banjuwangi, Java 63 Fm
Banka, India 71 Fc
Banka Pahari, India 71 Cc
Banki, India 69 Gd
Bankipore, India 71 Ec
Banks I., N.-W. Territories 80 Gb
Banks I., Queensland 95 Hb
Banks Is., Pacific Ocean 98 Fj
Banks Pen., New Zealand 93 De
Banks Str., Tasmania 95 Jh
Bankura, India 71 Fd
Bann R., N. Ireland 31 Cf
Banningville, Congo 76 De
Bannu, W. Pakistan 70 Bd
Baños, Spain 50 Dc
Baños de Montemayor, Spain 50 Bb
Ban-pot, Siam 67 Bc
Bansda, India 68 Dd
Bansi, India 71 Db
Banswara, India 68 Dd
Bantalor, New Brunswick 82 Ec
Ban Thakham, Siam 67 Be
Ban tha U, Siam 67 Cc
Bantry & B., Eire 31 Aj
Banu, Afghanistan 73 Jb
Banur, India 70 Ee
Banyo, Cameroon 79 Hg
Banzare Coast, Antarctica 100 Jb
Banzyville, Congo 76 Ed
Bapaume, France 52 Ea
Baq'a, Arabia 72 Dd
Ba'qubah, Iraq 72 Dc
Bar, Yugoslavia 56 Bc
Bara, Sudan 79 Mf
Barabanki, India 71 Cb
Barabinsk, Russia 58 Gc
Baraboo, Wisconsin 83 Bd
Baracoa, Cuba 89 Eb
Barad, Syria 74 Fb
Barahona, Rep. Dominicana 89 Db
Barahona, Spain 51 Ec
Barail Ra., India 69 Hc
Barak R., India 69 Hd
Baramula, Kashmir 70 Dc
Baranagar, India 71 Gd
Baranof I., Alaska 85 Zm
Baranovichi, Russia 60 Ee
Baranów, Poland 49 Jc
Baraque Michel, Belgium 44 Ed
Baraunda, India 71 Cc
Baraut, India 70 Ef
Barbacena, Brazil 91 Jh
Barbacoas, Colombia 90 Bc
Barbadillo del Mercada, Sp. 50 Da
Barbados, I., Windward Is. 89 Hd
Barbastro, Spain 51 Fa
Barbezieux, France 52 Cd
Barbuda, I., Leeward Is. 89 Gc
Barca d'Alva, Portugal 50 Bb
Barcaldine, Queensland 95 Jd
Barcarrota, Spain 50 Bc
Barce. See Marj, el
Barcellona Pozza di Gotto, Sicily 55 Ef
Barcelona, Spain 51 Gb
Barcelona, Venezuela 90 Ea
Barcelonnette, France 53 Gd
Barcelos, Brazil 90 Ed
Barcelos, Portugal 50 Ab
Barco de Avila, El, Spain 50 Cb
Barcoo, R., Queensland 95 Hd
Bardera, Somalia 77 Jd
Bardi, India 71 Dc
Bardia, Libya 79 Lb
Bardsey, I., Wales 31 Dh
Bareilly, India 71 Ba
Barents Sea, Arctic Ocean 58 Ba
Barentsöya, I., Arctic Ocean 58 Ba
Barfurush. See Babōl
Bargal, Somalia 77 Lb
Barh, India 71 Ec
Barhaj, India 71 Db
Bar Harbor, Maine 82 Dd
Bari, India 71 Ab
Bari, Italy 55 Fe
Bari Doab, W. Pakistan 70 Ce
Barinas, Venezuela 90 Cb
Baring, C., N.-W. Terr. 80 Hb
Barisal, East Pakistan 69 Hd
Barito, R., Borneo 63 Fl
Barkald, Norway 47 Df
Barkhan, W. Pakistan 70 Af
Barkly Tableland, Australia 95 Gc
Bârlad, Rumania 56 Fa
Bar le Duc, France 52 Fb
Barlee L., W. Australia 94 Ce
Barlee Ra., W. Australia 94 Cd
Barletta, Italy 55 Fe
Barmer, India 68 Dc
Barmouth, Wales 31 Eh
Barn, Mt., Quebec 82 Eb
Barnaby River, N.B. 82 Fc
Barnard Castle, England 31 Ff
Barnaul, Russia 58 Hc
Barne Inlet, Antarctica 100 La
Barnegat B., New Jersey 83 Jf
Barneveld, Netherlands 44 Db
Barnsley, England 31 Gg
Barnstable, Massachusetts 86 Eb
Barnstaple, England 31 Ej
Baroda, India 68 Dd
Barpeta, India 69 Hc
Barquinha, Portugal 50 Ac
Barquisimeto, Venezuela 90 Da
Barra, Arabia 72 Ee
Barra, Brazil 91 Jf
Barra Hd., Scotland 30 Bd
Barra, I., Scotland 30 Bc
Barra, Sd. of, Scotland 30 Bc
Barrackpore, India 71 Gd
Barra do Corda, Brazil 91 He
Barra do Piraí, Brazil 91 Jh
Barra do Bugres, Brazil 90 Ff
Barra Mansa, Brazil 91 Jh
Barran, Somalia 77 Kb
Barranca, Peru 90 Bd
Barranca Bermeja, Colombia 90 Cb
Barrancas, Venezuela 90 Eb
Barrancos, Portugal 50 Bc
Barranqueras, Argentina 92 Ec
Barranquilla, Colombia 90 Ca
Barre, Vermont 83 Kc
Barreiras, Brazil 91 Jf
Barreirinha, Brazil 91 Fd
Barreirinhas, Brazil 91 Jd
Barreiro, Portugal 50 Ac
Barreiros, Brazil 91 Ke
Barrême, France 53 Ge
Barrie, Ontario 83 Gc
Barrier I., Great, N.Z. 93 Eb
Barrier I., Little, N.Z. 93 Eb
Barrington, Mt., N.S.W. 95 Kf
Barringun, N.S.W. 95 Je
Barrow, Argentina 92 De
Barrow, England 31 Ef
Barrow R., Eire 31 Ch
Barrow Str., N.-W. Terr. 80 Mb
Barrow Creek, N.T., Aust. 95 Fd
Barry, Wales 31 Ej
Barsaloi, Kenya 77 Hd
Barsi, India 68 Ee
Bar-sur-Aube, France 52 Fb
Bar-sur-Seine, France 52 Fb
Bartibog, New Brunswick 82 Fc
Bartica, Guyana 90 Fb
Bartle Frere Mt., Queensland 95 Hc
Bartlesville, Oklahoma 84 Gd
Baruva, India 69 Fe
Barvaux, Belgium 44 Dd
Barwa, India 71 Ed
Barwani, India 68 Ed
Barwon, R., New S. Wales 95 Je
Basel (Basle), Switzerland 45 Ca
Baselland, canton, Switz. 45 Ca
Bashi, Persia 73 Fd
Bashi Chan., Phil.-Taiwan 65 Ke
Bashkirskaya, aut. rep., Russ. 58 Ec
Basia, India 71 Ed
Basilan, I., Philippines 63 Hj
Basilicata, reg., Italy 55 Ee
Basingstoke, England 31 Gj
Baskatong L., Quebec 83 Hb
Båsmo, Norway 46 Fc
Basongo, Congo 76 Ee
Basra, Iraq 72 Ec
Bas-Rhin, dep., France 52 Gb
Bass Str., Tasmania-Vict. 95 Jg
Bassac, Laos 67 Dd
Bassein, Burma 69 He
Bassein, India 68 Dd
Basses, Gt. & Lit., Ceylon 68 Fg
Basses-Alpes, dep., France 53 Gd
Basses-Pyrénées, dep., Fr. 53 Ce
Basse Terre, Leeward Is. 89 Gc
Bassevelde, Belgium 44 Bc
Båstad, Sweden 47 Eh
Bastak, Persia 73 Fd
Baştam, Persia 73 Dc
Basti, India 71 Db
Bastia, Corsica 54 Bd
Bastogne, Belgium 44 De
Basutoland. See Lesotho 75 De
Bata, Rio Muni 76 Bd
Bataan, Philippines 63 Hh
Batacosa, Mexico 88 Cb
Batala, India 70 De
Batalha, Portugal 50 Ac
Batan Is., Philippines 62 Hf
Batangas, Philippines 63 Hh
Batavia, Argentina 92 Cd
Batavia. See Djakarta
Batavia, New York 86 Aa
Bataysk, Russia 61 Eg
Batchawana, Ontario 83 Db
Batchelor, N. Terr., Aust. 94 Fb
Batenburg, Netherlands 44 Dc
Bath, England 31 Fj
Bath, Maine 82 De
Bath, New York 86 Ba
Bathurst, Gambia 78 Bf
Bathurst, New Brunswick 82 Fc
Bathurst, New S. Wales 95 Jf
Bathurst Inl., N.-W. Terr. 80 Kc
Bathurst I., N. Terr., Aust. 94 Eb
Bathurst I., N.-W. Terr. 80 La
Batie, Volta 78 Eg
Batiscan, Quebec 83 Kb
Batjan, I., Indonesia 63 Jl
Batna, Algeria 78 Ga
Baton Rouge, Louisiana 85 He
Batopilas, Mexico 88 Cb
Batraki, Russia 61 Jd
Batrun, Lebanon 74 Dc
Battambang, Cambodia 67 Cd
Batticaloa, Ceylon 68 Fg
Battice, Belgium 44 Dd
Battih, S. Yemen 72 Ef
Battle Creek, Michigan 83 Dd
Battleford, Saskatchewan 80 Kf
Battleford, N., Sask. 80 Kf
Battle Harbour, Labrador 81 Vf
Battle Mountain, Nevada 87 Ee
Batu, Indonesia 63 Cl
Batumi, Gruzinskaya S.S.R. 58 Dd
Baturadja, Sumatra 63 Dl
Baturite, Brazil 91 Kd
Baubau, Celebes 63 Hm
Bauchi, Nigeria 79 Gf
Baud, India 69 Fd
Baudo, Colombia 90 Bb
Baudouinville, Congo 77 Ff
Bauge, France 52 Cc
Baunt, Russia 59 Lc
Baures, Bolivia 90 Ef
Bauru, Brazil 91 Hh
Baus, Brazil 91 Gg
Bauska, Latvia 47 Lh
Bautzen, Germany 48 Fc
Bavispe, Mexico 88 Ca
Bawal, India 70 Ef
Bawean, I., Indonesia 63 Fm
Bawiti, Egypt 79 Lc
Bawku, Ghana 78 Ef
Bay Is., Honduras 89 Bc
Bayamo, Cuba 89 Db
Bayana, India 71 Ab
Bayan Aul, Kazakh. 58 Gc
Bayan Dzurihe, Mongolia 62 Ea
Bayan Kara Shan, China 62 Cd
Bayburt, Turkey 72 Da
Bay City, Michigan 83 Ed
Baydaratskaya B., Russia 58 Fa
Bayern, Germany 48 Dd
Bayeux, France 52 Cb
Bayir, Jordan 74 Eg
Baykal, Oz., Russia 59 Kc
Baykit, Russia 59 Jb
Baykonur, Kazakh. 58 Fd
Bayona, Spain 50 Aa
Bayonne, France 53 Ce
Bayovar, Peru 90 Ae
Bayram Ali, Turkmenistan 58 Fe
Bayreuth, Germany 48 Dd
Bayrischer Wald, Germany 48 Ed
Bays, L. of, Ontario 83 Gc
Baytag Bogdo, China 62 Bb
Baza, Sa. de, Spain 51 Dd
Bazaruto, I., Moçambique 75 Fd
Bazas, France 53 Cd
Bazias, Rumania 56 Cb
Bazman, Persia 73 Hd
Beachy Head, England 31 Hk
Beacon, New York 86 Db
Beal Ra., Queensland 95 He
Bear Is. See Medvezhi Osa.
Beardmore Gl., Antarctica 100 La
Bearn, prov., France 53 Ce
Beata, I., Rep. Dominicana 89 Ec
Beatenberg, Switzerland 45 Cb
Beatrice, Nebraska 84 Gc
Beauceville, Quebec 83 Lb
Beaufort Sea, Arctic Ocean 39 Tb
Beaufort West, Cape Prov. 75 Cf
Beaugency, France 52 Dc
Beauly, Scotland 30 Dc
Beaumont, Belgium 44 Cd
Beaumont, France 52 Eb
Beaumont, New Zealand 93 Bf
Beaumont, Texas 85 Ge
Beaune, France 52 Fc
Beauport, Quebec 83 Lb
Beauraing, Belgium 44 Cd
Beauvais, France 52 Eb
Beauvoir-sur-Mer, France 52 Bc
Beaver, Utah 87 Gf
Beaver I., Michigan 83 Dc
Beaver R., Saskatchewan 80 Kf
Beaver R., Utah 87 Gf
Beaver Dam, Wisconsin 83 Bd
Beaver Falls, Pennsylvania 83 Fe
Beaverhead Mts., Idaho 87 Gc
Beawar, India 68 Dc
Bebedero, Argentina 92 Cd
Bebedouro, Brazil 91 Hh
Becej, Yugoslavia 56 Bb
Becerrea, Spain 50 Ba
Bechuanaland. See Botswana
Becleau, Rumania 49 Le
Bedak, Afghanistan 73 Jc
Bédar, Spain 51 Ed
Bedford, Pennsylvania 86 Ac
Bedford, Quebec 83 Kc
Bedford & co., England 31 Gh
Bedourie, Qnsld. 95 Gd
Bedretto, Switzerland 45 Db
Bedr Honein, Arabia 72 Ec
Beduval, Saskatchewan 80 Ce
Bedzin, Poland 49 Hc
Beechey, L., N.-W. Terr. 80 Kc
Beek, Netherlands 44 Dc
Beek, Netherlands 44 Dd
Beekbergen, Netherlands 44 Db
Beeringen, Belgium 44 Dc
Beerlegem, Belgium 44 Bd
Beer Menuha, Israel 74 Dg
Beernem, Belgium 44 Bc
Beers, Netherlands 44 Dc
Beersheba, Israel 74 Cf
Befale, Congo 76 Ed
Befandriana, Madagascar 77 Nk
Bega, N.S.W. 95 Kg
Behbehan, Persia 73 Fc
Beho, Belgium 44 Dd
Beidha, Arabia 72 Ce
Beilen, Netherlands 44 Eb
Beilul, Eritrea 77 Jb
Beinwil, Switzerland 45 Da
Beira, Moçambique 75 Fc
Beirūt (Beyrouth), Lebanon 74 Dd
Beitbridge, Rhodesia 75 Ed
Beit-et-Din, Lebanon 74 Dd
Beius, Rumania 56 Da
Beja, Portugal 50 Bc
Bejaia & G. of (Bougie), Algeria 53 Ph
Béjar, Spain 50 Cb
Bejestan, Persia 73 Gc
Bejucal, Cuba 89 Cb
Békéscsaba, Hungary 49 Je
Bela, W. Pakistan 68 Cc
Belagunj, India 71 Dc
Belang, Celebes 63 Hk
Bela Palanka, Yugoslavia 56 Dc
Belaya Tserkov, Ukraine 60 Gg
Belcher Is., N.-W. Territories 81 Re
Belchirag, Afghanistan 73 Jb
Belchite, Spain 51 Eb
Beldanga, India 71 Gd
Belebey, Russia 61 Mc
Belem, Mexico 88 Bb
Belém. See Pará
Belen, Argentina 92 Cc
Belen, Panama 89 Ce
Belfast, Maine 82 Dd
Belfast & L., N. Ireland 31 Df
Belfeld, Netherlands 44 Ec
Belford, England 30 Fe
Belfort, France 52 Gc
Belgaum, India 68 De
Belgium, Central Europe 43 Jf
Belgorod, Russia 60 Kf
Belgorod Dnestrovskiy, Ukraine 60 Gh
Belgrade. See Beograd
Belgrano, Argentina 92 Ee
Belin, France 53 Cd
Belitung, I., Indonesia 63 El
Belize, British Honduras 89 Bc
Bell I., Newfoundland 82 La
Bellac, France 52 Dc
Bella Coola, Brit. Columbia 80 Ff
Bellaire, Michigan 83 Dc
Bellaire, Ohio 83 Fe
Bellary, India 68 Ee
Bellavista, Peru 90 Be
Belledune, New Brunswick 82 Fc
Bellefontaine, Ohio 83 Ee
Bellefonte, Pennsylvania 86 Bb
Belle Ile, France 52 Bc
Belle Isle, New Brunswick 82 Fd
Belle Isle, Newfoundland 81 Vf
Belle Isle, Str. of, Nfd.-Can. 81 Vf
Belleme, France 52 Db
Belleville, France 52 Fc
Belleville, Illinois 83 Af
Belleville, Ontario 83 Hc
Bellevue, Ohio 83 Ee
Bellevue, Ontario 83 Db
Belley, France 52 Fd
Belle Yella, Liberia 78 Cg
Bellin, Quebec 81 Td
Bellingham, England 30 Fe
Bellingham, Washington 84 Bb
Bellinghausen Sea, Antarc. 100 Rc
Bellinzona, Switzerland 45 Eb
Bellows Falls, Vermont 86 Da
Belluno, Italy 54 Db
Bell Ville, Argentina 92 Dd
Bélmez, Spain 50 Cc
Belmont, New York 86 Ba
Belmont L., Pennsylvania 86 Cb
Belmonte, Brazil 91 Kg
Belmonte, Portugal 50 Bb
Belmonte, Spain 51 Dc
Belmullet, Eire 31 Af
Belo Horizonte, Brazil 91 Jg
Beloit, Kansas 84 Gd
Beloit, Wisconsin 83 Bd
Belomorsk, Russia 58 Cb
Belopol'ye, Ukraine 60 Jf
Belorado, Spain 50 Da
Beloretsk, Russia 61 Pd
Belorussia, rep., U.S.S.R. 60 Ee
Belostok. See Bialystok
Beloye Oz., Russia 60 Ka
Beloye More, Russia 58 Cb
Belp, Switzerland 45 Cb
Belt, Lille, Denmark 47 Cj
Belt, Store, Denmark 47 Dj
Belterra, Brazil 91 Gd
Belvedere Marittimo, Italy 55 Ef
Belver, Portugal 50 Bc
Belvidere, New Jersey 86 Cb
Belvidere, Illinois 83 Bd
Belyy, Os., Russia 58 Fa
Bemidji, Minnesota 85 Hb
Benalla, Victoria 95 Jg
Benapol, India 71 Gd
Benares. See Varanasi
Benavente, Spain 50 Cb
Benbecula, I., Scotland 30 Cc
Bencubbin, W. Australia 94 Cf
Bend, Oregon 87 Cc
Ben Dearg, Scotland 30 Dc
Bendery, Moldavia 60 Fh
Bendigo, Victoria 95 Hg
Benevento, Italy 55 Ee
Bengal, B. of, India, etc. 69 Ge
Bengal, East, E. Pakistan 71 Gc
Bengal, West, India 71 Fd
Ben Gardane, Tunisia 79 Hb
Benghazi, Libya 79 Kb
Benguela, Angola 76 Cg
Benha, Egypt 79 Mb
Ben Hope, Scotland 30 Db
Beni, R., Bolivia 90 Df
Beni-Abbés, Algeria 78 Eb
Benicarló, Spain 51 Fb
Beni Mazar, Egypt 79 Mc
Benin, Bight of, W. Africa 78 Fh
Benin City, Nigeria 78 Gg
Beni Saf, Algeria 78 Ea
Beni Suef, Egypt 79 Mc
Benito, Rio Muni 76 Bd
Benjamin Constant, Brazil 90 Cd
Benkovac, Yugoslavia 54 Ec
Ben Lomond, N.S.W. 95 Ke
Ben Macdhui, Scotland 30 Ec
Ben More Assynt, Scotland 30 Db
Bennett, Brit. Columbia 80 De
Ben Nevis, Scotland 30 Dd
Bennington, Vermont 86 Da
Benson Mines, New York 83 Jc
Bent, Persia 73 Gd
Bentinck I., Burma 69 Jf
Bento Goncalves, Brazil 92 Fc
Benton Harbor, Michigan 83 Cd
Benue R., Nigeria 79 Gg
Benwee Hd., Eire 31 Af
Ben Wyvis, Scotland 30 Dc
Beograd, Yugoslavia 56 Cb
Beppu, Japan 66 Bh
Berar, India 68 Ed
Berat, Albania 57 Bd
Berber, Sudan 79 Me
Berbera, Somalia 77 Kb
Berberati, Cent. Afr. Rep. 79 Jh
Berdichev, Ukraine 60 Fg
Berdigyastyakh, Russia 59 Mb
Berdyansk, Ukraine 60 Kh
Beresti, Rumania 56 Fa
Berezniki, Russia 58 Ec
Berezovo, Russia 58 Fb
Berg, Norway 46 Gb
Berga, Spain 51 Fa
Bergamo, Italy 54 Bc
Bergen, Germany 48 Cb
Bergen, Germany 48 Ea
Bergen, Norway 47 Af
Bergen-op-Zoom, Netherlands 44 Cc
Bergerac, France 53 Dd
Bergisch Gladbach, Germany 48 Bc
Bergün, Switzerland 45 Eb
Berhampur, India 71 Gc
Berhampur, India 69 Fe
Beri, India 70 Ef
Bering, Russia 59 Tb
Bering Sea, Asia-America 85 Ul
Bering Str., Asia-America 85 Vl
Berislavl, Ukraine 60 Hh
Berjeik, Netherlands 44 Dc
Berkåk, Norway 46 De
Berkeley, California 87 Bg
Berkovitsa, Bulgaria 56 Dc
Berkshire (Berks), co., Eng. 31 Gj
Berkshire Hills, Mass. 86 Da
Berlin, Germany 48 Eb
Berlin, New Hampshire 83 Lc
Berlin, Wisconsin 83 Bd
Bermillo de Sayago, Spain 50 Bb
Bermudas, Is., Atlantic Oc. 85 Ne
Bern & canton, Switzerland 45 Cb
Bernasconi, Argentina 92 De
Bernay, France 52 Db
Bernburg, Germany 48 Dc
Berne. See Bern
Berneau, Belgium 44 Dd
Berneck, Switzerland 45 Ea
Berner Alpen, Switzerland 45 Cb
Bernina, Passo del, Switz. 45 Eb
Beromünster, Switz. 45 Da
Berri, prov., France 52 Ec
Berry Is., Bahama Is. 89 Da
Berryville, Virginia 86 Ac
Bersillies, Belgium 44 Cd
Berthierville, Quebec 83 Kb
Bertoua, Cameroon 79 Hh
Bertraghboy B., Eire 31 Ag
Bertrix, Belgium 44 De
Beru, I., Gilbert Is. 98 Gh
Berwick, Pennsylvania 86 Bb
Berwick, co., Scotland 30 Fe
Berwick-upon-Tweed., Eng. 30 Fe
Berwyn Mts., Wales 31 Eh
Berzee, Belgium 44 Cd
Besançon, France 52 Gc
Beskidy Zachodnie, Mts., Central Europe 49 Hd
Besni, Turkey 72 Cb
Bessemer, Alabama 85 Je
Best, Netherlands 44 Dc
Betanzos, Spain 50 Aa
Betbetti, Sudan 79 Ke
Bethanie, S.-W. Africa 75 Be
Bethel, Maine 82 Cd
Bethlehem, O.F.S. 75 De
Bethlehem, Jordan 74 Df
Bethlehem, Pennsylvania 86 Cb
Betling Sib, India 69 Hd
Betsiamites, Quebec 82 Db
Betsiamites R., Quebec 82 Db
Bettiah, India 71 Eb
Beugen, Netherlands 44 Dc
Beveland, Noord, I., Netherlands 44 Bc
Beveland, Zuid, I., Netherlands 44 Bc
Beveren, Belgium 44 Cc
Beverloo, Belgium 44 Dc
Beverly, Massachusetts 86 Ea
Beverst, Belgium 44 Dd
Bex, Switzerland 45 Cb
Beyla, Guinea 78 Dg
Beypazari, Turkey 72 Ba
Beypore, India 68 Ef
Beysehir, Turkey 72 Bb
Beyt Guvrin, Israel 74 Cf
Beyt Shean, Israel 74 De
Bezdán, Yugoslavia 56 Bb
Bezhitsa, Russia 60 He
Béziers, France 53 Ee
Bhabua, India 71 Dc
Bhadarwah, Kashmir 70 Dd
Bhadaur, India 70 De
Bhadaura, India 71 Ac
Bhadohi, India 71 Dc
Bhadra, India 70 Df

Bhadreswar, India 71 Gd
Bhagalpur, India 71 Fc
Bhakkar, W. Pakistan 70 Be
Bhamo, Burma 69 Jd
Bhandara, India 68 Ed
Bhannis, Lebanon 74 Dd
Bhanrer Ra., India 71 Bd
Bharatpur, India 71 Ab
Bhatgaon, Nepal 71 Eb
Bhatinda, India 70 De
Bhatnair, India 70 Df
Bhatpara, India 71 Gd
Bhavnagar, India 68 Dd
Bhawani Patna, India 69 Fe
Bhera, W. Pakistan 70 Cd
Bhilwara, India 68 Dc
Bhima R., India 68 Ee
Bhind, India 71 Bb
Bhir (Bir), India 68 Ee
Bhiwani, India 70 Ef
Bhojpur, India 71 Ec
Bhong Chu, R., Tibet 69 Gc
Bhopal, India 71 Ad
Bhuj, India 68 Cd
Bhusawal, India 68 Ed
Bhutan, Himalayas 69 Hc
Biafra, Bight of, W. Africa 76 Bd
Biak, I., W. Irian 63 Ll
Białogard, Poland 49 Ga
Białowieza, Poland 49 Kb
Białystok, Poland 49 Kb
Biarritz, France 53 Ce
Biberach, Germany 48 Cd
Bibon, Wisconsin 83 Ab
Bic, Quebec 82 Db
Bicknell, Indiana 83 Cf
Bida, Nigeria 78 Gg
Bidar, India 68 Ee
Biddeford, Maine 86 Ea
Bideford & B., England 31 Ej
Bidesir, India 70 Dg
Biel, Switzerland 45 Ca
Bielefeld, Germany 48 Cb
Bieler See, Switzerland 45 Ca
Bielsk, Poland 49 Kb
Bienne. See Biel
Bière, Switzerland 45 Bb
Bietschhorn, Mt., Switz. 45 Cb
Big I., N.-W. Territories 81 Sd
Biga, Turkey 72 Aa
Big Bell, W. Australia 94 Ce
Big Belt Mts., Montana 87 Hb
Big Bend Nat. Park, Texas 84 Ff
Bigelow, Maine 83 Lc
Biggar, Saskatchewan 80 Kf
Bighorn Mts., Wyoming 84 Ec
Bighorn R., Montana-Wy. 84 Ec
Bignona, Senegal 78 Bf
Big Rapids, Michigan 83 Dd
Big Salmon R., Yukon 80 Ed
Big Spring, Texas 84 Fe
Big Trout L., Ontario 81 Pf
Bihac, Yugoslavia 54 Ec
Bihar, India 71 Ec
Bihar, state, India 69 Gd
Biharamulo, Tanzania 77 Ge
Bihorului, Mts., Rumania 56 Da
Bijagos, Arqui. Dos., Portuguese Guinea 78 Bf
Bijapur, India 68 Ee
Bijar, Persia 72 Eb
Bijawar, India 71 Bc
Bijeljina, Yugoslavia 56 Bb
Bijna, India 71 Bc
Bijnabad, Persia 73 Gd
Bijnor, India 70 Ff
Bikaner, India 70 Cf
Bikin, Russia 59 Nd
Bikini, I., Marshall Is. 98 Ff
Bikoro, Congo 76 De
Bilaspur, India 70 Ee
Bilaspur, India 71 Cd
Bilauktaung Ra., Burma-Siam 63 Ch
Bilbao, Spain 50 Da
Bileća, Yugoslavia 56 Bc
Bilecik, Turkey 72 Aa
Bilé Karpaty, Czechoslovakia 49 Gd
Bilin, Burma 69 Je
Bilisht, Albania 57 Cd
Billabong, R. See Moulmein
Billings, Montana 84 Eb
Billiton, I. See Belitung
Bilma, Niger 79 He
Biloela, Qnsld. 95 Jd
Bilo Goro, Yugoslavia 54 Fc
Biloxi, Mississippi 85 Je
Bilsen, Belgium 44 Dd
Bilsi, India 71 Ba
Bilta, Norway 46 Jb
Bilthoven, Netherlands 44 Db
Bilugyun, I., Burma 69 Je
Bilyarsk, Russia 61 Kc
Bimbe, Angola 76 Dg
Bimini Is., Bahama Is. 85 Lf
Bimlipatam, India 69 Fe
Bina, India 71 Bc
Binaija, Mt., Ceram I., Indon. 63 Jl
Binalud, Mt., Persia 73 Gb
Binche, Belgium 44 Cd
Bindki, India 71 Cb
Bindura, Rhodesia 75 Ec
Binefar, Spain 51 Fb
Binga, Rhodesia 75 Dc
Bingen, Germany 48 Bd
Bingerville, Ivory Coast 78 Eg
Bingham, Maine 82 Dd
Binghamton, New York 86 Ca
Bingol, Turkey 72 Db
Binh Dinh, Indo-China 67 Dd
Binn, Switzerland 45 Db
Bintan, I., Riouw Arch., Indon. 63 Dk
Bint Jubeil, Lebanon 74 Dd
Bir Ali, S. Yemen 72 Eg
Birao. See Hiroo
Birchwood, New Zealand 93 Af
Birdsboro, Pennsylvania 86 Cb
Birdsville, Queensland 95 Ge
Birdum, N. Terr., Australia 94 Fc
Birecik, Turkey 72 Cb
Birein, Syria 74 Eb
Bir Fadhil, Arabia 72 Ee
Bir Gara, Chad 79 Jf
Birhan, Mt., Ethiopia 77 Hb
Birjand, Persia 73 Gc
Birkah, Muscat & Oman 73 Ge
Birkenhead, England 31 Eg
Bir Malusi, Iraq 72 Cc
Bir Maqran, Arabia 72 Ee
Birmingham, Alabama 85 Je
Birmingham, England 31 Fh
Birmingham, Michigan 83 Ed
Birni-n-Kebbi, Nigeria 78 Ff
Birni-n' Konni, Niger 78 Gf
Birobidzhan, Russia 59 Nd
Biroo. See Hiro
Birq, Arabia 72 Df
Birr, Eire 31 Bg
Birsilpur, India 70 Cf
Birsk, Russia 61 Mc
Biryusa R., Russia 59 Jc
Biržhay (Birzhay), Lithuania 47 Lh
Bisalpur, India 71 Ba
Bisauli, India 71 Ba
Bisbal, la, Spain 51 Gb
Bisbee, Arizona 84 Ee
Biscay, B. of, France-Spain 43 Fg
Bischofszell, Switzerland 45 Ea
Biscoe, B., Antarctica 100 Nb
Biscoe, Is., Antarctica 100 Sc
Biscotasing, Ontario 83 Eb
Bisha, Arabia 72 De
Bishnath, India 69 Hc
Bishnupur, India 71 Fd
Bishop Auckland, England 31 Ff
Bishop's Falls, Nfd. 82 Lb
Bishops Stortford, England 31 Hj
Bishri, Jebel el, Syria 72 Cb
Bisisthal, Switzerland 45 Db
Biskia, Eritrea 77 Ha
Bismarck, N. Dakota 84 Fb
Bismarck Arch., Pacific Oc. 98 Dh
Bismarck C., Greenland 39 Mb
Bissau, India 70 Df
Bissau, Port. Guinea 78 Bf
Bissett, Manitoba 80 Mf
Bistcho, L., Alberta 80 He
Biswan, India 71 Cb
Bithur, India 71 Cb
Bitlis, Turkey 72 Db
Bitola, Yugoslavia 56 Cd
Bitonto, Italy 55 Fe
Bitterfeld, Germany 48 Ec
Bitter Root Mts., Idaho 87 Fb
Bivio, Switzerland 45 Eb
Biwa Ko, Japan 66 Dg
Biysk, Russia 58 Hc
Bizerte, Tunisia 79 Ga
Bjelovar, Yugoslavia 54 Fc
Björkö, Sweden 47 Hg
Bjorli, Norway 46 Ce
Björna, Sweden 46 He
Björnör, Norway 46 Dd
Björnöya, I., Barents Sea 58 Aa
Black Hills, S. Dakota 84 Fc
Black Isle, Scotland 30 Ec
Black Mt., W. Pakistan 70 Cc
Black Mts., Arizona 87 Fh
Black Mts., Wales 31 Ej
Black Sea, Europe-Asia 40 Cd
Blackall, Queensland 95 Jd
Blackburn, England 31 Fg
Blackburn, Mt., Alaska 80 Cd
Blackdown Hills, England 31 Ek
Blackfoot, Idaho 87 Gd
Blackpool, England 31 Eg
Blackriver, Michigan 83 Ec
Black River Falls, Wisconsin 83 Ac
Black Rock Des., Nevada 87 De
Blacksod B., Eire 31 Af
Black Sugar Loaf, Mt., New South Wales 95 Kf
Blackville, New Brunswick 82 Fc
Black Volta R., Ghana 78 Eg
Blackwater L., N.-W. Terr. 80 Gd
Blackwater R., Eire 31 Bh
Blagoveshchensk, Russia 59 Mc
Blagoveshchensk, Russia 61 Mc
Blagoevgrad, Bulgaria 56 Dc
Blair Atholl, Scotland 30 Ed
Blairgowrie, Scotland 30 Ed
Blairmore, Alberta 80 Jg
Blaj, Rumania 56 Da
Blanc, C., Mauritania 78 Bd
Blanc, le, France 52 Dc
Blanc, Mt., France-Italy 52 Gd
Blanca, B., Argentina 92 De
Blanca Pk., Colorado 84 Ed
Blanca, Sierra, New Mexico 84 Ee
Blanche, L., S. Australia 95 Ge
Blanco, C., Oregon 87 Ad
Blanco, Pico, Costa Rica 89 Ce
Blandford, England 31 Fk
Blanes, Spain 51 Gb
Blangpidie, Sumatra 63 Ck
Blangy, France 52 Db
Blankenberge, Belgium 44 Bc
Blantyre, Malawi 77 Hh
Blaregnies, Belgium 44 Bd
Blaton, Belgium 44 Bd
Blaye, France 53 Cd
Blazowa, Poland 49 Kd
Bleharies, Belgium 44 Bd
Blenheim, New Zealand 93 Dd
Blenheim, Ontario 83 Ed
Blida, Algeria 78 Fa
Blind River, Ontario 83 Eb
Blitta, Togo 78 Fg
Block I., Rhode Island 86 Eb
Bloemfontein, O.F.S. 75 De
Blois, France 52 Dc
Blokzijl, Netherlands 44 Eb
Bloody Foreland, Eire 30 Be
Bloomfield, Indiana 83 Cf
Bloomington, Illinois 83 Cf
Bloomington, Indiana 85 Jd
Bloomsburg, Pennsylvania 86 Bb
Blossburg, Pennsylvania 86 Bb
Blue Mt., India 69 Hd
Blue Mts., Jamaica 89 Dc
Blue Mts., New S. Wales 95 Kf
Blue Mts., Oregon 87 Dc
Blue Mts., Pennsylvania 86 Cb
Bluefield, W. Virginia 85 Kd
Bluefields, Nicaragua 89 Cd
Blue Lake, Michigan 83 Dc
Blue Ridge, Mts., U.S.A. 85 Kd
Blue Stack Mts., Eire 31 Bf
Bluff, New Zealand 93 Bg
Bluff, Utah 84 Ed
Bluff Knoll, W. Australia 94 Cf
Blumenau, Brazil 92 Gc
Blyth, England 30 Ge
Blytheville, Arkansas 85 Hd
Bo, Sierra Leone 78 Cg
Boac, Philippines 63 Hh
Boaco, Nicaragua 89 Bd
Boa Fé, Brazil 90 Ce
Boa Vista, Brazil 90 Ec
Bobo Dioulasso, Upper Volta 78 Ef
Bobolice, Poland 49 Gb
Bobrov, Russia 61 Ee
Bobruysk, White Russia 60 Fe
Boca do Acre, Brazil 90 De
Boca do Copana, Brazil 90 Ee
Bocas del Toro, Panama 89 Ce
Bochnia, Poland 49 Jd
Bocholt, Belgium 44 Dc
Bocholt, Germany 48 Bc
Bochum, Germany 48 Bc
Bocota, Moçambique 75 Ed
Bodaybo, Russia 59 Lc
Boden, Sweden 46 Jd
Boden See, Switz.-Germany 45 Ea
Boderg L., Eire 31 Bg
Bodmin & Moors, England 31 Dk
Bodö, Norway 46 Fc
Boende, Congo 76 Ee
Boertange, Netherlands 44 Ea
Bogalusa, Louisiana 85 Je
Bogandé, Upper Volta 78 Ef
Bogbonga, Congo 76 Dd
Bogdarin, Russia 59 Lc
Bogdo Ula, China 62 Ab
Boggeragh Mts., Eire 31 Ah
Bogong, Mt., Victoria 95 Jg
Bogar, Java 63 Em
Bogorodsk, Russia 61 Jd
Bogorodskoye, Russia 59 Pc
Bogotá, Colombia 90 Cc
Bogotol, Russia 58 Hc
Bogra, E. Pakistan 71 Gc
Bohemia, Czechoslovakia 48 Ed
Böhmer Wald, Ger.-Czech. 48 Ed
Bohol, I., Philippines 63 Hj
Boiaçu, Brazil 90 Ed
Boiestown, New Brunswick 82 Ec
Boigu, I., Torres Str., Qnsld. 95 Ha
Boim, Brazil 91 Fd
Bois, L. des, N.-W. Terr. 80 Gc
Bois Blanc I., Michigan 83 Dc
Boisé, Idaho 87 Ed
Bois-le-Duc. See 's Hertogenbosch
Boissevain, Manitoba 80 Mg
Bojnurd, Persia 73 Gb
Bokaro, India 71 Ed
Boké, Guinea 78 Cf
Bokki, Cameroon 79 Hg
Bokn Fd., Norway 47 Ag
Bokoro, Chad 79 Jf
Boksmeer, Netherlands 44 Dc
Bokstel, Netherlands 44 Dc
Bolan, W. Pakistan 68 Cc
Bolan Pass, W. Pakistan 68 Cc
Bolangir, India 69 Fd
Bolbec, France 52 Db
Bole, Ghana 78 Eg
Bolebyn, Sweden 46 Jd
Bolgrad, Ukraine 60 Fj
Bolintin, Rumania 56 Eb
Bolivar, Argentina 92 De
Bolivar, Colombia 90 Bc
Bolivia, rep., S. America 90 Dg
Bollon, Queensland 95 Je
Bollstabruk, Sweden 46 Ge
Bolmen, L., Sweden 47 Eh
Bolobo, Congo 76 De
Bologna, Italy 54 Cc
Bologoye, Russia 60 Jc
Bolomba, Congo 76 Dd
Bolotnoye, Russia 58 Hc
Bolsena, L. di, Italy 54 Cd
Bolshevik, Ostrov, Russia 59 Ka
Bolshoy Lyakhovskiy, Ostrov, Russia 59 Pa
Boltana, Spain 51 Fa
Bolton, England 31 Fg
Bolu, Turkey 72 Ba
Bolzano, Italy 54 Cb
Bomal, Belgium 44 Dd
Bomba, & Gulf of, Libya 79 Kb
Bombala, New S. Wales 95 Jg
Bombarral, Portugal 50 Ac
Bombay, India 68 De
Bom Futuro, Brazil 90 Ef
Bomhus, Sweden 47 Gf
Bom Jesus, Brazil 91 Je
Bömlo, I., Norway 47 Ag
Bomnak, Russia 59 Mc
Bomoseen, L., Vermont 86 Da
Bonaduz, Switzerland 45 Eb
Bonaire I., Neth. Antilles 89 Fd
Bonanza, Nicaragua 89 Cd
Bonaventure I., Quebec 82 Fb
Bonavista & B., Newfoundland 82 Mb
Bondo, Congo 76 Ed
Bône. See Annaba
Bone, G. of, Celebes 63 Hl
Bongor, Chad 79 Jf
Bonifacio & B. de, Corse 55 Be
Bonin Is., Pacific 62 Me
Bonn, Germany 48 Bc
Bonne Bay, Newfoundland 82 Jb
Bonneval, France 52 Db
Bonnie Rock, W. Australia 94 Cf
Bonny, France 52 Ec
Bonny, Nigeria 78 Gh
Bonom Mhai, Mts., S. Vietnam 67 Dd
Boom, Belgium 44 Cc
Boon Tsagan Nur, Mongolia 62 Ca
Boonville, New York 86 Ca
Boothia, G. of, N.-W. Terr. 81 Pc
Boothia Pen., N.-W. Terr. 81 Nb
Bopeechee, S. Aust. 95 Ge
Boqueron, Cuba 89 Dc
Boquete, Panama 89 Ce
Boramo, Somalia 77 Jc
Borås, Sweden 47 Eh
Borba, Brazil 90 Fd
Bordeaux, France 53 Cd
Bordertown, S. Australia 95 Gg
Borga, Sweden 46 Fd
Börge Fjell, Norway 46 Ed
Borger, Netherlands 44 Eb
Borger, Texas 84 Fd
Borgholm, Sweden 47 Gh
Borgne, Haiti 89 Ec
Borisoglebsk, Russia 61 Ee
Borisov, White Russia 60 Fd
Bo River Post, Sudan 79 Lg
Borja, Spain 51 Eb
Borjas Blancas, Spain 51 Fb
Borkum, I., Germany 48 Bb
Borlänge, Sweden 47 Ff
Borneo, Indonesia 63 Fk
Bornholm, I., Denmark 47 Fj
Borodino, Russia 60 Jd
Borogontsy, Russia 59 Nb
Borongan, Philippines 63 Jh
Borovichi, Russia 60 Hb
Borroloola, N. Terr., Aust. 95 Gc
Borskoye, Russia 61 Kd
Borüjerd, Persia 72 Ec
Bor Yuryakh, Russia 59 La
Borzya, Russia 59 Lc
Bosaso, Somalia 77 Kb
Bosco, Switzerland 45 Db
Boscobel, Wisconsin 83 Ad
Bosiljgrad, Yugoslavia 56 Dc
Boskoop, Netherlands 44 Cb
Bosna-Hercegovina, Yugosl. 56 Ab
Böso Pen., Japan 66 Gg
Bosobolo, Congo 76 Dd
Bosoli, Botswana 75 Dd
Bosporus, Turkey 72 Aa
Bosso, Niger 79 Hf
Bostan, W. Pakistan 68 Cb
Boston, England 31 Hh
Boston, Massachusetts 83 Ld
Boston Mts., Arkansas 85 Hd
Botera, Angola 76 Cg
Bothaville, O.F.S. 75 De
Bothnia, G of, N.-W. Europe 47 Hf
Botswana (Bechuanaland), S. Africa 75 Cd
Botucatu, Brazil 91 Hh
Bouake, Ivory Coast 78 Eg
Bouar, Cent. Afr. Rep. 79 Jg
Bou Arfa, Morocco 78 Eb
Bouches-du-Rhône, dep., France 53 Fe
Bou Djébéha, Mali 78 Ee
Boudoukou, Ivory Coast 78 Eg
Boudry, Switzerland 45 Bb
Bougainville, I., Solomon Is. 98 Eh
Bougaroun C., Algeria 78 Ga
Bougie & G. of. See Bejaia
Bougouni, Mali 78 Df
Bouillon, Belgium 44 De
Boularderie I., Nova Scotia 82 Hc
Boulder, Colorado 84 Ec
Boulder, W. Australia 94 Df
Boulia, Queensland 95 Gd
Boulogne, France 52 Da
Bouna, Ivory Coast 78 Eg
Bounty Is., Pacific Ocean 98 Gm
Bourbonnais, prov., France 52 Ec
Bourem, Mali 78 Ee
Bourg, France 52 Fc
Bourg Argental, France 53 Fd
Bourges, France 52 Ec
Bourget, L. du, France 52 Fd
Bourgogne, prov., France 52 Fc
Bourg St. Pierre, Switz. 45 Cc
Bourke, New S. Wales 95 Jf
Bourkes, Ontario 83 Fa
Bournemouth, England 31 Fk
Bouvet I., Atlantic Ocean 100 Cd
Bovigny, Belgium 44 Dd
Bovino, Italy 55 Ee
Bow R., Alberta 80 Jf
Bowen, Queensland 95 Jc
Bowling Green, Kentucky 85 Jd
Bowling Green, Ohio 83 Ee
Bowman B., N.-W. Terr. 81 Sc
Bowman I., Antarctica 100 Hc
Bowmanville, Ontario 83 Gd
Boxholm, Sweden 47 Fg
Boyne, R., Eire 31 Cg
Boyne City, Michigan 83 Dc
Bozeman, Montana 84 Db
Bozok. See Yozgat
Bozoum, Cent. Afr. Rep. 79 Jg
Bra, Italy 54 Ac
Brabant, prov., Belgium 44 Cd
Brabant, Noord, prov., Netherlands 44 Dc
Brac, I., Yugoslavia 54 Fd
Bracadale L., Scotland 30 Cc
Bracebridge, Ontario 83 Gc
Bräcke, Sweden 46 Fe
Brad, Rumania 56 Da
Braddock, Pennsylvania 86 Ab
Bradford, England 31 Fg
Bradford, Pennsylvania 86 Ab
Braemar, Scotland 30 Ed
Braga, Portugal 50 Ab
Bragado, Argentina 92 De
Bragança, Portugal 50 Bb
Bragança Paulista, Brazil 91 Hh
Brahmanbaria, E. Pakistan 69 Hd
Brahmaputra R., India 69 Hc
Braidwood, Illinois 83 Be
Brail, Switzerland 45 Fb
Brăila, Rumania 56 Fb
Braine l'Alleud, Belgium 44 Cd
Braine le Comte, Belgium 44 Cd
Brak, Libya 79 Hc
Brampton, Ontario 83 Fd
Brandenburg, Germany 48 Eb
Brandon, Manitoba 80 Mg
Brandon Head, Eire 31 Ah
Brandsen, Argentina 92 Ee
Brandvlei, Cape Province 75 Cf
Braniewo, Poland 49 Ha
Bransfield Str., Antarctica 100 Tc
Bransk, Poland 49 Kb
Brantford, Ontario 83 Fd
Brantôme, France 53 Dd
Bras d'or L., Nova Scotia 82 Hd
Brasília, Brazil 91 Hg
Brasília Legal, Brazil 91 Fd
Brasov, Rumania 56 Eb
Brassus, le, Switzerland 45 Bb
Bratislava, Czechoslovakia 49 Gd
Bratsk, Russia 59 Kc
Brattleboro, Vermont 86 Da
Braunau, Austria 48 Ed
Braunlage, Germany 48 Dc
Braunschweig, Germany 48 Db
Braunwald, Switzerland 45 Db
Brava, Somalia 77 Jd
Brawley, California 87 Fj
Bray, Eire 31 Cg
Brazil, Indiana 83 Cf
Brazil, rep., S. America 90-91
Brazos R., Texas 84 Ge
Brazzaville, French Congo 76 De
Brčko, Yugoslavia 56 Bb
Bream B., New Zealand 93 Ea
Brechin, Scotland 30 Fd
Brecknock, Pen., Chile 92 Bh
Brecknock, co., Wales 31 Eh
Břeclav, Czechoslovakia 49 Gd
Brecon, Wales 31 Ej
Brecon Beacons, Wales 31 Ej
Breda, Netherlands 44 Cc
Bredasdorp, Cape Province 75 Cf
Bredy, Russia 61 Qd
Bree, Belgium 44 Dc
Breedene, Belgium 44 Ac
Breidha fjördhur, Iceland 46 Tm
Breil, France 53 Ge
Breithorn, Mt., Switzerland 45 Cb
Brejo, Brazil 91 Jd
Bremangerland, Norway 46 A
Bremen, Germany 48 Cb
Bremerhaven, Germany 48 Cb
Bremerton, Washington 87 Bb
Bremgarten, Switzerland 45 Da
Brenner Pass, Austria-Italy 54 Cb
Breno, Italy 54 Cc
Brent, Ontario 83 Gb
Brescia, Italy 54 Cc
Breskens, Netherlands 44 Bc
Breslau. See Wroclaw
Bressay I., Scotland 30 Qb
Bressuire, France 52 Cc
Brest, France 52 Ab
Brest (Brest-Litovsk), White Russia 60 Ce
Bretagne, prov., France 52 Bb
Breţcu, Rumania 56 Fa
Breugel, Netherlands 44 Dc
Brevik, Norway 47 Cg
Brewarrina, New S. Wales 95 Je
Brewer, Maine 82 Dd
Brewster Mt., Antarctica 100 Lb
Brežice, Yugoslavia 54 Ec
Brezova, Czechoslovakia 49 Gd
Březová, Czechoslovakia 49 Gd
Bria, Cent. Afr. Rep. 79 Kg
Briançon, France 53 Gd
Briare, France 52 Ec
Bridgehampton, New York 86 Db
Bridgeport, Connecticut 83 Ke
Bridgeton, New Jersey 86 Cc
Bridgetown, Nova Scotia 82 Fd
Bridgman C., Arctic Ocean 39 Na
Bridgton, Maine 82 Ce
Bridgwater & B., England 31 Ej
Bridlington, England 31 Gf
Brielle, Netherlands 44 Cc
Brienz, Switzerland 45 Db
Brienzer See, Switzerland 45 Cb
Brier I., Nova Scotia 82 Ed
Brig, Switzerland 45 Cb
Brigels, Switzerland 45 Eb
Brigham, Utah 87 Ge
Brighton, England 31 Gk
Brignoles, France 53 Ge
Brindaban, India 70 Eg
Brindisi, Italy 55 Ge
Brione, Switzerland 45 Db
Brioude, France 53 Ed
Brisbane, Queensland 95 Ke
Brissago, Switzerland 45 Db
Bristol, England 31 Fj
Bristol, New Brunswick 82 Ec
Bristol, Pennsylvania 86 Cb
Bristol, Rhode Island 86 Eb
Bristol, Tennessee 85 Kd
Bristol B., Alaska 85 Wm
Bristol Channel, England 31 Dj
Bristol I., South Sandwich Is. 100 Ad
British Columbia, prov., Canada 80 Ff
British Guiana. See Guyana
British Honduras, Central America 88 Gd
British Isles, N.-W. Europe 42 Ee
Brito, Nicaragua 89 Bd
Britstown, Cape Province 75 Cf
Brive, France 53 Dd
Briviesca, Spain 50 Da
Brno, Czechoslovakia 49 Gd
Broach, India 68 Dd
Broad B., Scotland 30 Cb
Broadalbin, New York 83 Jd
Broadford, Pennsylvania 86 Ab
Broadford, Scotland 30 Dc
Brock I., N.-W. Territories 80 Ha
Brockton, Massachusetts 86 Ea
Brockville, Ontario 83 Jc
Brod, Yugoslavia 56 Ab
Brod, Yugoslavia 56 Cd
Brodeur Pen., N.-W. Terr. 81 Pb
Brodhead, Wisconsin 83 Bd
Brodick, Scotland 30 De
Broek-in-Waterland, Netherlands 44 Db
Broglio, Switzerland 45 Db
Broken Hill, New S. Wales 95 Hf
Bromberg. See Bydgoszcz
Bromptonville, Quebec 83 Lc
Brönnöysund, Norway 44 Ed
Bronte, Sicily 55 Eg
Brookings, Oregon 87 Ad
Brookings, S. Dakota 84 Gc
Brooklyn, New York 86 Db
Brooklyn, Nova Scotia 82 Fd
Brooks Ra., Alaska 80 Cb
Brook's Point, Philippines 63 Gj
Brookville, Pennsylvania 86 Ab
Broom, L., Scotland 30 Dc
Broome, W. Australia 94 Dc
Brora, Scotland 30 Eb
Brothers, The, Is., Red Sea 72 Bd
Broughty Ferry, Scotland 30 Fd
Broumov, Czechoslovakia 49 Gc
Brouwershaven, Netherlands 44 Bc
Brown, Mt., S. Australia 95 Gf
Brownsville, Texas 84 Gf
Brownville, Maine 82 Dd
Brownwood, Texas 84 Ge
Brozas, Spain 50 Bc
Bruce, Mt., W. Australia 94 Cd
Bruce Mines, Ontario 83 Eb
Bruck, Austria 48 Ee
Bruck an der Mur, Austria 48 Fe
Bruges, Belgium 44 Bc
Brugg, Switzerland 45 Da
Brugge. See Bruges
Bruly, Belgium 44 Ce
Brumado, Brazil 91 Jf
Brummen, Netherlands 44 Eb
Brunei & state, Borneo 63 Fk
Brunette Downs, N.T., Aust. 95 Gc
Brunflo, Sweden 46 Fe
Brunn. See Brno
Brunnen, Switzerland 45 Da
Brunner, New Zealand 93 Ce
Brunssum, Netherlands 44 Dd
Brunswick. See Braunschweig
Brunswick, Georgia 85 Ke
Brunswick, Maine 82 Ce
Brunswick, Maryland 86 Bc
Brunswick B., W. Australia 94 Dc
Brunswick, Pen. de, Chile 92 Bh
Bruny I., Tasmania 95 Jh
Brusa. See Bursa
Brusartsi, Bulgaria 56 Dc
Brusio, Switzerland 45 Eb
Brussels, Belgium 44 Cd
Bruxelles (Brussel). See Brussels
Bruzual, Venezuela 90 Db
Bryansk, Russia 60 Je
Bryce Canyon Nat. Park, Utah 87 Gg
Bryson, Quebec 83 Hc
Brzeg, Poland 49 Gc
Brzesko, Poland 49 Jc
Bsharri, Lebanon 74 Dc
Bua, Angola 76 Cf
Buayan, Philippines 63 Jj
Bubasa, Ethiopia 77 Jc
Bubiyan I., Persian Gulf 72 Ed
Bubulu, Uganda 77 Gd
Bucaramanga, Colombia 90 Cb
Buchach, Ukraine 60 Dg
Buchan Ness, Scotland 30 Fc
Buchanan, Liberia 78 Cg
Buchanan, L., Queensland 95 Jd
Buchardo, Argentina 92 Dd
Bucharest. See Bucureşti
Buchs, Switzerland 45 Ea
Buckhannon, West Virginia 83 Ff
Buckie, Scotland 30 Fc
Buckingham, Quebec 83 Jc
Buckingham & co., England 31 Gj
Bucksport, Maine 82 Dd
Buctouche, New Brunswick 82 Fc
Bucureşti, Rumania 56 Fb
Bud, Norway 46 Be
Budaia, Arabia 72 De
Budapest, Hungary 49 He
Budaun, India 71 Ba
Bud Bud, India 71 Fd
Buddh Gaya, India 71 Ec
Bude, England 31 Dk
Budeşti, Rumania 56 Fb
Budhana, India 70 Ef
Budva, Yugoslavia 56 Bc
Buea, Nigeria 79 Gh
Buenaventura, Colombia 90 Bc
Buenaventura, Mexico 88 Cb
Buenavista, Mexico 88 Cb
Buenos Aires, Argentina 92 Ed
Buenos Aires, Colombia 90 Cd
Buenos Aires, L., Chile-Argentina 92 Cg
Bufa, Mt., Mexico 88 Dc
Buffalo, Missouri 86 Ba
Buffalo, New York 83 Gd
Buffalo L., N.-W. Terr. 80 Hd
Bug, R., Poland-W. Russia 49 Jb
Buga, Colombia 90 Bc
Buganda, Uganda 77 Gd
Bugti, W. Pakistan 68 Cc
Bugulchan, Russia 61 Md
Bugulma, Russia 61 Lc
Buguruslan, Russia 61 Ld
Builth Wells, Wales 31 Eh
Buinsk, Russia 61 Jc
Buique, Brazil 91 Ke
Buitenpost, Netherlands 44 Ea
Bujumbura, Burundi 77 Fe
Buka, I., Solomon Is. 98 Eh
Bukama, Congo 76 Ff
Bukavu, Congo 77 Fe
Bukene, Tanzania 77 Ge
Bukhara, Uzbek. 58 Fe
Bukoba, Tanzania 77 Ge
Bukwimba, Tanzania 77 Ge
Bula, Seram I., Indonesia 63 Kl
Bülach, Switzerland 45 Da
Bulagan, Mongolia 62 Da
Bulan, Philippines 63 Hh
Bulandshahr, India 70 Ef
Bulawayo, Rhodesia 75 Dd
Bulgaria, Central Europe 43 Nh
Bullange, Belgium 44 Ed
Buller R., New Zealand 93 Cd
Bullfinch, W. Australia 94 Cf
Bulloo Cr., Queensland 95 He
Bulnes, Chile 92 Be
Bulo Burti, Somalia 77 Kd
Bulsar, India 68 Dd
Bulu, Mt., Borneo 63 Gk
Bulun, Russia 59 Ma
Bumba, Congo 76 Ed
Buna, Kenya 77 Hd
Buna, Papua 95 Ja
Bunbury, W. Australia 94 Cf
Buncrana, Eire 30 Ce
Bundaberg, Queensland 95 Kd
Bundi, India 68 Ec
Bundooma, N. Terr., Aust. 95 Fd
Bundoran, Eire 31 Bf
Bungay, England 31 Hh
Bungo, Angola 76 Df
Bungo Str., Japan 66 Ch
Bunguran Kep., Indonesia 63 Ek
Bunschoten, Netherlands 44 Db
Buntok, Borneo 63 Gl
Buochs, Switzerland 45 Db
Buol, Celebes 63 Hk
Buolkalakh, Russia 59 La
Buorkhaya, Guba, Russia 59 Na
Buraimi, Trucial States 73 Ge
Bur Akaba, Somalia 77 Jd
Buram, Sudan 79 Lf
Burao, Somalia 77 Kc
Buraq, Syria 74 Ed
Burayda, Arabia 72 Dd
Burazjun, Persia 73 Fd
Burchun, China 62 Aa
Burd, Jebel, Arabia 72 Cd
Burdekin, R., Queensland 95 Jc
Burdia, Sudan 79 Lf
Burdur, Turkey 72 Bb
Burdwan, India 71 Fd
Bureå, Sweden 46 Jd
Bureinskiy Khrebet, Russia 59 Nd
Buren, Netherlands 44 Dc
Büren, Switzerland 45 Ca
Bureya, Russia 59 Nd
Burg, Netherlands 44 Db
Burgas, Bulgaria 56 Fc
Bur Gavo, Somalia 77 Je
Burgdorf, Switzerland 45 Ca
Burgenland, prov., Austria 49 Ge
Burghersdorp, Cape Prov. 75 Df
Burgos, Spain 50 Da
Burhanpur, India 68 Ed
Buria, India 70 Ee
Burias I., Philippines 63 Hb
Buriti, Brazil 91 Jd
Burketown, Queensland 95 Gc
Burks Falls, Ontario 83 Gc
Burley, Idaho 87 Gd
Burlington, Iowa 85 Hc
Burlington, New Jersey 86 Cb
Burlington, Ontario 83 Gd
Burlington, Vermont 83 Kc
Burlington, Wisconsin 83 Bd
Burlyuk, Russia 60 Hj
Burma, S. Asia 69 Hd

Cheju Do, Korea 62 Jd
Chekiang, prov., China 65 Jh
Chekunda, Russia 59 Nc
Chelforó, Argentina 92 Ce
Chelkar, Kazakh. 58 Ed
Chełm, Poland 49 Kc
Chelmsford, England 31 Hj
Chelsea, Vermont 83 Kc
Chelsea, Wisconsin 83 Ac
Cheltenham, England 31 Fj
Chelva, Spain 51 Ec
Chelyabinsk, Russia 61 Qc
Chemba, Moçambique 75 Ec
Chembar, Russia 61 Fd
Chemnitz. See Karl Marx Stadt
Chenab R., W. Pakistan 70 Be
Chenchow. See Hwaiyang
Chenesht, Persia 73 Gc
Chengchow, China 64 Fe
Chengho, China 65 Jj
Chengshan Tow, China 62 Hc
Chêngtêhshih, China 64 Hb
Chengtu, China 64 Bg
Chenhsien, China 65 Fk
Chennan. See Tchpao
Chenoa, Illinois 83 Be
Chenting, China 64 Gc
Chenyüan, China 65 Dj
Cheongkong, Hainan I. 62 Eg
Chepen, Peru 90 Be
Chepes, Argentina 92 Cd
Cher, R. & dep., France 52 Ec
Cherbourg, France 52 Cb
Cherchell, Algeria 78 Fa
Cheremkhovo, Russia 59 Kc
Cherepovets, Russia 60 Lb
Cherkassy, Ukraine 60 Gg
Chermoz, Russia 58 Fc
Chernigov, Ukraine 60 Gf
Chernikovsk, Russia 61 Nc
Chernovsk, Russia 61 Ja
Chernovtsy, Ukraine 60 Dg
Chernyakhovsk, Russia 47 Jj
Cherokee, Iowa 84 Gc
Cherrapungi, India 69 Hc
Cherryfield, Maine 82 Ed
Cherskogo, Khrebet, Russia 59 Pb
Chertkovo, Ukraine 60 Lg
Cherven Bryag, Bulgaria 56 Ec
Chesapeake B., Maryland 85 Ld
Cheshire, co., England 31 Fg
Cheshskaya Guba, Russia 58 Db
Chesley, Ontario 83 Fc
Chester, England 31 Fg
Chester, Pennsylvania 86 Cc
Chesterfield, England 31 Gg
Chesterfield Inl., N.-W. Terr. 81 Nd
Chesterfield Inlet, N.-W. Terr. 81 Nd
Chesterfield Is., Pacific Oc. 98 Ej
Chestertown, Maryland 86 Bc
Chesuncook L., Maine 82 Dc
Chethang, Tibet 69 Hc
Chetumal, Mexico 88 Gd
Chetumal B., Mexico 89 Bc
Cheviot, New Zealand 93 De
Cheviot, The, England 30 Fe
Cheviot Hills, Eng.-Scot. 30 Fe
Cheyenne, Wyoming 84 Fc
Cheyenne R., S. Dakota 84 Fc
Chhachrauli, India 70 Ee
Chhata, India 70 Eg
Chhatarpur, India 71 Bc
Chhibramau, India 71 Bb
Chhindwara, India 71 Bd
Chhiai, Taiwan 65 Kl
Chia-mu-ssu. See Kiamusze
Chiang-hsi. See Kiangsi
Chiang-kan, Siam 67 Cc
Chiang Mai, Siam 67 Bc
Chiang Rai, Siam 67 Bc
Chiang-su. See Kiangsu
Chiapa, Mexico 88 Fd
Chiapas R. & state, Mexico 88 Fd
Chiasso, Switzerland 45 Ec
Chiavari, Italy 54 Bc
Chiba, Japan 66 Gg
Chibia, Angola 75 Ac
Chibougamau & L., Quebec 82 Ab
Chicago, Illinois 83 Ce
Chichagof I., Alaska 85 Zm
Chichester, England 31 Gk
Ch'i-ch'i-ha-erh. See Tsitsihar
Chickasha, Oklahoma 84 Ge
Chiclayo, Peru 90 Bf
Chico, California 87 Cf
Chicoana, Argentina 92 Cc
Chicopee, Massachusetts 86 Da
Chicoutimi, Quebec 82 Cb
Chicuma, Angola 76 Dd
Chicundo, Transvaal 75 Ed
Chidambaram, India 68 Ef
Chidley, C., Quebec 81 Ud
Chiengue, Angola 76 Dg
Chien-ou. See Kienow
Chieti, Italy 54 Ed
Chièvres, Belgium 44 Bd
Chignecto B., N.B.-N.S. 82 Fd
Chihchow. See Kweichih
Chih-fêng, China 64 Ja
Chihkiang, China 65 Dj
Chihsien, China 64 Ge
Chihuahua & state, Mexico 88 Cb
Chikala, Malawi 77 Hg
Chik-Ballapur, India 63 Ef
Chikien, China 59 Mc
Chikmagalur, India 68 Ef
Chikwawa, Malawi 77 Gh
Chilant'ai, China 64 Bc
Chilas, Kashmir 70 Dc
Chilca, Pta. de, Peru 90 Bf
Chile, rep., S. America 92 Bf
Chilecito, Argentina 92 Cc
Chilete, Peru 90 Be
Chilia Veche, Rumania 56 Gb
Chi-lin. See Kirin
Chilka L., India 69 Ge
Chilko L., Brit. Columbia 80 Gf
Chilko R., Brit. Columbia 80 Gf
Chillan, Chile 92 Be
Chillicothe, Ohio 83 Ef
Chilliwack, Brit. Columbia 80 Gg
Chiloe, I. de, Chile 92 Bf
Chilonga, Zambia 77 Gg
Chilpancingo, Mexico 88 Ed
Chiltern Hills, England 31 Gj
Chilton, Wisconsin 83 Bc
Chiluane, Moçambique 75 Fd
Chilubula, Zambia 77 Gg
Chilumba, Malawi 75 Eb
Chilung, Taiwan 65 Kk
Chilwa L., Malawi 77 Hh
Chimay, Belgium 44 Cd
Chimbay, Uzbek. 58 Fd
Chimbote, Peru 90 Be
Chimkent, Kazakh. 58 Fd
China, Asia 41 Ke
Chi-nan. See Tsinan
Chinandega, Nicaragua 89 Bd
Chincha, Peru 90 Bf
Chinchaga R., Alberta 80 He
Chin-chiang. See Tsingkiang
Chinchón, Spain 50 Db
Chinchow, China 62 Hb
Chindwin R., Burma 69 Jc
Ching Hai, China 62 Dc
Chingleput, India 68 Ff
Ching Shan, China 64 Eg
Ch'ing-tao. See Tsingtao
Chinguetta, Mauritania 78 Cd
Ch'ing-yuan. See Paoting
Chinhai, China 65 Kh
Chin Hills, Burma 69 Hd
Chin-hua. See Kinhwa
Chini, India 70 Fe
Chi-ning. See Tsining
Chiniot, W. Pakistan 70 Ce
Chinju, Korea 62 Jc
Chinkiang, China 64 Jf
Chin Ling Shan, China 62 Ed
Chinsura, India 71 Gd
Chinwangtao, China 64 Jc
Chioggia, Italy 54 Dc
Chios, I. See Khios, I.
Chipili, Zambia 77 Fg
Chipman, New Brunswick 82 Fc
Chipoka, Malawi 75 Eb
Chippenham, England 31 Fj
Chippewa, R., Wisconsin 85 Hb
Chipping Norton, England 31 Fj
Chiputneticook Ls., Maine-New Brunswick 82 Ed
Chiquian, Peru 90 Bf
Chiquimula, Guatemala 88 Ge
Chiquinquira, Colombia 90 Cb
Chiras, Afghanistan 73 Jb
Chirawa, India 70 Df
Chiriqui, Lag. de, Panama 89 Ce
Chiriqui Grande, Panama 89 Ce
Chirpan, Bulgaria 56 Ec
Chirripo Grande, Mt., Costa Rica 89 Ce
Chisamba Falls, Zambia 77 Gg
Chishmy, Russia 61 Mc
Chisimaio, Somalia 77 Je
Chisinau. See Kishinev
Chistopol', Russia 61 Kc
Chita, Russia 59 Lc
Chitambo, Zambia 77 Gg
Chitila, Rumania 56 Fb
Chitipa, Malawi 75 Ea
Chitorgarh, India 68 Dd
Chitradurga, India 68 Ef
Chitral & R., W. Pakistan 70 Cc
Chitre, Panama 89 Ce
Chittagong, East Pakistan 69 Hd
Chittoor, India 68 Ef
Chiusi, Italy 54 Cd
Chiuta, L., Malawi 77 Hg
Chiva, Spain 51 Ec
Chivasso, Italy 54 Ac
Chivay, Peru 90 Cg
Chivilcoy, Argentina 92 Dd
Chiwanda, Tanzania 77 Gg
Chmielnik, Poland 49 Jc
Choapam, Mexico 88 Ed
Choban Bey, Syria 74 Fa
Chocaya, Bolivia 90 Dh
Chocen, Czechoslovakia 49 Gc
Cho-chow, China 64 Gc
Choco, Colombia 90 Bb
Choconta, Colombia 90 Cb
Choele Choel, Argentina 92 Ce
Choiseul, I., Solomon Islands 98 Eh
Choix, Mexico 88 Cb
Chojna, Poland 48 Fb
Choke Mts., Ethiopia 77 Hb
Cholet, France 52 Cc
Cholon, S. Vietnam 67 Dd
Choluteca, Honduras 89 Bd
Choma, Zambia 75 Dc
Chomutov, Czechoslovakia 48 Ec
Chone, Ecuador 90 Ad
Chongjin, Korea 62 Jb
Chong Kal, Cambodia 67 Cd
Chonos, Arch. de los, Chile 92 Bg
Chorillos, Peru 90 Bf
Chorrera, Panama 89 De
Chorzele, Poland 49 Jb
Chorzow, Poland 49 Hc
Choshi, Japan 66 Gg
Chos Malal, Argentina 92 Be
Chota, Peru 90 Be
Choushan I., China 65 Lh
Christchurch, New Zealand 93 De
Christianshaab, Greenland 81 Wc
Christie, Mt., Yukon 80 Fd
Christmas I., Indian Ocean 63 En
Christmas I., Pacific Ocean 99 Kg
Chrudim, Czechoslovakia 49 Fd
Chrzanów, Poland 49 Hc
Chuale L., Moçambique 75 Ed
Chuambara, Moçambique 75 Ed
Chuanchow, China 65 Jk
Chuanhsien, China 65 Ej
Chubut & R., Argentina 92 Cf
Chuchow, China 65 Fj
Chuchow. See Lishui
Chucul, Argentina 92 Dd
Chudovo, Russia 60 Gb
Chudskoye, Oz., Estonia-Russia 47 Mg
Chuhsien, China 64 Je
Chühsien, China 65 Jh
Chukai, W. Malaysia 63 Dk
Chukhloma, Russia 61 Fa
Chukotskiy Khrebet, Russ. 59 Sb
Chul'man, Russia 59 Mc
Chulym, Russia 58 Hc
Chumbi, Tibet 69 Gc
Chumikan, Russia 59 Nc
Chumporn, Siam 67 Bd
Chuna, R., Russia 59 Jc
Chunar, India 71 Dc
Chunchŏn, Korea 62 Jc
Chungan, China 65 Hj
Chung-ch'ing. See Chungking
Chunghsien, China 65 Cg
Chungking, China 65 Ch
Chungshan, China 65 Ek
Chungsiang, China 64 Fg
Chungtien, China 62 Ce
Chunian, W. Pakistan 70 Ce
Chunya, Tanzania 77 Gf
Chuquibambilla, Peru 90 Cf
Chuquicamata, Chile 92 Cb
Chur, Switzerland 45 Eb
Churapcha, Russia 59 Nb
Churchill, Manitoba 80 Ne
Churchill C., Manitoba 81 Ne
Churchill L., Saskatchewan 80 Ke
Churchill R., Manitoba 80 Me
Churia Ghati Hills, Nepal 71 Eb
Churu, India 70 Df
Chusovoy, Russia 58 Ec
Chuvashskaya, aut. rep., Russia 58 Dc
Chwan Ho. See Yangtze Kiang
Ciaris, I. de, Mexico 88 Bb
Cicero, Illinois 83 Be
Cidones, Spain 51 Db
Ciechanow, Poland 49 Jb
Ciego de Avila, Cuba 89 Db
Cienaga, Colombia 90 Ca
Cienfuegos, Cuba 89 Cb
Cierfs, Switzerland 45 Fb
Cieszyn, Poland 49 Hd
Cieza, Spain 51 Ec
Cifuentes, Spain 51 Db
Cimaltepec, Mexico 88 Ed
Cimarron R., Oklahoma, etc. 84 Fd
Cîmpulung, Rumania 56 Eb
Cincinnati, Ohio 83 Df
Cioara, Rumania 56 Fb
Ciotat, France 53 Fe
Circeo C., Italy 55 De
Circle, Alaska 85 Yl
Circleville, Ohio 83 Ef
Cirencester, England 31 Fj
Ciro, Italy 55 Ff
Cirque Mt., Labrador 81 Ue
Citlaltepetl, Mt., Mexico 88 Ed
Citrusdal, Cape Province 75 Bf
Cittanova, Italy 55 Ff
Ciudad Bolivar, Venezuela 90 Eb
Ciudad Bolivia, Venezuela 90 Cb
Ciudad Camargo, Mexico 88 Cb
Ciudad Juarez, Mexico 88 Ca
Ciudad Madero, Mexico 88 Ec
Ciudad Real, Spain 50 Dc
Ciudad Rodrigo, Spain 50 Bb
Ciudad Victoria, Mexico 88 Ec
Civitanova Marche, Italy 54 Dd
Civray, France 52 Dc
Civril, Turkey 72 Ab
Cizre, Turkey 72 Db
Clackmannan co., Scotland 30 Ed
Clacton, England 31 Hj
Claire, L., Alberta 80 Je
Clamecy, France 52 Ec
Clara I., Burma 69 Jf
Clare, Michigan 83 Dd
Clare, co., Eire 31 Ah
Clare I., Eire 31 Ag
Claremont, New Hampshire 86 Da
Claremorris, Eire 31 Bg
Clarence R., New Zealand 93 De
Clarence Hd., N.-W. Terr. 81 Ra
Clarence I., Antarctica 100 Tc
Clarence, I., Chile 92 Bh
Clarence Str., N. Terr., Aust. 94 Fb
Clarion, Pennsylvania 86 Ab
Clarion R., Pennsylvania 86 Ab
Clarksburg, West Virginia 83 Ff
Clarksdale, Mississippi 85 He
Clarksville, Tennessee 85 Jd
Claro, Switzerland 45 Eb
Clausthal, Germany 48 Dc
Clear, C., Eire 31 Aj
Clear L., California 87 Bf
Clearfield, Pennsylvania 86 Ab
Clearwater L., Quebec 81 Se
Clearwater R., Idaho 87 Fb
Cleburne, Texas 84 Ge
Clermont, Queensland 95 Jd
Clermont-Ferrand, France 52 Ed
Cleveland, Ohio 83 Fe
Cleveland, Tennessee 85 Kd
Clew Bay, Eire 31 Ag
Clifden, Eire 31 Ag
Clifton, Arizona 84 Ee
Clifton Hills, S. Australia 95 Ge
Clifton Ville, Wisconsin 83 Bc
Clinton, Illinois 83 Be
Clinton, Iowa 85 Hc
Clinton, Massachusetts 86 Ea
Clinton, Missouri 85 Hd
Clinton, Ontario 83 Fd
Clinton Colden L., N.-W.T. 80 Kd
Clipperton I., Pacific Ocean 99 Qf
Clisson, France 52 Cc
Cliza, Bolivia 90 Dg
Clonakilty & B., Eire 31 Bj
Cloncurry, Queensland 95 Hd
Clones, Eire 31 Cf
Clonmel, Eire 31 Bh
Clorinda, Argentina 92 Ec
Cloud Pk., Wyoming 84 Ec
Clovis, New Mexico 84 Fe
Cluj, Rumania 56 Da
Clusone, Italy 54 Bc
Clyde, New Zealand 93 Bf
Clyde, N.-W. Terr. 81 Tb
Clyde, Firth of, Scotland 30 De
Clyde Inlet, N.-W. Terr. 81 Tb
Clyde R., Scotland 30 Ee
Coahuila, state, Mexico 88 Db
Coalcoman, Mexico 88 Dd
Coamo, Puerto Rico 89 Fc
Coari, Brazil 90 Ed
Coast Mts., Brit. Columbia 80 Ff
Coast Ra., Oregon, etc. 80 Gh
Coatbridge, Scotland 30 Ee
Coatepec, Mexico 88 Ed
Coatepeque, Guatemala 88 Fe
Coatesville, Pennsylvania 86 Cc
Coaticook, Quebec 83 Jc
Coats I., N.-W. Terr. 81 Qd
Coats Ld., Antarctica 100 Bb
Coatzacoalcos, Mexico 88 Fd
Cobalt, Ontario 83 Gb
Coban, Guatemala 88 Fd
Cobar, New S. Wales 95 Jf
Cobb, Mt., New Zealand 93 Dd
Cobequid Mts., Nova Scotia 82 Fd
Cobh, Eire 31 Bj
Cobija, Bolivia 90 Df
Cobleskill, New York 83 Jd
Coboconk, Ontario 83 Gc
Cobourg, Ontario 83 Gd
Cobourg Pen., N. Terr., Australia 94 Fb
Cobre, El, Cuba 89 Dc
Coburg, Germany 48 Dc
Coburg I., N.-W. Terr. 81 Ra
Cocahacra, Peru 90 Cg
Cocamá, Peru 90 Cf
Cochabamba, Bolivia 90 Dg
Cochin, India 68 Eg
Cochin China, S. Vietnam 67 Dd
Cochinoca, Argentina 92 Cb
Cochrane, Ontario 81 Qg
Cochrane, L., Chile-Argent. 92 Bg
Cockburn, S. Aust. 95 Hf
Cockburn, Can., Chile 92 Bh
Cockburn I., Ontario 83 Ec
Coco, I. del, Pacific Ocean 99 Sg
Cocos Is., Indian Ocean 96 Hf
Cocula, Mexico 88 Dc
Cocumbi, Angola 76 Dg
Cocuy, Colombia 90 Cb
Cod, C., Massachusetts 86 Ea
Codajas, Brazil 90 Ed
Codfish I., New Zealand 93 Ag
Codó, Brazil 91 Jd
Codroy Pond, Newfoundland 82 Jb
Cod's Hd., Eire 31 Aj
Coe Hill, Ontario 83 Hc
Coen, Qnsld. 95 Hb
Cœur d'Alene, Idaho 87 Eb
Coevorden, Netherlands 44 Eb
Coeymans, New York 86 Da
Coffeyville, Kansas 84 Gd
Coff's Harbour, N.S.W. 95 Kf
Cognac, France 52 Cd
Cogolludo, Spain 50 Db
Cohoes, New York 86 Da
Coiba, I., Panama 89 Ce
Coihaique, Chile 92 Bg
Coimbatore, India 68 Ef
Coimbra, Portugal 50 Ab
Coin, Spain 50 Cd
Coire. See Chur
Cojimies, Ecuador 90 Ac
Colac, Victoria 95 Hg
Colair L., India 68 Fe
Colbeck Arch., Antarctica 100 Fc
Colcha, Bolivia 90 Dh
Colchester, England 31 Hj
Colebrook, New Hampshire 83 Lc
Coleman, Alberta 80 Jg
Colemerik. See Hakkâri
Coleraine, N. Ireland 30 Ce
Coleridge, L., New Zealand 93 Ce
Colgong, India 71 Fc
Colhué Huapi, L., Argentina 92 Cg
Colima & state, Mexico 88 Db
Colinas, Brazil 91 Je
Coll, I., Scotland 30 Cd
Collahuasi, Chile 92 Cb
Collie, W. Australia 94 Cf
Collier B., W. Australia 94 Dc
Collines-de-Normandie, France 52 Cb
Collingwood, Ontario 83 Fc
Collingwood, Queensland 95 Hd
Collinsville, Qnsld. 95 Jd
Collo, Algeria 78 Ga
Colmar, France 52 Gb
Colmars, France 53 Gd
Colmena, Argentina 92 Dc
Colmenar, Spain 50 Cd
Colmenar de Oreja, Spain 50 Db
Colmenar Viejo, Spain 50 Db
Colne R., England 31 Hj
Cologne, Germany 48 Bc
Colomb-Bechar, Algeria 78 Eb
Colombia, Brazil 91 Hh
Colombia, rep., S. America 90 Cc
Colombier, Switzerland 45 Bb
Colombo, Ceylon 68 Eg
Colon, Argentina 92 Ed
Colon, Argentina 92 Dd
Colon, Cuba 89 Cb
Colon, Panama 89 De
Colon, Venezuela 90 Cb
Colonelganj, India 71 Cb
Colonia, Uruguay 92 Ed
Colonia Alvear, Argentina 92 Cd
Colonsay I., Scotland 30 Cd
Colorado, state, U.S.A. 84 Ed
Colorado Des., California 87 Eh
Colorado Plat., Arizona 84 Dd
Colorado, R., Argentina 92 De
Colorado R., Texas 84 Gf
Colorado R., U.S.A. 84 Dd
Colorados, Arch. de los, Cuba 89 Cb
Colorado Springs, Colorado 84 Fd
Colotlan, Mexico 88 Dc
Colpoy B., Ontario 83 Fc
Colquechaca, Bolivia 90 Dg
Colton, California 87 Eh
Columbia, Indiana 83 De
Columbia, Mississippi 85 Je
Columbia, Missouri 85 Hd
Columbia, Pennsylvania 86 Bb
Columbia, S. Carolina 85 Ke
Columbia C., Canada 39 Qa
Columbia, Mt., Alberta 80 Hf
Columbia Plat., Wash., etc. 84 Cb
Columbia R., Wash., etc. 80 Gg
Columbus, Georgia 85 Ke
Columbus, Indiana 83 Df
Columbus, Mississippi 85 Je
Columbus, Nebraska 84 Gc
Columbus, Ohio 83 Ef
Colville L., N.-W. Terr. 80 Fc
Colville Ra., New Zealand 93 Eb
Colwyn Bay, Wales 31 Eg
Comacchio, & Valli di, Italy 54 Dc
Comalcalco, Mexico 88 Fd
Comana, Rumania 56 Fb
Comayagua, Honduras 89 Bd
Combarbala, Chile 92 Bd
Comblain, Belgium 44 Dd
Comeragh Mts., Eire 31 Bh
Comino C., Sardinia 55 Be
Comiso, Sicily 55 Eg
Comitan, Mexico 88 Fd
Commentry, France 52 Ec
Commissioners L., Quebec 82 Bb
Commonwealth Ra., Antarc. 100 Na
Como, Italy 54 Bc
Como, L. di, Italy 54 Bc
Comodoro Rivadavia, Argentina 92 Cg
Comondu, Mexico 88 Bb
Comores, Arch. des, Ind. Oc. 77 Jg
Comorin C., India 68 Eg
Compiègne, France 52 Eb
Comporta, Portugal 50 Ac
Compostela, Mexico 88 Dc
Conakry, Guinea 78 Cg
Conceicao do Araguaya, Braz. 91 He
Concepción, Argentina 92 Ec
Concepción, Bolivia 90 Df
Concepción, Chile 92 Be
Concepción, Paraguay 92 Eb
Concepción, Rio de la, Mex. 88 Ba
Concepción del Oro, Mex. 88 Dc
Concepción del Uruguay, Argentina 92 Ed
Conception B., Nfd. 81 Wg
Conception I., Bahama Is. 89 Db
Conception, Pt., California 84 Be
Conchas Res., New Mexico 84 Fd
Conchi, Chile 92 Cb
Concord, Massachusetts 86 Ea
Concord, New Hampshire 86 Ea
Concordia, Argentina 92 Ed
Concordia, Chile 92 Ba
Concordia, Kansas 84 Gd
Concordia, Mexico 88 Cc
Condobolin, New S. Wales 95 Jf
Condom, France 53 De
Condor, Cord. del, Peru 90 Bd
Conemaugh, Pennsylvania 86 Ab
Conesa, Argentina 92 Df
Coney I., New York 86 Db
Confolens, France 52 Dc
Congo R., Congo 76 De
Congo (French), Cent. Africa 76 Dd
Congo Rep., Cent. Africa 76 Ee
Coniston, England 31 Ef
Conn L., Eire 31 Af
Connacht, prov., Eire 31 Ag
Connecticut R., Verm., etc. 86 Da
Connecticut, state, U.S.A. 85 Mc
Connellsville, Pennsylvania 86 Ab
Connemara, Mts. of, Eire 31 Ag
Connors, New Brunswick 82 Dc
Conselheiro Lafaiete, Brazil 91 Jh
Conshohocken, Penn. 86 Cb
Constance. See Konstanz
Constance, L. See Boden See
Constancia do Baetas, Brazil 90 Ee
Constança, Rumania 56 Gb
Constantine, Algeria 78 Ga
Constitucion, Chile 92 Be
Consuegra, Spain 50 Dc
Contamana, Peru 90 Ce
Conthey, Switzerland 45 Cb
Contreras, I., Chile 92 Ah
Contwoyto L., N.-W. Terr. 80 Jc
Convención, Colombia 90 Cb
Conway, New Hampshire 83 Lc
Conway, Wales 31 Eg
Coober Pedy, S. Australia 95 Fe
Cooch Behar, India 71 Gb
Cook, B. de, Chile 92 Bj
Cook Inl., Alaska 85 Xm
Cook Is., Pacific Ocean 98 Jj
Cook, Mt., New Zealand 93 Ce
Cook Str., New Zealand 93 Ed
Cook's Passage, Queensland 95 Jb
Cookshire, Quebec 83 Lc
Cooktown, Queensland 95 Jc
Coolgardie, W. Australia 94 Df
Cooma, New South Wales 95 Jg
Coonamble, N.S.W. 95 Jf
Coondiwindi, Queensland 95 Ke
Coonor, India 68 Ef
Coopers Cr., S. Australia 95 Ge
Cooperstown, New York 86 Ca
Cooroy, Qnsld. 95 Ke
Coos Bay, Oregon 87 Ad
Cootamundra, N.S. Wales 95 Jf
Cootehill, Eire 31 Cf
Copenhagen, Denmark 47 Ej
Copetonas, Argentina 92 De
Copiapo, Chile 92 Bc
Coporaque, Peru 90 Cf
Copper Cliff, Ontario 83 Fb
Coppermine, N.-W. Terr. 80 Hc
Coppermine R., N.-W. Terr. 80 Hc
Coppet, Switzerland 45 Bb
Coquar, Quebec 83 Ja
Coquilhatville, Congo 76 Dd
Coquimbo & B. de, Chile 92 Bc
Corabia, Rumania 56 Ec
Coraçoes, Brazil 91 Hh
Corato, Italy 55 Fe
Coraigh. See Cork
Corcovado, G. del, Chile 92 Bf
Corcovado, Mt., Chile 92 Bf
Corcubión, Spain 50 Aa
Córdoba, Mexico 88 Ed
Córdoba, Spain 50 Cd
Córdoba & Sa. de, Argentina 92 Dd
Cordova, Alaska 85 Yl
Córdova, Peru 90 Cf
Corfu (Kérkira) I., Greece 57 Be
Corfu, Str. of, Greece 57 Ce
Coria, Spain 50 Bb
Corigliano Calabro, Italy 55 Ff
Coringa, India 69 Fe
Corinth (Korinthos), Greece 57 Df
Corinth, Mississippi 85 Je
Corinth, New York 86 Da
Corinto, Brazil 91 Jg
Corinto, Nicaragua 89 Bd
Coristine, Ontario 83 Gb
Cork & co., Eire 31 Bj
Cork Harb., Eire 31 Bj
Corleone, Sicily 55 Dg
Corner Brook, Nfd. 82 Jb
Corning, New York 86 Ba
Cornwall, New York 86 Cb
Cornwall, Ontario 83 Jc
Cornwall, co., England 31 Dk
Coro, Venezuela 90 Da
Coroata, Brazil 91 Jd
Corocoro, Bolivia 90 Dg
Coroico, Bolivia 90 Dg
Coromandel Ra., N. Zealand 93 Eb
Coronada, B., Costa Rica 89 Ce
Coronation G., N.-W. Terr. 80 Jc
Coronation I., Antarctica 100 Tc
Coronel, Chile 92 Be
Coronel Pringles, Argentina 92 De
Coronel Suarez, Argentina 92 De
Coronie, Surinam 91 Fb
Coropuna, Mt., Peru 90 Cg
Corozal, Brit. Honduras 89 Bc
Corpen Aike, Argentina 92 Cg
Corpus Christi, Texas 84 Gf
Corque, Bolivia 90 Dg
Corrales, Uruguay 92 Ed
Corralitos, Mexico 88 Ca
Corregidor, I., Philippines 63 Hh
Correze, dep., France 53 Dd
Corrib L., Eire 31 Ag
Corrientes, Argentina 92 Ec
Corrientes, C., Argentina 92 Ee
Corrientes, C., Mexico 88 Cc
Corrigin, W. Australia 94 Cf
Corry, Pennsylvania 86 Ab
Corse, I., France 54 Bd
Corsewall Pt., Scotland 30 De
Corsica (Corse), I., France 54 Bd
Corsicana, Texas 84 Ge
Cortes, G. de, Cuba 89 Cb
Cortessem, Belgium 44 Dd
Cortland, New York 86 Ba
Cortona, Italy 54 Dd
Coruche, Portugal 50 Ac
Coruh, R., Turkey 72 Da
Corum, Turkey 72 Ca
Corumba, Brazil 91 Fg
Corunna. See La Coruña
Corvallis, Oregon 87 Bc
Corwen, Wales 31 Eh
Corwin, Alaska 85 Wl
Cosalo, Mexico 88 Cc
Coscurita, Spain 51 Db
Coseguina, Vol., Nicaragua 89 Bd
Cosenza, Italy 55 Ff
Cosquin, Argentina 92 Dd
Cossonay, Switzerland 45 Bb
Costa Brava, Spain 51 Gb
Costa Rica, rep., Central America 89 Cd
Costermansville. See Bukavu
Cotabato, Philippines 63 Hj
Cotagaita, Bolivia 90 Dh
Cotahuasi, Peru 90 Cg
Côte-d'Or, dep., France 52 Fc
Côtes-du-Nord, dep., Fr. 52 Bb
Cotonou, Dahomey 78 Fg
Cotswold Hills, England 31 Fj
Cottbus, Germany 48 Fc
Cottica, Surinam 91 Gc
Coudersport, Pennsylvania 86 Bb
Coudres, I. aux, Quebec 83 Lb
Coulman, I., Antarctica 100 Lb
Council Bluffs, Iowa 84 Gc
Courantyne R., Guyana etc. 91 Fc
Couronne C., France 53 Fe
Courtenay, B.C. 80 Gg
Courtmacsherry, Eire 31 Bj
Courtrai, Belgium 44 Bd
Court St Etienne, Belgium 44 Cd
Couta Magalhães, Brazil 91 He
Couterne, France 52 Cb
Couthuin, Belgium 44 Dd
Couvin, Belgium 44 Cd
Covenas, Colombia 90 Bb
Coventry, England 31 Fh
Covilhã, Portugal 50 Bb
Covington, Kentucky 83 Df
Covington, Virginia 85 Ld
Cowan, L., W. Australia 94 Df
Cowdenbeath, Scotland 30 Ed
Cowell, S. Australia 95 Gf
Cowen, Mt., Montana 80 Jg
Cowes, I. of W., England 31 Gk
Cowra, New South Wales 95 Jf
Coxsackie, New York 86 Da
Cox's Bazar, E. Pakistan 69 Hd
Coyame, Mexico 88 Cb
Coyuca, Mexico 88 Dd
Cozumel, Mexico 88 Gc
Cozumel, I., Mexico 88 Gc
Cracow (Krakow), Poland 49 Hc
Craiova, Rumania 56 Db
Cranbrook, Brit. Columbia 80 Hg
Crandon, Wisconsin 83 Bc
Crans, Switzerland 45 Cb
Crater L., Oregon 87 Bd
Crater Lake Nat. Park, Oregon 87 Bd
Crateus, Brazil 91 Je
Crato, Brazil 90 Ee
Crato, Brazil 91 Ke
Crazy Mts., Montana 84 Db
Cree L., Saskatchewan 80 Ke
Cree R., Saskatchewan 80 Ke
Cremona, Italy 54 Cc
Cres, I., Yugoslavia 54 Ec
Crest, Quebec 83 Gb
Cresta, Switzerland 45 Eb
Creston, Iowa 85 Hc
Cresswell B., N.-W. Terr. 81 Nb
Crete (Kriti), Greece 57 Eg
Crete, Sea of, Greece 57 Eg
Creuse, dep., France 52 Dc
Creusot, le, France 52 Fc
Crewe, England 31 Fg
Crieff, Scotland 30 Ed
Crimea (Krym), Russia 60 Hj
Crimmitschau, Germany 48 Ec
Crisana, Rumania 56 Ca
Cristobal, Panama 89 De
CrnaGora, Yugoslavia 56 Bc
Croisic, le, France 52 Bc
Croker I., N. Terr., Aust. 94 Fb
Cromarty, Scotland 30 Ec
Cromer, England 31 Hh
Cromwell, New Zealand 93 Bf
Crooked I., Bahama Is. 89 Eb
Crooked Island Pass., Bahama Is. 89 Eb
Cross Fell, England 31 Ff
Crotone, Italy 55 Ff
Crown Prince Olav Land, Antarctica 100 Ec
Crown Princess Martha Ld., Antarctica 100 Bb
Crows Nest Pass, Alberta 80 Jg
Croydon, England 31 Gj
Croydon, Queensland 95 Hc
Crozet Is., Indian Ocean 96 Dj
Crozier, C., Antarctica 100 Lb
Cruz, Utah 87 Gf
Cruz Alta, Argentina 92 Dd
Cruz Alta, Brazil 92 Fc
Cruz del Eje, Argentina 92 Dd
Cruzeiro do Sul, Brazil 90 Ce
Cruz Grande, Chile 92 Bc
Cruz Grande, Mexico 88 Ed
Crystal Falls, Michigan 83 Bb
Cuangar, Angola 75 Bc
Cuango, Angola 76 Df
Cuanza R., Angola 76 Cf
Cuatro Cienegas, Mexico 88 Cb
Cuba, New York 83 Gd
Cuba, Portugal 50 Bc
Cuba, I., Caribbean S. 89 Cb
Cuchi, Angola 76 Dg
Cuchillo-Co, Argentina 92 De
Cuchillo Parado, Mexico 88 Cb
Cucuta, Colombia 90 Cb
Cudahy, Wisconsin 83 Cd
Cuddalore, India 68 Ef
Cuddapah, India 68 Ef
Cue, W. Australia 94 Ce
Cuéllar, Spain 50 Cb
Cuenca, Ecuador 90 Bd
Cuenca, Spain 51 Db
Cuencame, Mexico 88 Dc
Cuernavaca, Mexico 88 Ed

Fortaleza, *Brazil* 91 Kd
Fortaleza, *Terr. do Acre, Brazil* 90 De
Fort Ann, *New York* 86 Da
Fort Archambault, *Chad* 79 Jg
Fort Atkinson, *Wisconsin* 83 Bd
Fort Augustus, *Scotland* 30 Dc
Fort Beaufort, *Cape Province* 75 Df
Fort Bragg, *California* 87 Bf
Fort Chipewyan, *Alberta* 80 Je
Fort Collins, *Colorado* 84 Ec
Fort Coulonge, *Quebec* 83 Hc
Fort Crampel, *Central African Republic* 79 Jg
Fort Dauphin, *Madagascar* 77 Nm
Fort Dodge, *Iowa* 85 Hc
Fort Edward, *New York* 83 Kd
Fortescue, R., *W. Australia* 94 Cd
Fort Fairfield, *Maine* 82 Ec
Fort Fitzgerald, *Alberta* 80 Ge
Fort Flatters, *Algeria* 78 Gc
Fort Fraser, *Brit. Columbia* 80 Gf
Fort George, R., *Quebec* 81 Rf
Fort Gouraud, *Mauritania* 78 Cd
Fort Grahame, *B.C.* 80 Ge
Forth, Firth of, *Scotland* 30 Fd
Forth R., *Scotland* 30 Ed
Fort Henrique, *South-West Africa* 75 Ac
Fort Hertz, *Burma* 69 Jf
Fort Howard, *Wisconsin* 83 Bc
Fort Hunter, *New York* 86 Ca
Fortin Avalos Sanchez, *Paraguay* 92 Eb
Fortin General Diaz, *Paraguay* 92 Db
Fortin Teniente Montania, *Paraguay* 92 Db
Fortin Lopez, *Paraguay* 92 Db
Fort Jameson, *Zambia* 77 Gg
Fort Johnston, *Malawi* 77 Hg
Fort Kent, *Maine* 82 Dc
Fort Lallemand, *Algeria* 78 Gb
Fort Lamy, *Chad* 79 Jf
Fort Laperrine. See Tamanrasset
Fort Laramie, *Wyoming* 84 Fc
Fort McKenzie, *Quebec* 81 Te
Fort Madison, *Iowa* 85 Hc
Fort Morgan, *Colorado* 84 Fc
Fort Munro, *W. Pakistan* 70 Af
Fort Nelson & R., *B.C.* 80 Ge
Fort Peck Res., *Montana* 84 Eb
Fort Plain, *New York* 86 Ca
Fort Polignac, *Algeria* 78 Gg
Fort Portal, *Uganda* 77 Gd
Fortrose, *Scotland* 30 Ec
Fort Saint, *Algeria* 79 Gb
Fort St George. See Madras
Fort St John, *B.C.* 80 Ge
Fort Sandeman, *W. Pakistan* 70 Ae
Fort Saskatchewan, *Alberta* 80 Jf
Fort Scott, *Kansas* 85 Hd
Fort Sibut, *Cent. Afr. Rep.* 79 Jg
Fort Smith, *Arkansas* 85 Hd
Fort Smith, *N.-W. Terr.* 80 Jd
Fortuna, *California* 87 Ae
Fortuna, *Spain* 51 Ec
Fortune B., *Newfoundland* 82 Lc
Fort Vermilion, *Alberta* 80 He
Fort Victoria, *Rhodesia* 75 Ed
Fort Wayne, *Indiana* 83 De
Fort White, *Burma* 69 Hd
Fort William, *Ontario* 81 Pg
Fort William, *Scotland* 30 Dd
Fort Worth, *Texas* 84 Ge
Fort Yukon, *Alaska* 85 Yl
Forville, *Belgium* 44 Cd
Fosse, *Belgium* 44 Cd
Foster Ls., *Saskatchewan* 80 Ke
Fougères, *France* 52 Cb
Foul B., *Egypt* 79 Nd
Foul, I., *Burma* 69 He
Foula, I., *Scotland* 30 Ha
Foulness I., *England* 31 Hj
Fouly, la, *Switzerland* 45 Cc
Foúrnoi, Is., *Greece* 57 Ff
Foveaux Strait, *New Zealand* 93 Ag
Fowchow. See Fowling
Fowlers B., *S. Australia* 94 Ff
Fowling, *China* 65 Ch
Fowning, *China* 64 Jf
Fowyang, *China* 64 Gf
Fox Is., *Aleutian Is.* 85 Wm
Fox R., *Manitoba* 80 Ne
Foxe Basin, *N.-W Terr.* 81 Rc
Foxe Chan., *N.-W. Terr.* 81 Qc
Foxe Pen., *N.-W. Terr.* 81 Rd
Foxton, *New Zealand* 93 Ed
Foyle L., *N. Ireland* 30 Ce
Foynes, *Eire* 31 Ah
Foz do Aripuana, *Brazil* 90 Ee
Foz do Cunene, *Angola* 75 Ac
Foz Embira, *Brazil* 90 Ce
Foz do Jordão, *Brazil* 90 Ce
Foz do Jutai, *Brazil* 90 Dd
Foz do Pauini, *Brazil* 90 De
Fraire, *Belgium* 44 Cd
Framboise, *Nova Scotia* 82 Hd
Frameries, *Belgium* 44 Bd
Framingham, *Massachusetts* 86 Ea
Franca, *Brazil* 91 Hh
Francavilla Fontana, *Italy* 55 Fe
France, *W. Europe* 43 Hg
Frances L., *Yukon* 80 Fd
Franceville, *Gabon* 76 Ce
Franche-Comte, prov., *Fr.* 52 Gc
Francistown, *Botswana* 75 Dd
Francois L., *Brit. Columbia* 80 Ff
Frankfort, *Kentucky* 85 Kd
Frankfort, *Michigan* 83 Cc
Frankfurt-am-Main, *Ger.* 48 Cc
Frankfurt-an-der-Oder, *Ger.* 48 Fb
Fränkischer Jura, *Germany* 48 Dd
Franklin, *New Hampshire* 86 Ea
Franklin, *New Jersey* 86 Cb
Franklin, *Pennsylvania* 86 Ab
Franklin, *Tasmania* 95 Jh
Franklin Dist., *N.-W. Terr.* 80 Jb
Franklin, I., *Antarctica* 100 Lb
Franklin Mts., *North-West Territories* 80 Gd
Franklin Falls, *N.H.* 82 Ce
Frantsa Iosifa, Zemlya, *Arctic Ocean* 58 Da
Franz Josef Fd., *Greenland* 39 Nb
Franz Josef Land. See Frantsa Iosifa, Zemlya
Fraser R., *British Columbia* 80 Gf
Fraserburg, *Cape Province* 75 Cf
Fraserburgh, *Scotland* 30 Fc
Frasertown, *New Zealand* 93 Fc
Frasnes, *Belgium* 44 Bd
Frater, *Ontario* 83 Db
Frauenfeld, *Switzerland* 45 Da
Fray Bentos, *Uruguay* 92 Ed
Fredericia, *Denmark* 47 Cj
Frederick, *Maryland* 86 Bc
Fredericton, *New Brunswick* 82 Ed
Frederik Hendrik, I., *New Guinea* 63 Lm
Frederikshaab, *Greenland* 39 Pc
Frederikshavn, *Denmark* 47 Dh
Fredonia, *Colombia* 90 Bb
Fredonia, *New York* 86 Aa
Fredrika, *Sweden* 46 Hd
Fredrikstad, *Norway* 47 Dg
Freehold, *New Jersey* 86 Cb
Freeport, *Illinois* 83 Bd
Freeport, *Pennsylvania* 86 Ab
Freetown, *Sierra Leone* 78 Cg
Fregenal de la Sierra, *Spain* 50 Bc
Fréhel C., *France* 52 Bb
Freiberg, *Germany* 48 Ec
Freiburg, *Germany* 84 Bd
Freirina, *Chile* 92 Bc
Freistadt, *Austria* 48 Fd
Freital, *Germany* 48 Ec
Freixiel, *Portugal* 50 Bb
Freixo, *Portugal* 50 Bb
Fremantle, *W. Australia* 94 Cf
Fremont, *Nebraska* 84 Gc
Fremont, *Ohio* 83 Ee
Fremont Pk., *Wyoming* 84 Dc
Fremont Mts., *Oregon* 87 Cd
Fremont R., *Utah* 84 Dd
French R., *Ontario* 83 Fb
French Guiana, rep., *S. America* 91 Gc
Frenchman R., *Saskatchewan* 80 Kg
French River, *Ontario* 83 Fc
French Somaliland, *E. Afr.* 77 Jb
Fresco, *Ivory Coast* 78 Dg
Fresnillo, *Mexico* 88 Dc
Fresno, *California* 87 Dg
Frewena, *N.T., Aust.* 95 Gc
Frias, *Spain* 50 Da
Fribourg & canton, *Switz.* 45 Cb
Fridtjof Nansen Mt., *Antarc.* 100 La
Friedland, *Germany* 48 Eb
Friesische Is., Nord, *Ger.* 47 Cj
Friesische Is., Ost., *Germany* 48 Ab
Friesland, prov., *Netherland* 44 Da
Frio C., *S.-W. Africa* 75 Ac
Friuli-Venezia Giulia, reg., *Italy* 54 Db
Frobisher B., *N.-W. Terr.* 81 Td
Frobisher L., *Saskatchewan* 80 Ke
Frohavet, *Norway* 46 Ce
Frome, *England* 31 Fj
Frome, L., *S. Australia* 95 Hf
Fronteira, *Portugal* 50 Bc
Frontera, *Mexico* 88 Fd
Fronteras, *Mexico* 88 Ca
Front Royal, *Virginia* 86 Ac
Frosinone, *Italy* 55 De
Frostburg, *Maryland* 86 Ac
Fröya, *Norway* 46 Ce
Frozen Str., *N.-W. Terr.* 81 Qc
Frunze, *Kirgiz* 58 Gd
Frutigen, *Switzerland* 45 Cb
Frutuoso, *Brazil* 90 Ef
Frývaldov, *Czechoslovakia* 49 Gc
Fthiótis, *Greece* 57 De
Fuchin, *China* 62 Ka
Fu-chou. See Foochow
Fuchow. See Linchwan
Fu-chow, *China* 64 Kc
Fuente-Alamo de Murcia, *Sp.* 51 Ed
Fuente del Arco, *Spain* 50 Cc
Fuentes de Onoro, *Spain* 50 Bb
Fuertaventura I., *Canary Is.* 78 Cc
Fuerte, El, *Mexico* 88 Cb
Fuerte, R., *Mexico* 88 Cb
Fuji yama (Fuji san), *Japan* 66 Fg
Fukien, prov., *China* 65 Hj
Fuki Kaku, *Taiwan* 62 He
Fukui, *Japan* 66 Ef
Fukuoka, *Japan* 66 Bh
Fukushima, *Japan* 66 Gf
Fukuyama, *Japan* 66 Gd
Fukuyama, *Japan* 66 Cg
Fulda, R., *Germany* 48 Cc
Fulton, *New York* 86 Ba
Fulton Chain Ls., *New York* 86 Ca
Funchal, *Madeira I.* 78 Bb
Fundão, *Portugal* 50 Bb
Fundy, B. of, *N.S., N.B.* 82 Fd
Fünen. See Fyn
Fünfkurchen. See Pécs
Funing. See Siapu
Fure, *Japan* 66 Gb
Furg, *Persia* 73 Gd
Furneaux Grp., *Tasmania* 95 Jh
Furnes. See Veurne
Furqlus, *Syria* 74 Fc
Fürth, *Germany* 48 Dd
Furue. See Kanoya
Fusagasuga, *Colombia* 90 Cc
Fushih, *China* 64 Dd
Fushimi, *Japan* 66 Dg
Fu-shun, *China* 64 Lb
Fusin, *China* 64 Ka
Fusio, *Switzerland* 45 Db
Fuwa, *S. Yemen* 72 Eg
Fuyu, *China* 62 Ha
Fyn, *Denmark* 47 Dj
Fyne L., *Scotland* 30 Dd
Fyzabad. See Faizabad
Gaberones, *Botswana* 75 Dd
Gabès, & G. of, *Tunisia* 79 Hb
Gabin, *Poland* 49 Hb
Gabon, *Central Africa* 76 Ce
Gabrovo, *Bulgaria* 56 Ec
Gach Saran, *Persia* 73 Fc
Gadag, *India* 68 Ee
Gadsden, *Alabama* 85 Je
Gael Hamkes B., *Greenland* 39 Mb
Gaeşti, *Rumania* 56 Eb
Gaeta & G. di, *Italy* 55 Dd
Gafsa, *Tunisia* 79 Gb
Gagetown, *New Brunswick* 82 Ed
Gaibanda, *E. Pakistan* 71 Gc
Gaillac, *France* 53 De
Gaiman, *Argentina* 92 Cf
Gainseville, *Florida* 85 Kf
Gainsborough, *England* 31 Gg
Gairdner, L., *S. Australia* 95 Gf
Gairloch, *Scotland* 30 Dc
Galag. See Kalak
Galangue, *Angola* 76 Dg
Galapagos Is., *Pacific Ocean* 99 Rg
Galashiels, *Scotland* 30 Fe
Galatea, *New Zealand* 93 Fc
Galathea B., *Nicobar Is.* 69 Hg
Galati, *Rumania* 56 Gb
Galatz. See Galati
Galcaio, *Somalia* 77 Kc
Galch Dar, *Persia* 73 Fd
Galdhöpiggen, Mt., *Norway* 47 Cf
Galeana, *Mexico* 88 Ca
Galeana, *Mexico* 88 Ec
Galena, *Illinois* 83 Ad
Galesburg, *Illinois* 83 Ae
Galeton, *Pennsylvania* 86 Bb
Galich, *Russia* 61 Fa
Galilee, L., *Queensland* 95 Jd
Galilee, Sea of. See Tiberias L.
Galle, *Ceylon* 68 Fg
Gallegos R., *Argentina* 92 Bh
Gallipoli. See Gelibolu
Gallipoli, *Italy* 55 Fe
Gällivare, *Sweden* 46 Jc
Galloway, Mull of, *Scotland* 31 Df
Galt, *Ontario* 83 Fd
Galtee Mts., *Eire* 31 Bh
Galva, *Ilinois* 83 Ae
Galveston, *Texas* 85 Hf
Galvez, *Argentina* 92 Dd
Galway (Gaillimh), *Eire* 31 Ag
Galway B., *Eire* 31 Ag
Gambaga, *Ghana* 78 Ef
Gambia, The & R., *N.-W. Africa* 78 Bf
Gambo, *Newfoundland* 82 Lb
Gams, *Switzerland* 45 Ea
Gananoque, *Ontario* 83 Hc
Gand, *Belgium* 44 Bc
Gandak R., *India* 71 Eb
Gandava, *W. Pakistan* 68 Cc
Gander (Airport) & L., *Nfd.* 82 Lb
Gandesa, *Spain* 51 Fb
Gandía, *Spain* 51 Ec
Ganga. See Ganges
Ganganagar, *India* 70 Cf
Gangaw, *Burma* 69 Hd
Ganges (Ganga), R., *India* 71 Ec
Gangoh, *India* 70 Ef
Gangtok, *India* 71 Gb
Ganjam, *India* 69 Ge
Gannat, *France* 52 Ec
Gannett Pk., *Wyoming* 84 Dc
Gantheaume B., *W. Australia* 94 Be
Gao, *Mali* 78 Ee
Gaoual, *Guinea* 78 Cf
Gara L., *Eire* 32 Gf
Garachine, *Panama* 89 De
Garanhuns, *Brazil* 91 Ke
Garba Tula, *Kenya* 77 Hd
Gard, dep., *France* 53 Fd
Garda, L. di., *Italy* 54 Cc
Gardafui, C., *Somalia* 77 Lb
Garden, *Michigan* 83 Cc
Gardiner, *Maine* 82 Dd
Gardiner, *Oregon* 87 Ad
Gardiners, B. & I., *New York* 86 Db
Gardner I., *Hawaiian Is.* 98 Je
Gardò, *Somalia* 77 Kc
Gardula, *Ethiopia* 77 Hc
Gar Gunsa, *Tibet* 68 Fb
Garha, *India* 71 Bc
Garhmuktesar, *India* 70 Ff
Garhshankar, *India* 70 Ee
Garibaldi, *Brazil* 92 Fc
Garibaldi Park, *B.C.* 80 Gf
Garies, *Cape Province* 75 Bf
Garissa, *Kenya* 77 He
Garm, *Tadzhikskaya rep.* 58 Ge
Garmsar, *Persia* 73 Fb
Garo Hills, *India* 69 Hc
Garonne, R., *France* 53 De
Garoua, *Cameroon* 79 Hg
Garraway, *Liberia* 78 Dh
Garrison Res., *N. Dakota* 84 Fb
Garrovillas, *Spain* 50 Bc
Garry, L., *N.-W. Territories* 80 Mc
Garsen, *Kenya* 77 Je
Gartok, *Tibet* 68 Fb
Gary, *Indiana* 83 Ce
Garza, *Argentina* 92 Dc
Garzon, *Colombia* 90 Bc
Gasan Kuli, *Turkmenistan* 58 Ee
Gascogne, G. de, *Fr.-Sp.* 53 Be
Gascogne, prov., *France* 53 De
Gascoyne, R., *W. Australia* 94 Ce
Gasherbrum, Mt., *Kashmir* 70 Ec
Gasht, *Persia* 73 Hd
Gaspé, *Quebec* 82 Fb
Gaspé B. & C., *Quebec* 82 Fb
Gaspé Pen., *Quebec* 82 Fb
Gaspésia Park, *Quebec* 82 Eb
Gasselte, *Netherlands* 44 Eb
Gastonia, *N. Carolina* 85 Kd
Gastre, *Argentina* 92 Cf
Gat (Ghat), *Libya* 79 Hd
Gata, *Spain* 50 Bb
Gata, C., *Cyprus* 74 Bc
Gateshead, *England* 30 Ff
Gatineau R., *Quebec* 83 Jb
Gatooma, *Rhodesia* 75 Dc
Gatun L., *Panama* 89 Ce
Gaud-i-Zirreh, *Afghanistan* 73 Hd
Gauhati, *India* 69 Hc
Gaurihar, *India* 71 Cc
Gavbandi, *Persia* 73 Fd
Gavdhos, I., *Crete* 57 Eg
Gavião, *Portugal* 50 Bc
Gäv Koshi, *Persia* 73 Gd
Gävle, *Sweden* 47 Gf
Gävlebukten, *Sweden* 47 Gf
Gavur D., *Turkey* 72 Cb
Gawler Ra., *S. Australia* 95 Gf
Gaya, *India* 71 Ec
Gaya, *Niger* 78 Ff
Gayaza, *Uganda* 77 Ge
Gaylord, *Michigan* 83 Dc
Gaza, *Cent. Afr. Rep.* 79 Jh
Gaza, *Egypt* 74 Cf
Gazi Antep, *Turkey* 72 Cb
Gazik, *Persia* 73 Hc
Gdansk, *Poland* 49 Ha
Gdynia, *Poland* 49 Ha
Gebeit, *Sudan* 79 Ne
Gedaref, *Sudan* 79 Nf
Gedinne, *Belgium* 44 Ce
Geel, *Belgium* 44 Cc
Geelong, *Victoria* 95 Hg
Geelvink B., *W. Irian* 63 Ll
Geeraardsbergen. See Grammont
Geikie R., *Saskatchewan* 80 Le
Gela, *Sicily* 55 Eg
Gelderland, *Netherlands* 44 Db
Geldrop, *Netherlands* 44 Dc
Gelib, *Somalia* 77 Jd
Gelibolu, *Turkey* 72 Aa
Gelinden, *Belgium* 44 Dd
Gelsenkirchen, *Germany* 48 Bc
Gemas, *W. Malaysia* 67 Cf
Gembloux, *Belgium* 44 Cd
Gemena, *Congo* 76 Dd
Gemert, *Netherlands* 44 Dc
Gemmenich, *Belgium* 44 Dd
Gemmi Pass, *Switzerland* 45 Cb
Genappe, *Belgium* 44 Cd
Gendringen, *Netherlands* 44 Ec
Geneina, *Sudan* 79 Kf
Genemuiden, *Netherlands* 44 Eb
General Acha, *Argentina* 92 De
General Alvarado, *Arg.* 92 Ee
General Alvear, *Argentina* 92 De
General Capdevila, *Argent.* 92 Dc
General Carneiro, *Brazil* 91 Gg
General Guido, *Argentina* 92 Ee
General José de San Martin, *Argentina* 92 Ec
General La Madrid, *Argent.* 92 De
General Lavalle, *Argentina* 92 Ee
General Madariaga, *Argent.* 92 Ee
General Pico, *Argentina* 92 De
General Pinto, *Argentina* 92 Dd
General Roca, *Argentina* 92 Ce
General Viamonte, *Argent.* 92 De
General Villegas, *Argentina* 92 De
Geneseo, *New York* 86 Ba
Geneva, *New York* 86 Ba
Geneva, L. of. See Léman, Lac
Génève (Geneva), *Switz.* 45 Bb
Genkai Nada, *Japan* 66 Ah
Gennargentu, Mte. del, *Sard.* 55 Be
Gennep, *Netherlands* 44 Dc
Genoa. See Genova
Genova, *Italy* 54 Bc
Genova, G. di, *Italy* 54 Bc
Gent. See Gand
Geographe B., *W. Australia* 94 Cf
Geographe Chan., *W. Aust.* 94 Bd
Georga Zemlya, *Arctic Oc.* 58 Da
George L., *New York* 86 Da
George L., *New S. Wales* 95 Jg
George R., *Quebec* 81 Te
Georgetown, *Guyana* 90 Fb
Georgetown, *Delaware* 83 Jf
Georgetown, *Virginia* 86 Bc
George Town, *Gr. Cayman, West Indies* 89 Cc
George Town, *Penang I., W. Malaysia* 67 Ce
Georgetown, *Pr. Edward I.* 82 Gc
Georgetown, *Qnsld.* 95 Hc
Georgia, rep. See Gruzinskaya rep.
Georgia, state, *U.S.A.* 85 Ke
Georgian B., *Ontario* 83 Fc
Georgian B. Is. Nat. Pk., *Ont.* 83 Fc
Georgiyevsk, *Russia* 58 Dd
Georgina, R., *Queensland* 95 Gd
Gera, *Germany* 48 Ec
Geraardsbergen, *Belgium* 44 Bd
Geraldine, *New Zealand* 93 Cf
Geraldton, *Ont.* 81 Pg
Geraldton, *W. Australia* 94 Be
Gérgal, *Spain* 51 Dd
Gerlach, *Nevada* 87 De
Germania, *Argentina* 92 Dd
Germany, *Central Europe* 42 Kf
Gerona, *Spain* 51 Ga
Gers, dep., *France* 53 De
Gerze, *Turkey* 72 Ca
Getafe, *Spain* 50 Db
Gethsemani, *Quebec* 82 Ha
Gettysburg, *Pennsylvania* 86 Bc
Gevar. See Yuksekova
Gevgelija, *Yugoslavia* 56 Dd
Ghabaghib, *Syria* 74 Ed
Ghadames, *Libya* 79 Gb
Ghaghara, R., *India* 71 Db
Ghaida, *S. Yemen* 72 Eg
Ghail, *Arabia* 72 Ee
Ghana (Gold Coast), *W. Afr.* 78 Eg
Ghantur, *Syria* 74 Fc
Gharandal, *Jordan* 74 Dg
Ghardaia, *Algeria* 78 Fb
Gharian, *Libya* 79 Hb
Ghat, *Arabia* 72 Ed
Ghatal, *India* 71 Fd
Ghatampur, *India* 71 Cb
Ghatghat, *Arabia* 72 Ee
Ghats, Eastern, *India* 68 Fe
Ghats, Western, *India* 68 De
Ghauta, *Arabia* 72 Ee
Ghaziabad, *India* 70 Ef
Ghazipur, *India* 71 Dc
Ghazir, *Lebanon* 74 Dc
Ghazni, *Afghanistan* 73 Jc
Ghazouet, *Algeria* 78 Ea
Gheorgheni, *Rumania* 56 Ea
Ghislenghien, *Belgium* 44 Bd
Ghizao, *Afghanistan* 73 Jc
Ghorak, *Afghanistan* 73 Jc
Ghorian, *Afghanistan* 73 Hc
Ghotki, *W. Pakistan* 68 Cc
Ghubreh, *Muscat & Oman* 73 Ge
Giaour Dagh. See Gavur D.
Giarre, *Sicily* 55 Eg
Gibara, *Cuba* 89 Db
Gibeon, *S.-W. Africa* 75 Be
Gibraltar, *Spain* 50 Cd
Gibraltar, Str. of, *Spain* 50 Ce
Gibson Desert, *W. Aust.* 94 Dd
Gien, *France* 52 Ec
Giessen, *Germany* 48 Cc
Gifhorn, *Germany* 48 Db
Gifu, *Japan* 66 Eg
Giganta, La, *Mexico* 88 Bb
Gijón, *Spain* 50 Ca
Gila Des., *Arizona* 84 De
Gila R., *Arizona* 84 De
Gilau, *Rumania* 56 Da
Gilbert Is., *Pacific Ocean* 98 Gh
Gilbert, R., *Queensland* 95 Hc
Gilberton, *Qnsld.* 95 Hc
Gilbués, *Brazil* 91 Je
Gilgit & R., *Kashmir* 70 Dc
Gimel, *Switzerland* 45 Bb
Ginir, *Ethiopia* 77 Jc
Ginzo, *Spain* 50 Ba
Gioia, G. di, *Italy* 55 Ef
Giornico, *Switzerland* 45 Db
Girardot, *Colombia* 90 Cc
Girdle Ness, *Scotland* 34 Me
Giresun, *Turkey* 72 Ca
Girga, *Egypt* 79 Mc
Giridih, *India* 71 Fc
Girishk, *Afghanistan* 73 Hc
Gironde, dep., *France* 53 Cd
Gironde, R., *France* 52 Cd
Girvan & R., *Scotland* 35 Gj
Gisborne, *New Zealand* 93 Gc
Gisenyi, *Rwanda* 77 Fe
Gisors, *France* 52 Db
Giswil, *Switzerland* 45 Db
Gitch, Mt., *Ethiopia* 77 Hb
Giurgiu, *Rumania* 56 Ec
Givry, *Belgium* 44 Cd
Gizhiga, *Russia* 59 Rb
Giżycko, *Poland* 49 Ja
Gjirokastër, *Albania* 57 Cd
Gjoa Haven, *N.-W. Terr.* 80 Mc
Gjövik, *Norway* 47 Df
Glabbeek, *Belgium* 44 Cd
Glace Bay, *Nova Scotia* 82 Jc
Glacier, *British Columbia* 80 Hf
Gladstone, *Michigan* 83 Cc
Gladstone, *Queensland* 95 Kd
Gladwin, *Michigan* 83 Dd
Glamoc, *Yugoslavia* 54 Fc
Glamorgan, *Wales* 31 Ej
Glärnisch, Mt., *Switzerland* 45 Db
Glarus & canton, *Switz.* 45 Ea
Glasgow, *Kentucky* 85 Jd
Glasgow, *Scotland* 30 Ee
Glassboro, *New Jersey* 86 Cc
Glauchau, *Germany* 48 Ec
Glazov, *Russia* 61 La
Glen, *New Hampshire* 83 Lc
Glen Affric, *Scotland* 30 Dc
Glen Afton, *N.Z.* 93 Eb
Glendale, *California* 87 Dh
Glendive, *Montana* 84 Fb
Glen Garry, *Scotland* 30 Ed
Glenhope, *New Zealand* 93 Dd
Glen Innes, *New S. Wales* 95 Ke
Glen Falls, *New York* 83 Kd
Glenties, *Eire* 31 Bf
Glenville, *West Virginia* 83 Ff
Gletsch, *Switzerland* 45 Db
Glittertind, Mt., *Norway* 47 Cf
Gliwice, *Poland* 49 Hc
Globe, *Arizona* 84 De
Glogau. See Głogów
Głogów, *Poland* 49 Gc
Gloppen, *Norway* 46 Bf
Gloria, *Brazil* 91 Ke
Gloucester, *Massachusetts* 86 Ea
Gloucester, *New Jersey* 86 Cc
Gloucester & co., *England* 31 Fj
Gloversville, *New York* 86 Ca
Glukhov, *Ukraine* 60 Hf
Gmünd, *Austria* 48 Ee
Gmünd, *Germany* 48 Cd
Gmunden, *Austria* 48 Ee
Gniezno, *Poland* 49 Gb
Goa, *India* 68 De
Goalpara, *India* 69 Hc
Goalundo, *E. Pakistan* 71 Gd
Gobabis, *S.-W. Africa* 75 Bd
Gobi, The, *E. Asia* 59 Kd
Gobindpur, *India* 71 Fd
Godavari, R., *India* 68 Ee
Godda, *India* 71 Fc
Godech, *Bulgaria* 56 Dc
Goderich, *Ontario* 83 Fd
Godhra, *India* 68 Dd
Gods L., *Manitoba* 80 Mf
Gods R., *Manitoba* 81 Ne
Godthaab, *Greenland* 39 Pc
Goes, *Netherlands* 44 Bc
Goesi, *W. Irian* 63 Kl
Gogama, *Ontario* 83 Fb
Gog Magog Hills, *England* 31 Hh
Gogra R., *India* 71 Db
Gogrial, *Sudan* 79 Lg
Gohana, *India* 70 Ef
Goiânia, *Brazil* 91 Hg
Goias, *Brazil* 91 Hf
Gökçeağac, *Turkey* 72 Ba
Goksun, *Turkey* 72 Cb
Golaghat, *India* 69 Hc
Gol'chikha, *Russia* 58 Ha
Golconda, *India* 68 Ee
Goldap, *Poland* 49 Ka
Golden B., *New Zealand* 93 Dd
Golden Lake, *Ontario* 83 Hc
Goldfield, *Nevada* 87 Eg
Goleniow, *Poland* 48 Fb
Golmo, *China* 62 Cc
Goltva, *Ukraine* 60 Hg
Gomal Pass, *W. Pakistan* 70 Bd
Gombe, *Nigeria* 79 Hf
Gomel', *White Russia* 60 Ge
Gomera, I., *Canary Is.* 78 Bc
Gómez Farias, *Mexico* 88 Dc
Gómez Palacio, *Mexico* 88 Db
Gonaïves, *Haiti* 89 Ec
Gonave, I. de la, *Haiti* 89 Ec
Gonbad-e-Kavus, *Persia* 73 Gb
Gonda, *India* 71 Db
Gondal, *India* 68 Dd
Gondo, *Switzerland* 45 Db
Gönen, *Turkey* 57 Fd
Gongka Ling, *China* 62 De
Goniądz, *Poland* 49 Kb
Goodenough I., *New Guinea* 95 Ka
Gooderham, *Ontario* 83 Gc
Good Hope, *N.-W. Terr.* 80 Fc
Good Hope, C. of, *Cape Prov.* 75 Bf
Goodland, *Kansas* 84 Fd
Goodrich, *Wisconsin* 83 Ac
Goole, *England* 31 Gg
Goomalling, *W. Australia* 94 Cf
Goor, *Netherlands* 44 Eb
Goorle, *Netherlands* 44 Dc
Goose L., *Oregon-California* 87 Ce
Goose Bay, *Labrador* 81 Uf
Gopalpur, *India* 69 Fe
Göppingen, *Germany* 48 Cd
Gor, *Spain* 50 Dd
Gora, *China* 62 Ce
Gorakhpur, *India* 71 Db
Gordola, *Switzerland* 45 Db
Gordonvale, *Qnsld.* 95 Jc
Gore, *Ethiopia* 77 Hc
Goré, *Chad* 79 Jg
Gore, *New Zealand* 93 Bg
Gore Bay, *Ontario* 83 Ec
Gorey, *Eire* 31 Ch
Gorgan, *Persia* 73 Fb
Gorgona, I., *Italy* 54 Bd
Gorinchem, *Netherlands* 44 Cc
Gorizia, *Italy* 54 Dc
Gor'kiy, *Russia* 61 Gb
Gorlice, *Poland* 49 Jd
Görlitz, *Germany* 48 Fc
Gorlovka, *Ukraine* 60 Lg
Gorodetz, *Russia* 61 Fb
Gorodishche, *Russia* 61 Gd
Gorodnitsa, *Ukraine* 60 Ef
Gorontalo, *Celebes* 63 Hk
Gorrahei, *Ethiopia* 77 Jc
Gorsel, *Netherlands* 44 Eb
Gorzów (Wielkopolski), *Poland* 48 Fb
Gosainthan, Mt., *Nepal-Tibet* 69 Gc
Göschenen, *Switzerland* 45 Db
Goshanak, *W. Pakistan* 68 Bc
Goshen, *New York* 86 Cb
Gospić, *Yugoslavia* 54 Ec
Gosport, *England* 31 Gk
Gossau, *Switzerland* 45 Ea
Gosselies, *Belgium* 44 Cd
Gossen, *Norway* 46 Be
Gostivar, *Yugoslavia* 56 Cd
Göta Älv, *Sweden* 47 Eg
Göteborg, *Sweden* 47 Dh
Gotha, *Germany* 48 Dc
Gothenburg. See Göteborg
Gotland, I., *Sweden* 47 Hh
Goto Retto, *Japan* 66 Ah
Gotska Sandön, *Sweden* 47 Hg
Göttingen, *Germany* 48 Cc
Gottwaldov, *Czechoslovakia* 49 Gd
Gouda, *Netherlands* 44 Cb
Goudswaard, *Netherlands* 44 Cc
Gough I., *Atlantic Ocean* 97 Kn
Gouin Res., *Quebec* 82 Ab
Goulburn, *New South Wales* 95 Jf
Goundam, *Mali* 78 Ee
Gouré, *Niger* 79 Hf
Gournay, *France* 52 Db
Gouverneur, *New York* 83 Jc
Gowanda, *New York* 83 Gd
Gowna L., *Eire* 31 Bg
Goya, *Argentina* 92 Ec
Gozo, I., *Malta* 55 Eg
Graaff Reinet, *Cape Province* 75 Cf
Grabow, *Poland* 49 Hc
Gračac, *Yugoslavia* 54 Ec
Gracefield, *Quebec* 83 Hb
Gracias, *Honduras* 89 Bd
Gracias a Dios, *Nicaragua* 89 Cd
Gradets, *Bulgaria* 56 Fc
Grado, *Spain* 50 Ba
Grafton, *New South Wales* 95 Ke
Grafton, *W. Virginia* 83 Ff
Grafton, Is., *Chile* 92 Bh
Graham Ld., *Antarctica* 100 Sc
Graham Bell, Os., *Arctic Oc.* 58 Fa
Grahamstown, *Cape Province* 75 Df
Grajewo, *Poland* 49 Kb
Grammont, *Belgium* 44 Be
Grampian Mts., *Scotland* 30 Dd
Gramsbergen, *Netherlands* 44 Eb
Granada, *Nicaragua* 89 Bd
Granada, *Spain* 50 Dd
Granby, *Quebec* 83 Kc
Gran Canaria, I., *Canary Is.* 78 Bc
Gran Chaco, *Argentina* 92 Dc
Grand Can., *China* 62 Gc
Grand I., *Michigan* 83 Cb
Grand I., *New York* 86 Aa
Grand L., *Maine-N.B.* 82 Dd
Grand L., *New Brunswick* 82 Fd
Grand L., *Newfoundland* 82 Kb
Grand R., *Michigan* 83 Dd
Grand R., *S. Dakota* 84 Fb
Grand Bassa. See Buchanan
Grand Bassam, *Ivory Coast* 78 Eg
Grand Canyon, *Arizona* 84 Dd
Grand Canyon Nat. Park, *Arizona* 84 Dd
Grand Cayman, I., *W.I.* 89 Cc
Grand Coulee Dam, *Wash.* 84 Cb
Grande, B., *Argentina* 92 Ch
Grande, Rio, *Brazil* 91 Gg
Grande, Sa. See Sa da Ibiapaba
Grande Anse, *N.B.* 82 Fc
Grande Comore, I., *Comores, Archipel des* 77 Jg
Grande de Santiago, R., *Me.* 88 Dc
Grand Falls, *Labrador* 81 Uf
Grand Falls, *N.B.* 82 Ec
Grand Falls, *Newfoundland* 82 Lb
Grand Forks, *B.C.* 80 Hg
Grand Forks, *N. Dakota* 84 Gb
Grand Haven, *Michigan* 83 Cd
Grandin, L., *N.-W. Terr.* 80 Hd
Grand Island, *Nebraska* 84 Gc
Grand Junction, *Colorado* 84 Ed
Grand Lahou, *Ivory Coast* 78 Dg
Grand Ledge, *Michigan* 83 Dd
Grand Manan I., *N.B.* 82 Ed
Grand Marais, *Minnesota* 83 Ab
Grand Mère, *Quebec* 83 Kb
Grandola, *Portugal* 50 Ac
Grand Piles, *Quebec* 83 Kb
Grand Prairie, *Alberta* 80 He
Grand Rapids, *Michigan* 83 Dd
Grandrieu, *Belgium* 44 Cd
Grand River, *Quebec* 82 Fb
Grandson, *Switzerland* 45 Bb
Grand Teton Mt. & Nat. Park, *Wyoming* 84 Dc
Grane, *Norway* 46 Ed
Granity, *New Zealand* 93 Cd
Granja, *Brazil* 91 Jd
Grankulla, *Finland* 47 Lf
Granollers, *Spain* 51 Gb
Granön, *Sweden* 46 Hd
Grant, *Ontario* 81 Pf
Grant Ld., *Arctic Ocean* 39 Qa
Grant Ra., *Nevada* 87 Ff
Grantham, *England* 31 Gh
Grantown-on-Spey, *Scotland* 30 Ec
Grants Pass, *Oregon* 87 Bd
Granville, *New York* 86 Da
Granville L., *Manitoba* 80 Le
Gras, L. de, *N.-W. Terr.* 80 Jd
Graskop, *Transvaal* 75 Ed
Gräsö, *Sweden* 47 Hf
Grassano, *Italy* 55 Fe
Grasse, *France* 53 Ge
Grassett, *Ontario* 83 Da
Grassier, *Switzerland* 45 Bb
Graubünden, canton, *Switz.* 45 Eb
Graus, *Spain* 51 Fa
Gravberg, *Sweden* 47 Dg
Grave, *Netherlands* 44 Dc
Gravelbourg, *Saskatchewan* 80 Kg
's Gravenhage, *Netherlands* 44 Cb
Gravenhurst, *Ontario* 83 Gc
's Gravenzande, *Netherlands* 44 Cb
Gray, *France* 52 Fc
Grayling, *Michigan* 83 Dc
Graz, *Austria* 49 Fe
Great Australian Bight, *Aust.* 94 Ef
Great Barrier Reef, *Aust.* 95 Jc
Great Barrington, *Mass.* 86 Da
Great Basin, *Nevada* 84 Cc
Great Bear L., *N.-W. Terr.* 80 Gc
Great Bear R., *N.-W. Terr.* 80 Gc
Great Blasket I., *Eire* 31 Ah
Great Dividing Ra., *Aust.* 95 Jd

Great Falls, *Montana* 87 Hb
Great Geysir, *Iceland* 46 Vm
Great Lake. See Tonle Sap
Great N. Mts., *W.Va., etc.* 86 Ac
Great Pt., *Massachusetts* 86 Eb
Great Rapids, *Manitoba* 80 Mf
Great Salt L., *Utah* 87 Ge
Great Salt Lake Des., *Utah* 87 Ge
Great Sandy Des., *W. Aust.* 94 Dd
Great Sandy I. (Fraser I.), *Queensland* 95 Ke
Great Slave L., *N.-W. Terr.* 80 Jd
Great Smoky Mts. Nat. Park, *Tenn./N. Car.* 85 Kd
Great South B., *New York* 86 Db
Great Torrington, *England* 31 Ek
Great Victoria Des., *W. Aust.* 94 Ee
Great Wass I., *Maine* 82 Ed
Great Yarmouth, *England* 31 Jk
Grebbestad, *Sweden* 47 Dg
Greco C., *Cyprus* 74 Cc
Greece, *S. Europe* 43 Nj
Greeley, *Colorado* 84 Fc
Green B., *Wisconsin* 83 Cc
Green Mts., *Vermont* 83 Kd
Green R., *Utah* 84 Ed
Green Bay, *Wisconsin* 83 Cc
Greenfield, *Indiana* 83 Df
Greenfield, *Massachusetts* 83 Kd
Greenland, *N. America* 39 Pb
Greenland Sea, *Greenland* 39 Mb
Greenock, *Scotland* 30 De
Greenport, *New York* 83 Ke
Greensboro, *N. Carolina* 85 Ld
Greensburg, *Pennsylvania* 86 Ab
Greenville, *Alabama* 85 Je
Greenville, *Liberia* 78 Dg
Greenville, *Maine* 82 Dd
Greenville, *Michigan* 83 Dd
Greenville, *Mississippi* 85 He
Greenville, *S. Carolina* 85 Ke
Greenville, *Texas* 84 Ge
Greenwich, *Connecticut* 86 Db
Greenwich, *England* 31 Hj
Greenwich, *Rhode Island* 86 Eb
Greenwood, *Mississippi* 85 He
Greenwood, *S. Carolina* 85 Ke
Greenwood, *Wisconsin* 83 Ac
Greenwood L., *N.Y.-N.J.* 86 Cb
Gregory Ra., *Queensland* 95 Hc
Griefen See, *Switzerland* 45 Da
Greifswald, *Germany* 48 Ea
Grein, *Austria* 48 Fd
Greiz, *Germany* 48 Ec
Grenaa, *Denmark* 47 Dh
Grenada, I., *Windward Is.* 89 Gd
Grenadines, Is., *Windward Is.* 89 Gd
Grenchen, *Switzerland* 45 Ca
Grenoble, *France* 53 Fd
Grenville, C., *Queensland* 95 Hb
Gretna, *Louisiana* 85 Hf
Grevelingen, *Netherlands* 44 Cc
Grevenå, *Greece* 57 Cd
Grey Ra., *Qnsld.-N.S.W.* 95 He
Greylock Mt., *Massachusetts* 86 Da
Greymouth, *New Zealand* 93 Ce
Greys Butte. See Juniper Mt.
Greystones, *Eire* 31 Cg
Greytown, *New Zealand* 93 Ed
Greytown. See San Juan del Norte
Griesalp, *Switzerland* 45 Cb
Griffin, *Georgia* 85 Ke
Griffith, *N.S.W.* 95 Jf
Grim C., *Tasmania* 95 Hh
Grimsby, *England* 38 He
Grimstad, *Norway* 47 Cg
Grindelwald, *Switzerland* 45 Db
Grindstone, *Michigan* 83 Ec
Grinnell Ld., *Arctic Ocean* 39 Qa
Grinnell Pen., *N.-W. Terr.* 80 Na
Griquatown, *Cape Province* 75 Ce
Griva, *Latvia* 47 Mj
Grobiņa, *Latvia* 47 Jh
Gröbming, *Austria* 48 Ee
Grodno, *White Russia* 60 Ce
Grodzisk, *Poland* 49 Gb
Groenlo, *Netherlands* 44 Eb
Groix, I. de, *France* 52 Bc
Groningen & prov., *Netherlands* 44 Ea
Grono, *Switzerland* 45 Eb
Groote Eylandt, *N.Terr., Aust.* 95 Gb
Grootfontein, *S.-W. Africa* 75 Be
Grootfontein, *S.-W. Africa* 75 Bc
Groot Natuna I. See Bunguran Kep
Grossevichi, *Russia* 59 Nd
Gross Glockner, *Austria* 48 Ee
Grosswardein. See Oradea
Groton, *New York* 86 Ba
Groznyy, *Russia* 58 Dd
Grudziądz, *Poland* 49 Hb
Grüsch, *Switzerland* 45 Eb
Gruz, *Yugoslavia* 56 Bc
Gruzinskaya rep. (Georgia), *U.S.S.R.* 58 Dd
Grybów, *Poland* 49 Jd
Gsteig, *Switzerland* 45 Cb
Guabito, *Panama* 89 Ce
Guacanayabo, G. de, *Cuba* 89 Db
Guachipas, *Argentina* 92 Cc
Guadalaja, *Spain* 50 Db
Guadalajara, *Mexico* 88 Dc
Guadalcanal, *Spain* 50 Cc
Guadalcanal, I., *Solomon Is.* 98 Eh
Guadalcazar, *Mexico* 88 Dc
Guadalquivir, R., *Spain* 50 Cd
Guadalupe, *Mexico* 88 D
Guadalupe, I., *Leeward Is.* 89 Gc
Guadalupe I., *Mexico* 88 Ab
Guadalupe Mts., *New Mexico-Texas* 84 Ee
Guadalupe R., *Texas* 84 Gf
Guadalupe-y-Calvo, *Mexico* 88 Cb
Guadarrama, *Spain* 50 Cb
Guadarrama, Sa. de, *Spain* 50 Db
Guadiana, R., *Spain* 50 Bc
Guadix, *Spain* 50 Dd
Guafo & G. de, *Chile* 92 Bf
Guaitecas, Is., *Chile* 92 Bf
Guajar-á-Mirim, *Brazil* 90 Df
Guajaratuba, *Brazil* 90 Ee
Gualeguaychu, *Argentina* 92 Dd
Guam, I., *Pacific Ocean* 98 Df
Guamá, *Brazil* 91 Hd
Guamini, *Argentina* 92 Ce
Guamo, *Colombia* 90 Bc
Guanabaçoa, *Cuba* 89 Cb
Guanacevi, *Mexico* 88 Cb
Guanahani. See San Salvador
Guanajuato, *Mexico* 88 Dc
Guanare, *Venezuela* 90 Cb
Guanarito, *Venezuela* 90 Db
Guandacol, *Argentina* 92 Cc
Guane, *Cuba* 89 Cb
Guanica, *Puerto Rico* 89 Fc
Guanta. See Puerto La Cruz
Guantanamo, *Cuba* 89 Db
Guapi, *Colombia* 90 Bc
Guapiles, *Costa Rica* 89 Cd
Guapore, *Brazil* 92 Fc
Guapore (Rondonia), *Brazil* 90 Ef
Guapore, R., *Brazil-Bolivia* 90 Ef
Guaqui, *Bolivia* 90 Dg
Guarapuava, *Brazil* 92 Fc
Guarda, *Portugal* 50 Bb
Guasdualito, *Venezuela* 90 Cb
Guasipati, *Venezuela* 90 Eb
Guatemala, *Guatemala* 88 Fe
Guatemala, rep., *Cent. America* 88 Fe
Guatrache, *Argentina* 92 De
Guaviare, R., *Colombia* 90 Dc
Guaxupe, *Brazil* 91 Hh
Guayabal, *Venezuela* 90 Db
Guayama, *Puerto Rico* 89 Fc
Guayaquil, *Ecuador* 90 Bd
Guaymas, *Mexico* 88 Bb
Guben, *Germany* 48 Fc
Gubin. See Guben
Gudiyatam, *India* 68 Ef
Guelma, *Algeria* 78 Ga
Guelph, *Ontario* 83 Fd
Guemes, *Argentina* 92 Cb
Guéret, *France* 52 Dc
Guernsey, I., *Channel Is.* 52 Bb
Guernsey Res., *Wyoming* 84 Fc
Guerrero, *Mexico* 88 Cb
Guerrero, *Tamaulipas, Mex.* 88 Eb
Guerrero, state, *Mexico* 88 Dd
Gugera, *W. Pakistan* 70 Ce
Guiana Highlands, *S. America* 90 Ec
Guija, *Moçambique* 75 Ed
Guildford, *England* 31 Gj
Guilford, *Maine* 82 Dd
Guillaumes, *France* 53 Gd
Guimaraes, *Brazil* 91 Jd
Guimarães, *Portugal* 50 Ab
Guinea, *West Africa* 78 Cf
Guinea, G. of, *N.-W. Africa* 76 Ad
Guines, *Cuba* 89 Cb
Guingamp, *France* 52 Bb
Guiria, *Venezuela* 90 Ea
Guisanbourg, *Fr. Guiana* 91 Gc
Guise, *France* 52 Eb
Guisisil, Vol., *Nicaragua* 89 Bd
Gujar Khan, *W. Pakistan* 70 Cd
Gujranwala, *W. Pakistan* 70 Dd
Gujrat, *W. Pakistan* 70 Dd
Gulbarga, *India* 68 Ee
Gulbene, *Latvia* 47 Mh
Gulfport, *Mississippi* 85 Je
Gulistan, *W. Pakistan* 68 Cb
Gul Koh, *Afghanistan* 73 Jc
Gull L., *Quebec* 81 Rg
Gulpen, *Netherlands* 44 Dd
Gulran, *Afghanistan* 73 Hb
Gulu, *Uganda* 77 Gd
Gumel, *Nigeria* 79 Gf
Gummersbach, *Germany* 48 Bc
Gümüljina. See Komotini
Gümüsane, *Turkey* 72 Ca
Guna, *India* 71 Ac
Gunchu, *Japan* 66 Ch
Gunisao R., *Manitoba* 80 Mf
Gunnedah, *N.S.W.* 95 Kf
Guntakal, *India* 68 Ee
Guntur, *India* 68 Fe
Gurais, *Kashmir* 70 Dc
Gurdaspur, *India* 70 Dd
Gurgaon, *India* 70 Ef
Gurgl, *Austria* 48 De
Gurha, *India* 68 Dc
Gurkha, *Nepal* 71 Eb
Gurla Mandhata, Mt., *Tibet* 68 Fb
Gurnigel, *Switzerland* 45 Cb
Gursköy, *Norway* 46 Ae
Guru, *Tibet* 69 Gc
Gurupa, *Brazil* 91 Gd
Gurupa, I., *Brazil* 91 Gd
Guru Sikhar, *India* 68 Dd
Guryev, *Kazakh.* 58 Ed
Gusev, *Lithuania* 47 Kj
Guspini, *Sardinia* 55 Bf
Güstrow, *Germany* 48 Eb
Guthrie, *Oklahoma* 84 Gd
Guttannen, *Switzerland* 45 Db
Guyana, *S. America* 90 Fc
Guyenne, prov., *France* 53 Dd
Guzman, *Mexico* 88 Dd
Gwa, *Burma* 69 He
Gwadar, *Persia* 73 He
Gwadar, *W. Pakistan* 68 Bc
Gwalior *India* 71 Bb
Gwanda, *Rhodesia* 75 Dd
Gweebarra B., *Eire* 31 Bf
Gwelo, *Rhodesia* 75 Dc
Gyangtse, *Tibet* 69 Gc
Gydanskiy Pol., *Russia* 85 Ga
Gympie, *Queensland* 95 Ke
Györ, *Hungary* 49 Ge
Gypsumville, *Manitoba* 80 Mf
Gyula, *Hungary* 49 Je
Gzhatsk, *Russia* 60 Jd
Haag, *Switzerland* 45 Ea
Haaksbergen, *Netherlands* 44 Eb
Haarlem, *Netherlands* 44 Cb
Habana, *Cuba* 89 Cb
Habban, *S. Yemen* 72 Eg
Habbaniyah, *Iraq* 72 Dc
Habigang, *E. Pakistan* 69 Hd
Haboro, *Japan* 66 Gb
Hachinohe, *Japan* 66 Gc
Hachuman, *Japan* 66 Eg
Hadasan, *Mongolia* 62 Ba
Hadda, *Arabia* 72 Ce
Haddington, *Scotland* 30 Ee
Hadera, *Israel* 74 Ce
Haderslev, *Denmark* 47 Cj
Hadjin. See Saimbeyli
Haecht, *Belgium* 44 Cd
Haeju, *Korea* 62 Jc
Haelen, *Belgium* 44 Dd
Hafar, *Arabia* 72 Ed
Hafar al Ats, *Arabia* 72 Ed
Haffe. See Babenna
Hafnarfjördhur, *Iceland* 46 Vm
Hagen, *Germany* 48 Bc
Hageri, *Estonia* 47 Lg
Hagerstown, *Maryland* 86 Bc
Hagi, *Japan* 66 Bg
Hague, C. de la, *France* 52 Cb
Hague, The. See 's Gravenhage
Haibak, *Afghanistan* 73 Jb
Hai cheng, *China* 64 Lb
Haichow. See Tunghai
Haidar Pasha. See Kadiköy
Haifa, *Israel* 74 Ce
Haig, *W. Australia* 94 Ef
Hail, *Arabia* 72 Dd
Hailar, *China* 62 Ga
Haileybury, *Ontario* 83 Gb
Hailun, *China* 62 Ja
Hailuoto, *Finland* 46 Ld
Hainan I., *China* 65 En
Hainan Str., *China* 65 Dm
Hainaut, prov., *Belgium* 44 Bd
Haines, *Alaska* 80 De
Haipong, *N. Vietnam* 67 Db
Hair, *Arabia* 72 Ee
Haiten I., *China* 65 Jk
Haiti, rep., *West Indies* 89 Ec
Hajduböszörmény, *Hungary* 49 Je
Hajima, Jebel, *Arabia* 72 Ce
Hajipur, *India* 71 Ec
Hajjar, *China* 62 Bc
Haka, *Burma* 69 Hd
Hakkâri, *Turkey* 72 Db
Hakodate, *Japan* 66 Gd
Hal, *Belgium* 44 Cd
Hala, *W. Pakistan* 68 Cc
Halacho, *Mexico* 88 Fc
Halaib, *Sudan* 72 Ce
Halba, *Lebanon* 74 Ec
Halbe, *Arabia* 72 Df
Halberstadt, *Germany* 48 Dc
Halden, *Norway* 47 Dg
Haleb. See Aleppo
Halebiye, *Syria* 72 Cb
Hali, *Arabia* 72 Df
Halia, *India* 71 Dc
Haliburton, *Ontario* 83 Gc
Halifax, *England* 38 Ee
Halifax & Harb., *N.S.* 82 Gd
Halifax B., *Queensland* 95 Jc
Halkett C., *Alaska* 85 Xk
Hall, *Germany* 48 Cd
Hall Is., *Caroline Is.* 98 Eg
Hall Ld., *Greenland* 39 Pa
Halle, *Germany* 48 Ec
Halle. See Hal
Hallein, *Austria* 48 Ee
Halley, B., *Antarctica* 100 Ab
Halliste, *Estonia* 47 Lg
Hällnäss, *Sweden* 46 Hd
Hallowell, *Maine* 82 Cd
Halls Creek, *W. Australia* 94 Ec
Hallstavik, *Sweden* 47 Hf
Hallviken, *Sweden* 46 Fe
Halmahera, I., *Indonesia* 63 Jk
Halmstad, *Sweden* 47 Eh
Halsa, *Norway* 46 Ce
Hälsingborg, *Sweden* 47 Eh
Halys, C. See Bafra Br.
Hama, *Syria* 74 Eb
Hamada, *Japan* 66 Cg
Hamadan, *Persia* 72 Ec
Hamam, *Arabia* 72 Ee
Hamamatsu, *Japan* 66 Eg
Hamar, *Arabia* 72 Ee
Hamar, *Norway* 47 Df
Hambantota, *Ceylon* 68 Fg
Hamburg, *Germany* 48 Db
Hamburg, *New York* 86 Aa
Hamburg, *Pennsylvania* 86 Cb
Hamdānīya, *Syria* 74 Eb
Hämeenlinna, *Finland* 47 Lf
Hameln, *Germany* 48 Cb
Hamersley Ra., *W. Aust.* 94 Cd
Hami, *S. Yemen* 72 Eg
Hamidan, *Arabia* 73 Fe
Hamidiya, *Syria* 74 Dc
Hamilton, *New York* 86 Ca
Hamilton, *New Zealand* 93 Eb
Hamilton, *Ohio* 83 Df
Hamilton, *Ontario* 83 Gd
Hamilton, *Scotland* 30 Ee
Hamilton, *Victoria* 95 Hg
Hamilton Inl., *Labrador* 81 Vf
Hamilton R., *Labrador* 81 Uf
Hamina, *Finland* 47 Mf
Hamirpur, *India* 71 Cc
Hamm, *Germany* 48 Bc
Hammān, *Iraq* 72 Dc
Hamme, *Belgium* 44 Cc
Hammerdal, *Sweden* 46 Fe
Hammerfest, *Norway* 46 Ka
Hammond, *Indiana* 83 Ce
Hammond, *New Brunswick* 82 Fd
Hammonton, *New Jersey* 86 Cc
Hamont, *Belgium* 44 Dc
Hampden, *New Zealand* 93 Cf
Hampshire, co., *England* 31 Gj
Hampton, *New Brunswick* 82 Fd
Hampton, *New Hampshire* 82 Ce
Hamun-i-Helmand, *Persia-Afghanistan* 73 Hc
Hamun-i-Puzak, *Afghanistan* 73 Hc
Han, *Belgium* 44 Dd
Hanakiya, *Arabia* 72 Dd
Hanau, *Germany* 48 Cc
Hanchung, *China* 64 Cf
Hancock, *Michigan* 85 Jb
Hancock, *New York* 86 Cb
Handegg, *Switzerland* 45 Db
Handeni, *Tanzania* 77 Hf
Hanford, *California* 87 Dg
Hanford, *Washington* 87 Db
Hangchow, *China* 65 Kg
Hangchow B., *China* 64 Kg
Hangu, *W. Pakistan* 70 Bd
Han Kiang, *China* 62 Ed
Hankö & Fd., *Finland* 47 Kg
Hankow (Wuhan), *China* 64 Gg
Hanle, *Kashmir* 68 Eb
Hanmer, *New Zealand* 93 De
Hanna, *Alberta* 80 Jf
Hannibal, *Missouri* 85 Hd
Hannover, *Germany* 48 Cb
Hannut, *Belgium* 44 Dd
Hanöbukten, *Sweden* 47 Fj
Hanoi, *N. Vietnam* 67 Db
Hanover, *Ontario* 83 Fc
Hanover, *Pennsylvania* 86 Bc
Hanover, I., *Chile* 92 Bh
Hansi, *India* 70 Ef
Hansweert, *Netherlands* 44 Cc
Hanumangarh. See Bhatnair
Hanyang, *China* 65 Gg
Hanyin, *China* 64 Df
Hao, I., *Tuamotu Arch.* 99 Lj
Haparanda, *Sweden* 46 Ld
Hapur, *India* 70 Ef
Haqal, *Arabia* 72 Bd
Haraiya, *India* 71 Db
Harak, *Arabia* 72 Cd
Harar, *Ethiopia* 77 Jc
Harardera, *Somalia* 77 Kd
Hara Usu Nur, *Mongolia* 62 Ba
Harbin. See Pinkiang
Harbor Beach, *Michigan* 83 Ed
Harbor Spring, *Michigan* 83 Dc
Harburg Wilhelmsburg, *Ger.* 48 Cb
Harda, *India* 68 Ed
Hardanger Fd., *Norway* 47 Bf
Hardangervidder, *Norway* 47 Bf
Hardenberg, *Netherlands* 44 Eb
Harderwijk, *Netherlands* 44 Db
Harding, *Natal* 75 Ef
Hardoi, *India* 71 Cb
Hardwar, *India* 70 Ff
Hardy, Pen., *Chile* 92 Cj
Hare B., *Newfoundland* 82 La
Hare, I. See I. aux Lievres
Hareidland, *Norway* 46 Ae
Hare Indian R., *N.-W. Terr.* 80 Fc
Hargeisa, *Somalia* 77 Jc
Hari, R., *Sumatra* 63 Dl
Harian, *Persia* 73 Fb
Harib, *Arabia* 72 Ef
Harihar, *India* 68 Ef
Harim, *Syria* 74 Ea
Haripur, *W. Pakistan* 70 Cd
Hariq, *Arabia* 72 Ee
Harishpur, *India* 69 Gd
Harlan, *Kentucky* 85 Kd
Harlebeke, *Belgium* 44 Bd
Harlequin Hills, *Nevada* 87 De
Harlingen, *Netherlands* 44 Da
Harmanli. See Kharmanli
Harney, L., *Oregon* 87 Dd
Harney Basin, *Oregon* 84 Bc
Harnösand, *Sweden* 46 Ge
Harper, *Liberia* 78 Dh
Harran, *Turkey* 72 Cb
Harrington Harbour, *Quebec* 82 Ja
Harris, & Sd. of, *Scotland* 30 Cc
Harrisburg, *Pennsylvania* 86 Bb
Harrison, *Michigan* 83 Dc
Harrison, C., *Labrador* 81 Vf
Harrison, L., *Brit. Columbia* 80 Gg
Harrisonburg, *Virginia* 85 Ld
Harrisville, *Michigan* 83 Ec
Harrogate, *England* 31 Fg
Har Sagi, *Israel* 74 Cg
Hârşova, *Rumania* 56 Fb
Harspranget, *Sweden* 46 Jc
Harstad, *Norway* 46 Gb
Hart, *Michigan* 83 Cd
Hartford, *Connecticut* 86 Db
Hartland, *New Brunswick* 82 Ec
Hartlepool, *England* 31 Gf
Harvard, *Illinois* 83 Bd
Harvard, Mt., *Colorado* 84 Ed
Harvey, *New Brunswick* 82 Ed
Harwich, *England* 31 Hj
Haryana, state, *India* 70 Dd
Harz, Mts., *Germany* 48 Dc
Hasā, *Jordan* 74 Dg
Hasan D., *Turkey* 72 Bb
Hasanpur, *India* 71 Ba
Hasbaya, *Lebanon* 74 Dd
Hassan, *India* 68 Ef
Hasselt, *Belgium* 44 Dd
Hasselt, *Netherlands* 44 Eb
Hastiere, *Belgium* 44 Cd
Hastings, *England* 31 Hk
Hastings, *Michigan* 83 Dd
Hastings, *Minnesota* 85 Hc
Hastings, *Nebraska* 84 Gc
Hastings, *New Zealand* 93 Fc
Hatay, *Turkey* 72 Cb
Hateg, *Rumania* 56 Db
Hatha, *Arabia* 72 De
Hathras, *India* 71 Bb
Ha-tinh, *N. Vietnam* 67 Dc
Hatteras, C., *N. Carolina* 85 Md
Hattiesburg, *Mississippi* 85 Je
Hatton Headline, *N.-W. Terr.* 81 Ud
Hatvan, *Hungary* 49 He
Hat Yai, *Siam* 63 Dj
Haudères, les, *Switzerland* 45 Cb
Haugesund, *Norway* 47 Ag
Haukipudas, *Finland* 46 Ld
Hauki vesi, *Finland* 46 Ne
Haura, *S. Yemen* 72 Eg
Hauraki Gulf, *New Zealand* 93 Eb
Hauroko, L., *New Zealand* 93 Af
Hausa, *Jordan* 74 Fh
Hausstock, Mt., *Switzerland* 45 Eb
Haut, Isle, *Maine* 82 Dd
Hauta, *S. Yemen* 72 Eg
Hauta, *Arabia* 72 Ee
Haut Atlas, Mts., *Morocco* 78 Db
Haut-Garonne, dep., *France* 53 De
Haut-Loire, dep., *France* 53 Ed
Haut-Marne, dep., *France* 52 Fb
Hautes, Alpes, dep., *France* 53 Gd
Haute-Saône, dep., *France* 52 Gc
Haute-Savoie, dep., *France* 52 Gc
Hautes-Pyrénées, dep., *Fr.* 53 De
Haute Vienne, dep., *France* 53 Dc
Haute Volta, *W. Africa* 78 Ef
Haut-Rhin, dep., *France* 52 Gc
Havana. See Habana
Havasu L., *Cal.-Ariz.* 87 Fh
Havelange, *Belgium* 44 Dd
Havelland, *Germany* 48 Eb
Havelock, *New Brunswick* 82 Fc
Havelock I., *Andaman Is.* 69 Hf
Havelock North, *N.Z.* 93 Fc
Haverfordwest, *Wales* 31 Dj
Haverhill, *Massachusetts* 86 Ea
Haverstraw, *New York* 86 Cb
Havre, *Belgium* 44 Cd
Havre, *Montana* 84 Eb
Havre de Grace, *Maryland* 86 Bc
Havre-St. Pierre, *Quebec* 81 Uf
Hawaii, I., *Hawaiian Is.* 99 Kf
Hawaiian Is., *Pacific Ocean* 98 Je
Hawea Flat, *New Zealand* 93 Bf
Hawera, *New Zealand* 93 Ec
Hawick, *Scotland* 30 Fe
Hawke B., *New Zealand* 93 Fc
Hawkesbury, *Ontario* 83 Jc
Hawr al Hammar, *Iraq* 72 Ec
Hawr Saniya, *Iraq* 72 Ec
Hay, *New South Wales* 95 Hf
Hay R., *Alberta* 80 He
Hayatpur, *India* 71 Fc
Hayes Pen., *Greenland* 39 Qb
Hay River, *N.-W. Terr.* 80 Hd
Hazara Highlands, *Afghan.* 73 Hc
Hazard, *Kentucky* 85 Kd
Hazaribagh, *India* 71 Ed
Hazaribagh Ra., *India* 71 Dd
Hazarjuft, *Afghanistan* 73 Hc
Hazawza, *Arabia* 72 Cc
Hazelton, *British Columbia* 80 Fe
Hazeva, *Israel* 74 Dg
Hazil, *Arabia* 72 Dd
Hazleton, *Pennsylvania* 86 Cb
Hazro, *W. Pakistan* 70 Cd
Heard I., *Indian Ocean* 96 Fk
Hearst, *Ontario* 81 Qg
Hebrides, Outer, *Scotland* 30 Bc
Hebron, *Labrador* 81 Ue
Hebron, *Jordan* 74 Df
Hecate Str., *Brit. Columbia* 80 Ef
Hecelchakan, *Mexico* 88 Fc
Hechingen, *Germany* 48 Cd
Hechtel, *Belgium* 44 Dc
Hector, Mt., *New Zealand* 93 Ed
Hede, *Sweden* 46 Ee
Hedemora, *Sweden* 47 Ff
Heemstede, *Netherlands* 44 Cb
Heer, *Netherlands* 44 Dd
Heerenveen, *Netherlands* 44 Db
Heerlen, *Netherlands* 44 Dd
Hegemann, C., *Greenland* 39 Nc
Heide, *Germany* 48 Ca
Heidelberg, *Germany* 48 Cd
Heidelberg, *Transvaal* 75 De
Heiden, *Switzerland* 45 Ea
Heijen, *Netherlands* 44 Dc
Heilbronn, *Germany* 48 Cd
Heinola, *Finland* 47 Mf
Heist, *Belgium* 44 Bc
Hejaz, *Arabia* 72 Ce
Hekla, Mt., *Iceland* 46 Wn
Helchteren, *Belgium* 44 Dc
Helder, Den, *Netherlands* 44 Cb
Helena, *Arkansas* 85 He
Helena, *Montana* 87 Gb
Helensburgh, *Scotland* 30 Dd
Helensville, *New Zealand* 93 Eb
Helgoland, I., *Germany* 48 Ba
Helgoländer Bucht, *Ger.* 48 Ba
Hell Gate, *British Columbia* 80 Fe
Hellin, *Spain* 51 Ec
Helmand Des., *Afghanistan* 73 Hc
Helmand R., *Afghanistan* 73 Hc
Helme, *Estonia* 47 Lh
Helmond, *Netherlands* 44 Dc
Helmsdale, *Scotland* 30 Eb
Helsingfors. See Helsinki
Helsingör, *Denmark* 47 Eh
Helsinki, *Finland* 47 Lf
Helston, *England* 31 Dk
Hemelum, *Netherlands* 44 Db
Hemnes, *Norway* 46 Ec
Hemse, *Sweden* 47 Hh
Hendaye, *France* 53 Ce
Henderson, *Kentucky* 85 Jd
Henderson, *New York* 83 Hd
Henderson I., *Pacific Ocean* 99 Nk
Hengam, I., *Persia* 73 Gd
Hengchow. See Hengyang
Hengelo, *Netherlands* 44 Eb
Henghsien, *China* 65 Dl
Hengshan, *China* 65 Fj
Hengyang, *China* 65 Fj
Henley-on-Thames, *England* 31 Gj
Henlopen, C., *New Jersey* 86 Cc
Hennebont, *France* 52 Bc
Henrietta Maria C., *Ontario* 81 Qf
Henrique de Carvalho, *Angola* 76 Ef
Henzada, *Burma* 69 Je
Heran, *Yemen* 72 Df
Herat, *Afghanistan* 73 Hc
Herau. See Herowabad
Hérault, dep., *France* 53 Ee
Herbert, *N.Z.* 93 Cf
Herbertville, *New Zealand* 93 Fd
Herbertville, *Quebec* 82 Cb
Herbesthal, *Belgium* 44 Ed
Herceg Novi, *Yugoslavia* 56 Bc
Heredia, *Costa Rica* 89 Cd
Hereford & co., *England* 31 Fh
Hereheretue, I., *Pacific Oc.* 99 Lj
Herford, *Germany* 48 Cb
Herinnes, *Belgium* 44 Cd
Heriot. See Edievale
Herisau, *Switzerland* 45 Ea
Herkimer, *New York* 86 Ca
Herma Ness, *Zetland* 30 Ja
Hermil, *Lebanon* 74 Ec
Hermitage B., *Newfoundland* 82 Kc
Hermite, Is., *Chile* 92 Cj
Hermon, Mt. See Sheikh
Hermosillo, *Mexico* 88 Bb
Herning, *Denmark* 47 Ch
Héron, *Belgium* 44 Dd
Heron I., *Qnsld.* 95 Kd
Herowabad, *Persia* 72 Eb
Herräng, *Sweden* 47 Hf
Herrera, *Argentina* 92 Dc
Herrera di Pisuerga, *Spain* 50 Ca
Hersey, *Michigan* 83 Dd
Herselt, *Belgium* 44 Cc
Hertford & co., *England* 31 Gj
's Hertogenbosch, *Netherl'd.* 44 Dc
Herval. See Joacaba
Hervás, *Spain* 50 Cb
Hervé, *Belgium* 44 Dd
Hervey, B., *Queensland* 95 Kd
Hervey Is., *Cook Is.* 98 Jj
Herzberg, *Germany* 48 Ec
Herzliya, *Israel* 74 Ce
Herzogenbuchsee, *Switz.* 45 Ca
Hesdin, *France* 52 Ea
Heught, Mt., *N. Terr. Aust.* 94 Fd
Heusden, *Netherlands* 44 Dc
Hève, C. de la, *France* 52 Db
Hexham, *England* 30 Ff
Hiakiang, *China* 65 Dk
Hibbing, *Minnesota* 85 Hb
Hicks Bay, *N.Z.* 93 Gc
Hidalgo, *Mexico* 88 Eb
Hidalgo, state, *Mexico* 88 Ec
Hieflau, *Austria* 48 Fe
Hierro, I., *Canary Is.* 78 Bc
Highland Park, *Illinois* 83 Cd
High Point, *N. Carolina* 85 Ld
Hiimeji, *Japan* 66 Dg
Hiiumaa, *Estonia* 47 Kg
Hijar, *Spain* 51 Eb
Hikon, *Japan* 66 Eg
Hildesheim, *Germany* 48 Cb
Hillah, al, *Iraq* 72 Dc
Hillman, *Michigan* 83 Ec
Hillsborough, *N.B.* 82 Fd
Hillsdale, *Michigan* 83 De
Hillston, *N.S.W.* 95 Jf
Hilversum, *Netherlands* 44 Db
Hilyan, *Arabia* 72 De
Himachel Pradesh, *India* 70 Ee
Himalaya Mts., *India, etc.* 68 Eb
Himanka, *Finland* 46 Kd
Himare, *Albania* 57 Bd
Hindeloopen, *Netherlands* 44 Db
Hindubagh, *W. Pakistan* 68 Cb
Hindu Kush, Mts., *Afghanistan-W. Pakistan* 68 Da
Hindupur, *India* 68 Ef
Hingan. See Ankang
Hingan, *China* 64 Ea
Hinganghat, *India* 68 Ed
Hingho, *China* 64 Fb
Hinghwa, *China* 64 Jf
Hinghwa. See Putien
Hingi, *China* 65 Bk
Hinglaj, *W. Pakistan* 68 Cc
Hingol R., *W. Pakistan* 68 Cc
Hingoli, *India* 68 Ee
Hinis, *Turkey* 72 Db
Hinnöy, *Norway* 46 Fb
Hinsdale, *New Hampshire* 86 Da
Hiroo, *Japan* 66 Hc
Hirosaki, *Japan* 66 Gd
Hiroshima, *Japan* 66 Cg
Hisaronu, *Turkey* 72 Ba
Hisban, *Jordan* 74 Df
Hispaniola, I., *West Indies* 89 Ec
Hissar, *India* 70 Df
Hissmofors, *Sweden* 46 Fe
Hisua, *India* 71 Ec
Hisya, *Syria* 74 Ec
Hit, *Iraq* 72 Dc
Hitra, *Norway* 46 Ce
Hivaoa, I., *Marquesas Is.* 99 Mh
Hiwasa, *Japan* 66 Dh
Hjälmaren, L., *Sweden* 47 Fg
Hjörring, *Denmark* 47 Ch
Hkamti, *Burma* 69 Jc
Hobart, *Tasmania* 95 Jh
Hoboken, *Belgium* 44 Cc
Hobro, *Denmark* 47 Ch
Hobsogol, *Mongolia* 59 Kc
Hochwan, *China* 65 Cg
Hodal, *India* 70 Eg
Hodeida, *Yemen* 72 Dg
Hodgson, *Manitoba* 80 Mf
Hódmezövásárhely, *Hungary* 49 Je
Hoek van Holland, *Netherlands* 44 Cc
Hof, *Germany* 48 Dc
Hofei, *China* 64 Hg
Höfs Jökull, *Iceland* 46 Wm
Hofuf, *Arabia* 72 Ed
Höganäs, *Sweden* 47 Eh
Hohe Tauern, *Austria* 48 Ee
Hohsien, *China* 65 Ek
Hoihong, *China* 65 Em
Hoihow, *Hai-Nan I.* 65 Em
Hokianga Harb., *N.Z.* 93 Da
Ho-kien-fu, *China* 64 Hc
Hokitika, *New Zealand* 93 Ce
Hokkaido I., *Japan* 66 Gc
Holbæk, *Denmark* 47 Dj
Holberg, *British Columbia* 80 Ff
Holguin, *Cuba* 89 Db
Holinkoerh, *China* 64 Eb
Holland, *Michigan* 83 Cd
Holland, *New York* 86 Aa
Holland, Noord, prov., *Netherlands* 44 Cb
Holland, Parts of, Lincs., *England* 31 Gh
Holland, Zuid, prov., *Netherlands* 44 Cb
Hollange, *Belgium* 44 De
Hollidaysburg, *Pennsylvania* 86 Ab
Hollogne, *Belgium* 44 Dd
Holly, *Michigan* 83 Ed
Hollywood, *California* 87 Dh
Holman Island, *N.-W. Terr.* 80 Hb
Holmestrand, *Norway* 47 Dg
Holmsund, *Sweden* 46 Je
Holstebro, *Denmark* 47 Ch
Holstein, *Germany* 48 Cb
Holsteinsborg, *Greenland* 39 Pc
Holten, *Netherlands* 44 Eb
Holwerd, *Netherlands* 44 Da
Holy I., *England* 30 Fe
Holy I., *Wales* 31 Dg
Holy Cross, *Alaska* 85 Wl
Holy Cross, Mt. of the, *Colo.* 84 Ed
Holyhead, *Wales* 31 Dg
Holyoke, *Massachusetts* 83 Kd
Home B., *N.-W. Territories* 81 Tc
Homer, *Alaska* 85 Xm
Homer, *New York* 83 Hd
Homestead, *Pennsylvania* 86 Ab
Homfray Str., *Andaman Is.* 69 Hf
Hommelvik, *Norway* 46 Ce
Homs, *Libya* 79 Hb
Homs, *Syria* 74 Ec
Honan. See Loyang
Honan, prov., *China* 64 Fe
Honda, *Colombia* 90 Cb
Honda, B., *Cuba* 89 Cb
Hondo, *Mexico* 88 Db
Honduras, rep., *C. America* 89 Bd
Honduras, C., *Honduras* 89 Bc
Honduras, G. of, *Brit. Hon.* 89 Bc
Hönefoss, *Norway* 47 Df
Honesdale, *Pennsylvania* 86 Cb
Honfleur, *France* 52 Db
Honghai B., *China* 65 Gl
Hong Kong (Gt. Br.), *China* 65 Gl
Honolulu, I., *Hawaiian Is.* 99 Ke
Honor, *Michigan* 83 Cc
Honshu I., *Japan* 66 Cg
Hood, Mt., *Oregon* 87 Cc
Hoofdplaat, *Netherlands* 44 Bc
Hooger Smilde, *Netherlands* 44 Eb
Hoogeveen, *Netherlands* 44 Eb
Hoogezand, *Netherlands* 44 Ea
Hooghalen, *Netherlands* 44 Eb
Hooghly, *India* 71 Gd
Hooghly R., *India* 71 Ge
Hook Hd., *Eire* 31 Ch
Hoopeston, *Illinois* 83 Ce
Hoorn, *Netherlands* 44 Db
Hoosick Falls, *New York* 86 Da
Hoover Dam, *Arizona* 87 Fh
Hope, *British Columbia* 80 Gg
Hopedale, *Labrador* 81 Ue
Hopeh, prov., *China* 64 Gc
Hopen, I., *Barents Sea* 58 Ba
Hopes Advance C., *Quebec* 81 Td
Hopetoun, *W. Australia* 94 Df
Hope Town, *Andaman Is.* 69 Hf
Hopetown, *Cape Province* 75 Ce
Hopkinsville, *Kentucky* 85 Jd
Hoppo, *China* 65 Dm
Hoquiam, *Washington* 87 Bb
Horaždovice, *Czechoslovakia* 48 Ed
Horcasitas, *Mexico* 88 Bb
Horgen, *Switzerland* 45 Da
Horka, *Germany* 48 Fc

Hormoz, *Persia* 73 Fd
Hormoz I., *Persia* 73 Gd
Hormuz, Str. of, *Arabia-Persia* 73 Gd
Horn, *Austria* 49 Fd
Horn, *Iceland* 46 Ul
Horn, C. See Hornos, C. de
Horn Mts., *N.-W. Terr.* 80 Hd
Hornavan, *Sweden* 46 Gc
Hornby, *N.Z.* 93 De
Hörnefors, *Sweden* 46 He
Hornell, *New York* 86 Ba
Hornopiren, Mt., *Chile* 92 Bf
Hornos, C. de, *Chile* 92 Cj
Hornsea, *England* 31 Gg
Horo, *Netherlands* 44 Dc
Horonobe, *Japan* 66 Gb
Horqueta, *Paraguay* 92 Eb
Horseheads, *New York* 86 Ba
Horsens, *Denmark* 47 Cj
Horse Shoe, *W. Australia* 94 Ce
Horsham, *England* 31 Gj
Horsham, *Victoria* 95 Hg
Horšovský Týn, *Czech.* 48 Ed
Horst, *Netherlands* 44 Ec
Horten, *Norway* 47 Dg
Horton R., *N.-W. Terr.* 80 Gc
Hoşap, *Turkey* 72 Db
Hose Ra., *Sarawak* 63 Fk
Hoshangabad, *India* 71 Ad
Hoshiarpur, *India* 70 De
Hospel, *India* 68 Ee
Hospenthal, *Switzerland* 45 Db
Hossegor, *France* 53 Ce
Hoste, I., *Chile* 92 Cj
Hosur, *India* 68 Ef
Hotagen, *Sweden* 46 Fe
Hotseh, *China* 64 Ge
Hot Springs, *S. Dakota* 84 Fc
Hot Springs Nat. Park, *Ark.* 85 He
Hotton, *Belgium* 44 Dd
Houdelaincourt, *France* 52 Fb
Houffalize, *Belgium* 44 Dd
Houghton L., *Michigan* 83 Dc
Houlton, *Maine* 82 Ec
Hourn L., *Scotland* 34 Ee
Housatonic, R., *Connecticut* 86 Db
Houston, *Texas* 84 Gf
Houten, *Netherlands* 44 Db
Houtman Abrolhos, *W. Aust.* 94 Be
Howard, *Michigan* 83 Dd
Howard, *Pennsylvania* 86 Bb
Howell, *Michigan* 83 Ed
Howick, *Natal* 75 Ee
Howland I., *Pacific Ocean* 98 Hg
Howley, *Newfoundland* 82 Kb
Howrah, *India* 71 Gd
Hoy I., *Orkney* 30 Eb
Hoyes, *Spain* 50 Bb
Hoyt, *New Brunswick* 82 Ed
Hoyun, *China* 62 Ff
Hozat, *Turkey* 72 Cb
Hrubieszów, *Poland* 49 Kc
Hsawnghsup. See Thaungdut
Hsenwi, *Burma* 69 Jd
Hsiachwan Shan, *China* 65 Fm
Hsi-an. See Sian
Hsi-ch'ang. See Sichang
Hsinchu, *Taiwan* 65 Kk
Hsi-ning. See Sining
Hsinking. See Changchun
Hsipaw, *Burma* 69 Jd
Hsüchang, *China* 64 Ff
Hsuchow. See Hsüchang
Huachi, *Bolivia* 90 Dg
Huacho, *Peru* 90 Bf
Huacrachuco, *Peru* 90 Be
Hualgayoc, *Peru* 90 Be
Hualien, *Taiwan* 65 Kl
Huanay, *Bolivia* 90 Dg
Huancabamba, *Peru* 90 Be
Huancane, *Peru* 90 Dg
Huancavelica, *Peru* 90 Bf
Huancayo, *Peru* 90 Bf
Huanchaca, *Bolivia* 90 Dh
Huanchaco, *Peru* 90 Be
Huanta, *Peru* 90 Cf
Huanuco, *Peru* 90 Be
Huaonta, *Nicaragua* 89 Cd
Huara, *Chile* 92 Ca
Huaras, *Peru* 90 Be
Huards, L. aux, *Quebec* 82 Cb
Huariaca, *Peru* 90 Bf
Huario, *Peru* 90 Bf
Huarmey, *Peru* 90 Bf
Huasco, *Chile* 92 Bc
Huatusco. See Coatepec
Huaylas, *Peru* 90 Be
Hubli, *India* 68 Ee
Huchow, *China* 64 Kg
Huddersfield, *England* 31 Fg
Hudiksvall, *Sweden* 47 Gf
Hudson, *Maine* 82 Dd
Hudson, *New York* 86 Da
Hudson B., *Canada* 81 Pe
Hudson B., *Saskatchewan* 80 Lf
Hudson R., *New York* 86 Da
Hudson Str., *Canada* 81 Sd
Hudson Falls, *New York* 83 Kd
Hue, *S. Vietnam* 67 Dc
Huedin, *Rumania* 56 Da
Huehuetenango, *Guatemala* 88 Fd
Huejutla, *Mexico* 88 Ec
Huelva, *Spain* 50 Bd
Huércal Overa, *Spain* 51 Ed
Huete, *Spain* 51 Db
Hughenden, *Queensland* 95 Hd
Huhehot, *China* 64 Eb
Huiarau Ra., *New Zealand* 93 Fc
Hüichŏn, *Korea* 62 Jb
Hukawng Valley, *Burma* 69 Jc
Hukow, *China* 62 Ge
Hukuntsi, *Botswana* 75 Cd
Hula L., *Israel* 74 Dd
Hulin. See Linkiang
Hull, *England* 31 Gg
Hull, *Quebec* 83 Jc
Hulst, *Netherlands* 44 Cc
Hulun. See Hailar
Hulun Chih, *China* 62 Ga
Hulutao, *China* 62 Hb
Huma, *China* 59 Mc
Humacao, *Puerto Rico* 89 Fc
Humaita, *Paraguay* 92 Ec
Humaita, *Brazil* 90 Ee
Humansdorp, *Cape Prov.* 75 Cf
Humay, *Peru* 90 Bf
Humbe. See Mutano
Humber R., *England* 31 Hg
Humbermouth, *Nfd.* 82 Kb
Humboldt, *Saskatchewan* 80 Kf
Humboldt B., *California* 84 Bc
Humboldt Glacier, *Greenl'd.* 39 Qb
Humboldt R., *Nevada* 87 De
Hume Res., *New S. Wales* 95 Jg
Humenne, *Czechoslovakia* 49 Jd
Humphreys, Mt., *California* 87 Dg
Hun, *Libya* 79 Jc
Hunafloi, *Iceland* 46 Vm
Hunan, prov., *China* 65 Ej
Hungary, *Central Europe* 43 Mg
Hungnam, *Korea* 62 Jc
Hungtze Hu, *China* 64 Jf
Hunsrück, Mts., *Germany* 48 Bd
Hunter Is., *Tasmania* 95 Hh
Huntingdon, *England* 31 Gh
Huntingdon & Peterborough, co., *England* 31 Gh
Huntingdon, *Pennsylvania* 86 Ab
Huntington, *Indiana* 83 De
Huntington, *New York* 86 Db
Huntington, *W. Virginia* 85 Kd
Huntly, *New Zealand* 93 Eb
Huntly, *Scotland* 30 Fc
Huntsville, *Alabama* 85 Je
Huntsville, *Ontario* 83 Gc
Hunucma, *Mexico* 88 Fc
Hun-yüan-chow, *China* 64 Fc
Hunza, *Kashmir* 70 Db
Huon Is., *Pacific Ocean* 98 Fj
Huon Pen., *New Guinea* 95 Ja
Hupeh, prov., *China* 64 Fg
Hurd, C., *Ontario* 83 Fc
Hurghada, *Egypt* 79 Mc
Huron, *S. Dakota* 84 Gc
Huron, L., *U.S.A.-Canada* 85 Kc
Huskvarna, *Sweden* 47 Fh
Husum, *Germany* 48 Ca
Hutchinson, *Kansas* 84 Gd
Hüttenberg, *Austria* 48 Fe
Huttwil, *Switzerland* 45 Ca
Huy, *Belgium* 44 Dd
Hvar, I., *Yugoslavia* 54 Fd
Hwahsien, *China* 65 Fl
Hwaian, *China* 64 Jf
Hwaijen, *China* 64 Fc
Hwaiking. See Tsinyang
Hwaining, *China* 65 Hg
Hwaiyang, *China* 64 Gf
Hwaiyn. See Tsingkiang
Hwangchow. See Hwangkang
Hwang-Hai. See Yellow Sea
Hwang Ho, *China* 62 Gc
Hwang Ho, Mouth of, *China* 64 Jc
Hwanghsien, *China* 64 Kd
Hwangkang, *China* 64 Gg
Hweichow. See Sihsien
Hweimin, *China* 64 Hd
Hweinan, *China* 62 Jb
Hweitseh, *China* 65 Aj
Hwohsien, *China* 64 Ed
Hyden, *Kentucky* 86 Fb
Hyden, *W. Australia* 94 Cf
Hyde Park, *Vermont* 83 Kc
Hyderabad, *India* 68 Ee
Hyderabad, *W. Pakistan* 68 Cc
Hyères, *France* 53 Ge
Hyères, Is d', *France* 53 Ge
Hyland R., *Yukon* 80 Fd
Hyndman Pk., *Idaho* 84 Dc
Hyogo, *Japan* 66 Dg
Hyrynsalmi, *Finland* 46 Nd
Hythe, *England* 31 Hj
Iasi, *Rumania* 60 Eh
Iauarete, *Colombia* 90 Dc
I. aux Lievres, *Quebec* 83 Lb
Ibadan, *Nigeria* 78 Fg
Ibague, *Colombia* 90 Bc
Ibarra, *Ecuador* 90 Bc
Ibb, *Yemen* 72 Dg
Ibembo, *Congo* 76 Ed
Ibicui, *Brazil* 92 Ec
Ibiza I., *Balearic Is.* 51 Fc
Ibresi, *Russia* 61 Hc
Ibri, *Muscat & Oman* 73 Ge
Ibwe Munyama, *Zambia* 75 Dc
Íca, *Peru* 90 Bf
Ica, R., *Brazil* 90 Dd
Içana, *Brazil* 90 Dc
Içel, *Turkey* 72 Bb
Iceland, I., *N. Atlantic Oc.* 42 Cb
Ichak, *India* 71 Ec
Ichang, *China* 64 Eg
Icheng, *China* 64 Fg
Ichow. See Lini
Ichun, *China* 65 Gj
Idah, *Nigeria* 78 Gg
Idaho, state, *U.S.A.* 84 Cc
Idaho Falls, *Idaho* 87 Gd
Ideles, *Algeria* 78 Gd
Idfu, *Egypt* 79 Md
Idhra, I., *Greece* 57 Df
Idirtu, *China* 62 Cc
Idlib, *Syria* 74 Eb
Idutywa, *Cape Province* 75 Df
Ieper, *Belgium* 44 Ad
Ierissós, G. of, *Greece* 57 Dd
Ifakara, *Tanzania* 77 Hf
Iférouane, *Niger* 78 Ge
Ifni, terr., *N.-W. Africa* 78 Cc
Igan, *Sarawak* 63 Fk
Igarapé Miri, *Brazil* 91 Hd
Igarka, *Russia* 58 Hb
Ighil-Izane, *Algeria* 78 Fa
Iglesias, *Sardinia* 55 Bf
Igli, *Algeria* 78 Eb
Igloolik, *N.-W. Terr.* 81 Qc
Igoma, *Tanzania* 77 Gf
Igra, *Russia* 61 Lb
Iguaçú & R., *Brazil* 92 Fc
Iguala, *Mexico* 88 Ed
Iguapé, *Brazil* 92 Gb
Iguatu, *Brazil* 91 Ke
Igumira, *Tanzania* 77 Gf
Ihosy, *Madagascar* 77 Nl
Ihtiman, *Bulgaria* 56 Dc
Iida, *Japan* 66 Eg
Iisalmi, *Finland* 46 Me
Ijebu-Ode, *Nigeria* 78 Fg
Ijselmonde, *Netherlands* 44 Cc
Ijselmuiden, *Netherlands* 44 Db
Ijselstein, *Netherlands* 44 Db
Ijssel Meer, *Netherlands* 44 Db
Ijssel R., *Netherlands* 44 Eb
Ijui, *Brazil* 92 Fc
Ijzendijke, *Netherlands* 44 Bc
Ikaria, I., *Greece* 57 Ff
Ikisu, *Tanzania* 77 Ge
Ikla, *Estonia* 47 Lh
Ikushumbet, *Japan* 66 Gc
Ilagan, *Philippines* 63 Hg
Ilam, *Nepal* 71 Fb
Ilam, *Persia* 72 Ec
Ilanz, *Switzerland* 45 Eb
Iława, *Poland* 49 Hb
Iławka, *Poland* 49 Ja
Ilbunga, *S. Aust.* 95 Ge
Ile-á-la Crosse, L., *Sask.* 80 Ke
Ile-de-France, prov., *France* 52 Eb
Ile Mayotte, I., *Archipel des Comores* 77 Kg
Ilfracombe, *England* 31 Ej
Ilhavo, *Portugal* 50 Ab
Ilhéus, *Brazil* 91 Ef
Ili, *Kazakh.* 58 Gd
Ilía, *Greece* 57 Cf
Ilic, *Turkey* 72 Cb
Ilich, *Kazakh.* 58 Fd
Ilikotu (Hingan), *China* 62 Ha
Ilimsk, *Russia* 59 Kc
Iliodhrómia, I., *Greece* 57 De
Ilion, *New York* 86 Ca
Illapel, *Chile* 92 Bd
Ille-et-Vilaine, dep., *France* 52 Cb
Illescas, *Spain* 50 Db
Illimani, Mt., *Bolivia* 90 Dg
Illinois, state, *U.S.A.* 85 Hd
Illora, *Spain* 50 Dd
Il'men', Oz., *Russia* 60 Gb
Ilo, *Peru* 90 Cg
Iloilo, *Philippines* 63 Hh
Ilorin, *Nigeria* 78 Fg
Ilpi, *Russia* 59 Sb
Imabari, *Japan* 66 Cg
Iman, *Russia* 59 Nd
Imandra, Oz., *Russia* 58 Cb
Imerimandroso, *Madagascar* 77 Nk
Imi, *Ethiopia* 77 Jc
Immendingen, *Germany* 48 Ce
Imperatriz, *Brazil* 90 De
Imperatriz, *Brazil* 91 He
Imperia, *Italy* 54 Bd
Imperial Dam, *Arizona* 84 De
Imphal, *India* 69 Hd
Imroz, I., *Turkey* 72 Aa
Imtan, *Syria* 74 Ee
Inagua, I. Gt., *Bahama Is* 89 Eb
Inagua, I. Lit., *Bahama Is.* 89 Eb
Inari & L., *Finland* 46 Mb
Inchkeith, *Scotland* 30 Ed
Inchŏn, *Korea* 62 Jc
Incourt, *Belgium* 44 Cd
Indaal, L., *Scotland* 30 Ce
Indalsälven, *Sweden* 46 Ge
Indaw, *Burma* 69 Jd
Indawgyi L., *Burma* 69 Jc
Independence, *Kansas* 84 Gd
Independencia, *Argentina* 92 Cd
India, rep., *S. Asia* 68-69
Indian Des. See Thar Des.
Indiana, *Pennsylvania* 86 Ab
Indiana, state, *U.S.A.* 85 Jc
Indianapolis, *Indiana* 83 Cf
Indian Head, *Saskatchewan* 80 Lf
Indian House L., *Quebec* 81 Ue
Indian L., *New York* 86 Ca
Indiga, *Russia* 58 Db
Indigirka, R., *Russia* 59 Pb
Indonesia, *S.-E. Asia* 63 Fl
Indore, *India* 68 Ed
Indre, dep., *France* 52 Dc
Indre-et-Loire, dep., *France* 52 Dc
Indur (Nizamabad), *India* 68 Ee
Indus, R., *W. Pakistan, etc.* 68 Cd
Inebolu, *Turkey* 72 Ba
Ingelmunster, *Belgium* 44 Bd
Ingersoll, *Ontario* 83 Fd
Ingham, *Queensland* 95 Jc
Inglefield Inlet, *Greenland* 39 Qb
Inglefield Ld., *Greenland* 39 Qb
Inglewood, *New Zealand* 93 Ec
Ing Luiggi, *Argentina* 92 De
Ingolstadt, *Germany* 48 Dd
Ingrid Christensen Coast, *Antarctica* 100 Fb
Inhambane, *Moçambique* 75 Fd
Inishark I., *Eire* 31 Ag
Inishbofin, I., *Eire* 31 Ag
Inishkea I., *Eire* 31 Af
Inishman, I., *Eire* 31 Ag
Inishmore, I., *Eire* 31 Ag
Inishmurray, I., *Eire* 31 Bf
Inishtrahull, *Eire* 30 Ce
Inishturk, I., *Eire* 31 Ag
Injune, *Qnsld.* 95 Je
Inklin R., *British Columbia* 80 Ee
Innertkirchen, *Switzerland* 45 Db
Innisfail, *Queensland* 95 Jc
Innsbruck, *Austria* 48 De
Inoucdjouac, *Quebec* 81 Re
Inowrocław, *Poland* 49 Hb
Inquisivi, *Bolivia* 90 Dg
Ins, *Switzerland* 45 Ca
In Salah, *Algeria* 78 Fc
Insar, *Russia* 61 Gd
Insein, *Burma* 69 Je
In Shan. See Yin Shan
Insterburg. See Chernyakhovsk
Intelewa, *Surinam* 91 Fc
Interlaken, *Switzerland* 45 Cb
Interview I., *Andaman Is.* 69 Hf
Intragna, *Switzerland* 45 Db
Inutil, B., *Chile* 92 Ch
Inuvik, *Yukon* 80 Ec
Inveraray, *Scotland* 30 Dd
Invercargill, *New Zealand* 93 Bg
Inverell, *N.S.W.* 95 Ke
Inverness, *Nova Scotia* 82 Hc
Inverness & co., *Scotland* 30 Ec
Inverurie, *Scotland* 30 Fc
Investigator Str., *S. Aust.* 95 Gg
Inyati, *Rhodesia* 75 Dc
Inza, *Russia* 61 Hd
Inzer, *Russia* 61 Nc
Ioannina, *Greece* 57 Ce
Iola, *Kansas* 84 Gd
Iona, *Nova Scotia* 82 Hd
Iona I., *Scotland* 30 Cd
Ionia, *Michigan* 83 Dd
Ionian Is., *Greece* 57 Be
Ionian Sea, *Italy, etc.* 43 Mj
Ionishkis, *Lithuania* 47 Kh
Ios, I., *Greece* 57 Ef
Iowa, state, *U.S.A.* 85 Hc
Ipala, *Mexico* 88 Cc
Ipameri, *Brazil* 91 Hg
Ipen. See Ypres
Ipiales, *Colombia* 90 Bc
Ipin, *China* 65 Bh
Ipiros, *Greece* 57 Ce
Ipoh, *W. Malaysia* 67 Cf
Ippy, *Cent. Afr. Rep.* 79 Kg
Ipswich, *England* 31 Hh
Ipswich, *Queensland* 95 Ke
Ipu, *Brazil* 91 Jd
Iquique, *Chile* 92 Bb
Iquitos, *Peru* 90 Cd
Iracoubo, *French Guiana* 91 Gb
Iráklia, I., *Greece* 57 Ef
Iráklion, *Crete* 57 Eg
Iran (Persia), *Asia* 73 Fc
Irapa, *Venezuela* 90 Ea
Irapuato, *Mexico* 88 Dc
Iraq, *Asia* 72 Dc
Irazu, Vol., *Costa Rica* 89 Cd
Irbid, *Jordan* 74 De
Irbit, *Russia* 61 Rb
Ireland, Rep. of (Eire) 31 Bg
Irendyk Mts., *Russia* 61 Ne
Irgiz, *Kazakh.* 58 Fd
Irian Barat, *Indonesia* 41 Nj
Irikinskiy, *U.S.S.R.* 61 Pe
Iringa, *Tanzania* 77 Hf
Irish Sea, *British Isles* 31 Dg
Irkutsk, *Russia* 59 Kc
Irondale, *Ontario* 83 Gc
Iron Knob, *S. Australia* 95 Gf
Iron Mountain, *Michigan* 83 Cc
Iron River, *Michigan* 83 Bb
Ironton, *Ohio* 85 Kd
Ironwood, *Michigan* 83 Ab
Iroquois, *Ontario* 83 Jc
Iroquois Chute, *Quebec* 83 Kb
Irrawaddy, *Burma* 69 He
Irrawaddy, R., *Burma* 69 He
Irtysh, R., *Russia* 58 Fc
Irumu, *Congo* 77 Fd
Isabela I., *Galapagos Is.* 99 Rh
Isaccea, *Rumania* 56 Gb
Isafjördhur, *Iceland* 46 Ul
Isai Kalat, *W. Pakistan* 68 Bc
Isa Khel, *W. Pakistan* 70 Bd
Isangi, *Congo* 76 Ed
Isari, *Greece* 57 Df
Ischia, I., *Italy* 55 De
Ise, *Japan* 66 Eg
Ise B., *Japan* 66 Eg
Iseghem, *Belgium* 44 Bd
Iselin, *Pennsylvania* 86 Ab
Iseltwald, *Switzerland* 45 Cb
Isère, dep. & R., *France* 53 Fd
Isernia, *Italy* 55 Ee
Isfandaqeh. See Gāv Koshī
Isha Baidao, *Somalia* 77 Jd
Ishan, *China* 65 Dk
Ishikari, *Japan* 66 Hc
Ishim, *Russia* 58 Fc
Ishimbai, *Russia* 61 Nd
Ishinomaki B., *Japan* 66 Ge
Ishkamish, *Afghanistan* 73 Jb
Ishkanan, *Persia* 73 Fd
Ishkasham, *Afghanistan* 73 Kb
Ishpeming, *Michigan* 83 Cb
Isil Kul, *Russia* 58 Gc
Isiolo, *Kenya* 77 Hd
Isisford, *Queensland* 95 Hd
Iskenderun, *Turkey* 72 Cb
Iskilip, *Turkey* 72 Ba
Iskitim, *Russia* 58 Hc
Iskut R., *British Columbia* 80 Ee
Islamabad, *Kashmir* 70 Dd
Islamabad, *W. Pakistan* 70 Cd
Islampur, *India* 71 Ec
Island L., *Manitoba* 80 Nf
Island Pond, *Vermont* 83 Lc
Islands, B. of, *Newfoundland* 82 Jb
Islands, B. of, *New Zealand* 93 Ea
Islay I., *Scotland* 35 Dh
Isle of Man, *British Isles* 31 Ef
Isle Verte, *Quebec* 82 Dc
Ismailia, *Egypt* 79 Mb
Isna, *Egypt* 79 Mc
Isoka, *Zambia* 77 Gg
Isparta, *Turkey* 72 Bb
Israel, *W. Asia* 74 Ce
Isriya, *Syria* 74 Fb
Issoudun, *France* 52 Dc
Issyk Kul, Oz., *Kirgiz.* 58 Gd
Istanbul, *Turkey* 72 Aa
Istmina, *Colombia* 90 Bb
Istra, *Yugoslavia* 54 Dc
Itabaiana, *Brazil* 91 Ke
Itacare, *Brazil* 91 Kf
Itacoatiara, *Brazil* 90 Fd
Itaete, *Brazil* 91 Jf
Itaituba, *Brazil* 91 Fd
Itajai, *Brazil* 92 Gc
Itajui, *Brazil* 91 Hf
Italy, *Central Europe* 43 Kh
Itapaci, *Brazil* 91 Hf
Itapajé, *Brazil* 91 Kd
Itapecuru-mirim, *Brazil* 91 Jd
Itapemirim, Cachoeiro de, *Brazil* 91 Jh
Itapetininga, *Brazil* 91 Hh
Itapeva, *Brazil* 91 Hh
Itaqui, *Brazil* 92 Ec
Itarsi, *India* 68 Ed
Itasca, L., *Minnesota* 84 Gb
Itatubu, *Brazil* 90 Ee
Itauna, *Brazil* 91 Jh
Itéa, *Greece* 57 De
Ithaca, *Michigan* 83 Dd
Ithaca, *New York* 86 Ba
Itháci. See Ithaka
Ithaka, *Greece* 57 Ce
Itiés, *Greece* 57 Cd
Ituaçu, *Brazil* 91 Jf
Itubera, *Brazil* 91 Kf
Itula, *Congo* 77 Fe
Iturbe, *Argentina* 92 Cb
Iturup, I., *Kuril Is.* 39 De
Ivailovgrad, *Bulgaria* 56 Fd
Ivanhoe, *New South Wales* 95 Hf
Ivanic Grad, *Yugoslavia* 54 Fc
Ivano-Frankovsk (Stanislav), *Russia* 60 Dg
Ivanovka, *Russia* 61 Kd
Ivanovo, *Russia* 60 Mc
Ivdel, *Russia* 58 Fb
Iviza I. See Ibiza I.
Ivory Coast, *West Africa* 78 Dg
Ivugivik, *Quebec* 81 Rd
Iwakuni, *Japan* 66 Cg
Iwaniska, *Poland* 49 Jc
Ixiamas, *Bolivia* 90 Df
Ixtla, *Mexico* 88 Ed
Ixtlan de Juarez, *Mexico* 88 Ed
Iyang, *China* 65 Hh
Iyo Nada, *Japan* 66 Bh
Izabal & L., *Guatemala* 88 Gd
Izegem (Iseghem), *Belgium* 44 Bd
Izhevsk, *Russia* 61 Lb
Izhma & R., *Russia* 58 Eb
Izki, *Muscat & Oman* 73 Ge
Izmail, *Ukraine* 60 Fj
Izmir, *Turkey* 72 Ab
Izmit, *Turkey* 72 Aa
Izra, *Syria* 74 Ee
Iztapa, *Guatemala* 88 Fe
Izu Pen, *Japan* 66 Fg
Izu Shichito, *Japan* 66 Fg
Izyum, *Ukraine* 60 Kg
Jääski. See Svetogorsk
Jabalpur, *India* 71 Cd
Jabbeke, *Belgium* 44 Bc
Jabbul, *Syria* 74 Fa
Jablonec, *Czechoslovakia* 48 Fc
Jaboti, *Brazil* 90 Fd
Jabrin Oasis, *Arabia* 72 Ee
Jaburú, *Brazil* 90 Dd
Jaca, *Spain* 51 Ea
Jacarezinho, *Brazil* 91 Hh
Jachal, *Argentina* 92 Cd
Jaci Paraná, *Brazil* 90 Ee
Jackson, *Michigan* 83 Dd
Jackson, *Mississippi* 85 He
Jackson, *Ohio* 83 Ef
Jackson, *Tennessee* 85 Jd
Jackson Mts., *Nevada* 87 De
Jacksonville, *Florida* 85 Ke
Jacksonville, *Illinois* 83 Af
Jacmel, *Haiti* 89 Ec
Jacobabad, *W. Pakistan* 68 Cc
Jacobina, *Brazil* 91 Jf
Jacques Cartier, Mt., *Que.* 82 Fb
Jacquet River, *N.B.* 82 Ec
Jade Mines, *Burma* 69 Jc
Jadib, *S. Yemen* 73 Ff
Jadotville, *Congo* 76 Fg
Jaén, *Spain* 50 Dd
Jafarabad, *India* 68 Dd
Jaffna, *Ceylon* 68 Eg
Jagadhri, *India* 70 Ee
Jagdispur, *India* 71 Ec
Jaghbub, *Libya* 79 Kc
Jagraon, *India* 70 De
Jaguarão, *Brazil* 92 Fd
Jaguari, *Brazil* 92 Fc
Jaguariaiva, *Brazil* 91 Hh
Jaguaruna, *Brazil* 92 Gc
Jahanabad, *India* 71 Ec
Jahangirabad, *India* 70 Ff
Jahra, *Kuwait* 72 Ed
Jahrom, *Persia* 73 Fd
Jaicos, *Brazil* 91 Je
Jaipur, *India* 68 Ec
Jaipur, *India* 69 Jc
Jais, *India* 71 Cb
Jaisalmer, *India* 68 Dc
Jajarm, *Persia* 73 Gb
Jajpur, *India* 69 Gd
Jäkkvik, *Sweden* 46 Gc
Jakobi, *Estonia* 47 Mg
Jalalabad, *Afghanistan* 70 Bc
Jalalpur, *India* 71 Db
Jalalpur, *W. Pakistan* 70 Bf
Jalalpur, *W. Pakistan* 70 Dd
Jalapa, *Nicaragua* 89 Ed
Jalapa Enriquez, *Mexico* 88 Ed
Jalasjärvi, *Finland* 46 Ke
Jalaun, *India* 71 Bb
Jaldak, *Afghanistan* 73 Jc
Jalgaon, *India* 68 Ed
Jalisco, state, *Mexico* 88 Dd
Jalor, *India* 68 Dc
Jalpaiguri, *India* 71 Gb
Jalq, *Persia* 73 Hd
Jaluit, I., *Marshall Is.* 98 Fg
Jam, *Persia* 73 Fd
Jamaica, I., *West Indies* 89 Dc
Jamaja, *Estonia* 47 Kg
Jamalabad, *Persia* 72 Eb
Jamalpur, *E. Pakistan* 71 Hc
Jamalpur, *India* 71 Fc
Jamdena, I., *Indonesia* 63 Km
James B., *Canada* 81 Qt
James Ras., *N. Terr., Aust.* 94 Fd
James R., *S. Dakota* 84 Gc
Jamesburg, *California* 87 Cg
James Ross, I., *Antarctica* 100 Tc
Jameston, *New York* 86 Aa
Jamestown, *New York* 83 Gd
Jamestown, *N. Dakota* 84 Gb
James W. Ellsworth Ld., *Antarctica* 100 Rb
Jamiltepec, *Mexico* 88 Ed
Jammer Bugt, *Denmark* 47 Ch
Jammu, *Kashmir* 70 Dc
Jamnagar, *India* 68 Dd
Jampur, *W. Pakistan* 70 Bf
Jamrad, *Afghanistan* 73 Jc
Jamrao, *W. Pakistan* 68 Cc
Jämsä, *Finland* 47 Lf
Jamshedpur, *India* 71 Fd
Jamui, *India* 71 Fc
Jamuna R., *E. Pakistan* 71 Gc
Jamundi, *Colombia* 90 Bc
Jandaq, *Persia* 73 Fc
Jandiala, *India* 70 De
Janesville, *Wisconsin* 80 Ph
Janeville, *New Brunswick* 82 Fc
Jangipur, *India* 71 Gc
Jani Khel, *W. Pakistan* 70 Bd
Janjira, *India* 68 De
Jan Mayen I., *Arctic Ocean* 58 Aa
Janos, *Mexico* 88 Ca
Jansath, *India* 70 Ef
Jansenville, *Cape Province* 75 Cf
Januaria, *Brazil* 91 Jg
Janze, *France* 52 Cc
Jaora, *India* 68 Ed
Japan & Sea of, *E. Asia* 41 Ne
Japen, I., *W. Irian* 63 Ll
Japura, *Brazil* 90 Dd
Japvo Mt., *India* 69 Hc
Jaragua, *Brazil* 91 Hg
Jaragua, *Brazil* 92 Gc
Jaramillo, *Argentina* 92 Cg
Jarandilla, *Spain* 50 Cb
Jardim, *Brazil* 91 Ke
Jardines de la Reina, *Cuba* 89 Db
Jarji, *Nigeria* 78 Gf
Jarocin, *Poland* 49 Gc
Jaromer, *Czechoslovakia* 49 Fc
Jaroslaw, *Poland* 49 Kc
Järpen, *Sweden* 46 Ee
Jarvis I., *Pacific Ocean* 98 Jh
Järvsö, *Sweden* 47 Gf
Jashpurnagar, *India* 71 Ed
Jask, *Persia* 73 Gd
Jason I., *Falkland Is.* 92 Dh
Jasper & Park, *Alberta* 80 Hf
Jassy. See Iasi
Jastrowie, *Poland* 49 Gb
Jaswantnagar, *India* 71 Bb
Jaszberény, *Hungary* 49 He
Jataí, *Brazil* 91 Gg
Jath, *India* 68 Ee
Jativa, *Spain* 51 Ec
Jatobá, *Brazil* 91 Hd
Jaú, *Brazil* 91 Hh
Jauche, *Belgium* 44 Cd
Jauf. See Al Jawf
Jauja, *Peru* 90 Bf
Jaumave, *Mexico* 88 Ec
Jaunpur, *India* 71 Dc
Java, I., *Indonesia* 63 Em
Javari, R., *Peru-Brazil* 90 Ce
Javier, I., *Chile* 92 Bg
Jawa, *Nigeria* 79 Hf
Jawalamukhi, *India* 70 Ee
Jazir, *Muscat & Oman* 73 Gf
Jebba, *Nigeria* 78 Fg
Jeble, *Syria* 74 Db
Jech Doab, *W. Pakistan* 70 Cd
Jedburgh, *Scotland* 30 Fe
Jedede, *Arabia* 72 De
Jefferson, *Wisconsin* 83 Bd
Jefferson City, *Missouri* 85 Hd
Jefferson, Mt., *Oregon* 87 Cc
Jehol. See Chêngtehshih
Jekabpils, *Latvia* 47 Lh
Jelgava (Yelgava), *Latvia* 47 Kh
Jelsava, *Czechoslovakia* 49 Jd
Jemeppe, *Belgium* 44 Cd
Jena, *Germany* 48 Dc
Jenin, *Jordan* 74 De
Jenipapo, *Brazil* 90 Fe
Jeppo, *Finland* 46 Ke
Jerablus, *Syria* 74 Fa
Jerash, *Jordan* 74 De
Jeremie, *Haiti* 89 Ec
Jeremoabo, *Brazil* 91 Kf
Jerez, *Mexico* 88 Dc
Jerez de la Frontera, *Spain* 50 Bd
Jericho, *Jordan* 74 Df
Jericho, *Queensland* 95 Jd
Jerome, *Arizona* 84 De
Jerruck, *W. Pakistan* 68 Cc
Jersey, I., *Channel Is.* 52 Bb
Jersey City, *New Jersey* 86 Cb
Jerseyshore, *Pennsylvania* 86 Bb
Jerusalem, *Israel-Jordan* 74 Df
Jervois Ra., *N. Terr., Aust.* 95 Gd
Jesselton, *N. Borneo* 63 Gj
Jessore, *E. Pakistan* 71 Gd
Jesup, *Georgia* 85 Ke
Jesus I., *Quebec* 83 Kc
Jetalsar, *India* 68 Dd
Jeypore, *India* 69 Fe
Jezzin, *Lebanon* 74 Dd
Jhal, *W. Pakistan* 68 Cc
Jhalrapatan, *India* 68 Ed
Jhang Maghiana, *W. Pakistan* 70 Ce
Jhansi, *India* 71 Bc
Jhau, *W. Pakistan* 68 Cc
Jhazaouet (Nemours), *Algeria* 78 Ea
Jhelum, *W. Pakistan* 70 Cd
Jhelum R., *W. Pakistan* 70 Cd
Jhudo, *W. Pakistan* 68 Cc
Jhunjhunu, *India* 70 Df
Jiachan, *Tibet* 68 Fb
Jiaupur, *India* 71 Db
Jibhalanta, *Mongolia* 59 Jd
Jicaro, *Nicaragua* 89 Bd
Jičin, *Czechoslovakia* 48 Fc
Jidd, *Iraq* 72 Cc
Jiddah, *Arabia* 72 Ce
Jiggitai L., *Tibet* 69 Ga
Jihlava, *Czechoslovakia* 49 Fd
Jildiah, Jebel, *Arabia* 72 Dd
Jimena de la Frontera, *Spain* 50 Cd
Jimenez, *Mexico* 88 Db
Jimma, *Ethiopia* 77 Hc
Jim Thorpe, *Pennsylvania* 86 Cb
Jinnah Barrage, *W. Pakistan* 70 Bd
Jinotega, *Nicaragua* 89 Bd
Jipijapa, *Ecuador* 90 Ad
Jirgalanta, *Mongolia* 59 Jd
Jishah, *Arabia* 72 Ed
Jisr esh Shughur, *Syria* 74 Eb
Jiul R., *Rumania* 56 Db
Jiza, *Jordan* 74 Df
Jizan, *Arabia* 72 Df
Joacaba, *Brazil* 92 Fc
João Pessoa, *Brazil* 91 Le
Jobson, *Argentina* 92 Dc
Jodhpur, *India* 68 Dc
Joensuu, *Finland* 46 Ne
Jofane, *Moçambique* 75 Ed
Jogjakarta, *Java* 63 Fm
Johannesburg, *Transvaal* 75 De
John o' Groats, *Scotland* 30 Eb
Johnson City, *Tennessee* 85 Kd
Johnsonburg, *Pennsylvania* 86 Ab
Johnston I., *Pacific Ocean* 98 Jf
Johnstown, *New York* 86 Ca
Johnstown, *Pennsylvania* 86 Ab
Johore Bahru, *W. Malaysia* 67 Cf
Joinville, *Brazil* 92 Gc
Joinville, *France* 52 Fb
Joinville I., *Antarctica* 100 Tc
Jokkmökk, *Sweden* 46 Hc
Joliet, *Illinois* 83 Be
Joliette, *Quebec* 83 Kc
Jolo, I., *Philippines* 63 Hj
Jol Plat, *Arabia* 72 Ef
Jonava, *Lithuania* 47 Lj
Jonesboro, *Arkansas* 85 Hd
Jonesport, *Maine* 82 Ed
Jönköping, *Sweden* 47 Fh
Jonquière, *Quebec* 82 Cb
Jonuta, *Mexico* 88 Fd
Joplin, *Missouri* 85 Hd
Jordan, *W. Asia* 72 Cc
Jordan, R., *Israel-Jordan* 74 De
Jorhat, *India* 69 Hc
Jorje Montt, I., *Chile* 92 Bh
Joseph Bonaparte Gulf, *W. Australia* 94 Eb
Jotun Fjell, *Norway* 47 Cf
Jotunheimen, *Norway* 42 Kc
Joux, L. de, *Switzerland* 45 Bb
Jowai, *India* 69 Hc
Juan de Fuca Str., *U.S.A.-Canada* 84 Bb
Juan Fernandez I., *Pac. Oc.* 99 Sl
Juan Stuven, I., *Chile* 92 Ag
Juárez, *Argentina* 92 Ee
Juba, *Sudan* 79 Mh
Juba R., *Somalia* 77 Jd
Jubba, *Arabia* 72 Dd
Jubbulpore. See Jabalpur
Jubeil, *Lebanon* 74 Dc
Jucaro, *Cuba* 89 Db
Juchitan, *Mexico* 88 Ed
Judeidat el Wādī, *Syria* 74 Ed
Judenburg, *Austria* 48 Fe
Jugoslavia. See Yugoslavia

King Leopold Ra., W. Aust. 94 Ec
King Leopold & Queen Astrid Coast, Antarctica 100 Gc
Kingmen, China 64 Fg
King Oscar II Ld., Antarc. 100 Tc
Kingsbridge, England 31 Ek
King's Canyon Nat. Park, California 87 Dg
Kingscourt, Eire 31 Cg
King's Lynn, England 31 Hh
King Sound, W. Australia 94 Dc
Kingston, Jamaica 89 Dc
Kingston, New York 86 Cb
Kingston, New Zealand 93 Bf
Kingston, Ontario 83 Hc
Kingston-on-Thames, Eng. 31 Gj
Kingtung, China 62 Df
Kingushi, Congo 76 Df
Kingussie, Scotland 30 Ec
King William I., N.-W. Terr. 80 Mc
King William Ld., Greenland 39 Nb
Kingwood, W. Virginia 83 Gf
Kingyang, China 64 Cd
Kingyüan. See Ishan
Kinhsien, China 64 Kc
Kinhwa, China 65 Jh
Kinki, China 64 Cd
Kinleith, New Zealand 93 Ec
Kinross & co., Scotland 30 Ed
Kinsale, Eire 31 Bj
Kinshasa (Leopoldville), Congo 76 De
Kintap, Borneo 63 Gl
Kintyre, Scotland 30 De
Kinyangiri, Tanzania 77 Ge
Kiparissia, Greece 57 Cf
Kiparissía, G. of, Greece 57 Cf
Kipawa & L., Quebec 83 Gb
Kipini, Kenya 77 Je
Kirá Panayiá. See Pelagos, I.
Kirchberg, Switzerland 45 Ca
Kirensk, Russia 59 Kc
Kirgizskaya rep., U.S.S.R. 58 Gd
Kiri, Congo 76 De
Kirin, China 62 Jb
Kirit, Somalia 77 Kc
Kiriwina, I. See Trobriand I.
Kirkağaç, Turkey 72 Ab
Kirkby Lonsdale, England 31 Ff
Kirkcaldy, Scotland 30 Ed
Kirkcudbright & co., Scot. 30 Ee
Kirkee, India 68 De
Kirkenes, Norway 46 Na
Kirkland Lake, Ontario 83 Fa
Kirksville, Missouri 85 Hc
Kirkuk, Iraq 72 Db
Kirkwall, Orkney 30 Fb
Kirong Dzong, Nepa 71 Ea
Kirov, Russia 60 Jd
Kirov, Russia 61 Ja
Kirovgrad, Russia 61 Pb
Kirovograd, Ukraine 60 Hg
Kirovsk, Russia 58 Cb
Kirriemuir, Scotland 30 Ed
Kirsanov, Russia 61 Fd
Kirsehir, Turkey 72 Bb
Kirthar Ra., W. Pakistan 68 Cc
Kirun. See Chilung
Kiruna, Sweden 46 Jc
Kisamba, Congo 76 Ef
Kisangani, Congo 76 Fd
Kisbér, Hungary 49 He
Kishan, China 64 Ce
Kishanganj, India 71 Gb
Kishangarh, India 68 Dc
Kishangarh, India 70 Bg
Kishi, Nigeria 78 Fg
Kishinev, Moldavia 60 Fh
Kishtwar, Kashmir 70 Dd
Kisii, Kenya 77 Ge
Kisiju, Tanzania 77 Hf
Kiska, I., Aleutian Is. 85 Um
Kiskisink, Quebec 82 Bc
Kiskunfélégyháza, Hungary 49 He
Kismayu. See Chisimaio
Kispest, Hungary 49 He
Kissaraing I., Burma 69 Jf
Kissidougou, Guinea 78 Cg
Kistna R., India 68 Ee
Kisujszállás, Hungary 49 Je
Kisumu, Kenya 77 Ge
Kisvárda, Hungary 49 Kd
Kiswe, Syria 74 Ed
Kita, Mali 78 Df
Kitab, Uzbek. 58 Fe
Kitakyushu, Japan 62 Kd
Kitale, Kenya 77 Hd
Kitchener, Ontario 83 Fd
Kitchioh, China 65 Gl
Kitgum, Uganda 77 Gd
Kithira I., Greece 57 Df
Kithirai Chan., Greece 57 Dg
Kithnos, I., Greece 57 Ef
Kitimat, B.C. 80 Ff
Kittanning, Pennsylvania 86 Ab
Kittatinny Mts., New Jersey 86 Cb
Kittila, Finland 46 Lc
Kitui, Kenya 77 He
Kityang, China 65 Hl
Kitzingen, Germany 48 Dd
Kiuchuan, China 62 Cc
Kiukiang, China 65 Hh
Kiumbi, Congo 76 Ff
Kiungchow. See Kiungshan
Kiungchow Str. See Hainan Str.
Kiungshan, Hainan I. 65 En
Kiuruvesi, Finland 46 Me
Kivi Järvi, Finland 46 Le
Kivu L., Congo 77 Fe
Kiwai I., Papua 95 Ha
Kiyev, Ukraine 60 Gf
Kiyma, Kazakh. 58 Fc
Kizel, Russia 58 Ec
Kizil Irmak, Turkey 72 Ba
Kizyl Arvat, Turkmenistan 58 Ee
Kizyl Jilga, Kashmir 68 Ea
Kjerringöy, Norway 46 Fc
Kjöge, B., Greenland 39 Nc
Kladanj, Yugoslavia 56 Bb
Kladno, Czechoslovakia 48 Fc
Klagenfurt, Austria 48 Fe
Klaipeda, Lithuania 47 Jj
Klamath R., California 87 Be
Klamath Falls, Oregon 87 Cd
Klamath Mts., California 87 Be
Klamono, W. Irian 63 Kl
Klang, W. Malaysia 67 Cf
Klar Älv, Sweden 46 Ef
Klausenburg. See Cluj
Klerksdorp, Transvaal 75 De
Kleszczele, Poland 49 Kb
Klimpfjall, Sweden 46 Fd
Klisura, Bulgaria 56 Ec
Kliuchi, Russia 61 Gd
Ključ, Yugoslavia 54 Fc
Klodawa, Poland 49 Hb
Klofta, Norway 47 Df
Klomnice, Poland 49 Hc
Klondike R., Yukon 80 Dd
Kloosterzande, Netherlands 44 Cc
Klosters, Switzerland 45 Eb
Kluane, L., Yukon 80 Dd
Klundert, Netherlands 44 Cc
Klyuchyevskaya Sopka, Russ. 59 Rc
Knighton, Wales 31 Eh
Knin, Yugoslavia 54 Fc
Knob, C., W. Australia 94 Cf
Knockmealdown Mts., Eire 31 Bh
Knokke, Belgium 44 Bc
Knox, Pennsylvania 86 Ab
Knox Coast, Antarctica 100 Hc
Knoxville, Tennessee 85 Kd
Knysna, Cape Province 75 Cf
Knyszyn, Poland 49 Kb
Koartak, Quebec 81 Td
Kobarid, Yugoslavia 54 Db
Kobe, Japan 66 Dg
København, Denmark 47 Dj
Koblenz, Germany 48 Bc
Kobrin, White Russia 60 De
Kobroör, I., Indonesia 63 Km
Kocaeli. See Izmit
Kočani, Yugoslavia 56 Dd
Kočevje, Yugoslavia 54 Ec
Ko Chang, Siam 67 Cd
Kochi, Japan 66 Ch
Kochow. See Mowming
Kochumdek, Russia 59 Jb
Kodavere. See Kallaste
Kodiak & I., Alaska 85 Xm
Koekelare, Belgium 44 Ac
Koffiefontein, O.F.S. 75 De
Koforidua, Ghana 78 Eg
Kofu, Japan 66 Fg
Kogaluk R., Quebec 81 Re
Kohat, W. Pakistan 70 Bd
Kohima, India 69 Hc
Kojonup, W. Australia 94 Cf
Kokand, Uzbek. 73 Ka
Kokchetav, Kazakh. 58 Fc
Kokhtla Yarva, Estonia 47 Mg
Kokkola, Finland 46 Ke
Kokoda, Papua 95 Ja
Kokomo, Indiana 83 Ce
Kokoshili Ra., Tibet 69 Ga
Kokpekty, Kazakh. 58 Hd
Koksijde, Belgium 44 Ac
Kokstad, Cape Province 75 Df
Kokura, Japan 66 Bh
Ko Kut, Siam 67 Cd
Kokyar, China 70 Eb
Ko-lan-chow, China 64 Ec
Kolar, India 68 Ef
Kolari, Finland 46 Kc
Kolarovgrad, Bulgaria 56 Fc
Kolberg. See Kolobrzeg
Kolda, Senegal 78 Bf
Kolding, Denmark 47 Cj
Kole, Belgian Congo 76 Fd
Kolguyev Ostrov, Russia 58 Db
Kolhapur, India 68 De
Kolin, Czechoslovakia 48 Fc
Kolkas Rags, Latvia 47 Kh
Köln, Germany 48 Bc
Kolno, Poland 49 Jb
Kolo, Poland 49 Hb
Kolo, Tanzania 77 He
Kołobrzeg, Poland 49 Fa
Kologriv, Russia 61 Ga
Kolokani, Mali 78 Df
Kolomna, Russia 60 Ld
Kolomyya, Ukraine 60 Dg
Kolossia, Kenya 77 Hd
Kolpakovskiy, Russia 59 Qc
Kolpashevo, Russia 58 Hc
Kolwezi, Congo 76 Fg
Kolyma, R., Russia 59 Qb
Kolymskiy, Khrebet, Russia 59 Qb
Komandorskiye Ostr., Russ. 59 Rc
Komariya, Ceylon 68 Fg
Komarno, Czechoslovakia 49 He
Komatsu, Japan 66 Ef
Komi, aut. rep., Russia 58 Eb
Kommunisma Pk., Tadzhikskaya S.S.R. 58 Ge
Komoran, I., W. Irian 63 Lm
Komotini, Greece 56 Ed
Kompong Cham, Cambodia 67 Dd
Kompong Chhnang, Cambodia 67 Cd
Kompong-thom, Cambodia 67 Cd
Komsomolets Ostrov, Russia 59 Ja
Komsomolsk, Russia 59 Nc
Kondinskoe, Russia 58 Fb
Kondoa, Tanzania 77 He
Kong, Ivory Coast 78 Eg
Kong Karl's Land, Arctic Oc. 58 Ba
Kongmoon, China 65 Fl
Kongor, Sudan 79 Mg
Kongsberg, Norway 47 Cg
Kongsmoen, Norway 46 Ed
Kongsvinger, Norway 47 Ef
Kongwa, Tanzania 77 Hf
Königsberg. See Kaliningrad
Königshütte. See Chorzow
Konispol, Albania 57 Ce
Konjic, Yugoslavia 56 Ac
Konotop, Ukraine 60 Hf
Konstantinovka, Ukraine 60 Kg
Konstantinovsk, Russia 61 Eg
Konstanz, Germany 48 Ce
Kontiomäki, Finland 46 Nd
Konya, Turkey 72 Bb
Konza, Kenya 77 He
Kootenay Park, B.C. 80 Hf
Kootwijk, Netherlands 44 Db
Kopeisk, Russia 61 Qc
Kopervik, Norway 47 Ag
Köping, Sweden 47 Fg
Kopparberg, Sweden 47 Fg
Koppigen, Switzerland 45 Ca
Koprivnica, Yugoslavia 54 Fb
Kora, India 71 Cb
Korangi, W. Pakistan 73 Je
Korçë, Albania 57 Cd
Korčula, I., Yugoslavia 54 Fd
Korea, N., E. Asia 62 Jb
Korea, S., E. Asia 62 Jc
Korea B., Korea 62 Hc
Korea Kaikyo, Korea 62 Jd
Korinthia & Argolis, Greece 57 Df
Kórinthos, Greece 57 Df
Korinthos, G. of, Greece 57 De
Koritza. See Korçë
Kormakiti, C., Cyprus 74 Ab
Kornat, I., Yugoslavia 54 Ed
Korneuburg, Austria 49 Gd
Korogwe, Tanzania 77 Hf
Körös, Hungary 56 Ca
Korosten, Ukraine 60 Ff
Koro Toro, Chad 79 Je
Korpo, Finland 47 Jf
Korsakov, Russia 59 Pd
Korsnas, Finland 46 Je
Korsnes, Norway 46 Gb
Kortgem, Netherlands 44 Bc
Korthpulé, Albania 56 Bd
Korti, Sudan 79 Me
Kortrijk. See Courtrai
Korwai, India 71 Bc
Koryakskiy Khrebet, Russia 59 Rb
Kos, I., Greece 57 Ff
Koscierzyna, Poland 49 Ga
Kosha, Sudan 79 Md
Koshchagyl, Kazakh. 58 Ed
Koshiki Retto, Japan 66 Aj
Kosi, India 70 Eg
Košice, Czeckoslovakia 49 Jd
Kosima, Kuwait 72 Ed
Koslan, Russia 58 Db
Köslin. See Koszalin
Kosovo Metohija, Yugoslavia 56 Cc
Kostainica, Yugoslavia 54 Fc
Kosti, Sudan 79 Mf
Kostino, Russia 58 Hb
Kostroma, Russia 60 Mc
Koszalin, Poland 49 Gb
Kota Bharu, W. Malaysia 67 Ce
Kotah, India 68 Ec
Kota Kota, Malawi 77 Gg
Kotalpur, India 71 Fd
Kota Tinggi, W. Malaysia 67 Cf
Kotcha L., British Columbia 80 Ge
Kotehandpur, E. Pakistan 71 Gd
Kotel, Bulgaria 56 Fc
Kotelnich, Russia 61 Ja
Kotelnyy, Ostrov, Russia 59 Na
Köthen, Germany 48 Dc
Kotido, Uganda 77 Gd
Kotka, Finland 47 Mf
Kot Kapura, India 70 De
Kot Kasim, India 70 Ef
Kotkhai, India 70 Ee
Kotlas, Russia 58 Db
Kotli, Kashmir 70 Cd
Kotonkoro, Nigeria 78 Gf
Kotri, W. Pakistan 68 Cc
Kotturu, India 68 Ef
Kotzebue Sd., Alaska 85 Wl
Kouango, Cent. Afr. Rep. 79 Kg
Koudougou, Volta 78 E
Koulikoro, Mali 78 Df
Koundé, Cent. Afr. Rep. 79 Hg
Kourou, French Guiana 91 Gb
Koutiala, Mali 78 Df
Kouvola, Finland 47 Mf
Kovel, Ukraine 60 Df
Kovno. See Kaunas
Kovrov, Russia 61 Eb
Kowloon, China 65 Gl
Koyiu, China 65 Fl
Koyukuk, R., Alaska 85 X
Kozan, Turkey 72 Cb
Kozani, Greece 57 Cd
Kozhikode (Calicut), India 68 Ef
Kra & Isthmus of, Siam 67 Bc
Krabi, Thailand 67 Be
Kragerö, Norway 47 Cg
Kragujevac, Yugoslavia 56 Cb
Kraków, Poland 49 He
Kramatorsk, Ukraine 60 Kg
Kranj, Yugoslavia 54 Eb
Kranystaw, Poland 49 Kc
Krapina, Yugoslavia 54 Eb
Krasino, Novaya Zemlya 58 Ea
Krasnobród, Poland 49 Kc
Krasnodar, Russia 58 Cd
Krasnograd, Ukraine 60 Jg
Krasnoufimsk, Russia 61 Nb
Krasnovishersk, Russia 58 Eb
Krasnovodsk, Turkmenistan 58 Ed
Krasnoyarsk, Russia 59 Jc
Krasnyy Kholm, Russia 60 Kb
Krasnyy Kut, Russia 61 He
Krasnyy Uzel, Russia 61 Gc
Krasnyy Yar, Russia 61 Ge
Kratie, Indo-China 67 Dd
Krefeld, Germany 48 Bc
Kremenchug, Ukraine 60 Hg
Kremensk, Russia 61 Ff
Krems, Austria 48 Fd
Kretinga, Lith. 47 Jj
Kreuzlingen, Switzerland 45 Ea
Kribi, Cameroon 79 Gh
Krimml, Austria 48 Ee
Krishnanagar, India 71 Gd
Krishnaraja Res., India 68 Ef
Kristiansand, Norway 47 Cg
Kristianstad, Sweden 47 Fh
Kristiansund, Norway 46 Be
Kristiinankaupunki, Finland 46 Je
Kristinehamn, Sweden 47 Fg
Kriti, I. See Crete, I.
Kriva Palanka, Yugoslavia 56 Dc
Krivoy Rog, Ukraine 60 Hh
Krizevči, Yugoslavia 54 Fb
Krk, I., Yugoslavia 54 Ec
Krnov, Czechoslovakia 49 Gc
Kroken, Norway 46 Fd
Kroměříž, Czechoslovakia 49 Gd
Kronoby, Finland 46 Ke
Kronshtadt, Russia 60 Fa
Kroonstad, Orange Free State 75 De
Kropotkin, Russia 58 Dd
Krotoszyn, Poland 49 Gc
Krško, Yugoslavia 54 Ec
Krugersdorp, Transvaal 75 De
Kruishoutem, Belgium 44 Bd
Krujë, Albania 56 Bd
Krumbach, Germany 48 Dd
Krumlov, Czechoslovakia 48 Fd
Krung Thep, Siam 67 Cd
Krupnik, Bulgaria 56 Dd
Krusevac, Yugoslavia 56 Cc
Kruševo, Yugoslavia 56 Cd
Krustpils, Latvia 47 Lh
Krzyz, Poland 49 Gb
Ksabi, Algeria 78 Ec
Ksar El Boukhari, Algeria 78 Fa
Ksar-el-Kebir, Morocco 78 Da
Ktima, Cyprus 74 Ac
Kuala, Sumatra 63 Ck
Kuala Kangsar, W. Malaysia 67 Cf
Kuala Klawang, W. Malaysia 67 Cf
Kuala Krai, W. Malaysia 63 Dj
Kuala Lipis, W. Malaysia 67 Cf
Kuala Lumpur, W. Malaysia 67 Cf
Kuandang, Celebes 63 Hk
Kuangchow (Canton), China 65 Fl
Kuang-hsi. See Kwangsi
Kuang-tung. See Kwangtung
Kuantan, W. Malaysia 63 Dk
Kub, S.-W. Africa 75 Bd
Kucha, China 58 He
Kuching, Sarawak 63 Fk
Kuchow. See Jungkiang
Kudat, N. Borneo 63 Gj
Kudymkar, Russia 58 Ec
Kuei-chou. See Kweichow
Kuei-lin. See Kweilin
Kueiteh, China 62 Dc
Kuhak, Persia 73 Hd
Kuh Banan, Persia 73 Gc
Kuh-e-Bul, Persia 73 Fc
Kuh Furgan, Persia 73 Gd
Kuh-i-Dinar, Persia 73 Fc
Kuhmo, Finland 46 Nd
Kuhpayeh, Persia 73 Fc
Kuhrud. See Qohoud
Kuhsan, Afghanistan 73 Hc
Kuibis, S.-W. Africa 75 Be
Kuikang, China 65 Hh
Kuilenburg, Netherlands 44 Dc
Kuinre, Netherlands 44 Db
Kui Nua, Siam 67 Bd
Kukatush, Ontario 83 Ea
Kukawa, Nigeria 79 Hf
Kukës, Albania 56 Cc
Kukong, China 65 Fk
Kulachi, W. Pakistan 70 Be
Kuldiga, Latvia 47 Kh
Kuldja, China 58 Hd
Kulgera, N. Territory, Australia 95 Fe
Kulhakangri Mt., Tibet 69 Hc
Kulin, China 65 Bh
Kulmbach, Germany 48 Dc
Kulu, India 70 Ee
Kulunda, Russia 58 Gc
Kumai, Borneo 63 Fl
Kumamoto, Japan 66 Bh
Kumara, New Zealand 93 Ce
Kumara, Russia 59 Mc
Kumasi, Ghana 78 Eg
Kumbakonam, India 68 Ef
Kumher, India 71 Ab
Kumora, Russia 59 Lc
Kumta, India 68 Df
Kunda, Estonia 47 Mg
Kunduz, Afghanistan 73 Jb
Kungchang. See Lungsi
Kungnang, India 69 Hd
Kungrad, Uzbek. 58 Ed
Kungur, Russia 61 Nb
Kunhsien, China 64 Ef
Kunlun Shan, China-Tibet 40 He
Kunming, China 62 De
Kunsan, Korea 62 Jc
Kuopio, Finland 46 Me
Kupa R., Yugoslavia 54 Ec
Kupang, Timor I. 63 Hn
Kupiškis, Lithuania 47 Lj
Kupyansk, Ukraine 60 Kg
Kure, Japan 66 Cg
Kure, I., Hawaiian Is. 98 He
Kureika, Russia 58 Hb
Kurgan, Russia 58 Fc
Kuria Muria Is., Arabian Sea 73 Gf
Kurigram, E. Pakistan 71 Gc
Kuril'skiye Ostrova, Russia 59 Pd
Kurnool, India 68 Ee
Kurram, W. Pakistan 70 Bd
Kurskiy Zaliv, Russia 47 Jj
Kursky, Russia 60 Kf
Kurtalan, Turkey 72 Db
Kuru, Finland 47 Kf
Kuruman, Cape Province 75 Ce
Kurume, Japan 66 Bh
Kurunegala, Ceylon 68 Fg
Kusa, Russia 61 Pc
Kusaie, I., Caroline Is. 98 Fg
Kushersk, Russia 61 Ma
Kushiro, Japan 66 Jc
Kushk, Afghanistan 73 Hc
Kushka, Turkmenistan 58 Fe
Kushtia, E. Pakistan 71 Gd
Kushva, Russia 61 Pa
Kuskokwim B., Alaska 85 Wm
Kusma, Nepal 71 Da
Kustanay, Kazakh. 58 Fc
Kütahya, Turkey 72 Ab
Kutai R., Borneo 63 Gk
Kut-al-Hai. See Al Hayy
Kutaradja, Sumatra 63 Cj
Kutch, Gt. Rann of, India 68 Cd
Kutch & Gulf of, India 68 Cd
Kutchian, Japan 66 Gc
Kutina, Yugoslavia 54 Fc
Kutno, Poland 49 Hb
Kütsing, China 65 Ak
Kutu, Ethiopia 77 Gc
Kutum, Sudan 79 Kf
Kuusamo, Finland 46 Nd
Kuusjärvi, Finland 46 Ne
Kuwait & state, Persian G. 72 Ed
Kuyang, China 64 Eb
Kuybyshev, Russia 61 Kd
Kuybyshev, Russia 58 Gc
Kuybyshevskoye Vdkhr., Russia 61 Jc
Kuytan, Russia 59 Kc
Kuzhbal, Russia 61 Ga
Kuzino, Russia 61 Pb
Kuzmin, Yugoslavia 56 Bb
Kuznetsk, Russia 61 Hd
Kuzovatovo, Russia 61 Hd
Kvalöy, N., Norway 46 Ha
Kvalöy, S., Norway 46 Hb
Kvarken, Ostra, Sweden 46 Je
Kvarner, G. of, Yugoslavia 54 Ec
Kvarnerolo, G. of, Yugosl. 54 Ec
Kvesmenes, Norway 46 Jb
Kwajalein, Is., Marshall Is. 98 Fg
Kwakhanai, Botswana 75 Cd
Kwakoegron, Surinam 91 Fb
Kwangchang, China 65 Hj
Kwangchow Wan, China 65 Em
Kwangnan, China 65 Bk
Kwangping. See Yungnien
Kwangshun, China 65 Cj
Kwangsi, prov., China 65 Cl
Kwangsin. See Shangjao
Kwangtung, prov., China 65 Fl
Kwang-Tung (Luta) Pen., China 64 Kc
Kwania L., Uganda 77 Gd
Kweichih, China 65 Hg
Kweichow. See Fengkieh
Kweichow, prov., China 65 Bj
Kweihwa. See Kweisui
Kweihwa. See Tzeyun
Kweiki, China 65 Hh
Kweilin, China 65 Ek
Kweiping, China 65 El
Kweisui. See Huhehot
Kweiteh. See Shangkiu
Kweiyang, China 65 Cj
Kweiyang, China 65 Fk
Kwi-chu. See Phu Qui
Kwidzyń, Poland 49 Hb
Kwitao, Burma 69 Jc
Kwoka, Mt., W. Irian 63 Kl
Kyakhta, Russia 59 Kc
Kyancutta, S. Australia 95 Gf
Kyangin, Burma 69 Je
Kyaukpadaung, Burma 69 Jd
Kyaukpyu, Burma 69 He
Kyaukse, Burma 69 Jd
Kyauktaw, Burma 69 Hd
Kyelang, India 70 Ed
Kyi R., Tibet 69 Hc
Kymi, Finland 47 Mf
Kynšperk, Czechoslovakia 48 Ec
Kynuna, Queensland 95 Hd
Kyoga L., Uganda 77 Gd
Kyoto, Japan 66 Dg
Kyrenia, Cyprus 74 Bb
Kyshtym, Russia 61 Qc
Kythrea, Cyprus 74 Bb
Kyushu, I., Japan 66 Bh
Kyustendil, Bulgaria 56 Dc
Kyusyur, Russia 59 Ma
Kyzyl, Russia 59 Jc
Kyzyl Kum, Uzbek., etc. 58 Fd
Kyzylsk, Russia 61 Pd
Kzyl Orda, Kazakh. 58 Fd
Laanila, Finland 46 Mb
La Asencion, Mexico 88 Ca
La Asuncion, Margarita I., Venezuela 90 Ea
Laban, Jordan 74 Dg
La Banda, Argentina 92 Dc
Labang, Sarawak 63 Fk
Labé, Guinea 78 Cf
Labelle, Quebec 83 Jb
Laberge, L., Yukon 80 Dd
Labouheyre, France 53 Cd
Laboulaye, Argentina 92 Dd
Labrador, Canada 81 Uf
Labrea, Brazil 90 Ee
La Brea, Trinidad 90 Ea
Labuan, I., N.-W. Borneo 63 Gj
Labuk B., N. Borneo 63 Gj
Labytnangi, Russia 40 Fb
La Canoa, Venezuela 90 Eb
La Carlota, Argentina 92 Dd
La Carolina, Spain 50 Dc
Laccadive Is., Indian Ocean 68 Df
La Ceiba, Venezuela 90 Cb
Lac Frontiere, Quebec 82 Cc
Lachen, Switzerland 45 Da
Lachine, Quebec 83 Kc
Lachlan R., New S. Wales 95 Jf
Lachmangarh, India 70 Dg
Lachute, Quebec 83 Jc
Lackawanna, New York 86 Aa
Lackawaxen, Pennsylvania 86 Cb
La Cocha, Argentina 92 Cc
Lacombe, Alberta 80 Jf
Laconia, New Hampshire 86 Ea
La Copelina, Argentina 92 Ce
La Coruña, Spain 50 Aa
Lac-Rémi, Quebec 83 Jb
La Crosse, Wisconsin 85 Hc
La Cruz, Colombia 90 Bc
La Cruz, Mexico 88 Cb
Ladakh Ra., Tibet/Kashmir 68 Eb
Ladiz, Persia 73 Hd
Ladoga L. See Ladozhskoye Oz.
La Dorada, Colombia 90 Cb
Ladozhskoye Oz., Russia 60 Ga
Ladwa, India 70 Ef
Lady Neunes B., Antarctica 100 Lb
Ladysmith, British Columbia 80 Gg
Ladysmith, Natal 75 De
Lae, New Guinea 95 Ja
Laeken, Belgium 44 Cd
Læsö, I., Denmark 47 Dh
La Esperanza, Honduras 89 Bd
La Estrada, Spain 50 Aa
La Fayette, Indiana 83 Ce
Lafayette, Louisiana 85 He
Lafontaine, Quebec 82 Dc
Lages, Brazil 91 Ke
Laggan L., Scotland 30 Ed
Laghouat, Algeria 78 Fb
Lagonegro, Italy 55 Ee
Lagos, Mexico 88 Dc
Lagos, Nigeria 78 Fg
Lagos, Portugal 50 Ad
La Grande, Oregon 87 Dc
La Grange, Georgia 85 Ke
Lagrange, Indiana 83 Cd
La Grange, W. Australia 94 Dc
La Granja, Spain 50 Cb
La Guaira, Venezuela 90 Da
La Guardia, Argentina 92 Cc
La Guardia, Spain 50 Ab
Laguna, Brazil 92 Gc
Lagunas, Peru 90 Be
Lagunillas, Bolivia 90 Eg
Laharpur, India 71 Cb
Lahej, S. Yemen 72 Dg
Lahijan, Persia 73 Fb
Laholm, Sweden 47 Eh
Lahore, W. Pakistan 70 De
Lahti, Finland 47 Lf
Laibach. See Ljubljana
Lai, C., N. Vietnam 67 Dc
Lai-chau, N. Vietnam 67 Cb
Laichow. See Yehsien
Laigle, France 52 Db
Laila, Arabia 72 Ee
Laingsburg, Cape Province 75 Cf
Lairg, Scotland 30 Eb
Laisamis, Kenya 77 Hd
Laishev, Russia 61 Jc
Laives, Italy 45 Gb
Laja, L., Chile 92 Be
La Japonesa, Argentina 92 Ce
Lajes, Brazil 92 Fc
La Junquera, Spain 51 Ga
La Junta, Colorado 84 Fd
Lakatrask, Sweden 46 Jc
Lake Charles, Louisiana 85 Hf
Lake City, Michigan 83 Bc
Lake Edward, Quebec 83 Kb
Lakefield, Ontario 83 Gc
Lake Geneva, Wisconsin 83 Bd
Lake George, New York 86 Da
Lake Grace, W. Aust. 94 Cf
Lake Harbour, N.-W. Terr. 81 Td
Lake King, W. Australia 94 Cf
Lakeland, Florida 85 Kf
Lake Majella, California 87 Cg
Lake Nash, N. Terr., Aust. 95 Gd
Lake Pleasant, New York 86 Ca
Lake Pukaki, N.Z. 93 Cf
Lake Victoria Res., Quebec 83 Hb
Lakeview, Oregon 87 Cd
Lakewood, New Jersey 86 Cb
Lakewood, New York 86 Aa
Lakewood, Ohio 83 Fe
Lakhimpur, India 71 Cb
Lakhimpur, India 69 Hc
Lakki, W. Pakistan 70 Bd
Lakkor Tso, Tibet 69 Fb
Lakonia, Greece 57 Df
Lakonia, G. of, Greece 57 Df
Lakota, Ivory Coast 78 Dg
Lakse Fd., Norway 46 Ma
Lakselv, Norway 46 La
Laktsang, Tibet 69 Fb
Lala Musa, W. Pakistan 70 Dd
Lalbagh, India 71 Gc
Lalganj, India 71 Ec
La Libertad, Ecuador 90 Ad
La Libertad, Guatemala 88 Fd
La Libertad, Nicaragua 89 Bd
La Ligua, Chile 92 Bd
Lalin, Spain 50 Aa
Lalitpur, India 71 Bc
La Maddalena, I., Sardinia 55 Be
La Malbaie, Quebec 83 Lb
La Manche, Newfoundland 82 Mc
Lamastre, France 53 Fd
Lambach, Austria 48 Ed
Lamballe, France 52 Bb
Lambayeque, Peru 90 Be
Lambert's Ld., Greenland 39 Mb
Lambertville, New Jersey 86 Cb
Lámbia, Greece 57 Cf
Lambton, C., N.-W. Terr. 81 Gb
Lamé, Chad 79 Hg
Lamego, Portugal 50 Bb
Lamia, Greece 57 De
Lammermuir Hills, Scotland 30 Fe
Lamotrek Is., Caroline Is. 98 Dg
Lampazos, Mexico 88 Db
Lampedusa, I., Medit. Sea 79 Ha
Lampeter, Wales 31 Eh
Lamphun, Siam 67 Bc
Lampi, I., Burma 69 Jf
Lamu, Kenya 77 Je
Lamud, Peru 90 Be
Lanark & co., Scotland 30 Ee
Lancashire, co., England 31 Fg
Lancaster, England 31 Ff
Lancaster, New Brunswick 81 Tg
Lancaster, New Hampshire 83 Lc
Lancaster, New York 86 Aa
Lancaster, Pennsylvania 86 Bb
Lancaster, Wisconsin 83 Ad
Lancaster Sd., N.-W. Terr. 81 Pb
Lanchow, China 64 Dc
Landeck, Austria 48 De
Landen, Belgium 44 Dd
Landerneau, France 52 Ab
Landes, dep., France 53 Cd
Landfall, I. See Recalada
Landi Khana. See Tor Khama
Landi Kotal, W. Pakistan 70 Bc
Landon, Sweden 46 Fe
Landsberg, Germany 48 Dd
Landsberg. See Gorzów
Land's End, England 31 Dk
Landshut, Germany 48 Ed
Landskrona, Sweden 47 Ej
Langaa, Denmark 47 Ch
Langadhas, Greece 57 Dd
Langana L., Ethiopia 77 Hc
Langchung, China 64 Cg
Langeac, France 53 Ed
Langeland, I., Denmark 47 Dj
Längelmavesi, Finland 47 Lf
Langenthal, Switzerland 45 Ca
Langholm, Scotland 30 Fe
Lang Jökull, Iceland 46 Vm
Langkawi, I., W. Malaysia 67 Be
Langlade, Quebec 83 Ja
Langogne, France 53 Ed
Langon, France 53 Cd
Langöy, Norway 46 Fb
Langres, France 52 Fc
Langsa, Sumatra 63 Ck
Långsele, Sweden 46 Ge
Lang-Son, N. Vietnam 67 Db
Långträsk, Sweden 46 Jd
Languedoc, prov., France 53 Ee
Lanklaer, Belgium 44 Dc
Lankor Tso, Tibet 69 Fb
Lannion, France 52 Bb
Lansdale, Pennsylvania 86 Cb
Lansing, Michigan 83 Dd
Lanusei, Sardinia 55 Bf
Lanzarote, I., Canary Is. 78 Cc
Laoag, Philippines 63 Hg
Lao Bao, Laos 67 Dc
Lao-chang-Ho R., China 64 Hd
Lao Kay, N. Vietnam 67 Cb
Laon, France 52 Eb
La Oroya, Peru 90 Bf
Laos, S.-E. Asia 67 Cc
Lao shan, China 64 Kd
Lapalisse, France 52 Ec
La Paragua, Venezuela 90 Eb
La Paz, Argentina 92 Ed
La Paz, Argentina 92 Cd
La Paz, Bolivia 90 Dg
La Paz, Honduras 89 Bd
La Paz, Mexico 88 Bc
Lapchung L., Tibet 69 Gb
Lapeer, Michigan 83 Ed
La Pelada, Argentina 92 Dd
La Pérouse, str., U.S.S.R.-Japan 66 Gb
Lapinlahti, Finland 46 Me
Lapithos, Cyprus 74 Bb
La Plata, Argentina 92 Ed
La Porte, Indiana 83 Ce
Laporte, Pennsylvania 86 Bb
Lapovo, Yugoslavia 56 Cb
Lappa Järvi, Finland 46 Ke
Lappeenranta, Finland 47 Nf
Lappland, N. Europe 46 Jb
Lapptrask, Sweden 46 Kc
Laprida, Argentina 92 De
Laptevykh Sea, Russia 59 La
Lăpuşul Românesc. See Tîrgu Lăpuş
Łapy, Poland 49 Kb

La Quiaca, Argentina 92 Cb
Lar, Persia 73 Fd
Larache, Morocco 78 Da
Laragne, France 53 Fd
Laramate, Peru 90 Cf
Laramie, Wyoming 84 Ec
Laramie Mts., Wyoming 84 Ec
Laranjeiras, Brazil 91 Kf
La Rasse, Switzerland 45 Ba
Larchwood, Ontario 83 Fb
Laredo, Texas 84 Gf
Largeau (Faya), Chad 76 Da
Largs, Scotland 30 De
Larino, Italy 55 Ee
La Rioja, Argentina 92 Cc
Larisa, Greece 57 De
Larkana, W. Pakistan 68 Cc
Larnaca & B., Cyprus 74 Bc
Larne, N. Ireland 31 Df
La Robla, Spain 50 Ca
Laroche, Belgium 44 Dd
La Rochelle, France 52 Cc
La Roda, Spain 51 Dc
Larrimah, N.Terr., Aust. 94 Fc
Lars Christensen Coast, Antarctica 100 Fc
Laruns, France 53 Ce
Larvik, Norway 47 Dg
Laryak, Russia 58 Gb
La Salle, Illinois 83 Be
Las Anod, Somalia 77 Kc
La Sarre, Quebec 81 Rg
Las Cejas, Argentina 92 Dc
Las Colorados, Argentina 92 Be
Las Cruces, Mexico 88 Cb
Las Cruces, New Mexico 84 Ee
La Serena, Chile 92 Bc
Las Flores, Argentina 92 Ee
Lash. See Khash
Las Heras, Argentina 92 Cg
Lashio, Burma 69 Jd
Lashkar, India 71 Bb
Lashkar Gah, Afghanistan 68 Bb
Lasithi, Crete 57 Eg
Lasjerd, Persia 73 Fb
Las Khoreh, Somalia 77 Kb
Las Lajas, Argentina 92 Be
Las Lomitas, Argentina 92 Db
Las Palmas, Canary Is. 78 Bc
Las Plumas, Argentina 92 Cf
Lassen Pk., California 87 Ce
Lassen Vol. Nat. Park, Cal. 87 Ce
Las Tablas, Panama 89 Ce
Last Mountain L., Sask. 80 Kf
Lastovo, I., Yugoslavia 54 Fd
Las Vegas, Nevada 87 Fg
Las Vegas, New Mexico 84 Ed
Latacunga, Ecuador 90 Bd
Latakia, Syria 74 Db
Laterrière, Quebec 82 Cb
Latina, Italy 55 De
Latrobe, Pennsylvania 86 Ab
Latrun, Jordan 74 Cf
La Tuque, Quebec 83 Kb
Latvia, rep., U.S.S.R. 47 Kh
Laufen, Switzerland 45 Ca
Lauhkaung. See Launggyang
Launceston, England 31 Ek
Launceston, Tasmania 95 Jh
Launggyang, Burma 69 Jc
La Unión, Chile 92 Bf
La Unión, Mexico 88 Dd
La Unión, Salvador 89 Bd
La Unión, Spain 51 Ed
Laura, Queensland 95 Hc
La Urbana, Venezuela 90 Db
Laurel, Maryland 86 Bc
Laurel, Mississippi 85 Je
Laurel Hill, Pennsylvania 86 Ab
Laurent, Quebec 83 Kb
Laurentide Mts., Quebec 82 Bc
Laurentides Park, Quebec 82 Cc
Lauria, Italy 55 Ee
Laurie, I., South Orkneys 100 Tc
Lausanne, Switzerland 45 Bb
Lautaro, Chile 92 Be
Lautem. See Vila Nova de Malaca
Lauzon, Quebec 83 Lb
Lavacherie, Belgium 44 Dd
Laval, France 52 Cb
Laval B., Quebec 82 Db
Lavalle, Argentina 92 Cd
Lavalleja. See Minas
Lavamünd, Austria 48 Fe
Lavardac, France 53 Dd
La Vega, Rep. Dominicana 89 Ec
La Vela, Venezuela 90 Da
Laverton, W. Australia 94 De
Lavongai. See New Hanover
Lavos, Portugal 50 Ab
Lavras, Brazil 91 Hh
Lavras, Brazil 92 Fd
Lavras, Brazil 91 Ke
Lavrentiya, Russia 59 Tb
Lávrion, Greece 57 Ef
Lawk Sawk, Burma 69 Jd
Lawlers, W. Australia 94 De
Lawra, Ghana 78 Ef
Lawrence, Massachusetts 86 Ea
Lawrence, New Zealand 93 Bf
Lawton, Oklahoma 84 Ge
Laysan I., Hawaiian Is. 98 He
Lazarevac, Yugoslavia 56 Cb
Lazio, reg., Italy 55 Dd
Lead, S. Dakota 84 Fc
Leadville, Colorado 84 Ed
Leaf R., Quebec 81 Se
Leamington, England 31 Fh
Leamington, Ontario 83 Ed
Learmonth, W. Aust. 94 Bd
Leavenworth, Kansas 84 Gd
Łeba, Poland 49 Ga
Lebanon, New Hampshire 86 Da
Lebanon, Pennsylvania 86 Bb
Lebanon, W. Asia 72 Cc
Lebesby, Norway 46 Ma
Lebombo Mts., S. Africa 75 Ee
Lebork, Poland 49 Ga
Lebu, Chile 92 Be
Lebwa, Lebanon 74 Ec
Lecce, Italy 55 Ge
Lecco, Italy 54 Bc
Lectoure, France 53 Dd
Ledbury, England 31 Fh
Ledesma, Argentina 92 Db
Ledesma, Spain 50 Cb
Ledo, India 69 Jc
Lee R., Eire 31 Bj
Leeds, England 31 Fg
Leende, Netherlands 44 De
Leerbeek, Belgium 44 Cd
Leerdam, Netherlands 44 Dc
Leesburg, Virginia 86 Bc
Leeuwarden, Netherlands 44 Da
Leeuwin, C., W. Australia 94 Bf
Leeward Is., West Indies 89 Gc
Lefka, Cyprus 74 Ab
Lefkara, Cyprus 74 Bc
Lefkoniko, Cyprus 74 Bb
Lefroy, L., W. Australia 94 Df
Legaspi, Philippines 63 Hh
Legge Pk., Tasmania 95 Jh
Leghorn. See Livorno
Legnica, Poland 49 Gc
Leh, Kashmir 70 Ec
Le Havre, France 52 Db
Lehi, Utah 84 Dc
Lehututu, Botswana 75 Cd
Leiah, W. Pakistan 70 Be
Leicester & co., England 31 Gh
Leichhardt, R., Queensland 95 Gc
Leiden, Netherlands 44 Cb
Leigh Creek, S. Australia 95 Gf
Leighton Buzzard, England 31 Gj
Leignon, Belgium 44 Dd
Leimuiden, Netherlands 44 Cb
Leinster, prov., Eire 31 Cg
Leipzig, Germany 48 Ec
Leith, Scotland 30 Ee
Leitrim, co., Eire 31 Bf
Leix (Laoighis), co., Eire 31 Ch
Leiyang, China 65 Fj
Leka, Norway 46 Dd
Le Kef, Tunisia 79 Ga
Leksands Noret, Sweden 47 Ff
Leksvik, Norway 46 De
Leland, Michigan 83 Dc
Leleque, Argentina 92 Bf
Le Maire, Estrecho de, Argentina 92 Dh
Léman, Lac, Switzerland 45 Bb
Le Mans, France 52 Db
Lemberg. See Lvov
Lemnos. See Limnos, I.
Lemyethna, Burma 69 Je
Lena, R., Russia 59 Mb
Lenina, Pk., Kirgiz. 58 Ge
Leninabad, Uzbek. 58 Fd
Leninakan, Armyanskaya S.S.R. 58 Dd
Leningrad, Russia 60 Gb
Leninka, Russia 59 Sb
Leninogorsk, Kazakh. 58 Hc
Leninsk Kuznetskiy, Russia 58 Hc
Lenk, Switzerland 45 Cb
Lennox, I., Chile & Argent. 92 Cj
Lens, France 52 Ea
Lent, Netherlands 44 Dc
Lentiira, Finland 46 Nd
Lenvik, Norway 46 Hb
Lenya, Burma 69 Jf
Lenz, Switzerland 45 Eb
Lenzerheide, Switzerland 45 Eb
Leoben, Austria 48 Fe
Leominster, England 31 Fh
Leominster, Massachusetts 86 Ea
Léon, France 53 Ce
León, Mexico 88 Dc
León, Nicaragua 89 Bd
León, Spain 50 Ca
León, Monts. de, Spain 50 Ba
Leonforte, Sicily 55 Eg
Leonidhion, Greece 57 Df
Leonora, W. Australia 94 De
Leontevo, Russia 60 Kb
Léopold II L., Congo 76 De
Leopoldsburg, Belgium 44 Dc
Leopoldville. See Kinshasa
Lephepe, Botswana 75 Dd
Lepontine, Alpi, Switz.-Italy 45 Db
Lepreau, New Brunswick 82 Ed
Lercara Friddi, Sicily 55 Dg
Lerdo, Mexico 88 Db
Lerida, Spain 51 Fb
Lerma, Argentina 92 Cb
Lerma, Spain 50 Da
Lermoos, Austria 48 De
Léros, I., Greece 57 Ff
Le Roy, New York 86 Aa
Lerwick, Scotland 30 Ja
Lesbos. See Lesvos I.
Les Escoumins, Quebec 82 Db
Leskovac, Yugoslavia 56 Cc
Lesnoy, Russia 58 Cb
Lesotho, S. Africa 75 De
Lesozavodsk, Russia 59 Nd
Lesparre, France 53 Cd
Lesser Slave L., Alberta 80 He
Lessines, Belgium 44 Bd
Lestijärvi, Finland 46 Le
Lesvos, I., Greece 57 Ee
Leszno, Poland 49 Gc
Letea I., Rumania 56 Gb
Lethbridge, Alberta 80 Jg
Leti Kep., Indonesia 63 Jm
Leticia, Colombia 90 Dd
Letpadan, Burma 69 Jc
Letterkenny, Eire 30 Bf
Letty Harbour, N.-W. Terr. 80 Gc
Letur, Spain 51 Dc
Leucate, France 53 Ee
Leuk, Switzerland 45 Cb
Leuser, Mt., Sumatra 63 Ck
Leuven. See Louvain
Leuze, Belgium 44 Bd
Levádhia, Greece 57 De
Levanger, Norway 46 De
Leven L., Scotland 30 Ed
Levêque, C., W. Australia 94 Dc
Levice, Czechoslovakia 49 Hd
Levick, Mt., Antarctica 100 Lb
Levin, New Zealand 93 Ed
Levis, Quebec 83 Lb
Levitha, I., Greece 57 Ff
Levkás, I., Greece 57 Ce
Levoča, Czechoslovakia 49 Jd
Lewes, England 31 Hk
Lewes R., Yukon 80 Dd
Lewis I., Scotland 30 Cb
Lewis Ra., Montana 84 Db
Lewisburg, Pennsylvania 83 He
Lewiston, Idaho 87 Eb
Lewiston, Maine 82 Cd
Lewiston, Michigan 83 Dc
Lewistown, Illinois 83 Ae
Lewistown, Montana 84 Eb
Lewistown, Pennsylvania 86 Bb
Lexington, Kentucky 85 Kd
Leydsdorp, Transvaal 75 Ed
Leysele, Belgium 44 Ad
Leyte, I., Philippines 63 Hh
Lezajsk, Poland 49 Kc
Lha-kang Dzong, Tibet 69 Hc
Lhasa, Tibet 69 Hc
Lha-tse Dzong, Tibet 69 Gc
Lhontse Dzong, Tibet 69 Hc
Liangchow. See Wuwei
Liangsiang, China 64 Hc
Liant, C., Siam 67 Cd
Liao R., China 62 Hb
Liaocheng, China 64 Hd
Liaohsien, China 64 Fd
Liao-tung, G. of, China 64 Kc
Liaoyang, China 64 Lb
Liard, N.-W. Territories 80 Gd
Liard R., N.-W. Territories 80 Gd
Liari, W. Pakistan 68 Cc
Liberec, Czechoslovakia 48 Fc
Liberia, Costa Rica 89 Bd
Liberia, W. Africa 78 Cg
Libertad, Mexico 88 Bb
Libnan, Jebel, Lebanon 74 Dc
Libourne, France 53 Cd
Libreville, Gabon 76 Bd
Libya, N. Africa 79 Hc
Licata, Sicily 55 Dg
Licheng. See Tsinan
Lichfield, England 31 Fh
Lida, White Russia 60 De
Liddes, Switzerland 45 Cc
Liddon G., N.-W. Terr. 81 Hb
Lidköping, Sweden 47 Eg
Lido-di-Roma, Italy 55 De
Lidzbark, Poland 49 Ja
Liechtenstein, Europe 45 Ea
Liège & prov., Belgium 44 Dd
Liegnitz. See Legnica
Lieksa, Finland 46 Pe
Lienkong, China 65 Jj
Lienyunkang, China 64 Je
Lienz, Austria 48 Ee
Liepāja, Latvia 47 Jh
Lier, Belgium 44 Cc
Lierneux, Belgium 44 Dd
Liestal, Switzerland 45 Ca
Lievre R. du, Quebec 83 Jb
Lifu, I., Loyalty Is. 98 Fk
Ligure, Appennino, Italy 54 Bc
Liguria, reg., Italy 54 Bc
Ligurian Sea, Italy 54 Bd
Lihsien, China 65 Eh
Likiang, China 62 De
Likimi, Congo 76 Ed
Liling, China 65 Fj
Lilla Edet, Sweden 47 Eg
Lille, Belgium 44 Cc
Lille, France 52 Ea
Lillehammer, Norway 47 Df
Lillesand, Norway 47 Cg
Lillo, Belgium 44 Cc
Lillo, Spain 50 Dc
Lillooet, British Columbia 80 Gf
Lilongwe, Malawi 77 Gg
Lim-Fjorden, Denmark 47 Ch
Lima, Ohio 83 De
Lima, Peru 90 Bf
Limache, Chile 92 Bd
Limassol, Cyprus 74 Bc
Limay, R., Argentina 92 Ce
Limay Mahuida, Argentina 92 Ce
Limbazi, Latvia 47 Lh
Limbourg, Belgium 44 Dd
Limburg, Germany 48 Cc
Limburg, prov., Belgium 44 Dd
Limchow. See Hoppo
Limeira, Brazil 91 Hh
Limerick (Luimneach), Eire 31 Bh
Limes, Belgium 44 Dd
Limestone, Maine 82 Ec
Limmavady, N. Ireland 30 Ce
Limmen, Netherlands 44 Cb
Limmen Bight, N. Territory, Australia 95 Gb
Limni, Greece 57 De
Limnos, I., Greece 57 Ee
Limoges, France 52 Dd
Limon, Costa Rica 89 Cd
Limousin, prov., France 52 Dd
Limoux, France 53 Ee
Limpopo R., Moçamb., etc. 75 Ed
Linares, Chile 92 Be
Linares, Mexico 88 Ec
Linares, Spain 50 Dc
Lincheng, China 64 He
Linchwan, China 65 Hj
Lincoln, Argentina 92 Dd
Lincoln, Maine 82 Dd
Lincoln, Michigan 83 Ec
Lincoln, Nebraska 84 Gc
Lincoln, New Zealand 93 De
Lincoln & co., England 31 Gg
Lincoln Sea, Arctic Ocean 39 Qa
Lincoln Wolds, England 31 Gg
Lindau, Germany 48 Ce
Lindesay, Mt., Queensland 95 Ke
Lindesnes, Norway 47 Bh
Lindi, Tanzania 77 Hf
Lindley, Orange Free State 75 De
Lindos, Greece 57 Gf
Lindsay, Ontario 83 Gc
Lindsey, Lincs., England 31 Gg
Line Is., Pacific Ocean 99 Kg
Linfen, China 62 Fc
Lingchwan, China 65 Ek
Lingen, Germany 48 Bb
Lingga, I., Riouw Arch., Indon. 63 El
Lingling, China 62 Fe
Linguéré, Senegal 78 Be
Lingyun, China 65 Ck
Linhai, China 63 He
Linhares, Brazil 91 Jg
Linho, China 64 Cb
Linhsien, China 65 Fk
Lini, China 62 Gc
Linkiang, China 62 Jb
Linkiang, China 62 Ka
Linkiang. See Tsingkiang
Linköping, Sweden 47 Fg
Linkuva, Lithuania 47 Kh
Linnhe L., Scotland 30 Dd
Linosa, I., Medit. Sea 55 Dh
Linping, China 65 Gk
Lins, Brazil 92 Gb
Linsi, China 62 Gb
Lintan. See Kadiger
Linth, R., Switzerland 45 Eb
Linthal, Switzerland 45 Db
Linton, Quebec 83 Kb
Linyu, China 64 Jb
Linz, Austria 48 Fd
Lion, G. du, France 53 Fe
Lion Pt., N.-W. Territories 80 Gb
Lio Porgyul, Tibet 68 Eb
Liouesso, Fr. Congo 76 Dd
Lipa, Yugoslavia 54 Fc
Lipari Is. (Eolie, Isole), Italy 55 Ef
Lipetsk, Russia 60 Le
Liping, China 65 Dj
Lipovets, Ukraine 60 Fg
Lippstadt, Germany 48 Cc
Lipsói, I., Greece 57 Ff
Lira, Uganda 77 Gd
Lircay, Peru 90 Cf
Liria, Spain 51 Ec
Lisala, Congo 76 Ed
Lisboa, Portugal 50 Ac
Lisbon. See Lisboa
Lisburn, N. Ireland 31 Cf
Lisburne C., Alaska 85 Wl
Liscannor B., Eire 31 Ah
Lisdoonvarna, Eire 31 Ag
Lishih, China 64 Ed
Lishui, China 65 Jh
Lisianski, I., Hawaiian Is. 98 He
Lisieux, France 52 Db
L'Isle, Switzerland 45 Bb
L'Islet, Quebec 83 Lb
Liski, Russia 61 De
Lismore, Eire 31 Bh
Lismore, New South Wales 95 Ke
Listowel, Eire 31 Ah
Listowel, Ontario 83 Fd
Lith, Al, Arabia 72 De
Lithgow, New South Wales 95 Kf
Lithinon, C., Crete 57 Eg
Lithuania (Litovskaya S.S.R.), U.S.S.R. 47 Kj
Litoměrice, Czechoslovakia 48 Fc
Litovskaya S.S.R. See Lithuania
Little America, Antarctica 100 Mb
Little Belt Mts., Montana 84 Db
Little Current, Ontario 83 Fc
Little Falls, Minnesota 85 Hb
Little Falls, New York 86 Ca
Little Horn Mts., Arizona 87 Gj
Little River, New Zealand 93 De
Little Rock, Arkansas 85 He
Little Smoky R., Alberta 80 Hf
Little Valley, New York 86 Aa
Littleton, New Hampshire 83 Lc
Liuan, China 62 Gd
Liuchow, China 64 Ef
Liupan Shan, China 64 Be
Liusvaara, Russia 46 Pe
Liverpool, New South Wales 95 Kf
Liverpool, Nova Scotia 82 Fd
Liverpool & B., England 31 Eg
Liverpool Coast, Greenland 39 Nb
Liverpool Ra., New S. Wales 95 Jf
Livingston, Guatemala 89 Bc
Livingston, Montana 84 Db
Livingston, I., S. Shetlands 100 Sc
Livingstone, Zambia 75 Dc
Livingstonia, Malawi 75 Eb
Livno, Yugoslavia 54 Fd
Livny, Russia 60 Ke
Livo Joki, Finland 46 Md
Livorno, Italy 54 Cd
Livramento, Brazil 92 Ed
Liwa, Muscat & Oman 73 Ge
Liwale, Tanzania 77 Hf
Liyepaya, Latvia 47 Jh
Lizard Pt., England 31 Dl
Ljubljana, Yugoslavia 54 Eb
Ljubuški, Yugoslavia 54 Fd
Ljungdalen, Sweden 46 Ee
Ljusdal, Sweden 47 Gf
Llandovery, Wales 31 Ej
Llandrindod Wells, Wales 31 Eh
Llandudno, Wales 31 Eg
Llanelli, Wales 36 Fe
Llanes, Spain 50 Ca
Llangollen, Wales 31 Eh
Llanguihue, L., Chile 92 Bf
Llano Estacado, New Mexico-Texas 84 Fe
Llano Grande, Mexico 88 Cc
Llerena, Spain 50 Bc
Llico, Chile 92 Bd
Lloydminster, Saskatchewan 80 Jf
Lluchmayor, Balearic Is. 51 Gc
Loango, Fr. Congo 76 Ce
Lobbes, Belgium 44 Cd
Loberia, Argentina 92 Ee
Lobito, Angola 76 Cg
Lobos, Argentina 92 Ee
Lobstick L., Labrador 81 Tf
Locarno, Switzerland 45 Db
Lochalsh, Ontario 83 Da
Lochalsh, Kyle of, Scotland 30 Dc
Lochem, Netherlands 44 Eb
Lochinver, Scotland 30 Db
Lochnagar, Scotland 30 Ed
Lochy L., Scotland 30 Dd
Lock Haven, Pennsylvania 86 Bb
Lockerbie, Scotland 30 Ee
Lockport, New York 86 Aa
Locle, le, Switzerland 45 Ba
Loc Ninh, S. Vietnam 63 Eh
Lodeynoye Pole, Russia 60 Ha
Lodhran, W. Pakistan 70 Bf
Lodi, Wisconsin 83 Bd
Lödingen, Norway 46 Fb
Lodwar, Kenya 77 Hd
Łódź, Poland 49 Hc
Loenen, Netherlands 44 Eb
Loewoek (Luwuk), Celebes 63 Hl
Lofer, Austria 48 Ee
Lofoten, Is., Norway 46 Ec
Logan, Utah 84 Dc
Logan, Mt., Quebec 82 Eb
Logan, Mt., Yukon 80 Cd
Logansport, Indiana 83 Ce
Logone R., Cameroun/Chad 76 Cb
Logrono, Spain 51 Da
Lohardaga, India 71 Ed
Loharu, India 70 Df
Loikaw, Burma 69 Je
Loir, R., France 52 Cc
Loire, dep., France 52 Ed
Loire R., France 52 Fc
Loire-Atlantique, dep., Fr. 52 Cc
Loiret, dep., France 52 Ec
Loir-et-Cher, dep., France 52 Dc
Loja, Ecuador 90 Bd
Loja, Spain 50 Cd
Loka, Sudan 79 Mh
Lokeren, Belgium 44 Cc
Lokka, Finland 46 Mc
Lökken, Denmark 47 Ch
Lökken, Norway 46 Ce
Loko, Nigeria 78 Gg
Loks I., N.-W. Territories 81 Ud
Lola, Angola 76 Cg
Lolland, Denmark 47 Dj
Lom, Bulgaria 56 Dc
Lomas, Argentina 92 Ed
Lomas, Peru 90 Cg
Lombardia, reg., Italy 54 Bc
Lomblem, I., Indonesia 63 Hm
Lombok, I. & Str., Indonesia 63 Gm
Lomé, Togo 78 Fg
Lomela, Congo 76 Ee
Lomié, Cameroun 79 Hh
Lommel, Belgium 44 Dc
Lomond L., Scotland 30 Dd
Łomża, Poland 49 Kb
Loncoche, Chile 92 Be
Loncopue, Argentina 92 Be
Londiani, Kenya 77 He
London, England 31 Gj
London, Ontario 83 Fd
Londonderry & co., N. Ire. 30 Cf
Londonderry, C., W. Aust. 94 Eb
Londonderry, I., Chile 92 Bj
Long B., S. Carolina 85 Le
Long I., Bahama Is. 89 Db
Long I., New York 86 Db
Long I., Nova Scotia 82 Ed
Long L., Maine 82 Dc
Long L., Ontario 81 Pg
Long, L., Scotland 30 Dd
Long Ra., Newfoundland 82 Kb
Longa, Brazil 91 Je
Long Beach, California 87 Dj
Long Beach, New Jersey 86 Cc
Long Branch, New Jersey 86 Cb
Longchamps, Belgium 44 Dd
Longford & co., Eire 31 Bg
Long Island City, New York 86 Db
Long Island Sd., N.Y., etc. 86 Db
Long Point, Ontario 83 Fd
Longreach, Queensland 95 Hd
Longs Pk., Colorado 84 Ec
Longtown, England 30 Fe
Longué, France 52 Cc
Longueuil, Quebec 83 Kc
Longuyon, France 52 Fb
Longview, Washington 87 Bb
Longwy, France 52 Fb
Long-Xuyen, S. Vietnam 67 Dd
Lonneker, Netherlands 44 Eb
Lons-le-Saunier, France 52 Fc
Loochristi, Belgium 44 Bc
Looe, England 31 Ek
Lookout, C., N. Carolina 85 Le
Loolmalasin, Mt., Tanzania 77 He
Loop Hd., Eire 31 Ah
Lopez C., Gabon 76 Be
Lopik, Netherlands 44 Cc
Lop Nor, China 62 Bb
Lopphavet, Norway 46 Ja
Lora Hamun, W. Pakistan 68 Bc
Lorain, Ohio 83 Ee
Loralai, W. Pakistan 68 Cb
Lorca, Spain 51 Ed
Lord Howe I., Pacific Ocean 98 El
Lordsburg, New Mexico 84 Ee
Lorena, Brazil 91 Jh
Loreto, Brazil 91 He
Loreto, Mexico 88 Bb
Lorica, Colombia 90 Bb
Lorient, France 52 Bc
Lorn, Firth of, Scotland 30 Dd
Lorrach, Germany 48 Be
Lorraine, prov., France 52 Fb
Los Andes, Chile 92 Bd
Los Angeles, California 87 Dh
Los Angeles, Chile 92 Be
Los Blancos, Argentina 92 Db
Loshan, China 65 Ah
Lošinj, I., Yugoslavia 54 Ec
Los Lamentos. See Felix U Gomez
Los Menucos, Argentina 92 Cf
Los Pozos, Chile 92 Bc
Los Santos, Panama 89 Ce
Los Santos de Maimona, Sp. 50 Bc
Lossiemouth, Scotland 30 Ec
Los Teques, Venezuela 90 Da
Los Tigres, Argentina 92 Dc
Los Vilos, Chile 92 Bd
Lot, dep., France 53 Dd
Lot, R., France 53 Dd
Lota, Chile 92 Be
Lotbinière, Quebec 83 Lb
Lot-et-Garonne, dep., Fr. 53 Dd
Lottigna, Switzerland 45 Db
Loubet Coast, Antarctica 100 Sc
Loudéac, France 52 Bb
Loudima, Fr. Congo 76 Ce
Loudon, Malawi 77 Gg
Loudun, France 52 Dc
Louga, Senegal 78 Be
Loughborough, England 31 Gh
Loughborough's I., Burma 69 Jf
Loughrea, Eire 31 Bg
Louhans, France 52 Fc
Louiseville, Quebec 83 Kb
Louisiade Arch., Papua 95 Kb
Louisiana, state, U.S.A. 85 He
Louis Philippe Ld., Antarc. 100 Tc
Louis Trichardt, Transvaal 75 Dd
Louisville, Kentucky 85 Jd
Loulé, Portugal 50 Ad
Lourdes, France 53 Ce
Lourenço Marques, Moçamb. 75 Ee
Louriçal, Portugal 50 Ab
Lourinhã, Portugal 50 Ac
Louth, England 31 Hg
Louth, New South Wales 95 Jf
Louth, co., Eire 31 Cg
Louvain, Belgium 44 Cd
Louveigne, Belgium 44 Dd
Louviers, France 52 Db
Lövånger, Sweden 46 Jd
Loviisa, Finland 47 Mf
Lövlid, Sweden 46 Gd
Low, C., N.-W. Territories 81 Pd
Lowa, Congo 76 Fe
Lowell, Massachusetts 86 Ea
Lowell, Michigan 83 Dd
Lowestoft, England 31 Jh
Łowicz, Poland 49 Hb
Lowville, New York 86 Ca
Loyalty Is., Pacific Ocean 98 Fk
Loyang, China 64 Fe
Loyung, China 65 Dk
Lozère, dep., France 53 Ed
Loznica, Yugoslavia 56 Bb
Luan. See Changchih
Luang Prabang, Laos 67 Cc
Luarca, Spain 50 Ba
Luashi, Congo 76 Eg
Lubaczów, Poland 49 Kc
Lubana, Latvia 47 Mh
Lubartów, Poland 49 Kc
Lübben, Germany 48 Ec
Lubbock, Texas 84 Fe
Lübeck, Germany 48 Db
Lübecker B., Germany 48 Da
Lubefu, Congo 76 Ee
Lubin, Poland 49 Gc
Lublin, Poland 49 Kc
Lubliniec, Poland 49 Hc
Lubuklinggau, Sumatra 63 Dl
Lubumbashi (Elisabethville), Congo 75 Db
Luc, le, France 53 Ge
Lucala, Angola 76 Df
Lucania. See Basilicata
Lucca, Italy 54 Cd
Lucea, Jamaica 89 Dc
Lucena, Spain 50 Cd
Lučenec, Czechoslovakia 49 Hd
Lucera, Italy 55 Ee
Lucerne (Luzern), Switz. 45 Da
Luch, Russia 61 Fb
Luchenya, Malawi 77 Hh
Luchow, China 65 Bh
Luchow (Hofei), China 64 Hg
Lucinda, Pennsylvania 86 Ab
Luckau, Germany 48 Ec
Luckenwalde, Germany 48 Eb
Lucknow, India 71 Cb
Lucknow, Ontario 83 Fd
Luçon, France 52 Cc
Luderitz, S.-W. Africa 75 Ae
Ludhiana, India 70 De
Ludington, Michigan 83 Cc
Ludlow, England 31 Fh
Ludvika, Sweden 47 Ff
Ludwigshafen, Germany 48 Cd
Ludwigslust, Germany 48 Db
Ludza, Latvia 47 Mh
Luebo, Congo 76 Ef
Luga, Russia 60 Fb
Lugano & L. di, Switz. 45 Db
Lugansk, Ukraine 60 Lg
Lugh Ganane, Somalia 77 Jd
Lugo, Spain 50 Ba
Lugoj, Rumania 56 Cb
Lugovay, Kazakh. 58 Gd
Luhit R., India 69 Jc
Luhsien. See Luchow
Luhwang Shan, I., China 65 Lh
Luichow. See Hoihong
Luichow Pen., China 62 Ef
Luime, Angola 76 Dg
Luitpold Cst., Antarctica 100 Ab
Luján, Argentina 92 Ed
Luján, Argentina 92 Cd
Lukachek, Russia 59 Nc
Lukala, Congo 76 Cf
Lukovit, Bulgaria 56 Ec
Lukoyanov, Russia 61 Gc
Lukula, Congo 76 Cf
Lule Älv, Sweden 46 Jc
Luleå, Sweden 46 Kd
Luluabourg, Congo 76 Ef
Lulung, China 64 Jc
Lumbres, France 52 Ea
Lummen, Belgium 44 Dd
Lumsden, New Zealand 93 Bf
Lund, Sweden 47 Ej
Lundy I., England 31 Dj
Lüneburg, Germany 48 Db
Lunel, France 53 Fe
Lunéville, France 52 Gb
Lungan. See Pingwu
Lungki, China 65 Hk
Lungnan, China 65 Gk
Lungsi, China 64 Be
Lungyen, China 65 Hk
Luni, India 68 Dc
Lunino, Russia 61 Gd
Lunz, Austria 48 Fe
Lupeh, China 62 Hb
Lupiro, Tanzania 77 Hf
Lupkow, Poland 49 Kd
Luputa, Congo 76 Ef
Luque, Paraguay 92 Ec
Luray, Virginia 83 Gf
Lurgan, N. Ireland 31 Cf
Luribay, Bolivia 90 Dg
Luröy, Norway 46 Ec
Lusaka, Zambia 75 Dc
Lusambo, Congo 76 Ee
Lusambo, Congo 76 Ef
Lushai Hills. See Mizo Hills
Lushnjë, Albania 57 Bd
Lushun, China 64 Kc
Lussanvira, Brazil 91 Gh
Lut Des., Persia 73 Gc
Lutembo, Angola 76 Eg
Luther, Michigan 83 Dc
Luton, England 31 Gj
Lutsen, Minnesota 83 Ab
Lutsk, Ukraine 60 Df
Luttre, Belgium 44 Cd
Luvia, Finland 47 Jf
Luwuk (Loewoek), Celebes 63 Hl
Luxembourg, and Grand-duchy, N.-W. Europe 52 Gb
Luxembourg, prov., Belg. 52 Fb
Luxeuil, France 52 Gc
Luxor, Egypt 79 Mc
Luzern & canton, Switz. 45 Da
Luziânia, Brazil 91 Hg
Luzilândia, Brazil 91 Jd
Luzon, I., Philippines 63 Hg
Luzon Str., Philippines 62 Hf
Luzy, France 52 Ec
Lvov, Ukraine 60 Dg
Lwanhsien, China 64 Jc
Lwan-ping, China 64 Hb
Lyallpur, W. Pakistan 70 Ce
Lybster, Scotland 30 Eb
Lycksele, Sweden 46 Hd
Lydavėnai, Lithuania 47 Kj
Lydda, Israel 74 Cf
Lydenburg, Transvaal 75 Ee
Lyell, Mt., Brit. Columbia 80 Hf
Lyell, Mt., California 87 Dg
Lyell Ra., New Zealand 93 Dd
Lykens, Pennsylvania 86 Bb
Lyme B., England 31 Fk
Lyme Regis, England 31 Fk
Lynchburg, Virginia 85 Ld
Lynn, Massachusetts 86 Ea
Lynn Lake, Manitoba 80 Le
Lynton, England 31 Ej
Lyon, France 52 Fd
Lyonnais, prov., France 52 Ed
Lyons, New York 86 Ba
Lyons, R., W. Australia 94 Cd
Lys, R., Belgium, etc. 44 Bd
Lyse, Poland 49 Jb
Lysekil, Sweden 47 Dg

Lyss, *Switzerland* 45 Ca
Lyster, *Quebec* 83 Lb
Lysva, *Russia* 61 Na
Lyttelton, *New Zealand* 93 De
Lytton, *British Columbia* 80 Gf
Ma'an, *Jordan* 74 Dg
Maarheeze, *Netherlands* 44 Dc
Maarianhamina. See Mariehamn
Ma'arret en Numan, *Syria* 74 Eb
Maas, R., *Netherlands* 44 Dc
Maasbree, *Netherlands* 44 Ec
Maaseik, *Belgium* 44 Dc
Ma'asir. See Hazawza
Maassluis, *Netherlands* 44 Cc
Maastricht, *Netherlands* 44 Dd
Mabote, *Moçambique* 75 Ed
Mabrouk, *Mali* 78 Ee
Mabuki, *Tanzania* 77 Ge
McAdam, *New Brunswick* 82 Ed
Macaé, *Brazil* 91 Jh
Macaíba, *Brazil* 91 Ke
McAlester, *Oklahoma* 84 Ge
Macao (Port.), *China* 65 Fl
Macapá, *Brazil* 91 Gc
Macás, *Ecuador* 90 Bd
Macau, *Brazil* 91 Ke
Macauba, *Brazil* 91 Gf
Macclesfield, *England* 31 Fg
McClintock Channel, *N.-W. Terr.* 80 Lb
McCluer G., *New Guinea* 63 Kl
McClure, C., *N.-W. Terr.* 80 Hb
McClure Str., *N.-W. Terr.* 80 Hb
McComb, *Mississippi* 85 He
McConnellsburg, *Pa.* 86 Ac
Macdonald, L., *W. Australia* 94 Ed
Macdonnell Ras., *N.T., Aust.* 94 Fd
McDouall Ra., *N. Terr., Aust.* 95 Fc
Maceió, *Brazil* 91 Ke
Macerata, *Italy* 54 Dd
McGill, *Nevada* 87 Ff
Macgillycuddy's Reeks, *Eire* 31 Aj
McGregor Ra., *Queensland* 95 He
Mach, *W. Pakistan* 68 Cc
Machala, *Ecuador* 90 Bd
Macharetí, *Bolivia* 90 Eh
Machias, *Maine* 82 Ed
Machias B., *Maine* 82 Ed
Machiasport, *Maine* 82 Ed
Machicha, *Moçambique* 75 Fd
Machiques, *Venezuela* 90 Ca
Machiwara, *India* 70 Ee
Măcin, *Rumania* 56 Gb
Mackay, *Alberta* 80 Je
Mackay, *Queensland* 95 Jd
Mackay L., *N.-W. Terr.* 80 Jd
Mackay, L., *W. Australia* 94 Ed
McKeesport, *Pennsylvania* 86 Ab
Mackenna, *Argentina* 92 Dd
Mackenzie, *Guyana* 90 Fb
Mackenzie Dist., *N.-W. Terr.* 80 Gd
Mackenzie B., *N.-W. Terr.* 80 Dc
Mackenzie Mts., *N.-W. Terr.* 80 Ed
Mackenzie R., *N.-W. Terr.* 80 Fc
Mackenzie Sea, *Antarctica* 100 Fc
Mackenzie King I., *N.-W. T.* 80 Ja
Mackinac I. & Str. of, *Mich.* 83 Dc
Mackinaw, *Michigan* 83 Dc
McKinley, Mt., *Alaska* 85 Xl
Macleod, *Alberta* 80 Jg
McLeod B., *N.-W. Terr.* 80 Jd
Macloutsie, *Botswana* 75 Dd
Mac-Mahon, Fort, *Algeria* 78 Fc
McMillan, L., *New Mexico* 84 Fe
Macmillan Ra., *Yukon* 80 Dd
Macmillan R., *Yukon* 80 Ed
McMurdo Sd., *Antarctica* 100 Lb
Macomer, *Sardinia* 55 Be
Macon, *Belgium* 44 Cd
Mâcon, *France* 52 Fc
Macon, *Georgia* 85 Ke
Macouria, *Fr. Guiana* 91 Gc
McPherson, *Kansas* 84 Gd
McPherson, *N.-W. Terr.* 80 Dc
Macpherson Ra., *Queensland* 95 Ke
Macquarie Harb., *Tasmania* 95 Jh
Macquarie I., *Pacific Ocean* 98 En
Macquarie, R., *N.S.W.* 95 Jf
Mac-Robertson Ld., *Antarc.* 100 Fb
Macroom, *Eire* 31 Bj
Macuje, *Colombia* 90 Cc
Macusani, *Peru* 90 Cf
McVicar Arm, *N.-W. Terr.* 80 Hc
Madaba, *Jordan* 74 Df
Madadi, *Chad* 79 Ke
Madagascar I., *Indian Oc.* 77 Nl
Madain Salih, *Arabia* 72 Cd
Madan, *Persia* 73 Gb
Madaripur, *E. Pakistan* 69 Hd
Madawaska, *Ontario* 83 Gc
Madeira, Is., *Atlantic Ocean* 78 Bb
Madeira, R., *Brazil* 90 Ee
Madeleine, C. de la, *Quebec* 82 Fb
Madhepur, *India* 71 Fb
Madhipura, *India* 71 Fc
Madhopur, *India* 68 Ec
Madhopur, *India* 70 Dd
Madhubani, *India* 71 Fb
Madhupur, *India* 71 Fc
Madhya Pradesh, *India* 68 Ed
Madison, *New Jersey* 86 Cb
Madison, *S. Dakota* 84 Gc
Madison, *Wisconsin* 83 Bd
Madisonville, *Kentucky* 85 Jd
Madoc, *Ontario* 83 Hc
Madona, *Latvia* 47 Mh
Madras, *India* 68 Ff
Madre, Sa., *Mexico* 88 Cb
Madre Austral, Lag. de la, *Mexico* 88 Ec
Madre de Dios, I., *Chile* 92 Ah
Madre de Dios, R., *Peru-Bolivia* 90 Df
Madre del Sur, Sa., *Mexico* 88 Dd
Madrid, *Spain* 50 Db
Madridejos, *Spain* 50 Dc
Madura, I., *Indonesia* 63 Fm
Madurai, *India* 68 Eg
Maebashi, *Japan* 66 Ff
Maestra, Sa., *Cuba* 89 Db
Maevatanana, *Madagascar* 77 Nk
Mafeking, *Cape Province* 75 De
Mafia I., *Tanzania* 77 Hf
Mafra, *Portugal* 50 Ac
Mafraq, *Jordan* 74 Ee
Magad Plat. See Jol Plat.
Magadan, *Russia* 59 Qc
Magadi & L., *Kenya* 77 He
Magadino, *Switzerland* 45 Db
Magallanes, & Estrecho de, *Chile* 92 Bh
Magangué, *Colombia* 90 Cb
Magas. See Panäh
Magaz, *Spain* 50 Cb
Magburaka, *Sierra Leone* 78 Cg
Magdagachi, *Russia* 59 Mc
Magdala, *Ethiopia* 77 Hb
Magdalen Is., *Quebec* 82 Hc
Magdalena, *Bolivia* 90 Ef
Magdalena, *Mexico* 88 Ba
Magdalena, B., *Mexico* 88 Bc
Magdalena, I., *Chile* 92 Bf
Magdalena, R., *Colombia* 90 Cb
Magdeburg, *Germany* 48 Db
Magellan, Str. of, *Chile* 92 Ch
Mageröya, *Norway* 46 Ma
Maggia, *Switzerland* 45 Db
Maggiore, L., *Italy* 54 Bb
Maghang Tsangpo, R., *Tibet* 69 Gc
Maghara, Geb., *Egypt* 74 Bg
Magherafelt, *N. Ireland* 31 Cf
Maglaj, *Yugoslavia* 56 Bb
Maglie, *Italy* 55 Ge
Magnetic I., *Queensland* 95 Jc
Magnetic Pole, N., *N.-W. T.* 81 Lb
Magnitogorsk, *Russia* 61 Pd
Magog, *Quebec* 83 Kc
Magpie, *Quebec* 82 Fa
Magpie L., & R., *Quebec* 82 Fa
Magwe, *Burma* 69 Jd
Mahabad, *Persia* 72 Eb
Mahabaleshwar, *India* 68 De
Mahaban, *India* 70 Eg
Mahabharat Ra., *Nepal* 71 Eb
Mahaddei Uen, *Somalia* 77 Kd
Mahadeo Hills, *India* 71 Ad
Mahail, *Arabia* 72 Df
Mahajamba, B. de, *Madag.* 77 Nk
Mahajan, *India* 70 Cf
Mahalapye, *Botswana* 75 Dd
Mahallat, *Persia* 73 Fc
Maham, *India* 70 Ef
Mahanadi R., *India* 69 Fd
Mahanoro, *Madagascar* 77 Nk
Mahanoy City, *Pennsylvania* 86 Bb
Mahbubnagar, *India* 68 Ee
Mahdia, *Tunisia* 79 Ha
Mahé, *India* 68 Ef
Mahendragiri, Mt., *India* 69 Fe
Mahia Pen., *New Zealand* 93 Fc
Mahmed-Hussein-magala. See Shahsavar
Mahmudabad, *India* 71 Cb
Mahmudabad, *Persia* 73 Fb
Mahua, *Moçambique* 77 Hg
Mahuva, *India* 68 Dd
Maida, *Yemen* 72 Df
Maidan, *Afghanistan* 73 Jc
Maidstone, *England* 31 Hj
Maiduguri, *Nigeria* 79 Hf
Maienfeld, *Switzerland* 45 Ea
Maihar, *India* 71 Cc
Maikal Ra., *India* 71 Cd
Maikop, *Russia* 58 Dd
Maimana, *Afghanistan* 73 Hb
Main R., *Germany* 48 Cd
Main Barrier Ra., *N.S.W.* 95 Hf
Maine, prov., *France* 52 Cb
Maine, state, *U.S.A.* 85 Nb
Maine, G. of, *Maine, etc.* 82 De
Maine-et-Loire, dep., *France* 52 Cc
Maing Kaing, *Burma* 69 Jd
Maingkwan, *Burma* 69 Jc
Mainpuri, *India* 68 Ec
Mainstream, *Maine* 82 Dd
Mainz, *Germany* 48 Cd
Maipo, Mt., *Argentina* 92 Cd
Maipu, *Argentina* 92 Ee
Maissin, *Belgium* 44 De
Mait & I., *Somalia* 77 Kb
Maitland, *New South Wales* 95 Kf
Maitland, L., *W. Australia* 94 De
Maiz, *Mexico* 88 Ec
Maizuru, *Japan* 66 Dg
Maja, I., *Indonesia* 63 El
Majagual, *Colombia* 90 Cb
Majdanpek, *Yugoslavia* 56 Cb
Majitha, *India* 70 De
Majmaa, *Arabia* 72 Ed
Majorca, *Balearic Is.* 51 Gc
Majunga, *Madagascar* 77 Nk
Majuro, Is., *Marshall Is.* 98 Gg
Makale, *Ethiopia* 77 Hb
Makania, *Tanzania* 77 He
Makariev, *Russia* 61 Fb
Makarvey, *Russia* 61 Gb
Makassar, *Celebes* 63 Gm
Makassar Str., *Indonesia* 63 Gl
Makatea, I., *Tuamotu Arch.* 99 Lj
Makedhonia, *Greece* 57 Cd
Makemo, I., *Tuamotu Arch.* 99 Lj
Makeyevka, *Ukraine* 60 Kg
Makhach Kala, *Russia* 58 Dd
Makhai, *China* 62 Bc
Makikihi, *New Zealand* 93 Cf
Makindu, *Kenya* 77 He
Makkinga, *Netherlands* 44 Eb
Makla, Jebel el, *Arabia* 72 Cd
Makó, *Hungary* 56 Ca
Makongolosi, *Tanzania* 77 Gf
Makorako, Mt., *N.Z.* 93 Fc
Makram, *Arabia* 72 Ce
Makri, *India* 68 Fe
Makri. See Fethiye
Maksmo. See Maksamaa
Maksamaa, *Finland* 46 Ke
Maku, *Persia* 72 Db
Makum, *India* 69 Jc
Makurdi, *Nigeria* 78 Gg
Makwiro, *Rhodesia* 75 Ec
Mal B., *Quebec* 82 Fb
Malá, *Peru* 90 Bf
Malabang, *Philippines* 63 Hj
Malabar Coast, *India* 68 Df
Malabu, *Nigeria* 79 Hg
Malacca, *W. Malaysia* 63 Dk
Malacca, Str. of, *Sumatra-W. Malaysia* 63 Dk
Malad City, *Idaho* 84 Dc
Maladeta, Mt., *Spain* 51 Fa
Málaga, *Spain* 50 Cd
Malagasy Rep., *Indian Oc.* 77 Nl
Malaita, *Solomon Is.* 98 Fh
Malakal, *Sudan* 79 Mg
Malakand & Pass, *W. Pakistan* 70 Bc
Malån, *Sweden* 46 Hd
Malang, *Java* 63 Fm
Malanje, *Angola* 76 Df
Mälaren, L., *Sweden* 47 Gg
Malargue, *Argentina* 92 Ce
Malathia, *Kenya* 77 He
Malatya, *Turkey* 72 Cb
Malaut, *India* 70 De
Malawi (Nyasaland), *Cent. Africa* 77 Gg
Malaya. See West Malaysia
Malayer, *Persia* 72 Ec
Malaysia, *S.-E. Asia* 57 De
Malazgirt, *Turkey* 72 Db
Malbork, *Poland* 49 Ha
Malchow, *Germany* 48 Eb
Malda, *India* 71 Gc
Maldegem, *Belgium* 44 Bc
Malden, *Massachusetts* 86 Ea
Malden, I., *Pacific Ocean* 99 Kh
Maldive Is., *Indian Ocean* 40 Gh
Maldon, *England* 31 Hj
Maldonado, *Uruguay* 92 Fd
Maléa, C., *Greece* 57 Df
Malé Karpaty, *Czech.* 49 Gd
Malekula, I., *New Hebrides* 98 Fj
Máleme, *Crete* 57 Dg
Maler Kotla, *India* 70 De
Malesherbes, *France* 52 Eb
Malgache, Rep., *Indian Oc.* 77 Pl
Malheur L., *Oregon* 8[illegible] Dd
Mali, *W. Africa* 78 Ee
Malihabad, *India* 71 Cb
Malin Hd., *Eire* 30 Ce
Malinau, *Borneo* 63 Gk
Malindi, *Kenya* 77 Je
Malines, *Belgium* 44 Cc
Malkangiri, *India* 69 Fe
Malko Tŭrnovo, *Bulgaria* 56 Fd
Mallaig, *Scotland* 30 Dc
Mállia G., *Crete* 57 Eg
Mallorca I., *Balearic Is.* 51 Gc
Mallow, *Eire* 31 Bh
Malmberget, *Sweden* 46 Jc
Malmédy, *Belgium* 44 Ed
Malmesbury, *England* 31 Fj
Malmö, *Sweden* 47 Ej
Malmyzh, *Russia* 61 Kb
Maloggia, *Switzerland* 45 Eb
Malombe L., *Malawi* 77 Hg
Malone, *New York* 83 Jc
Malonga, *Congo* 76 Eg
Malpeque B., *P.E.I.* 82 Gc
Malta, *Montana* 84 Eb
Malta Chan., *Medit. Sea* 55 Eg
Malta I., *Mediterranean Sea* 55 Eh
Malters, *Switzerland* 45 Da
Malton, *England* 31 Cf
Malung, *Sweden* 47 E[illegible]
Malvaglia, *Switzerland* 45 Eb
Malvan, *India* 68 De
Malvern Hills, *England* 31 Fh
Malvina, *Quebec* 83 L[illegible]
Malvinas, Isles. See Falkland Is.
Mama, *Russia* 59 L[illegible]
Mamantel, *Mexico* 88 F[illegible]
Mambasa, *Congo* 77 F[illegible]
Mamonal, *Colombia* 90 B[illegible]
Mamou, *Guinea* 78 C[illegible]
Mampoko, *Congo* 76 D[illegible]
Mamu, *Afghanistan* 73 H[illegible]
Mamudju, *Celebes* 63 G
Man, *Ivory Coast* 78 D[illegible]
Man, I. of, *Irish Sea* 31 Ef
Manacapuru, *Brazil* 90 Ed
Manacor, *Balearic Is.* 51 Gc
Manado, *Celebes* 63 Hk
Managua, *Nicaragua* 89 Bd
Managua L., *Nicaragua* 89 Bd
Manakha, *Yemen* 72 Df
Manamah, *Bahrein I.* 73 Fd
Mananjary, *Madagascar* 77 Nl
Manantenina, *Madagascar* 77 Nl
Manapouri L., *New Zealand* 93 Af
Manasarowar L., *Tibet* 68 Fb
Manasquan, *New Jersey* 83 Je
Manassas, *Virginia* 83 Hf
Manaus, *Brazil* 90 Ed
Mancelona, *Michigan* 83 Dc
Manche, dep., *France* 52 Cb
Manchester, *England* 31 Fg
Manchester, *New Hampshire* 83 Ld
Manchouli, *China* 62 Ga
Manchuria, *China* 62 Ha
Mancora, *Peru* 90 Ad
Manda, *Tanzania* 77 Gg
Mandal, *Norway* 47 Bg
Mandalay, *Burma* 69 Jd
Mandal Gobi, *Mongolia* 62 Ea
Mandan, *N. Dakota* 84 Fb
Mandarin B., *China* 65 Em
Mander, *Netherlands* 44 Eb
Mandera, *Kenya* 77 Jd
Mandi, *India* 70 Ee
Mandih, *Philippines* 63 Hj
Mandla, *India* 71 Cd
Mandritsara, *Madagascar* 77 Nk
Mandvi, *India* 68 Cd
Manfredonia, G. di, *Italy* 55 Fe
Manfuha, *Arabia* 72 Ee
Mangaia, I., *Cook Is.* 99 Kk
Mangaldai, *India* 69 Hc
Mangalme, *Chad* 79 Jf
Mangalore, *India* 68 Df
Mangareva, I., *Tuamotu Arch.* 99 Mk
Mangaweka, *New Zealand* 93 Ec
Mangfall Geb., *Germany* 48 De
Mangiaralto, *Ecuador* 90 Ad
Mangonui, *New Zealand* 93 Da
Mangrol, *India* 68 Dd
Mangualde, *Portugal* 50 Bb
Mangueira, L. da, *Brazil* 92 Fd
Manhattan, *Kansas* 84 Gd
Manhay, *Belgium* 44 Dd
Manhuaçu, *Brazil* 91 Jh
Manicoré, *Brazil* 90 Ee
Manicouagan R., *Quebec* 81 Tf
Manifold, C., *Queensland* 95 Kd
Manihi, *India* 71 Ec
Manihiki, I., *Pacific Ocean* 98 Jj
Manikarchar, *India* 71 Gc
Manikganj. See Dasara
Manikpur, *E. Pakistan* 69 Hd
Manila, *Philippines* 63 Hh
Manipur (Imphal), *India* 69 Hc
Manisa, *Turkey* 72 Ab
Manistee, *Michigan* 83 Cc
Manistee R., *Michigan* 83 Dc
Manistique, *Michigan* 83 Cb
Manitoba, prov., *Canada* 80 Mf
Manitoba, L., *Manitoba* 80 Mf
Manitou Gorge, *Quebec* 81 Te
Manitou Is., *Michigan* 83 Cc
Manitoulin I., *Ontario* 83 Ec
Manitowaning, *Ontario* 83 Fc
Manitowoc, *Wisconsin* 83 Cc
Maniwaki, *Quebec* 83 Hb
Maniyah, *Iraq* 72 Dc
Manizales, *Colombia* 90 Bb
Manja, *Madagascar* 77 Ml
Manjimup, *W. Australia* 94 Cf
Manka, *Taiwan* 65 Kk
Mankato, *Minnesota* 85 Hc
Mankheri, *India* 71 Ed
Manlleu, *Spain* 51 Ga
Manmad, *India* 68 Dd
Mannar, *Ceylon* 68 Eg
Mannar, G. of, *India* 68 Eg
Mannargudi, *India* 68 Ef
Mannheim, *Germany* 48 Cd
Manoa, *Bolivia* 90 De
Manokwari, *W. Irian* 63 Kl
Manono, *Congo* 76 Ff
Manosque, *France* 53 Fe
Manresa, *Spain* 51 Fb
Mansa, *Zambia* 75 Db
Mansehra, *W. Pakistan* 70 Cc
Mansel I., *North-West Territories* 81 Qd
Mansfield, *England* 31 Gg
Mansfield, *Massachusetts* 83 Ld
Mansfield, *Ohio* 83 Ee
Mansfield, *Pennsylvania* 86 Bb
Mansfield, Mt., *Vermont* 83 Kc
Mansi, *Burma* 69 Jd
Mansilla de Las Mulas, *Spain* 50 Ca
Manta, *Ecuador* 90 Ad
Mantova, *Italy* 54 Cc
Mantua. See Mantova
Manú, *Peru* 90 Cf
Manua, I., *Samoa Is.* 98 Jj
Manuel Rodriguez, I., *Chile* 92 Bh
Manujan, *Persia* 73 Gd
Manus I., *Admiralty Is.* 98 Dh
Manyoni, *Tanzania* 77 Gf
Manzala L., *Egypt* 79 Mb
Manzanares, *Spain* 50 Dc
Manzanillo, *Cuba* 89 Db
Manzanillo, *Mexico* 88 Dd
Manzanillo, Pta., *Panama* 89 Dd
Mao, *Chad* 79 Jf
Mapia Is., *Pacific Ocean* 98 Cg
Mapimí, *Mexico* 88 Db
Mapire, *Venezuela* 90 Eb
Maple Creek, *Saskatchewan* 80 Kg
Maqainama, *Arabia* 72 Ee
Maqatin, *S. Yemen* 72 Eg
Maqna, *Arabia* 72 Bd
Maquela do Zombo, *Angola* 76 Df
Maquinchao, *Argentina* 92 Cf
Mara, *Transvaal* 75 Dd
Maraã, *Brazil* 90 Dd
Marabá, *Brazil* 91 He
Maracá, I. de, *Brazil* 91 Gc
Maracaibo, *Venezuela* 90 Ca
Maracaibo, L. de, *Venezuela* 90 Cb
Maracanã, *Brazil* 91 Hd
Maracaçume, *Brazil* 91 Hd
Maracay, *Venezuela* 90 Da
Marada, *Libya* 79 Jc
Maradi, *Niger* 78 Gf
Maragheh, *Persia* 72 Eb
Maragogi, *Brazil* 91 Ke
Marakei, I., *Gilbert Is.* 98 Gg
Marakwet, *Kenya* 77 Hd
Maralinga, *S. Australia* 94 Ff
Maramures, *Rumania* 49 Ke
Marand, *Persia* 72 Eb
Maranguape, *Brazil* 91 Kd
Marañón, R., *Peru* 90 Cd
Maraş, *Turkey* 72 Cb
Maraú, *Brazil* 91 Kf
Maravilha, *Brazil* 90 De
Marbella, *Spain* 50 Cd
Marble Bar, *W. Australia* 94 Cd
Marblehead, *Massachusetts* 86 Ea
Marcelino, *Brazil* 90 Dd
Marche, *Belgium* 44 Dd
Marche, reg., *Italy* 54 Dd
Marchena, *Spain* 50 Cd
Marchin, *Belgium* 44 Dd
Mar Chiquita, *Argentina* 92 Dd
Marcus I., *Pacific Ocean* 98 Ee
Marcy, Mt., *New York* 83 Kc
Mardan, *W. Pakistan* 70 Cc
Mar del Plata, *Argentina* 92 Ee
Mardin, *Turkey* 72 Db
Mare, I., *Loyalty Is.* 98 Fk
Marechal Deodoro. See Alagoas
Maree, L., *Scotland* 30 Dc
Mareeba, *Queensland* 95 Jc
Marengo, *Wisconsin* 83 Ab
Margarita, I., *Venezuela* 90 Ea
Margarites, *Crete* 57 Eg
Margate, *England* 31 Hj
Marianao, *Cuba* 89 Cb
Marianas, Is., *Pacific Ocean* 98 Df
Marianna, *Arkansas* 85 He
Mariánské Lázně, *Czech.* 48 Ed
Marias R., *Montana* 84 Db
Marib, *Yemen* 72 Df
Maribor, *Yugoslavia* 54 Eb
Maridi, *Sudan* 79 Lh
Marie Byrd Ld., *Antarctica* 100 Pb
Mariefred, *Sweden* 47 Gg
Marie Galante, I., *Leeward Is.* 89 Gc
Mariehamn, *Finland* 47 Hf
Marienbad. See Mariánské L.
Marienberg, *Netherlands* 44 Eb
Marienbourg, *Belgium* 44 Cd
Marienburg. See Malbork
Mariental, *S.-W. Africa* 75 Bd
Marienthal, *Russia* 61 Kc
Marienville, *Pennsylvania* 86 Ab
Mariestad, *Sweden* 47 Eg
Marietta, *Ohio* 83 Ff
Mari Indus, *W. Pakistan* 70 Bd
Marina Fall, *Guyana* 90 Fb
Marine City, *Michigan* 83 Ed
Marinette, *Wisconsin* 83 Cc
Marinha Grande, *Portugal* 50 Ac
Marion, *Indiana* 83 De
Marion, *Ohio* 83 Ee
Maritsa R., *Bulgaria, etc.* 56 Ed
Mariyampole. See Kapsukas
Mariyskaya A.S.S.R., *Russia* 58 Dc
Marj, el, *Libya* 79 Kb
Märjamaa, *Estonia* 47 Lg
Markala, *Mali* 78 Df
Markapur, *India* 68 Ee
Markelo, *Netherlands* 44 Eb
Marken, I., *Netherlands* 44 Db
Market Drayton, *England* 31 Fh
Market Harborough, *Eng.* 31 Gh
Markham, L., *Tibet* 69 Fa
Markham, Mt., *Antarctica* 100 Ka
Markovo, *Russia* 59 Sb
Marks, *Russia* 61 He
Markstay, *Ontario* 83 Fb
Marlboro, *Massachusetts* 86 Ea
Marlborough, *Guyana* 90 Fb
Marlette, *Michigan* 83 Ed
Marmagão, *Goa* 68 De
Marmande, *France* 53 Dd
Marmara, Sea of, *Turkey* 72 Aa
Marmaris, *Turkey* 72 Ab
Marne, dep., *France* 52 Fb
Maroua, *Cameroon* 79 Hf
Marouini, R., *Fr. Guiana* 91 Gc
Marquesas, Is., *Pac. Oc.* 99 Mh
Marquette, *Michigan* 83 Cb
Marquina, *Spain* 51 Da
Marrakech (Marrakesh), *Morocco* 78 Db
Marree, *S. Australia* 95 Ge
Marsabit, *Kenya* 77 Hd
Marsa Hali, *Arabia* 72 Df
Marsala, *Sicily* 55 Dg
Marseille, *France* 53 Fe
Marshall, *Illinois* 83 Cf
Marshall, *Michigan* 83 Dd
Marshall, *Texas* 85 He
Marshall Is., *Pacific Ocean* 98 Fg
Marshall Pass. See Monarch Pass
Marshalltown, *Iowa* 85 Hc
Marshfield. See Coos Bay
Marshfield, *Wisconsin* 83 Ac
Mars Hill, *Maine* 82 Ec
Marstrand, *Sweden* 47 Dh
Marsum, *Netherlands* 44 Da
Martaban, *Burma* 69 Je
Martaban, G. of, *Burma* 69 Je
Martelange, *Belgium* 44 De
Martha's Vineyard, I., *Mass.* 86 Eb
Martigny-Ville, *Switzerland* 45 Cb
Martina, *Switzerland* 45 Fb
Martinborough, *N.Z.* 93 Ed
Martinho, *Brazil* 91 Fe
Martinique, I., *Windward Is.* 89 Gd
Martinsburg, *W. Virginia* 86 Bc
Marton, *New Zealand* 93 Ed
Martos, *Spain* 50 Dd
Martre, Lac la, *N.-W.Terr.* 80 Hd
Maruf, *Afghanistan* 73 Jc
Marugame, *Japan* 66 Cg
Marum, *Netherlands* 44 Ea
Marutea, I., *Tuamotu Arch.* 99 Lj
Marvejols, *France* 53 Ed
Mary, *Turkmenistan* 58 Fe
Maryborough, *Queensland* 95 Ke
Maryborough. See Portlaoise
Maryborough, *Victoria* 95 Hg
Marydale, *Cape Province* 75 Ce
Mary Kathleen, *Qnsld.* 95 Hd
Maryland, state, *U.S.A.* 85 Ld
Maryport, *England* 31 Ef
Marysville, *California* 84 Bd
Marysville, *New Brunswick* 82 Ed
Más Afuera, I., *Pacific Ocean* 99 Sl
Masaka, *Uganda* 77 Ge
Masangena, *Moçambique* 75 Ed
Masara, *Moçambique* 75 Ec
Masasi, *Tanzania* 77 Hg
Masaya, *Nicaragua* 89 Bd
Masbate, I., *Philippines* 63 Hh
Mascara, *Algeria* 78 Fa
Maseru *Lesotho* 75 De
Mashaki, *Afghanistan* 73 Jc
Masharbrum, Mt., *Kashmir* 70 Ec
Mashhad, *Persia* 73 Gb
Mashkol, Hamun-i-, *W. Pak.* 68 Bc
Masi-Manimba, *Congo* 76 De
Masindi, *Uganda* 77 Gd
Masira Chan, *Arabia* 73 Ge
Masira, G. of, *Arabia* 73 Gf
Masira I., *Muscat & Oman* 73 Ge
Masjed Soleyman, *Persia* 72 Ec
Mask L., *Eire* 32 Ef
Masoala C., *Madagascar* 77 Pk
Mason, *Michigan* 83 Dd
Mason City, *Iowa* 85 Hc
Masöy, *Norway* 46 La
Massa, *Italy* 54 Cc
Massachusetts B., *Mass.* 86 Ea
Massachusetts, state, *U.S.A.* 85 Mc
Massafra, *Italy* 55 Fe
Massakori, *Chad* 79 Jf
Massapê, *Brazil* 91 Jd
Massawa, *Eritrea* 77 Ha
Massena, *New York* 83 Jc
Massénya, *Chad* 79 Jf
Masseube, *France* 53 De
Massey, *Ontario* 83 Eb
Massillon, *Ohio* 83 Fe
Massinga, *Moçambique* 75 Fd
Masterton, *New Zealand* 93 Ed
Mastuj, *W. Pakistan* 70 Cb
Mastung, *W. Pakistan* 68 Cc
Mastura, *Arabia* 72 Ce
Masulipatnam, *India* 68 Fe
Masyaf, *Syria* 74 Eb
Mat, *India* 70 Eg
Mata Amarilla, *Argentina* 92 Bg
Matagalpa, *Nicaragua* 89 Bd
Matagorda B., I., & *Texas* 84 Gf
Matakana I., *New Zealand* 93 Fb
Matale, *Ceylon* 68 Fg
Matam, *Senegal* 78 Ce
Matamata, *N.Z.* 93 Eb
Matamoros, *Mexico* 88 Db
Matamoros, *Mexico* 88 Eb
Matane, *Quebec* 82 Eb
Matanzas, *Cuba* 89 Cb
Matapedia, *Quebec* 82 Ec
Matapedia, L., *Quebec* 82 Eb
Matapozuelos, *Spain* 50 Cb
Matara, *Ceylon* 68 Fg
Mataram, *Lombok I., Indon.* 63 Gm
Mataranka, *N. Terr., Aust.* 94 Fb
Mataró, *Spain* 51 Gb
Matatiele, *Cape Province* 75 Df
Matauale, *Brazil* 91 Gc
Mataura, *New Zealand* 93 Bg
Matehuala, *Mexico* 88 Dc
Matera, *Italy* 55 Fe
Mátészalka, *Hungary* 49 Ke
Mateur, *Tunisia* 79 Ga
Matfors, *Sweden* 46 Ge
Mathura, *India* 68 Ec
Matiara, *India* 71 Fc
Matlock, *England* 31 Fg
Matna, *Sudan* 79 Nf
Mato Grosso, *Brazil* 90 Ff
Matrah, *Muscat & Oman* 73 Ge
Matruh, *Egypt* 79 Lb
Matsue, *Japan* 66 Cg
Matsumoto, *Japan* 66 Ff
Matsushima, *Japan* 66 Ge
Matsuyama, *Japan* 66 Ch
Mattawa, *Ontario* 83 Gb
Matterhorn, Mt., *Switz.-It.* 45 Cc
Matthew Town, *Bahama Is.* 89 Eb
Mattoon, *Illinois* 83 Bf
Matucana, *Peru* 90 Bf
Matun, *Afghanistan* 73 Jc
Matura, *Brazil* 90 Dd
Maturín, *Venezuela* 90 Eb
Matvaieva, *Russia* 61 Nb
Mau, *India* 68 Ec
Mau Aimma, *India* 71 Cc
Maubeuge, *France* 52 Ea
Maubin, *Burma* 69 Je
Maubourguet, *France* 53 De
Maudaha, *India* 71 Cc
Mauele, *Moçambique* 75 Ed
Maués, *Brazil* 91 Fd
Mauganj, *India* 71 Cc
Maugerville, *New Brunswick* 82 Ed
Maui, I., *Hawaiian Is.* 99 Ke
Mauleon Licharre, *France* 53 Ce
Maurawan, *India* 71 Cb
Maurice, L., *S. Australia* 94 Fe
Mauriceville, *N.Z.* 93 Ed
Mauritania, *W. Africa* 78 Cd
Mauritius, I., *Indian Ocean* 96 Df
Maurs, *France* 53 Ed
Mauston, *Wisconsin* 83 Ad
Mawk Mai, *Burma* 69 Jd
Mawlaik, *Burma* 69 Hd
Mawson, *Antarctica* 100 Fc
Maxcanu, *Mexico* 88 Gc
May, C., *New Jersey* 86 Cc
May, I. of, *Scotland* 30 Fd
Mayaguana I., *Bahamas Is.* 89 Eb
Mayaguez, *Puerto Rico* 89 Fc
Mayari, *Cuba* 89 Db
Mayen, *Germany* 48 Bc
Mayenne, dep., *France* 52 Cb
Mayfield, *Kentucky* 85 Jd
Maymyo, *Burma* 69 Jd
Maynooth, *Ontario* 83 Hc
Mayno Pyl'gino, *Russia* 59 Sb
Mayo, co., *Eire* 31 Ag
Mayoumba, *Gabon* 76 Ce
Mayran, L., *Mexico* 88 Db
Mays Landing, *New Jersey* 86 Cc
Mayuram, *India* 68 Ef
Mayville, *New York* 86 Aa
Maza, *Argentina* 92 De
Mazabuka, *Zambia* 75 Dc
Mazagan, *Morocco* 78 Db
Mazagão, *Brazil* 91 Gd
Mazamet, *France* 53 Ee
Mazan, *Argentina* 92 Cc
Mazan, *Peru* 90 Cd
Mazapil, *Mexico* 88 Dc
Mazara del Vallo, *Sicily* 55 Dg
Mazaredo, *Argentina* 92 Cg
Mazar-i-Sharif, *Afghanistan* 73 Jb
Mazarron, *Spain* 51 Ed
Mazatenango, *Guatemala* 88 Fe
Mazatlán, *Mexico* 88 Cc
Mažeikiai, *Lithuania* 47 Kh
Mbabane, *Swaziland* 75 Ee
Mbale, *Uganda* 77 Gd
Mbamba Bay, *Kenya* 75 Fb
Mbarangandu, *Tanzania* 77 Hg
Mbarara, *Uganda* 77 Ge
Mbeya, *Tanzania* 77 Gf
Mead L., *Nevada, etc.* 87 Fg
Meadow L., *Saskatchewan* 80 Kf
Meadville, *Pennsylvania* 83 Fe
Meaford, *Ontario* 83 Fc
Meath, co., *Eire* 32 Kf
Mecatina I., Gt., *Quebec* 82 Ja
Mecatina, I., Lit., *Quebec* 82 Ja
Mecca, *Arabia* 72 Ce
Mechanicville, *New York* 86 Da
Mechelen, *Belgium* 44 Dd
Mechelen. See Malines
Mécheria, *Algeria* 78 Eb
Medak, *India* 68 Ee
Medak, *Yugoslavia* 54 Ec
Medan, *Sumatra* 63 Ck
Médanos, *Argentina* 92 De
Medellín, *Colombia* 90 Bb
Medemblik, *Netherlands* 44 Db
Médenine, *Tunisia* 79 Hb
Meder, *Eritrea* 77 Jb
Medford, *Oregon* 87 Bd
Medford, *Wisconsin* 83 Ac
Medgidia, *Rumania* 56 Gb
Media, *Pennsylvania* 86 Cc
Medias, *Rumania* 56 Ea
Medicine Bow Pk., *Wyoming* 84 Ec
Medicine Hat, *Alberta* 80 Jg
Medina, *Arabia* 72 Ce
Medina, *New York* 86 Aa
Medina, *Ohio* 83 Fe
Medinaceli, *Spain* 51 Db
Medina del Campo, *Spain* 50 Cb
Medina de Rioseco, *Spain* 50 Cb
Medina Sidonia, *Spain* 50 Cd
Médine, *Mali* 78 Cf
Mediterranean Sea, *S. Europe, etc.* 43 Jj
Medvezhegorsk, *Russia* 58 Cb
Medvezhi Osa., *Russia* 59 Ra
Medvezhiy Yar., *Russia* 59 Ja
Meekatharra, *W. Australia* 94 Ce
Meenin. See Menin
Meerle, *Belgium* 44 Cc
Meerlo, *Netherlands* 44 Eb
Meersburg, *Germany* 48 Ce
Meersen, *Netherlands* 44 Dd
Meerut, *India* 70 Ef
Meeuwen, *Belgium* 44 Cc
Mega, *Ethiopia* 77 Hd
Megalópolis, *Greece* 57 Df
Mégantic, & L., *Quebec* 83 Lc
Mégara, *Greece* 57 De
Megiskan, *Quebec* 83 Ha
Mehar, *W. Pakistan* 68 Cc
Meherpur, *E. Pakistan* 71 Gd
Mehin, *Syria* 74 Fc
Mehndawal, *India* 71 Db
Meihsien, *China* 65 Hk
Meiktila, *Burma* 69 Jd
Meiningen, *Germany* 48 Dc
Meiringen, *Switzerland* 45 Db
Meissen, *Germany* 48 Ec
Meitene, *Latvia* 47 Kh
Mejillones, *Chile* 92 Bb
Mekatina, *Ontario* 83 Db
Meknès, *Morocco* 78 Db
Mekong, R., *Cambodia, etc.* 63 Dh
Melanesia, *Pacific Ocean* 98 Dg
Melbourne, *Victoria* 95 Jg
Melfi, *Italy* 55 Ee
Melfort, *Saskatchewan* 80 Lf
Meligalá, *Greece* 57 Cf
Melilla, *Morocco* 78 Ea
Melipilla, *Chile* 92 Bd
Melitopol, *Ukraine* 60 Jh
Melk, *Austria* 49 Fd
Melle, *France* 52 Cc

Mellier, *Belgium* 44 De
Mellingen, *Switzerland* 45 Da
Melo, *Uruguay* 92 Fd
Melona, *Israel* 74 De
Melreux, *Belgium* 44 Dd
Melton Mowbray, *England* 31 Gh
Melun, *France* 52 Eb
Melut, *Sudan* 79 Mf
Melville, *Saskatchewan* 80 Lf
Melville B., *Greenland* 39 Qb
Melville, C., *Queensland* 95 Hb
Melville I., *N. Terr., Aust.* 94 Fb
Melville I., *N.-W. Terr.* 80 Ja
Melville L., *Labrador* 81 Yf
Melville Pen., *N.-W. Terr.* 81 Qc
Melvin L., *Ireland* 31 Bf
Memba & B., *Moçambique* 77 Jg
Membij, *Syria* 74 Fa
Memel. *See* Klaipeda
Memphis, *Tennessee* 85 Jd
Memphremagog, L., *Quebec* 83 Kc
Memramcook, *N.B.* 82 Fd
Menai Str., *Wales* 31 Eg
Menairi, *Chad* 79 Ke
Ménaka, *Mali* 78 Fe
Menasha, *Wisconsin* 83 Bc
Mendak, *Arabia* 72 De
Mendawai, R., *Borneo* 63 Fl
Mende, *France* 53 Ed
Mendebo Mts., *Ethiopia* 77 Hc
Menderes, R., *Turkey* 72 Ab
Mendip Hills, *England* 31 Fj
Mendocino, C., *California* 87 Ae
Mendota, *Illinois* 83 Be
Mendota, L., *Wisconsin* 83 Bd
Mendoza, *Argentina* 92 Cd
Mendrisio, *Switzerland* 45 Dc
Menfi, *Sicily* 55 Dg
Meng Chai Nat, *Siam* 67 Cc
Meng Chumporn. *See* Chumporn
Meng Fang, *Siam* 67 Bc
Meng Khemmarat, *Siam* 67 Dc
Meng Krabin. *See* Aranya
Meng Kuwi. *See* Kui Nua
Meng Phrae, *Siam* 67 Bc
Meng Thoen, *Siam* 67 Bc
Mengtsz, *China* 62 Df
Meng Uthen. *See* Ban tha U
Menin, *Belgium* 44 Bd
Menindee, *New S. Wales* 95 Hf
Menjapa, Mt., *Borneo* 63 Gk
Menominee & R., *Michigan* 83 Cc
Menomonie, *Wisconsin* 85 Hc
Menorca I., *Balearic Is.* 51 Hb
Mentawai Is., *Indonesia* 41 Jj
Menton, *France* 53 Ge
Menzelinsk, *Russia* 61 Lc
Menzies, *W. Australia* 94 De
Me'ona, *Israel* 74 De
Meoqui, *Mexico* 88 Cb
Me-ping, R., *Siam* 67 Bc
Meppel, *Netherlands* 44 Eb
Merabello G., *Crete* 57 Eg
Merano, *Italy* 54 Cb
Merasheen I., *Nfd.* 82 Lc
Meratus Peg., *Borneo* 63 Gl
Merauke, *W. Irian* 63 Mm
Merca, *Somalia* 77 Jd
Mercara, *India* 68 Ef
Merced, *California* 87 Cg
Mercedaria, Mt., *Argentina* 92 Bd
Mercedes, *Argentina* 92 Ed
Mercedes, *Argentina* 92 Ec
Mercedes, *Bolivia* 90 Df
Mercedes, *Uruguay* 92 Ed
Mercer, *New Zealand* 93 Eb
Mercer, *Pennsylvania* 83 Fe
Merchtem, *Belgium* 44 Cd
Mercy, C., *N.-W. Terr.* 81 Uc
Meredith, *Michigan* 83 Dc
Meredith, C., *Falkland Is.* 92 Dh
Meregh, *Somalia* 77 Kd
Mergentheim, *Germany* 48 Cd
Mergui, *Burma* 69 Jf
Mergui Arch., *Burma* 69 Jf
Merida, *Mexico* 88 Gc
Merida, *Spain* 50 Bc
Merida & Cord. de, *Venez.* 90 Cb
Meriden, *Connecticut* 86 Db
Meridian, *Mississippi* 85 Je
Merioneth, co., *Wales* 31 Eh
Merj Uyun, *Lebanon* 74 Dd
Merowe, *Sudan* 79 Me
Merredin, *W. Australia* 94 Cf
Merrill, *Wisconsin* 83 Bc
Merrimack R., *New Hamp.-Mass.* 86 Ea
Mersey R., *England* 31 Fg
Mersin, *Turkey* 72 Bb
Mersing, *W. Malaysia* 63 Dk
Mersis, *Somalia* 77 Kd
Mersrags, *Latvia* 47 Kh
Merta, *India* 68 Dc
Merthyr Tydfil, *Wales* 31 Ej
Mertola, *Portugal* 50 Bd
Meru, *Kenya* 77 Hd
Merxplas, *Belgium* 44 Cc
Merzig, *W. Germany* 48 Bd
Mesa, *Arizona* 84 De
Mesagne, *Italy* 55 Fe
Mesará B., *Crete* 57 Eg
Mesa Verde Nat. Park, *Colo.* 84 Ed
Meshchovsk, *Russia* 60 Jd
Meshghara, *Lebanon* 74 Dd
Meskene, *Syria* 74 Fa
Mesmiye, *Syria* 74 Ed
Mesocco, *Switzerland* 45 Eb
Mesolóngion, *Greece* 57 Ce
Messancy, *Belgium* 44 De
Messina, *Sicily* 55 Ef
Messina, Str. di, *Italy* 55 Ef
Messines, *Belgium* 44 Ad
Messinia, *Greece* 57 Cf
Messinia, G. of, *Greece* 57 Df
Mesudiye, *Turkey* 72 Ca
Metan, *Argentina* 92 Dc
Metangula, *Moçambique* 77 Gg
Méthana Pen., *Greece* 57 Df
Methil, *Scotland* 30 Ed
Methven, *New Zealand* 93 Ce
Metis Ls., *Quebec* 82 Eb
Metis Beach, *Quebec* 82 Db
Metkovic, *Yugoslavia* 56 Ac
Metlakatla, *Alaska* 85 Zm
Metlika, *Yugoslavia* 54 Ec
Metorica, *Moçambique* 77 Hg
Metropolitan, *Michigan* 83 Cb
Métsovon, *Greece* 57 Ce
Mettet, *Belgium* 44 Cd
Mettlen, *Switzerland* 45 Cb
Mettur Dam, *India* 68 Ef
Metulla, *Israel* 74 Dd
Metz, *France* 52 Gb
Meulebeke, *Belgium* 44 Bd
Meurthe-et-Moselle, dep., *Fr.* 52 Gb
Meuse, dep. & R., *France* 52 Fb
Meuse R., *Belgium* 44 Dd
Mexcala & R., *Mexico* 88 Ed
Mexiana, I., *Brazil* 91 Hd
Mexicali, *Mexico* 88 Aa
Mexico, *Mexico* 88 Ed
Mexico, *New York* 86 Ba
Mexico B., *New York* 86 Ba
Mexico, G. of, *Mexico, etc.* 88 Fb
Mexico, rep., *Cent. America* 88 Dc
Meyadin, *Syria* 72 Db
Meybod, *Persia* 73 Fc
Meyersdale, *Pennsylvania* 86 Ac
Meymac, *France* 52 Ed
Mèze, *France* 53 Ee
Mezen', *Russia* 58 Db
Mézières, *France* 52 Fb
Mezöbereny Békés, *Hungary* 49 Je
Mezökövesd, *Hungary* 49 Je
Mezötúr, *Hungary* 49 Je
Mezquitic, *Mexico* 88 De
Mgori, *Tanzania* 77 Ge
Mhow, *India* 68 Ed
Miahuatlan, *Mexico* 88 Ed
Miajadas, *Spain* 50 Cc
Miami, *Arizona* 84 De
Miami, *Florida* 85 Kf
Miandowab, *Iraq* 72 Eb
Miandrivazo, *Madagascar* 77 Nk
Mianeh, *Persia* 72 Eb
Miani, *India* 70 De
Miani, *W. Pakistan* 70 Cd
Mian Kalai, *W. Pakistan* 70 Bc
Mianwali, *W. Pakistan* 70 Bd
Miao-tao I., *China* 64 Kc
Miass, *Russia* 61 Qc
Miastko, *Poland* 49 Ga
Micay, *Colombia* 90 Bc
Michailovsk, *Russia* 61 Qd
Michailovsk, *Russia* 61 Ld
Micheh, *China* 64 Ed
Michigan, state, *U.S.A.* 85 Jb
Michigan, L., *U.S.A.-Canada* 85 Jc
Michigan City, *Indiana* 83 Ce
Michikamau, L., *Labrador* 81 Uf
Michipicoten, *Ontario* 81 Qg
Michipicoten I. & B., *Ont.* 83 Db
Michoacan, state, *Mexico* 88 Dd
Michurinsk, *Russia* 61 Ed
Mickelson, *Michigan* 83 Dc
Micronesia, *Pacific Ocean* 98 Df
Middelburg, *Netherlands* 44 Bc
Middelburg, *Transvaal* 75 De
Middelharnis, *Netherlands* 44 Cc
Middelkerke, *Belgium* 44 Ac
Middleboro, *Massachusetts* 86 Eb
Middleburg, *New York* 83 Jd
Middleburg, *Pennsylvania* 86 Bb
Middlebury, *Vermont* 83 Kd
Middlemarch, *New Zealand* 93 Bf
Middleport, *New York* 86 Aa
Middlesboro, *Kentucky* 85 Kd
Middlesbrough, *England* 31 Gf
Middleton, *Nova Scotia* 82 Fd
Middleton, *England* 31 Ff
Middletown, *Connecticut* 86 Db
Middletown, *Delaware* 83 Ge
Middletown, *New York* 86 Cb
Middletown, *Ohio* 83 Df
Middletown, *Pennsylvania* 86 Bb
Midland, *Michigan* 83 Dd
Midland, *Ontario* 83 Gc
Midlothian, co., *Scotland* 30 Ee
Midnapore, *India* 71 Fc
Midway Is., *Hawaiian Is.* 98 He
Midye, *Turkey* 72 Aa
Miécourt, *Switzerland* 45 Ca
Miedzyrzec, *Poland* 49 Kc
Mienning, *China* 62 Df
Mienyang, *China* 65 Fg
Mienyang, *China* 64 Bg
Mier, *Mexico* 88 Eb
Mieres, *Spain* 50 Ca
Mifflintown, *Pennsylvania* 86 Bb
Migdal Gad. *See* Ashqelon
Mikhaylovgrad, *Bulgaria* 56 Dc
Mikhaylovka, *Russia* 61 Fe
Mikkeli, *Finland* 47 Mf
Mikonos I., *Greece* 57 Ef
Milan, *New Hampshire* 83 Lc
Milan. *See* Milano
Milano, *Italy* 54 Bc
Milas, *Turkey* 72 Ab
Milazzo, *Sicily* 55 Ef
Mildura, *Victoria* 95 Hf
Miléai, *Greece* 57 De
Miles, *Queensland* 95 Ke
Miles City, *Montana* 84 Eb
Milesburg, *Pennsylvania* 86 Bb
Milford, *Delaware* 86 Cc
Milford, *Massachusetts* 86 Ea
Milford. *See* Shubenacadie
Milford, *Pennsylvania* 86 Cb
Milford, *Utah* 87 Gf
Milford Haven, *Wales* 31 Dj
Milford Sound, *N.Z.* 93 Af
Milgun, *W. Australia* 94 Ce
Mili, Is., *Marshall Islands* 98 Gg
Miliana, *Algeria* 78 Fa
Milk R., *Montana* 84 Eb
Milkovo, *Russia* 59 Qc
Mill, *Netherlands* 44 Dc
Mill I., *Antarctica* 100 Hc
Mill Is., *N.-W. Territories* 81 Rd
Millau, *France* 53 Ed
Millbridge, *Ontario* 83 Hc
Millerovo, *Russia* 61 Ef
Millersburg, *Ohio* 83 Fe
Miller's Flat, *New Zealand* 93 Bf
Mille Vaches, *Quebec* 82 Db
Millicent, *S. Australia* 95 Hg
Millinocket, *Maine* 82 Dd
Millridge, *Maine* 82 Ed
Millville, *New Jersey* 86 Cc
Milne B., *Papua* 95 Kb
Milo, *Maine* 83 Ed
Milos, I., *Greece* 57 Ef
Milparinka, *New S. Wales* 95 He
Milton, *New Zealand* 93 Bg
Milton, *Ontario* 83 Gd
Milton, *Pennsylvania* 86 Bb
Miltown Malbay, *Eire* 31 Ah
Milwaukee, *Wisconsin* 83 Cd
Mimika, *W. Irian* 63 Ll
Mina al Ahmadi, *Kuwait* 73 Ed
Minab, *Persia* 73 Gd
Mina Hassan Tani (Kenitra), *Morocco* 78 Db
Minaki, *Ontario* 80 Nf
Minas, *Uruguay* 92 Ed
Minas de Riotinto, *Spain* 50 Bd
Minas Novas, *Brazil* 91 Jg
Minatitlan, *Mexico* 88 Fd
Minbu, *Burma* 69 Hd
Minch, Little, *Scotland* 30 Cc
Minch, North, *Scotland* 30 Cb
Mindanao, I., *Philippines* 63 Jj
Minden, *Germany* 48 Cb
Mindoro, I. & Str., *Phil.* 63 Hh
Mîneciu, *Rumania* 56 Fb
Mine Hd., *Eire* 31 Bj
Minehead, *England* 31 Ej
Mineola, *New York* 86 Db
Mineral Ra., *Michigan* 83 Bb
Mineral Point, *Wisconsin* 83 Ad
Mineral Wells, *Texas* 84 Ge
Minga, *Zambia* 77 Gg
Mingan, Is. & Pass, *Quebec* 82 Ga
Mingenew, *W. Australia* 94 Ce
Mingin, *Burma* 69 Hd
Minglanilla, *Spain* 51 Ec
Mingoyo, *Tanzania* 77 Hg
Mingshui, *China* 62 Cb
Minhla, *Burma* 69 Je
Minhow, *China* 65 Jj
Minicoy, I., *India* 68 Dg
Minilya, *W. Australia* 94 Bd
Minna, *Nigeria* 78 Gg
Minneapolis, *Minnesota* 85 Hb
Minnedosa, *Manitoba* 80 Mf
Minnesota, state, *U.S.A.* 84 Gb
Minnesota R., *Minn., etc.* 84 Gc
Minnik, *Syria* 74 Fa
Miño, *Spain* 50 Aa
Miño (Minho), R., *Spain-Portugal* 50 Aa
Minorca. *See* Menorca
Minot, *N. Dakota* 84 Fb
Min Shan, *China* 64 Ae
Minsk, *White Russia* 60 Ee
Minsk Mazowiecki, *Poland* 49 Jb
Minto Inl., *N.-W. Terr.* 80 Hb
Minto L., *Quebec* 81 Re
Minusinsk, *Russia* 59 Jc
Minya Konka, *China* 62 De
Mio, *Michigan* 83 Dc
Miracema do Norte, *Brazil* 91 He
Mirador, *Brazil* 91 Je
Miraflores, *Colombia* 90 Cb
Miraj, *India* 68 De
Mirambeau, *France* 53 Cd
Miramichi B., *N.B.* 82 Fc
Miramont, *France* 53 Dd
Miram Shah, *W. Pakistan* 70 Bd
Miranda, *Argentina* 92 Ee
Miranda, *Brazil* 91 Fh
Miranda. *See* Bonanza
Miranda de Ebro, *Spain* 50 Da
Miranda do Corvo, *Portugal* 50 Ab
Miranda do Douro, *Portugal* 50 Bb
Mirande, *France* 53 De
Mirandela, *Portugal* 50 Bb
Mirandilla, *Spain* 50 Bc
Mirbat, *Muscat & Oman* 73 Ff
Mirdum, *Netherlands* 44 Db
Mirebeau, *France* 52 Dc
Mirim, L., *Brazil* 92 Fd
Mirjaveh, *Persia* 73 Hd
Mirnoye, *Russia* 58 Hb
Mirosi, *Rumania* 56 Eb
Mirpur, *Kashmir* 70 Cd
Mirpur Khas, *W. Pakistan* 68 Cc
Mirtoan Sea, *Greece* 57 Df
Mirtos, *Crete* 57 Eg
Mirt Padam, *India* 69 Jc
Mirzapur, *India* 71 Dc
Miscou I., *New Brunswick* 82 Fc
Mishrif, *Arabia* 72 De
Misis, *Turkey* 72 Cb
Miska, *Arabia* 72 De
Miskolc, *Hungary* 49 Jd
Misoöl, I., *W. Irian* 63 Kl
Misquah Hills, *Minnesota* 83 Ab
Mississippi, state, *U.S.A.* 85 He
Mississippi R., *U.S.A.* 85 Hd
Missolónghin. *See* Mesolóngion
Missoula, *Montana* 87 Fb
Missouri, state, *U.S.A.* 85 Hd
Missouri R., *U.S.A.* 84 Gc
Mistassini L., *Quebec* 81 Sf
Mistretta, *Sicily* 55 Eg
Misurata, *Libya* 79 Jb
Mitala Maria, *Uganda* 77 Gd
Mitchell, *Ontario* 83 Fd
Mitchell, *Queensland* 95 Je
Mitchell, *S. Dakota* 84 Gc
Mitchell, Mt., *N. Carolina* 85 Kd
Mitchell, R., *Queensland* 95 Hc
Mitchell River, *Qnsld.* 95 Hc
Mitchelstown, *Eire* 33 Gj
Mithankot, *W. Pakistan* 70 Bf
Mithi, *W. Pakistan* 68 Cd
Mithimna, *Greece* 57 Fe
Mitilini, *Lesvos, I., Greece* 57 Fe
Mito, *Japan* 66 Gf
Mitsiz, *Gabon* 76 Cd
Mittelmark, *Germany* 48 Eb
Mitu, *Colombia* 90 Dc
Mitumba Mts., *Congo* 77 Fe
Miyako, *Japan* 66 He
Miyandowab, *Persia* 72 Eb
Miyazaki, *Japan* 66 Bj
Mizda, *Libya* 79 Hb
Mizen Hd., *Eire* 31 Aj
Mizil, *Rumania* 56 Fb
Mizo Hills, *India* 69 Hd
Mizque, *Bolivia* 90 Dg
Mjölby, *Sweden* 47 Fg
Mjosa, L., *Norway* 47 Df
Mladá Boleslav, *Czech.* 48 Fc
Mlanje, Mt., *Malawi* 77 Hh
Mlawa, *Poland* 49 Jb
Mljet, I., *Yugoslavia* 54 Fd
Mo, *Norway* 46 Ed
Mo Ångsåg, *Sweden* 46 He
Moapa, *Nevada* 87 Fg
Moberly, *Missouri* 85 Hd
Mobile, *Alabama* 85 Je
Mobridge, *S. Dakota* 84 Fb
Mocajuba, *Brazil* 91 Hd
Moçambique, *E. Afr.* 77 Jh
Moçâmedes, *Angola* 76 Ch
Mocha, *Yemen* 72 Dg
Mocimboa-da-Praia, *Moçambique* 77 Jg
Mocoa, *Colombia* 90 Bc
Mocorito, *Mexico* 88 Cb
Moctezuma, *Mexico* 88 Cb
Moctezuma, *Mexico* 88 Cb
Mocuba, *Moçambique* 75 Fc
Mocuburi, *Moçambique* 77 Hg
Modane, *France* 53 Gd
Modave, *Belgium* 44 Dd
Modena, *Italy* 54 Cc
Modesto, *California* 87 Cg
Modica, *Sicily* 55 Eg
Modjamboli, *Congo* 76 Ed
Mo-duc, *S. Vietnam* 67 Dd
Modung, *China* 62 Ce
Moengo, *Surinam* 91 Gb
Mofa, *Ethiopia* 77 Jb
Moffat, *Scotland* 30 Ee
Mogadiscio (Mogadishu), *Somalia* 77 Kd
Mogador, *Morocco* 78 Db
Mogadouro, *Portugal* 50 Bb
Mogar, *Ethiopia* 77 Hc
Mogaung, *Burma* 69 Jc
Mogilev, *White Russia* 60 Ge
Mogilev Podol'skiy, *Ukraine* 60 Eg
Mogocha, *Russia* 59 Lc
Mogochin, *Russia* 58 Hc
Mogok, *Burma* 69 Jd
Mogu, *Ethiopia* 77 Jd
Moguer, *Spain* 50 Bd
Mohacs, *Hungary* 56 Bb
Mohaka, R., *New Zealand* 93 Fc
Mohammedia, *Algeria* 78 Fa
Mohawk & R., *New York* 86 Ca
Moheli I., *Comores Arch.* 77 Jg
Moho, *China* 59 Mc
Mohoro, *Tanzania* 77 Hf
Moine, L. du, *Quebec* 83 Hb
Moirang, *India* 69 Hd
Moisie, B., *Quebec* 82 Fa
Moissac, *France* 53 Dd
Mojave, *California* 87 Dh
Moji, *Brazil* 91 Hh
Moju & R., *Brazil* 91 Hd
Mokai, *New Zealand* 93 Ec
Mokameh, *India* 71 Ec
Mokolo, *Cameroon* 79 Hf
Mokpo, *Korea* 62 Jd
Mokshany, *Russia* 61 Gd
Moldava, *Czechoslovakia* 49 Jd
Moldavia, *Rumania* 56 Fa
Moldavia, rep., *U.S.S.R.* 60 Fh
Molde & Fd., *Norway* 46 Be
Moldova Nouă, *Rumania* 56 Cb
Molepolole, *Botswana* 75 Dd
Môle St Nicolas, *Haiti* 89 Ec
Molfetta, *Italy* 55 Fe
Molina, *Chile* 92 Be
Molina, *Spain* 51 Ec
Molina, *Spain* 51 Eb
Moline, *Illinois* 85 Hc
Moliro, *Congo* 77 Gf
Moll, *Belgium* 44 Dc
Mollendo, *Peru* 90 Cg
Mollis, *Switzerland* 45 Ea
Mollösund, *Sweden* 47 Dg
Molndal, *Sweden* 47 Eh
Molotov. *See* Perm
Molotovsk, *Russia* 58 Cb
Molotovsk, *Russia* 61 Jb
Molucca Pass, *Indonesia* 63 Jk
Moluccas, Is., *Indonesia* 63 Jl
Moma, *Moçambique* 77 Hh
Mombasa, *Kenya* 77 He
Mombetsu, *Japan* 66 Hb
Mombuey, *Spain* 50 Ba
Momchilgrad, *Bulgaria* 56 Ed
Momeik. *See* Mong-mit
Momignies, *Belgium* 44 Cd
Momotombo, *Nicaragua* 89 Bd
Mompós, *Colombia* 90 Cb
Mön, I., *Denmark* 47 Ej
Monå Fd., *Finland* 46 Ke
Mona, I., *Puerto Rico* 89 Fc
Mona Pass., *West Indies* 89 Fc
Monach I., *Scotland* 34 Ad
Monaco, princip., *S. Europe* 53 Ge
Monadhliath Mts., *Scotland* 30 Ec
Monaghan & co., *Eire* 31 Cf
Monarch Pass, *Colorado* 84 Ed
Monasterace Marina, *Italy* 55 Ff
Monastir, *Sardinia* 55 Bf
Monastir. *See* Bitola
Monastir, *Tunisia* 79 Ha
Monção, *Portugal* 50 Aa
Monchique, *Portugal* 50 Ad
Monclova, *Mexico* 88 Db
Moncton, *New Brunswick* 82 Fc
Mondoñedo, *Spain* 50 Ba
Mondul, *Tanzania* 77 He
Monemvasia, *Greece* 57 Df
Monessen, *Pennsylvania* 86 Ab
Monetny, *Russia* 61 Qb
Moneva, *Spain* 51 Eb
Monforte, *Portugal* 50 Bc
Monga, *Congo* 76 Ed
Mongalla, *Sudan* 79 Mg
Monger, L., *W. Australia* 94 Ce
Möng-Hsu, *Burma* 69 Jd
Monghyr, *India* 71 Fc
Möng Kiang. *See* Mong Yai
Mongkol-borey, *Cambodia* 67 Cd
Möng Kung, *Burma* 69 Jd
Mong-mit, *Burma* 69 Jd
Mongo, *Chad* 79 Jf
Mongolia, *E. Asia* 41 Jd
Mongolia, Inner, *China* 41 Kd
Mongonu, *Nigeria* 79 Hf
Mongoumba, *Cent. Afr. Rep.* 79 Jh
Möng-pai, *Burma* 69 Je
Möng Pan, *Burma* 69 Jd
Möng Pawn, *Burma* 69 Jd
Möng-Sit, *Burma* 69 Jd
Mongu, *Zambia* 75 Cc
Mong Yai, *Burma* 69 Jd
Moniquira, *Colombia* 90 Cb
Monkey Bay, *Malawi* 75 Eb
Monkira, *Queensland* 95 Hd
Monmouth & co., *Britain* 31 Fj
Monnikendam, *Netherlands* 44 Db
Mono L., *California* 87 Df
Monomoy I. & Pt., *Mass.* 86 Eb
Monopoli, *Italy* 55 Fe
Monóvar, *Spain* 51 Ec
Monreal del Campo, *Spain* 51 Eb
Monroe, *Louisiana* 85 He
Monroe, *Michigan* 83 Ee
Monroe, *Wisconsin* 83 Bd
Monrovia, *Liberia* 78 Cg
Mons, *Belgium* 44 Bd
Monsanto, *Portugal* 50 Bb
Monserrato, *Sardinia* 55 Bf
Monson, *Massachusetts* 86 Da
Monster, *Netherlands* 44 Cb
Mönsterås, *Sweden* 47 Gh
Mont, *Belgium* 44 Dd
Montagne Tremblante Park, *Quebec* 83 Jb
Montague, *Michigan* 83 Cd
Montague I., *S. Sandwich Is.* 100 Ad
Montalbán, *Spain* 51 Eb
Montana, state, *U.S.A.* 84 Db
Montánchez, *Spain* 50 Bc
Montargis, *France* 52 Ec
Montauban, *France* 53 Dd
Montbard, *France* 52 Fc
Montblanch, *Spain* 51 Fb
Montbrison, *France* 52 Fd
Montclair, *New Jersey* 86 Cb
Montcornet, *France* 52 Fb
Mont de Marsan, *France* 52 Ee
Montdidier, *France* 52 Eb
Mont Dore, le, *France* 52 Ed
Monte Alegre, *Brazil* 91 Gd
Monte Alegre, *Brazil* 91 Hg
Montebello, *Quebec* 83 Jc
Monte Carlo, *Monaco* 53 Ge
Monte Carmelo, *Brazil* 91 Hg
Monte Caseros, *Argentina* 92 Ed
Monte Coman, *Argentina* 92 Cd
Monte Cristi, *Rep. Dom.* 89 Ec
Monte Cristi, Sa de, *Rep. Dominicana* 89 Ec
Montecristo, I., *Italy* 54 Cd
Montefrío, *Spain* 50 Cd
Montego Bay, *Jamaica* 89 Dc
Montélimar, *France* 53 Fd
Montello, *Wisconsin* 83 Bd
Montemorelos, *Mexico* 88 Eb
Montenegro, *Yugoslavia* 56 Bc
Montereau, *France* 52 Eb
Monterey, *California* 87 Cg
Monterey, B. of, *California* 87 Cg
Monteria, *Colombia* 90 Bb
Montero, *Bolivia* 90 Eg
Monteros, *Argentina* 92 Cc
Monterrey, *Mexico* 88 Db
Monte Sant' Angelo, *Italy* 55 Ee
Montes Claros, *Brazil* 91 Jg
Montevideo, *Uruguay* 92 Ed
Montfort-sur-Meu, *France* 52 Bb
Montgomery, *Alabama* 85 Je
Montgomery, *W. Pakistan* 70 Ce
Montgomery & co., *Wales* 31 Eh
Monthey, *Switzerland* 45 Bb
Monticello, *Maine* 82 Ec
Monticello, *New York* 83 Je
Montijo, B. de, *Panama* 89 Ce
Montilla, *Spain* 50 Cd
Mont Joli, *Quebec* 82 Db
Mont Laurier, *Quebec* 83 Jb
Montluçon, *France* 52 Ec
Montmagny, *Quebec* 82 Cc
Montmédy, *France* 52 Fb
Montmirail, *France* 52 Eb
Montmorency, *Quebec* 83 Lb
Montoro, *Spain* 50 Cc
Montoursville, *Pennsylvania* 86 Bb
Montpelier, *Idaho* 84 Dc
Montpelier, *Vermont* 83 Kc
Montpellier, *France* 53 Ee
Montreal, *Quebec* 83 Kc
Montreal L., *Saskatchewan* 80 Kf
Montrégeau, *France* 53 De
Montreuil, *France* 52 Da
Montreuil Bellay, *France* 52 Cc
Montreux, *Switzerland* 45 Bb
Montrose, *Pennsylvania* 86 Bb
Montrose, *Scotland* 30 Fd
Monts, Pt. des, *Quebec* 82 Eb
Mont-St Jean, *Belgium* 44 Cd
Mont-St-Michel & B., *Fr.* 52 Cb
Montserrat, I., *Leeward Is.* 89 Gc
Monywa, *Burma* 69 Jd
Monza, *Italy* 54 Bc
Monze, *Zambia* 75 Dc
Monzón, *Spain* 51 Fb
Moora, *W. Australia* 94 Cf
Moore, L., *W. Australia* 94 Ce
Moorefield, *W. Virginia* 86 Ac
Moorfoot Hills, *Scotland* 30 Ee
Moorhead, *Minnesota* 84 Gb
Moorsel, *Belgium* 44 Cd
Moorslede, *Belgium* 44 Bd
Moose R., *Ontario* 81 Qf
Moosehead L., *Maine* 82 Dd
Moose Jaw, *Saskatchewan* 80 Kf
Moosic, Mts., *Pennsylvania* 86 Cb
Moosomin, *Saskatchewan* 80 Lf
Moosonee, *Ontario* 81 Qf
Mopti, *Mali* 78 Ef
Moquegua, *Peru* 90 Cg
Mora, *Ethiopia* 77 Hb
Mora, *Cameroon* 79 Hf
Mora, *Portugal* 50 Ac
Mora, *Spain* 50 Dc
Mora, *Sweden* 46 Ff
Moradabad, *India* 71 Ba
Mora de Rubielos, *Spain* 51 Eb
Moramanga, *Madagascar* 77 Nk
Morano Calabro, *Italy* 55 Ff
Morar, *India* 71 Bb
Morar L., *Scotland* 30 Dd
Morat. *See* Murten
Moratalla, *Spain* 51 Ec
Morava, *Czechoslovakia* 49 Gd
Morava R., *Yugoslavia* 56 Cb
Moravska Trebova, *Czech.* 49 Gd
Morawhanna, *Guyana* 90 Fb
Moray, co., *Scotland* 30 Ec
Moray Firth, *Scotland* 30 Ec
Morbihan, dep., *France* 52 Bc
Morden, *Manitoba* 80 Mg
Mordova, *Russia* 61 Ed
Mordovskaya, aut. rep. *Russ.* 58 Dc
Moreau R., *S. Dakota* 84 Fb
Morecambe & B., *England* 31 Ff
Moreda, *Spain* 50 Dd
Moree, *New South Wales* 95 Je
Moreira, *Brazil* 90 Ed
Mörel, *Switzerland* 45 Db
Morelia, *Mexico* 88 Dd
Morella, *Spain* 51 Eb
Morelos, *Mexico* 88 Db
Morelos, *Mexico* 88 Eb
Morelos, state, *Mexico* 88 Ed
Morena, Sa., *Spain* 50 Cc
Morere, *New Zealand* 93 Fc
Moreton B., *Queensland* 95 Ke
Morez, *France* 52 Gc
Morgan, *S. Australia* 95 Gf
Morgan City, *Louisiana* 85 Hf
Morgat, *France* 52 Ab
Morges, *Switzerland* 45 Bb
Morgins, *Switzerland* 45 Bb
Morian, *India* 69 Hc
Morice L., *Brit. Columbia* 80 Ff
Morinville, *Alberta* 80 Jf
Morioka, *Japan* 66 Ge
Morlaix, *France* 52 Bb
Mornington, I., *Chile* 92 Ag
Moro G., *Philippines* 63 Hj
Morobe, *New Guinea* 95 Ja
Morocco, *N.-W. Africa* 78 Db
Morogoro, *Tanzania* 77 Hf
Morokwen, *Cape Province* 75 Ce
Moron, *Cuba* 89 Db
Morona, *Ecuador* 90 Bd
Morondava, *Madagascar* 77 Ml
Morón de la Frontera, *Spain* 50 Cd
Morotai, I., *Indonesia* 63 Jk
Moroto, *Uganda* 77 Gd
Morpeth, *England* 30 Fe
Morphou & B., *Cyprus* 74 Ab
Morrinhos, *Brazil* 91 Hg
Morrinsville, *New Zealand* 93 Eb
Morris, *Manitoba* 80 Mg
Morrisburg, *Ontario* 83 Jc
Morris Jesup C., *Arctic Oc.* 39 Na
Morrison, *Illinois* 83 Be
Morristown, *New Jersey* 86 Cb
Morristown, *Tennessee* 85 Kd
Morrisville, *New York* 83 Jd
Morrosquillo, G. de, *Colomb.* 90 Bb
Mors, *Denmark* 47 Ch
Morshansk, *Russia* 61 Ed
Mortagne, *France* 52 Db
Mortagua, *Portugal* 50 Ab
Mortain, *France* 52 Cb
Morven, *New Zealand* 93 Cf
Morven, *Queensland* 95 Je
Morvi, *India* 68 Dd
Moscow, *Idaho* 87 Eb
Moscow. *See* Moskva
Moselle, dep., *France* 52 Gb
Moselle, R., *France* 52 Gb
Mosera, I. *See* Masira I.
Mosgiel, *New Zealand* 93 Cf
Moshupa, *Botswana* 75 Dd
Mosjöen, *Norway* 46 Ed
Moskenesöy, *Norway* 46 Ec
Moskva, *Russia* 60 Kd
Mosonmagyarovar, *Hungary* 49 Ge
Mosqueiro, *Brazil* 91 Hd
Mosquera, *Colombia* 90 Bc
Moss, *Norway* 47 Dg
Mossamedes, *Angola* 75 Ac
Mossburn, *New Zealand* 93 Bf
Mosselbaai, *Cape Province* 75 Cf
Mossendjo, *Fr. Congo* 76 Ce
Mossoro, *Brazil* 91 Ke
Mossuma, *Angola* 76 Eg
Mossurize, *Moçambique* 75 Ed
Most, *Czechoslovakia* 48 Ec
Mostaganem, *Algeria* 78 Fa
Mostar, *Yugoslavia* 56 Ac
Mostardas, *Brazil* 92 Fd
Mostrim, *Eire* 32 Ff
Mosul, *Iraq* 72 Db
Mota del Marqués, *Spain* 50 Cb
Motala, *Sweden* 47 Fg
Motatan, *Venezuela* 90 Cb
Motherwell, *Scotland* 30 Ee
Môtier, *Switzerland* 45 Cb
Môtiers, *Switzerland* 45 Bb
Motihari, *India* 71 Eb
Motôt, *Switzerland* 45 Cb
Motril, *Spain* 50 Dd
Motueka, *New Zealand* 93 Dd
Motul, *Mexico* 88 Gc
Moudhros, *Greece* 57 Ee
Moudon, *Switzerland* 45 Bb
Mouila, *Gabon* 76 Ce
Moukden. *See* Shenyang
Mould Bay, *N.-W. Terr.* 80 Ha
Moulins, *France* 52 Ec
Moulmein, *Burma* 69 Je
Moulouya R., *Morocco* 78 Eb
Mount Bellew, *Eire* 31 Bg
Mount Carmel, *Pennsylvania* 86 Bb
Mount Carroll, *Illinois* 83 Bd
Mount Clemens, *Michigan* 83 Ed
Mount Desert I. (Acadia Nat. Park), *Maine* 82 Dd
Mount Dutton, *S. Aust.* 95 Ge
Mount Forest, *Ontario* 83 Fc
Mount Gambier, *S. Aust.* 95 Hg
Mount Holly, *New Jersey* 86 Cc
Mount Jewett, *Pennsylvania* 86 Ab
Mount Lofty Ra., *S. Aust.* 95 Gf
Mount Magnet, *W. Aust.* 94 Ce
Mount Morgan, *Queensland* 95 Kd
Mount Morris, *New York* 86 Ba
Mount Murray, *Alberta* 80 Je
Mount Pleasant, *Michigan* 83 Dd
Mount Pleasant, *Pa.* 86 Ab
Mount Robson Park, *B.C.* 80 Hf
Mounts B., *England* 31 Dk
Mount Stewart, *P.E.I.* 82 Gc
Mount Union, *Pennsylvania* 86 Bb
Mount Vernon, *Virginia* 83 Hf
Mount Vernon, *W. Australia* 94 Cd
Moura, *Brazil* 90 Ed
Moura, *Portugal* 50 Bc
Mourão, *Portugal* 50 Bc
Mourne Mts., *N. Ireland* 31 Cf
Moussoro, *Chad* 79 Jf
Moutier, *Switzerland* 45 Ca
Moutohora, *New Zealand* 93 Fc
Mowming, *China* 65 Em
Mowping, *China* 64 Kd
Moyale, *Kenya* 77 Hd
Moyobamba, *Peru* 90 Be
Mozambique, *See* Moçambique
Mozhga, *Russia* 61 Lb
Mozyr, *White Russia* 60 Fe
Mpanda, *Tanzania* 77 Gf
Mporokoso, *Zambia* 77 Gf
Mstislavl, *White Russia* 60 Gd
Mtakuja, *Tanzania* 77 Gf
Mtito Andei, *Kenya* 77 He
Mtoko, *Rhodesia* 75 Ec
Mtsensk, *Russia* 60 Ke
Mu, R., *Burma* 69 Jd
Muádhdham, el, *Arabia* 72 Cd
Muang Chaiya, *Siam* 67 Be
Muang Chana, *Siam* 67 Ce
Muang Langsuan, *Siam* 67 Be
Muang Nan, *Siam* 67 Cc
Muang Palien, *Siam* 67 Be
Mubarraz, *Arabia* 72 Ed
Mubende, *Uganda* 77 Gd
Muchinga Mts., *Zambia* 77 Gg
Mucuri, *Brazil* 91 Kg
Mudanya, *Turkey* 72 Aa
Mudawwara, *Jordan* 74 Dh
Muddus Järvi, *Finland* 46 Mb
Mudgee, *New S. Wales* 95 Jf
Mudhnib, *Arabia* 72 Dd
Mueda, *Moçambique* 77 Hg
Mugford C., *Labrador* 81 Ue
Muggendorf, *Germany* 48 Dd

167

Norrsundet, Sweden 47 Gf
Norrtalje, Sweden 47 Hg
Norseman, W. Australia 94 Df
Norsholm, Sweden 47 Fg
North C., Antarctica 100 Lb
North C., New Zealand 93 Da
North, C., Nova Scotia 82 Hc
North Chan., Ontario 83 Eb
North Chan., Scot.-N. Ire. 30 De
North Downs, England 31 Hj
North I., New Zealand 93 Dc
North Pt., Prince Edward I. 82 Gc
North Sea, W. Europe 42 Gd
North Adams, Massachusetts 86 Da
Northallerton, England 31 Gf
Northam, W. Australia 94 Cf
Northampton, Mass. 86 Da
Northampton, W. Aust. 94 Be
Northampton & co., Eng. 31 Gh
North Bay, Ontario 83 Gb
North Bend, Oregon 87 Ad
North Berwick, Scotland 30 Fd
North Borneo. See Sabah
Northbridge, Massachusetts 86 Ea
North Carolina, state, U.S.A. 85 Kd
North Creek, New York 83 Jd
North Dakota, state, U.S.A. 84 Fb
North-East Foreland, Greenland 39 Ma
Northern Circars, India 68 Fe
Northern Ireland, Brit. Isles 31 Cf
Northern Rhodesia. See Zambia.
Northern Territory, Aust. 94 Fc
North Land. See Severnaya Zemlya
North Little Rock, Ark. 85 He
North Magnetic Pole 80 La
North Platte & R., Neb. 84 Fc
North Pole, Arctic Ocean 39 a
North Riding, Yorks, Eng. 31 Ff
North Ronaldsay, I., Orkney 30 Fa
North Sydney, Nova Scotia 82 Hc
North Tonawanda, N.Y. 86 Aa
Northumberland, co., Eng. 30 Fe
Northumberland Str., New Brunswick, etc. 82 Fc
Northumberland, Pa. 86 Bb
North Vancouver, B.C. 80 Gg
North Vietnam, S.-E. Asia 65 Bm
Northville, New York 83 Jd
North West C., W. Aust. 94 Bd
North-West River, Labrador 81 Uf
North-West Territories, Canada 80 Jd
Norton, New Brunswick 82 Fd
Norton Sd., Alaska 85 Wl
Norwalk, Connecticut 86 Db
Norwalk, Ohio 83 Ee
Norway, Michigan 83 Cc
Norway, kingdom, North-West Europe 42 Kc
Norwich, Connecticut 86 Db
Norwich, England 31 Hh
Norwich, New York 86 Ca
Norwood, Massachusetts 86 Ea
Norwood, New York 83 Jc
Noshiro, Japan 66 Fd
Nosseghem, Belgium 44 Cd
Nossi Bé, I., Madagascar 77 Nj
Noto, Sicily 55 Eg
Noto Pen., Japan 66 Ef
Notodden, Norway 47 Cg
Notre Dame B., Nfd. 82 Lb
Notre Dame Mts., Quebec 82 Cc
Notre Dame-du-Lac, Quebec 82 Dc
Nottawasaga B., Ontario 83 Fc
Nottingham & co., England 31 Gh
Nottingham I., N.-W. Terr. 81 Rd
Nouakchott, Mauritania 78 Be
Nova Becej, Yugoslavia 56 Cb
Nova Chaves, Angola 76 Eg
Nova Cruz, Brazil 91 Ke
Nova Freixo, Moçambique 77 Hg
Nova Gaia, Angola 76 Dg
Nova Goa, Goa 68 De
Nova Iorque, Brazil 91 Je
Nova Lisboa, Angola 76 Dg
Novara, Italy 54 Bc
Nova Scotia, prov., Canada 81 Th
Nova Sofala, Moçambique 75 Ed
Nova Venecia, Brazil 91 Jg
Novaya Sibir, Ostrov, Russ. 59 Qa
Novaya Zemlya, Russia 58 Ea
Nové Zámky, Czech. 49 He
Novgorod, Russia 60 Gb
Novi, Yugoslavia 54 Ec
Novi Pazar, Bulgaria 56 Fc
Novi Pazar, Yugoslavia 56 Cc
Novi Sad, Yugoslavia 56 Bb
Novocherkassk, Russia 61 Eg
Novokuznetsk, Russia 58 Hc
Novo Mesto, Yugoslavia 54 Ec
Novomoskovsk, Russia 60 Ld
Novomoskovsk, Ukraine 60 Jg
Novo Redondo, Angola 76 Cg
Novorossiysk, Russia 58 Cd
Novoshakhtinsk, Russia 61 Dg
Novosibirsk, Russia 58 Hc
Novosibirskiye Ostrova, Russia 59 Na
Novourgench. See Urgench
Novska, Yugoslavia 54 Fc
Novy Jičin, Czechoslovakia 49 Hd
Novy Port, Russia 58 Gb
Nowa Wilejka. See Naujoji Vilnia
Nowgong, India 69 Hc
Nowra, New South Wales 95 Kf
Nowshera, W. Pakistan 70 Ce
Nowy Sacz, Poland 49 Jd
Nowy Targ, Poland 49 Jd
Nowy Tomysl, Poland 49 Gb
Noya, Spain 50 Aa
Nozay, France 52 Cc
Nsanje, Malawi 75 Fc
Ntungamo, Uganda 77 Ge
Nuanetsi, Rhodesia 75 Ed
Nuassuak Pen., Greenland 39 Pb
Nueces R., Texas 84 Gf
Nueltin L., N.-W. Terr. 81 Md
Nueva, I., Chile & Argent. 92 Cj
Nueva Imperial, Chile 92 Be
Nueva Lubeca, Argentina 92 Bf
Nuevo, G., Argentina 92 Df
Nuevo Laredo, Mexico 88 Eb
Nuevo Leon, state, Mexico 88 Db
Nuits St Georges, France 52 Fc
Nukuhiva, I., Marquesas, I. 99 Lh
Nukuoro, I., Caroline Is. 98 Eg
Nukus, Uzbek. 58 Ed
Nules, Spain 51 Ec
Nullagine, W. Australia 94 Dd
Nullarbor, S. Australia 94 Ff
Nullarbor Plain, S. W. Aust. 94 Ef
Numata, Japan 66 Ff
Numazu, Japan 66 Fg
Nunchia, Colombia 90 Cb
Nunivak I., Alaska 85 Wl
Nunkiang, China 62 Ja
Nuoro, Sardinia 55 Be
Nuquí, Colombia 90 Bb
Nuri, Mexico 88 Cb
Nurmes, Finland 46 Ne
Nürnberg, Germany 48 Dd
Nurpur, India 70 Dd
Nurri, Sardinia 55 Bf
Nusaybin, Turkey 72 Db
Nushki, W. Pakistan 68 Cc
Nutak, Labrador 81 Ue
Nutrias, Venezuela 90 Db
Nuwara Eliya, Ceylon 68 Fg
Nyada, Sweden 46 Ge
Nyåker, Sweden 46 He
Nyala, Sudan 79 Kf
Nyalikungu, Tanzania 77 Ge
Nyamlell, Sudan 79 Lg
Nyandoma, Russia 58 Db
Nyantakara, Tanzania 77 Ge
Nyanza, Rwanda 77 Fe
Nyasa, L., Malawi 77 Gg
Nyasaland. See Malawi
Nyazepetrovsk, Russia 61 Pb
Nyda, Russia 58 Gb
Nyeri, Kenya 77 He
Nyhammar, Sweden 47 Ff
Nyiregyháza, Hungary 49 Je
Nykøbing, Denmark 47 Dj
Nykøbing, Denmark 47 Ch
Nykøbing, I., Denmark 42 Le
Nyköping, Sweden 47 Gg
Nylstroom. Transvaal 75 Dd
Nymagee, N.S.W. 95 Jf
Nyngan, New South Wales 95 Jf
Nyon, Switzerland 45 Bb
Nyonga, Tanzania 77 Gf
Nyons, France 53 Fd
Nysa, Poland 49 Gc
Nysted, Denmark 47 Dj
Nyurba, Russia 59 Lb
Nyuya, Russia 59 Lb
Nzega, Tanzania 77 Ge
Oahu, I., Hawaii 99 Ke
Oak Ridge, Tennessee 85 Kd
Oakan, Japan 66 Jc
Oakham, England 31 Gh
Oakland, California 87 Bg
Oakland, Maryland 83 Gf
Oakville, Ontario 83 Gd
Oamaru, New Zealand 93 Cf
Oates Ld., Antarctica 100 Kc
Oaxaca & state, Mexico 88 Ed
Ob, R., Russia 58 Fb
Obama, Japan 66 Dg
Oban, New Zealand 93 Bg
Oban, Scotland 30 Dd
Obatogamau L., Quebec 82 Ab
Obbia, Somalia 77 Kc
Obeh, Afghanistan 73 Hc
Oberammergau, Germany 48 De
Oberhausen, Germany 48 Bc
Oberriet, Switzerland 45 Ea
Oberwald, Switzerland 45 Db
Obi, I., Indonesia 63 Jl
Obidos, Brazil 91 Fd
Obidos, Portugal 50 Ac
Obihiro, Japan 66 Hc
Obo, Cent. Afr. Rep. 79 Lg
Obo, Mongolia 62 Db
Obock, Fr. Somaliland 77 Jb
Oborona, Russia 61 Ed
Obrayera, Nicaragua 89 Cd
Obskaya Guba, Russia 58 Gb
Ocampo, Mexico 88 Ec
Ocana, Colombia 90 Cb
Ocana, Spain 50 Dc
Occidental, Cord., Colombia 90 Bc
Ocean I., Pacific Ocean 98 Fh
Ocean City, New Jersey 86 Cc
Ochil Hills, Scotland 30 Ed
Ocland, Rumania 56 Ea
Ocoa, B. de, Rep. Dom. 89 Ec
Ocona, Peru 90 Cg
Oconto, Wisconsin 83 Cc
Ocos, Guatemala 88 Fe
Ocotal, Nicaragua 89 Bd
Ocumare, Venezuela 90 Da
Ocussi Ambeno, Port. Timor 94 Da
Oda, Ghana 78 Eg
Odaka, Japan 66 Gf
Odate, Japan 66 Gd
Odawara, Japan 66 Fg
Odemira, Portugal 50 Ad
Ödemiş, Turkey 72 Ab
Odense, Denmark 47 Dj
Oder R., Germany 48 Fb
Odessa, Ukraine 60 Gh
Odienné, Ivory Coast 78 Dg
Odoorn, Netherlands 44 Eb
Odorhei, Rumania 56 Ea
Odra R., Poland 48 Fb
Odzala, Fr. Congo 76 Cd
Oedelem, Belgium 44 Bc
Oeiras, Brazil 91 Je
Of, Turkey 72 Da
Offaly (Ui Failghe), co., Eire 31 Bg
Offenbach, Germany 48 Cc
Ogaki, Japan 66 Eg
Ogden, Utah 87 He
Ogdensburg, New York 83 Jc
Ogilvie Ra., Yukon 80 Dd
Ogoja, Nigeria 78 Gg
Ogoki R., Ontario 81 Pf
Ogr, Sudan 79 Lf
Ogulin, Yugoslavia 54 Ec
Ohakune, New Zealand 93 Ec
Ohau, L., New Zealand 93 Be
Ohey, Belgium 44 Dd
O'Higgins, Mt., Chile 92 Bg
Ohio, state, U.S.A. 85 Kc
Ohio R., U.S.A. 85 Jd
Ohrid, Yugoslavia 56 Cd
Ohridsko Jezero, Yugoslavia 56 Cd
Ohura, New Zealand 93 Ec
Oiapoque, R., Brazil, etc. 91 Gc
Oignies, Belgium 44 Cd
Oil City, Pennsylvania 86 Ab
Oil Springs, Ontario 83 Ed
Oirschot, Netherlands 44 Dc
Oise, dep., France 52 Eb
Oita, Japan 66 Bh
Oiticica, Brazil 91 Je
Ojinaga, Mexico 88 Db
Ojiya, Japan 66 Ff
Ojocaliente, Mexico 88 Dc
Ojo de Agua, Argentina 92 Dc
Ojo del Toro, Pico, Cuba 89 Dc
Oka R., Russia 61 Fc
Okahandja, S.-W. Africa 75 Bd
Okanagan Lake, B.C. 80 Gg
Okanogan R., Washington 84 Cb
Okaukuejo, S.-W. Africa 75 Bc
Okavango, R., Angola 75 Bc
Okayama, Japan 66 Cg
Okeechobee, L., Florida 85 Kf
Okehampton, England 31 Ek
Okha, Russia 59 Pc
Okhansk, Russia 61 Mb
Okhotsk, Russia 59 Pc
Okhotsk, Sea of, Russia 59 Pc
Okinawa Gunto, Japan 66 Mp
Oki gunto, Japan 66 Cf
Okkak. See Nutak
Oklahoma, state, U.S.A. 84 Gd
Oklahoma City, Oklahoma 84 Gd
Okmulgee, Oklahoma 84 Gd
Oktyabrskoy Revolyutsiy, Os., Russia 59 Ja
Okučani, Yugoslavia 54 Fc
Okuru, New Zealand 93 Be
Okushiri I., Japan 66 Fc
Olaine, Latvia 47 Kh
Olanchito, Honduras 89 Bc
Öland, I., Sweden 47 Gh
Olasan, Ethiopia 77 Kc
Olavarria, Argentina 92 De
Olawa, Poland 49 Gc
Olbia, Sardinia 55 Be
Olcott, New York 86 Aa
Oldcastle, Eire 31 Cg
Oldenburg, Germany 48 Da
Oldenburg, Germany 48 Cb
Oldenzaal, Netherlands 44 Eb
Old Forge, Pennsylvania 86 Cb
Oldham, England 31 Fg
Old Orchard Beach, Maine 86 Ea
Oldtown, Maine 82 Dd
Olean, New York 86 Aa
Olecko, Poland 49 Ka
Olekminsk, Russia 59 Mb
Olenek, Russia 59 Lb
Olenek, R., Russia 59 Ma
Olenekskiy Zaliv, Russia 59 Ma
Oléron, I. d', France 52 Cd
Olga, Russia 59 Nd
Olifants Kloof, Botswana 75 Cd
Olimbos, Mts., Greece 57 Dd
Oliva de Jerez, Spain 50 Bc
Olivares, Spain 51 Dc
Olivares, Cerro de, Argent. 92 Cd
Oliveira, Brazil 91 Jf
Olivenza, Spain 50 Bc
Olivone, Switzerland 45 Db
Ollague, Chile 90 Dh
Ollague, Mt., Bolivia 90 Dh
Olmedo, Spain 50 Cb
Olney, Illinois 83 Bf
Olomouc, Czechoslovakia 49 Gd
Olot, Spain 51 Ga
Olovyannaya, Russia 59 Lc
Olpe, Germany 48 Bc
Olst, Netherlands 44 Eb
Olsztyn, Poland 49 Jb
Olten, Switzerland 45 Ca
Oltu, Turkey 72 Da
Oltul R., Rumania 56 Eb
Olvera, Spain 50 Cd
Olympia, Greece 57 Cf
Olympia, Washington 87 Bb
Olympic Nat. Park, Wash. 84 Bb
Olympus. See Olimbos
Olympus, Mt., Washington 84 Bb
Olyutorskiy Zaliv, Russia 59 Rb
Omagh, N. Ireland 31 Cf
Omaguas, Peru 90 Cd
Omaha, Nebraska 84 Gc
Oman, Arabia 73 Ge
Oman, G. of, Arabia-Persia 73 Ge
Omarama, N.Z. 93 Cf
Omaruru, S.-W. Africa 75 Bd
Ombombo, S.-W. Africa 75 Ac
Omdurman, Sudan 79 Me
Omer, Michigan 83 Ec
Ometepec, Mexico 88 Ed
Ommen, Netherlands 44 Eb
Omoa, Honduras 89 Bc
Omsk, Russia 58 Gc
Omuta, Japan 66 Bh
Omutninsk, Russia 61 La
Onaway, Michigan 83 Dc
Öndör Hän, Mongolia 62 Fa
Onega & R., Russia 58 Cb
Onehunga, New Zealand 93 Eb
Oneida, New York 86 Ca
Oneida L., New York 86 Ca
Oneonta, New York 86 Ca
Onezhskoye Oz., Russia 58 Cb
Ongole, India 68 Fe
Ongudai, Russia 58 Hc
Oniipa, S.-W. Africa 75 Bc
Onitsha, Nigeria 78 Gg
Onjül, Mongolia 62 Ea
Onoto, Venezuela 90 Db
Onotoa, I., Gilbert Islands 98 Gh
Onslow, W. Australia 94 Bd
Onslow B., N. Carolina 85 Le
Ontario, prov., Canada 81 Qg
Ontario, L., U.S.A.-Canada 85 Lc
Onteniente, Spain 51 Ec
Ontiñena, Spain 51 Fb
Oodnadatta, S. Australia 95 Ge
Ooldea, S. Australia 94 Ff
Oostburg, Netherlands 44 Bc
Oostcamp, Belgium 44 Bc
Oostende. See Ostende
Ooster Schelde, Netherlands 44 Bc
Oosterwolde, Netherlands 44 Eb
Oosthuizen, Netherlands 44 Db
Oostmalle, Belgium 44 Cc
Oostvoorne, Netherlands 44 Cc
Ootacamund, India 68 Ef
Opala, Russia 59 Qc
Opari, Sudan 79 Mh
Opatija, Yugoslavia 54 Ec
Opava, Czechoslovakia 49 Gd
Ophir, Mt., W. Malaysia 67 Cf
Ophoven, Belgium 44 Dc
Opochka, Russia 60 Fc
Opodepe, Mexico 88 Ba
Opole, Poland 49 Gc
Oporto. See Porto
Opotiki, New Zealand 93 Fc
Oppa B., Japan 66 Ge
Oppeln. See Opole
Opunake, New Zealand 93 Dc
Oputo, Mexico 88 Ca
Oqair. See Uqair
Oradea, Rumania 56 Ca
Orai, India 71 Bc
Oran, Algeria 78 Ea
Orange, France 53 Fd
Orange, Massachusetts 86 Da
Orange, Texas 85 He
Orange R., S. Africa 75 Be
Orange Free State, S. Africa 75 De
Orangeburg, S. Carolina 85 Ke
Orangeville, Ontario 83 Fd
Oranje Geb., Surinam 91 Fc
Oras, Philippines 63 Jh
Orăştie, Rumania 56 Db
Oraşul Stalin. See Brasov
Oravita, Rumania 56 Cb
Oravská Magura, Czech. 49 Hd
Orbe, Switzerland 45 Bb
Orcera, Spain 51 Dc
Orchha, India 71 Bc
Ord, Mt., W. Australia 94 Ec
Ordenes, Spain 50 Aa
Ord River, W. Australia 94 Ec
Ordu, Turkey 72 Ca
Ordzhonikidze, Russia 58 Dd
Ordzhonikidzegrad. See Bezhitsa
Örebro, Sweden 47 Fg
Oregon, Illinois 83 Bd
Oregon, state, U.S.A. 84 Bc
Oregon City, Oregon 87 Bc
Öregrund, Sweden 47 Hf
Orekhovo Zuyevo, Russia 60 Ld
Orel, Russia 60 Ke
Orellana, Peru 90 Be
Orellana, Spain 50 Cc
Orenburg, Russia 61 Me
Orense, Spain 50 Ba
Orepuki, New Zealand 93 Ag
Öresund, Denmark-Sweden 47 Ej
Orgaña, Spain 51 Fa
Orgaz, Spain 50 Dc
Orhon R., Mongolia 62 Da
Oriental, Cord., Colombia 90 Cb
Oriental, Cord., Peru 90 Be
Orihuela, Spain 51 Ec
Orillia, Ontario 83 Gc
Orinoco, R., Venezuela 90 Eb
Orissa, state, India 69 Fd
Oristano & G. di., Sardinia 55 Bf
Orivesi, Finland 46 Ne
Oriximiná, Brazil 91 Fd
Orizaba, Mexico 88 Ed
Orizare, Bulgaria 56 Fc
Orizona, Brazil 91 Hg
Orkanger, Norway 46 Ce
Orkney, Scotland 30 Fb
Orland, Norway 46 Ce
Orlando, Florida 85 Kf
Orléanais, prov., France 52 Dc
Orléans, France 52 Dc
Orleans, I. of, Quebec 83 Lb
Orléansville. See El-Asnam
Orman, Syria 74 Ee
Ormara, W. Pakistan 68 Bc
Ormondville, New Zealand 93 Fd
Ornach, W. Pakistan 68 Cc
Orne, dep., France 52 Cb
Örnsköldsvik, Sweden 46 He
Orochen, Russia 59 Mc
Orocue, Colombia 90 Cc
Oroluk, I., Caroline Islands 98 Eg
Oron. See Kochumdek
Orono, Maine 82 Dd
Orontes, R., Syria 72 Cb
Orosei, G. di, Sardinia 55 Be
Orosi, Vol., Costa Rica 89 Bd
Orsa, Sweden 47 Ff
Orsha, White Russia 60 Gd
Orsières, Switzerland 45 Cb
Orsk, Russia 61 Pe
Orsova, Rumania 56 Db
Ortegal, C., Spain 50 Ba
Orthez, France 53 Ce
Ortiz, Mexico 88 Cb
Ortiz, Venezuela 90 Db
Orugueira, Spain 50 Ba
Orulgan Khrebet, Russia 59 Mb
Oruro, Bolivia 90 Dg
Orust, Sweden 47 Dg
Oryekhovo, Russia 61 Ge
Osa, Russia 61 Mb
Osaka, Japan 66 Dg
Oschiri, Sardinia 55 Be
Oscoda, Michigan 83 Ec
Osen, Norway 46 Dd
Osh, Kirgiz. 58 Gd
Oshawa, Ontario 83 Gd
O Shima, Japan 66 Fg
Oshkosh, Wisconsin 83 Bc
Oshnoviyeh, Persia 72 Eb
Osijek, Yugoslavia 56 Bb
Osilo, Sardinia 55 Be
Osipenko. See Berdyansk
Osipovichi, White Russia 60 Fe
Osire Sud, S.-W. Africa 75 Bd
Oskarshamn, Sweden 47 Gh
Oslo, Norway 47 Dg
Oslo Fd., Norway 47 Dg
Osmanabad, India 68 Ee
Osmancik, Turkey 72 Ba
Osnabrück, Germany 48 Cb
Osorio, Brazil 92 Fc
Osorno, Chile 92 Bf
Osorno, Spain 50 Ca
Osowiec, Poland 49 Kb
Oss, Netherlands 44 Dc
Ossining, New York 86 Db
Östavall, Sweden 46 Fe
Ostende, Belgium 44 Ac
Österreich, Nieder, prov., Austria 49 Fd
Österreich, Ober, prov., Austria 48 Fd
Östersund, Sweden 46 Fe
Östhammar, Sweden 47 Hf
Ostrava, Czechoslovakia 49 Hd
Ostroda, Poland 49 Hb
Ostrołęka, Poland 49 Jb
Ostrov, Rumania 56 Gb
Ostrov, Russia 60 Fc
Ostrovno, Russia 59 Rb
Ostrowiec, Poland 49 Jc
Ostrów Mazowiecka, Poland 49 Jb
Ostuni, Italy 55 Fe
Östvågöy, Norway 46 Fb
Ōsumi Kaikyō, Japan 66 Bj
Osuna, Spain 50 Cd
Oswego & R., New York 86 Ba
Oswestry, England 31 Eh
Ota, Japan 66 Cg
Otago Peninsula, N.Z. 93 Cf
Otaki, New Zealand 93 Ed
Otaru & B., Japan 66 Gc
Otasuts, Japan 66 Gc
Otavalo, Ecuador 90 Bc
Otepää, Estonia 47 Mg
Othris, Mts., Greece 57 De
Otira, New Zealand 93 Ce
Otis, New Brunswick 82 Ec
Otjiwarongo, S.-W. Africa 75 Bd
Otoçac, Yugoslavia 54 Ec
Otoineppu, Japan 66 Hb
Otorohanga, New Zealand 93 Ec
Otradnyy, Russia 61 Kd
Otranto, Str. of, It.-Albania 57 Bd
Otsego, L., New York 86 Ca
Otsu, Japan 66 Dg
Ottawa, Illinois 83 Be
Ottawa, Kansas 84 Gd
Ottawa, Ontario 83 Jc
Ottawa Is., Hudson B., Canada 81 Qe
Ottawa R., Quebec, etc. 83 Hb
Otterlo, Netherlands 44 Db
Otteröy, Norway 46 Be
Ottignies, Belgium 44 Cd
Otting, Germany 48 Ed
Ottumwa, Iowa 85 Hc
Otus, Russia 60 Jj
Otway, B., Chile 92 Bh
Otway, C., Victoria 95 Hg
Otwock, Poland 49 Jb
Ötz, Austria 48 De
Ötztaler Alpen, Italy/Austria 54 Cb
Ouachita Mts., Arkansas, etc. 85 He
Ouachita R., Arkansas 85 He
Ouagadougou, Volta 78 Ef
Ouahigouya, Volta 78 Ef
Ouangolodougou, Iv. Cst. 78 Dg
Ouargla, Algeria 78 Gb
Oubangui R., Congo 76 Dd
Ouddorp, Netherlands 44 Bc
Oudecappelle, Belgium 44 Ac
Oudenaarde. See Audenarde
Oudenbosch, Netherlands 44 Cc
Oudtshoorn, Cape Province 75 Cf
Ouessant, I. d', France 52 Ab
Ouezzane, Morocco 78 Db
Ouidah, Dahomey 78 Fg
Oulu, Finland 46 Ld
Oulu Järvi, Finland 46 Md
Oulu Joki, Finland 46 Md
Oum Chalouba, Chad 79 Ke
Ounas Joki, Finland 46 Lc
Ouricuri, Brazil 91 Je
Ourinhos, Brazil 91 Hh
Ouro Preto, Brazil 91 Jh
Ouse R., England 31 Gf
Ouse R., England 31 Hh
Outarde B., Quebec 82 Db
Outardes, R. aux, Quebec 82 Db
Outjo, S.-W. Africa 75 Bd
Ouyen, Victoria 95 Hg
Ovalle, Chile 92 Bd
Ovar, Portugal 50 Ab
Over Flakkee I., Netherlands 44 Cc
Overijssel, prov., Netherlands 44 Eb
Överkalix, Sweden 46 Kc
Övermark, Finland 46 Je
Overpelt, Belgium 44 Dc
Övertornea, Sweden 46 Kc
Oviedo, Spain 50 Ca
Ovruch, Ukraine 60 Ff
Owaka, New Zealand 93 Bg
Owasco L., New York 86 Ba
Owatonna, Minnesota 85 Hc
Owego, New York 86 Ba
Owen I., Burma 69 Jf
Owen, Wisconsin 83 Ac
Owensboro, Kentucky 85 Jd
Owens L., California 87 Eg
Owen Sound, Ontario 83 Fc
Owen Stanley Ra., Papua 95 Ja
Owerri, Nigeria 78 Gg
Owo, Nigeria 78 Gg
Owosso, Michigan 83 Dd
Owyhee R., Oregon 87 Ed
Oxford, Maryland 83 Hf
Oxford, New York 83 Jd
Oxford & co., England 31 Gj
Oxley's Pk., New S. Wales 95 Jf
Oyem, Gabon 76 Cd
Oymyakon, Russia 59 Pb
Oyo, Nigeria 78 Fg
Oyster B., Tasmania 95 Jh
Ozark Plat., Missouri, etc. 85 Hd
Ozarks, L. of the, Missouri 85 Hd
Ozd, Hungary 49 Jd
Ozerki, Russia 61 Gd
Ozhogino, Russia 59 Pb
Ozieri, Sardinia 55 Be
Ozun, Rumania 56 Eb
Paan, Burma 69 Je
Paan, China 62 Ce
Paarl, Cape Province 75 Bf
Pabaži, Latvia 47 Lh
Pabianice, Poland 49 Hc
Pabna, E. Pakistan 71 Gd
Pacaraima, Sa., Brazil, etc. 90 Ec
Pacasmayo, Peru 90 Be
Pachbhadra, India 70 Cg
Pachen, Tibet 62 Bd
Pachow. See Pachung
Pachuca, Mexico 88 Ec
Pachung, China 64 Cg
Paços, Portugal 50 Ab
Padam, Kashmir 70 Ed
Padang, Sumatra 63 Dl
Paderborn, Germany 48 Cc
Padilla, Bolivia 90 Eg
Padova, Italy 54 Cc
Padrauna, India 71 Eb
Padre I., Texas 84 Gf
Padstow, England 31 Dk
Padua. See Padova
Paducah, Kentucky 85 Jd
Padul, Spain 50 Dd
Paeroa, New Zealand 93 Eb
Pafuri, Moçambique 75 Ed
Pagai Is., Indonesia 63 Dl
Pagan, Burma 69 Hd
Pagan I., Mariana Is. 98 Df
Pagasai, G. of, Greece 57 De
Pago, I., Yugoslavia 54 Ec
Pagong L., Kashmir-Tibet 68 Eb
Paharpur, W. Pakistan 70 Bd
Pahiatua, New Zealand 93 Ed
Pahlavi Dezh, Persia 73 Fb
Pahsien, China 64 Hc
Pahsien. See Chungking
Paignton, England 31 Ek
Paiho, China 64 Ef
Paijanne, L., Finland 47 Lf
Pai-Khoi Khrebet, Russia 58 Fb
Pailingmiao, China 62 Fb
Pailani, India 71 Cc
Paimpol, France 52 Bb
Painted Des., Arizona 84 Dd
Paisley, Ontario 83 Fc
Paisley, Scotland 30 Ee
Paita, Peru 90 Ae
Pai Tu Hu, China 64 Hg
Paiz do Vinho, Portugal 50 Bb
Pajakumbuh, Sumatra 63 Dl
Pajala, Sweden 46 Kc
Pajares, Spain 50 Ca
Pajde, Estonia 47 Lg
Pakanbaru, Sumatra 63 Dk
Pakaur, India 71 Fc
Pakchan, Burma 69 Jf
Pak-hoi, China 65 Dm
Pakistan, S. Asia 68 Cc
Pak-lay, Laos 67 Cc
Pakokku, Burma 69 Jd
Pakpattan, W. Pakistan 70 Ce
Pakrac, Yugoslavia 54 Fc
Paks, Hungary 49 He
Pakse, Laos 67 Dc
Pakwach, Uganda 77 Gd
Palafrugell, Spain 51 Gb
Palaiokhóra, Crete 57 Dg
Palamau, India 71 Ed
Palamcottah, India 68 Eg
Palamós, Spain 51 Gb
Palamuse, Estonia 47 Mg
Palana, Russia 59 Rc
Palanpur, India 68 Dd
Palapye Rd., Botswana 75 Dd
Palau Is., Pacific Ocean 63 Kj
Palaw, Burma 67 Bd
Palawan, I., Philippines 63 Gj
Paldiski, Estonia 47 Lg
Palembang, Sumatra 63 Dl
Palena, Chile 92 Bf
Palencia, Spain 50 Ca
Palenque, Mexico 88 Fd
Paleokhorio, Cyprus 74 Bc
Palermo, Argentina 92 Db
Palermo, Sicily 55 Df
Palestina, Chile 92 Cb
Palestine, Texas 84 Ge
Palestine, W. Asia 72 Cc
Paletwa, Burma 69 Hd
Palghat, India 68 Ef
Palgrave Pt., S.-W. Africa 75 Ad
Palgu Tso, Tibet 69 Gc
Palhoça, Brazil 92 Gc
Pali, India 68 Dc
Palimé, Togo 78 Fg
Palisade, Nevada 87 Ee
Paliseul, Belgium 44 De
Palizada, Mexico 88 Fd
Palk Str., India 68 Eg
Palkot, India 71 Ed
Palliser B., New Zealand 93 Ed
Palm I., Qnsld. 95 Jc
Palma, Balearic Is. 51 Gc
Palma, Moçambique 77 Jg
Palma, I., Canary Is. 78 Bc
Palmares, Brazil 92 Fd
Palmas, Brazil 92 Fc
Palmas, B., Mexico 88 Cc
Palmas C., Liberia 78 Dh
Palmas, G. of, Sardinia 55 Bf
Palma Sola, Venezuela 90 Da
Palm Beach, West, Florida 85 Kf
Palmeira, Brazil 92 Fc
Palmer Arch., Antarctica 100 Sc
Palmerston, Ontario 83 Fd
Palmerston I., Cook Islands 98 Jj
Palmerston North, N.Z. 93 Ed
Palmerston South, N.Z. 93 Cf
Palmira, Colombia 90 Bc
Palms, Michigan 83 Ed
Palmyra, Syria 72 Cc
Palmyra I., Pacific Ocean 98 Jg
Palni Hills, India 68 Ef
Paloh, Borneo 63 Ek
Paloich, Sudan 79 Mf
Palo Santo, Argentina 92 Ec
Palpa, Nepal 71 Db
Palu, Turkey 72 Db
Palwal, India 70 Ef
Pamban Chan., India 68 Eg
Pamekasan, Indonesia 63 Fm
Pamiers, France 53 De
Pamir, Mts., Russia 58 Ge
Pamlico Sd., N. Carolina 85 Ld
Pampias, Peru 90 Cf
Pamplona, Colombia 90 Cb
Pamplona, Spain 51 Ea
Panache L., Ontario 83 Fb
Panagyurishte, Bulgaria 56 Ec
Panāh, Persia 73 Hd
Panama & rep., Central America 89 De
Panama, G. of, Panama 89 De
Panama Canal, Cent. America 89 Gb
Panama City, Florida 85 Je
Panarea, I., Italy 55 Ef
Panay, I., Philippines 63 Hh
Pančevo, Yugoslavia 56 Cb
Panciu, Rumania 56 Fb
Pandan, Philippines 63 Hh
Pan de Azucar, Chile 92 Bc
Pandharpur, India 68 Ee
Pando, Uruguay 92 Ed
Pandora, Costa Rica 89 Ce
Panevezys, Lithuania 47 Lj
Panfilov, Kazakh. 58 Hd
Panfilovo, Russia 61 Fe
Pangala, Fr. Congo 76 Ce
Pangkiang, China 62 Fb
Panguitch, Utah 84 Dd
Pania Mutombo, Congo 76 Ef
Panipat, India 70 Ef
Panja, China 62 Bc
Panjim. See Nova Goa
Panjnad R., W. Pakistan 70 Bf
Pannerden, Netherlands 44 Ec
Panruti, India 68 Ef
Pantanaw, Burma 69 Je
Pantar, I., Indonesia 63 Hm
Pantelleria, I., Medit. Sea 55 Dg
Pao-an-chow, China 64 Gb
Paochang, China 64 Ga
Paochi. See Paoki
Pão de Açúcar, Brazil 91 Ke
Paoki, China 64 Ce
Paoking. See Shaoyang
Paola, Italy 55 Ff
Paoning. See Langchung
Paosham, China 62 Ce
Paoting, China 64 Gc

Port Taufiq, Egypt 79 Mc
Portugal, W. Europe 43 Ej
Portugalia, Angola 76 Ef
Portuguese Guinea, N.-W. Africa 78 Bf
Portumna, Eire 31 Bg
Port Vendres, France 53 Ee
Port Victoria, Kenya 77 Gd
Port Washington, Wisconsin 83 Cd
Port Weller, Ontario 83 Gd
Poru Tso, Tibet 69 Fb
Porvenir, Chile 92 Bh
Porvoo, Finland 47 Lf
Posadas, Argentina 92 Ec
Posadowsky, B., Antarctica 100 Gc
Poschiavo, Switzerland 45 Fb
Poseh, China 65 Cl
Posen. See Poznan
Poshan, China 64 Hd
Posht-e-Badam, Persia 73 Gc
Poso, Celebes 63 Hl
Poso Danau, Celebes 63 Gl
Possession I., Antarctica 100 Lb
Poste M. Cortier, Algeria 78 Fd
Poste Weygand, Algeria 78 Fd
Posušje, Yugoslavia 54 Fd
Potapovo, Russia 58 Hb
Potchefstroom, Transvaal 75 De
Potemkino, Russia 61 Ge
Potenza, Italy 55 Ee
Poti, Gruzinskaya S.S.R. 58 Dd
Potiskum, Nigeria 79 Hf
Potomac R., Maryland, etc. 86 Ac
Potosi, Bolivia 90 Dg
Potrerillos, Chile 92 Cc
Potsdam, Germany 48 Eb
Pottstown, Pennsylvania 83 Je
Pottsville, Pennsylvania 83 He
Pouce Coupe, B.C. 80 Ge
Poughkeepsie, New York 83 Ke
Poulo Condore, I. de 67 De
Pouso Alegre, Brazil 91 Ff
Pouso Alegre, Brazil 91 Hh
Povenets, Russia 58 Cb
Poverty B., New Zealand 93 Gc
Povoa de Varzim, Portugal 50 Ab
Povorino, Russia 61 Fe
Povungnituk & R., Quebec 81 Rd
Powassan, Ontario 83 Gb
Powder R., Montana 84 Eb
Powell Creek, N.T., Aust. 95 Fc
Powell River, B.C. 80 Gf
Poyang, China 65 Hh
Poyang Hu, China 65 Hh
Poza de la sal, Spain 50 Da
Požarevac, Yugoslavia 56 Cb
Požega, Yugoslavia 56 Ab
Poznan, Poland 49 Gb
Pozo Almonte, Chile 92 Cb
Pozoblanco, Spain 50 Cc
Prachin Buri, Siam 67 Cd
Prado, Brazil 91 Kg
Praga, Poland 49 Jb
Prague. See Praha
Praha, Czechoslovakia 48 Fc
Prai, W. Malaysia 67 Ce
Praid, Rumania 56 Ea
Prainha, Brazil 90 Ee
Prainha, Brazil 91 Gd
Prairie, Queensland 95 Hd
Prairie du Chien, Wisconsin 85 Hc
Prairie du Sac, Wisconsin 83 Bd
Prang, Ghana 78 Eg
Pratapgarh, India 71 Cc
Prato, Italy 54 Cd
Pravia, Spain 50 Ba
Pregolya, R., Russia 47 Jj
Prenay, Lithuania 47 Kj
Prentice, Wisconsin 83 Ac
Přerov, Czechoslovakia 49 Gd
Prescott, Arizona 87 Gh
Prescott, Ontario 83 Jc
President R. Sáenz-Pena, Argentina 92 Dc
Presidente Hermes, Brazil 90 Ef
Prešov, Czechoslovakia 49 Jd
Prespansko, Jezero, Albania, etc. 57 Cd
Presque Isle, Maine 82 Dc
Pressburg. See Bratislava
Přeštice, Czechoslovakia 48 Ed
Preston, England 31 Fg
Prestwick, Scotland 30 De
Pretoria, Transvaal 75 De
Pretty Boy L., Maryland 86 Bc
Préveza, Greece 57 Ce
Pribilof Is., Bering Sea 85 Vm
Příbram, Czechoslovakia 48 Fd
Priego, Spain 50 Cd
Prieska, Cape Province 75 Ce
Prignitz, Germany 48 Db
Prijedor, Yugoslavia 54 Fc
Prijepolje, Yugoslavia 56 Bc
Prilep, Yugoslavia 56 Cd
Priluki, Ukraine 60 Hf
Prim Pt., Prince Edward I. 82 Gc
Primrose L., Saskatchewan 80 Kf
Prince Albert, Cape Prov. 75 Cf
Prince Albert, Saskatchewan 80 Kf
Prince Albert Mts., Antarc. 100 Lb
Prince Albert Park, Sask. 80 Kf
Prince Albert Pen., N.-W.T. 80 Hb
Prince Albert Sd., N.-W.T. 80 Hb
Prince Alfred, C., N.-W.T. 80 Fb
Prince Charles I., N.-W.T. 81 Rc
Prince Edward I., Canada 81 Ug
Prince Edward Is., Indian Oc. 96 Bj
Prince Edward Pen., Ont. 83 Hd
Prince George, B.C. 80 Gf
Prince Harald Ld., Antarc. 100 Db
Prince of Wales, C., Alaska 85 Wl
Prince of Wales I., Alaska 80 Ee
Prince of Wales I., N.-W.T. 80 Lb
Prince of Wales I., Qnsld. 95 Hb
Prince of Wales Str., N.-W.T. 80 Hb
Prince Patrick I., N.-W.T. 80 Hb
Prince Regent Inl., N.-W.T. 81 Pb
Prince Rupert, B.C. 80 Ef
Princes Lake, Ontario 83 Gc
Princess Astrid Ld., Antarc. 100 Cb
Princess Charlotte B., Queensland 95 Hb
Princess Elizabeth Ld., Antarctica 100 Fb
Princess Ragnhild Ld., Antarctica 100 Db
Princess Royal I., B.C. 80 Ff
Princeton, Illinois 83 Be
Princeton, Kentucky 85 Jd
Princeton, Maine 82 Ed
Princeton, Wisconsin 83 Bd
Princetown, Pr. Edward I. 82 Ed
Prince William Sd., Alaska 85 Yl
Príncipe I., G. of Guinea 76 Bd
Principe da Beira, Brazil 90 Ef
Pringles, Argentina 92 Df
Prins Karls Forland, Arctic Ocean 58 Aa
Prinzapolca, Nicaragua 89 Cd
Pripyat (Pripet) Marshes, White Russia 60 Ee
Pripyat (Pripet), R., White Russia 60 Ff
Pristina, Yugoslavia 56 Cc
Pritzwalk, Germany 48 Eb
Privolnoye, Russia 61 He
Prizren, Yugoslavia 56 Cc
Prizzi, Sicily 55 Dg
Progreso, Mexico 88 Gc
Prokop'yevsk, Russia 58 Hc
Prokuplje, Yugoslavia 56 Cc
Prome, Burma 69 Je
Propria, Brazil 91 Kf
Prosperine, Qnsld. 95 Jd
Provence, prov., France 53 Fe
Providence, N.-W. Terr. 80 Hd
Providence, Rhode Island 83 Le
Providence, C., N.-W. Terr. 80 Jb
Providence I., Indian Ocean 96 Ed
Provins, France 52 Eb
Provo, Utah 84 Dc
Prozor, Yugoslavia 54 Fd
Prudentopolis, Brazil 92 Fc
Prudhoe Ld., Greenland 39 Qb
Prüm, Germany 48 Bc
Prut, R., Russia, etc. 60 Fj
Przasnysz, Poland 49 Jb
Przemyśl, Poland 49 Kd
Przhevalsk, Kirgiz. 58 Gd
Psará, I., Greece 57 Ee
Pskov, Russia 60 Fb
Pskovskoye Oz., Russia 60 Fb
Ptuj, Yugoslavia 54 Eb
Puan, Argentina 92 De
Pucacuro, Peru 90 Bd
Pucallpa, Peru 90 Ce
Puchezh, Russia 61 Fb
Puchow. See Yungtsi
Puck, Poland 49 Ha
Pudasjärvi, Finland 46 Md
Pudukkottai, India 68 Ef
Puebla & state, Mexico 88 Ed
Puebla Bonito, New Mexico 84 Ed
Puebla de Alcocer, Spain 50 Cc
Puebla de Sanabria, Spain 50 Ba
Puebla de Trives, Spain 50 Ba
Pueblo, Colorado 84 Fd
Pueblo Hundido, Chile 92 Cc
Puelches, Argentina 92 Ce
Puenteareas, Spain 50 Aa
Puente Caldelas, Spain 50 Aa
Puentedeume, Spain 50 Aa
Puerh, China 62 Df
Puerhken, Mongolia 59 Jd
Puerto Aisen, Chile 92 Bg
Puerto Armuelles, Panama 90 Ab
Puerto Asis, Colombia 90 Bc
Puerto Ayacucho, Venezuela 90 Db
Puerto Barrios, Guatemala 89 Gd
Puerto Bermudez, Peru 90 Cf
Puerto Berrio, Colombia 90 Cb
Puerto Cabello, Venezuela 90 Da
Puerto Cabezas, Nicaragua 89 Cd
Puerto Carreno, Colombia 90 Db
Puerto Casado, Paraguay 92 Eb
Puerto Chicama, Peru 90 Be
Puerto Colombia, Colombia 90 Ca
Puerto Córdoba, Colombia 90 Dd
Puerto Cortes, Honduras 89 Bc
Puerto Coyle, Argentina 92 Ch
Puerto Cumarebo, Venez. 90 Da
Puerto de Carrizal, Chile 92 Bc
Puerto de Chanaral, Chile 92 Bc
Puerto de Santa Maria, Sp. 50 Bd
Puerto Deseado, Argentina 92 Cg
Puerto Gaiba. See Puerto Quijarro
Puerto Grether, Bolivia 90 Eg
Puerto Harberton, Argent. 92 Ch
Puerto Heath, Bolivia 90 Df
Puerto La Cruz, Venezuela 90 Ea
Puerto Leguizamo, Colombia 90 Cd
Puerto Libertad, Salvador 89 Bd
Puertollano, Spain 50 Cc
Puerto Lobos, Argentina 92 Cf
Puerto Madryn, Argentina 92 Cf
Puerto Maldonado, Peru 90 Df
Puerto Montt, Chile 92 Bf
Puerto Morelos, Mexico 88 Gc
Puerto Natales, Chile 92 Ch
Puerto Nuevo, Colombia 90 Db
Puerto Pirámides, Argentina 92 Df
Puerto Plata, Rep. Dom. 89 Ec
Puerto Princesa, Phil. 63 Gj
Puerto Quellen, Chile 92 Bf
Puerto Quijarro, Bolivia 90 Fg
Puerto Rico, I., W. Indies 89 Fc
Puerto Suarez, Bolivia 91 Fg
Puerto Sucre, Bolivia 90 Df
Puerto Varas, Chile 92 Bf
Puerto Victoria, Peru 90 Ce
Puerto Villamizar, Colombia 90 Cb
Puerto Visser, Argentina 92 Cg
Puerto Wilches, Colombia 90 Cb
Pueyrredón, L., Argentina 92 Bg
Pugachev, Russia 61 Jd
Pugal, India 70 Cf
Puget, France 53 Ge
Puget Sd., Washington 84 Bb
Puglia, dep., Italy 55 Fe
Pühalepa, Estonia 47 Kg
Puigcerdá, Spain 51 Fa
Puimro, Brazil 91 Gc
Pukaki, L., New Zealand 93 Cf
Pukapuka I., Pacific Ocean 98 Jj
Pukapuka I., Tuamotu Arch. 99 Mj
Pukchong, Korea 62 Jb
Pukekohe, New Zealand 93 Eb
Pukow, China 64 Jf
Pula, Yugoslavia 54 Dc
Pulacayo, Bolivia 92 Cb
Pulap, I., Caroline Islands 98 Dg
Pulaski, New York 83 Hd
Pulicat L., India 68 Ff
Pulkkila, Finland 46 Ld
Pullen I., N.-W. Terr. 80 Ec
Pultneyville, New York 86 Ba
Puma, Tanzania 77 Ge
Puna, I., Ecuador 90 Ad
Punakha, Bhutan 71 Gb
Punch, Kashmir 70 Dd
Pundri, India 70 Ef
Punjab, India 70 De
Puno, Peru 90 Cg
Punta Alta, Argentina 92 De
Punta Arenas, Chile 92 Bh
Punta Colorado, Chile 92 Bc
Punta del Faro, Sicily 55 Ef
Punta de Pedras, Brazil 91 Hd
Punta Gorda, Brit. Hond. 89 Bc
Puntarenas, Costa Rica 89 Ce
Punta Salinas, Venezuela 90 Ca
Punxsutawney, Pennsylvania 86 Ab
Punyu. See Canton
Puolanka, Finland 46 Md
Puquio, Peru 90 Cf
Purang Chaka, Tibet 69 Fb
Puri, India 69 Ge
Purificacion, Colombia 90 Cc
Purna, India 68 Ee
Purnea, India 71 Fc
Pursat, Cambodia 67 Cd
Purulia, India 71 Fd
Purus, R., Brazil, etc. 90 De
Purwa, India 71 Cb
Pusan, Korea 62 Jc
Pushchino, Russia 59 Kc
Pusht-e-Kuh, Mts., Persia 72 Ec
Putao. See Fort Hertz
Putaruru, N.Z. 93 Ec
Putbus, Germany 48 Ea
Putien, China 65 Jk
Putignano, Italy 55 Fe
Putnam, Connecticut 86 Eb
Putnok, Hungary 49 Jd
Putorana, Gory, Russia 59 Jb
Puttalam, Ceylon 68 Eg
Putte, Belgium 44 Cc
Putte, Belgium 44 Cc
Putten, Netherlands 44 Db
Putumayo, R., Colombia, etc. 90 Cd
Putussibau, Borneo 63 Fk
Puula Vesi, Finland 47 Mf
Puurs, Belgium 44 Cc
Puy, le, France 53 Ed
Puyallup, Washington 87 Bb
Puy-de-Dôme, dep., France 52 Ed
Pyapon, Burma 69 Je
Pyatistennoye, Russia 59 Rb
Pyhä Järvi, Finland 46 Le
Pyhä Järvi, Finland 47 Kf
Pyhäntä, Finland 46 Md
Pyinmana, Burma 69 Je
Pyöngyang, Korea 62 Jc
Pyramid L., Nevada 87 De
Pyramid Pk., California 87 Cf
Pyrénées, Mts., France-Sp. 51 Ea
Pyrénées-Orientales, dep., France 53 Ee
Pyrzyce, Poland 48 Fb
Pyu, Burma 69 Je
Pyzdry, Poland 49 Gb
Qabatiya, Israel 74 De
Qafar, Arabia 72 Dd
Qaiya, Arabia 72 Ee
Qala Mashiz, Persia 73 Gd
Qal'at al Akhdhar, Arabia 72 Cd
Qal'at Dar al Hamra, Arabia 72 Cd
Qal'at ed Dab'a, Jordan 74 Ef
Qal'at el Marqah, Syria 74 Db
Qal'at el Mudiq. See Ma'arret en Numan
Qal'at Uneiza, Jordan 74 Dg
Qalqiliya, Jordan 74 Ce
Qamr B., S. Yemen 73 Ff
Qara, Egypt 79 Lc
Qardaha, Syria 74 Eb
Qartaba, Lebanon 74 Dc
Qasab, Trucial States 73 Gd
Qasim, Arabia 72 Dd
Qasr Amij, Iraq 72 Dc
Qasr el Azraq, Jordan 74 Ef
Qasr e Qand, Persia 73 Hd
Qasr Haiyaniya, Arabia 72 Dd
Qasr ibn Aliya, Arabia 72 Dd
Qasr-i-Shirin, Persia 72 Ec
Qa'taba, Yemen 72 Dg
Qatana, Syria 74 Ed
Qatar, Persian Gulf 73 Fd
Qatif, Arabia 72 Ed
Qayen, Persia 73 Gc
Qazvin, Persia 73 Fb
Qena, Egypt 79 Mc
Qeshm I., Persia 73 Gd
Qeys I., Persia 73 Fd
Qishn, S. Yemen 73 Ff
Qishran, I., Arabia 72 Ce
Qohoud, Persia 73 Fc
Qom, Persia 73 Fc
Qotur, Persia 72 Db
Qoz Bal 'Air, Arabia 72 Df
Quabbin Res., Massachusetts 86 Da
Quakenbrück, Germany 48 Bb
Quang Tri., S. Vietnam 63 Eg
Quarai, Brazil 92 Ed
Quatre Bras, Belgium 44 Cd
Qubeiyat, Lebanon 74 Ec
Quchan, Persia 73 Gb
Quebec, Quebec 82 Cc
Quebec, prov., Canada 81 Sf
Queen Alexandra Ra., Antarctica 100 Ka
Queen Anne, Maryland 86 Cc
Queen Charlotte B., Falkland Islands 92 Dh
Queen Charlotte Is., B.C. 80 Ef
Queen Charlotte Sd., B.C. 80 Ff
Queen Charlotte Str., B.C. 80 Ff
Queen Elizabeth Is., N.-W.T. 80 Ka
Queen Mary Ld., Antarctica 100 Gc
Queen Maud G., N.-W. T. 80 Lc
Queen Maud Ld., Antarc. 100 Cb
Queen Maud Ra., Antarc. 100 Pa
Queen's Chan., N. Terr., Australia 94 Eb
Queensland, state, Australia 95 Hd
Queenstown, Cape Province 75 Df
Queenstown, New Zealand 93 Bf
Queenstown. See Cobh
Queenstown, Tasmania 95 Jh
Queimadas, Brazil 91 Kf
Quelimane, Moçambique 75 Fc
Quemu Quemú, Argentina 92 De
Quequen, Argentina 92 Ee
Queretaro, Mexico 88 Dc
Quesnel, Brit. Columbia 80 Gf
Quesnel L., Brit. Columbia 80 Gf
Quetta, W. Pakistan 68 Cb
Quezaltenango, Guatemala 88 Fe
Quezon City, Philippines 63 Hh
Quibdo, Colombia 90 Bb
Quiberon de B., France 52 Bc
Quievrain, Belgium 44 Bd
Quila, Mexico 88 Cc
Quilca, Peru 90 Cg
Quilino, Argentina 92 Dd
Quillabamba, Peru 90 Cf
Quillan, France 53 Ee
Quillota, Chile 92 Bd
Quilon (Kollam), India 68 Eg
Quilpie, Queensland 95 He
Quimper, France 52 Ab
Quimperle, France 52 Bc
Quince Mil, Peru 90 Cf
Quincy, Illinois 85 Hd
Quincy, Massachusetts 83 Ld
Quines, Argentina 92 Cd
Quincy, Michigan 83 De
Quintana de la Serena, Sp. 50 Cc
Quintanar de la Orden, Sp. 50 Dc
Quintana Roo, state, Mexico 88 Gd
Quipapa, Brazil 91 Ke
Quiriquire, Venezuela 90 Ea
Quiroga, Spain 50 Ba
Quissanga, Moçambique 77 Jg
Quissico, Moçambique 75 Ed
Quitapa, Angola 76 Dg
Quito, Ecuador 90 Bd
Quixada, Brazil 91 Kd
Quixeramobim, Brazil 91 Ke
Qunsuliye, Arabia 72 De
Quorn, S. Australia 95 Gf
Quryat, Muscat & Oman 73 Ge
Qus, Egypt 79 Mc
Qusaiba, Arabia 72 Dd
Qusayar, S. Yemen 73 Fg
Quseir, Egypt 79 Mc
Qusuriya, Arabia 72 De
Quteifa, Syria 74 Ed
Quyon, Quebec 83 Hc
Raahe, Finland 46 Ld
Raasay & Sd of, Scotland 30 Cc
Rab, I., Yugoslavia 54 Ec
Raba, Sumbawa I., Indon. 63 Gm
Rabat, Morocco 78 Db
Rabat Kerim, Persia 73 Fb
Rabigh, Arabia 72 Ce
Rabkob. See Dharmjaygarh
Rabkor, Russia 60 Fe
Race, C., Newfoundland 82 Mc
Race, The, Conn.-New York 86 Db
Rach-Gia, S. Vietnam 67 Dd
Raciborz, Poland 49 Hc
Racine, Wisconsin 83 Cd
Rada, Yemen 72 Dg
Radak Chain, Marshall Is. 98 Gf
Rădăuti, Rumania 60 Dh
Radhanpur, India 68 Dd
Radhwa, Jebel, Arabia 72 Ce
Radnevo, Bulgaria 56 Ec
Radnor, co., Wales 31 Eh
Radom, Poland 49 Jc
Radomir, Bulgaria 56 Dc
Radomsko, Poland 49 Hc
Radstadt, Austria 48 Ee
Radviliskis, Lithuania 47 Kj
Radzyn, Poland 49 Kc
Rae, N.-W. Territories 80 Hd
Rae Isthmus, N.-W. Terr. 81 Pc
Rae R., N.-W. Territories 80 Hc
Rae Bareli, India 71 Cb
Raeside, L., W. Australia 94 De
Raetihi, New Zealand 93 Ec
Rafaela, Argentina 92 Dd
Rafah, Egypt 74 Cf
Rafsanjan, Persia 73 Gc
Raga, Sudan 79 Lg
Ragaz, Bad, Switzerland 45 Ea
Raghugarh, India 71 Ac
Raghunathpur, India 71 Fd
Raglan, New Zealand 93 Eb
Raglan Ra., New Zealand 93 De
Ragunda, Sweden 46 Ge
Ragusa (Dubrovnik), Yugosl. 54 Gd
Ragusa, Sicily 55 Eg
Rahaerg. See Tak
Raheita, Eritrea 77 Jb
Rahhyut, Muscat & Oman 73 Ff
Raiatea, I., Society Islands 99 Kj
Raichur, India 68 Ee
Raida, S. Yemen 72 Eg
Raigarj, India 71 Gc
Raikot, India 70 De
Raingarh, India 70 Ee
Rainier, Mt., Washington 87 Bb
Rainy L., Ontario-Minn. 81 Ng
Raipur, India 68 Fd
Raivavae, I., Austral Is. 99 Lk
Raiwind, W. Pakistan 70 De
Raja, Mt., Borneo 63 Fl
Rajahmundry, India 68 Fa
Rajakhera, India 71 Bb
Rajang, R., Sarawak 63 Fk
Rajanpur, W. Pakistan 70 Bf
Rajapalaiyam, India 68 Eg
Rajasthan, state, India 68 Dc
Rajgarh, India 70 Df
Rajkot, India 68 Dd
Rajmahal, India 71 Fc
Rajmahal Hills, India 71 Ec
Rajura, India 68 Ee
Rakahanga, I., Pacific Oc. 98 Jh
Rakaposhi, Mt., Kashmir 70 Db
Raka Tsangpo, R., Tibet 69 Gc
Rakvere, Estonia 47 Mg
Raleigh, N. Carolina 85 Ld
Raleigh B., N. Carolina 85 Le
Ralik Chain, Marshall Is. 98 Fg
Ram, Jordan 74 Dh
Rama, Ethiopia 77 Jb
Rama, Israel 74 De
Ramadi, Iraq 72 Dc
Ramah, Labrador 81 Ue
Ramallah, Jordan 74 Df
Ramallo, Argentina 92 Dd
Ramanthapuran, India 68 Eg
Rambouillet, France 52 Db
Rameswaram, India 68 Eg
Ramgarh, India 70 Df
Ramgarh, India 71 Cd
Ramgarh, India 71 Ed
Ram Hormuz, Persia 72 Ec
Ramkola, India 71 Dd
Ramla, Israel 74 Cf
Ramnagar, India 71 Cd
Ramnagar, Kashmir 70 Dd
Ramnagar, W. Pakistan 70 Dd
Ramore, Ontario 83 Fa
Ramoutsa, Botswana 75 Dd
Rampart House, Yukon 80 Cc
Rampur, India 69 Fd
Rampur, India 70 Ee
Rampur, India 71 Ba
Rampur Boalia, E. Pakistan 71 Gc
Ramree, Burma 69 He
Ramscappelle, Belgium 44 Ac
Ramsele, Sweden 46 Ge
Ramsey, Isle of Man 31 Ef
Ramsey I., Wales 31 Dj
Ramsey, Ontario 83 Eb
Ramsgate, England 31 Hj
Ramsjö, Sweden 47 Fe
Ramtha, Jordan 74 Ee
Ramtok, India 68 Ed
Ran Fd., Norway 46 Ec
Ranaghat, India 71 Gd
Rancagua, Chile 92 Bd
Rance, Belgium 44 Cd
Ranchi, India 71 Ed
Randazzo, Sicily 55 Eg
Randers, Denmark 47 Dh
Randolph, Vermont 83 Kd
Random I., Newfoundland 82 Mb
Randsfjord, Norway 46 Df
Ranenburg, Russia 61 Ed
Ranfurly, New Zealand 93 Cf
Rangamati, E. Pakistan 69 Hd
Rangeley, Maine 82 Cd
Rangeley Ls., Maine 82 Cd
Ranger, Texas 84 Ge
Rangiora, New Zealand 93 De
Rangitaiki, R., New Zealand 93 Fc
Rangitikei, R., New Zealand 93 Ed
Rangitoto Ra., New Zealand 93 Ec
Rangoon & R., Burma 69 Je
Rangpur, E. Pakistan 71 Gc
Rania, India 70 Df
Ranibennur, India 68 Ef
Raniganj, India 71 Fc
Raniganj, India 71 Fd
Ranikhet, India 71 Ba
Rankin Inl., N.-W. Terr. 81 Nd
Rannoch L., Scotland 30 Ed
Rantauparapap, Sumatra 63 Ck
Rantekombola, Mt., Celebes 63 Gh
Rantsila, Finland 46 Ld
Ranua, Finland 46 Md
Rapa, I., Austral Islands 99 Lk
Rapadama, Volta 78 Ef
Rapid City, S. Dakota 84 Fc
Rapla, Estonia 47 Lg
Rapperswil, Switzerland 45 Da
Raqqa, Syria 72 Cb
Rarotonga, I., Cook Island 99 Kk
Ras al Had, Muscat & Oman 73 Ge
Ras al Khaymah, Trucial States 73 Gd
Ras Dashan, Mt., Ethiopia 77 Hb
Rashad, Sudan 79 Mf
Rashadiya, Jordan 74 Dg
Rasheiya, Lebanon 74 Dd
Rashm, Persia 73 Fb
Rasht, Persia 72 Eb
Raška, Yugoslavia 56 Cc
Rason, L., W. Australia 94 De
Rasova, Rumania 56 Fb
Rasskazovo, Russia 61 Ed
Ratangarh, India 70 Df
Rat Buri, Siam 67 Bd
Rathlin I., N. Ireland 30 Ce
Ratibor. See Raciborz
Ratikon, Mts., Switz.-Austria 45 Ea
Ratnagiri, India 68 De
Raton, New Mexico 84 Fd
Rättvik, Sweden 47 Ff
Rauch, Argentina 92 Ee
Raudha, Yemen 72 Df
Raukumara Ra., N.Z. 93 Fc
Rauma, Finland 47 Jf
Rautas, Sweden 46 Hb
Rautavaara, Finland 46 Ne
Rautio, Finland 46 Ld
Ravar, Persia 73 Gc
Ravenna, Italy 54 Dc
Ravi R., W. Pakistan 70 De
Rawaidha, Arabia 72 De
Rawalpindi, W. Pakistan 70 Cd
Rawandiz, Iraq 72 Db
Rawatsar, India 70 Df
Rawene, New Zealand 93 Da
Rawlinna, W. Australia 94 Ef
Rawlins, Wyoming 84 Ec
Rawson, Argentina 92 Cf
Ray, C., Newfoundland 82 Jc
Rays Hill, Pennsylvania 86 Ac
Rayadrug, India 68 Ef
Raymond, Alberta 80 Jg
Rayon. See Cardenas
Rayon, Mexico 88 Bb
Razan, Persia 72 Eb
Razelm L., Rumania 56 Gb
Razgrad, Bulgaria 56 Fc
Razmak, W. Pakistan 70 Ad
Ré, I. de, France 52 Cc
Read Island, N.-W. Terr. 80 Jc
Reading, England 31 Gj
Reading, Pennsylvania 83 Je
Real, Cord., Bolivia 90 Dg
Real, Cord., Ecuador, etc. 90 Bd
Real Castillo, Mexico 88 Aa
Realico, Argentina 92 De
Realp, Switzerland 45 Db
Reata, Mexico 88 Db
Rebun, I., Japan 66 Gb
Recalada, Chile 92 Ah
Recalde, Argentina 92 De
Recherche Arch., W. Aust. 94 Df
Rechna Doab, W. Pakistan 70 Ce
Recht, Belgium 44 Ed
Recife, Brazil 91 Le
Reconquista, Argentina 92 Ec
Recreio, Brazil 91 Fe
Red L., Minnesota 85 Hb
Red R., Louisiana, etc. 85 He
Red R., Minnesota, etc. 84 Gb
Red R. See Song-koi
Redbank, New Jersey 86 Cb
Red Deer, Alberta 80 Jf
Red Deer R., Alberta 80 Jf
Redding, California 87 Be
Redfield, S. Dakota 84 Gc
Red Indian L., Nfd. 82 Kb
Redlands, California 87 Eh
Red Lodge, Montana 84 Eb
Redon, France 52 Bc
Redondela, Spain 50 Aa
Red Pine, New Brunswick 82 Ec
Redruth, Michigan 83 Bb
Red Sea, Africa-Arabia 40 Cf
Ree L., Eire 31 Bg
Reed City, Michigan 83 Cd
Reedsburg, Wisconsin 83 Ad
Reefton, New Zealand 93 Ce
Refresco, Chile 92 Cc
Regencia, Brazil 91 Kg
Regensburg, Germany 48 Ed
Reggan, Algeria 78 Fc
Reggio Calabria, Italy 55 Ef
Reggio nell'Emilia, Italy 54 Cc
Reghin, Rumania 56 Ea
Regina, Saskatchewan 80 Lf
Registro do Araguaia, Brazil 91 Gg
Rehoboth, S.-W. Africa 75 Bd
Rehovot, Israel 74 Cf
Reichenbach, Germany 48 Ec
Reigate, England 31 Gj
Reigi, Estonia 47 Kg
Reims, France 52 Fb
Reina Adelaide, Arch. de la, Chile 92 Bh
Reindeer L., Saskatchewan 80 Le
Reinosa, Mexico 88 Eb
Reinosa, Spain 50 Ca
Reitan, Norway 46 De
Reitz, Orange Free State 75 De
Rekinniki, Russia 59 Rb
Remansão, Brazil 91 Hd
Remanso, Brazil 91 Je
Rembang, Java 63 Fm
Remedios, Cuba 89 Db
Remedios, Panama 89 Ce
Remeshk, Persia 73 Gd
Remiremont, France 52 Gb
Remoulins, France 53 Fe
Remscheid, Germany 48 Bc
Remüs, Switzerland 45 Fb
Rena, Norway 47 Df
Renaix. See Ronse
Renca, Argentina 92 Cd
Rendsburg, Germany 48 Ca
Renfrew, Ontario 83 Hc
Renfrew, co., Scotland 30 Ee
Rengat, Sumatra 63 Dl
Reni (Taranagar), India 76 Df
Renigunta, India 68 Ef
Renk, Sudan 79 Mf
Renkum, Netherlands 44 Dc
Renmark, S. Australia 95 Hf
Rennell, I., Solomon Islands 98 Fj
Rennes, France 52 Cb
Reno, Nevada 87 Df
Renovo, Pennsylvania 83 He
Rensselaer, New York 83 Kd
Renswoude, Netherlands 44 Db
Reo, Flores I., Indonesia 63 Hm
Réole la, France 53 Cd
Republica Dominicana, W.I. 89 Ec
Republican, R., Nebraska 84 Gc
Rep. of South Africa, Afr. 75 Ce
Repulse B., N.-W. Terr. 81 Pc
Repulse B., Queensland 95 Jd
Requena, Peru 91 Cd
Requena, Spain 51 Ec
Resita, Rumania 56 Cb
Resistencia, Argentina 92 Ec
Resolution I., New Zealand 93 Af
Resolution, Fort, N.-W. T. 80 Jd
Resolution I., N.-W. Terr. 81 Ud
Rethel, France 52 Fb
Réthimnon, Crete 57 Eg
Rethy, Belgium 44 Dc
Réunion, I., Indian Ocean 96 Dg
Reusel, Netherlands 44 Dc
Reutlingen, Germany 48 Cd
Reutte, Austria 48 De
Revda, Russia 61 Qb
Revel. See Tallinn
Revelstoke, B.C. 80 Hf
Revilla Gigedo Is., Mexico 88 Bd
Revivim, Israel 74 Cf
Rewa, India 71 Cc
Rewari, India 70 Ef
Rey, I. del, Panama 89 De
Reydharfjord, Iceland 46 Zm
Reyes, Mexico 88 Dd
Reykjavik, Iceland 46 Um
Reynard, R. au, Quebec 82 Fb
Rezā'iyeh, Persia 72 Db
Rēzekne, Latvia 47 Mh
Rheden, Netherlands 44 Eb
Rhein R., Germany 48 Bc
Rheine, Germany 48 Bb
Rheinland-Pfalz, Germany 48 Bd
Rhenen, Netherlands 44 Dc
Rheydt, Germany 48 Bc
Rhine R. See Rhein R.
Rhinelander, Wisconsin 83 Bc
Rhode Island, state, U.S.A. 86 Eb
Rhodes (Rodhos), I., Gr. 57 Gf
Rhodesia, Cent. Africa 75 Dc
Rhodesia, N. See Zambia.
Rhön Geb., Germany 48 Cc
Rhondda, Wales 31 Ej
Rhône, dep., France 52 Fd
Rhône, R., France, etc. 53 Fd
Rhyl, Wales 31 Eg
Riaño, Spain 50 Ca
Riau Arch., Indonesia 63 Dk
Riaza, Spain 50 Db
Ribadeo, Spain 50 Ba
Ribadesella, Spain 50 Ca
Ribble R., England 31 Fg
Ribe, Denmark 47 Cj
Ribeirão Preto, Brazil 91 Hh
Ribera, Sicily 55 Dg
Riberalta, Bolivia 90 Df
Richards C., Arctic Ocean 39 Ra
Richardson Mts., N.Z. 93 Bf
Richfield, Utah 87 Gf
Richibucto, New Brunswick 82 Fc
Richland, Washington 87 Db
Richland Center, Wisconsin 83 Ad
Richmond, California 87 Bg
Richmond, Cape Province 75 Cf
Richmond, Indiana 83 Df
Richmond, Maine 82 Cd
Richmond, New York 83 Je
Richmond, New Zealand 93 Dd
Richmond, Quebec 83 Kc
Richmond, Queensland 95 Hd
Richmond, Virginia 85 Ld
Ricla, Spain 51 Eb
Riddes, Switzerland 45 Cb
Ridgetown, Ontario 83 Fd
Ridgway, Pennsylvania 83 Ge
Ridi, Nepal 71 Db
Riding Mount Park, Man. 80 Lf
Ridout, Ontario 83 Eb
Riesa, Germany 48 Ec
Rietavas, Lithuania 47 Jj
Rieti, Italy 54 Dd
Riga, Latvia 47 Lh
Riga, G. of, Latvia 47 Kh
Rigan, Persia 73 Gd
Rigmati, Persia 73 Gd
Rignasco, Switzerland 45 Db
Rigolet, Labrador 81 Vf
Rig-Rig, Chad 79 Hf
Rijeka, Yugoslavia 54 Ec
Rijswijk, Netherlands 44 Cb
Rimatara, I., Austral Is. 99 Kk

Rimini, *Italy* 54 Dc
Rîmnicu Sărat, *Rumania* 56 Fb
Rîmnicu Vîlcea, *Rumania* 56 Eb
Rimousici, *Quebec* 82 Db
Rincon, *Cuba* 89 Cb
Rincón, *New Mexico* 84 Ee
Rindal, *Norway* 46 Ce
Ringelspitz, Mt., *Switz.* 45 Eb
Ringköbing, *Denmark* 47 Ch
Ringvassöy, I., *Norway* 46 Hb
Rinihue, *Chile* 92 Be
Riobamba, *Ecuador* 90 Bd
Rio Bonito, *Brazil* 91 Jh
Rio Branco, *Brazil* 92 Gc
Rio Branco, *Brazil* 90 De
Rio Branco, *Uruguay* 92 Fd
Rio Bueno, *Chile* 92 Bf
Rio Chico, *Argentina* 92 Cg
Rio Chico, *Venezuela* 90 Da
Rio Colorado, *Argentina* 92 De
Rio Cuarto, *Argentina* 92 Dd
Rio de Janeiro, *Brazil* 91 Jh
Rio de Oro. See Convención
Rio-de-Oro, (*Sp. W. Africa*) 78 Bd
Rio do Sul, *Brazil* 92 Gc
Rio Gallegos & R., *Argent.* 92 Ch
Rio Grande, *Brazil* 92 Fd
Rio Grande, *Mexico* 88 Dc
Rio Grande del Norte, *Mexico-U.S.A.* 88 Db
Riohacha, *Colombia* 90 Ca
Rio Hondo, *Argentina* 92 Dc
Rio Muerto, *Argentina* 92 Dc
Rio Mulato, *Bolivia* 90 Dg
Rio Muni, *W. Africa* 76 Cd
Rio Negro, *Brazil* 92 Gc
Rionero in Vulture, *Italy* 55 Ee
Rio Pardo, *Brazil* 91 Gh
Rio Verde, *Brazil* 91 Gg
Rio Verde, *Ecuador* 90 Bc
Rio Verde, *Mexico* 88 Ec
Rioz, *France* 52 Gc
Ripats, *Sweden* 46 Jc
Ripley, *California* 87 Fj
Ripley, *New York* 86 Aa
Ripley, *W. Virginia* 83 Ff
Ripon, *England* 31 Ff
Ripon, *Quebec* 83 Jc
Ripon, *Wisconsin* 83 Bd
Risafe, *Syria* 72 Cb
Risalpur, *W. Pakistan* 70 Cc
Risbäck, *Sweden* 46 Jc
Rishiri, I., *Japan* 66 Gb
Rishon-le-Zion, *Israel* 74 Cf
Risör, *Norway* 47 Cg
Ristijärvi, *Finland* 46 Nd
Ritchie's Arch., *Andaman Is.* 69 Hf
Rivadavia, *Argentina* 92 Db
Rivas, *Nicaragua* 89 Bd
Rivera, *Argentina* 92 De
Rivera, *Uruguay* 92 Ed
Riverhead, *New York* 83 Ke
Rivero, I., *Chile* 92 Bg
Riversdale, *New Zealand* 93 Bf
Riverside, *California* 87 Ej
Riverside Mt., *California* 87 Fh
Riverton, *New Zealand* 93 Bg
Riviera di Levante, *Italy* 54 Bc
Riviera di Ponente, *Italy* 54 Ad
Rivière à Pierre, *Quebec* 83 Kb
Rivière du Loup, *Quebec* 82 Dc
Riyadh (Ar Riyadh), *Arabia* 72 Ee
Riyaq, *Lebanon* 74 Ed
Rizaiyeh. See Rezā'īyeh
Rize, *Turkey* 72 Da
Rizokarpaso, *Cyprus* 74 Cb
Rizzuto C., *Italy* 55 Ff
Roa, *Spain* 50 Db
Roanne, *France* 52 Fc
Roanoke, *Virginia* 85 Ld
Roaringwater B., *Eire* 31 Aj
Roatan I., *Honduras* 89 Bc
Robat Thana, *W. Pakistan* 68 Bc
Robertsfors, *Sweden* 46 Jd
Robertsganj, *India* 71 Dc
Robertsport, *Liberia* 78 Cg
Roberval, *Quebec* 82 Bb
Robeson Ch., *Arctic Ocean* 39 Qa
Robinson's, *Newfoundland* 82 Jb
Robore, *Bolivia* 90 Fg
Robson, Mt., *B.C.* 80 Hf
Roca, la, *Spain* 50 Bc
Rocafuerte, *Ecuador* 90 Bd
Rocha, *Uruguay* 92 Fd
Rochdale, *England* 31 Fg
Rochefort, *Belgium* 44 Dd
Rochefort, *France* 52 Cd
Rochester, *England* 31 Hj
Rochester, *Michigan* 83 Ed
Rochester, *Minnesota* 85 Hc
Rochester, *New Hampshire* 83 Ld
Rochester, *New York* 83 Hd
Roche-sur-Yon, la, *France* 52 Cc
Rockall, I., *Atlantic Ocean* 46 Dd
Rockefeller Plateau, *Antarc.* 100 Pb
Rockford, *Illinois* 83 Bd
Rockhampton, *Queensland* 95 Kd
Rock Hill, *S. Carolina* 85 Ke
Rock Island, *Illinois* 83 Ae
Rockland, *Maine* 82 Dd
Rockland, *Massachusetts* 86 Ea
Rockland, *Ontario* 83 Jc
Rock Pt., *New Zealand* 93 Dd
Rock Springs, *Wyoming* 84 Ec
Rockstone, *Guyana* 90 Fb
Rockville, *Maryland* 86 Bc
Rocky Mount, *N. Carolina* 85 Ld
Rocky Mts., *N. America* 84 Db
Rocky Mountain Nat. Park, *Colorado* 84 Ec
Rocroi, *France* 52 Fb
Rödby, *Denmark* 47 Dj
Rodchevo, *Russia* 59 Qb
Rodez, *France* 53 Ed
Rodhopi, *Greece* 56 Ed
Rodhos & I., *Greece* 57 Gf
Rodkhan, *W. Pakistan* 68 Bc
Rodopi Planina, *Bulg.-Greece* 56 Dd
Rodosto. See Tekirdag
Rodriquez, I., *Indian Ocean* 96 Ef
Roebourne, *W. Australia* 94 Cd
Roermond, *Netherlands* 44 Dc
Roeselare (Roulers), *Belg.* 44 Bd
Roes Welcome, *N.-W. Terr.* 81 Pd
Rœulx, *Belgium* 44 Cd
Rogachev, *White Russia* 60 Ge
Rogers City, *Michigan* 83 Ec
Rogersville, *New Brunswick* 82 Fc
Rogliano, *Corsica* 53 Kh
Rohri, *W. Pakistan* 68 Cc
Rohtak, *India* 70 Ef
Roi Et, *Siam* 67 Cc
Roisin, *Belgium* 44 Bd
Rojas, *Argentina* 92 Dd
Rokiškis, *Lithuania* 47 Lj
Rolde, *Netherlands* 44 Eb
Rolle, *Switzerland* 45 Bb
Rolvsöy, *Norway* 46 Ka
Roma, *Queensland* 95 Je
Roma, *Sweden* 47 Hh
Roma, *Italy* 55 De
Roma, I., *Indonesia* 63 Jm
Romaine R., *Quebec* 82 Ga
Roman, *Rumania* 56 Fa
Romans, *France* 53 Fd
Romanshorn, *Switzerland* 45 Ea
Romanzof, C., *Alaska* 85 Wl
Rome, *Georgia* 85 Je
Rome, *New York* 83 Jd
Rome (Roma), *Italy* 55 De
Romerée, *Belgium* 44 Cd
Romford, *England* 31 Hj
Romney, *W. Virginia* 83 Gf
Romny, *Ukraine* 60 Hf
Römö, I., *Denmark* 47 Cj
Romont, *Switzerland* 45 Bb
Romsdalshorn, *Norway* 46 Be
Ron, *N. Vietnam* 67 Dc
Ronda, *Kashmir* 70 Dc
Ronda, *Spain* 50 Cd
Rondeau, *Ontario* 83 Fd
Rondônia, *Brazil* 90 Ef
Ronehamn, *Sweden* 47 Hh
Ronge, Lac la, *Sask.* 80 Le
Rönne, *Bornholm, I., Den.* 47 Fj
Ronne B., *Antarctica* 100 Sb
Ronneby, *Sweden* 47 Fh
Ronse, *Belgium* 44 Bd
Roosendaal, *Netherlands* 44 Cc
Roosevelt, I., *Antarctica* 100 Mb
Roosevelt Res., *Arizona* 84 De
Rooseveltown, *New York* 83 Jc
Roper, R., *N. Terr., Aust.* 95 Fb
Roquefort, *France* 53 Cd
Rori, *India* 70 Df
Röros, *Norway* 46 De
Rorschach, *Switzerland* 45 Ea
Rös Vatn, *Norway* 46 Fd
Rosa, la, *Switzerland* 45 Fb
Rosa, Monte, *Switz.-Italy* 45 Cc
Rosablanche, Mt., *Switz.* 45 Cb
Rosarinho. See Axinim
Rosario, *Argentina* 92 Dd
Rosario, *Brazil* 91 Jd
Rosario, *Chile* 92 Bb
Rosario, *Mexico* 88 Aa
Rosario, *Mexico* 88 Cc
Rosario de la Frontera, *Argentina* 92 Dc
Rosario Oeste, *Brazil* 91 Ff
Rosario Tala, *Argentina* 92 Ed
Rosas, *Spain* 51 Ga
Rosas, G. of, *Spain* 51 Ga
Roscommon, *Michigan* 83 Dc
Roscommon & co., *Eire* 31 Bg
Roscrea, *Eire* 31 Bh
Rose, I., *Samoa* 98 Jj
Roseburg, *Oregon* 87 Bd
Roseires, *Sudan* 79 Mf
Rosenheim, *Germany* 48 Ee
Rosetown, *Saskatchewan* 80 Kf
Rosetta (Rashid), *Egypt* 79 Mb
Rosier, C., *Quebec* 82 Fb
Rosignano Marittamo, *Italy* 54 Cd
Rosignol, *Guyana* 90 Fb
Roslavl, *Russia* 60 He
Rosport, *Luxembourg* 44 Ee
Ross, *England* 31 Fj
Ross, *New Zealand* 93 Ce
Ross Ice Shelf, *Antarctica* 100 Ma
Ross, I., *Antarctica* 100 Lb
Ross I., *Burma* 69 Jf
Ross R., *Yukon* 80 Ed
Ross Sea, *Antarctica* 100 Mb
Rossa, *Switzerland* 45 Eb
Ross & Cromarty, co., *Scot.* 30 Dc
Rossano, *Italy* 55 Ff
Rosseau L., *Ontario* 83 Gc
Rossel I., *Papua* 95 Kb
Rossignol, *Belgium* 44 De
Rossignol L., *Nova Scotia* 82 Fd
Rossland, *British Columbia* 80 Hg
Rosslare Harb., *Eire* 31 Ch
Rosslyn, *Virginia* 86 Bc
Rosta, *Norway* 46 Hb
Rosthern, *Saskatchewan* 80 Kf
Rostock, *Germany* 48 Ea
Rostov, *Russia* 61 Dg
Rostov, *Russia* 60 Lc
Roswell, *New Mexico* 84 Fe
Rota, I., *Mariana Islands* 98 Df
Rothenburg, *Germany* 48 Dd
Rotherham, *England* 31 Gg
Rothesay, *Scotland* 30 De
Roti, I., *Indonesia* 63 Hn
Rotorua, *New Zealand* 93 Fc
Rotterdam, *Netherlands* 44 Cc
Rotuma, I., *Fiji* 98 Gj
Roubaix, *France* 52 Ea
Rouen, *France* 52 Db
Rõuge, *Estonia* 47 Mh
Roulers, *Belgium* 44 Bd
Roundup, *Montana* 84 Eb
Roura, *Fr. Guiana* 91 Gc
Rous, Pen., *Chile* 92 Cj
Rousay I., *Orkney, Scotland* 30 Ea
Rousbrugge, *Belgium* 44 Ad
Roussillon, prov., *France* 53 Ee
Rouveen, *Netherlands* 44 Eb
Rouyn, *Quebec* 83 Ga
Rovaniemi, *Finland* 46 Lc
Roveredo, *Switzerland* 45 Eb
Rovigo, *Italy* 54 Cc
Rovinari, *Rumania* 56 Db
Rovno, *Ukraine* 60 Ef
Roxas, *Philippines* 63 Hh
Roxburgh, *New Zealand* 93 Bf
Roxburgh, co., *Scotland* 30 Fe
Roxbury, *New York* 86 Ca
Royal Canal, *Eire* 31 Cg
Royale, I., *Michigan* 83 Bb
Royan, *France* 52 Cd
Rožňava, *Czechoslovakia* 49 Jd
Rtishchevo, *Russia* 61 Fd
Ruahine Ra., *New Zealand* 93 Fc
Ruapehu, Mt., *New Zealand* 93 Ec
Ruawai, *N.Z.* 93 Eb
Rubtsovsk, *Russia* 58 Hc
Ruby, *Alaska* 85 Xl
Rudauli, *India* 71 Cb
Rudbar, *Afghanistan* 73 Hc
Ruddervoorde, *Belgium* 44 Bc
Rudköbing, *Denmark* 47 Dj
Rudok, *Tibet* 68 Eb
Rudolf L., *Kenya* 77 Hd
Ruel, *Ontario* 83 Fb
Ruffec, *France* 52 Dc
Rufino, *Argentina* 92 Dd
Rugby, *England* 31 Gh
Rügen, I., *Germany* 48 Ea
Rui Barbosa, *Brazil* 91 Jf
Rujiena, *Latvia* 47 Lh
Ruk, *W. Pakistan* 68 Cc
Rukumkot, *Nepal* 71 Da
Rukwa, L., *Tanzania* 77 Gf
Rum Cay, *Bahama Islands* 89 Eb
Rum, I., *Scotland* 30 Cd
Rumania, *Central Europe* 43 Pg
Rumbek, *Sudan* 79 Lg
Rumburk, *Czechoslovakia* 48 Fc
Rumegies, *France* 44 Bd
Rumford Falls, *Maine* 82 Cd
Rumigny, *France* 44 Ce
Rumillies, *Belgium* 44 Bd
Rum Jungle, *N. Terr., Aust.* 94 Eb
Rumoi, *Japan* 66 Gc
Rumuruti, *Kenya* 77 Hd
Runanga, *New Zealand* 93 Ce
Rungwa, *Tanzania* 77 Gf
Rungwe Mt., *Tanzania* 77 Gf
Rupar, *India* 70 Ee
Rupbas, *India* 71 Ab
Rurrenabaque, *Bolivia* 90 Df
Rurutu, I., *Austral Islands* 99 Kk
Rusape, *Rhodesia* 75 Ec
Ruse (Ruschuk), *Bulgaria* 56 Ec
Ruseifa, *Jordan* 74 Ee
Rusele, *Sweden* 46 Hd
Rusne, R., *Lithuania* 47 Jj
Russas, *Brazil* 91 Kd
Russel, C., *N.-W. Terr.* 80 Ha
Russelkonda, *India* 69 Fe
Russell, *New Zealand* 93 Ea
Russell Pt., *N.-W. Terr.* 80 Hb
Russian Socialist Federated Soviet Rep. (Russia) 58-59
Russkoye Ust'ye, *Russia* 59 Pa
Russo, *Switzerland* 45 Da
Rustak, *Afghanistan* 73 Jb
Rutbah, *Iraq* 72 Dc
Ruthi, *Switzerland* 45 Ea
Ruthin, *Wales* 31 Eg
Rutland, *Vermont* 83 Kc
Rutland, co., *England* 31 Gh
Rutland I., *Andaman Is.* 69 Hf
Ruurlo, *Netherlands* 44 Eb
Ruvuma R., *Moçambique* 77 Hg
Ruweiba, *Sudan* 79 Le
Ruwenzori, Mt., *Uganda* 77 Gd
Ružomberok, *Czechoslovakia* 49 Hd
Rvazhsk, *Russia* 60 Me
Rwanda, *Cent. Afr.* 77 Fe
Ryan, L., *Scotland* 30 Df
Ryazan, *Russia* 60 Ld
Rybachiy, Pol., *Russia* 58 Cb
Rybinsk, *Russia* 60 Lb
Rybinskoye Res., *Russia* 60 Lb
Rybnoye, *Russia* 59 Ka
Ryde, *I. of W., England* 31 Gk
Rye, *England* 31 Hk
Rye Patch Res., *Nevada* 87 De
Rymarov, *Czechoslovakia* 49 Gd
Rypin, *Poland* 49 Hb
Ryukyu Retto, *Japan* 62 Hf
Rzeszów, *Poland* 49 Jc
Rzhev, *Russia* 60 Jc
Saalfeld, *Germany* 48 Dc
Saanen, *Switzerland* 45 Cb
Saarbrucken, *W. Germany* 48 Bd
Saaremaa, Os., *Lithuania* 47 Kg
Saari Selkä, *Finland* 46 Nb
Saarland, *Europe* 48 Bd
Saarlouis, *W. Germany* 48 Bd
Saas Grund, *Switzerland* 45 Cb
Saavedra, *Argentina* 92 De
Saavedra, *Chile* 92 Be
Sabac, *Yugoslavia* 56 Bb
Sabadell, *Spain* 51 Gb
Sabah (North Borneo), *Malaysia* 63 Gj
Sabalan, Mt., *Persia* 72 Eb
Sabalgarh, *India* 68 Ec
Sabana, Arch. de, *Cuba* 89 Cb
Sabanalarga, *Colombia* 90 Ca
Sabancuy, *Mexico* 88 Fd
Sab Biyar, *Syria* 74 Fd
Sabha, *Jordan* 74 Ee
Sabile, *Latvia* 47 Kh
Sabiñánigo, *Spain* 51 Ea
Sabinas, *Mexico* 88 Db
Sabine, *Texas* 85 Hf
Sabine R., *Louisiana/Texas* 85 He
Sabine Mt., *Antarctica* 100 Lb
Sable, *France* 52 Cc
Sable, C., *Florida* 85 Kf
Sable, C., *Nova Scotia* 82 Fe
Sable I., *Nova Scotia* 82 He
Sables d'Olonne, les, *France* 52 Cc
Sabrina Coast, *Antarctica* 100 Hc
Sabzawar (Shindand), *Afghan.* 73 Hc
Sabzevar, *Persia* 73 Gb
Sacaca, *Bolivia* 90 Dg
Sacandaga Res., *New York* 86 Ca
Sacedon, *Spain* 51 Db
Sachigo R., *Ontario* 81 Nf
Sackets Harbor, *New York* 83 Hd
Sackville, *New Brunswick* 82 Fd
Saco, *Maine* 82 Ce
Sacramento, *Brazil* 91 Hg
Sacramento, *California* 87 Cf
Sacramento R., *California* 87 Cf
Sada, *Yemen* 72 Df
Sádaba, *Spain* 51 Ea
Sadabad, *India* 71 Bb
Sa da Bandeira, *Angola* 76 Cg
Sadad, *Syria* 74 Ec
Sa da Ibiapaba, *Brazil* 91 Jd
Sadaich. See Sadij
Sadhaura, *India* 70 Ee
Sadij, *Persia* 73 Gd
Sadiya, *India* 69 Jc
Sa 'diya, Jebel, *Arabia* 72 De
Sadmarda, *Afghanistan* 73 Jb
Sado, I., *Japan* 66 Fe
Sadra, *India* 68 Dd
Saeki, *Japan* 66 Bh
Safad, *Israel* 74 Ed
Safed Koh Ra., *Afghanistan-W. Pakistan* 70 Bc
Safi, *Morocco* 78 Db
Safi, *Syria* 74 Df
Safidabeh, *Persia* 73 Hc
Safita, *Syria* 74 Ec
Safranbolu, *Turkey* 72 Ba
Saga, *Japan* 66 Bh
Sagaing, *Burma* 69 Jd
Sagami B., *Japan* 66 Fg
Sagar, *India* 71 Bd
Sagar I., *India* 71 Ge
Sagauli, *India* 71 Eb
Saginaw, *Michigan* 83 Dd
Saginaw B., *Michigan* 83 Ed
Saglouc, *Quebec* 81 Rd
Sagone, G. de, *Corsica* 54 Bd
Sagres, *Portugal* 50 Ad
Sagua la Grande, *Cuba* 89 Cb
Saguenay R., *Quebec* 82 Cb
Sagunto, *Spain* 51 Ec
Saham, *Muscat & Oman* 73 Ge
Sahand, Mt., *Persia* 72 Eb
Sahara, *N. Africa* 78 Ec
Sahara Des., *Africa* 78-79
Saharanpur, *India* 70 Ef
Saharien Atlas, Mts., *Algeria* 78 Fb
Sahaswan, *India* 71 Ba
Sahiadriparvat Ra., *India* 68 Ed
Sahibganj, *India* 71 Fc
Sahiwal, *W. Pakistan* 70 Ce
Sahuayo, *Mexico* 88 Dc
Sahuaripa, *Mexico* 88 Cb
Sahugun, *Spain* 50 Ca
Sahun, *S. Yemen* 72 Eg
Sahy, *Czechoslovakia* 49 Hd
Sahyadri Mts., *India* 68 Dd
Saibai, I., Torres Str., *Qnsld.* 95 Ha
Saida. See Sidon
Saidabad, *Persia* 73 Gd
Saidapet, *India* 68 Ff
Said Bundas, *Sudan* 79 Kg
Saidpur, *India* 71 Dc
Saignelégier, *Switzerland* 45 Ba
Saigon, *S. Vietnam* 67 Dd
Sailana, *India* 68 Dd
Saimaa Kanal, *Fin.-Russ.* 47 Nf
Saimaa, L., *Finland* 47 Mf
Saimbeyli, *Turkey* 72 Bc
St Abbs Hd., *Scotland* 30 Fe
St Affrique, *France* 53 Ee
St Agatha, *Maine* 82 Dc
St Agrève, *France* 53 Fd
St Albans, *England* 31 Gj
St Albans, *Vermont* 83 Kc
St Amour, *France* 52 Fc
St Andre, *Quebec* 82 Dc
St André C., *Madagascar* 77 Mk
St Andrews, *New Brunswick* 82 Ed
St Andrew's, *Newfoundland* 82 Jc
St Andrews, *New Zealand* 93 Cf
St Andrews, *Scotland* 30 Fd
Ste Anne, *Quebec* 82 Cc
Ste Anne de Beaupré, *Que.* 83 Kb
Ste Anne de la Pérade, *Que.* 83 Kb
Ste Anne des Monts, *Quebec* 82 Eb
St Anns Bay, *Jamaica* 89 Dc
St Anthony, *Idaho* 84 Dc
St Antönien, *Switzerland* 45 Eb
St Antonis, *Netherlands* 44 Dc
St Augustin, C. de., *Madag.* 77 Ml
St Augustine, *Florida* 85 Kf
St Austell, *England* 31 Dk
Ste Barbara, *Venezuela* 90 Eb
St Barthélemy, I., *Leeward I.* 89 Gc
St Béat, *France* 53 De
St Bernard Pass, Gd., *Switzerland-Italy* 54 Ac
St Boniface, *Manitoba* 80 Mf
St Bride's B., *Wales* 31 Dj
St Brieuc, *France* 52 Bb
St Calais, *France* 52 Dc
St Catherines, *Ontario* 83 Gd
Ste Cécile, *Quebec* 83 Lc
St Chamond, *France* 52 Fd
St Charles, *Michigan* 83 Dd
St Charles, C., *Labrador* 81 Vf
St Chély d'Apcher, *France* 53 Ed
St Christopher, I. (St Kitts), *Leeward Islands* 89 Gc
St Clair, *Michigan* 83 Ed
St Clair, L., *Mich.-Ont.* 83 Ed
St Cloud, *Minnesota* 85 Hb
Ste Croix, *Switzerland* 45 Bb
St Croix, I., *West Indies* 89 Gc
St Croix, R., *Wisconsin* 85 Hb
St Davids Hd., *Wales* 31 Dj
St Denis, *France* 52 Eb
St di Nova Siri, *Italy* 55 Fe
St Dizier, *France* 52 Fb
St Elias Mt., *Alaska* 85 Yl
St Elias Ra., *Yukon* 80 Cd
Saintes, *France* 52 Cd
St Étienne, *France* 52 Fd
St Eustatius, I., *Leeward Is.* 89 Gc
St Fabien, *Quebec* 82 Db
St Fargeau, *France* 52 Ec
St Felicien, *Quebec* 82 Bb
St Filipsland, *Netherlands* 44 Cc
St Florent & G. de, *Corsica* 54 Bd
St Florentin, *France* 52 Eb
St Flour, *France* 53 Ed
St Francis, *Maine* 82 Dc
St Francis B., *S.-W. Africa* 75 Ae
St Francis, L., *Quebec* 83 Jc
St François, L., *Quebec* 83 Kc
St Fulgent, *France* 52 Cc
St Gabriel de Brandon, *Que.* 83 Kb
St Gallen & canton, *Switz.* 45 Ea
St Gaudens, *France* 53 De
St Gédéon, *Quebec* 82 Cb
St George, *New Brunswick* 82 Ed
St George I., *Bering Sea* 85 Vm
St Georges, *Fr. Guiana* 91 Gc
St George's B., *Nfd.* 82 Jb
St George's Chan., *Ireland-Wales* 31 Cj
St Georges, *Quebec* 82 Cc
St Gérard, *Belgium* 44 Cd
St Germain, *France* 52 Eb
St German, *Puerto Rico* 89 Fc
St Gheorghe I., *Rumania* 56 Gb
St Ghislain, *Belgium* 44 Bd
St Gilgen, *Austria* 48 Ee
St Gilles, *Belgium* 44 Cc
St Gilles, *France* 53 Fe
St Gillis-Waas, *Belgium* 44 Cc
St Gingolph, *Switzerland* 45 Bb
St Girons, *France* 53 De
St Gotthard, pass, *Switz.* 45 Db
St Guenolé, *France* 52 Ac
St Helena, *Atlantic Ocean* 97 Kk
St Helena B., *Cape Province* 75 Bf
St Helens, *England* 31 Eg
St Helens, Mt., *Washington* 87 Bb
St Hilaire, *New Brunswick* 82 Dc
St Hubert, *Belgium* 44 Dd
St Hyacinthe, *Quebec* 83 Kc
St Ignace, *Michigan* 83 Dc
St Imier, *Switzerland* 45 Ba
St Irénée, *Quebec* 83 Lb
St Ives, *England* 31 Dk
St Jacques, *New Brunswick* 82 Dc
St James, C., *B.C.* 80 Ef
St Jean, *Belgium* 44 Ad
St Jean, *France* 52 Gd
St Jean, *Quebec* 83 Kc
St Jean d'Angély, *France* 52 Cd
St Jean de Luz, *France* 53 Ce
St Jérôme, *Quebec* 83 Kc
St Joachim, *Quebec* 83 Lb
St John, *New Brunswick* 82 Ed
St John B., *Newfoundland* 82 Ka
St John, L., *Quebec* 82 Cb
St John, Mt., *Quebec* 82 Ga
St John's, *Michigan* 83 Dd
St John's, *Newfoundland* 82 Mc
St Johnsbury, *Vermont* 83 Kc
St John's I., *Red Sea* 72 Ce
St Joris-Winge, *Belgium* 44 Cd
St Joseph, *Michigan* 83 Cd
St Joseph, *Missouri* 85 Hd
St Joseph, *Quebec* 82 Cc
St Joseph I., *Ontario* 83 Eb
St Joseph L., *Ontario* 81 Nf
Ste Justine, *Quebec* 83 Lb
St Kilda, I., *Scotland* 30 Bc
St Laurent, *Fr. Guiana* 91 Gb
St Lawrence, *Queensland* 95 Jd
St Lawrence, G. of, *Canada* 82 Gb
St Lawrence I., *Alaska* 85 Vl
St Lawrence, R., *Quebec etc.* 81 Tg
St Lawrence Seaway, *N. America* 83 Jc
St Leger, *Belgium* 44 De
St Leonard, *Belgium* 44 Cc
St Léonard, *France* 52 Dd
St Leonard, *New Brunswick* 82 Ec
St Lewis, C., *Labrador* 81 Vf
St Lin, *Quebec* 83 Kc
St Lô, *France* 52 Cb
St Louis, *Mauritania* 78 Be
St Louis, *Michigan* 83 Dd
St Louis, *Missouri* 85 Hd
St Louis, L., *Quebec* 83 Kc
St Louis de Kent, *N.B.* 82 Fc
St Lucia C., *Natal* 75 Ee
St Lucia, I., *Windward Is.* 89 Gd
St Lucia L., *Natal* 75 Ee
St Luke's I., *Burma* 69 Jf
St Maartensdijk, *Netherlands* 44 Cc
St Magnus B., *Shetland* 30 Ha
St Maixent, *France* 52 Cc
St Malo & Gulf, *France* 52 Bb
St Marc, *Haiti* 89 Ec
St Mard, *Belgium* 44 De
Ste Marie C., *Madagascar* 77 Nm
Ste Marie I., *Madagascar* 77 Nk
St Martin, I., *Leeward Is.* 89 Gc
St Martins, *New Brunswick* 82 Fd
St Mary B., *Nova Scotia* 82 Ed
St Mary Is., *India* 68 Df
St Mary's, *Ontario* 83 Fd
St Marys, *Pennsylvania* 86 Ab
St Marys, *Tasmania* 95 Jh
St Mary's B., *Newfoundland* 82 Mc
St Mary's I., *Scotland* 30 Ee
St Mary's Pk., *S. Australia* 95 Gf
St Matthew I., *Alaska* 85 Vl
St Matthew's I., *Burma* 69 Jg
St Maurice, *Switzerland* 45 Bb
St Maurice de Labrieville, *Quebec* 82 Db
St Maurice R., *Quebec* 83 Kb
St Maximin, *France* 53 Fe
St Meen, *France* 52 Bb
St Michael, *Alaska* 85 Wl
St Michaels, *Maryland* 83 Hf
St Moritz, *Switzerland* 45 Eb
St Nazaire, *France* 52 Bc
St Nicolaasga, *Netherlands* 44 Db
St Nicolas. See St Niklaas
St Niklaas, *Belgium* 44 Cc
St Niklau, *Switzerland* 45 Cb
St Odilienberg, *Netherlands* 44 Ec
St Omer, *France* 52 Ea
Saintonge, prov., *France* 52 Cd
St Paul, *Minnesota* 85 Hc
St Paul I., *Bering Sea* 85 Vm
St Paul, I., *Indian Ocean* 96 Fh
St Paul de Fenouillet, *France* 53 Ee
St Peter, *Prince Edward I.* 82 Gc
St Peter, L., *Quebec* 83 Kb
St Petersburg, *Florida* 85 Kf
St Petersburg, *Pennsylvania* 86 Ab
St Pierre, *Martinique, W.I.* 89 Gd
St Pierre, *Quebec* 83 Lb
St Pierre, I., *Atlantic Ocean* 82 Kc
St Pol, *France* 52 Ea
St Polten, *Austria* 49 Fd
St Pons, *France* 53 Ee
St Pourçain, *France* 52 Ec
St Quentin, *France* 52 Eb
St Raymond, *Quebec* 83 Lb
St Rémi d'Amherst. See Lac-Rémi
St Roch, *Quebec* 82 Dc
St Sébastien C., *Madagascar* 77 Nj
St Sernin-sur-Rance, *France* 53 Ee
St Servan, *France* 52 Bb
St Sever, *France* 53 Ce
St Simeon, *Quebec* 83 Lb
St Simon, *Quebec* 82 Dc
St Stephen, *New Brunswick* 82 Ed
St Thecle, *Quebec* 83 Kb
Ste Thérèse, L., *N.-W. Terr.* 80 Gd
St Thomas, *Ontario* 83 Fd
St Thomas, I., *Virgin Is.* 89 Gc
St Trond. See St Truiden
St Tropez, *France* 53 Ge
St Truiden, *Belgium* 44 Dd
St Valery, *France* 52 Da
St Valery-en-Caux, *France* 52 Db
St Veit, *Austria* 48 Fe
St Vincent, *Windward Is.* 89 Gd
St Vincent C., *Madagascar* 77 Ml
St Vincent, G., *S. Australia* 95 Gg
St Vith, *Belgium* 44 Ed
Saipan, I., *Mariana Is.* 98 Df
Saiping. See Sinyang
Saiun (Saywūn), *S. Yemen* 72 Ef
Saivomuotka, *Sweden* 46 Kb
Saiyidwala, *W. Pakistan* 70 Ce
Saka Dzong, *Tibet* 69 Gc
Sakai, *Japan* 66 Dg
Sakakah, *Arabia* 72 Dd
Saka Kalat, *W. Pakistan* 68 Cc
Sakania, *Congo* 77 Fg
Sakarya, R., *Turkey* 72 Bb
Sakata, *Japan* 66 Fe
Sakesar, *W. Pakistan* 70 Cd
Sakha, *Arabia* 72 De
Sakhalin, *Russia* 59 Pc
Sakahlinskiy Zaliv, *Russia* 59 Pc
Saki, *Russia* 60 Hj
Sakiai, *Lithuania* 47 Kj
Sakishima Gunto, Is., *Japan* 66 Kk
Sakti, *India* 71 Db
Sakylä, *Finland* 47 Kf
Sala, *Czechoslovakia* 49 Gd
Šala, *Sweden* 47 Gg
Salacgriva, *Latvia* 47 Lh
Sala Consilina, *Italy* 55 Ee
Salada, L., *Mexico* 88 Aa
Salado, R., *Argentina* 92 Dc
Salaga, *Ghana* 78 Eg
Salahiya, *Syria* 72 Dc
Salajar, I., *Indonesia* 63 Hm
Salala, *Muscat & Oman* 73 Ff
Salama, *Guatemala* 88 Fd
Salamanca, *Mexico* 88 Dc
Salamanca, *New York* 83 Gd
Salamanca, *Spain* 50 Cb
Salamaua, *New Guinea* 95 Ja
Salamina, *Colombia* 90 Bb
Salamís & I., *Greece* 57 Df
Salangen, *Norway* 46 Gb
Salas, *Spain* 50 Ba
Salas de los Infantes, *Spain* 50 Da
Salatsgriva. See Salacgriva
Salaverry, *Peru* 90 Be
Sala-y-Gomez I., *Pacific Oc.* 99 Qk
Salbris, *France* 52 Ec
Saldana, *Spain* 50 Ca
Saldus, *Latvia* 47 Kh
Sale, *Victoria* 95 Jg
Salekhard, *Russia* 58 Fb
Salem, *India* 68 Ef
Salem, *Massachusetts* 83 Ld
Salem, *New Jersey* 83 Jf
Salem, *Oregon* 87 Bc
Salemi, *Sicily* 55 Dg
Sälen, *Sweden* 47 Ef
Salerno, *Italy* 55 Ee
Salerno, G. di., *Italy* 55 Ee
Salford, *England* 31 Fg
Salgueiro, *Brazil* 91 Ke
Salida, *Colorado* 84 Ed
Salina, *Kansas* 84 Gd
Salina, I., *Italy* 55 Ef
Salina Cruz, *Mexico* 88 Ed
Salinas. See Salinópolis
Salinas, *California* 87 Cg
Salinas, *Ecuador* 90 Ad
Salinas, *Mexico* 88 Dc
Salinas, *Mexico* 88 Db
Salinas R., *California* 87 Cg
Saline R., *Kansas* 84 Gd
Salinitas, *Chile* 92 Bb
Salinópolis, *Brazil* 91 Hd
Salisbury, *England* 31 Fj
Salisbury, *Maryland* 85 Kd
Salisbury, *New Brunswick* 82 Fc
Salisbury, *N. Carolina* 85 Kd
Salisbury, *Rhodesia* 75 Ec
Salisbury I., *N.-W. Terr.* 81 Rd
Salisbury L., *Uganda* 77 Gd
Salisbury Plain, *England* 31 Fj
Salkhad, *Syria* 74 Ee
Sallyana, *Nepal* 71 Da
Salmon R., *Idaho* 87 Fc
Salmon Gums, *W. Aust.* 94 Df
Salmon River Mts., *Idaho* 87 Ec
Salo, *Finland* 47 Kf
Salon, *France* 53 Fe
Salon, *India* 71 Cb
Salonica. See Thessaloníki
Salonta, *Rumania* 56 Ca
Salqin, *Syria* 74 Ea
Salsette I., *India* 68 De
Salt Fd., *Norway* 46 Fc
Salt L., *W. Australia* 94 Bd
Salt Ls., *W. Australia* 94 Ee
Salt R., *Arizona* 84 De
Salt Ra., *W. Pakistan* 68 Db
Salta, *Argentina* 92 Cb
Saltdal, *Norway* 46 Fc
Saltee, Is., *Eire* 31 Ch
Saltillo, *Mexico* 88 Db
Salt Lake City, *Utah* 87 He
Salto, *Argentina* 92 Dd
Salto, *Uruguay* 92 Ed
Salto da Divisa, *Brazil* 91 Kg
Salton Sea, *California* 87 Fj
Saltrou, *Haiti* 89 Ec
Salûm & G. of, *Egypt* 79 Lb
Salur, *India* 69 Fe
Salut, Is du, *Fr. Guiana* 91 Gb
Saluzzo, *Italy* 54 Ac
Salvador (Bahia), *Brazil* 91 Kf
Salvador, El, rep., *C. Amer.* 89 Bd
Salvaterra, *Portugal* 50 Ac
Salvatierra, *Mexico* 88 Dc
Salzburg, *Austria* 48 Ee
Salzgitter, *Germany* 48 Db
Salzwedel, *Germany* 48 Db
Samahala, *Botswana* 75 Cc
Samalut, *Egypt* 79 Mc
Samana & B. de, *Rep. Dom.* 89 Fc
Samar, I., *Philippines* 63 Jh
Samarai, *Papua* 95 Kb
Samarinda, *Borneo* 63 Gl
Samarkand, *Uzbek.* 58 Fe
Samarra Balad, *Iraq* 72 Dc
Samastipur, *India* 71 Ec
Samāwa, *Iraq* 72 Ec
Sambalpur, *India* 71 Dd
Sambava, *Madagascar* 77 Pj
Sambeek, *Netherlands* 44 Dc
Sambhal, *India* 71 Ba
Sambhar, *India* 71 Ab
Sambor, *Ukraine* 60 Cg
Samborombón, B., *Argent.* 92 Ee
Sambre, R., *Belgium* 44 Cd
Samedan, *Switzerland* 45 Eb
Sameminato, *Japan* 66 Gd
Sami, *W. Pakistan* 68 Bc
Samira, *Arabia* 72 Dd
Sam Ka, *Burma* 69 Jd
Sam-nua, *Laos* 67 Cb
Samoa, Is., *Pacific Ocean* 98 Hj
Samokov, *Bulgaria* 56 Dc
Samorogouan, *Upper Volta* 78 Ef
Samos, I., *Greece* 57 Ff
Samothrace. See Samothráki I.
Samothráki I., *Greece* 57 Ed
Sampacho, *Argentina* 92 Dd
Sampit, *Borneo* 63 Fl
Samrée, *Belgium* 44 Dd
Samsat, *Turkey* 72 Cb
Samshui, *China* 65 Fl
Samsö, I., *Denmark* 47 Dj

Shasta Res., California 87 Ce
Shatra, Iraq 72 Ec
Shatt-al-Arab, Iraq 72 Ec
Shaubek, Jordan 74 Dg
Shawano, Wisconsin 83 Bc
Shawinigan, Quebec 83 Kb
Shawnee, Oklahoma 84 Gd
Shchors, Ukraine 60 Gf
Sheboygan, Wisconsin 83 Cd
Shediac, New Brunswick 82 Fc
Sheelin L., Eire 31 Cg
Sheenjik R., Alaska 80 Cc
Sheep Haven, Eire 30 Be
Sheerness, England 31 Hj
Sheffield, England 31 Gg
Sheffield, New Zealand 93 Ce
Sheikh, Jeb. esh, Syria 74 Dd
Sheikh 'Abd er Rahman, S. Yemen 72 Eg
Sheikh Miskin, Syria 74 Ee
Sheikh 'Othman, S. Yemen 72 Eg
Sheik Seraq, Syria 74 Fd
Shekha, S. Yemen 72 Ef
Shekhupura, W. Pakistan 70 Ce
Sheklung, China 65 Fl
Shelburne, Nova Scotia 82 Fe
Shelburne, Ontario 83 Fc
Shelby, Michigan 83 Cd
Shelby, Montana 84 Db
Shelikhova, Zaliv, Russia 59 Qc
Shelter I., New York 86 Db
Shenandoah, Pennsylvania 86 Bb
Shenandoah Junct., W. Va. 86 Bc
Shenandoah Nat. Park, Virginia 85 Ld
Shenandoah R., Virginia 86 Bc
Shenchow. See Yüanling
Shendam, Nigeria 79 Gg
Shendi, Sudan 79 Me
Shëngjin, Albania 56 Bd
Shenkursk, Russia 58 Db
Shensi, prov., China 64 De
Shenyang, China 64 Lb
Sheopur, India 68 Ed
Shepetovka, Ukraine 60 Ef
Shepparton, Victoria 95 Jg
Sherada, Ethiopia 77 Hc
Sherard Osborn Fd., Greenland 39 Pa
Sherbro I., Sierra Leone 78 Cg
Sherbrooke, Quebec 83 Lc
Sheridan, Wyoming 84 Ec
Sherman, Texas 84 Ge
Sherpur, E. Pakistan 71 Gc
Sherridon, Manitoba 80 Le
Shetland (Zetland), Scotland 34 Qb
Shevaroy Hills, India 68 Ef
Shiant Is., Scotland 30 Cc
Shibam, S. Yemen 72 Ef
Shibarghan, Afghanistan 73 Jb
Shibata, Japan 66 Ff
Shibetsi, Japan 66 Jc
Shibin el Kom, Egypt 79 Mb
Shickshock Mts., Quebec 82 Eb
Shiel L., Scotland 30 Dd
Shigatse, Tibet 69 Gc
Shihnan. See Enshih
Shih Pao Shan, China 62 Ee
Shihshow, China 65 Fh
Shihtao, China 64 Ld
Shihtsien, China 65 Dj
Shikarpur, W. Pakistan 68 Cc
Shikohabad, India 71 Bb
Shikoku, I., Japan 66 Ch
Shilka & R., Russia 59 Lc
Shillelagh, Eire 31 Ch
Shillong, India 69 Hc
Shilongol. See Silinhot
Shimoga, India 68 Ef
Shimo Jima, Japan 66 Ah
Shimoni, Kenya 77 He
Shimonoseki, Japan 66 Bg
Shin L., Scotland 30 Eb
Shinas, Muscat & Oman 73 Ge
Shinghar, W. Pakistan 70 Ae
Shingshal & Pass, Kashmir 70 Db
Shingu, Japan 66 Dh
Shinjo, Japan 66 Ge
Shinshar, Syria 74 Ec
Shinyanga, Tanzania 77 Ge
Shipets. See Shibetsi
Shippigan, New Brunswick 82 Fc
Shippigan I., New Brunswick 82 Fc
Shiraishi, Japan 66 Gf
Shiraz, Persia 73 Fd
Shireza, W. Pakistan 68 Cc
Shisur, Arabia 73 Ff
Shiuhing. See Koyiu
Shivpuri, India 71 Ac
Shizugawa, Japan 66 Ge
Shizuoka, Japan 66 Fg
Shklov, White Russia 60 Gd
Shkodër, Albania 56 Bc
Shoal Harbour, Nfd. 82 Lb
Shoka. See Changhua
Sholapur, India 68 Ee
Shonai. See Tsuruoka
Shorkot, W. Pakistan 70 Ce
Short Mts., W. Virginia 86 Ac
Shoshone Falls, Idaho 84 Dc
Shoshone Res., Wyoming 84 Ec
Shovo Tso, Tibet 69 Fb
Shreveport, Louisiana 85 He
Shrewsbury, England 31 Fh
Shropshire (Salop), co., England 31 Fh
Shtora, Lebanon 74 Dd
Shubenacadie, Nova Scotia 82 Gd
Shuikow, China 65 Jj
Shujaabad, W. Pakistan 70 Bf
Shumagin Is., Alaska 85 Xm
Shumaisa, Arabia 72 Ee
Shumen. See Kolaovgrad
Shumerlya, Russia 61 Hc
Shunking. See Nanchung
Shunteh. See Singtai
Shuqra, S. Yemen 72 Eg
Shurab, Persia 73 Gc
Shurma, Arabia 72 De
Shuru Tso, Tibet 69 Gb
Shusf, Persia 73 Hc
Shushal, Kashmir 68 Eb
Shushtar, Persia 72 Ec
Shuya, Russia 61 Eb
Shuyang, China 64 Je
Shwebo, Burma 69 Jd
Shwedaung, Burma 69 Je
Shwegyin, Burma 69 Je
Shweli R., Burma 69 Jd
Sialkot, W. Pakistan 70 Dd
Siam. See Thailand
Siam, G. of. See Thailand, G. of
Sian, China 64 De
Siangtan, China 65 Fj
Siangyang, China 64 Ff
Siangyin, China 65 Fh
Siapu, China 65 Jj
Siargao, I., Philippines 63 Jj
Siaton, Philippines 63 Hj
Šiauliai, Lithuania 47 Kj
Sib, Muscat & Oman 73 Ge
Sibenik, Yugoslavia 54 Ed
Siberut, I., Indonesia 63 Cl
Sibi, W. Pakistan 68 Cc
Sibiu, Rumania 56 Eb
Sibolga, Sumatra 63 Ck
Sibsagar, India 69 Hc
Sibu, Sarawak 63 Fk
Sicasica, Bolivia 90 Dg
Sichang, China 62 De
Sicie C., France 53 Fe
Sicilia. I. See Sicily
Sicilian Chan., Medit. Sea 55 Cg
Sicily (Sicilia), I., Italy 55 Dg
Sicuani, Peru 90 Cf
Sid, Yugoslavia 56 Bb
Sideby, Finland 47 Je
Siderno Marina, Italy 55 Ff
Sidhout, India 68 Ef
Sidi Barrani, Egypt 79 Lb
Sidi-bel-Abbès, Algeria 78 Ea
Sidi Ifni, Ifni, N.-W. Africa 78 Cc
Sidlaw Hills, Scotland 30 Ed
Sidnaw, Michigan 83 Bb
Sidney, New York 83 Jd
Sidon, Lebanon 74 Dd
Sidri, Gulf of, Libya 79 Jb
Siedlce, Poland 49 Kb
Siegen, Germany 48 Cc
Siem-reap, Cambodia 67 Cd
Siena, Italy 54 Cd
Sieradz, Poland 49 Hc
Siero, Spain 50 Ca
Sierra Colorada, Argentina 92 Cf
Sierra Grande, Argentina 92 Cf
Sierra Leone, W. Africa 78 Cg
Sierra Madre, Mexico 88 Cb
Sierra Mojada, Mexico 88 Db
Sierra Rosaria, Argentina 92 Cf
Sifnos, I., Greece 57 Ef
Sigean, France 53 Ee
Sighet, Rumania 49 Ke
Sighisoara, Rumania 56 Ea
Siglufjördhur, Iceland 46 Wl
Sigmaringen, Germany 48 Cd
Sigsig, Ecuador 90 Bd
Sigüenza, Spain 50 Db
Siguiri, Guinea 78 Df
Sigulda, Latvia 47 Lh
Sihanoukville, Cambodia 63 Dh
Sihl See, Switzerland 45 Da
Sihsien, China 65 Jh
Siilinjärvi, Finland 46 Me
Sikandarabad, India 70 Ef
Sikandra Rao, India 71 Bb
Sikar, India 70 Dg
Sikasso, Mali 78 Df
Si Kiang, R., China 62 Ff
Siking. See Sian
Sikinos, I., Greece 57 Ef
Sikkim, India 71 Gb
Sila, La, Italy 55 Ff
Silairsk, Russia 61 Nd
Silao, Mexico 88 Dc
Silchar, India 69 Hd
Silenen, Switzerland 45 Db
Silenrieux, Belgium 44 Cd
Sil Garhi, Nepal 71 Ca
Silifke, Turkey 72 Bb
Silinhot, China 62 Gb
Silistra, Bulgaria 56 Fb
Siljan, L., Sweden 47 Ff
Silkeborg, Denmark 47 Ch
Silloth, England 30 Ef
Silv, Switzerland 45 Eb
Silvânia, Brazil 91 Hg
Silvaplana, Switzerland 45 Eb
Silva Porto, Angola 76 Dg
Silver L., Oregon 87 Cd
Silvercreek, New York 83 Gd
Silves, Brazil 90 Fd
Silves, Portugal 50 Ad
Silvretta, Mts., Austria-Switz. 48 Ce
Simard, L., Quebec 83 Gb
Simcoe, Ontario 83 Fd
Simcoe, L., Ontario 83 Gc
Simeulue, I., Indonesia 63 Ck
Simferopol, Russia 60 Jj
Simi, I., Greece 57 Ff
Simla, India 70 Ee
Simleul Silvaniei, Rumania 49 Ke
Simo, Finland 46 Ld
Simola, Finland 47 Nf
Simon, L., Quebec 83 Jc
Simpelveld, Netherlands 44 Dd
Simplon and Pass, Switz. 45 Db
Simpson, Fort, N.-W. Terr. 80 Gd
Simpson, C., Alaska 80 Ac
Simpson Des., Australia 95 Ge
Simpson, I., Chile 92 Bg
Simuna, Estonia 47 Mg
Sinai, pen., Egypt 79 Mc
Sinaloa, state, Mexico 88 Cb
Sinaloa & R., Mexico 88 Cb
Sinamaica, Venezuela 90 Ca
Sinbo, Burma 69 Jd
Sinchang, China 65 Kh
Sin-chow, China 64 Gc
Sindel, Bulgaria 56 Fc
Sindhuli Garhi, Nepal 71 Eb
Sind Sagar Doab, W. Pakistan 70 Be
Sines, Portugal 50 Ad
Singa, Sudan 79 Mf
Singapore, & Str., S.-E. Asia 67 Cf
Singaradja, Bali I., Indon. 63 Gm
Singen, Germany 48 Ce
Singhana, India 70 Df
Singida, Tanzania 77 Ge
Singitic G., Greece 57 Dd
Singkawang, Borneo 63 Ek
Singkep, I., Riouw Arch., Indon. 63 Dl
Singora. See Songkhla
Singsingsia, China 62 Bb
Singtai, China 64 Gd
Singtze, China 65 Hh
Sinho, China 64 Gd
Sinhsien, China 62 Fc
Sinhwa, China 65 Ej
Sining, China 62 Dc
Siniscola, Sardinia 55 Be
Sinj, Yugoslavia 56 Ac
Sinjar, & Jebel, Iraq 72 Db
Sinjil, Palestine 74 De
Sinkiang, China 40 Hd
Sin-min-fu, China 64 Lb
Sinnamary, Fr. Guiana 91 Gb
Sinning, China 65 Ej
Sinoe L., Rumania 56 Gb
Sinoia, Rhodesia 75 Ec
Sinop, Turkey 72 Ca
Sintra, Portugal 50 Ac
Sinuiju, Korea 62 Hb
Sinyang, China 62 Fd
Sion, Switzerland 45 Cb
Sioux City, Iowa 84 Gc
Sioux Falls, S. Dakota 84 Gc
Sioux Lookout, Ontario 81 Nf
Siparia, Trinidad 90 Ea
Sipolilo, Rhodesia 75 Ec
Sipora, I., Indonesia 63 Cl
Siquisique, Venezuela 90 Da
Sira, India 68 Ef
Sira. See Siros, I.
Siracusa, Sicilia 55 Eg
Sirajganj, E. Pakistan 71 Gc
Sir Douglas, Mt., Alberta 80 Jf
Sir Edward Pellew Group, N. Territory, Australia 95 Gc
Siretul, R., Rumania 56 Fa
Sirhind, India 70 Ee
Siri, Ethiopia 77 Hc
Sirjan, Persia 73 Gd
Sirna, I., Greece 57 Ff
Sironcha, India 68 Ee
Sironj, India 68 Ed
Siros, I., Greece 57 Ef
Sirsa, India 70 Df
Sirsi, India 71 Ba
Sirsi, India 68 Df
Sirte & G. of, Libya 79 Jb
Sisak, Yugoslavia 54 Fc
Sisaket, Siam 67 Cc
Sisal, Mexico 88 Fc
Sisi, Botswana 75 Dd
Sisopon, Cambodia 67 Cd
Sisteron, France 53 Fd
Sitamarhi, India 71 Eb
Sitamau, India 68 Ed
Sitapur, India 71 Cb
Sitara, Arabia 72 Ee
Sithonia, Greece 57 Dd
Sitía, Crete 57 Fg
Sitka, Alaska 85 Zm
Sitpur, W. Pakistan 70 Bf
Sittang, Burma 69 Je
Sittang, R., Burma 69 Je
Sittard, Netherlands 44 Dd
Sitten. See Sion
Sivand, Persia 73 Fc
Sivas, Turkey 72 Cb
Siverek, Turkey 72 Cb
Sivrihisar, Turkey 72 Bb
Sivry, Belgium 44 Cd
Siwa, Egypt 79 Lc
Siwalik Hills, India 68 Eb
Siwan, India 71 Eb
Sjælland, Denmark 47 Dj
Sjötorp, Sweden 47 Eg
Skadarsko Jezero, Yugosl.-Alb. 56 Bc
Skagafjord, Iceland 46 Wl
Skagen, Denmark 47 Dh
Skagerrak, Norway-Denmark 47 Bh
Skagway, Alaska 85 Zm
Skaneateles, L., New York 86 Ba
Skara, Sweden 47 Eg
Skardu, Kashmir 70 Dc
Skarnes, Norway 47 Df
Skeena R., Brit. Columbia 80 Ff
Skegness, England 31 Hg
Skellefte Älv, Sweden 46 Hd
Skellefteå, Sweden 46 Jd
Skiathos, I., Greece 57 De
Skibbereen, Eire 31 Aj
Skien, Norway 47 Cg
Skierniewice, Poland 49 Jc
Skiftet Kihti, Finland 47 Jf
Skikda (Philippeville), Algeria 53 Qh
Skipton, England 31 Fg
Skíros, I., Greece 57 Ee
Skive, Denmark 47 Ch
Skofja Loka, Yugoslavia 54 Eb
Skópelos, I., Greece 57 De
Skopin, Russia 60 Le
Skopje, Yugoslavia 56 Cc
Skövde, Sweden 47 Eg
Skovorodino, Russia 59 Mc
Skowhegan, Maine 82 Dd
Skradin, Yugoslavia 54 Ed
Skrunda, Latvia 47 Kh
Skudeneshavn, Norway 47 Ag
Skuodas, Lithuania 47 Jh
Skye, I., Scotland 30 Cc
Slagelse, Denmark 47 Dj
Slamet, Mt., Java 63 Em
Slaney R., Eire 31 Ch
Slatina, Yugoslavia 56 Ab
Slatina, Rumania 56 Eb
Slatington, Pennsylvania 86 Cb
Slave R., N.-W. Territories 80 Jd
Släveni, Rumania 56 Eb
Slavgorod, Russia 58 Gc
Slavonia, Yugoslavia 56 Ab
Slavyansk, Ukraine 60 Kg
Slea Hd., Eire 31 Ah
Sleat, Sd. of, Scotland 30 Dc
Sleepers, The, Hudson Bay, Canada 81 Qe
Sleydinge, Belgium 44 Bc
Slide Mt., New York 83 Jd
Sliedrecht, Netherlands 44 Cc
Slieve Aughty, Mts., Eire 31 Bg
Slieve Bloom Mts., Eire 31 Bg
Slieve Mish, Mts., Eire 31 Ah
Sligo & co., Eire 31 Bf
Sligo B., Eire 31 Bf
Slite, Sweden 47 Hh
Sliven, Bulgaria 56 Fc
Slobodskoy, Russia 61 Ka
Sloka, Latvia 60 Cc
Slonim, White Russia 60 De
Sloten, Netherlands 44 Db
Slough, England 31 Gj
Slovakia, Czechoslovakia 49 Hd
Slovenija, Yugoslavia 54 Ec
Slovensko, Czechoslovakia 49 Hd
Sluis, Netherlands 44 Bc
Sluiskil, Netherlands 44 Bc
Slunj, Yugoslavia 54 Ec
Slupsk, Poland 49 Ga
Slussfors, Sweden 46 Gd
Slutsk, White Russia 60 Ee
Slyne Hd., Eire 31 Ag
Slyudyanka, Russia 59 Kc
Smethport, Pennsylvania 86 Ab
Smilde, Netherlands 44 Eb
Smiltene, Latvia 47 Lh
Smith, Alberta 80 Je
Smith B., N.-W. Territories 81 Ra
Smith B., Gt. Bear L., N.-W. Territories 80 Gc
Smith I., Quebec 81 Rd
Smith, I., South Shetlands 100 Sc
Smithers, British Columbia 80 Ff
Smith Falls, Ontario 83 Hc
Smithton, Tasmania 95 Hh
Smoky R., Alberta 80 He
Smoky Hill R., Kansas 84 Fd
Smöla, Norway 46 Be
Smolensk, Russia 60 Hd
Smoothstone L., Sask. 80 Kf
Smyrna (Izmir), Turkey 72 Ab
Snaefell, Isle of Man 31 Df
Snake, R., & Canyon, Washington, etc. 87 Db
Snake R., Yukon 80 Ec
Snares Is., New Zealand 93 Ah
Snåsa, Norway 46 Ed
Snåsa Vatn, Norway 46 Dd
Sneek, Netherlands 44 Da
Sneen, Eire 31 Aj
Sneeuw Gebergte, W. Irian 63 Ll
Snizort L., Scotland 30 Cc
Snöhetta, Mt., Norway 46 Ce
Snow Pk. See Medicine Bow Pk.
Snowdon, Wales 31 Eg
Snow Water L., Nevada 84 Dc
Snowy Mts., Vict.-N.S.W. 95 Jg
Soasiu, Moluccas 63 Jk
Soazza, Switzerland 45 Eb
Sobakin, Russia 61 Jd
Sobrado, Brazil 91 Ge
Sobral, Brazil 91 Jd
Sobrance, Czechoslovakia 49 Kd
Sobraon, India 70 De
Society Is., Pacific Ocean 99 Kj
Socorro, Colombia 90 Cb
Socorro, New Mexico 84 Ee
Socorro I., Mexico 88 Bd
Socotra I., Indian Ocean 77 Lb
Soc-trang, S. Vietnam 67 De
Sodankylä, Finland 46 Mc
Söderfors, Sweden 47 Gf
Söderhamn, Sweden 47 Gf
Söderköping, Sweden 47 Gg
Södertälje, Sweden 47 Gg
Sodiri, Sudan 79 Lf
Sodus, New York 86 Ba
Sodus Pt., New York 86 Ba
Soepiori, I., W. Irian 63 Ll
Soest, Germany 48 Cc
Soest, Netherlands 44 Db
Sofiya (Sofia), Bulgaria 56 Dc
Sogamosa, Colombia 90 Cb
Sogndal, Norway 47 Bg
Sognefjord, Norway 47 Af
Söğut, Turkey 72 Ba
Sohag, Egypt 79 Mc
Sohagpur, India 71 Cd
Sohan R., W. Pakistan 70 Cd
Sohar, Muscat & Oman 73 Ge
Sohawal, India 71 Cc
Soheb, S. Yemen 72 Eg
Sohna, India 70 Ef
Soignies, Belgium 44 Cd
Soissons, France 52 Eb
Soke, Turkey 72 Ab
Sok Gomba. See Pachen
Sok Karmalinsk, Russia 61 Lc
Sokode, Togo 78 Fg
Sokol, Russia 60 Lb
Sokolo, Mali 78 Df
Sokota, Ethiopia 77 Hb
Sokoto, Nigeria 78 Ff
Solai, Kenya 77 Hd
Solbad Hall, Austria 48 De
Soledad, Venezuela 90 Eb
Soledade, Brazil 90 De
Solent, The, England 31 Gk
Solenzara, Corsica 55 Be
Sol Iletsk, Russia 58 Ec
Solimoes, R. See Amazonas
Solingen, Germany 48 Bc
Solleftea, Sweden 46 Ge
Sollum. See Salûm
Solok, Sumatra 63 Dl
Solomon Is., Pacific Ocean 98 Eh
Solomon R., Kansas 84 Gd
Solon, India 70 Ee
Solothurn & canton, Switz. 45 Ca
Solsona, Spain 51 Fa
Solstad, Norway 46 Dd
Soltau, Germany 48 Cb
Solund, I., Norway 47 Af
Solway Firth, Eng.-Scot. 30 Ef
Solwezi, Zambia 76 Fg
Soma, Turkey 72 Ab
Somali Republic, E. Africa 77 Jd
Sombor, Yugoslavia 56 Bb
Sombreiro Chan., Nicobar I. 69 Hg
Sombrerete, Mexico 88 Dc
Sombrero, I., Leeward Is. 89 Gc
Somcuţa Mare, Rumania 49 Ke
Someren, Netherlands 44 Dc
Somerset, Pennsylvania 83 Ge
Somerset, Queensland 95 Hb
Somerset, co., England 31 Ej
Somerset I., N.-W. Terr. 80 Nb
Somerset Res., Vermont 86 Da
Somerville, New Jersey 86 Cb
Somme, Belgium 44 Dd
Somme, dep., France 52 Eb
Somme, R., France 52 Da
Sommieres, France 53 Fe
Somoto, Nicaragua 89 Bd
Somovit, Bulgaria 56 Ec
Somzee, Belgium 44 Cd
Son R., India 71 Ec
Sonamukhi, India 71 Fd
Sonbarsa, India 71 Fc
Sönderborg, Denmark 47 Cj
Sonepat, India 70 Ef
Song-Cau, S. Vietnam 67 Dd
Songea, Tanzania 77 Hg
Songkhla, Siam 67 Ce
Song-koi, R., N. Vietnam 67 Cb
Sonhat, India 71 Dd
Sonkajärvi, Finland 46 Me
Sonkovo, Russia 60 Kc
Sonmiani, W. Pakistan 68 Cc
Sonneberg, Germany 48 Dc
Sonogno, Switzerland 45 Db
Sonora, state & R., Mexico 88 Bb
Sonoyta, Mexico 88 Ba
Sonpur, India 69 Fd
Sonpur, India 71 Ec
Sonson, Colombia 90 Bb
Soochow, China 64 Kg
Soping. See Yuyu
Soppero, Sweden 46 Jb
Sopron, Hungary 54 Fb
Sopur, Kashmir 70 Dc
Sora, Italy 55 De
Sorata, Bolivia 90 Dg
Sorbas, Spain 51 Dd
Sorell, Tasmania 95 Jh
Sörenberg, Switzerland 45 Db
Sörfold, Norway 46 Fc
Sorgono, Sardinia 55 Be
Soria, Spain 51 Db
Soriano, Uruguay 92 Ed
Sornico, Switzerland 45 Db
Sorocaba, Brazil 91 Hh
Soroka, Russia 61 Ld
Soroki, Moldavia 60 Fg
Sorol, I., Caroline Is. 98 Cg
Soromesis, Botswana 75 Cc
Soron, India 71 Bb
Sorong, W. Irian 63 Kl
Sororoca, Brazil 90 Ec
Soroti, Uganda 77 Gd
Söröy, I., Norway 46 Ka
Sorrento, Italy 55 Ee
Sorsele, Sweden 46 Gd
Sortavala, Karelia 46 Pf
Sosnovka, Russia 61 Ed
Sosnovo Ozerskoye, Russia 59 Lc
Sosnowiec, Poland 49 Hc
Sosva, Russia 58 Fc
Soto la Marina, Mexico 88 Ec
Sotra, I., Norway 47 Af
Sotuta, Mexico 88 Gc
Souanke, Fr. Congo 76 Cd
Soudan, W. Africa 78 De
Soudan, N. Terr., Aust. 95 Gd
Souflion, Greece 56 Fd
Souillac, France 53 Dd
Söul, Korea 62 Jc
Sour El Ghozlane, Algeria 78 Fa
Soure, Brazil 91 Hd
Soure, Portugal 50 Ab
Souris, Manitoba 80 Lg
Souris, Prince Edward I. 82 Gc
Sousel, Brazil 91 Gd
Sousse, Tunisia 79 Ha
Souterraine, la, France 52 Dc
South B., N.-W. Territories 81 Qd
South Downs, England 31 Gk
South I., New Zealand 93 Be
South Africa, Rep. of, Africa 75 Ce
Southampton, England 31 Fk
Southampton, New York 83 Ke
Southampton, Ontario 83 Fc
Southampton, C., N.-W. Territories 81 Qd
Southampton I., N.-W. Terr. 81 Qd
South Arabia, Federation & Protectorate 72 Eg
South Australia, state, Aust. 94 Fe
South Bend, Indiana 83 Ce
South Bend, Washington 87 Bb
Southbridge, Massachusetts 86 Da
Southbridge, New Zealand 93 De
South Carolina, state, U.S.A. 85 Ke
South China Sea, Asia 41 Kh
South Dakota, state, U.S.A. 84 Fc
South-East C., Tasmania 95 Jh
Southend, England 31 Hj
Southern Alps, New Zealand 93 Bf
Southern Cross, W. Aust. 94 Cf
Southern Ocean, Antarctica 100 Cc
Southern Rhodesia. See Rhodesia
Southern Yemen (Aden, col. & prot.) S.-W. Asia 72 Dg
South Georgia, I., Atlantic Ocean 100 Ad
South Hadley Falls, Mass. 86 Da
South Haven, Michigan 83 Cd
South Indian L., Manitoba 80 Me
South Magnetic Pole 100 Jc
South Milwaukee, Wisconsin 83 Cd
South Nahanni R., N.-W. Territories 80 Fd
South Orkneys, Is., Atl. Oc. 100 Tc
South Paris, Maine 82 Cd
South Polar Plateau, Antarc. 100 Ma
South Pole, Antarctica 100 a
Southport, England 31 Eg
Southport, Prince Edward I. 82 Gc
Southport, Queensland 95 Ke
South River, New Jersey 86 Cb
South River, Ontario 83 Gc
South Ronaldsay I., Orkney 30 Fb
South Sandwich, Is., Atl. Oc. 100 Ad
South Shetlands, Is., Antarc. 100 Tc
South Shields, England 30 Gf
South Thule, I., South Sandwich Is. 100 Ad
South-West C., Tasmania 95 Jh
South-West Africa, S. Africa 75 Bd
Southwold, England 31 Jh
Souza, Brazil 91 Ke
Souzel, Portugal 50 Bc
Sovetsk, Russia 47 Jj
Sovetskaya Gavan, Russia 59 Pd
Sovietsk, Russia 61 Jb
Soy, Kenya 77 Hd
Soya & B., Japan 66 Gb
Soya Str., Japan 66 Gb
Soya Misaki, Japan 66 Hb
Soyopa, Mexico 88 Cb
Spa, Belgium 44 Dd
Spain, W. Europe 43 Fh
Spalato. See Split
Spalding, England 31 Gh
Spandau, Germany 48 Eb
Spanish, Ontario 83 Eb
Spanish Fork, Utah 84 Dd
Spanish Guinea, Cent. Afr. 76 Bd
Spanish Sahara, W. Africa 78 Cc
Spanish Town, Jamaica 89 Dc
Sparks, Nevada 87 Df
Sparta. See Sparti
Sparta, Wisconsin 83 Ad
Spartanburg, S. Carolina 85 Ke
Sparti, Greece 57 Df
Spartivento C., Italy 55 Fg
Spassk, Russia 61 Fd
Spassk Dal'niy, Russia 59 Nd
Spassk, Russia 62 Kb
Spassk-Ryazanskiy, Russia 61 Ec
Spence Bay, N.-W. Terr. 81 Nc
Spencer G., S. Australia 95 Gf
Spenser Mts., New Zealand 93 De
Sperrin Mts., N. Ireland 31 Cf
Spétsai I., Greece 57 Df
Spey R., Scotland 30 Ec
Speyer, Germany 48 Cd
Spezand, W. Pakistan 68 Cb
Spezia, La, Italy 54 Bc
Spinazzola, Italy 55 Fe
Spiringen, Switzerland 45 Db
Spitsbergen, Arctic Ocean 58 Aa
Spitsbergen, Vest, Arctic Oc. 58 Aa
Spittal, Austria 48 Ee
Split, Yugoslavia 54 Fd
Split L., Manitoba 80 Me
Splügen, Switzerland 45 Eb
Splügen Pass, Switz.-Italy 45 Eb
Spokane, Washington 87 Eb
Spoleto, Italy 54 Dd
Spontin, Belgium 44 Cd
Sporadhes, Aegean Sea 57 Ff
Sporadhes, Voriai, Aegean Sea 57 Ee
Spree R., Germany 48 Eb
Spremberg, Germany 48 Fc
Sprimont, Belgium 44 Dd
Springbok, Cape Province 75 Be
Springburn, N.Z. 93 Ce
Springfield, Illinois 83 Bf
Springfield, Massachusetts 83 Kd
Springfield, Missouri 85 Hd
Springfield, Ohio 83 Ef
Springfield, Vermont 86 Da
Springfontein, O.F.S. 75 Df
Springhill, Nova Scotia 82 Hd
Springsure, Queensland 95 Jd
Springville, New York 83 Gd
Springville, Utah 84 Dc
Spruce Brook, Nfd. 82 Jb
Spruce Knob, W. Virginia 86 Ac
Spruga, Switzerland 45 Db
Squillace, G. di, Italy 55 Ff
Srbija (Serbia), Yugoslavia 56 Cc
Srebrenica, Yugoslavia 56 Bb
Srednyy, Khrebet, Mts., Russia 59 Rc
Sredne Kamchatsk, Russia 59 Rc
Sredne Kolymsk, Russia 59 Qb
Sredne Vilyuysk, Russia 59 Mb
Srem, Poland 49 Gb
Srepok, Cambodia 67 Dd
Sretensk, Russia 59 Lc
Srikakulam, India 69 Fe
Sri Madhopur, India 70 Dg
Srinagarh, Kashmir 70 Dc
Srirangapatna, India 68 Ef
Srivilliputtur, India 68 Eg
Srnetica, Yugoslavia 56 Ab
Sroda, Poland 49 Gb
Stackpool, Ontario 83 Fb
Stadacona, Quebec 83 Kb
Staden, Belgium 44 Ad
Staffa I., Scotland 30 Cd
Stafford & co., England 31 Fh
Stalingrad. See Volgograd
Stalino, Russia 59 Jb
Stambaugh, Michigan 83 Bb
Stamford, Connecticut 83 Ke
Stamproi, Netherlands 44 Dc
Stanchik, Russia 59 Qa
Standerton, Transvaal 75 De
Standish, Michigan 83 Dd
Stanislav. See Ivano-Frankovsk
Stanley, Falkland Is. 92 Eh
Stanley Falls, Congo 76 Ed
Stanleyville. See Kisangani
Stann Creek, Brit. Honduras 89 Bc
Stanovoy Khrebet, Mts., Russia 59 Mc
Stans, Switzerland 45 Db
Stansmore Ra., W. Australia 94 Ed
Stanthorpe, Queensland 95 Ke
Stanton, Michigan 83 Dd
Stanton, N.-W. Terr. 80 Fc
Staphorst, Netherlands 44 Eb
Starachowice, Poland 49 Jc
Stara Planina, Bulgaria 56 Ec
Staraya Russa, Russia 60 Gc
Stara Zagora, Bulgaria 56 Ec
Starbuck, I., Pacific Ocean 99 Kh
Stargard, Poland 48 Fb
Star'obelks, Ukraine 60 Lg
Starodub, Russia 60 He
Starogard, Poland 49 Hb
Staro Konstantinov, Ukraine 60 Eg
Staryy Oskol, Russia 60 Kf
Staten I., New York 86 Cb
Staten I. See Estados, I.
Stattlandet, Norway 46 Ae
Staunton, Virginia 85 Ld
Stavanger, Norway 47 Ag
Stavelot, Belgium 44 Dd
Stavenisse, Netherlands 44 Cc
Stavern, Norway 47 Dg
Staveren, Netherlands 44 Db
Stavropol, Russia 58 Dd
Steckborn, Switzerland 45 Da
Steelton, Pennsylvania 86 Bb
Steenbergen, Netherlands 44 Cc
Steenkool, W. Irian 63 Kl
Steensel, Netherlands 44 Dc
Steenwijk, Netherlands 44 Eb
Stefanie L., Ethiopia 77 Hd
Stefansson I., N.-W. Terr. 80 Kb
Steiermark, prov., Austria 48 Fe
Stein, Switzerland 45 Da
Steinkjer, Norway 46 Dd
Stekene, Belgium 44 Cc
Stellarton, Nova Scotia 82 Gd
Stenay, France 52 Fb
Stendal, Germany 48 Db
Stenträsk, Sweden 46 Hc
Stephenson, Michigan 83 Cc
Stephenville, Newfoundland 82 Jb
Stepnoy. See Elista
Stepnyak, Kazakh. 58 Gc
Sterea, Greece 57 Ce
Sterling, Colorado 84 Fc
Sterling, Illinois 83 Be
Sterlitamak, Russia 61 Md
Sternberk, Czechoslovakia 49 Gd
Sterrebeek, Belgium 44 Cd
Stettin (Szczecin), Poland 48 Fb
Stettler, Alberta 80 Jf
Steubenville, Ohio 83 Fe
Stevens Point, Wisconsin 83 Bc
Stewart, Brit. Columbia 80 Ff
Stewart I., Chile 92 Bh
Stewart Is., New Zealand 93 Ag
Stewart R., Yukon 80 Dd
Stewart River, Yukon 80 Dd
Stewart Sd., Andaman Is. 69 Hf
Steyr, Austria 48 Fd
Stia, Italy 54 Cd
Stikine R., Brit. Columbia 80 Ee
Stillwater, Minnesota 85 Hb
Stimlje, Yugoslavia 56 Cc
Stip, Yugoslavia 56 Cd
Stirling & co., Scotland 30 Ed
Stirling Ra., W. Australia 94 Cf
Stjernöy, Norway 46 Ka

Thetford Mines, Quebec 83 Lb
Theux, Belgium 44 Dd
Thief River Falls, Minnesota 84 Gb
Thielsen, Mt., Oregon 87 Cd
Thielt, Belgium 44 Bc
Thiers, France 52 Ed
Thies, Senegal 78 Bf
Thimbu, Assam 69 Gc
Thingvalla vatn, Iceland 46 Vm
Thio, Eritrea 77 Jb
Thionville, France 52 Gb
Thira, I., Greece 57 Ef
Thirsk, England 31 Gf
Thirtyone Mile L., Quebec 83 Jb
Thisted, Denmark 47 Ch
Thistilfjord, Iceland 46 Yl
Thityabin, Burma 69 Jd
Thiviers, France 52 Dd
Thjórsá, R., Iceland 46 Wm
Thok Jalung, Tibet 68 Fb
Thomastown, Eire 31 Ch
Thomasville, Georgia 85 Ke
Thompson, Manitoba 80 Me
Thompsonville, Connecticut 86 Db
Thomson, R., Queensland 95 Hd
Thomson Ville, Michigan 83 Cc
Thongwa, Burma 69 Je
Thorn. See Torun
Thornhill, Scotland 30 Ee
Thorshavn, Færöe Is. 42 Fc
Thórshöfn, Iceland 46 Yl
Thouars, France 52 Cc
Thourout, Belgium 44 Bc
Thousand Isles, New York 83 Jc
Thraki, Dhitiki, Greece 56 Ed
Three Kings Is., N.Z. 93 Da
Three Points C., Ghana 78 Eh
Three Rivers, Michigan 83 Cd
Three Rivers. See Trois Rivières
Throssel Ra., W. Australia 94 Dd
Thueyts, France 53 Fd
Thuin, Belgium 44 Cd
Thule, Greenland 81 Ta
Thun, Switzerland 45 Cb
Thunder B., Michigan 83 Ec
Thuner See, Switzerland 45 Cb
Thur, R., Switzerland 45 Da
Thurgau, canton, Switz. 45 Da
Thüringer Wald, Germany 48 Dc
Thurles, Eire 31 Bh
Thursday I., Queensland 95 Hb
Thurso, Scotland 30 Eb
Thusis, Switzerland 45 Eb
Tiassale, Ivory Coast 78 Dg
Tibati, Cameroon 79 Hg
Tiber, R., Italy 54 Dd
Tiberias & L., Israel 74 De
Tibet, S. Asia 40 He
Tiburon, Haiti 89 Ec
Tiburon I., Mexico 88 Bb
Ticino, canton, Switzerland 45 Db
Ticonderoga, New York 83 Kd
Ticul, Mexico 88 Gc
Tidjikja, Mauritania 78 Ce
Tiebissou, Ivory Coast 78 Dg
Tiefencastel, Switzerland 45 Eb
Tieh-ling, China 64 La
Tiel, Netherlands 44 Dc
Tielt, Belgium 44 Bc
Tien Chih, China 62 Df
Tien-ching. See Tientsin
Tien-chwang-tai, China 64 Kb
Tienen. See Tirlemont
Tienpao, China 65 Cl
Tienpaoshan, China 64 Hb
Tiensha Pass, China 64 Ce
Tienshai, China 64 Be
Tien Shan, Central Asia 58 Gd
Tienshui, China 62 Ed
Tientsin, China 64 Hc
Tiermas, Spain 51 Ea
Tierra del Fuego, Chile-Argentina 92 Ch
Tiffin, Ohio 83 Ee
Tigănesti, Rumania 56 Fb
Tighina. See Bendery
Tigil, Russia 59 Qc
Tignish, Prince Edward I. 82 Gc
Tigris, R., Iraq 72 Ec
Tijoca, Brazil 91 Hd
Tijuana, Mexico 84 Ce
Tikhvin, Russia 60 Hb
Tikrit, Iraq 72 Dc
Tiksi, Russia 59 Ma
Tilburg, Netherlands 44 Dc
Tilbury, England 31 Hj
Tilcara, Argentina 92 Cb
Tilichiki, Russia 59 Rb
Tillamook, Oregon 87 Ac
Tillangchong I., Nicobar Is. 69 Hg
Tillsonburg, Ontario 83 Fd
Tilos, I., Greece 57 Ff
Tilsit. See Sovetsk
Timanski Kryazh, Russia 58 Eb
Timaru, New Zealand 93 Cf
Timbuktu. See Tombouctou
Timiskaming, Quebec 83 Gb
Timisoara, Rumania 56 Cb
Timmins, Ontario 83 Fa
Timor, I. & Sea, Indonesia 63 Hn
Timote, Argentina 92 De
Tinaca Pt., Philippines 63 Jj
Tindouf, Algeria 78 Dc
Tineo, Spain 50 Ba
Tingchow. See Changting
Tinghsien, China 64 Gc
Tingnan, China 65 Gk
Tingo Maria, Peru 90 Be
Tingri Dzong, Tibet 69 Gc
Tinian, I., Mariana Is. 98 Df
Tinkhannock, Pennsylvania 86 Cb
Tinnevelly. See Tirunelveli
Tinogasta, Argentina 92 Cc
Tinos, I., Greece 57 Ef
Tinsukia, India 69 Jc
Tintigny, Belgium 44 De
Tintina, Argentina 92 Dc
Tinwald, New Zealand 93 Ce
Tioman Pulau, I., W. Malaysia 67 Cf
Tionesta, Pennsylvania 86 Ab
Tipperary & co., Eire 31 Bh
Tiracumba, Sa. de, Brazil 91 Hd
Tiran, I., Arabia 72 Bd
Tirana. See Tiranë
Tiranë, Albania 56 Bd
Tiraspol, Moldavia 60 Fh
Tire, Turkey 72 Ab
Tireboli, Turkey 72 Ca
Tiree I., Scotland 30 Cd
Tirgu Jiu, Rumania 56 Db
Tirgu Mures, Rumania 56 Ea
Tirgu Lăpuş, Rumania 49 Ke
Tirgu Ocna, Rumania 56 Fa
Tirich Mir, W. Pakistan 70 Bb
Tirlemont, Belgium 44 Cd
Tirlyanski, Russia 61 Pc
Tirnavos, Greece 57 De
Tirol, Austria 48 De
Tiruchchendur, India 68 Eg
Tiruchirappalli, India 68 Ef
Tiru Kona Malai. See Trincomalee
Tirunelvelei, India 68 Eg
Tirupati, India 68 Ef
Tiruvannamalai, India 68 Ef
Tisa R., Yugoslavia 56 Cb
Tisiye, Syria 74 Ee
Tissa, Nigeria 79 Hg
Tisza R., Hungary 49 Je
Titalyah, E. Pakistan 71 Gb
Titicaca, L., Bolivia-Peru 90 Dg
Titisee, Germany 48 Ce
Titograd, Yugoslavia 56 Bc
Titov-Veles, Yugoslavia 56 Cd
Titovo Uzice, Yugoslavia 56 Bc
Titu, Rumania 56 Eb
Titusville, Pennsylvania 83 Ge
Tiverton, England 31 Ek
Tiwi, Muscat & Oman 73 Ge
Tixkokob, Mexico 88 Gc
Tixtla, Mexico 88 Ed
Tizimin, Mexico 88 Gc
Tizi Ouzou, Algeria 78 Fa
Tjalang, Sumatra 63 Ck
Tjilatjap, Java 63 Em
Tjirebon, Java 63 Em
Tjörn, I., Sweden 47 Dg
Tlacotalpan, Mexico 88 Ed
Tlaltenango, Mexico 88 Dc
Tlapa, Mexico 88 Ed
Tlaxcala, Mexico 88 Ed
Tlaxiaco, Mexico 88 Ed
Tlemcen, Algeria 78 Eb
Tméssa, Libya 79 Jc
Toay, Argentina 92 De
Toba, Japan 66 Eg
Tobago, I., Windward Is. 89 Gd
Toba, Donau, Sumatra 63 Ck
Tobarra, Spain 51 Ec
Tobel, Switzerland 45 Ea
Tobelo, Halmahera I. 63 Jk
Tobermory, Ontario 83 Fc
Tobermory, Scotland 30 Cd
Toboali, Bangka I., Indonesia 63 El
Tobol, Russia 61 Rd
Toboli, Celebes 63 Hl
Tobolsk, Russia 58 Fc
Tobruk, Libya 79 Kb
Tocantinópolis, Brazil 91 He
Tocina, Spain 50 Cd
Toco, Chile 92 Cb
Tocopilla, Chile 92 Bb
Tocuyo, Venezuela 90 Cb
Todenyang, Kenya 77 Hd
Todos Santos, Mexico 88 Bc
Todos Santos, B., Mexico 88 Aa
Togarakaikyo, Japan 66 Aj
Toghraqbulaq, China 62 Bb
Togo, West Africa 78 Fg
To Huping Tso, Tibet 69 Fb
Tojo, Japan 66 Cg
Tokachi Dake, Japan 66 Hc
Tokanga, Russia 58 Db
Tokanui, New Zealand 93 Bg
Tokar, Sudan 77 Ha
Tokara Retto, Japan 66 Nn
Tokat, Turkey 72 Ca
Tokelau Is., Pacific Ocean 98 Hh
Tokmak, Kirgiz. 58 Gd
Toko, New Zealand 93 Ec
Tokomaru, New Zealand 93 Gc
Tokoto, China 64 Eb
Tokushima, Japan 66 Dh
Tokuyama, Japan 66 Bg
Tokyo & B., Japan 66 Fg
Tolaga Bay, New Zealand 93 Gc
Tolbukhin, Bulgaria 56 Fc
Toledo, Chile 92 Bc
Toledo, Ohio 83 Ee
Toledo, Spain 50 Cc
Toledo, Mtes. de, Spain 50 Cc
Tolen & I., Netherlands 44 Cc
Tolmin, Yugoslavia 54 Db
Tolo, G. of, Celebes 63 Hl
Toluca, Mexico 88 Ed
Tolun, China 64 Ha
Tölz, Bad, Germany 48 De
Tomah, Wisconsin 83 Ac
Tomahawk, Wisconsin 83 Bc
Tomar, Portugal 50 Ac
Tomari, Russia 59 Pd
Tomaszów Mazowiecki, Pol. 49 Jc
Tomatumari, Guyana 90 Fb
Tombigbee R., Alabama 85 Je
Tombouctou, Mali 78 Ee
Tome, Chile 92 Be
Tomiko, Ontario 83 Gb
Tomini, G. of, Celebes 63 Hl
Tomkinson Ra., W. Aust. 94 Ee
Tommot, Russia 59 Mc
Tomsk, Russia 59 Hc
Tom's River New Jersey 83 Jf
Tonala, Mexico 88 Fd
Tonawanda, New York 86 Aa
Tönder, Denmark 47 Cj
Tondi, India 68 Eg
Tonga, Sudan 79 Mg
Tonga, Is., Pacific Ocean 98 Hk
Tongareva, I., Pacific Ocean 99 Kh
Tongeren, Belgium 44 Dd
Tongobory, Madagascar 77 Ml
Tongoy, Chile 92 Bd
Tongres. See Tongeren
Tongue, Scotland 30 Eb
Tongue R., Montana 84 Eb
Tonichi, Mexico 88 Cb
Tonk, India 68 Ec
Tonkhil, Mongolia 62 Ba
Tonking, N. Vietnam 67 Cb
Tonking, G. of, N. Vietnam 67 Db
Tonkova, Russia 58 Hb
Tonle Sap, Cambodia 67 Cd
Tonneins, France 53 Dd
Tonnerre, France 52 Fc
Tonopah, Nevada 87 Ef
Tönsberg, Norway 47 Dg
Tooele, Utah 87 Ge
Toowoomba, Queensland 95 Ke
Top Oz., Karel.-Fin. 58 Cb
Topeka, Kansas 84 Gd
Topoľčany, Czechoslovakia 49 Hd
Topolobampo & B., Mexico 88 Cb
Torbat-e-Heydariyeh, Persia 73 Gb
Torbat-e-Jam, Persia 73 Hb
Torhout. See Thourout
Tori, India 71 Ed
Torino. See Turin
Toriñana, C., Spain 50 Aa
Torit, Sudan 79 Mh
Tor Khama, W. Pakistan 70 Bc
Torma, Estonia 47 Mg
Torne Älv, Sweden 46 Kc
Torne Träsk, Sweden 46 Hb
Torneträsk, Sweden 46 Hb
Tornio, Finland 46 Ld
Tornquist, Argentina 92 De
Törökszentmiklós, Hungary 49 Je
Toroni, G. of, Greece 57 Dd
Toronto, Ontario 83 Gd
Tororo, Uganda 77 Gd
Toros Dağlari, Mts., Turkey 72 Bb
Torquay, England 31 Ek
Torre Annunziata, Italy 55 Ee
Torreblanca, Spain 51 Fb
Torre del Greco, Italy 55 Ee
Torrelaguna, Spain 50 Db
Torrelapaja, Spain 51 Eb
Torrelavega, Spain 50 Da
Torrens, L., S. Australia 95 Gf
Torrente, Spain 51 Ec
Torreon, Mexico 88 Db
Torres, Mexico 88 Bb
Torres Is., Pacific Ocean 98 Fj
Torres Str., Queensland 95 Hb
Torres Novas, Portugal 50 Ac
Torres Vedras, Portugal 50 Ac
Torrevieja, Spain 51 Ed
Torridon L., Scotland 30 Dc
Torrijos, Spain 50 Cc
Torrington, Connecticut 86 Db
Torrox, Spain 50 Dd
Torsby, Sweden 47 Ef
Tortola, I., Virgin Is. 89 Gc
Tortorici, Sicily 55 Ef
Tortosa, Spain 51 Fb
Tortue, I., Haiti 89 Eb
Tortuga I., Mexico 88 Bb
Torud, Persia 73 Gb
Torun, Poland 49 Hb
Törva, Estonia 47 Mh
Tory, I., Eire 30 Be
Torzhok, Russia 60 Jc
Tosa B., Japan 66 Ch
Tosashimizu, Japan 66 Ch
Toscana, dep., Italy 54 Cd
Tosco-Emiliano, Appennino, Mts., Italy 54 Cc
Tossa, Spain 51 Gb
Tostado, Argentina 92 Dc
Totana, Spain 51 Ed
Totling, Tibet 68 Eb
Totma, Russia 58 Dc
Totnes, England 31 Ek
Totonicapam, Guatemala 88 Fd
Totsk, Russia 61 Ld
Tottori, Japan 66 Dg
Touba, Ivory Coast 78 Dg
Toubkal, Mt., Morocco 78 Db
Touggourt, Algeria 78 Gb
Toul, France 52 Fb
Toulon, France 52 Fe
Toulouse, France 53 De
Toungoo, Burma 69 Je
Touquet, le, France 52 Da
Touraine, prov., France 52 Dc
Tourakom, Laos 69 Ke
Tourbis L., Quebec 83 Jb
Tourcoing, France 52 Ea
Tour-du-Pin, la, France 52 Fd
Tournai, Belgium 44 Bd
Tournon, France 53 Fd
Tournus, France 52 Fc
Tours, France 52 Dc
Touwsrivier, Cape Province 75 Cf
Towanda, Pennsylvania 86 Bb
Towari, Celebes 63 Hl
Townsville, Queensland 95 Jc
Towson, Maryland 86 Cc
Towuti Danau, Celebes 63 Hl
Towy R., Wales 31 Ej
Towyn, Wales 31 Eh
Toyama & B., Japan 66 Ef
Tozeur, Tunisia 79 Gb
Trabzon, Turkey 72 Ca
Tracadie, New Brunswick 82 Fc
Tradom, Tibet 69 Fc
Trairi, Brazil 91 Kd
Traiguen, Chile 92 Be
Traiguen, I., Chile 92 Bg
Trail, British Columbia 80 Hg
Traipú, Brazil 91 Ke
Tralee & B., Eire 31 Ah
Tramore, Eire 31 Ch
Tranås, Sweden 47 Fg
Trancas, Argentina 92 Cc
Trancoso, Portugal 50 Bb
Trang, Siam 67 Be
Trangan, I., Indonesia 63 Km
Tranquebar, India 68 Ef
Transcona, Manitoba 80 Mg
Transvaal, S. Africa 75 Dd
Transylvania, Rumania 56 Da
Transylvanian Alps, Rumania 56 Db
Trapani, Sicily 55 Df
Traralgon, Victoria 95 Jg
Trasimeno, L., Italy 54 Dd
Trasparga, Spain 50 Ba
Traunstein, Germany 48 Ee
Traverse, B., Michigan 83 Dc
Traverse Is., Atlantic Ocean 100 Ad
Traverse City, Michigan 83 Dc
Třebíč, Czechoslovakia 49 Fd
Trebinje, Yugoslavia 56 Bc
Trebizond (Trabzon), Turkey 72 Ca
Treinta-y-Tres, Uruguay 92 Fd
Trelew, Argentina 92 Cf
Trelleborg, Sweden 47 Ej
Tremadoc B., Wales 31 Eh
Trembling Mt., Quebec 83 Jb
Tremiti Is., Italy 54 Ed
Tremont, Maine 82 Dd
Tremp, Spain 51 Fa
Trencin, Czechoslovakia 49 Hd
Trenel, Argentina 92 De
Trenque Lauquen, Argentina 92 De
Trent. See Trento
Trent Canal, Ontario 83 Gc
Trent R., England 31 Gg
Trentino-Alto Adige, reg., It. 54 Cb
Trento, Italy 54 Cb
Trenton, Michigan 83 Ed
Trenton, Missouri 85 Hc
Trenton, New Jersey 86 Cb
Trenton, Ontario 83 Hc
Tréport, le, France 52 Da
Tres Arroyos, Argentina 92 De
Tres Lomas, Argentina 92 De
Tres Marias, Is., Mexico 88 Cc
Tres Montes, Pen., Chile 92 Ag
Três Rio, Brazil 91 Jh
Tres Virgenes, Las, Mexico 88 Bb
Treves. See Trier
Treviso, Italy 54 Dc
Triana, Spain 50 Bd
Tricase, Italy 55 Gf
Trichinopoly. See Tiruchirappalli
Trichur, India 68 Ef
Trier, Germany 48 Bd
Trieste, Italy 54 Dc
Trikeri Str., Greece 57 De
Trikkala, Greece 57 Ce
Trikomo, Cyprus 74 Bb
Trim, Eire 33 Kf
Trincomalee, Ceylon 68 Fg
Trindade, I., Atlantic Ocean 97 Gl
Trinidad, Bolivia 90 Ef
Trinidad, Colorado 84 Fd
Trinidad, Cuba 89 Db
Trinidad, Uruguay 92 Ed
Trinidad, I., Argentina 92 De
Trinidad I., West Indies 90 Ea
Trinity & B., Newfoundland 82 Mb
Trinity R., Texas 84 Ge
Trionto C., Italy 55 Ff
Tripoli, Lebanon 74 Dc
Tripoli, Libya 79 Hb
Trípolis, Greece 57 Df
Tripolitania, Libya 79 Hc
Tripura, India 69 Hd
Tristan da Cunha, Atl. Oc. 97 Jm
Triunfo, Mexico 88 Bc
Trivandrum, India 68 Eg
Trn, Bulgaria 56 Dc
Trnava, Czechoslovakia 49 Gd
Trobriand Is., Papua 95 Ka
Trogir, Yugoslavia 54 Fd
Trois Pistoles, Quebec 82 Db
Trois Ponts, Belgium 44 Dd
Trois Rivières, Quebec 82 Bc
Troitsk, Russia 61 Qc
Troitsk, Russia 61 Fc
Troitsko Pechorsk, Russia 58 Eb
Trollhättan, Sweden 47 Eg
Trollheimen, Norway 46 Ce
Tromen, Mt., Argentina 92 Be
Tromsö, Norway 46 Hb
Tronchiennes, Belgium 44 Bc
Trondheim & Fd., Norway 46 De
Troödos, Cyprus 74 Ac
Troon, Scotland 30 De
Tropea, Italy 55 Ef
Troppau. See Opava
Trosa, Sweden 47 Gg
Trout Lake, Michigan 83 Db
Troy, New York 83 Kd
Troy, Turkey 72 Ab
Troyes, France 52 Fb
Truba, Arabia 72 Dd
Trubia, Spain 50 Ba
Trucial States, Persian Gulf 73 Fe
Truer Ra., N. Terr., Aust. 94 Fd
Trujillo, Honduras 89 Bc
Trujillo, Peru 90 Be
Trujillo, Rep. Dominicana 89 Ec
Trujillo, Spain 50 Cc
Trujillo, Venezuela 90 Cb
Truk I., Caroline Is. 98 Eg
Truksum, Tibet 69 Fb
Trumbull, Mt., Arizona 87 Gg
Truns, Switzerland 45 Db
Truro, England 31 Dk
Truro, Nova Scotia 82 Gd
Trutnov, Czechoslovakia 49 Fc
Tryavna, Bulgaria 56 Ec
Trzebnica, Poland 49 Gc
Tržič, Yugoslavia 54 Eb
Tsabong, Botswana 75 Ce
Tsagan Olom, Mongolia 62 Ca
Tsahura, S. Yemen 72 Eg
Tsamkong, China 67 Eb
Tsangbe, Bhutan 71 Gb
Tsanghsien, China 64 Hc
Tsangwu. See Wuchow
Tsaochow. See Hotseh
Tsaokiang, China 64 Gd
Tsaring Nor, China 62 Cd
Tsaritsyn. See Volgograd
Tschenstochau. See Czestochowa
Tschiertschen, Switzerland 45 Eb
Tsehchow. See Tsincheng
Tsengshing, China 65 Fl
Tses, S.-W. Africa 75 Be
Tsesis. See Cesis
Tshikapa, Congo 76 Ef
Tsho Mirari L., Kashmir 70 Fd
Tsimlyanskoye Vdkhr., Russ. 61 Ff
Tsinan, China 64 Hd
Tsincheng, China 64 Fe
Tsinchow. See Tienshai
Tsin-chow, China 64 Gc
Tsingchow. See Yitu
Tsing Hai. See Ching Hai
Tsingkiang, China 65 Gh
Tsingkiang, China 64 Jf
Tsingkow, China 64 Je
Tsingtao, China 64 Kd
Tsingyüan. See Paoting
Tsingyün, China 65 Fl
Tsining, China 62 Gc
Tsinkiang, China 65 Jk
Tsinyang, China 64 Fe
Tsitsihar, China 62 Ha
Tsivory, Madagascar 77 Nl
Tsivylsk, Russia 61 Hc
Tskhinvali, Gruzinskaya S.S.R. 58 Dd
Tso-motre-tung, L., Tibet 69 Gc
Tsu, Japan 66 Eg
Tsugaru Str., Japan 66 Gd
Tsugitaka, Mt. See Tsukao Shan
Tsukao Shan, Mt., Taiwan 62 Hf
Tsungfa, China 65 Fl
Tsungming, China 64 Kg
Tsungtso, China 62 Ef
Tsunhwa, China 64 Hb
Tsunyi, China 65 Cj
Tsuruga, Japan 66 Eg
Tsuruoka, Japan 66 Fe
Tsuyama, Japan 66 Dg
Tsuyung, China 62 De
Tua, Congo 76 De
Tua, Portugal 50 Bb
Tuakau, New Zealand 93 Eb
Tuamarino, New Zealand 93 Dd
Tuamotu Arch., Pacific Oc. 99 Mj
Tuao, Philippines 63 Hg
Tuapse, Russia 58 Cd
Tuatapere, New Zealand 93 Ag
Tuba, R, Russia 59 Jc
Tubai, I., Society Islands 99 Lj
Tubarão, Brazil 92 Gc
Tubas, Jordan 74 De
Tubeiq, Jeb. el, Jordan 74 Fh
Tübingen, Germany 48 Cd
Tubize, Belgium 44 Cd
Tubuai, I., Austral Islands 99 Lk
Tubutama, Mexico 88 Ba
Tucacas, Venezuela 90 Da
Tuckernuck I., Mass. 86 Eb
Tuckerton, New Jersey 83 Jf
Tucson, Arizona 84 De
Tucumcari, New Mexico 84 Fd
Tucupare, Brazil 91 Fe
Tucupita, Venezuela 90 Eb
Tucurui, Brazil 91 Hd
Tudela, Spain 51 Ea
Tufi, Papua 95 Ja
Tug, Turkey 72 Db
Tuguegarao, Philippines 63 Hg
Tugur, Russia 59 Nc
Tukums, Latvia 47 Kh
Tula, Mexico 88 Ec
Tula, Mexico 88 Ec
Tula, Russia 60 Kd
Tulagi, I., Solomon Islands 98 Eh
Tulan. See Dulan
Tulancingo, Mexico 88 Ec
Tularosa, New Mexico 84 Ee
Tulcan, Ecuador 90 Bc
Tulcea, Rumania 56 Gb
Tulchin, Ukraine 60 Fg
Tulear, Madagascar 77 Ml
Tuli, Rhodesia 75 Dd
Tulkarm, Jordan 74 De
Tullamore, Eire 31 Cg
Tulle, France 53 Dd
Tulsa, Oklahoma 84 Gd
Tulua, Colombia 90 Bc
Tulun, Russia 59 Kc
Tumaco & Rada de, Colomb. 90 Bc
Tumany, Russia 59 Qb
Tumbes, Peru 90 Ad
Tumkur, India 68 Ef
Tumlong, India 71 Gb
Tummel R., Scotland 30 Ed
Tummo, Libya 79 Hd
Tump, W. Pakistan 68 Bc
Tumu, Ghana 78 Ef
Tumucumaque, Sa., Brazil 91 Gc
Tumupasa, Bolivia 90 Df
Tunas de Zaza, Cuba 89 Db
Tunbridge Wells, England 31 Hj
Tundla, India 68 Ec
Tundubai, Sudan 79 Kf
Tunduru, Tanzania 77 Hg
Tüngan, China 65 Ej
Tungchang. See Liaocheng
Tungchow, China 64 De
Tungchwan. See Hweitseh
Tungchwan. See Santai
Tunghai, China 64 Je
Tungho, China 62 Ja
Tunghsien, China 64 Hc
Tunghwa, China 62 Jb
Tungjen, China 65 Dj
Tungkun, China 65 Fl
Tungkwan, China 64 Ee
Tungkwan, China 64 De
Tungliao, China 62 Hb
Tungshan (Suchow), China 64 He
Tungtai, China 64 Kf
Tung Ting Hu, China 65 Fh
Tunguska, R., Russia 59 Jb
Tunhwang, China 62 Bb
Tuni, India 69 Fe
Tunis, Tunisia 79 Ha
Tunisia, N. Africa 79 Gb
Tunja, Colombia 90 Cb
Tunnsjö, Norway 46 Ed
Tunuyan & R., Argentina 92 Cd
Tuoy Khaya, Russia 59 Lb
Tuparoa, New Zealand 93 Gb
Tupelo, Mississippi 85 Je
Tupik, Russia 60 Hd
Tupilco, Mexico 88 Fd
Tupinambaranas, I., Brazil 90 Fd
Tupiza, Bolivia 90 Dh
Tupper Lake, New York 83 Jc
Tuquerres, Colombia 90 Bc
Tura, India 69 Hc
Tura, Russia 59 Jb
Turabah, Arabia 72 De
Turan, Persia 73 Gb
Turbo, Colombia 90 Bb
Turda, Rumania 56 Da
Tureia I., Tuamotu Arch. 99 Mk
Turfan & Depression, China 62 Ab
Turgay, Kazakh 58 Fd
Turgutlu, Turkey 72 Ab
Türi, Estonia 47 Lg
Turiaçu, Brazil 91 Hd
Turiamo, Venezuela 90 Da
Turin (Torino), Italy 54 Ac
Turkestan, Kazakh, etc. 58 Fd
Turkey, Europe-Asia 40 Be
Turkmenskaya rep., U.S.S.R. 58 Ed
Turks Is., Bahamas Is. 89 Eb
Turku, Finland 47 Kf
Turneffe Is., Brit. Honduras 89 Bc
Turnhout, Belgium 44 Cc
Tŭrnovo, Bulgaria 56 Ec
Turnu Măgurele, Rumania 56 Ec
Turnu Severin, Rumania 56 Db
Turquino, Pico de, Cuba 89 Dc
Turrialba, Costa Rica 89 Ce
Turshiz. See Kāshmar
Turtkul, Uzbek. 58 Fd
Turukta, Russia 59 Lb
Turukhansk, Russia 58 Hb
Turzovka, Czechoslovakia 49 Hd
Tus, Persia 73 Gb
Tuscaloosa, Alabama 85 Je
Tuscarora Mts., Pa. 86 Bb
Tuscola, Illinois 83 Bf
Tuticorin, India 68 Eg
Tuttlingen, Germany 48 Ce
Tutuila, I., Samoa 98 Hj
Tuwairifa, Arabia 72 Ee
Tuxpan, Mexico 88 Ec
Tuxpan, Mexico 88 Cc
Tuxtepec, Mexico 88 Ed
Tuxtla & Vol. de, Mexico 88 Ed
Tuxtla Gutierrez, Mexico 88 Fd
Tuy, Spain 50 Aa
Tuyen-Quang, N. Vietnam 67 Db
Tuy-hoa, S. Vietnam 67 Dd
Tuyun, China 65 Cj
Tuz Golu, Turkey 72 Bb
Tuzla, Yugoslavia 56 Bb
Tvärån, Sweden 46 Jd
Tvurditsa, Bulgaria 56 Ec
Twante, Burma 69 Je
Tweed, Ontario 83 Hc
Tweed, R., Scotland 30 Fe
Tweedsmuir Hills, Scotland 30 Ee
Tweedsmuir Park, B.C. 80 Ff
Twenty-five de Mayo, Argent. 92 Ce
Twenty-five de Mayo, Argent. 92 De
Twin Falls, Idaho 87 Fd
Two Harbors, Minnesota 85 Hb
Two Mountains, L. of, Que. 83 Jc
Two Rivers, Wisconsin 83 Cc
Tylar, Texas 84 Ge
Tygda, Russia 59 Mc
Tyndinskiy, Russia 59 Mc
Tyndall, Mt., New Zealand 93 Ce
Tyne R., England 30 Ff
Tynemouth, England 30 Ge
Tynset, Norway 46 De
Tyre (Sur), Lebanon 74 Dd
Tyrone, Pennsylvania 86 Ab
Tyrone, co., N. Ireland 31 Cf
Tyrrhenian Sea, Italy 55 Ce
Tyumen, Russia 58 Fc
Tzechung, China 64 Gd
Tzeli, China 65 Eh
Tzeya Ho, China 62 Gc
Tzeyang, China 64 Gd
Tzeyun, China 65 Ck
Uau el Chebir. See Wau el Kebir
Uaupés & R., Brazil 90 Dc
Uba, Brazil 91 Jh
Ubait, Arabia 72 Cd
Ubari, Libya 79 Hc
Uberaba, Brazil 91 Hg
Uberlandia, Brazil 91 Hg
Überlingen, Germany 48 Ce
Ubon, Muang, Siam 67 Cc
Ubsa Nur, Mongolia 59 Jc
Ucayali, R., Peru 90 Ce
Uch, W. Pakistan 70 Bf
Uchiura wan, Japan 66 Gc
Uchiza, Peru 90 Be
Uckermark, Germany 48 Eb
Udain, Yemen 72 Dg
Udaipur, India 68 Dd
Uddevalla, Sweden 47 Dg
Udd Jaur, Sweden 46 Gd
Uden, Netherlands 44 Dc
Udine, Italy 54 Db
Udon Thani, Siam 67 Cc
Udskaya Guba, Russia 59 Nc
Udzha. See Bor Yuryakh
Uelen, Russia 59 Tb
Ueno, Japan 66 Eg
Ufa, Russia 61 Mc
Uganda, E. Africa 77 Gd
Ugwashi-Uku, Nigeria 76 Bc
Uherske Hradiště, Czech. 49 Gd
Ui Failghe, co., Eire 31 Bg
Uinta Mts., Utah 84 Dc
Uist, North, I., Scotland 30 Cc
Uist, South, I., Scotland 30 Cc
Uitenhage, Cape Province 75 Df
Uitgeest, Netherlands 44 Cb
Ujhani, India 71 Bb
Ujpest, Hungary 49 He
Ukerewe Is., Tanzania 77 Ge
Ukhta, Russia 58 Cb
Ukiah, California 87 Bf
Ukmerge, Lithuania 47 Lj
Ukraine, rep., U.S.S.R. 60 Eg
Ulan, Mongolia 59 Jd
Ulan Bator, Mongolia 62 Ea
Ulanhot, China 62 Ha
Ulan Ude, Russia 59 Kc
Ulcinj, Yugoslavia 56 Bd
Ulithi, I., Pacific Ocean 98 Cf
Ullapool, Scotland 30 Dc
Ullared, Sweden 47 Eh
Ulldecona, Spain 51 Fb
Ullswater L., England 31 Ff
Ullung Do, Sea of Japan 66 Bf
Ulm, Germany 48 Cd
Ulster, prov., Eire-N. Ire. 31 Bf
Ulua, R., Honduras 89 Bc
Ulukişla, Turkey 72 Bb
Ulverston, England 31 Ef
Ulyanovsk, Russia 61 Jc
Ulzen, Germany 48 Db
Uman, Ukraine 60 Gg
Umanak Fd., Greenland 39 Pb
Umarkot, W. Pakistan 68 Cc
Umbria, dep., Italy 54 Dd
Umeå, Sweden 46 Je
Umm ar Rusuys, Muscat & Oman 73 Ge
Umm el Qulban, Arabia 72 Dd
Umm Kuteira, Sudan 79 Lf
Umm Lej, Arabia 72 Cd
Umm Qasr, Iraq 72 Ec
Umm Rasas. See Umm ar Rusuys
Umm Ruwaba, Sudan 79 Mf
Umnak I., Aleutian Is. 85 Wm
Umtali, Rhodesia 75 Ec
Umtata, Cape Province 75 Df
Umvuma, Rhodesia 75 Ec
Una, India 70 Ee
Una R., Yugoslavia 54 Fc
Unadilla, New York 86 Ca
Ualakleet, Alaska 85 Wl
Unalaska, Aleutian Is. 85 Wm
Unayzah, Arabia 72 Dd
Uncastillo, Spain 51 Ea
Uncia, Bolivia 90 Dg
Undzhul. See Onjül
Ungava B., Quebec 81 Te
União, Brazil 91 Jd
União da Vitoria, Brazil 92 Fc
Uniejów, Poland 49 Hc
Unimak I., Aleutian Is. 85 Wm
Unini, Peru 90 Cf
Union, Argentina 92 Ce
Union, Argentina 92 Cc
Union, S. Carolina 85 Ke
Union of Soviet Socialist Republics, Europe-Asia 40-41
Uniontown, Pennsylvania 86 Ac
Unionville, Nevada 87 De
United Arab Rep. See Egypt
United Kingdom of Great Britain and N. Ireland 30-31
United States of America 84-85
Unnao, India 71 Cb
Unst I., Shetland, Scotland 30 Ja
Unterwalden, canton, Switz. 45 Db
Unzha, Russia 61 Ga
Uozu, Japan 66 Ef
Upata, Venezuela 90 Eb
Upemba L., Congo 76 Ff
Upernivik, Greenland 39 Pb
Upington, Cape Province 75 Ce

Upolu, I., *Samoa* 98 Hj
Upper Marlboro, *Maryland* 86 Bc
Upper Sandusky, *Ohio* 83 Ee
Upper Seal L., *Quebec* 81 Se
Upper Volta, *W. Africa* 78 Ef
Uppsala, *Sweden* 47 Gg
Uqair, *Arabia* 72 Ed
Ur, *Iraq* 72 Ec
Uracoa, *Venezuela* 90 Eb
Urakawa, *Japan* 66 Hc
Ural, R., *Kazakh., etc.* 58 Ec
Ural'sk, *Kazakh.* 58 Ec
Ural'skiy Khrebet, *Russia* 58 Ec
Uranium City, *Saskatchewan* 80 Ke
Urapunga, *N. Terr., Aust.* 95 Fb
Ura Tyube, *Tadzhikskaya rep.* 58 Fe
Urawa, *Japan* 66 Fg
Urbakh, *Russia* 61 He
Urcos, *Peru* 90 Cf
Urda, *Kazakh.* 58 Dd
Urdzhar, *Kazakh.* 58 Hd
Ures, *Mexico* 88 Bb
Urfa, *Turkey* 72 Cb
Urga. See Ulan Bator
Urgench, *Uzbek.* 58 Ed
Urgun, *Afghanistan* 73 Jc
Uri, canton, *Switzerland* 45 Db
Uribe, *Colombia* 90 Cc
Uribia, *Colombia* 90 Ca
Urnäsch, *Switzerland* 45 Ea
Urtazymsk, *Russia* 61 Pd
Urtein, *Mongolia* 62 Ga
Uruapan, *Mexico* 88 Dd
Urubamba & R., *Peru* 90 Cf
Urucará, *Brazil* 90 Fd
Uruçui, *Brazil* 91 Je
Urucuia, *Brazil* 91 Hg
Urudangi, *Qnsld.* 95 Gd
Uruguaiana, *Brazil* 92 Ec
Uruguay, rep., *S. America* 92 Ed
Uruguay, R., *Uruguay, etc.* 92 Ed
Urumchi, *China* 58 Hd
Urumes Sughra, *Syria* 74 Ea
Urussanga, *Brazil* 92 Gc
Urville, T. d', *W. Irian* 63 Ll
Uryupinsk, *Russia* 61 Fe
Urzhum, *Russia* 61 Kb
Urziceni, *Rumania* 56 Fb
Usak, *Turkey* 72 Ab
Usakos, *S.-W. Africa* 75 Bd
Usborne, Mt., *Falkland Is.* 92 Eh
Usedom, *Germany* 48 Ea
Ushant I. See Ouessant, I. d'
Ushirombo, *Tanzania* 77 Ge
Ush Tobe, *Kazakh.* 58 Gd
Ushuaia, *Argentina* 92 Ch
Uska, *India* 71 Db
Uskedal, *Norway* 47 Ag
Uskub. See Skopje
Uskudar, *Turkey* 72 Aa
Usole Siberskoye, *Russia* 59 Kc
Uspenskiy, *Kazakh.* 58 Gd
Usquil, *Peru* 90 Be
Ussel, *France* 52 Ed
Ussuri, R., *Russia-China* 59 Nd
Ussuriysk, *Russia* 59 Nd
Ust' Aldan, *Russia* 59 Mb
Ust' Amginskoye, *Russia* 59 Nb
Ust' Apuka, *Russia* 59 Rb
Ust' Belaya, *Russia* 59 Sb
Ust' Bolsheretsk, *Russia* 59 Qc
Ust' Chaun, *Russia* 59 Sb
Uster, *Switzerland* 45 Da
Usti nad Labem, *Czech.* 48 Fc
Ust' Ishim, *Russia* 58 Gc
Ust' Kamenogorsk, *Kazakh.* 58 Hc
Ust' Khayryuzovo, *Russia* 59 Qc
Ust' Kut, *Russia* 59 Kc
Ust' Maya, *Russia* 59 Nb
Ust' Port, *Russia* 58 Hb
Ust' Sopochnoye, *Russia* 59 Qc
Ust' Tsilma, *Russia* 58 Eb
Ust' Uda, *Russia* 59 Kc
Ust' Usa, *Russia* 58 Eb
Ust' Uyskoye, *Russia* 61 Rc
Ustyurt, plat., *Kazakh.* 58 Ed
Ustyuzhna, *Russia* 60 Kb
Usu. See Abuta
Usumacinta, R., *Mexico* 88 Fd
Utah, state, *U.S.A.* 84 Dd
Utah L., *Utah* 84 Dc
Utajarvi, *Finland* 46 Md
Utena, *Lithuania* 47 Lj
Utete, *Tanzania* 77 Hf
Uthal, *W. Pakistan* 68 Bc
Utiariti, *Brazil* 90 Ff
Utica, *New York* 83 Jd
Utiel, *Spain* 51 Ec
Utikuma L., *Alberta* 80 He
Utraula, *India* 71 Db
Utrecht, *Natal* 75 Ee
Utrecht & prov., *Neth.* 44 Db
Utrera, *Spain* 50 Cd
Utrillas, *Spain* 51 Eb
Utsjoki, *Finland* 46 Mb
Utsunomiya, *Japan* 66 Ff
Uttar Pradesh, *India* 68 Ec
Uttaradit, *Siam* 67 Cc
Uusikaarlepyy, *Finland* 46 Ke
Uusikaupunki, *Finland* 47 Jf
Uvac, *Yugoslavia* 56 Bc
Uvat, *Russia* 58 Fc
Uvea, I., *Loyalty Islands* 98 Fk
Uvira, *Congo* 77 Fe
Uwajima, *Japan* 66 Ch
Uxbridge, *Massachusetts* 86 Ea
Uxbridge, *Ontario* 83 Gc
Uxmal, *Mexico* 88 Gc
Uyu Chaung R., *Burma* 69 Jc
Uyuni, *Bolivia* 90 Dh
Uzbekskaya rep., *U.S.S.R.* 58 Fd
Uzdin, *Yugoslavia* 56 Cb
Uzgen, *Kirgiz.* 58 Gd
Uzhgorod, *Ukraine* 60 Cg
Uzyansk, *Russia* 61 Nd
Vaal R., *S. Africa* 75 Dd
Vaalwater, *Transvaal* 75 Dd
Vaasä, *Finland* 46 Je
Vac, *Hungary* 49 He
Vache, I. La, *Haiti* 89 Ec
Vadsö, *Norway* 46 Na
Vaduz, *Liechtenstein* 45 Ea
Væröy, *Norway* 46 Ec
Vags Fd., *Norway* 46 Gb
Vah, R., *Czechoslovakia* 49 Gd
Vaila I., *Shetland, Scotland* 30 Ha
Vairowal, *India* 70 Da
Valais, canton, *Switzerland* 45 Cb
Val Brillant, *Quebec* 82 Eb
Valcheta, *Argentina* 92 Cf
Valday, *Russia* 60 Hc
Valday Hills, *Russia* 60 Hc
Valdepeñas, *Spain* 50 Dc
Valderredible, *Spain* 50 Da
Valderrobres, *Spain* 51 Fb
Valdés, Pen., *Argentina* 92 Df
Valdez, *Alaska* 85 Yl
Valdivia, *Chile* 92 Be
Valdosta, *Georgia* 85 Ke
Valea-lui-Mihai, *Rumania* 49 Ke
Valença, *Brazil* 91 Je
Valença, *Brazil* 91 Kf
Valençay, *France* 52 Dc
Valence, *France* 53 Fd
Valencia, *Spain* 51 Ec
Valencia, *Venezuela* 90 Da
Valencia, Gulf of, *Spain* 51 Fc
Valencia de Alcántara, *Spain* 50 Bc
Valencia de Don Juan, *Spain* 50 Ca
Valenciennes, *France* 52 Ea
Văleni de Munte, *Rumania* 56 Fb
Valentia I., *Eire* 33 Ck
Valentin, Mt., *Chile* 92 Bg
Valera, *Venezuela* 90 Cb
Valga, *Estonia* 47 Mh
Valjala, *Estonia* 47 Kg
Valjevo, *Yugoslavia* 56 Bb
Valkeakoshi, *Finland* 47 Lf
Valkenburg, *Netherlands* 44 Dd
Valladolid, *Mexico* 88 Gc
Valladolid, *Spain* 50 Cb
Valldemosa, *Balearic Is.* 51 Gc
Valle-D'Aosta, reg., *Italy* 54 Ac
Valle de La Pascua, *Venez.* 90 Db
Valle de Santiago, *Mexico* 88 Dc
Valledupar, *Colombia* 90 Ca
Vallejo, *California* 87 Bf
Vallenar, *Chile* 92 Bc
Valletta, *Malta* 55 Eh
Valley City, *N. Dakota* 84 Gb
Valleyfield, *Quebec* 83 Jc
Vallgrund, *Finland* 46 Je
Vallorbe, *Switzerland* 45 Bb
Valmaseda, *Spain* 50 Da
Valmiera, *Latvia* 47 Lh
Valognes, *France* 52 Cb
Valona (Vlorë), *Albania* 57 Bd
Valona B., *Albania* 57 Bd
Valoria la Buena, *Spain* 50 Cb
Valparaiso, *Chile* 92 Bd
Valparaiso, *Mexico* 88 Dc
Vals Platz, *Switzerland* 45 Eb
Valtimo, *Finland* 46 Ne
Valverde de Júcar, *Spain* 51 Dc
Valverde del Camino, *Spain* 50 Bd
Van & Gölu, *Turkey* 72 Db
Van Vändra, *Estonia* 47 Lg
Vanavara, *Russia* 59 Kb
Van Buren, *Arkansas* 85 Hd
Van Buren, *Maine* 82 Ec
Vanceboro, *Maine* 82 Ed
Vancouver, *Brit. Columbia* 80 Gg
Vancouver, *Washington* 87 Bc
Vancouver I., *Brit. Columbia* 80 Fg
Vancouver, Mt., *Yukon* 80 Dd
Van Diemen, C., *N.T., Aust.* 94 Fb
Van Diemen G., *N.T. Aust.* 94 Fb
Vanegas, *Mexico* 88 Dc
Vänern, L., *Sweden* 47 Eg
Vänersborg, *Sweden* 47 Eg
Vangaindrano, *Madagascar* 77 Nl
Vankarem, *Russia* 59 Tb
Vannes, *France* 52 Bc
Vannöy, *Norway* 46 Ha
Van Rhyns Dorp, *Cape Prov.* 75 Bf
Vansittart I., *N.-W. Terr.* 81 Qc
Vanua Levu, I., *Fiji* 98 Gj
Var, dep., *France* 53 Ge
Varanasi, *India* 71 Dc
Varanger Fd., *Norway* 46 Pb
Varanger Halvöya, *Norway* 46 Na
Varaždin, *Yugoslavia* 54 Fb
Varberg, *Sweden* 47 Eh
Vardar R., *Greece, etc.* 56 Dd
Vardö, *Norway* 46 Pa
Vares, C. de, *Spain* 50 Ba
Varese, *Italy* 54 Bc
Varkaus, *Finland* 46 Me
Varna, *Bulgaria* 56 Fc
Varnavin, *Russia* 61 Gb
Värtsilä, *Finland* 46 Pe
Vasht. See Gasht
Vasknarva, *Estonia* 47 Mg
Vassar, *Michigan* 83 Ed
Vastanfors, *Sweden* 47 Fg
Västerås, *Sweden* 47 Gg
Väster Dal Älv, *Sweden* 47 Ef
Västervik, *Sweden* 47 Gh
Vasvar, *Hungary* 49 Ge
Vatican City, *Italy* 55 De
Vaticano C., *Italy* 55 Ef
Vatna Jökull, *Iceland* 46 Xm
Vatomandry, *Madagascar* 77 Nk
Vättern, L., *Sweden* 47 Fg
Vättis, *Switzerland* 45 Eb
Vaucluse, dep., *France* 53 Fd
Vaud, canton, *Switzerland* 45 Bb
Växjö, *Sweden* 47 Fh
Vaygach Ostrov, *Russia* 58 Fa
Vechel, *Netherlands* 44 Dc
Vedia, *Argentina* 92 Dd
Vedrin, *Belgium* 44 Cd
Veere, *Netherlands* 44 Bc
Vega & Fd., *Norway* 46 Dd
Vegorrítis, L., *Greece* 57 Cd
Vegreville, *Alberta* 80 Jf
Vejle, *Denmark* 47 Cj
Vela, *Argentina* 92 Ee
Velaines, *Belgium* 44 Bd
Velebit Planina, *Yugoslavia* 54 Ec
Velestinon, *Greece* 57 De
Vélez Rubio, *Spain* 51 Dd
Velikiy Ustyug, *Russia* 58 Db
Velikiye Luki, *Russia* 60 Gc
Velizh, *Russia* 60 Gd
Velletri, *Italy* 55 Dd
Vellore, *India* 68 Ef
Velp, *Netherlands* 44 Db
Velsen, *Netherlands* 44 Cb
Velsk, *Russia* 60 Na
Venado, *Mexico* 88 Dc
Venado Tuerto, *Argentina* 92 Dd
Vendee, dep., *France* 52 Cc
Vendôme, *France* 52 Dc
Venendaal, *Netherlands* 44 Db
Veneto, reg., *Italy* 54 Cc
Venezia, & G. di, *Italy* 54 Dc
Venezuela, rep., *S. America* 90 Db
Venezuela, G. de, *Venezuela* 90 Ca
Vengurla, *India* 68 De
Venice (Venezia), *Italy* 54 Dc
Venlo, *Netherlands* 44 Ec
Venraij, *Netherlands* 44 Dc
Ventotene, I., *Italy* 55 De
Ventspils, *Latvia* 47 Jh
Ventura, *California* 87 Dh
Vera. See Jobson
Vera, *Spain* 51 Ed
Veracruz and state, *Mexico* 88 Ed
Veramin, *Persia* 73 Fb
Veraval, *India* 68 Dd
Verbania, *Switzerland* 45 Dc
Vercelli, *Italy* 54 Bc
Verde C. (Vert C.), *Senegal* 78 Bf
Verdun, *France* 52 Fb
Verdun, *Quebec* 83 Kc
Vereshchagino, *Russia* 58 Hb
Vereshchagino, *Russia* 61 Ma
Vereya, *Russia* 61 Cc
Verga C., *Guinea* 78 Cf
Vergara, *Uruguay* 92 Fd
Vergennes, *Vermont* 83 Kc
Verín, *Spain* 50 Bb
Verkhne Imbatskoye, *Russia* 58 Hb
Verkhne Uralsk, *Russia* 61 Pd
Verkhne Vilyuysk, *Russia* 59 Mb
Verkhoturye, *Russia* 58 Fc
Verkhoyansk, *Russia* 59 Nb
Verkhoyanskiy Khr., *Russia* 59 Mb
Vermillion, *S. Dakota* 84 Gc
Vermont, state, *U.S.A.* 85 Mc
Verneuil, *France* 52 Db
Vernon, *British Columbia* 80 Hf
Veroia, *Greece* 57 Dd
Verona, *Italy* 54 Cc
Verrieres, les, *Switzerland* 45 Bb
Versailles, *France* 52 Eb
Versam, *Switzerland* 45 Eb
Vert C., *Senegal* 78 Bf
Verte, I., *Quebec* 82 Dc
Vertryck, *Belgium* 44 Cd
Verviers, *Belgium* 44 Dd
Vervins, *France* 52 Eb
Vesanto, *Finland* 46 Me
Vesoul, *France* 52 Gc
Vessem, *Netherlands* 44 Dc
Vesta. See Pandora
Vesterålen, Is., *Norway* 46 Fb
Vestfjorden, *Norway* 46 Ec
Vest Spitsbergen, *Arctic Oc.* 58 Aa
Vest Vågöy, *Norway* 46 Eb
Vesyegonsk, *Russia* 60 Kb
Veszprem, *Hungary* 49 Ge
Vetluga & R., *Russia* 61 Gb
Veurne, *Belgium* 44 Ac
Vevey, *Switzerland* 45 Bb
Vex, *Switzerland* 45 Cb
Veys, *Persia* 72 Ec
Viacha, *Bolivia* 90 Dg
Viana, *Brazil* 91 Jd
Viborg, *Denmark* 47 Ch
Vibo Valentia, *Italy* 55 Ff
Vicente de la Barquera, S., *Spain* 50 Ca
Vicenza, *Italy* 54 Cc
Vich, *Spain* 51 Gb
Vichuquen, *Chile* 92 Bd
Vichy, *France* 52 Ec
Vicksburg, *Mississippi* 85 He
Vicosa, *Brazil* 91 Jd
Victor Harbour, *S. Australia* 95 Gg
Victoria, *Argentina* 92 Dd
Victoria, *British Columbia* 80 Gg
Victoria, *Hong Kong* 62 Ff
Victoria, state, *Australia* 95 Hg
Victoria Falls, *Rhodesia* 75 Dc
Victoria I., *N.-W. Territories* 80 Jb
Victoria L., *Uganda, etc.* 77 Ge
Victoria Ld., *Antarctica* 100 Lb
Victoria Mt., *Burma* 69 Hd
Victoria, Mt., *Papua* 95 Ja
Victoria, R., *N. Terr., Aust.* 94 Fc
Victoria Point, *Burma* 69 Jf
Victoria River Downs, *N. Territory, Australia* 94 Ec
Victoriaville, *Quebec* 83 Kb
Victoria West, *Cape Province* 75 Cf
Victorica, *Argentina* 92 Ce
Vicuna, *Chile* 92 Bd
Vidago, *Portugal* 50 Bb
Vidin, *Bulgaria* 56 Db
Viedma, *Argentina* 92 Df
Viedma, L., *Argentina* 92 Bg
Vienna (Wien), *Austria* 49 Gd
Vienne, *France* 52 Fd
Vienne, dep., *France* 52 Dc
Vienne R., *France* 52 Dc
Vientiane, *Laos* 67 Cc
Vieques, I. de, *West Indies* 89 Fc
Vierlingsbeek, *Netherlands* 44 Dc
Vierwaldstatter See, *Switz.* 45 Da
Vierzon Ville, *France* 52 Ec
Viesite, *Latvia* 47 Lh
Vietnam, *S.-E. Asia* 67 Dc
Vif, *France* 53 Fd
Vigan, *Philippines* 63 Hg
Vigan, le, *France* 53 Ee
Vigia, *Brazil* 91 Hd
Vigia Chico, *Mexico* 88 Gd
Vigo & R., *Spain* 50 Aa
Vigrestad, *Norway* 47 Ag
Vihanti, *Finland* 46 Ld
Vijayanagar, *India* 68 Ee
Vijayavada, *India* 68 Fe
Vijosë R., *Albania* 57 Bd
Vikaviskis, *Lithuania* 47 Kj
Vikna, *Norway* 46 Dd
Vila Arriaga, *Angola* 76 Cg
Vila de Cangombe, *Angola* 76 Cg
Vila de João Belo, *Moçamb.* 75 Ee
Vila Lugela. See Mocuba
Vila Luso, *Angola* 76 Dg
Vila Machado, *Moçambique* 75 Ec
Vila Manica, *Moçambique* 75 Ec
Vilanculos, *Moçambique* 75 Fd
Vilane, *Latvia* 47 Mh
Vila Nova de Cerveira, *Port.* 50 Ab
Vila Nova de Famalicão, *Port.* 50 Ab
Vila Nova de Malaca, *Timor I., Indonesia* 63 Jm
Vila Pery, *Moçambique* 75 Ec
Vila Real, *Portugal* 50 Bb
Vilar Formoso, *Portugal* 50 Bb
Vila Serpa Pinto, *Angola* 76 Dg
Vila Velha de Rodao, *Port.* 50 Bc
Vila Verissimo, *Angola* 76 Ef
Vila Viçosa, *Portugal* 50 Bc
Vilcheka, Os., *Arctic Ocean* 58 Fa
Vilhelmina, *Sweden* 46 Gd
Vilhena, *Brazil* 90 Ef
Viljandi, *Estonia* 47 Lg
Villa Angela. See Santa Sylvina
Villa Bella, *Bolivia* 90 Df
Villa Bens, *Sp. Sahara* 78 Cc
Villablino, *Spain* 50 Ba
Villacañas, *Spain* 50 Dc
Villacarriedo, *Spain* 50 Da
Villach, *Austria* 48 Ee
Villa Cisneros, *Sp. Sahara* 78 Bd
Villa Constitución, *Argentina* 92 Dd
Villa del Rosario, *Paraguay* 92 Eb
Villa de Rosario, *Argentina* 92 Dd
Villa Dolores, *Argentina* 92 Cd
Villafranca, *Spain* 50 Ba
Villafranca del Cid, *Spain* 51 Eb
Villafranca del Panadés, *Sp.* 51 Fb
Villaggio-Duca-Abruzzi, *Somalia* 77 Kd
Villaguay, *Argentina* 92 Ed
Villa Guillermina, *Argentina* 92 Ec
Villa Hermosa, *Mexico* 88 Fd
Villa Hidalgo, *Mexico* 88 Db
Villa Ingavi, *Bolivia* 90 Eh
Villa Iris, *Argentina* 92 De
Villajoyosa, *Spain* 51 Ec
Villalba, *Spain* 50 Ba
Villaldama, *Mexico* 88 Db
Villalón de Campos, *Spain* 50 Ca
Villalonga, *Argentina* 92 De
Villalpando, *Spain* 50 Cb
Villa Maria, *Argentina* 92 Dd
Villa Mercedes, *Argentina* 92 Cd
Villa Montes, *Bolivia* 90 Eh
Villa Murtinho, *Brazil* 90 Df
Villanueva de Córdoba, *Sp.* 50 Cc
Villanueva de la Serena, *Sp.* 50 Cc
Villanueva de los Infantes, *Spain* 50 Dc
Villanueva -y Geltrú, *Spain* 51 Fb
Villaodrid, *Spain* 50 Ba
Villaputzu, *Sardinia* 55 Bf
Villarcayo, *Spain* 50 Da
Villareal, *Spain* 51 Ec
Villarrica, *Chile* 92 Be
Villarrica, *Paraguay* 92 Ec
Villarrobledo, *Spain* 51 Dc
Villavicencio, *Colombia* 90 Cc
Villaviciosa, *Spain* 50 Ca
Villa Viejo, *Colombia* 90 Bc
Villazon, *Bolivia* 90 Dh
Villefort, *France* 53 Ed
Villefranche-de-Rouergue, *France* 53 Dd
Ville Marie, *Quebec* 83 Gb
Villena, *Spain* 51 Ec
Villeneuve-sur-Lot, *France* 53 Dd
Villeurbanne, *France* 52 Fd
Villingen, *Germany* 48 Cd
Villupuram, *India* 68 Ef
Vilna. See Vilnyus
Vilnyus, *Lithuania* 47 Lj
Vilvoorde, *Belgium* 44 Cd
Vilyuysk, *Russia* 59 Mb
Vimioso, *Portugal* 50 Bb
Vimperk, *Czechoslovakia* 48 Ed
Viña del Mar, *Chile* 92 Bd
Vinal Haven I., *Maine* 82 Dd
Vinaroz, *Spain* 51 Fb
Vincennes, *Indiana* 83 Cf
Vinchiaturo, *Italy* 55 Ee
Vinde Alv, *Sweden* 46 Hd
Vindhya Ra., *India* 68 Ed
Vineland, *New Jersey* 86 Cc
Vineyard Sd., *Mass.* 86 Eb
Vinga, *Rumania* 56 Cb
Vinh, *N. Vietnam* 67 Dc
Vinkovci, *Yugoslavia* 56 Bb
Vinnitsa, *Ukraine* 60 Fg
Vintes, *Ecuador* 90 Bd
Viranşehir, *Turkey* 72 Cb
Virden, *Manitoba* 80 Lg
Virgin Is., *West Indies* 89 Gc
Virginia, *Minnesota* 85 Hb
Virginia, state, *U.S.A.* 85 Ld
Virginia Falls, *N.-W. Terr.* 80 Fd
Viroqua, *Wisconsin* 83 Ad
Virovitica, *Yugoslavia* 56 Ab
Virpazar, *Yugoslavia* 56 Bc
Virtasalmi, *Finland* 46 Me
Virton, *Belgium* 44 De
Virtsu, *Estonia* 47 Kg
Viru, *Peru* 90 Be
Vis, I., *Yugoslavia* 54 Fd
Visalia, *California* 87 Dg
Visby, *Gotland, Sweden* 47 Hh
Viscount Melville Sd., *N.-W. Territories* 80 Jb
Visé, *Belgium* 44 Dd
Viseu, *Brazil* 91 Hd
Viseu, *Portugal* 50 Bb
Vishakhapatnam, *India* 69 Fe
Viški, *Latvia* 47 Mh
Viso, Mte., *Italy* 54 Ac
Visoko, *Yugoslavia* 56 Bc
Visp, *Switzerland* 45 Cb
Vista Alegre, *Brazil* 90 Ec
Vistula (Wisła), R., *Poland* 49 Jc
Vitebsk, *White Russia* 60 Gd
Viterbo, *Italy* 54 Dd
Vitigudino, *Spain* 50 Bb
Viti Levu, I., *Fiji* 98 Gj
Vitim, R., *Russia* 59 Lc
Vitoria, *Brazil* 91 Jh
Vitoria, *Spain* 51 Da
Vitoria do Mearim, *Brazil* 91 Jd
Vitry-le-François, *France* 52 Fb
Vittangi, *Sweden* 46 Jc
Vitteaux, *France* 52 Fc
Vittoria, *Sicily* 55 Eg
Viver, *Spain* 51 Ec
Vivero, *Spain* 50 Ba
Vivi, *Russia* 59 Jb
Vivoratá, *Argentina* 92 Ee
Vizianagram, *India* 69 Fe
Viziru, *Rumania* 56 Fb
Vizovice, *Czechoslovakia* 49 Gd
Vizzini, *Sicily* 55 Eg
Vlaanderen, Oost, *Belgium* 44 Bd
Vlaanderen, West, *Belgium* 44 Bd
Vlaardingen, *Netherlands* 44 Cc
Vladimir, *Russia* 60 Mc
Vladimirovka, *Russia* 61 Hf
Vladivostok, *Russia* 59 Nd
Vlieland I., *Netherlands* 44 Ca
Vlissingen, *Netherlands* 44 Bc
Vlorë, *Albania* 57 Bd
Vltava R., *Czechoslovakia* 48 Fc
Voghera, *Italy* 54 Bc
Vohemar, *Madagascar* 77 Pj
Võhma, *Estonia* 47 Lg
Voi, *Kenya* 77 He
Voiotia, *Greece* 57 De
Voiron, *France* 52 Fd
Voitsberg, *Austria* 48 Fe
Voivis, L., *Greece* 57 De
Vojvodina, *Yugoslavia* 56 Bb
Volcano B. See Uchiura wan
Volga, R., *Russia* 58 Dd
Volgograd, *Russia* 61 Gf
Volissos, *Greece* 57 Ee
Volkhov, R., *Russia* 60 Gb
Vollenhove, *Netherlands* 44 Db
Volochanka, *Russia* 59 Ja
Volochisk, *Ukraine* 60 Eg
Vologda, *Russia* 60 Lb
Volokolamsk, *Russia* 60 Jc
Vólos, *Greece* 57 De
Volovets, *Ukraine* 60 Cg
Volozhin, *White Russia* 60 Ed
Volsk, *Russia* 61 Hd
Volta. See Upper Volta
Volta, L., *Ghana* 78 Eg
Volta, White, R., *Ghana* 78 Eg
Voltveti, *Estonia* 47 Lg
Vonêche, *Belgium* 44 Cd
Voorburg, *Netherlands* 44 Cb
Voorschoten, *Netherlands* 44 Cb
Voorst, *Netherlands* 44 Eb
Voorthuizen, *Netherlands* 44 Db
Vopnafjordhur, *Iceland* 46 Ym
Vorab, Mt., *Switzerland* 45 Eb
Vorarlberg, *Austria* 48 Ce
Vorauen, *Switzerland* 45 Da
Vorkuta, *Russia* 58 Fb
Vormsi, I., *Estonia* 47 Kg
Voronezh, *Russia* 60 Lf
Vosges, dep. & mts., *France* 52 Gb
Voss, *Norway* 47 Bf
Vostok I., *Pacific Ocean* 99 Kj
Votkinsk, *Russia* 61 Lb
Vouvry, *Switzerland* 45 Bb
Vouziers, *France* 52 Fb
Voxna, *Sweden* 47 Ff
Voyampolka, *Russia* 59 Qc
Voznesensk, *Ukraine* 60 Gh
Vrancv, *Czechoslovakia* 49 Jd
Vrangelya Ostrov, *Russia* 59 Sa
Vranje, *Yugoslavia* 56 Cc
Vratsa, *Bulgaria* 56 Dc
Vrbas, *Yugoslavia* 56 Bb
Vrchovina Českomoravska, *Czechoslovakia* 49 Fd
Vredefort, *O.F.S.* 75 De
Vrin, *Switzerland* 45 Eb
Vrindavan, *India* 71 Ab
Vroomshoop, *Netherlands* 44 Eb
Vršac, *Yugoslavia* 56 Cb
Vrútky, *Czechoslovakia* 49 Hd
Vryburg, *Cape Province* 75 Ce
Vučitrn, *Yugoslavia* 56 Cc
Vukovar, *Yugoslavia* 56 Bb
Vulcano, I., *Italy* 55 Ef
Vulpera, *Switzerland* 45 Fb
Vuolijoki, *Finland* 46 Md
Vurbitsa, *Bulgaria* 56 Fc
Vyatka (Kirov), *Russia* 61 Ja
Vyatka, R., *Russia* 58 Dc
Vyazemskiy, *Russia* 59 Nd
Vyazma, *Russia* 60 Jd
Vyazniki, *Russia* 61 Fb
Vyborg, *Russia* 60 Fa
Vyrtsyarv Oz., *Estonia* 47 Mg
Vyru, *Estonia* 47 Mh
Vyshniy Volochek, *Russia* 60 Jc
Vyskov, *Czechoslovakia* 49 Gd
Vytegra, *Russia* 60 Ka
Wa, *Ghana* 78 Ef
Waalhaven, *Netherlands* 44 Cc
Waalwijk, *Netherlands* 44 Dc
Wabasca R., *Alberta* 80 Je
Wabash & R., *Indiana* 83 De
Waboose Dam, *Ontario* 81 Pf
Wabos. See Searchmont
Wabra, *Arabia* 72 Ed
Wabuda, I., *New Guinea* 95 Ha
Waco, *Texas* 84 Ge
Wad, *W. Pakistan* 68 Cc
Wadden Zee, *Netherlands* 44 Da
Waddington Mt., *B.C.* 80 Ff
Wad Hamid, *Sudan* 79 Me
Wadi-es-Sir, *Jordan* 74 Df
Wadi Gemal I., *Egypt* 79 Nd
Wadi Halfa, *Sudan* 79 Md
Wadi Musa, *Jordan* 74 Dg
Wad Medani, *Sudan* 79 Mf
Wafi, *Arabia* 72 De
Wageningen, *Netherlands* 44 Dc
Wager B., *N.-W. Territories* 81 Pc
Wagga Wagga, *N.S.W.* 95 Jg
Wagin, *W. Australia* 94 Cf
Wahla, *Arabia* 72 Df
Wahpeton, *N. Dakota* 80 Mg
Waiau, *New Zealand* 93 De
Waichow. See Waiyeung
Waigeo, I., *W. Irian* 63 Kl
Waiheke I., *New Zealand* 93 Eb
Waihi, *New Zealand* 93 Eb
Waikaia, *New Zealand* 93 Bf
Waikare, Moana, *N.Z.* 93 Fc
Waikari, *New Zealand* 93 De
Waikato, R., *New Zealand* 93 Ec
Waikouaiti, *New Zealand* 93 Cf
Waimakariri, R., *New Zealand* 93 De
Waimate, *New Zealand* 93 Cf
Waimes, *Belgium* 44 Ed
Wainganga R., *India* 68 Ed
Waingapu, *Sumba I., Indon.* 63 Hm
Wainwright, *Alaska* 85 Xk
Waipara, *New Zealand* 93 De
Waipawa, *New Zealand* 93 Fc
Waipukurau, *New Zealand* 93 Fd
Wairarapa, L., *New Zealand* 93 Ed
Wairau, R., *New Zealand* 93 Dd
Wairoa, *New Zealand* 93 Fc
Waitara, *New Zealand* 93 Ec
Waitomo, *New Zealand* 93 Ec
Waiuku, *New Zealand* 93 Eb
Waiyeung, *China* 65 Gl
Wajir, *Kenya* 77 Jd
Wakamatsu, *Japan* 66 Ff
Wakasa B., *Japan* 66 Dg
Wakatipu, L., *N.Z.* 93 Bf
Wakayama, *Japan* 66 Dg
Wakba. See El Jafr
Wake I., *Pacific Ocean* 98 Ff
Wakefield, *England* 31 Gg
Wakonichi L., *Quebec* 82 Aa
Wakrah, *Qatar* 73 Fd
Wakuan Hu, *China* 64 Hf
Walachia, *Rumania* 56 Eb
Walbrzych, *Poland* 49 Gc
Walcheren I., *Netherlands* 44 Bc
Wald, *Switzerland* 45 Da
Waldia, *Ethiopia* 77 Hb
Waldoboro, *Maine* 82 Dd
Waldport, *Oregon* 87 Ac
Walen See, *Switzerland* 45 Ea
Walenstadt, *Switzerland* 45 Ea
Wales, *Great Britain* 31 Eh
Walgett, *N.S.W.* 95 Jf
Walgreen Coast, *Antarctica* 100 Qb
Walker L., *Nevada* 87 Df
Walkerton, *Ontario* 83 Fc
Walkerville, *Ontario* 83 Ed
Wallace, *Idaho* 87 Fb
Wallaceburg, *Ontario* 83 Ed
Wallaroo, *S. Australia* 95 Gf
Wallaston, Mt., *N.T., Aust.* 94 Fc
Walla-Walla, *Washington* 87 Db
Wallenpaupack, L., *Pa.* 86 Cb
Wallowa Mts., *Oregon* 87 Ec
Walsall, *England* 31 Fh
Walsh, *Queensland* 95 Hc
Walsoorden, *Netherlands* 44 Cc
Waltham, *Massachusetts* 86 Ea
Waltham, *Quebec* 83 Hc
Walton, *New York* 86 Ca
Walvis Bay, *S.-W. Africa* 75 Ad
Walwale, *Ghana* 78 Ef
Wamba, *Congo* 77 Fd
Wamel, *Netherlands* 44 Dc
Wampsville, *New York* 83 Jd
Wana, *W. Pakistan* 70 Ad
Wanaaring, *N.S.W.* 95 He
Wanaka & L., *New Zealand* 93 Bf
Wandiwash, *India* 68 Ef
Wandoan, *Qnsld.* 95 Je
Wandre, *Belgium* 44 Dd
Wandsbek, *Germany* 48 Db
Wan Fou Shan, *China* 65 Gh
Wanganui & R., *N.Z.* 93 Ec
Wangaratta, *Victoria* 95 Jg
Wanhsien, *China* 62 Ed
Wankie, *Rhodesia* 75 Dc
Wanning, *Hainan* 65 En
Wanping, *China* 64 Hc
Wanyuan, *China* 64 Df
Wapiti R., *Alberta* 80 Hf
Warandab, *Ethiopia* 77 Jc
Warangal, *India* 68 Ee
Wardair, *Ethiopia* 77 Kc
Wardha & R., *India* 68 Ed
Waremme, *Belgium* 44 Dd
Waren, *Germany* 48 Eb
Warka, *Poland* 49 Jc
Warmbad, *S.-W. Africa* 75 Be
Warmbaths, *Transvaal* 75 Dd
Warnemünde, *Germany* 48 Ea
Warner Valley, *Oregon* 87 Dd
Warner's Ra., *Oregon* 87 Cd
Warneton, *Belgium* 44 Ad
Warora, *India* 68 Ed
Warragul, *Victoria* 95 Jg
Warren, *Illinois* 83 Bd
Warren, *Ohio* 83 Fe
Warren, *Pennsylvania* 86 Ab
Warrenpoint, *N. Ireland* 31 Cf
Warrenton, *Virginia* 86 Bc
Warri, *Nigeria* 78 Gg
Warrington, *England* 31 Fg
Warrnambool, *Victoria* 95 Hg
Warsaw, *Indiana* 83 De
Warsaw, *New York* 86 Aa
Warsaw. See Warszawa
Warszawa, *Poland* 49 Jb
Warta, *Poland* 49 Hc
Warta R., *Poland* 49 Hb
Warwick, *Queensland* 95 Ke
Warwick, *Rhode Island* 86 Eb
Warwick & co., *England* 31 Fh
Wasatch Mts., *Utah* 84 Dd
Wasen, *Switzerland* 45 Ca
Wash, The, *England* 31 Hh
Washakie Needles, *Wyoming* 84 Ec
Washington, *Dist. of Columb.* 83 Hf
Washington, *New Jersey* 86 Cb
Washington, *Ohio* 83 Ef
Washington, *Pennsylvania* 83 Fe
Washington, *Virginia* 86 Ac
Washington, state, *U.S.A.* 84 Bb
Washington I., *Pacific Ocean* 98 Jg
Washington Ld., *Greenland* 39 Qa
Washington, Mt., *N.H.* 82 Cd
Washir, *Afghanistan* 70 Aa
Washuk, *W. Pakistan* 68 Bc
Wasmes, *Belgium* 44 Bd
Wassen, *Switzerland* 45 Db
Waterbury, *Connecticut* 86 Db
Waterford, *New Brunswick* 82 Ec
Waterford (Port Láirge), *Eire* 31 Ch
Waterford Harb., *Eire* 31 Ch
Waterloo, *Belgium* 44 Cd
Waterloo, *Iowa* 85 Hc
Waterloo, *Ontario* 83 Fd
Waterloo, *Quebec* 83 Kc
Watertown, *New York* 83 Jd
Watertown, *S. Dakota* 84 Gc
Watertown *Wisconsin* 83 Bd
Waterville, *Maine* 82 Dd
Watervliet, *New York* 86 Da
Waterways, *Alberta* 80 Je
Watford, *England* 31 Gj
Watkins Glen, *New York* 86 Ba
Watlings I., *Bahama Is.* 89 Eb
Watou, *Belgium* 44 Ad
Watrous, *Saskatchewan* 80 Kf
Watsa, *Congo* 77 Fd
Watson Lake, *Yukon* 80 Fe
Watsonville, *California* 87 Cg
Watt, *New Brunswick* 82 Ed
Wau, *New Guinea* 95 Ja
Wau, *Sudan* 79 Lg
Wauchope, *N. Terr., Aust.* 95 Fd
Wau el Kebir, *Libya* 79 Jc
Waukegan, *Illinois* 83 Cd
Waukesha, *Wisconsin* 83 Bd
Waupaca, *Wisconsin* 83 Bc
Waupun, *Wisconsin* 83 Bd
Wausau, *Wisconsin* 83 Bc
Wautoma, *Wisconsin* 83 Bc
Wauwatosa, *Wisconsin* 83 Bd
Wave Hill, *N. Terr., Aust.* 94 Fc
Waveney R., *England* 31 Hh
Waverly, *New York* 86 Ba
Waverly, *Ohio* 83 Ef
Wavre, *Belgium* 44 Cd
Wawa (Jamestown), *Ontario* 83 Eb
Waycross, *Georgia* 85 Ke
Wayland. See Nicholson
Waynesboro, *Pennsylvania* 86 Bc
Waynesburg, *Pennsylvania* 83 Ff
Wazirabad, *W. Pakistan* 70 Dd
Waziristan, N. & S. *Pakistan* 70 Ad
Weald, The, *England* 31 Hj
Wear R., *England* 31 Ff
Weatherly, *Pennsylvania* 86 Cb
Webbwood, *Ontario* 83 Fb
Wechelderzande, *Belgium* 44 Cc
Weda B., *Halmahera, Indon.* 63 Jk
Weddell I., *Falkland Island* 92 Dh
Weddell Sea, *Antarctica* 100 Ac

Wedgeport, Nova Scotia 82 Fe
Weed, California 87 Be
Weedon, Quebec 83 Lc
Weedsport, New York 86 Ba
Weert, Netherlands 44 Dc
Weesen, Switzerland 45 Ea
Weesp, Netherlands 44 Db
Weichang, China 64 Jb
Weiden, Germany 48 Ed
Weifang, China 64 Jd
Wei-hai, China 64 Ld
Wei Ho., R., China 62 Ed
Weihwei. See Chihsien
Weimar, Germany 48 Dc
Weinfelden, Switzerland 45 Ea
Weiser, Idaho 87 Ec
Wei Shan Hu, China 64 He
Weissenfels, Germany 48 Dc
Weisshorn, Mt., Switzerland 45 Cb
Weissmies, Mt., Switzerland 45 Db
Weisstannen, Switzerland 45 Ea
Wejh. See Al Wajh
Welford, Queensland 95 He
Welland, Ontario 83 Gd
Wellesley Is., Queensland 95 Gc
Wellin, Belgium 44 Dd
Wellingborough, England 31 Gh
Wellington, New Zealand 93 Ed
Wellington, I., Chile 92 Bg
Wells, England 31 Hh
Wells, England 31 Fj
Wells, Nevada 87 Fe
Wellsboro, Pennsylvania 86 Bb
Wellsville, New York 86 Ba
Wels, Austria 48 Ed
Welsford, New Brunswick 82 Ed
Welshpool, Wales 31 Eh
Wema, Congo 76 Ee
Wembo Niama, Congo 76 Ee
Wenatchee, Washington 87 Cb
Wenchow, China 65 Kh
Wenshan, China 65 Bl
Wensi, China 64 Ee
Wernhout, Netherlands 44 Cc
Wervershoof, Netherlands 44 Db
Wervica, Belgium 44 Bd
Wesel, Germany 48 Bc
Wesenberg, Germany 48 Eb
Weser R., Germany 48 Cb
Wessel Is., N. Terr., Aust. 95 Gb
West Allis, Wisconsin 83 Bd
West Barra, Shetland 30 Ja
West Bend, Wisconsin 83 Bd
West Bengal, India 69 Gd
West Branch, Michigan 83 Dc
West Bromwich, England 31 Fh
Westbrook, Maine 82 Ce
West Chester, Pennsylvania 86 Cc
Westende, Belgium 44 Ac
Westerloo, Belgium 44 Cc
Westerly, Rhode Island 86 Eb
Western Australia, state,
Australia 94 Dd
Wester Schelde, Netherlands 44 Bc
Westfalen, Germany 48 Cc
Westfield, Massachusetts 83 Kd
Westfield, New Brunswick 82 Ed
Westfield, New York 86 Aa
Westfield, Pennsylvania 86 Bb
West Hartlepool, England 31 Gf
West Indies, Caribbean Sea 97 Cg
West Irian, prov., N. Guinea 63 Kl
Westkapelle, Netherlands 44 Bc
West Lothian, co., Scotland 30 Ee
West Malaysia (Malaya),
S.-E. Asia 63 Dk
Westmeath, co., Eire 31 Cg
Westminster, Maryland 86 Bc
Westmorland, co., England 31 Ff
West Nicholson, Rhodesia 75 Dd
Weston, N. Borneo 63 Gj
Weston, West Virginia 83 Ff
Weston-super-Mare, Eng. 31 Fj
West Pakistan, S. Asia 68 Cc
West Palm Beach, Florida 85 Lf
West Point, New York 86 Db
Westport, Eire 31 Ag
Westport, New Zealand 93 Cd
Westport, Ontario 83 Hc
Westray I., Orkney 31 Ea
Westree, Ontario 83 Fb
West St. John, N.B. 82 Ed
West Riding, Yorks, Eng. 31 Gg
West Virginia, state, U.S.A. 85 Kd
Westwoud, Netherlands 44 Db
Wetar, I. & Str., Indonesia 63 Jm
Wetaskiwin, Alberta 80 Jf
Wetterhorn, Mt.,Switzerland 45 Db
Wexford & co., Eire 31 Ch
Weyburn, Saskatchewan 80 Lg
Weymont, Quebec 83 Kb
Weymouth, England 31 Fk
Weymouth, Nova Scotia 82 Fd
Whakataki, New Zealand 93 Fd
Whakatane, New Zealand 93 Fb
Whale R., Quebec 81 Te
Whale, R., Gt. & Lit. Quebec 81 Re
Whales, B. of, Antarctica 100 Mb
Whalsay I., Shetland 30 Ja
Whangarei, New Zealand 93 Ea
Wharanui, New Zealand 93 Ed
Whataroa, New Zealand 93 Ce
Wheeler Pk., Nevada 87 Ff
Wheeling, W. Virginia 83 Fe
Whitbourne, Newfoundland 82 Mc
Whitby, England 31 Gf
Whitby, Ontario 83 Gd
White, B., Newfoundland 82 Ka
White Mts., New Hampshire 83 Lc
White R., Arkansas 85 Hd
White R., S. Dakota 84 Fc
White R., Yukon 80 Cd
Whitefish, Montana 84 Db
Whitefish B., Michigan 83 Db
Whitehall, Michigan 83 Cd
Whitehall, New York 83 Kd
Whitehaven, England 31 Ef
Whitehorse, Yukon 80 Dd
White Oil Springs. See Naft
White Pass, Brit. Columbia 80 Ee
White Plains, New York 86 Db
White River, Ontario 81 Qg
White River Junction, Vt. 85 Mc
White Russia, rep. See Belorussia
White Volta, R., Ghana 78 Eg
Whiting, New Jersey 83 Jf
Whitney, Ontario 83 Gc
Whitney, Mt., California 87 Dg
Whittier, California 87 Dj
Wholdaia L., N.-W. Terr. 80 Ld
Wiarton, Ontario 83 Fc
Wichita, Kansas 84 Gd
Wichita Falls. Texas 84 Ge
Wick, Scotland 30 Eb
Wicklow & co., Eire 31 Ch
Wicklow Head, Eire 31 Ch
Wicklow Mts., Eire 31 Cg
Wielbark, Poland 49 Jb
Wielen, Poland 49 Gb
Wieliczka, Poland 49 Jd
Wielun, Poland 49 Hc
Wien, Austria 49 Gd
Wiener Neustadt, Austria 49 Ge
Wiesbaden, Germany 48 Cc
Wiesen, Switzerland 45 Eb
Wigan, England 31 Fg
Wight, I. of, England 31 Gk
Wigtown & co., Scotland 31 Ef
Wigtown B., Scotland 31 Ef
Wijhe, Netherlands 44 Eb
Wijk, Netherlands 44 Dd
Wijk, Netherlands 44 Dc
Wil, Switzerland 45 Ea
Wilcannia, New. S. Wales 95 Hf
Wildhorn, Mt., Switzerland 45 Cb
Wildstrubel, Mt., Switzerland 45 Cb
Wildwood, New Jersey 83 Jf
Wilhelmshaven, Germany 48 Cb
Wilkes Coast, Antarctica 100 Jc
Wilkes Ld., Antarctica 100 Hb
Wilkes Barre, Pennsylvania 86 Cb
Wilkin's Str., Antarctica 100 Sb
Wilkolaz, Poland 49 Kc
Willamette R., Oregon 87 Bc
Willemsdorp, Netherlands 44 Cc
Willemstad, Curaçao I. 90 Da
Willemstad, Netherlands 44 Cc
Williambury, W. Aust. 94 Bd
William Creek, S. Aust. 95 Ge
Williams, Arizona 84 Dd
Williams Pt., N.-W. Terr. 80 Hc
Williamsport, Pennsylvania 86 Bb
Willimantic, Connecticut 86 Db
Williston, N. Dakota 84 Fb
Williston, Cape Province 75 Cf
Willmar, Minnesota 84 Gb
Willow L., N.-W. Terr. 80 Gd
Willow Lake R., N.-W. Terr. 80 Gd
Willowmore, Cape Province 75 Cf
Wills Mt., Pennsylvania 86 Ac
Wilmette, Illinois 83 Cd
Wilmington, California 87 Dj
Wilmington, Delaware 86 Cc
Wilmington, N. Carolina 85 Le
Wilnis, Netherlands 44 Cb
Wilno, Ontario 83 Hc
Wilson, N. Carolina 85 Ld
Wiltshire (Wilts), co., Eng. 31 Fj
Wiluna, W. Australia 94 De
Winburg, Orange Free State 75 De
Winchendon, Massachusetts 83 Kd
Winchester, England 31 Gj
Winchester, Ontario 83 Jc
Winchester, Virginia 86 Ac
Wind R., Yukon 80 Dc
Wind Cave Nat. Park,
S. Dakota 84 Fc
Windermere & L., England 31 Ff
Windhoek, S.-W. Africa 75 Bd
Windorah, Queensland 95 He
Wind River Pk. & Mts., Wyo. 84 Ec
Windsor, Connecticut 86 Db
Windsor, England 31 Gj
Windsor, Nova Scotia 82 Fd
Windsor, Ontario 83 Ed
Windsor, Vermont 83 Kd
Windsor Mills, Quebec 83 Lc
Windward Is., West Indies 89 Gd
Windward Pass, West Indies 89 Ec
Wingham, Ontario 83 Fd
Winisk R., Ontario 81 Pf
Winnebago L., Wisconsin 83 Bc
Winnemucca, Nevada 87 Ee
Winnemucca L., Nevada 87 De
Winner, S. Dakota 84 Gc
Winning Pool, W. Aust. 94 Bd
Winnipeg, Manitoba 80 Mg
Winnipeg, L., Manitoba 80 Mf
Winnipegosis, Manitoba 80 Mf
Winnipegosis, L., Manitoba 80 Lf
Winnipesaukee, L., N.H. 83 Ld
Winschoten, Netherlands 44 Ea
Winslow, Arizona 84 Dd
Winsted, Connecticut 86 Db
Winston-Salem, N. Carolina 85 Kd
Winter Ra. See Fremont Mts.
Winterhaven, California 87 Fj
Winterport, Maine 82 Dd
Winterswijk, Netherlands 44 Ec
Winterthur, Switzerland 45 Da
Winton, New Zealand 93 Bg
Winton, Queensland 95 Hd
Wisbech, England 31 Hh
Wisconsin, state, U.S.A. 85 Hc
Wisconsin R., Wisconsin 83 Bc
Wisconsin Rapids, Wisconsin 83 Bc
Wisla R., Poland 49 Jc
Wismar, Germany 48 Db
Witham R., England 31 Gg
Withlacoochee B., Florida 85 Kf
Witputs, S.-W. Africa 75 Be
Witry, Belgium 44 De
Witten, Germany 48 Bc
Wittenberg, Germany 48 Ec
Wittenberge, Germany 48 Db
Wittenoom, Western Aust. 94 Cd
Wittingen, Germany 48 Db
Wittstock, Germany 48 Eb
Włocławek, Poland 49 Hb
Woerden, Netherlands 44 Cb
Wognum, Netherlands 44 Db
Wohlen, Switzerland 45 Da
Wokam, I., Indonesia 63 Km
Wolbrom, Poland 49 Hc
Woleai, I., Caroline Islands 98 Dg
Wolfe I., Ontario 83 Hc
Wolfeboro, New Hampshire 83 Ld
Wolfsberg, Austria 48 Fe
Wolfville, Nova Scotia 82 Fd
Wolgast, Germany 48 Ea
Wolhusen, Switzerland 45 Ca
Wollal, W. Australia 94 Dc
Wollaston Foreland,Greenland 39 Mb
Wollaston Is., Chile 92 Cj
Wollaston L., Saskatchewan 80 Le
Wollongong, New S. Wales 95 Kf
Wolstenholme, C., Quebec 81 Rd
Wolvega, Netherlands 44 Eb
Wolverhampton, England 31 Fh
Wolverthem, Belgium 44 Cd
Wolverton, England 31 Gh
Woman River, Ontario 83 Eb
Wŏnsan, Korea 62 Jc
Wonthaggi, Victoria 95 Jg
Wood R., Saskatchewan 80 Kg
Wood Buffalo Park, Alberta 80 Je
Woodbury, New Jersey 86 Cc
Woodlark I., New Guinea 95 Ka
Woodroffe, Mt., S. Australia 94 Fe
Woods Hole, Massachusetts 86 Eb
Woods, L., N. Terr., Aust. 94 Fc
Woods, L. of the, Ontario 80 Ng
Woodside, Victoria 95 Jg
Woodstock, Illinois 83 Bd
Woodstock, New Brunswick 82 Ec
Woodstock, Ontario 83 Fd
Woodstock, Vermont 83 Kd
Woodstock, Virginia 86 Ac
Woodsville, New Hampshire 88 Kc
Woodville, New Zealand 93 Ed
Woomera, S. Australia 95 Gf
Woonsocket, Rhode Island 86 Eb
Wooramel, W. Aust. 94 Be
Worcester, Cape Province 75 Bf
Worcester, Massachusetts 83 Ld
Worcester & co., England 31 Fh
Workington, England 31 Ef
Workum, Netherlands 44 Db
Worms, Germany 48 Cd
Worthington, Minnesota 84 Gc
Worthington, Ontario 83 Fb
Wotho, I., Marshall Islands 90 Ff
Woudenberg, Netherlands 44 Db
Woudrichem, Netherlands 44 Cc
Wounta. See Huaonta
Wour, Chad 79 Jd
Wouw, Netherlands 44 Cc
Wowoni, I., Indonesia 63 Hl
Wrangel I. (Os. Vrangelya),
Arctic Ocean 59 Sa
Wrangell, Alaska 85 Zm
Wrangell, Mt., Alaska 85 Yl
Wrath C., Scotland 30 Db
Wrexham, Wales 31 Fg
Wright, Philippines 63 Jh
Wrigley, N.-W. Territories 80 Jd
Wrocław, Poland 49 Gc
Wubin, W. Aust. 94 Cf
Wuchang, China 62 Jb
Wuchang, China 65 Gg
Wuchih, Hainan Island 62 Eg
Wuchow, China 65 El
Wuchwan, China 64 Eb
Wudam, Muscat & Oman 73 Ge
Wuestwezel, Belgium 44 Cc
Wuhan, China 64 Gg
Wuhing. See Huchow
Wuhsien. See Soochow
Wuhu, China 64 Jg
Wukang, China 65 Ej
Wukari, Nigeria 79 Gg
Wukiang, China 64 Gd
Wu Kiang, R., China 62 Ee
Wular L., Kashmir 70 Dc
Wuntho, Burma 69 Jd
Wuppertal, Germany 48 Bc
Württemberg, Germany 48 Cd
Wurung, Queensland 95 Hc
Wurzburg, Germany 48 Cd
Wurzen, Germany 48 Ec
Wusiang, China 64 Fd
Wusih, China 64 Kg
Wuti, China 64 Hd
Wutsin, China 64 Kg
Wuwei, China 64 Ad
Wu Yi Shan, China 65 Hj
Wuyüan, China 64 Db
Wuyun, China 62 Ja
Wyandotte, Michigan 83 Ed
Wyandra, Queensland 95 Je
Wye R., England-Wales 31 Fh
Wyk, Germany 48 Ca
Wyndham, New Zealand 93 Bg
Wyndham, W. Australia 94 Ec
Wynghene, Belgium 44 Bc
Wyoming, state, U.S.A. 84 Ec
Wyoming Pk., Wyoming 84 Dc
Wysokie Mazowieckie,Poland 49 Kb
Wyszkow, Poland 49 Jb
Xanthi, Greece 56 Ed
Xanxere, Brazil 92 Fc
Xapuri, Brazil 90 Df
Xeró. See Peristéra I.
Xilókastron, Greece 57 De
Xingu, Brazil 90 De
Xique Xique, Brazil 91 Jf
Yaan, China 62 Dd
Yaate, Lebanon 74 Ec
Yablonovy Khrebet, Russia 59 Lc
Yabrud, Syria 74 Ed
Yagvildino, Russia 61 Nc
Yakhtul, Yemen 72 Dg
Yakima, Washington 87 Cb
Yako, Volta 78 Ef
Yakoma, Congo 76 Ed
Yaku Jima, Japan 66 Aj
Yaku Kaikyo. See Tanegashima
Kaikyo
Yakutsk, Russia 59 Mb
Yale, British Columbia 80 Gg
Yale, Michigan 83 Ed
Yalgoo, W. Australia 94 Ce
Yalinga, Cent. Afr. Rep. 76 Ec
Yalouke, Cent. Afr. Rep. 76 Dc
Yalta, Russia 60 Jj
Yalu, China 62 Ha
Yalu R., China, etc. 62 Hb
Yalung R., China 62 Dd
Yalutorovsk, Russia 58 Fc
Yamada. See Ise
Yamagata, Japan 66 Fe
Yamaguchi, Japan 66 Bg
Yamal, Pol., Russia 58 Fa
Yambol, Bulgaria 56 Fc
Yamdok Tso, Tibet 69 Hc
Yamethin, Burma 69 Jd
Yampol, Ukraine 60 Fg
Yampol, Ukraine 60 Eg
Yamsk, Russia 59 Qc
Yamuna R., India 71 Aa
Yanam, India 69 Fe
Yanaoca, Peru 90 Cf
Yanbu 'al Bahr, Arabia 72 Ce
Yandoon, Burma 69 Je
Yangchow. See Kiangtu
Yangi Hissar, China 70 Ea
Yang-kao, China 64 Fb
Yangku. See Taiyuan
Yangtze Kiang, China 64 Eg
Yangyuan, China 64 Gb
Yankton, S. Dakota 84 Gc
Yannina. See Ioannina
Yaouiba, Bolivia 90 Eh
Yaoundé, Cameroon 79 Hh
Yap, I., Pacific Ocean 98 Cg
Yaraka, Queensland 95 Hd
Yarda, Chad 79 Je
Yarensk, Russia 58 Db
Yarim, Yemen 72 Dg
Yarkand, China 70 Ea
Yarmouth, Maine 82 Ce
Yarmouth, Nova Scotia 82 Ee
Yaroslavl, Russia 60 Lc
Yartsevo, Russia 59 Jb
Yarumal, Colombia 90 Bb
Yarylgach, Russia 60 Hj
Yasin, Kashmir 70 Cb
Yasothon, Siam 63 Dg
Yass, New S. Wales 95 Jf
Yatakala, Niger 78 Ff
Yathkyed L., North-West
Territories 80 Md
Yatsushiro, Japan 66 Bh
Yatung, Tibet 69 Gc
Yauca, Peru 90 Cg
Yauri, Peru 90 Cf
Yautepec, Mexico 88 Ed
Yawata, Japan 66 Bh
Yazd, Persia 73 Fc
Yazdan, Persia 73 Hc
Yazd-e-Khrast, Persia 73 Fc
Ybbs, Austria 48 Fd
Ye, Burma 69 Je
Yecla, Spain 51 Ec
Yecora, Mexico 88 Cb
Yéfira, Greece 57 Dd
Yefremov, Russia 60 Le
Yegros, Paraguay 92 Ec
Yehkiatsi, China 62 Gd
Yehpaishow, China 64 Jb
Yehsien, China 64 Jd
Yelabuga, Russia 61 Lc
Yelan, Russia 61 Fe
Yelatma, Russia 61 Ec
Yeldyak, Russia 61 Nc
Yelets, Russia 60 Le
Yelizarovo, Russia 58 Fb
Yell I. & Sd., Scotland 30 Ja
Yellandu, India 68 Fe
Yellow R. See Hwang Ho
Yellow Sea, China 64 Ke
Yellowhead Pass, Alberta 80 Hf
Yellowstone, L., Wyoming 84 Dc
Yellowstone Nat. Park,
Wyoming 84 Dc
Yellowstone R., Montana 84 Eb
Yelwa, Nigeria 78 Ff
Yemanzhelinka, Russia 61 Qc
Yemen, S.-W. Asia 72 Df
Yenakiyevo, Ukraine 60 Lg
Yenan. See Fushih
Yenangyaung. See Kyaukpadating
Yen-Bay, N. Vietnam 67 Cb
Yenbo. See Yanbu 'al Bahr
Yencheng, China 64 Kf
Yenchih. See Mingshui
Yenchow. See Kienteh
Yenchow. See Tzeyang
Yenisey, R., Russia 58 Hb
Yeniseysk, Russia 59 Jc
Yeniseyskiy Zaliv, Russia 58 Ha
Yenkishih, China 62 Jb
Yenping. See Nanping
Yentai, China 64 Kd
Yeovil, England 31 Fk
Yeppoon, Qnsld. 95 Kd
Yeráki, Greece 57 Df
Yerbogachen, Russia 59 Kb
Yerevan, Armyanskaya S.S.R. 58 Dd
Yerofei Pavlovich, Russia 59 Mc
Yeropol, Russia 59 Rb
Yeshbum, S. Yemen 72 Eg
Yesseiy, Russia 59 Kb
Yeste, Spain 51 Dc
Yesud ha Ma'ala, Israel 74 Dd
Ye-u, Burma 69 Jd
Yeu, I. d', France 52 Bc
Yeungkong, China 62 Ff
Yeysk, Russia 58 Cd
Yhu, Paraguay 92 Ec
Yi, R., Uruguay 92 Ed
Yianisadhes Is., Crete 57 Fg
Yiannitsá, Greece 57 Dd
Yiáros. See Yioúra, I.
Yibna, Israel 74 Cf
Yidha, Greece 57 Dd
Yihsien, China 64 Gc
Yingchow. See Fowyang
Yingchwan, China 64 Cc
Yinghsien, China 64 Fc
Yingkisha. See Yangi Hissar
Yingkow, China 64 Lb
Yingtak, China 65 Fk
Yin Shan, China 64 Cb
Yioúra, I., Greece 57 Ef
Yithion, Greece 57 Df
Yitu, China 64 Jd
Yiyang, China 65 Fh
Yocalla, Bolivia 90 Dg
Yochow. See Yoyang
Yogovsk, Russia 61 Nb
Yoho Park, Brit. Columbia 80 Hf
Yokkaichi, Japan 66 Eg
Yoko, Cameroon 79 Hg
Yokohama, Japan 66 Fg
Yokosuku, Japan 66 Fg
Yokote, Japan 66 Ge
Yola, Nigeria 79 Hg
Yonago, Japan 66 Cg
Yone Zawa, Japan 66 Gf
Yonkers, New York 86 Db
Yonne, dep., France 52 Ec
York, England 31 Gg
York, Nebraska 84 Gc
York, Pennsylvania 86 Bc
York, W. Australia 94 Cf
York, C., Greenland 39 Qb
York, C., Queensland 95 Hb
York Factory, Manitoba 81 Ne
York Harbour, Maine 82 Ce
York Sd., W. Australia 94 Db
Yorke Pen., S. Australia 95 Gf
Yorkshire (Yorks), co.,
England 31 Ff
Yorkshire Moors, England 31 Gf
Yorkshire Wolds, England 31 Gf
Yorkton, Saskatchewan 80 Lf
Yoro, Honduras 89 Bd
Yosemite Nat. Park, Cal. 87 Dg
Yoshkar Ola, Russia 61 Hb
Youghal & Harb., Eire 31 Bj
Youghiogheny River Res.,
Penn, etc. 86 Ac
Youkadouma, Cameroon 79 Jh
Young, N.S.W. 95 Jf
Young I., Balleny Islands 100 Lc
Youngstown, Ohio 83 Fe
Yoyang, China 65 Fh
Yozgat, Turkey 72 Bb
Ypres, Belgium 44 Ad
Ypsilanti, Michigan 83 Ed
Yreka, California 87 Be
Yssingeaux, France 53 Fd
Ystad, Sweden 47 Ej
Ytterhogdal, Sweden 46 Fe
Yüanchow. See Chihkiang
Yüanchow. See Ichun
Yüanling, China 65 Eh
Yubi C., Morocco 78 Cc
Yucamani, Mt., Peru 90 Cg
Yucatán, state, Mexico 88 Gd
Yucatán Chan., Mex.-Cuba 89 Bb
Yugoslavia, Cent. Europe 54 Fc
Yuhsien, China 64 Gc
Yuhwan, China 65 Kh
Yukhnov, Russia 60 Jd
Yukon Terr., Canada 80 Dd
Yukon, R., Alaska 85 Wl
Yuksekova, Turkey 72 Db
Yulin, China 64 Dc
Yulin, Hainan 65 De
Yuma, Arizona 84 Dd
Yumen, China 59 Jd
Yungchow. See Lingling
Yungfu, China 65 Ek
Yungki. See Kirin
Yungkia. See Wenchow
Yungnien, China 64 Gd
Yungning, China 65 Dl
Yungning, China 62 De
Yungping. See Lulung
Yungshun, China 65 Dh
Yungsin, China 65 Gj
Yungsui, China 65 Dh
Yungtsi, China 64 Ee
Yunhsien, China 64 Ef
Yunsi, China 64 Ef
Yurievets, Russia 61 Fb
Yurimaguas, Peru 90 Be
Yurlovka, Russia 61 Hd
Yurmysh, Russia 61 Rb
Yushu, China 62 Cd
Yuta, Jordan 74 Df
Yutai, Bolivia 90 Eg
Yütze, China 64 Fd
Yuyang, China 65 Dh
Yuyu, China 64 Fb
Yverdon, Switzerland 45 Bb
Zaachila, Mexico 88 Ed
Zaandam, Netherlands 44 Cb
Zabaykal'sk, Russia 59 Ld
Zabid, Yemen 72 Dg
Zabol, Persia 73 Hc
Zabrze, Poland 49 Hc
Zacapa, Guatemala 88 Ge
Zacapoaxtla, Mexico 88 Ed
Zacatecas & state, Mexico 88 Dc
Zader, Yugoslavia 54 Ec
Zadonsk, Russia 60 Le
Zafarwal, W. Pakistan 70 Dd
Zafra, Spain 50 Bc
Zagazig, Egypt 79 Mb
Zagreb, Yugoslavia 54 Ec
Zahedan, Persia 73 Hd
Zahle, Lebanon 74 Dd
Zahran, Arabia 72 Df
Zaidiya, Yemen 72 Df
Zainsk, Russia 61 Lc
Zaječar, Yugoslavia 56 Dc
Zakho, Iraq 72 Db
Zakin, Afghanistan 73 Hc
Zakinthos, I., Greece 57 Cf
Zakroczyn, Poland 49 Jb
Zákros Crete 57 Fg
Zălău, Rumania 49 Ke
Zalew Wislany, Poland 49 Ha
Zalt Bommel, Netherlands 44 Dc
Zambezi R., S.-E. Africa 75 Ec
Zambia, Cent. Africa 75 Db
Zamboanga, Philippines 63 Hj
Zamora, Ecuador 90 Bd
Zamora, Mexico 88 Dd
Zamora, Spain 50 Cb
Zandberg, Netherlands 44 Eb
Zandvoort, Netherlands 44 Cb
Zanesville, Ohio 83 Ef
Zangla, Kashmir 70 Ed
Zanjan, Persia 72 Eb
Zank, Muscat & Oman 73 Ge
Zante. See Zakinthos I.
Zanthus, W. Australia 94 Df
Zanzibar & I., E. Africa 77 Hf
Zapala, Argentina 92 Be
Zapallar. See General José de
San Martin
Zapata Pen., Cuba 89 Cb
Zaporozhye, Ukraine 60 Jh
Zara, Turkey 72 Cb
Zara. See Zader
Zaragoza, Colombia 90 Cb
Zaragoza, Mexico 88 Ec
Zaragoza, Spain 51 Eb
Zaragoza, Mexico 88 Db
Zarand, Persia 73 Gc
Zarasai, Lithuania 47 Mj
Zarauz, Spain 51 Da
Zaraza, Venezuela 90 Db
Zaria, Nigeria 78 Gf
Zarki, Poland 49 Hc
Zarqa, Jordan 74 Ee
Zaruma, Ecuador 90 Bd
Zarzis, Tunisia 79 Hb
Zatec, Czechoslovakia 48 Ec
Zavitinsk, Russia 59 Mc
Zawiercie, Poland 49 Hc
Zaysan, Kazakh. 58 Hd
Zaysan, Oz., Kazakh. 58 Hd
Zbaszyn, Poland 49 Fb
Zduńska Wola, Poland 49 Hc
Zealand, New Brunswick 82 Ec
Zealand. See Sjælland
Zebak, Afghanistan 73 Kb
Zebdani, Syria 74 Ed
Zebid Qadhima, Arabia 72 Ce
Zeebrugge, Belgium 44 Bc
Zeeland, prov., Netherlands 44 Bc
Zeerust, Transvaal 75 De
Zegharta, Lebanon 74 Dc
Zeila, Somalia 77 Jb
Zeist, Netherlands 44 Db
Zeitz, Germany 48 Ec
Zele, Belgium 44 Cc
Zelenogradsk, Russia 47 Jj
Železná Ruda, Czech. 48 Ed
Zella, Libya 79 Jc
Zelman, Russia 61 Ge
Zelzate, Belgium 44 Bc
Zemio, Cent Afr. Rep. 79 Lg
Zemun, Yugoslavia 56 Cb
Zenica, Yugoslavia 56 Ab
Zepce, Yugoslavia 56 Ab
Zermatt, Switzerland 45 Cb
Zernez, Switzerland 45 Eb
Zetland (Shetland), Scotland 30 Ja
Zevenbergen, Netherlands 44 Cc
Zeya, Russia 59 Mc
Zeyma, Arabia 72 De
Zgierz, Poland 49 Hc
Zgorzelec. See Görlitz
Zhdanov, Ukraine 60 Kh
Zhigansk, Russia 59 Mb
Zhitomir, Ukraine 60 Ff
Zhmerinka, Ukraine 60 Fg
Ziarat, W. Pakistan 68 Cb
Ziba. See Dhaba
Zidani Most, Yugoslavia 54 Eb
Zierikzee, Netherlands 44 Bc
Zijpe, Netherlands 44 Cc
Zikhron Ya'aqov, Israel 74 Ce
Zilaf, Syria 74 Fe
Zile, Turkey 72 Ca
Zilfi, Arabia 72 Dd
Zilina, Czechoslovakia 49 Hd
Zima, Russia 59 Kc
Zimapan, Mexico 88 Ec
Zindajan, Afghanistan 73 Hc
Zinder, Niger 79 Gf
Zingst, pen., Germany 48 Ea
Zion Nat. Park, Utah 87 Gg
Zipaquira, Colombia 90 Cb
Zira, India 70 De
Zirc, Hungary 49 Ge
Zitacuaro, Mexico 88 Dd
Zittau, Germany 48 Fc
Zizers, Switzerland 45 Eb
Zlatoust, Russia 61 Pc
Zmeinogorsk, Russia 58 Hc
Znin, Poland 49 Gb
Znojmo, Czechoslovakia 49 Gd
Zofingen, Switzerland 45 Ca
Zohab, Persia 72 Ec
Zoisa, Tanzania 77 Hf
Zolder, Belgium 44 Dc
Zollino, Italy 55 Ge
Zomba, Malawi 77 Hh
Zonguldak, Turkey 72 Ba
Zorita, Spain 50 Cc
Zoute, le, Belgium 44 Bc
Zoutkamp, Netherlands 44 Ea
Zrenjanin, Yugoslavia 56 Cb
Zuara, Libya 79 Hb
Zuevka, Russia 61 Ka
Zug & canton, Switzerland 45 Da
Zuger See, Switzerland 45 Da
Zuid Beijerland, Netherlands 44 Cc
Zuider Zee. See Ijssel Meer
Zuidland, Netherlands 44 Cc
Zuidwolde, Netherlands 44 Eb
Zuila, Libya 79 Jc
Zukur, Jab., Yemen 72 Dg
Zula, Eritrea 77 Ha
Zulfikar, Afghanistan 73 Hb
Zumbo, Moçambique 75 Ec
Zumpango, Mexico 88 Ed
Zundert, Netherlands 44 Cc
Zungeru, Nigeria 78 Gg
Zürich & canton, Switz. 45 Da
Zürich See, Switzerland 45 Da
Zurzach, Switzerland 45 Da
Zutphen, Netherlands 44 Eb
Zwai L., Ethiopia 77 Hc
Zwartsluis, Netherlands 44 Eb
Zweelo, Netherlands 44 Eb
Zweibrucken, W. Germany 48 Bd
Zweisimmen, Switzerland 45 Cb
Zwickau, Germany 48 Ec
Zwoleń, Poland 49 Jc
Zwolle, Netherlands 44 Eb
Zyrardów, Poland 49 Jb
Zyryanka, Russia 59 Pb
Zyryanovsk, Kazakh. 58 Hd
Zyyi, Cyprus 74 Bc

TABLE OF DISTANCES
(STATUTE MILES)

	Vienna	Tokyo	Sydney	Singapore	San Francisco	Rome	Rio de Janeiro	Peking	Paris	Ottawa	Oslo	New York	Nairobi	Moscow	Madrid	London	Lisbon	Lagos	Johannesburg	Istanbul	Hong Kong	Hamburg	Geneva	Delhi	Darwin	Colombo	Cologne	Chicago	Cape Town	Canberra	Calcutta	Cairo	Buenos Aires	Brasilia	Bombay	Beirut	Bahamas (Nassau)	Baghdad
Athens	793	5,906	9,522	5,627	6,791	648	6,035	4,737	1,306	4,820	1,625	4,921	2,833	1,402	1,466	1,501	1,772	2,544	4,434	345	5,310	1,268	1,068	3,110	7,676	4,103	1,212	5,446	4,976	9,452	3,925	693	7,274	5,937	3,211	716	5,737	1,199
Baghdad	1,764	5,196	8,324	4,431	7,460	1,824	6,939	3,914	2,394	5,837	2,386	5,985	2,442	1,599	2,660	2,554	2,970	3,208	4,245	1,004	5,879	2,186	2,192	1,960	5,550	4,258	2,225	6,418	4,967	8,252	2,767	796	8,143	6,942	2,012	513	6,880	
Bahamas (Nassau)	5,126	7,596	9,477	10,613	2,761	5,072	4,025	7,868	4,486	1,404	4,670	1,096	7,779	5,673	4,301	4,335	4,102	5,454	7,879	5,879	9,070	4,740	4,692	8,364	10,399	9,783	4,666	1,297	7,492	9,590	9,037	6,382	4,318	3,457	8,792	6,458		
Beirut	1,390	5,594	8,813	4,934	7,299	1,361	6,481	4,336	1,981	5,483	2,123	5,604	2,430	1,533	2,180	2,163	2,484	2,786	4,173	614	4,752	1,849	1,761	2,470	6,998	3,388	1,847	6,090	4,811	8,739	3,279	350	7,700	6,449	2,508			
Bombay	3,703	4,183	6,312	2,432	8,392	3,831	8,339	2,945	4,353	7,569	4,129	7,786	2,819	3,139	4,671	4,481	4,981	4,737	4,327	2,995	2,672	4,057	4,173	709	4,508	949	4,151	8,042	5,116	6,246	1,035	2,698	9,287	8,546				
Brasilia	5,928	10,996	8,777	9,863	6,072	5,523	569	10,531	5,421	4,571	6,157	4,242	5,852	6,945	4,820	5,456	4,531	3,832	3,876	5,876	11,187	5,888	5,448	8,845	10,464	8,855	5,678	4,738	4,281	8,730	9,543	6,158	1,456					
Buenos Aires	7,358	11,403	7,311	9,863	6,465	6,945	1,213	12,001	6,878	5,639	7,624	5,303	6,473	8,388	6,266	6,919	5,985	5,044	4,933	7,616	11,467	7,348	6,892	9,815	9,117	9,167	7,135	5,624	4,279	7,272	10,279	7,356						
Cairo	1,470	5,939	8,950	5,129	7,458	1,321	6,153	4,678	1,992	5,500	2,271	5,602	2,203	1,809	2,080	2,195	2,365	2,443	3,893	763	5,048	1,946	1,755	2,736	7,206	3,513	1,900	6,137	4,507	8,863	3,533							
Calcutta	4,245	3,187	5,679	1,801	7,816	4,482	9,372	2,018	4,876	7,619	4,456	7,918	3,840	3,449	5,318	4,962	5,637	5,734	5,263	3,647	1,642	4,504	4,747	816	3,756	1,232	4,646	7,966	6,026	5,640								
Canberra	9,885	4,933	148	3,863	7,572	10,093	8,339	5,594	10,515	10,007	9,937	10,090	7,407	9,013	10,915	10,569	11,221	9,503	5,703	9,237	4,556	10,107	10,385	6,440	1,952	5,350	10,276	9,379	6,685									
Cape Town	5,673	9,147	6,830	6,001	10,252	5,251	3,784	8,040	5,803	8,026	6,503	7,804	2,548	6,313	5,339	6,010	5,333	2,974	790	5,224	7,372	6,074	5,597	5,769	6,962	4,890	5,903	8,520										
Chicago	4,701	6,307	9,233	9,355	1,851	4,826	5,309	6,585	4,140	651	4,044	723	8,022	4,956	4,192	3,945	3,997	5,980	8,712	5,476	7,788	4,249	4,385	7,472	9,345	8,977	4,248											
Cologne	463	5,809	10,292	6,441	5,600	677	5,942	4,860	247	3,072	639	3,765	4,008	1,284	883	331	1,149	3,069	5,475	1,239	5,729	227	323	3,862	8,334	5,102												
Colombo	4,658	4,261	5,430	1,698	9,047	4,739	8,508	3,208	5,295	8,530	5,098	8,755	3,019	4,106	5,569	5,416	5,870	5,247	3,916	4,141	2,523	5,019	5,105	1,513	3,746													
Darwin	8,008	3,365	1,960	2,079	7,652	8,238	9,970	3,727	8,583	9,683	7,990	9,983	6,466	7,062	9,070	8,619	9,390	8,847	6,602	7,404	2,656	8,151	8,480	4,571														
Delhi	3,448	3,640	6,483	2,580	7,692	3,669	8,740	2,352	4,091	7,055	3,724	7,304	3,366	2,702	4,509	4,183	4,828	5,019	4,960	2,833	2,344	3,732	3,946															
Geneva	507	6,094	10,425	6,523	5,823	444	5,680	5,104	245	3,754	962	3,852	3,782	1,498	627	468	929	2,745	5,189	1,190	5,918	540																
Hamburg	476	5,584	10,114	6,306	5,523	826	6,160	4,645	459	3,652	433	3,801	4,100	1,096	1,107	463	1,366	3,273	5,619	1,236	5,536																	
Hong Kong	5,418	1,787	4,585	1,606	6,900	5,764	10,998	1,213	5,986	7,722	5,341	8,055	5,441	4,444	6,540	5,993	6,847	7,357	6,661	4,989																		
Istanbul	779	5,575	9,297	5,383	6,709	843	6,377	4,394	1,393	4,872	1,522	5,003	2,966	1,106	1,686	1,562	2,003	2,849	4,637																			
Johannesburg	5,181	8,414	6,851	5,378	10,552	4,799	4,433	7,259	5,414	8,132	6,028	7,972	1,809	5,698	5,034	5,638	5,093	2,811																				
Lagos	2,971	8,380	9,647	6,935	7,801	2,494	3,745	7,119	2,913	5,363	3,704	5,249	2,381	3,886	2,300	3,109	2,359																					
Lisbon	1,432	6,931	11,294	7,385	5,669	1,161	4,794	6,009	894	3,345	1,694	3,358	4,023	2,419	319	972																						
London	791	5,959	10,575	6,760	5,354	908	5,750	5,077	215	3,323	723	3,441	4,250	1,565	774																							
Madrid	1,122	6,699	10,980	7,068	5,800	844	5,062	5,729	641	3,541	1,474	3,580	3,848	2,126																								
Moscow	1,033	4,656	9,020	5,249	5,862	1,491	7,169	3,607	1,542	4,437	1,012	4,660	3,944																									
Nairobi	3,624	6,992	7,541	4,631	9,600	3,346	5,553	5,719	4,026	7,369	4,456	7,352																										
New York	4,227	6,747	9,949	9,534	2,580	4,281	4,804	6,842	3,621	328	3,668																											
Oslo	848	5,237	9,918	6,251	5,189	1,253	6,486	4,374	822	3,480																												
Ottawa	4,095	6,427	9,863	9,213	2,440	4,176	5,131	6,509	3,518																													
Paris	648	6,037	10,534	6,666	5,578	689	5,688	5,116																														
Peking	4,636	1,308	5,558	2,770	5,922	5,068	10,764																															
Rio de Janeiro	6,136	11,538	8,403	9,781	6,612	5,713																																
Rome	477	6,135	10,137	6,224	6,250																																	
San Francisco	5,997	5,148	7,424	8,445																																		
Singapore	6,027	3,296	3,915																																			
Sydney	9,923	4,058																																				
Tokyo	5,681																																					

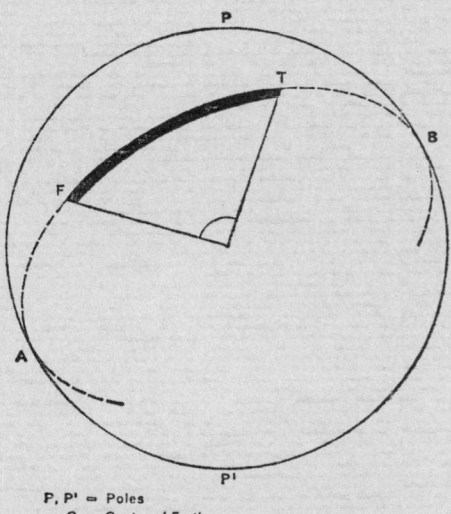

P, P' = Poles
C = Centre of Earth
AB = Great Circle
FT = Two points on Great Circle AB. Thick line is the shortest distance between F and T

GREAT CIRCLE DISTANCES

Our Chart shows the shortest distance between any two places, calculated by the "great circle" method.

A great circle described on the surface of a globe is a circle which divides the globe into two exactly equal parts. If two points are marked on the globe and a great circle is described so as to pass through both points (and only one great circle can do so), then the length of the shorter of the two arcs of this great circle which lie between the two points is the shortest distance that can be measured between them. By using this method, the shortest distance between any two places on the Earth can be calculated.

On the various map projections in this Atlas, the great circle will appear in different shapes: it is important to appreciate the properties of the particular map in use if a great circle distance is to be measured from it.

A close degree of accuracy in obtaining a great circle distance can be achieved by the solution of a spherical trigonometry problem, the sides and angles of the triangle being made up from the relevant values from the sphere.

A great circle is the path of the rays detected by radio direction finders. All meridians are great circles.

WEATHER CHART

\	\	\	HOW HOT IS IT? Average monthly temperatures — in degrees Fahrenheit at sea-level									Height in feet above sea-level		HOW WET IS IT? Average monthly rainfall — in inches											Total for year
JAN	FEB	MAR	APR	MAY	JUNE	JULY	AUG	SEP	OCT	NOV	DEC		City	JAN	FEB	MAR	APR	MAY	JUNE	JULY	AUG	SEP	OCT	NOV	DEC	
-18.0	-16.5	-8.5	8.5	31.0	49.0	56.5	50.0	38.0	20.0	-3.0	-16.0	30	Aklavik	.5	.5	.4	.5	.5	.8	1.4	1.4	.9	.9	.8	.4	9.0
83.5	82.0	76.5	67.5	59.5	54.0	53.0	58.0	65.0	73.0	78.5	82.0	1,901	Alice Springs	1.7	1.3	1.1	.4	.6	.5	.3	.3	.3	.7	1.2	1.5	9.9
48.0	49.0	53.0	59.5	68.5	76.0	81.0	81.0	74.5	67.0	58.0	51.5	351	Athens	2.2	1.6	1.4	.8	.8	.6	.2	.4	.6	1.7	2.8	2.8	15.9
49.5	53.0	59.5	71.0	82.0	89.0	93.0	93.0	87.0	76.5	64.0	53.0	111	Baghdad	.9	1.0	1.1	.5	.1	<1	<1	<1	<1	.1	.8	1.0	5.5
77.1	70.5	72.5	75.0	77.5	80.5	81.5	82.5	81.5	79.0	75.5	73.0	12	Bahamas (Nassau)	1.4	1.5	1.4	2.5	4.6	6.4	5.8	5.3	6.9	6.5	2.8	1.3	46.4
56.5	57.0	60.0	65.0	71.0	76.0	80.0	81.5	79.5	75.0	67.0	60.0	111	Beirut	7.5	6.2	3.7	2.2	.7	.1	<1	<1	.2	2.0	5.2	7.3	35.1
75.0	75.0	79.0	82.5	85.5	84.0	81.0	80.5	80.5	82.5	81.0	78.0	37	Bombay	.1	.1	.1	<1	.7	19.1	24.3	13.4	10.4	2.5	.5	.1	71.2
74.0	73.0	69.5	62.5	55.5	49.0	49.5	51.5	55.0	59.5	66.0	71.5	89	Buenos Aires	3.1	2.8	4.3	3.5	3.0	2.4	2.2	2.4	3.1	3.4	3.3	3.9	37.4
56.0	58.5	63.5	70.0	77.0	81.5	83.0	83.0	79.0	75.5	66.0	59.0	381	Cairo	.2	.2	.2	.1	.1	<1	0	0	<1	<1	.1	.2	1.1
67.5	71.5	81.0	86.0	86.5	85.5	84.0	83.5	84.0	81.5	74.0	67.0	21	Calcutta	.4	1.2	1.4	1.7	5.5	11.7	12.8	12.9	9.9	4.5	.8	.2	63.0
68.5	68.5	63.5	55.5	48.5	43.5	42.5	45.0	49.5	55.5	61.5	66.5	1,837	Canberra	1.9	1.7	2.2	1.6	1.8	2.1	1.8	2.2	1.6	2.2	1.9	2.0	23.0
69.0	69.5	67.5	62.5	58.0	55.5	54.0	55.0	57.0	61.0	64.0	67.0	56	Cape Town	.6	.3	.7	1.9	3.1	3.3	3.5	2.6	1.7	1.2	.7	.4	20.0
65.5	66.5	68.5	70.5	71.0	70.0	69.5	70.0	70.5	70.0	68.5	68.0	3,418	Caracas	.9	.4	.6	1.3	3.1	4.0	4.3	4.3	4.2	4.3	3.7	1.8	32.9
73.0	73.5	73.5	72.5	69.5	67.0	68.0	70.0	73.0	74.0	73.5	72.5	2,723	Catalão	11.8	10.2	8.8	3.8	1.1	.3	.5	.3	2.3	6.1	8.3	14.9	68.4
25.0	27.0	36.0	47.5	57.5	67.5	73.5	72.0	65.5	54.0	40.5	29.5	823	Chicago	2.0	2.0	2.6	2.8	3.4	3.5	3.3	3.2	3.1	2.6	2.4	2.0	32.9
61.5	61.0	58.0	53.5	48.0	43.5	42.5	44.0	48.5	53.0	56.5	60.0	32	Christchurch, N.Z.	2.2	1.7	1.9	1.9	2.6	2.6	2.7	1.9	1.8	1.7	1.9	2.2	25.1
36.0	38.0	43.0	49.5	57.5	62.5	65.5	64.5	59.0	51.0	43.0	38.0	184	Cologne	2.0	1.8	1.8	1.9	2.0	2.6	3.2	2.8	2.1	2.5	2.2	2.5	27.4
79.0	79.5	81.0	82.0	82.5	81.0	81.0	81.0	81.0	80.0	79.0	78.5	24	Colombo	3.5	3.5	5.8	9.1	14.6	8.8	5.3	4.3	6.3	13.7	12.4	5.8	93.1
83.5	83.5	84.0	84.0	82.0	78.5	77.0	79.5	82.5	85.0	86.0	85.0	97	Darwin	15.2	12.3	10.0	3.8	.6	.1	<1	.1	.5	2.0	4.7	9.4	58.7
57.0	62.0	72.5	82.0	92.0	92.5	88.5	86.0	84.0	79.0	68.0	59.5	714	Delhi	.9	.7	.5	.3	.5	2.9	7.1	6.8	4.6	.4	.1	.4	25.2
61.0	60.5	61.0	62.5	64.5	67.5	70.5	71.5	71.5	69.5	66.0	62.5	82	Funchal, Madeira	2.5	2.9	3.1	1.3	.7	.2	<1	<1	1.0	3.0	3.5	3.3	21.5
34.0	36.5	43.0	49.5	57.0	64.0	67.5	66.5	60.5	51.0	42.0	35.5	1,329	Geneva	1.9	1.8	2.2	2.5	3.0	3.1	2.9	3.6	3.6	2.8	3.1	2.4	32.9
63.0	62.5	62.5	65.0	70.0	75.0	79.0	80.0	78.0	74.0	68.5	65.0	151	Hamilton, Bermuda	4.4	4.7	4.8	4.1	4.6	4.4	4.5	5.4	5.2	5.8	5.0	4.7	57.6
-5.5	-5.0	6.0	18.0	31.5	40.0	47.0	48.0	40.5	31.0	20.0	4.0	49	Hebron, Labrador	.9	.7	.9	1.1	1.6	2.1	2.7	2.7	3.3	1.6	1.1	.6	19.3
60.0	59.0	63.5	71.0	78.0	81.5	82.5	82.5	81.0	77.0	69.5	63.5	109	Hong Kong	1.3	1.8	2.9	5.4	11.5	15.5	15.0	14.2	10.1	4.5	1.7	1.2	85.1
40.5	42.0	45.5	53.0	60.5	68.5	73.0	73.5	68.0	60.5	53.5	46.0	59	Istanbul	3.7	2.3	2.6	1.9	1.4	1.3	1.7	1.5	2.3	3.8	4.1	4.9	31.5
48.0	49.0	55.5	61.5	69.0	72.5	75.0	75.5	73.5	70.0	61.5	52.0	2,485	Jerusalem	5.2	5.2	2.5	1.1	.1	<1	0	0	<1	.5	2.8	3.4	20.8
68.0	67.5	65.0	61.0	54.5	50.5	51.0	55.5	60.5	65.0	66.0	67.5	5,463	Johannesburg	4.5	4.3	3.5	1.5	1.0	.3	.3	.3	.9	2.2	4.2	4.9	27.9
81.0	83.0	83.5	83.0	81.5	79.5	78.5	77.5	78.5	79.5	81.5	81.5	10	Lagos	1.1	1.8	4.0	5.9	10.6	18.1	11.0	2.5	5.5	8.1	2.7	1.0	72.3
74.0	75.0	74.5	71.5	67.0	63.0	62.0	61.0	62.5	64.5	67.0	70.0	394	Lima	<1	<1	<1	<1	.2	.2	.3	.3	.3	.1	.1	<1	1.6
75.5	75.5	74.5	72.5	66.5	61.0	61.0	66.0	74.5	80.5	79.0	76.5	3,161	Livingstone	5.7	6.0	4.3	1.0	.3	.1	0	<1	.1	.9	2.9	5.2	26.5
39.5	40.0	44.0	48.0	54.0	60.0	64.0	63.0	59.0	51.0	44.0	40.5	149	London	2.0	1.5	1.4	1.8	1.8	1.6	2.0	2.2	1.8	2.3	2.5	2.0	22.9
55.5	56.5	57.5	60.0	62.5	66.0	70.5	71.0	69.5	65.0	61.5	51.0	312	Los Angeles	3.1	3.0	2.8	1.0	.4	.1	<1	<1	.2	.6	1.2	2.6	15.0
49.5	51.0	53.5	57.5	64.0	70.5	75.0	76.5	72.5	65.5	57.5	51.5	75	Majorca	1.4	1.6	1.5	1.3	1.3	1.0	.2	.8	2.5	2.8	2.8	2.2	19.4
54.0	56.0	61.0	64.0	66.0	65.0	63.0	63.5	63.5	60.0	57.0	54.5	7,575	Mexico City	.5	.2	.4	.8	2.1	4.7	6.7	6.0	5.1	2.0	.7	.3	29.5
67.5	68.0	71.0	73.5	77.5	80.0	82.0	82.0	81.0	77.5	72.0	69.0	25	Miami	2.8	2.1	2.5	3.2	6.8	7.0	6.1	6.3	8.0	9.2	2.8	2.0	58.8
81.0	81.5	82.5	81.0	78.5	77.5	76.0	76.0	77.0	79.0	80.0	80.5	52	Mombasa	1.0	.7	2.5	7.7	12.6	4.7	3.5	2.5	2.5	3.4	3.8	2.4	47.3
15.0	16.5	24.5	39.0	54.5	62.0	65.5	62.0	52.0	40.0	27.0	18.0	505	Moscow	1.5	1.4	1.1	1.9	2.2	2.9	3.0	2.9	1.9	2.7	1.7	1.6	24.8
65.5	67.0	67.0	66.5	64.0	61.5	60.0	60.5	63.5	65.5	65.0	64.5	5,971	Nairobi	1.5	2.5	4.9	8.3	6.2	1.8	.6	.9	1.2	2.1	4.3	3.4	37.7
54.5	57.5	63.0	69.0	75.5	81.0	83.0	83.0	79.5	71.5	62.5	56.0	8	New Orleans	4.6	4.2	4.7	4.8	4.5	5.5	6.6	5.8	4.8	3.5	3.8	4.6	57.4
30.5	31.0	37.5	49.5	60.5	68.5	74.0	73.0	69.5	59.0	44.0	35.0	314	New York	3.7	3.8	3.6	3.2	3.2	3.3	4.2	4.3	3.4	3.5	3.0	3.6	42.8
25.0	26.0	32.5	42.0	52.5	60.0	64.5	61.0	52.5	43.0	33.0	27.5	308	Oslo	1.7	1.3	1.4	1.6	1.8	2.4	2.9	3.8	2.5	2.9	2.3	2.3	26.9
12.0	12.5	25.5	41.0	55.0	65.0	69.5	66.0	58.0	45.5	32.5	16.5	339	Ottawa	2.9	2.2	2.8	2.7	2.5	3.5	3.4	2.6	3.2	2.9	3.0	2.6	34.3
37.0	39.0	44.0	50.5	57.0	62.5	65.5	65.0	59.5	51.5	43.5	38.0	164	Paris	1.5	1.3	1.5	1.7	2.0	2.1	2.1	2.0	2.0	2.2	2.0	1.9	22.3
74.0	74.0	71.0	66.5	61.0	57.0	55.5	56.0	58.5	61.5	66.5	71.0	197	Perth, W. Australia	.3	.4	.8	1.7	5.1	7.1	6.7	5.7	3.4	2.2	.8	.5	34.7
78.5	79.0	77.5	74.5	71.5	70.0	69.0	70.0	70.0	71.5	73.5	76.5	201	Rio de Janeiro	4.9	4.8	5.1	4.2	3.1	1.6	1.6	1.7	2.6	3.1	4.1	5.4	42.7
64.0	63.5	61.5	56.5	51.0	47.5	45.5	47.0	50.5	54.5	57.5	61.5	980	Rotorua	4.4	4.4	3.5	4.6	5.5	5.3	4.9	5.0	4.8	4.9	4.3	3.7	55.0
46.5	47.5	52.0	57.0	64.5	71.0	76.0	76.0	72.0	63.0	54.5	48.5	377	Rome	2.7	2.3	1.5	1.7	2.0	1.0	.6	.9	2.7	3.7	3.8	2.8	25.7
23.5	22.0	27.5	35.5	42.5	52.5	59.5	61.0	54.5	46.5	37.0	29.0	243	St. John's, Newfoundland	5.3	4.9	4.6	4.2	3.6	3.5	3.5	3.7	3.8	5.3	5.9	5.5	53.8
50.0	53.0	54.5	56.5	57.0	59.0	59.0	59.0	62.0	61.0	57.0	52.0	52	San Francisco	4.7	3.8	3.1	1.5	.7	.1	<1	<1	.3	1.0	2.5	4.4	22.1
34.5	37.0	40.5	48.5	58.5	67.0	72.0	71.5	64.0	56.5	44.5	39.0	75	Sevastopol	1.1	1.1	1.1	.9	1.0	1.1	.8	.6	1.1	1.5	1.2	1.1	12.2
79.5	80.5	81.5	81.5	82.0	81.5	81.5	81.0	81.0	80.5	80.5	80.5	33	Singapore	9.9	6.8	7.6	7.4	6.8	6.8	6.7	7.7	7.0	8.2	10.0	10.1	95.0
71.5	71.5	69.5	64.5	59.0	54.5	53.0	55.5	59.0	63.5	67.0	70.0	138	Sydney	3.5	4.0	5.0	5.3	5.0	4.6	4.6	3.0	2.9	2.8	2.9	2.9	46.5
53.5	54.5	56.5	58.0	63.5	68.0	72.0	73.5	70.5	65.5	58.5	54.5	239	Tangier	4.5	4.2	4.8	3.5	1.7	.6	<1	<1	.7	3.9	5.8	5.4	35.3
24.5	30.0	41.5	56.5	68.5	77.5	81.5	79.5	70.5	56.0	41.0	28.5	13	Tientsin	.2	.1	.4	.5	1.1	2.4	7.4	6.0	1.7	.6	.4	.2	21.0
38.0	39.5	45.0	54.5	62.5	69.5	76.5	79.0	72.5	62.0	51.5	42.5	19	Tokyo	1.9	2.9	4.2	5.3	5.8	6.5	5.6	6.0	9.2	8.2	3.8	2.2	61.6
64.0	64.0	62.0	59.5	56.5	54.0	53.5	54.0	55.0	57.0	60.5	62.5	135	Valparaiso, Chile	.1	<1	.3	.6	4.1	5.9	3.9	2.9	1.3	.4	.2	.2	19.9
36.5	39.0	43.5	49.0	55.0	60.5	64.0	63.5	57.0	50.5	43.5	39.0	45	Vancouver	8.6	5.8	5.0	3.3	2.8	2.5	1.2	1.7	3.6	5.8	8.3	8.8	57.4
30.0	33.0	40.5	49.0	58.0	63.5	67.0	65.5	59.0	49.5	40.0	33.5	664	Vienna	1.5	1.4	1.8	2.0	2.8	2.7	3.0	2.7	2.0	2.0	1.9	1.8	25.6
-3.0	1.5	16.0	37.5	52.0	62.0	67.0	63.5	54.0	41.0	21.5	6.0	786	Winnipeg	.9	.9	1.2	1.4	2.3	3.1	3.1	2.5	2.3	1.5	1.1	.9	21.2

< = less than

179

THE READER'S DIGEST GREAT WORLD ATLAS

SECOND EDITION

Published by

THE READER'S DIGEST ASSOCIATION LIMITED
25 Berkeley Square, London, W.1, and Parkade, Strand Street, Cape Town

THE READER'S DIGEST ASSOCIATION PTY. LIMITED
Reader's Digest Building, 26-32 Waterloo Street, Surry Hills, Sydney

THE READER'S DIGEST ASSOCIATION (CANADA) LIMITED
215 Redfern Avenue, Montreal 6, Quebec

First Edition © THE READER'S DIGEST ASSOCIATION LIMITED 1961
First Revise November 1961
Second Revise March 1962
Third Revise July 1962
Fourth Revise November 1962
Fifth Revise August 1964
Sixth Revise January 1965
Seventh Revise November 1966
Second Edition © THE READER'S DIGEST ASSOCIATION LIMITED 1968

*All rights reserved,
including the right to reproduce this book
or parts thereof in any form*

Printing and Binding by

JOHN BARTHOLOMEW & SON LTD., EDINBURGH   BROWN KNIGHT & TRUSCOTT LTD., TONBRIDGE

HAZELL WATSON & VINEY LTD., AYLESBURY   BEN JOHNSON & CO. LTD., YORK

Relief maps, pages 8-28, 114-115 © Geographical Projects Limited, London, 1961